Chelsea McCracken
A Grammar of Belep

Mouton Grammar Library

Edited by
Georg Bossong
Bernard Comrie
Patience L. Epps
Irina Nikolaeva

Volume 78

Chelsea McCracken

A Grammar of Belep

DE GRUYTER
MOUTON

ISBN 978-3-11-076192-4
ISSN 0933-7636

Library of Congress Control Number: 2019950661

Bibliographic information published by the Deutsche Nationalbibliothek
The Deutsche Nationalbibliothek lists this publication in the Deutsche Nationalbibliografie;
detailed bibliographic data are available on the Internet at http://dnb.dnb.de.

© 2021 Walter de Gruyter GmbH, Berlin/Boston
This volume is text- and page-identical with the hardback published in 2019.
Printing and binding: CPI books GmbH, Leck

www.degruyter.com

Abstract

This book is a description of the grammar of Belep [yly], an Austronesian language variety spoken by about 1600 people in and around the Belep Isles in New Caledonia. The grammar begins with a summary of the cultural and linguistic background of Belep speakers, followed by chapters on Belep phonology and phonetics, morphology and word formation, nouns and the noun phrase, verbs and the verb group, basic clause structure, and clause combining.

The phonemic inventory of Belep consists of 18 consonants and 10 vowels and is considerably smaller than those of the surrounding languages. This is due to the fact that Belep consonants do not contrast in aspiration and Belep vowels do not contrast in length, unlike in Belep's closest relative Balade Nyelâyu. However, like-vowel hiatuses—sequences of heterosyllabic like vowels—are common in Belep, where the stress correlates of vowel length, intensity, and pitch do not generally coincide. Belep morphology is exclusively suffixing and fairly synthetic; it is characterized by a large disconnect between the phonological and the grammatical word and the existence of a number of proclitics and enclitics. Belep nouns fall into four noun classes, which are defined by their compatibility with the two available (alienable and inalienable) possessive constructions. Belep transitive verbs are divided into bound and free roots, while intransitive verbs are divided between those which require a nominative argument and those which require an absolutive argument. While the surrounding languages have a split-ergative argument structure, Belep has an unusual split-intransitive nominative-absolutive system, with the further complication that transitive subjects may be marked as genitive depending on the definiteness of the absolutive argument. Belep case marking is accomplished through the use of cross-linguistically unusual ditropic clitics; clitics marking the function of a Belep noun phrase are phonologically bound to whatever element precedes the noun phrase. In general, Belep lacks true complementation, instead making use of coordinate structures with unique linkers as a complementation strategy.

Acknowledgments

First and foremost, I want to say *ole pwalu* and *merci beaucoup* to the people of Belep for their extravagant welcome and their hard work and dedication to the project. Thanks especially to teâmaa WAHOULO Amabili and the cuuyama for their support, to WAHOULO Albert and the mairie staff for their invaluable assistance, and to BOUEDAOU Thérèse, the enseignantes, and the Comité de langue for their guidance. My work would have been impossible without the wisdom and patience of my primary consultants, TEANYOUEN Philippe, YARIK Darine, POITHILI Albert, and GUELEME Yasmine, and it also would have been impossible without the care and support provided by my two adoptive families, the MOILOU and DAYE clans—thanks especially to Ignacia, Gal, and Onis; Alice, Christophe, Kacaca, Magali, and Roro; Gabi, Pato, Larisa, and Eliane; Marjorie, the second Alice, Davy, Marie-France, and Mina; and wa Laurente. At the mairie, bisous to Apollonie, Maria, Didyme, and Ghislaine.

I want to extend my personal thanks to each and every Belema who participated in my work and allowed me to record or interview them—to my storytellers GUELEME Benjamin and Marie-Clothilde, TEANYOUEN Madeleine, THALE Elie, THALE Jean-Marie, TEAMBOUEON François, and POITHILI Allen; to songwriter POITHILI Pierre for sharing his original poetry with me; to grammar and vocabulary experts POITHILI Alexandrine, MOILOU Jean-Baptiste, WAHOULO Christine, TEAMBOUEON Eulalie, THALE Nazaire, YAMAMOTO Larisa, and GUELEME Simeon; to my interviewees YARIK Lisianne, PIDYO Lalita, PIDYO Bruno, and BOUEDAOU Edwin; and to all the people of Belep. All linguistic mistakes that remain are mine alone; Belema language experts are encouraged to offer critiques and corrections to my work.

Weniko Ihage, the director of the Académie des langues kanak, was an instrumental part of this project from the beginning, and I thank him for his support. He provided valuable introductions and was a strong defender of my project. Many thanks also to the Hoot ma whaap académicienne Scholastique Boiguivie and the chargée de mission Suzy Camoui for their collaborative efforts.

My love and gratitude to my friend and neighbor Alea Safier, who accompanied me on my 2009 trip. Thanks also to her parents for their financial assistance.

To my advisor, Dr. Christina Willis, thank you for taking me on in the middle of this project and for seeing it through to the end. Your help made me a better writer. To Dr. Robert Englebretson, thank you for your mentorship and encouragement, and for teaching me how to do linguistic analysis. Our discussions of morphosyntax were extremely helpful. To Dr. Fred Oswald, thank you for your help on my statistical analysis of Belep data, and for your willingness to lend your support to the project. To Dr. Laura Robinson, thank you for teaching me how to do field methods and for mentoring me in the early stages of this project. To Dr. Michel Achard, thank you for your wise advice and support through the first three years of grad school. The entire Linguistics Department faculty at Rice University provided a welcoming environment of intellectual pursuit, and the Linguistics graduate students formed a strong support system. Thanks especially to Katie Nelson for her friendship and wisdom, Michelle Morrison and Linda Lanz for their fieldwork tips, and Vica Papp and Chris Koops for their expertise on phon* and statistics.

This book is a revised version of my Ph.D. thesis. My grateful thanks to all the editors at De Gruyter who have played a role in shepherding it through the publication process. Thanks especially to Dr. Bernard Comrie for his detailed and thoughtful review of an earlier draft, and to Dr. Angela Terrill for her absolutely essential typesetting and editing work. I am also grateful to the College of Education and the Interdisciplinary Arts & Sciences Department at Dixie State University for their financial support of the project during the publication process.

Isabelle Bril originally directed me to Belep, and the staff of the Linguistics department at the Université de la Nouvelle-Calédonie, especially Véronique Fillol and Jacques Vernaudon, provided helpful avenues of research. TIDJINE Laea and his family hosted me during my 2009 visit and provided a kind and generous education in Kanak culture, assisted by PHADOM Rony and with the permission of the chefferie in Poum. WAHIO Gabriel and his wife, in the chefferie of Pouébo, graciously allowed me to record at their wedding.

I very much appreciated the collaboration and companionship of my friends Lara Giordana, Sophie Rendina, and Emma Sinclair-Reynolds while in New Caledonia. Thanks also to Thierry Pigeyre for his friendship. The UNESCO team provided me with useful information on bird species in Belep, the staff of the Centre Culturel Tjibaou was very helpful in locating various records, and the staff of the Auberge de Jeunesse in Nouméa was very helpful whenever I needed something.

Many thanks to the Lewis and Clark Fund for Exploration and Field Research, who funded this project in part. Funding was also provided by the Dolores Mitchell Trust Fund and the Rice University Linguistics Department Fellowship.

My parents, Jack and Debbie McCracken, provided a tremendous amount of support—financial, logistical, emotional—for this project, and it could not have happened without their help. To them, and to Joselle, Mackenzie, Apple, and the Kaweckis: Thank you for taking such good care of me. I love you.

Finally, to Jeremy C. Young, who called me every single day I was in New Caledonia and read and commented on every chapter draft: I am so grateful for your faithfulness, wise counsel, and unfailing support and love. Âyuang ngio and Bemelmans.

Preface

The following is a message for future generations of Belema from TEANYOUEN Philippe, the catechist of Belep in 2011.

TEANYOUEN Philippe, 14 September 2011
Waala, Belep

Enyixi yena to la comuli puluac, pulu Belep, ka âyuang ngi ame jua yavia wa înau ma a înaôeni puluac. Ka puluac, ka jia, tere jia ulayama lami cêboac, nilaac, lami ô cavac ka najiac. La cavac ka najiac ka naji pulu. Ka te ô ki a tao kâye pulu, ma te tao ce la puluac, te tao pan na puluac. Ma yena to name tiu u leac, ma te ô ki a jua yamayaap ma a înaôen, yamayaap ma a înaôeni puluac, yamayaap ma a comu la na puluac, ka tao kâye puluac, ma teme tao pan, ka u le lami me tame mwa la mon. Toven.

Yal-14092011-PT2-avenir

'If your language, the Belep language, is being studied, I would like you to truly search for a way to be an expert at your language. For your language, it is a gift—a true gift from your elders, your grandparents and great-grandparents, those who have gone away and left you. They went away and left you and left behind the language. So you must always keep your language, so that your language will always survive, always... your language will always continue. Now, as I am writing to you, you must truly concentrate on becoming experts, concentrate on becoming experts in your language, concentrate on exploring your language, and always keep your language, so that it will always continue, for all of those who will come after you. That's all.'

(1) *Enyixi yena to la comuli puluac, pulu Belep,*

enyixi	**yena=ro**	**la=**	**comu-li**	**pulu-ac**
if	now=when	3PL.SUBJ=	learn-TR	language-2PL.POSS

pulu	**Belep**
language	Belep

'If your language, the Belep language, is being studied,'

(2) *ka âyuang ngi ame jua yavia*

ka	âyua-ng=i	a=me	jua	yavi-a
LK	desire-1SG.POSS=GEN	2PL.SUBJ=IRR	very	search.TR-DA.IN

'I would like you to truly search for'

(3) *wa înau ma a înaôeni puluac.*

wa=	îna-u	ma	a=	înaôen-i
RESULT=	make-DETR	LK4	2PL.SUBJ=	be.expert-TR

pulu-ac
language-2PL.POSS

'a way to be an expert at your language.'

(4) *Ka puluac, ka jia, tere jia ulayama*

ka	pulu-aya=xa	jia	te=re
LK	language-2PL.POSS=LK	gift	3SG.SUBJ=ACT

jia   ulaya-ma
gift   old.man-AC

'For your language, it is a gift—a true gift from your elders'

(5) *lami cêboac, nilaac,*

la-mi	cêbo-ac
DEM.PL-DET.A.DST	grandparent-2PL.POSS

nila-ac
great.grandparent-2PL.POSS

'your grandparents and great-grandparents,'

(6) *lami ô cavac ka najiac.*

la-mi	ô	cavac	ka	naji-ac
DEM.PL-DET.A.DST	REAL	depart	LK	leave-2PL.ABS

'those who have gone away and left you.'

(7) *La cavac ka najiac ka naji pulu.*

la=	cavac	ka	naji-ac	ka	naji	pulu
3PL.SUBJ=	depart	LK	leave-2PL.ABS	LK	leave	language

'They went away and left you and left behind the language.'

(8) *Ka te ô ki a tao kâye pulu,*

ka	te=	ô=xi	a=	tao=	kâye
LK	3SG.SUBJ=	be.good=REL	2PL.SUBJ=	HAB=	keep

pulu
language

'So you must always keep your language,'

(9) *ma te tao ce la puluac, tao...*

ma=re=	tao=	ce=la	pulu-ac	tao=
LK4=3SG.SUBJ=	HAB=	settle=NOM	language-2PL.POSS	HAB=

'so that your language will always survive, always...'

(10) *te tao pan na puluac.*

te=	tao=	pan=a	pulu-ac
3SG.SUBJ=	HAB=	go.TV=NOM	language-2PL.POSS

'your language will always continue.'

(11) *Ma yena to name tiu u leac,*

ma	yena=ro	na=me	ti-u	u=le-ac
LK4	now=when	1SG.SUBJ=IRR	prick-DETR	toward=DAT-2PL.POSS

'Now, as I am writing to you,'

(12) *ma te ô ki a jua yamayaap ma a înaôen,*

ma	te=	ô=xi	a=	jua
LK4	3SG.SUBJ=	be.good=REL	2PL.SUBJ=	very

yamayava	ma	a=	înaôen
concentrate	LK4	2PL.SUBJ=	be.expert

'you must truly concentrate on becoming experts,'

(13) *yamayaap ma a înaôeni puluac,*

yamayava	ma	a=	înaôen-i	pulu-ac
concentrate	LK4	2PL.SUBJ=	be.expert-TR	language-2PL.POSS

'concentrate on becoming experts in your language,'

(14) *yamayaap ma a comu la na puluac,*

yamayava	ma	a=	comu=la
concentrate	LK4	2PL.SUBJ=	learn=LOC

na	pulu-ac
interior	language-2PL.POSS

'concentrate on exploring your language,'

(15) *ka tao kâye puluac, ma teme tao pan,*

ka	tao=	kâye	pulu-ac	ma	teme
LK	HAB=	keep	language-2PL.POSS	LK4	3SG.SUBJ=IRR

tao=	pan
HAB=	go.TV

'and always keep your language, so that it will always continue,'

(16) *ka u le lami me tame mwa la mon.*

ka	u=le	la-mi	me	ta=me
LK	toward=DAT	DEM.PL-DET.A.DST	IRR	go.UH=CTP

mwa=la	mon
again=LOC	side.DH

'for all of those who will come after you.'

(17) *Toven.*

toven
finish
'That's all.'

Contents

1	**Background information** —— 1	
1.1	Introduction —— 1	
1.2	Belep and its speakers —— 1	
1.3	The Belema people —— 3	
1.3.1	The clan in Belep —— 5	
1.3.2	*La coutume* —— 10	
1.3.3	History of Belep —— 14	
1.4	Belep within the Austronesian language family —— 16	
1.5	Previous research on the Belep language —— 18	
1.6	The Belep language —— 20	
1.6.1	Language name —— 20	
1.6.2	Linguistic profile of Belep —— 23	
1.7	Sociolinguistic situation —— 25	
1.7.1	Sociolinguistic variation —— 25	
1.7.2	Multilingualism and language contact —— 26	
1.7.3	Endangerment status and revitalization —— 29	
1.8	Methodology —— 30	
2	**Phonetics and phonology** —— 35	
2.1	Introduction —— 35	
2.2	Phonemic inventory —— 36	
2.2.1	Consonants —— 37	
2.2.1.1	Labial consonants —— 37	
2.2.1.2	Alveolar consonants —— 40	
2.2.1.3	Palatal consonants —— 42	
2.2.1.4	Velar consonants —— 43	
2.2.1.5	Nasal consonants —— 44	
2.2.1.6	Approximants —— 45	
2.2.2	Vowels —— 46	
2.3	Description of phonemes —— 48	
2.3.1	Consonants —— 49	
2.3.1.1	Labiovelar consonants —— 49	
2.3.1.2	Voiceless stops —— 51	
2.3.1.3	Prenasalized stops —— 54	
2.3.1.4	Approximants —— 59	
2.3.1.5	Neutralizations —— 60	
2.3.2	Vowels —— 63	
2.3.2.1	Vowel quality —— 64	
2.3.2.2	Vowel sequences —— 67	

2.3.2.3	Vowel nasality —— 74	
2.3.2.4	Neutralizations —— 76	
2.4	Allophony —— 76	
2.4.1	Consonants —— 77	
2.4.1.1	Phonetic labialization —— 77	
2.4.1.2	Voiceless stops —— 77	
2.4.1.3	Prestopped nasals —— 87	
2.4.1.4	Approximants —— 88	
2.4.2	Vowels —— 90	
2.4.2.1	Stress-induced vowel lengthening —— 90	
2.4.2.2	Devoicing and ingressive airstream —— 91	
2.5	Morphophonemic processes —— 93	
2.5.1	Lenition —— 93	
2.5.2	Phase shift —— 95	
2.5.3	Nasal spreading —— 97	
2.6	Orthographic conventions —— 98	
2.7	Phonotactics —— 100	
2.8	Prosody —— 104	
2.8.1	Disyllabic words —— 104	
2.8.2	Stress correlates —— 107	
2.8.3	The penultimate stress rule —— 108	
2.8.3.1	Distribution of like-vowel hiatus —— 109	
2.8.3.2	'Compounding' stress patterns —— 110	
2.8.4	Extrametricality —— 111	
2.8.5	Lexicality —— 112	
2.9	Other phonologies —— 113	
2.9.1	Belep SPECIAL stratum —— 114	
2.9.1.1	Sound symbolism —— 114	
2.9.1.2	Proper names —— 115	
2.9.2	Religious jargon —— 115	
2.9.3	FRENCH stratum —— 117	
2.9.3.1	Phonemic differences —— 119	
2.9.3.2	Phonetic influences —— 120	
2.9.3.3	Morphophonemics —— 120	
2.10	Summary —— 121	
3	**Architecture of the word —— 123**	
3.1	Introduction —— 123	
3.2	Definition of the word —— 123	
3.2.1	Phonological word —— 127	
3.2.1.1	Syllable structure —— 127	
3.2.1.2	Penultimate stress —— 128	

3.2.1.3	Conditioned allophony	129
3.2.1.4	Vowel epenthesis and phase shift	132
3.2.1.5	Morphophonemic stem alternations	133
3.2.1.6	Pause phenomena	133
3.2.2	Grammatical word	134
3.2.2.1	Grammatical words that are also phonological words	134
3.2.2.2	Grammatical words that are not phonological words	136
3.2.2.3	Intermediate units between grammatical words and syntactic constituents	139
3.2.2.4	Grammatical vs. phonological words	141
3.2.2.5	Affixes	142
3.2.2.6	Clitics	142
3.3	Word classes	147
3.3.1	Nouns	148
3.3.2	Verbs	150
3.3.3	Adverbs	152
3.3.4	Linkers	155
3.3.5	Interjections and discourse markers	156
3.4	Inflection and derivation	158
3.5	Inflectional morphology	159
3.5.1	Nouns	160
3.5.2	Verbs	161
3.5.3	Intermediate elements	163
3.6	Derivational morphology	165
3.6.1	Denominal nouns	165
3.6.1.1	Ordinal *ba=*	165
3.6.1.2	Dyadic *âma=*	166
3.6.2	Deverbal nouns	168
3.6.2.1	Agentive *â=*	168
3.6.2.2	Instrumental *ba=*	170
3.6.2.3	Resultative *wa=*	170
3.6.3	Deverbal verbs	172
3.6.4	Denominal verbs with *tu=*	173
3.7	Compounding	176
3.8	Non-concatenative morphology	178
3.9	Summary	179
4	**Nouns and the noun phrase**	**181**
4.1	Introduction	181
4.2	Nouns and possession	181
4.2.1	Noun classes	181
4.2.1.1	Noun class 1	182

4.2.1.2	Noun class 2 —— **184**	
4.2.1.3	Noun class 3 —— **187**	
4.2.1.4	Noun class 4 —— **188**	
4.2.2	Possessed nouns —— **190**	
4.2.2.1	Dependent possession —— **191**	
4.2.2.2	Possessive suffixes —— **192**	
4.2.2.3	Stem modification for type of possessor —— **194**	
4.2.2.4	Independent possession —— **198**	
4.2.3	Free (unpossessed) nouns and stem modification —— **200**	
4.2.4	Noun classifiers —— **202**	
4.2.5	Locative expressions using possessive constructions —— **206**	
4.3	Noun quantifiers —— **209**	
4.3.1	Associative plural *-ma* —— **211**	
4.3.2	Associative dual *-male* —— **212**	
4.3.3	General extender *-mene* —— **214**	
4.3.4	Total *-roven* —— **215**	
4.4	Determination and deixis —— **216**	
4.4.1	Conceptualization of space —— **217**	
4.4.2	Determiner suffixes —— **220**	
4.4.2.1	Deictic determiners —— **221**	
4.4.2.2	Anaphoric determiners —— **225**	
4.4.2.3	Interrogative determiners —— **227**	
4.4.3	Other determiners —— **227**	
4.5	The noun phrase —— **231**	
4.5.1	Noun phrase constituency —— **232**	
4.5.2	Binomial linker *le* —— **234**	
4.5.3	Noun phrase coordinator *ka* 'and' —— **235**	
4.5.4	Disjunctive linker *ai* 'or' —— **237**	
4.5.5	Inclusory *ma* 'with' —— **237**	
4.5.6	Comitative conjunction —— **239**	
4.6	Pronouns —— **240**	
4.6.1	Independent pronouns —— **241**	
4.6.2	Demonstrative pronouns —— **243**	
4.6.2.1	Table of demonstrative pronouns —— **252**	
4.6.3	Interrogative pronouns —— **255**	
4.7	Number system and numerals —— **256**	
4.7.1	Cardinal and ordinal numerals —— **257**	
4.7.2	Numerals in discourse —— **258**	
4.7.3	Numeral classifiers —— **262**	
4.8	Summary —— **264**	

5	**Verbs and the verb group** —— 265
5.1	Introduction —— 265
5.2	The verb word —— 265
5.2.1	Intransitive verbs with a nominative argument —— 266
5.2.1.1	Bound intransitives —— 267
5.2.2	Intransitive verbs with an absolutive argument —— 269
5.2.3	Transitive verbs —— 272
5.2.3.1	Free transitives —— 272
5.2.3.2	Bound transitives —— 274
5.2.3.3	Irregular transitives —— 275
5.2.4	Inflection for specificity —— 276
5.2.5	Patient valence —— 280
5.2.5.1	Transitivization with stem modification —— 280
5.2.5.2	Transitivizer -*li* —— 285
5.2.5.3	Detransitivizer -*u* —— 287
5.2.6	Differential absolutive suffixes —— 289
5.2.6.1	The suffix -*n* —— 290
5.2.6.2	The suffix -*a* —— 292
5.3	The verb group —— 293
5.4	Agent valence —— 295
5.4.1	Causative *pa=* —— 297
5.4.2	Reciprocal *pe=* —— 301
5.4.3	Reduced agentive *pu=* —— 302
5.5	Morphological aspect —— 304
5.5.1	Progressive *âga=* —— 306
5.5.2	Perfect *âmu=* —— 307
5.5.3	Subjunctive *ba=* —— 309
5.5.4	Continuative *bwa=* —— 310
5.5.5	Iterative *ca=* —— 312
5.5.6	Gnomic *da=* —— 312
5.5.7	Diminished *ma=* —— 313
5.5.8	Punctual *nyi=* —— 314
5.5.9	Habitual *tao=* —— 315
5.5.10	Dubitative *u=* —— 315
5.5.11	Completive -*roven* —— 316
5.5.12	General extender -*mene* —— 318
5.6	Morphological mood —— 318
5.6.1	Realis =*ô* —— 321
5.6.2	Irrealis =*me* —— 324
5.7	Absolutive suffixes —— 325
5.7.1	As verb inflections —— 326
5.7.2	Suffixes -*e* and -*er* —— 328

5.8	Subject agreement clitics —— 331	
5.9	Verb compounding —— 334	
5.10	Verb serialization —— 336	
5.10.1	Desiderative *jaar* 'to want to' —— 336	
5.10.2	Conative *cavi* 'to try to' —— 337	
5.10.3	Prospective *mo* 'to be about to' —— 338	
5.10.4	Inceptive *pan* 'to be going to' —— 339	
5.10.5	Concessive *ci* 'nonetheless' —— 340	
5.10.6	*koni* 'to never' —— 342	
5.10.7	Cessative *toveni* 'to finish' —— 344	
5.10.8	Other modal elements —— 345	
5.11	The verb phrase —— 347	
5.12	Directionals —— 348	
5.13	Locationals —— 351	
5.14	Summary —— 354	
6	**Basic clause structure —— 355**	
6.1	Introduction —— 355	
6.2	Basic word order and typology —— 355	
6.2.1	ADPOSITION + NOUN —— 359	
6.2.2	NOUN + RELATIVE CLAUSE —— 359	
6.2.3	NOUN + GENITIVE —— 360	
6.2.4	ADJECTIVE + STANDARD —— 360	
6.2.5	VERB + ADPOSITIONAL PHRASE —— 361	
6.2.6	VERB + MANNER ADVERB —— 361	
6.2.7	WANT + SUBORDINATE VERB —— 361	
6.3	Argument structure —— 362	
6.3.1	Nominative-accusative alignment —— 363	
6.3.2	Tripartite alignment —— 368	
6.3.3	Absolutive-ergative alignment —— 370	
6.3.4	Subjecthood in Belep —— 373	
6.3.4.1	Other candidates for subjecthood —— 375	
6.4	Case and grammatical relations —— 376	
6.4.1	Absolutive case —— 379	
6.4.2	Nominative case —— 381	
6.4.3	Genitive case —— 382	
6.4.4	Dative case —— 385	
6.4.5	Locative case —— 388	
6.4.6	Instrumental case —— 390	
6.5	Non-prototypical clause types —— 391	
6.5.1	Predicate nominals and the equative construction —— 392	
6.5.2	Existence and location —— 397	

6.5.3	Attribution —— 401
6.6	Question formation —— 403
6.6.1	Yes-no questions —— 403
6.6.2	Question-word questions —— 407
6.6.3	Answering, agreeing, and disagreeing —— 413
6.7	Imperatives and prohibitives —— 419
6.7.1	Imperatives —— 419
6.7.2	Prohibitives —— 422
6.8	Negation —— 424
6.8.1	Regular predicate negation —— 425
6.8.2	Inherently negative predicates —— 427
6.9	Topicalization and focalization —— 428
6.9.1	Topicalization —— 428
6.9.2	Focalization —— 430
6.9.2.1	Actual =*re* —— 431
6.9.2.2	Additive =*xa* —— 432
6.10	Voice and valency —— 432
6.10.1	Periphrastic causatives —— 433
6.10.2	Reflexives —— 434
6.10.3	Passives —— 435
6.10.4	Quotatives —— 436
6.11	Expression of temporal location —— 437
6.12	Comparison —— 440
6.12.1	Comparative construction —— 440
6.12.2	Expression of similarity —— 442
6.13	Summary —— 444
7	**Clause combining —— 445**
7.1	Introduction —— 445
7.2	Clausal coordination —— 446
7.2.1	Conjunctive linker *ka* —— 448
7.2.1.1	Event coordinator *ka* 'and' —— 448
7.2.1.2	*ka* in topicalization —— 452
7.2.1.3	Additive =*xa* 'ADD' in clause chaining —— 453
7.2.2	Disjunctive linker *ai* 'or' —— 456
7.2.3	Causal linker *mo* 'for' —— 457
7.2.4	Adversative linker *toma* 'but' —— 460
7.2.5	Linker *kara* 'well' —— 461
7.3	Complementation strategies —— 463
7.3.1	Linker *ka* in pseudocoordination —— 466
7.3.2	Linker *ma* in pseudocoordination —— 467
7.3.2.1	Purpose clauses with *ma* 'so that' —— 468

7.3.2.2	Correlational *ma* 'as' —— **471**	
7.3.3	Adverbial linker *to* 'when' —— **472**	
7.3.3.1	Adverbial *to* 'as' —— **473**	
7.3.3.2	Temporal *to* 'at the time of' —— **475**	
7.3.4	Conditional linker *enyi* 'if' —— **476**	
7.3.5	Sequential linker *ka me* 'then' —— **480**	
7.3.6	Linker *ki* as a complementation strategy —— **483**	
7.3.7	Genitive *=li* as a complementation strategy —— **484**	
7.3.7.1	Negative desiderative *kuar* 'to not want' —— **486**	
7.3.8	Reason clause marker *puu-r* 'origin' —— **487**	
7.3.8.1	Linkers and *puu-r* —— **491**	
7.3.9	Serialization as a complementation strategy —— **492**	
7.4	Relative clauses —— **495**	
7.4.1	Relative clauses with relativizer *ki* 'REL' —— **496**	
7.4.2	Relative clauses with a determiner —— **497**	
7.4.3	Relative clauses with a relative pronoun —— **499**	
7.4.4	Identification of the relativized noun phrase —— **501**	
7.5	Summary —— **502**	

Appendix A: Glossing conventions —— **505**
Appendix B: Cited texts —— **509**
Appendix C: Speakers —— **511**
Appendix D: Sample interlinearized text —— **512**

References —— **551**
Index —— **565**

List of Figures

Chapter 1
Figure 1: Map of the Far North, New Caledonia —— 2
Figure 2: Map of New Caledonia —— 4
Figure 3: Kin terms in Belep —— 10
Figure 4: A coutume to ask permission to enter. Photo by L. Giordana, 2009 —— 12
Figure 5: A coutume for a wake in Belep. Photo by L. Giordana, 2009 —— 13
Figure 6: A coutume for a wedding in Balade, 2010 —— 14
Figure 7: Subgrouping of New Caledonian languages —— 18

Chapter 2
Figure 1: Labiovelar consonant /p^w/ in /p^{w}a/ 'hole' —— 50
Figure 2: Consonant + /u/ sequence in /pua-/ 'side' —— 51
Figure 3: Mean VOT by place of articulation —— 52
Figure 4: Mean corrected VOT by aspiration class —— 53
Figure 5: Mean raw duration of nasal and stop portions by place of articulation —— 56
Figure 6: Mean raw duration of voiceless and prenasalized stops (in a carrier phrase) by place of articulation —— 57
Figure 7: Mean duration of nasals and prenasalized stops (in a carrier phrase) by place of articulation —— 58
Figure 8: Vowels before [r], male speaker (age 70), in Hz —— 64
Figure 9: Vowels before [r], female speaker (age 20s), in Hz —— 65
Figure 10: Average formant values, female speaker (age 20s), in Hz —— 66
Figure 11: Average formant values, male speaker (age 70), in Hz —— 67
Figure 12: Intensity and pitch contours for /pata/ 'to tell' —— 72
Figure 13: Intensity and pitch contours for /kaac/ 'bitter' —— 72
Figure 14: Intensity and pitch contours for /kic/ 'liver' —— 73
Figure 15: Oral vs nasal vowels for male speaker (age 70), in Hz —— 75
Figure 16: Oral vs nasal vowels for female speaker (age 20s), in Hz —— 75
Figure 17: Spectrogram of final unreleased /p/ in /tep/ 'to clack' —— 79
Figure 18: Spectrogram for /potae/ 'to massage' —— 80
Figure 19: Spectrogram for /poto/ [poro] 'to be white' —— 80
Figure 20: Spectrogram for /puti/ [puri] 'snake' —— 81
Figure 21: Spectrogram of /tutowie/ [tuɹowie] 'to insult' —— 81
Figure 22: Spectrogram showing final [r] in the word /cuut/ 'to stand' —— 82
Figure 23: Spectrogram showing final [t̚] in the word /cuut/ 'to stand' —— 82
Figure 24: Spectrogram and waveform for Belep co 'whale' —— 83
Figure 25: Spectrogram of final affricate [c͡ç] in /pic/ 'Alexandrian laurel' —— 84
Figure 26: Spectrogram of /cekeen/ 'sacred' —— 85
Figure 27: Spectrogram of /makeek/ (a person's name) —— 85
Figure 28: Spectrogram of /kaki/ 'to look' —— 86
Figure 29: Spectrogram of uvular place of articulation in /jeek/ 'plant' —— 86
Figure 30: Spectrogram for /ma^{m}bo/ 'honey' —— 87
Figure 31: Spectrogram showing a prestopped nasal in /m^{w}anok/ 'moon' —— 88
Figure 32: Pronunciation of /wo^{m}b^{w}an/ 'tomb-3SG.POSS' showing fricated initial [β] —— 89
Figure 33: Spectrogram for /la= juu-n/ [laɹuun] '3PL.SUBJ= dig-DA.NSG' —— 89
Figure 34: Spectrogram of /piju/ 'star' showing fricative [j] —— 90

Figure 35: Spectrogram for ingressive airstream —— 92
Figure 36: Spectrogram for /titu/ [tiru] 'stake' —— 105
Figure 37: Spectrogram for *nao* 'to sing' —— 106
Figure 38: Spectrogram for *baraap* 'evening' —— 107

Chapter 3
Figure 1: Spectrogram of *mwanao* 'to approach' —— 130
Figure 2: Spectrogram of nasalized =*a* after nasal consonant —— 131

Chapter 4
Figure 1: View from the church in Waala, looking down towards the harbor —— 218
Figure 2: Map of Belep showing spatial directions —— 219

Chapter 6
Figure 1: Argument structure in Belep —— 362
Figure 2: Intonation curve for *te dadabwa*, continuing intonation —— 404
Figure 3: Intonation curve for *te dadabwa*, final intonation —— 404
Figure 4: Intonation curve for *te ulo?*, a yes-no question —— 405
Figure 5: Intonation curve for *êê* 'yes' —— 415

Chapter 7
Figure 1: Keenan and Comrie's (1977: 66) accessibility hierarchy —— 495

List of Tables

Chapter 1
Table 1: Clans of Belep —— 6
Table 2: Examples of given names in Belep —— 9
Table 3: Belep flagging alignment system —— 24

Chapter 2
Table 1: Consonant inventory —— 36
Table 2: Vowel inventory —— 36
Table 3: Mean VOT by place of articulation —— 51
Table 4: Loss of aspiration contrasts in Northern languages —— 54
Table 5: Mean duration of nasal and stop portions by place of articulation —— 57
Table 6: Mean raw duration of stops (in a carrier phrase) by place of articulation —— 58
Table 7: Mean raw duration of nasals and prenasalized stops —— 59
Table 8: Central approximant contrasts with sequences of vowels —— 59
Table 9: Mean duration of vowels —— 70
Table 10: Sequences of unlike vowels —— 73
Table 11: Phonetic consonant inventory —— 77
Table 12: Production of /c/ as [s] —— 84
Table 13: Mean duration of vowels —— 92
Table 14: Complete and incomplete phases, type 1 —— 96
Table 15: Complete and incomplete phases, type 2 —— 96
Table 16: Complete and incomplete phases, type 3 —— 96
Table 17: Orthographic equivalents —— 99
Table 18: Monosyllabic structures in Belep —— 101
Table 19: Disyllabic structures in Belep —— 101
Table 20: Trisyllabic structures in Belep —— 102
Table 21: Attested consonant onsets —— 102
Table 22: Attested vowel onsets —— 103
Table 23: Attested coda consonants —— 103
Table 24: Impossible phonotactic structures —— 110
Table 25: Sound symbolic forms —— 114
Table 26: Proper names —— 115
Table 27: Religious jargon in Belep phonology —— 116
Table 28: LATIN stratum —— 116
Table 29: French borrowings into BELEP —— 117
Table 30: FRENCH stratum —— 119

Chapter 3
Table 1: Adverbs in Belep —— 152
Table 2: Linkers in Belep —— 155
Table 3: Interjections and discourse markers in Belep —— 157
Table 4: Inflectional and derivational morphology in Belep —— 159

Chapter 4
Table 1: Compatibility of noun classes with possessive constructions —— 182
Table 2: Examples of class 1 nouns —— 182

Table 3: Examples of stem modification in class 1 nouns —— 184
Table 4: Examples of class 2 nouns —— 185
Table 5: Examples of class 3 nouns —— 187
Table 6: Examples of class 4 nouns —— 188
Table 7: Types of possessive construction in Belep —— 190
Table 8: Possessive suffixes —— 192
Table 9: Stem modification in possessed noun stems depending on what the possessor is indexed by —— 194
Table 10: Stem modification depending on what the possessor is indexed by —— 196
Table 11: Stem modification of free noun stems —— 201
Table 12: Noun classifiers —— 202
Table 13: Locative words —— 207
Table 14: Spatial system of Belep —— 218
Table 15: Determiner suffixes —— 220
Table 16: Deictic determiners —— 222
Table 17: Independent pronouns —— 241
Table 18: Demonstrative pronominal stems —— 243
Table 19: Demonstrative pronouns —— 254
Table 20: Interrogative pronouns —— 255
Table 21: Belep cardinal numerals, 1-20 —— 257
Table 22: Belep cardinal numerals, above 20 —— 257
Table 23: Ordinal numerals —— 258
Table 24: Days of the week —— 261
Table 25: Bingo numerals —— 261
Table 26: Numeral classifiers —— 262
Table 27: Numeric determiners —— 263
Table 28: Numeral classifier NPs —— 264

Chapter 5
Table 1: Predicates requiring an absolutive S argument —— 269
Table 2: Free transitive verbs —— 272
Table 3: Inherently bound transitive verb roots —— 274
Table 4: Inflection for specificity —— 276
Table 5: Environments where generic and specific forms may appear —— 277
Table 6: Intransitive and transitivized verb stems —— 281
Table 7: Verbs transitivized with *-li* —— 285
Table 8: Examples of the usage of *-u* 'DETRANS' —— 287
Table 9: Examples of differential absolutive suffixes —— 290
Table 10: Verb clitic group position classes —— 296
Table 11: Causativized verbs —— 297
Table 12: Aspect clitics —— 304
Table 13: Classes of aspect formatives in Belep —— 305
Table 14: Belep greetings —— 309
Table 15: Frequencies of mood and aspect morphemes —— 319
Table 16: Reduction of realis =ô —— 323
Table 17: Anaphoric absolutive suffixes —— 325
Table 18: Subject agreement clitics —— 331
Table 19: Grammaticalized verb roots —— 334
Table 20: Verb phrase enclitics —— 347

Table 21: Belep directionals —— **348**
Table 22: Spatial directionals and corresponding full verbs —— **348**
Table 23: Belep locationals —— **351**

Chapter 6
Table1: Verbs requiring an absolutive S argument —— **371**
Table 2: Ditropic clitic case markers —— **377**
Table 3: Pronominal predicate locatives —— **392**
Table 4: Predicate existential and locative verbs —— **397**
Table 5: Interrogative verbs —— **410**
Table 6: Inherently negative predicates —— **427**
Table 7: Structure of periphrastic causatives —— **433**
Table 8: Reflexive verbs —— **435**
Table 9: Temporal nouns —— **437**
Table 10: Comparative construction —— **441**

Chapter 7
Table 1: Linkers used in combining clauses and noun phrases —— **446**
Table 2: Modality of morphemes indicating semantic dependency —— **465**

List of Abbreviations

1	first person
2	second person
3	third person
A	anaphoric
ABS	absolutive case
AC	associative plural
ACT	actual
ADD	additive
ADU	associative dual
AGT	agentive
CAUS	causative
CL	numeral classifier
COMPL	completive
CONT	continuative
CTF	centrifugal (away from the speaker)
CTP	centripetal (toward the speaker)
D	deictic
DA	differential absolutive
DAT	dative case
DC	deictic center
DEM	demonstrative pronoun
DET	determiner
DETR	detransitive
DH	downhill
DIM	diminished
DIR	directional
DST	distal
DU	dual number
DUB	dubitative
DYAD	dyadic
EX	existential
EXCL	exclusive
GE	general extender
GEN	genitive case
GNO	gnomic
GNR	generic
HAB	habitual
IA	inanimate
IDF	identifiable

IMPER	imperative
INCL	inclusive
INDEP	independent pronoun
INSTR	instrumental
IRR	irrealis
ITER	iterative
LK	linker
LN	loanword
LOC	locative
MAN	manner
MDS	medial-distal
MPX	medial-proximal
NDR	unmarked for direction
NEC	necessative
NEG	negative
NEW	new
NOM	nominative case
NSG	nonsingular
NTR	intransitive
ORD	ordinal
PA	paucal number
PL	plural number
POSS	possessive
PRES	presentative
PRF	perfect
PROG	progressive
PRX	proximal
PUNCT	punctual
Q	interrogative
RA	reduced agentive
REAL	realis
RECP	reciprocal
REL	relativizer
RESULT	resultative
SBJ	subjunctive
SG	singular number
SPC	specific
SUBJ	subject agreement
TR	transitive
TV	transverse
UH	uphill
VBLZ	verbalizer

1   Background information

1.1   Introduction

This work is a reference grammar of the Austronesian language variety known as Belep, Yalayu, or Nyelâyu of Belep ([yly]), which is spoken by approximately 1600 people in New Caledonia (Kanaky[1]), primarily on the island of Art. This introductory chapter will discuss the cultural context and history of the speakers of the Belep language variety (§1.3), differentiate Belep from other closely-related language varieties, and describe its unique characteristics (§1.6). Section §1.4 situates Belep with respect to the Austronesian language family as a whole; section §1.7 focuses on the sociolinguistic situation of Belep speakers; section §1.5 enumerates currently available scholarship on this language variety, and §1.8 discusses the methodology used for the collection of data for the reference grammar.

1.2   Belep and its speakers

The approximately 1600 speakers[2] of the Belep language variety, who are known as Belema, live in the Pacific archipelago of New Caledonia (*Nouvelle-Calédonie*), which is located 1500 km east of Australia and 2000 km north of New Zealand.[3] New Caledonia, formerly an overseas territory of France, was classified as a *collectivité sui generis* or 'special collectivity' in 1998. The archipelago consists of a main island (*Grande-Terre*, or 'Mainland'), the Loyalty Islands to the northeast, the Isle of Pines to the southeast, and the Belep Isles, located approximately 50 km off the northwest tip of the Mainland. The Belep Isles are the ancestral home of the Belema, and consist of: the main islet Art[4] (with an area of about 70 square km), where about 800 Belema live permanently (J.-B. Moilou, p. c., August 9, 2010); the abandoned islet of Pott[5] to the

---

[1] Indigenous Melanesians of New Caledonia refer to themselves as Kanaks and often prefer the term Kanaky for their country.
[2] A French census placed the number of speakers located in Belep at 930 in 2004 (ISEE 2004). According to former mayor Jean-Baptiste Moilou, the total population of Belema was 1676 people in 2010 (J.B. Moilou, p.c., August 9, 2010).
[3] http://www.nouvelle-caledonie.gouv.fr/site/La-Nouvelle-Caledonie/Presentation
[4] This islet is called /ⁿdau at/ [ⁿdau ar], translated as 'isle of the sun' in the Belep language. In most published sources, it is spelled <Art>.
[5] This islet is called /poc/ in the Belep language; in published sources, it tends to be spelled <Pott> or <Phwoc>. It was historically a kingdom separate from Belep and had its own language, which is now lost. It maintains great religious significance for all Belema.

northwest of Art, which still houses many active Belema plantations and sacred sites; and three uninhabitable islets to the southeast of Art (Dubois 1985). See Figure 1 for a detailed map of this area. The other approximately 800 Belema live on the Mainland—two permanent communities of Belema exist in Mont-Dore and the Jardins de Belep in the South, and many individual Belema live scattered throughout the rest of the country for school or work, or because they have married into a different community.

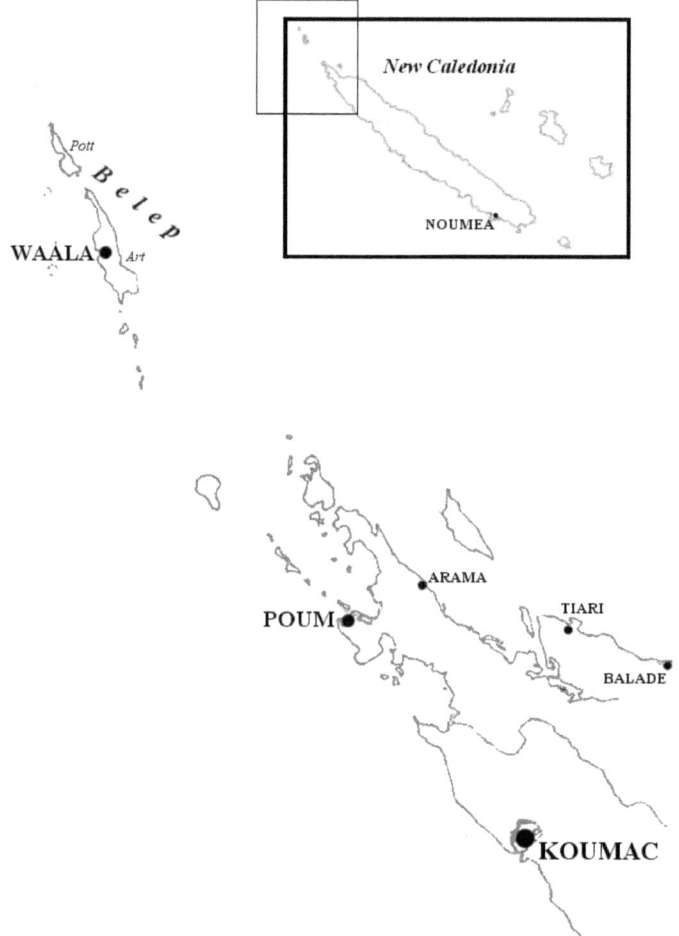

Fig. 1: Map of the Far North, New Caledonia. Adapted from DuBois (1985) and Bril (2002)

1.3 The Belema people

The culture of New Caledonian Kanaks sits at a crossroads between Melanesia and Polynesia, just as the archipelago itself sits at a nexus of these areas. New Caledonia was originally settled by Austronesians, though European observers (e.g. Dubois 1975a, Bensa 1988) have long sought evidence for earlier inhabitants. This search was largely motivated by Europeans' preoccupation with race—they were driven to posit that Melanesia and Polynesia were populated by different groups in order to explain the differing physical appearances of their inhabitants. Anthropologists are still divided over whether the distinction between Melanesia and Polynesia is a meaningful one, but have largely come to believe that a prolonged period of multifaceted interaction between the two regions and the existence of communities of practice among the peoples of the Pacific—rather than a single migration and subsequent divergent evolution—produced the large amount of cultural variation found in places such as New Caledonia (Thomas et al. 1989, Clark 2003).

Belep's location off the northwest tip of the Mainland (see Figure 1 above) places it within the purview of the Northern Province, a somewhat arbitrary French governmental division. Belep is incorporated as a *commune* (i.e. a 'town', with its own postal code) and has its own mayor elected from and by the local populace. Belep is also part of the Hoot ma Waap[6] *aire coutumière* 'customary area'—that is, a division chosen by Kanaks which more accurately reflects linguistic and cultural regions (this region is shaded on Figure 2 below).

Belep is one of many *tribus* 'tribes' in New Caledonia—a French word used by New Caledonians to mean 'reservation'. That is, in this nonstandard usage, *tribu* refers to 'a particular piece of land which is administered by Kanaks,' rather than to 'the people who live there'. Each *tribu* is under the authority of a distinct chieftain and contains the ancestral lands of several *clans* 'families'. Though several *tribus* may share a language, there is no Kanak term either for a *tribu* or for 'a group of people who share a language'. Language is a salient part of a person's identity, but it is most important as a signifier of his or her birthplace and natal clan—and thus as an indicator of which chieftain they are subject to. As a result, the ethnonyms used by the Belema consist largely of a chieftain's name followed by the suffix *-ma* (§4.3.1), which in this context indicates a group of people associated with the chieftain. For example, the *Bele-ma* are the subjects of *Teâ Belep*,[7] the high chief of Belep; the *Pu-ma* are the

---

6 The *Hoot ma Waap* region is named after two legendary brothers, called in Belep *Or* 'to spill' and *Waap* 'to topple'. The brothers gave their names to the two phratries (defined below) in the Far North; each *chefferie* in this region belongs either to the <Hoot> or the <Waap> (sometimes <Whaap>) phratry.

7 The Belep noun *teâ* has a variety of meanings; it may be a title for the chief of a group of people; it may refer to a *chef de clan* (the eldest man in a family), or to the chieftain's eldest son.

subjects of *Teâ Puma*,[8] the high chief of Balade; the *Nene-ma* are the subjects of *Teâ Nenemwa*, the high chief of Poum. There is no grammaticalized way to refer to a group of people who live in a particular place; for example, Belep speakers use the periphrastic *âju la Pwewo* 'people in Pouébo' to refer to all residents of Pouébo, where the high chief's dynasty is *Mwelebeng*.

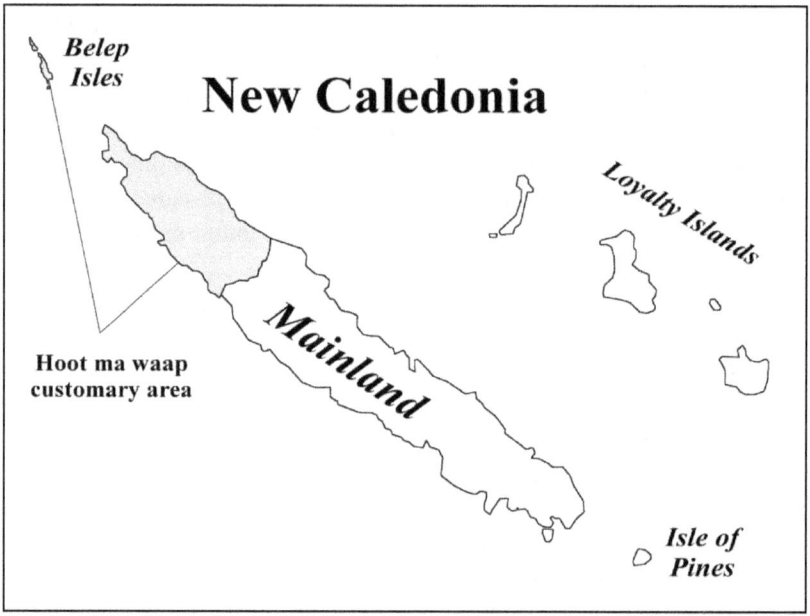

Fig. 2: Map of New Caledonia. Adapted from DuBois (1985) and Tschubby (2018).

It seems likely, then, that in Kanak society, a person's insoluble bonds to clan and family (and associated ancestral lands) are more important to their identity than the place they happen to live. Pre-colonized New Caledonia "was cross-cut geographically by long-standing patterns of alliance and enmity, which provided a context for constant small-scale movements of people and interrelationships of marriage and exchange," a state of affairs which at least existed in the Hoot ma Waap region, where Belep is located (Douglas 1990:26). These exchange networks were reinforced by patrilineal and patrilocal land ownership, as well as by a preference for exogamy in mar-

---

8 These are dynastic titles, rather than personal names; for example, the high chief of Koumac, *Teâ Kumwaak*, was César Boarat in 2012.

riage. In the North, "clans were divided between two mutually and permanently hostile networks" (Douglas 1982:393) called Hoot and Waap,[9] whose hostility was "complemented by similarly traditional and permanent marriage relationships" (Guiart 1957:23-24).[10] Guiart (1957) labeled these groups 'phratries' and observed that cross-phratry marriages were preferential. This situation is a likely contributor to the amount of linguistic diversity in New Caledonia (Grace 1991, 1995), and the maintenance of so many distinct language varieties in such a small area—there are at least 38 living languages in New Caledonia (Lewis et al. 2016). Stanford (2007:45-47) discusses several examples of linguistic exogamy contributing to the maintenance of distinct language varieties, including for the Sui people in China and several groups in Amazonia (Aikhenvald 2003). A comparable situation also exists among some groups in Arnhem Land (Warner 1937, Keen 2002, Hiscock 2008).

Within the wider culture of New Caledonia, Belep is often overlooked, left off of maps, and generally derided for its backwardness and independentism. For example, the website which advertises tourism in the Northern Province describes Belep thusly: "Far from everything, this little commune exists in a state of quasi-autarky, which has permitted it to remain authentic and to always champion a certain idea of independence." The article goes on to warn visitors of the lack of accommodations (Anonymous 2012).[11] In fact, Kanak culture is more strongly preserved in Belep than almost anywhere else in the country: most young Belema children are monolingual in Belep, nearly everyone still cultivates their ancestral yam plantations, and the cultural practices of *la coutume* (§1.3.2) are a major part of life. As the Northern Province website describes, "traditions are stronger [there] than elsewhere..."[12]

1.3.1 The clan in Belep

The basic unit of social organization in Belep society is the clan or extended family. The Belep word *âma naen* may be used narrowly to mean an individual nuclear family, with two parents and their children, or in its broader sense to mean a clan, a group of people sharing a last name and, crucially, a *totem* (Belep *janu* 'spirit'). Totems are

---

9 The Belema are part of the *Or* or <Hoot> phratry (Dubois 1975d, Guiart 1957), though the differentiation between the two phratries has become uncertain since French colonization.
10 « compensée par des relations matrimoniales, elles aussi traditionnelles et permanentes » (translation mine).
11 « Éloignée de tout, cette petite commune vit en quasi autarcie. Ce qui lui a permis de rester authentique et de toujours défendre une certaine idée de l'indépendance. Aujourd'hui, elle cherche pourtant à s'ouvrir davantage sur le monde et à casser cette image qui lui colle à la peau » (translation mine).
12 « Si vous vous y rendez, prévoyez une petite coutume pour le chef de tribu, car les traditions sont encore plus fortes ici qu'ailleurs...» (translation mine).

normally animals; their names are secret knowledge within the clan.[13] The Belep clan names (Belep *mewu-* 'variety')[14] are shown in Table 1, which is adapted from various sources (Menu et al. 2007-2008, L. Giordana, p.c., September 7, 2010).[15]

Tab. 1: Clans of Belep

Clan name	Belep form	Phonetic form	Possible etymology
BEALO	Bealo	[ᵐbealo]	
BELEP	Belep	[ᵐbelɛp]	
BOUANAOUE	Bwa na we	[ᵐbʷanāwe]	*bwa na we* 'head in water'
BOUEDAOU	Bwe dau	[ᵐbʷeⁿdau]	*bwe dau* 'on an island'
DAWILO	Dawilo	[ⁿdawilo]	
DAYE	Daye	[ⁿdaje]	
GUELEME	Geleme	[ᵑgelemē]	
(GUELE)	Gele	[ᵑgele]	
MOILOU	Mwalu	[mʷālu]	
OUALAIRI	Walairi	[walairi]	
OUIMO	Wimo	[wimō]	
PIDJO	Pijo	[piⁿɟo]	
PIGUIEPAT	-	-	-
POITHILI	Pwa cili	[pʷa cili]	*pwa cili* 'fruit of the thatch' or *pwa tili* 'fruit of attachment'
SHOUENE	Cuen	[cuɛn]	

---

13 Belep religious belief holds that people have two (or possibly three) souls: the *janu* 'spirit', the totem animal, which is the life-force given by one's ancestors, and which returns to one's ancestral homeland at death; and the *kânu* 'soul', the double, the carrier of the individual's personality, which goes to *Caviluumw* 'the Underworld' at death. Belema also have an *âyua-* 'desire', a person's will or the power of love, which is used to translate the Christian concept of the soul, and goes to the Christian Heaven at death (I. Moilou, p.c.).
14 The Belep noun *mewu-* 'variety' is used to refer both to a person's clan name and to a species of plant or animal; for example *mewu âju* 'a person's clan name'; *mewu pawi* 'species of hibiscus'. To inquire as to someone's given name, the locative question verb *iva* 'where?' is used, e.g. *iva naramw?* 'where is your given name?' The same construction is used to ask after a clan name, e.g. *iva mewuumw?* 'where is your clan name?'.
15 As is the custom in New Caledonia, surnames are written all in capital letters. The clan GUELE is shown in parentheses since the only remaining members are very old; it will end within a generation. The two TEAMBOUEON clans are distinguished from each other by the location of their clan lands, although this is not part of their surnames. There is also a YAMAMOTO family, composed of descendants of a single Japanese settler who arrived after French colonization.

Clan name	Belep form	Phonetic form	Possible etymology
TEANYOUEN	Teâ yuen	[teãjuɛn]	*teâ yuen* 'chief Yuen'
TEAMBOUEON (De Pairoome)	Teâ bwe ôn	[teãᵐbʷeõn]	*teâ bwe ôn* 'chief on the sand'
TEAMBOUEON (De Waala)	Teâ bwe ôn	[teãᵐbʷeõn]	*teâ bwe ôn* 'chief on the sand'
THALE	Cale	[cale]	
WAHOULO	Wa ulo	[waulo]	*wa ulo* [NOM= red] 'redness'
YARIK	Yarik	[jariq]	

Each clan owns its own lands throughout the Belep Isles, and these traditional homesteads (referred to as *plantations* in French and *nana pwang* 'bays' in Belep) are the sites where traditional agriculture and the transmission of folkways continue. The *plantations* are endowed with a mystical significance—a person cannot truly be a Kanak unless he plants and cultivates his own ancestral yam fields. This contrasts with the view of the clan's land holdings within the eight neighborhoods or *tribus* of Waala, which represent their (somewhat stifling) French identities, linked to the church, the school, and the government (Giordana 2014). The yam (*Dioscorea sp.*),[16] called *uvi* in Belep, is the most important crop for the Belema, and the cycle of the year is organized around its cultivation using swidden agriculture (Haudricourt 1964). A number of important strictures govern the cultivation of the yam due to its sacred nature and its symbolism (the yam symbolizes 'man', just as the *nu* 'coconut tree' symbolizes 'woman'). Yams cannot be wasted (leftovers must not be thrown away) and in older days it was forbidden to cut one with a knife. If a person 'insults' the yam by neglecting to follow these strictures, that person's yam fields could be cursed to never produce again, thus making that person unable to participate in cultural exchange networks (where yams are a necessity for wealth and status). Other major staples of traditional Belep agriculture are *manyook* 'manioc', *taro* 'taro', *kumwala* 'sweet potato', *walei* 'lesser yam/*Dioscorea esculenta*', and *bolao* 'banana'. This starchy diet was traditionally supplemented with fish and seafood, *bwak* 'flying fox' (French *roussette*),[17] and *puaxa* 'pork' from semi-domesticated pigs, likely a Polynesian import (Geraghty 1994). Although the domestic chicken (*Gallus gallus domesticus*) was introduced to New Caledonia by Europeans, there is some evidence for the presence of its wild counterpart, red junglefowl (*Gallus gallus*), prior to colonization (Lagarde & Ouetcho 2015); one or both of these birds are referred to by the native

---

16 At least three species of *Dioscorea* yam are habitually cultivated in Belep, although their scientific names are unknown.
17 The flying fox is the only mammal native to New Caledonia.

Belep word *jo* 'chicken'. Kava was unknown in New Caledonia prior to French colonization, though its use is now common (Russmann et al. 2003).

The traditional governance structure of Belep persists, despite the co-existence of French governance. Each clan has a male elder—a *chef de clan* (Belep *teâ* 'prince')—and a younger male representative. These two representatives from each clan serve in the *Conseil des anciens* (Belep *cuuyama*, from *cuuc* 'sage, judge'), the legislative body which supports the *grand-chef* (Belep *teâmaa* 'high chief'). Chieftaincy is hereditary in the WAHOULO clan, so-called because the legendary ancestor *Teâ Belep* was said to be red-headed.[18] A few other clans also have special roles in governance: the THALE serve as the official *porte-paroles* 'spokesmen' of the chief (Belep *teâ pulu* 'chief of words'); the POITHILI hunt the sacred *modap* 'manatee' and supply it to the chief; the BOUEDAOU are the guardians of the *chefferie* (Belep *kavebu* 'chief's home') and supply a new chief if there is a crisis of succession (A. Wahoulo, p.c., 20 Sept. 2011). In activities such as the construction of a new ceremonial hut for the *kavebu* and the yearly yam festival *Dao uvi*, all clans contribute or participate in some way. This balance between, on the one hand, the chief's absolute spiritual authority, and, on the other, his role as merely the 'first among equals', is found throughout New Caledonia (Bensa & Goromido 1997). The traditional Belep system of government is thus representative of both Polynesian and Melanesian traditions—hereditary chiefdom is a characteristic of Polynesia, while egalitarian societies depending on exchange networks are characteristic of Melanesia (Spriggs 1997).

New Caledonian custom is to write personal names in the format [CLANNAME Givenname] (*nara-* 'given name'). Many Belema have both an official French given name and a 'nickname' in the Belep language; however, some Belema have only one given name which suffices in both languages. Table 2 shows a few examples of given names.

Note that there is a phonetic correspondence between some of the pairs (e.g. French *Alice* [alis] and Belep *Aliic* [aliic]; French *Philippe* [filip] and Belep *Pilip* [pilip]), while others do not appear to be related. Belep names which also have lexical meanings tend to be bird names or other animal names (e.g. *Ileli* 'snipe', *Kolori* 'dark brown honeyeater', *Caivak* 'rat', *Gom* 'type of sea cucumber'). The children of the chief always receive the same names: the first son is *Teâ*, the second son is *Mweau*; the first daughter is *Kawo*, the second daughter *Ixe*; the last child is *Jegoloc*. In the past, it was taboo for Belema to say the given name of their opposite-sex sibling or cousin, and many elderly speakers still practice this custom.[19]

---

18 The etymology of the Belep clan name WAHOULO is likely /wa= ulo/ {RESULT= be.red} 'redness'.
19 There are a number of other taboos between opposite-sex siblings and cousins: they may not see each other naked, share clothing, sit on the same bench, etc.

Tab. 2: Examples of given names in Belep

French	Belep	French	Belep
Marie-Odile	Pato	-	Dao nu
Benjamin	Korowi	Philippe	Pilip
Jean-Baptiste	Gerâ	Yasmine	Mina
Hortense	Jajani	Cassandra	Kacaca
Albert	Weli	Gal	Gan
Magali	-	Ignacia	Acia
Eliane	-	Alice	Aliic
-	Weloo		

In Belep, a woman's children born before her marriage belong to her clan (they are usually formally adopted and raised by her maternal uncle or another male relative). When a woman marries, her husband's clan purchases her from her clan—she becomes a member of her husband's clan, and her subsequent children belong to her husband's clan. A person is seen as 'belonging' to his or her maternal uncle (French *tonton*), such that at death his or her clan makes a large ceremonial gift to the clan of the *tonton* (as elsewhere in New Caledonia; see Bensa & Goromido 1997). Given the importance of the *tonton* to Belep social structure, we would expect that there would be a unique word for this person (especially considering that the *tantine*—the wife of the *tonton* or the father's sister—has a special name, *âno* 'aunt'); however, most Belema use only the French term *tonton*, and one speaker told me that the maternal uncle is called *nya-* 'mother' in Belep. Dubois (1975f) seems to have found a different word *wânairiye-*, as shown in the chart of kin terminology in Figure 3 though it is no longer in use. The importance of the maternal uncle is a Melanesian characteristic (Panoff 1976). Figure 3 shows that mother's sisters are mothers (*nya-* 'mother'), and father's brothers are fathers (*cama-* 'father'). Mothers, fathers, and grandparents each have a separate vocative form: mother is *nyanya*, father is *caya*, and grandparent is *wa*. Parallel cousins are siblings (*ava-* 'sibling or parallel cousin', often referred to as *cousins germains* 'first cousins' in French), while cross-cousins (*bega-* 'cross-cousin') are noted by Dubois (1975f) as preferential spouses, a practice which seems to have fallen out of favor today, likely due to Christianization. Sibling's spouse and spouse's sibling are the same (*bee-* 'sibling-in-law'), and child's spouse and spouse's parent are the same (*moo-* 'parent/child-in-law'). Belep kin terms apart from 'mother' and 'father' do not distinguish between males and females; if this is necessary for clarity, speakers may modify a kin term with *tamwa* 'female' or *âc* 'male' as in e.g. *avang âc* [sibling-1SG.POSS male] 'my male sibling'.

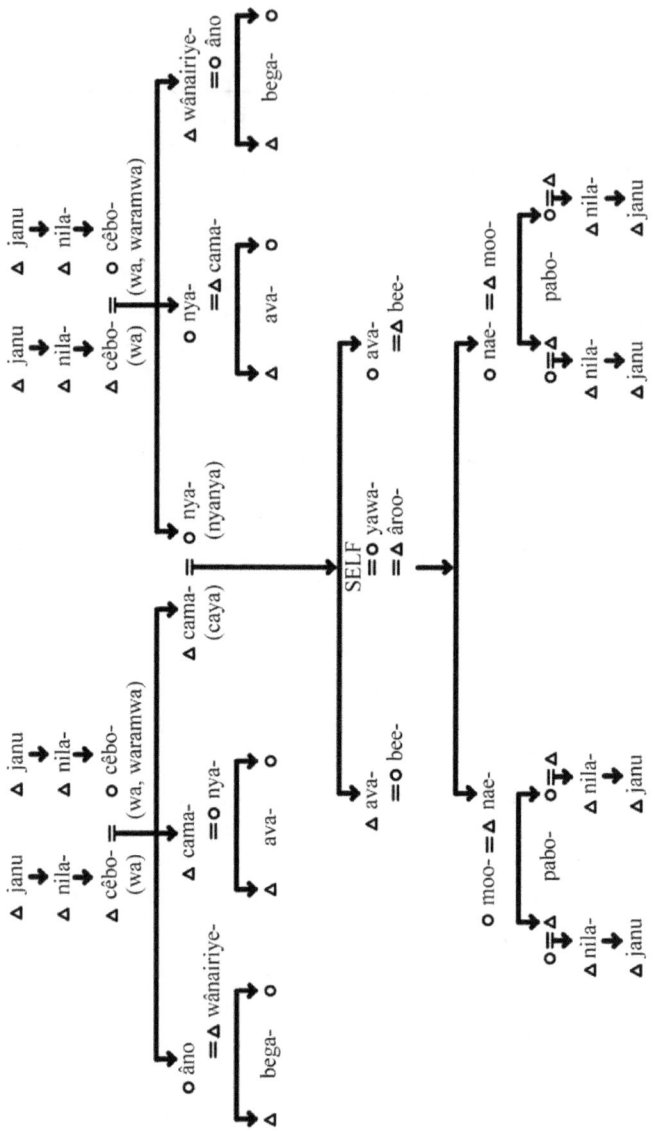

Fig. 3: Kin terms in Belep after Dubois (1975f)

1.3.2 *La coutume*

While the most important societal unit in Belep is the clan, the most important principle of social life is referred to in French as *la coutume*. This translates literally into English as 'the custom' (see similarities with Kastom in Vanuatu (Keesing 1982)) but there is no word in Belep for it. This is due to the fact that the French term *la coutume* subsumes a vast array of interrelated cultural practices in Belep society.

A great deal of anthropological literature describes exchange networks in Melanesia (Kirch 1991, Gell 1992, Brunton 1971, etc.). These networks are sustained by ritual gifting of culturally significant objects. In New Caledonia, "Melanesians set far greater store by acts of exchange and the relationships and meanings they mediated and expressed than by the objects as such, though objects were essential to maintain the flow and symbolize the rhythm of exchange relationships" (Douglas 1992:109).

La coutume places objects, and the social relationships they represent, in a constant flow of possession and reciprocity. Among New Caledonian Kanaks, to exchange ritual gifts is to *faire la coutume* 'to do the custom' (see §1.7 on the relationship between French and Belep), and it typically occurs in conjunction with all important social interactions: visiting someone's home, leaving someone's home, asking permission for something, asking for a favor, begging forgiveness, gathering to discuss something, gathering to have fun, etc. Kanaks believe, however, that it is not the gift itself which is important (this is merely a *geste* 'gesture' in French), but rather the words one speaks during the ritualized act of giving. Speech in *la coutume* is thus viewed as sacred.

In Belep, a specific set of discourse norms constrain such speech.[20] Speakers (as well as observers) in *la coutume* bow their heads, clasp their hands behind their backs (to indicate a lack of hostile intent), and lower their voices to just above a whisper, even if they are addressing a large crowd. This posture is intended as a gesture of respect to the *janu* 'spirits' of the ancestors, who are present whenever someone decides to *faire la coutume*. Public *coutumes* are limited to male speakers only, although women practice similar rituals in private among themselves. Speakers begin a *coutume* by addressing and naming their audience and describing the purpose of the *coutume*—that is, which social relationships and functions it is intended to address. Then they move into the functional portion, where they express their emotions about the relationship with uninhibited honesty. Finally, speakers mention their ritual gift, with a hope that it will be accepted as a token of their emotion, and terminate the *coutume* by saying *yet, toven* [end finish] 'that's all, I'm done'. The crowd of observers responds with *ole* [thank] 'thank you'. In all but the most fraught of circumstances, the speaker's gift will be accepted with a similar speech by his addressee; this may also be accompanied by a reciprocal gift. This 'return of *la coutume*' is called *yayila* in Belep.[21]

---

[20] These norms are highly variable from *tribu* to *tribu*; even in Balade, the discourse norms for *la coutume* are quite different.

[21] The scope of this word—whether it applies to all *coutumes* or merely some—is unknown.

Though there is not one individual word in Belep which subsumes all cultural practices referred to by *la coutume*, a number of words exist to identify particular types of *coutume*. A *daxu* is a small *coutume*, as one might give to ask permission to enter the home of a person or a sacred site, or to beg forgiveness for a small slight. This minimally consists of a bolt of fabric and a small amount of money, and often includes tobacco as well. Figure 4 shows the acceptance of such a *coutume* by the *grand-chef* WAHOULO Amabili.

Fig. 4: A *coutume* to ask permission to enter. Photo by L. Giordana, 2009.

One type of *daxu* is the *pwawak* or *âna pwawak*, where a visitor to a sacred site (such as Pott) offers tribute to the spirits of that site to avoid offending them. For example, one speaker described his tribute to the spirits of Pott[22] as sandals, a t-shirt, cigarettes, matches, and clothing. "I took them and placed them [on a sacred rock] like this, and said 'May you return the Tahitian that you took', and left them there."[23] As this story shows, people who do not perform a *pwawak* will be punished by the spirits; such a person is *wac* 'a denier, disrespectful of *la coutume*'.

---

22 This was a *coutume* of apology. The speaker's brother-in-law, an ignorant Tahitian, entered the sacred place without performing a *pwawak* and was punished by being turned invisible and held hostage by the spirits. This *pwawak* was performed to appease the spirits and apologize.
23 Yal-28072010-BGMCG-tahitian_0143-0170

A *pwaxu* is a large *coutume*, such as those assembled for major events like marriages and funerals.

Fig. 5: A *coutume* for a wake in Belep. Photo by L. Giordana, 2009.

Figure 5 shows the presentation of numerous yams as part of the *ola nuyan*, the gift from the deceased person's clan to the clan of their maternal uncles, a week after the person's death. The related *auvaa* is a ceremony which occurs at the end of a clan's official yearlong mourning period. This word is a loan from Nêlêmwa with the meaning 'good speech' and is performed by the *grand-chef*.

A modern French expression used often in Belep is: *on vit dans la coutume* 'we live in *la coutume*'. For the Belema, such cultural exchanges are seen not as confined to special occasions; they make up the fabric of daily life, securing and reifying people's social relationships and economic well-being, which are indistinguishable in Belema culture.

Fig. 6: A *coutume* for a wedding in Balade, 2010.

Figure 6 shows a *buac*, which is given by the man's clan to reserve a woman for marriage.[24] For such large *coutumes*, each person or family unit within a clan contributes his or her *paa-n* 'obligation-3SG.POSS', a small amount of rice, sugar, coffee, tea, yams, bananas, etc. which will be combined to form the large clan gift.

1.3.3 History of Belep

New Caledonia is believed to have been originally settled by the Austronesians around 1200 BCE, as suggested by Lapita[25] pottery evidence. By the first century of the Common Era, the long-distance exchange networks that characterized Austrone-

---

24 The word *buac* is also the name of a tree, *Fagraea berteroana* (French *bois tabou* 'taboo tree'), which is used to carve the rooftop spires that adorn and protect Kanak *cases* 'huts'.
25 'Lapita' is a term used by archeologists to refer to a certain type of pottery which is found throughout the Pacific and is considered to be evidence of a common material culture in the region. Lapita pottery has been linked with the Austronesian people (Spriggs 1997).

sian settlement in Melanesia had ceased to operate (Spriggs 1997). Following this period in Belep, oral histories suggest that the clans were largely autonomous, with independent governance and war between clans: in one story, Teâ Boa (presumably the chieftain of clan Boa) was killed by Teâ Polo, who later became the leader of several unified clans with his seat at Bweo (Dubois 1975d). At some point in the dynasty of Teâ Polo, a tsunami devastated the northeast coast of Art, destroying a village at Ono (Sousmarin). This may have been linked to the massive volcanic eruption of Kuwae in Vanuatu in 1452 CE (Spriggs 1997).

Around 1300 CE, power struggles in Polynesia led disaffected Polynesians to voyage west (Spriggs 1997). Oral histories suggest that some landed in New Caledonia near Hienghène (on the northeast coast of the Mainland) and dispersed to the north (Dubois 1985). Around 1540 CE, as a result of these migrations, Teâ Belep, the younger brother of a chief of Gomen (on the northwest coast of the Mainland), traveled north to Belep with two of his subjects after a dynastic struggle. Teâ Polo's alliance was still in effect in Belep; after a war between Teâ Polo and Teâ Belep, the two agreed to split the territory on the island of Art—Belep establishing his seat at Pairome—and rename the island group in Belep's honor (Dubois 1985, AW6).

Belep expanded his rule through marriage alliances, including one with the daughter of Teâ Pûnivaac, the clan chief of Mwan on the islet of Pott. Belep's son gained further dominance for the Belep dynasty by conquering Teâ Polo. By the 1700s CE, according to oral histories, the Belep dynasty had solidified its rule over all the clans of Art, and the chief began to call himself *teâmaa* 'high chief' (Dubois 1985).

Chief Waulo Chahup II Amabili, who lived from 1815 to 1877, led the united clans of Art in war against other groups on the Mainland, including the people of Balabio, Gomen, Koumac, and Hienghène. Around 1845-1850, Chahup also brought Pott under his rule when he killed Teâ Pûnivaac. Rejected by his people, Chahup fled to Balade, where he encountered the French missionaries Père Lambert and Père Montrouzier (Kasarhérou et al. 2007:33-34). (New Caledonia had been claimed as a French colony in 1853 (IEOM 2011).) On 9 January 1856, Chahup and the missionaries landed in Belep. Chahup moved his seat from Bweo to Waala, where a mission church was built, and was baptized in 1859, also encouraging his subjects to be baptized (Dubois 1975a).

The century that followed the first contact with European colonials was a painful and difficult one for the Belema, as shown by various historical records. From 1864-1897, about 22,000 French convicts and political prisoners arrived in New Caledonia (IEOM 2011). Under Chahup's successor, Alphonse Yââma Mweau (1842-1913), the islet of Pott was appropriated by the French government for colonization (from 1960-1975, the Belema would work to accumulate enough money to buy it back). In 1878, 350 dissidents from Boulouparis (on the Mainland) were exiled to Belep. From 1892-1898, the Belema were themselves exiled to Balade when Belep was designated as a leper colony (Kasarhérou et al. 2007). Leprosy among the returned Belema was not eliminated until the 1950s (Dubois 1975g:137).

In the past fifty years, the standard of living in Belep has risen considerably, with both an increase in colonial influence and the rise of a nascent Kanak identity. Around 1955, an airstrip was built in Waala (Dubois 1975a). A modern medical clinic, serviced by a French doctor and nurses, was also built. In 1961, Belep became a commune; its first mayor was elected in 1969 (Kasarhérou et al. 2007). In the 1980s, the movement for Kanak independence became violent (during a period called Les Evènements 'the Events'), and—according to my consultants—many Belema emigrated to the Mainland due to political divisions.

Today Belep struggles to obtain resources from the French administration (the boats and airplanes which service Belep are irregular at best), to provide support for its children (who must attend boarding school on the Mainland after age 12, a situation which causes many psychological and academic difficulties), and to establish more permanent settlements throughout Art. The *enclavement* 'ghettoization' of the entire population into the village of Waala—due to the presence there of the only church, school, and grocery stores—is viewed by the Belema as contributing to the widespread alcoholism and discontent among the population (as described in Hamelin et al. 2009).

1.4 Belep within the Austronesian language family

The language variety spoken in Belep (referred to here as 'Belep'; see §1.6.1) is a member of the Remote Oceanic branch of the Austronesian language family. The languages of Melanesia have been called "aberrant" due to the irregularity of sound changes from their presumed common ancestor with the Polynesian languages, Proto-Oceanic (Grace 1991). Subgrouping within these languages using the comparative method of phonological innovation has proved difficult in many cases, so linguists have used limited correspondence sets such as pronouns, kinship terms, and morphological affixes to make their hypotheses (Lynch & Tryon 1985, Geraghty 1988, Lynch & Ozanne-Rivierre 2001).

Several explanations have been put forward for the reasons behind this apparent resistance by Melanesian languages to the use of the comparative method. Early lexicostatistic argumentation by Dyen (1965) in particular claimed that Melanesia was in fact the homeland of the Austronesian family; this view has been discredited (Blust 2013). Other theories (Ray 1926, Capell 1962) tried to explain the aberrancy through the substratum influence of nearby language families (chiefly Papuan) and the idea of 'mixed' languages that were no longer Austronesian. This view has also been refuted (Grace 1985). The most likely explanation at this point seems to be that of Grace (1985)—that the Melanesian languages form a Sprachbund or a series of linguistic areas as well as being genetically related, and that this lack of boundaries between languages and between dialects has led to heavy borrowing and code-switching to the point that the original lines of descent are blurred. The obscuring of linguistic boundaries is also reflected in the fact that current disagreements exist over the precise number of languages in New Caledonia.

It seems fairly widely accepted that the languages of Mainland New Caledonia form two subgroups, North and South (Leenhardt 1946, Haudricourt 1971), where the North has been further divided into subgroups (Ozanne-Rivierre 1992, 1995, Rivierre 1993) and the South cannot be further subdivided based on current knowledge (Grace 1991, 1992, 1995). Ozanne-Rivierre's (1995) subgrouping of the Northern languages uses the comparative method to classify these languages into two subgroups, Far North and North. Of the five Far North languages, Nyelâyu alone in its subgroup underwent a number of phonological changes that its neighbors (Nêlêmwa/Nixumwak, Caaàc, and Yuanga) do not share (*k>Ø, *c>y *t>c) (Ozanne-Rivierre 1995:62). The most widely accepted subgrouping of the New Caledonian languages[26] is summarized in Figure 7. Belep is presumed to be subsumed under Nyelâyu in this classification; it is represented in parentheses.

Little documentation exists on most of the New Caledonian languages, and the Northern languages are particularly sparsely documented. Bril (2002) and Rivierre (1980) are the only complete reference grammars describing Northern languages (Nêlêmwa-Nixumwak and Cèmuhî respectively). A few other Northern languages have sketch grammars—the Voh-Koné varieties (Rivierre & Ehrhart 2006), 45 pages; Caaàc and other varieties spoken in the commune of Pouébo (Hollyman 1999), 18 pages; the languages of Hienghène: Pije, Fwâi, Nemi, and Jawe (Haudricourt & Ozanne-Rivierre 1982), 59 pages total; Yuanga (Bretteville 1993), 16 pages; Balade Nyelâyu (Ozanne-Rivierre et al. 1998), 42 pages. Rivierre (1983), a dictionary of Paicî, contains no grammatical information.

---

26 This work will use the term 'New Caledonian languages' to refer to the genetic subgrouping within Remote Oceanic. The term 'languages of New Caledonia' will be used to refer to all languages spoken in New Caledonia, including those outside the genetic subgroup.

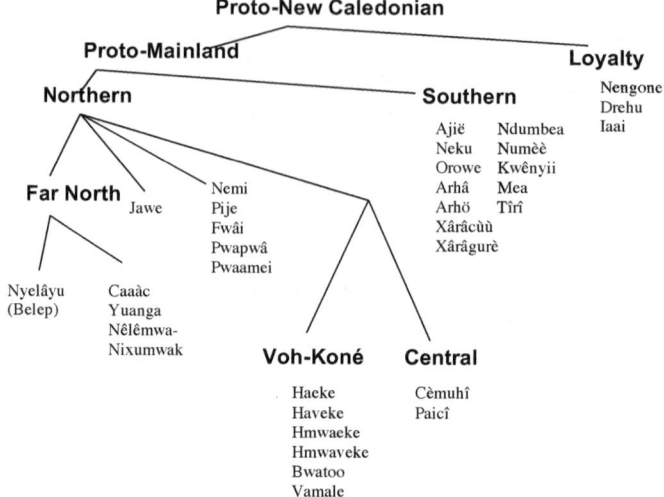

Fig. 7: Subgrouping of New Caledonian languages. Adapted from Ozanne-Rivierre (1995) and Haudricourt (1971).

1.5 Previous research on the Belep language

Prior to this research project, all linguistic data collection in the Belep Isles has been conducted by Marist missionaries of the Roman Catholic Church. The first text published in a Kanak language was the Belep narrative "Le chef de Touho", which was transcribed by one of the first missionaries to Belep, Père Pierre Lambert (who served from 1856-1863), and published in 1900 without glosses. Lambert also published a book of Belema religion and mythology (Lambert 1900) and kept a journal from 1855-1875 (Lambert 1855-1859, 1860-1875). These journals are stored on microfilm in the Archives of New Caledonia. Other texts, including a translated catechism, were transcribed by Lambert and his fellow missionaries in a mix of Belep and Balade Nyelâyu. These were copied in 1940 by Père Marie-Joseph Dubois. All of Dubois' copies but one were burned in 1955 by a "zealous priest" (since recitation of the Mass in the vernacular was officially forbidden prior to the Second Vatican Council, 1962-1965). Dubois's single surviving copy was given to Père Jean-Baptiste Neyret, who was still serving as priest there in 1973 when Dubois was sent to Belep on an ethnolinguistic mission by the Centre national de la recherche scientifique (CNRS), France's largest governmental research body.

A microfilmed manuscript collection catalogued under Neyret's name includes a year's worth of Masses, glossed and translated; a Belep/French dictionary; and a hymnal of translated hymns, which was also published in book form and is owned by most members of the Belema community. It is unclear how much of this work Neyret did himself, and how much of it is Lambert's work, if any (Neyret 1974 a-c).

This collection is owned by a few libraries, most of them in Australia, and is generally non-circulating.

Dubois's work, based on three field trips to Belep, was microfilmed as a manuscript collection in an edited version in 1975. This collection, a copy of which is owned by a few US libraries, includes: a Belep/French dictionary, a corpus of roughly glossed texts based on 8 hours of recordings on magnetic tape (the original recordings have not been located as of this writing), a dictionary of proper names of Belep, a genealogy of Belep, and a historical sketch (Dubois 1975 a-g). Various parts of these manuscripts were combined in a published book (Dubois 1985). Dubois's work also references the parish records of the Belep Mission (n.d.), which have not been located.

A few digital recordings of Far North languages are held in the Tjibaou Cultural Center in Nouméa. They include: a reading of a few lines from a well-known text that was part of Leenhardt's 1956-1958 linguistic survey, read by speakers from Belep, Pott, Poum, Tiari, and elsewhere (Leenhardt 1958); and recordings of several Belema music and dance performances interspersed with some Belep discourse (Dahl 1984, Ammann 1994, Nomoigne 1994).

In addition to these works on Belep, a great deal of other work has been done on the variety of Nyelâyu (§1.6.1) spoken in Balade, the site of the first European landing and the first Catholic Mission. Balade priests produced a constant stream of work on the local language beginning in the mid-19th century—mainly word lists and translations of Catholic texts into the vernacular. Many of these documents were reprinted in Ozanne-Rivierre et al. (1998), and those that were not reprinted were incorporated into the dictionary section of that work.

In the 20th century, historical reconstruction of Proto-New Caledonian and the establishment of its relationship to Proto-Oceanic has been one of the main focuses of linguists' research on the New Caledonian languages. The researchers carrying out this task have been mainly French linguists working for CNRS.

Leenhardt (1946) and Haudricourt (1971) contain comprehensive surveys of all the New Caledonian languages. Each spends only a few pages discussing the Far North languages as a whole, and neither provides any specifics about Belep or Balade Nyelâyu.

Ozanne-Rivierre and Mazaudon wrote a lexicon of Nyelâyu in 1986, but it is unpublished and stored only in the CNRS archive. Presumably[27] the data it contained was included in Ozanne-Rivierre et al. (1998), a 44-page sketch grammar, plus a dictionary and a collection of 6 texts (5 with interlinear glosses) in Balade Nyelâyu. This work contains useful information on phonology, although the grammatical sketch is understandably lacking in detail; as an illustration, the example sentences clearly

---

27 This presumption has yet to be verified.

show the language to be split-ergative, but there is no discussion of argument structure in the sketch grammar. Ozanne-Rivierre does, however, call the language split-ergative in her later article on complex predicates in Oceanic languages (2004).

Ozanne-Rivierre (1992, 1995, 2000), Rivierre (1993), and Ozanne-Rivierre & Rivierre (1989) primarily discuss the subgrouping of the New Caledonian languages, incorporating a few lexical items and data from Balade Nyelâyu. Hollyman (1999) is a collection of essays on the Far North languages, in particular on Polynesian loanwords in New Caledonia and the difference between personal and non-personal possession.

1.6 The Belep language

The Belema believe their language is extremely important for the preservation of cultural traditions and the wisdom of the elders. Speakers also believe their language is "easy to learn". In 1999, a committee of Belep teachers was formed in order to develop and formalize a writing system for use in the elementary school.[28] This *Comité de langue* 'Language Committee', though directed by the school, also had representatives from the *chefferie*,[29] the *mairie*,[30] and the church. The Committee adopted an official alphabet (based on orthographies developed for surrounding languages) and collected several wordlists, but was stymied in its efforts to continue by a delay in communication with the *Académie des langues kanak* (ALK) and the government of the Northern Province. In 2011, the ALK made its first official visit to Belep and gave its official sanction to the work of the Committee, stipulating that the Committee should become autonomous and open to all Belema. This was the first public recognition of the right of the Belema to linguistic self-determination.

1.6.1 Language name

The name of the language variety spoken in Belep is not agreed upon by all parties. In most authoritative existing literature, the Belep variety is classified as a dialect of Nyelâyu (or Nyâlayu, Yalayu [yly]), the language spoken in the Mainland villages of Balade, Arama, and Tiari (Lewis et al. 2016, Ozanne-Rivierre et al. 1998, Bril 2002). This classification is based on the findings of a linguistic survey of New Caledonia

---

28 Note that the Belep primary school is a private Catholic institution rather than one under the control of the French government.
29 French *chefferie* 'chiefdom' refers literally to the chief's home and metonymically to traditional Kanak governance structures.
30 French *mairie* 'city hall' refers literally to the building where the mayor's office is located and metonymically to colonial French government structures.

conducted in the 1970s; the results were published in Haudricourt (1971) and Haudricourt et al. (1979). The Belep data collected for that survey were gathered by Père Dubois, an ethnographer and priest with some training in linguistics, who made two field trips to Belep between 1940 and 1943 and another in 1973. His manuscript collection contains an account (Dubois 1975a) of his realization that the religious dialect he had learned was different from the language that the people were speaking in their daily communication, which they called *pulu Belep* 'language of Belep'. It is unclear how Dubois's findings were interpreted to posit an analysis whereby Belep was considered a dialect of Nyelâyu. Hollyman (1999), corroborating Leenhardt (1946), lists Belep and Nyelâyu as separate languages, with the latter being spoken in both Balade and Belep. This interpretation fits best with my findings.

Certainly, considerable cultural, religious, and familial ties exist between Belep and Balade. Balade was the site of the first Catholic mission in New Caledonia, and the priests who converted the Belema were sent from there (the surrounding villages of Koumac and Poum are, by contrast, largely Protestant). Marriage and familial ties between Belep and Balade date from at least the mid-1800s—the missionary translators of the catechism and other religious texts into the Belep vernacular used a Puma consultant (that is, someone originating from Balade; she was the mother of the *teâmaa* of Belep), which led to their being written in a mixed language variety (Dubois 1975a). Marriage ties may be more ancient, however; cultural practice encourages Kanaks to marry outside their phratry, and the Belema (who belong to the *Or* phratry) differ from the Puma (who belong to the *Waap* phratry), though this division (Dubois 1975a) is less clear today. From 1892-1898, the population of Belep was exiled to Balade to make way for a leper colony, further strengthening the relationship between the two groups (Kasarhérou et al. 2007). Ozanne-Rivierre's main consultant for the Balade variety (Ozanne-Rivierre et al. 1998), BOIGUIVIE Scholastique (the representative *académicienne* of the ALK in the Hoot ma Waap customary area), is a relative of several of my consultants in Belep. During Mme. BOIGUIVIE's official visit to Belep in 2011, her speech (in the Balade variety) before the Belep Language Committee was easily comprehensible for the Belema.

However, many differences exist between the two varieties. A cursory dictionary comparison[31] yields about one quarter of basic vocabulary that differs between the two varieties; Belep has a much reduced phonemic inventory from Balade Nyelâyu, and they have different basic word order, argument structure, and morphosyntactic organization. In 2010, I recorded speech in Balade and played it for several young people in Belep who lack significant ties to Balade; they could not understand

---

31 This comparison uses Belep words collected in my field work and Balade Nyelâyu words from Ozanne-Rivierre's (1998) dictionary. The wordlist used for comparison is a list of Austronesian basic vocabulary (Greenhill et al. 2008); in approximately 100 words, 25 tokens differed phonologically to a significant degree between the two language varieties.

it. Belema are fairly evenly divided on whether or not the varieties are "the same language"—consultants agree that a child from Balade and a child from Belep who have never visited the other place would not be able to communicate; however, many speakers feel strongly that the two varieties should be considered to be the same as a marker of identity.

My own observation is that, while the two varieties are not mutually intelligible to monolinguals, many speakers with familial ties to the other place learn both varieties from an early age, not realizing that they are learning multiple varieties. Thus, while purely linguistic evidence suggests that Belep and Balade should be classified as separate varieties, the decision whether to identify them as separate 'languages' is an ideological one which may take many other factors into account. Ultimately, it is the political responsibility of the Belep Language Committee, in consultation with the ALK, to decide the official standing and designation of their language variety in relation to Balade Nyelâyu.

Though some have proposed that the Belep variety should be called Belep Nyelâyu, I will refer to it only as 'Belep' throughout this work. This choice is based on current usage in Belep, in which *Belep* occurs as an autonym and in parallel to designations for other languages, as in (1) and (2).

(1)   *Mo tao pulu Belep !*
      mo   tao=   pulu   Belep
      LK3   HAB=   speak   Belep
      'Hey, keep speaking Belep!'

(2)   *Wara pulu français, pulu Belep !*
      wara=   pulu   [pɾãje]   pulu   Belep
      NEG.IMPER=   speak   French.LN   speak   Belep
      'Don't speak French, speak Belep!'

Speakers may also use *pulu Belep* as an autonym, as in (3).

(3)   *Iva naramw mwa na pulu Belep ?*
      iva   nara-mw=a   na   pulu   Belep
      be.where.GNR   name-2SG.POSS=LOC   interior   speech   Belep
      'What's your name in the language of Belep?'

Only Belep speakers who have read the existing literature on New Caledonian linguistics refer to their language variety as Nyelâyu. For these reasons, I will use 'Nyelâyu' in this description to refer strictly to the variety spoken in Balade. The term 'Belep' will refer to the variety spoken by the consultants who contributed to this study.

1.6.2 Linguistic profile of Belep

Belep grammar has much in common with that of other New Caledonian languages, as well as other neighboring languages of Island Melanesia and Fiji. It also has many characteristics that mark it as unusual, both cross-linguistically and within its subgroup (see §1.4) of Far North New Caledonian languages.

Belep has eighteen contrastive consonants and ten contrastive vowels in its phonology. This is a dramatically smaller number than in its sister languages—for example, Nêlêmwa has thirty consonants and twelve vowels (Bril 2000); Balade Nyelâyu has thirty-three consonants and twenty vowels (Ozanne-Rivierre et al. 1998). The major difference is that Belep lacks the aspiration contrast in voiceless stops, nasals, and approximants which exists in these other languages. Vowel-length contrasts do exist in Belep; however, "long" vowels should be considered to be sequences of like vowels. Belep is noteworthy for its unusual intonation pattern (referred to by observers as a "singing" intonation) whereby the first syllable carries the intensity peak, the penultimate syllable carries stress and stress-induced vowel lengthening, and the final syllable carries the pitch peak.

Belep morphology is considerably more complex than that of its neighboring languages, which are largely isolating. Belep morphosyntax relies heavily on clitics of three types: enclitics, which are phonologically indistinguishable from suffixes except that they may attach to various types of host; proclitics, which are indistinguishable from complete phonological words except for the fact that they do not carry stress and may only occur bound to a host; and ditropic enclitics (used solely for case-marking), a typologically unusual phenomenon (Cysouw 2005) whereby a clitic precedes its host but is bound phonologically to the word it follows. Belep is exclusively suffixing.

A major feature of Belep morphophonemics is the widespread existence of both 'bound' and 'free' forms of phonological words throughout the lexicon. This is realized in 'phase shift', wherein a word changes form depending on its position in the clause; it is also realized in the existence of meaningful alternations in nominal and verbal morphology. Many nouns have both possessed ('bound') and unpossessed ('free') phonological forms, and many transitive verbs are inherently 'bound' in that they cannot occur without a nominal or pronominal reference to their semantic patient. Other 'free' verbs inflect for whether the patient is generic or specific. In fact, the distinction between generic and specific noun phrases is highly grammaticalized in Belep into many aspects of the grammar; noun possession also distinguishes generic vs. specific possessors.

Noun classes are distinguished based on whether their members are compatible with inalienable or alienable possession, a common characteristic of Pacific Rim languages (Bickel & Nichols 2007). Many nouns are also inherently possessed; a nominal or pronominal reference to their possessor is obligatory. Determination of noun phrases is extremely complex as well, with demonstratives and determiners marking the number, animacy, proximity, direction, and discourse relevance of their referents. The most commonly marked verbal category in Belep is modality (with a highly grammaticalized distinction between realis and irrealis), and verbal aspect is also fairly complex. Tense is unmarked. Distinctions in clause combining are accomplished almost entirely by the semantics of particular linkers; the morphosyntax of main clauses and semantically dependent clauses is largely indistinguishable and may be considered a form of pseudocoordination (Ross 2016).

Belep has an unusual system for flagging core arguments which differs from the split-ergative systems of its close relatives. This system is summarized in Table 3.

Tab. 3: Belep flagging alignment system

Genitive	Nominative	Absolutive
—	S (most)	S (limited)
A (if P definite)	A (if P indefinite)	P

Table 3 shows that in Belep, most S arguments of intransitive verbs, as well as agent noun phrases in transitive clauses with an indefinite patient, are marked as in the nominative case. Agent noun phrases in transitive clauses with a definite patient are marked as genitive. Meanwhile, the patient noun phrase of a transitive verb is unmarked for case, as is the S argument of a limited number of intransitive verbs (these arguments are identified in this work as 'absolutive'). This system of grammatical relations thus qualifies as split-intransitive if P is indefinite ($A = S_a \neq S_p = P$) and a combination of split-intransitive and tripartite if P is definite ($A \neq S_a \neq S_p = P$).

Belep has a number of typologically unusual features. These include the fixed basic word order VOS (other word-order correlates are consistent with a head-initial language), and the ditropic clitics mentioned above. Belep's pronominal system is especially remarkable for its four grammatical numbers—singular, dual, paucal, and plural—which are unique in its geographical area (none of Belep's neighbors has a paucal number). Furthermore, Belep shares with its neighbors an unusual grammaticalized spatial system, where verbs, directionals, and noun determination all use the same three-way distinction between 'up', 'down', and 'transverse' axes—there is no basic verb 'to go', but rather three verbs 'to go up', 'to go down', and 'to go transverse'. Belep negation strategies are also fairly unusual, with a number of negative verbs: a negative locative verb, a negative existential verb, a verb meaning 'to not want', a verb meaning 'to not know', etc.

1.7 Sociolinguistic situation

The following sections discuss linguistic variation within the Belep community and the social factors which influence that variation.

1.7.1 Sociolinguistic variation

Age is the most salient sociolinguistic variable for Belep speakers. Young people's language use is remarked on by many speakers as different from that of other age groups (this was also noted by Dubois 1975c). The primary markers of young people's speech, according to Belep speakers, are increased code-mixing (see §1.7.2) and more frequent use of the characteristic 'singing' intonation pattern (§2.8). There are some lexical differences as well; speakers often cite elders' use of *pana manya* 'wait!', while young people use *waramen* 'wait!'. Young people also use argot from an invented language game (similar to Ubbi Dubbi in English) where /aŋ/ or /aⁿg/ is inserted before the rime of each syllable.

Other, less salient differences between the speech of older and younger speakers include: final [ṭ] in older speakers is regularized to final [r] in younger speakers; medial [ɣ] for older speakers is medial [ʁ] for younger speakers; and younger speakers are more likely than older ones to use the stylish [s] and [tʃ] pronunciations of /c/ (see chapter 2 for more information). Older speakers also have much larger vocabularies in Belep than do younger speakers, who are unlikely to know species names for flora and fauna, as well as words for certain cultural practices. Other relevant identity-based categories of sociolinguistic variation include gender,[32] clan background, and educational background/level of assimilation into French society. Though differences are noticeable within each of these variables, I was not able to collect data from a large enough sample size to be able to describe the differences conclusively.

Another source of sociolinguistic variation is register-based. Belep slow speech and fast speech differ to some degree, a common cross-linguistic phenomenon (Zwicky 1972) also noted by Dubois (1975c). This includes the reduction of approximants in fast speech: *maya-* [mãja] 'part' is often produced as [mãe] in fast speech; *ulayar* 'to be big' is often reduced to [ulaaɾ] in fast speech. Belep nasals may occasionally be affected by fast speech as well, being produced as prenasalized stops. For example, *naerama lami* 'those children' may be produced as [nãẽɾaᵐblamĩ], which also contains an instance of deletion of an unstressed vowel, another characteristic of fast speech.

---

[32] This was particularly noticeable in the speech of a few gender-variant people who exhibited both masculine and feminine speech patterns in Belep and French.

Choice of code is also a salient variation in register. Diglossic Belep speakers tend to use French (High) to refer to politics, economics, and education, while references to family, relationships, and cultural activities occur in Belep (Low) (see §1.7.2). However, this is not a hard and fast rule, and speakers use both of these codes in a complex interplay of the identities that they represent at any given moment.

La coutume (§1.3.2) is a particular speech genre that has its own sociolect. A considerable subset of Belep vocabulary is marked as normally occurring only in *la coutume*, such as the numerical classifiers (§4.4.1) which refer to quantities of ritual gifts such as yams and sugar cane. Some words have euphemistic counterparts for use in *la coutume*; for example, one speaker avoids use of the word *mwany* 'bad' in his *coutumes*, instead substituting the word *geek* 'dirty'. The honorific *â ô* 'great one' is used to refer to the *grand-chef* in *la coutume* rather than the usual *teâmaa* used in everyday speech. It is possible that *la coutume* is characterized by phonological or morphosyntactic patterns as well as these lexical ones—this would be a productive topic for further study.

1.7.2 Multilingualism and language contact

The Ethnologue lists 38 living languages for New Caledonia; of those, at least 29 belong to the New Caledonian language family (Lewis et al. 2016). By the time they are adults, most Belema speak more than one Kanak language.

A number of factors contribute to Kanak multilingualism. First, throughout New Caledonia, it is very common for women to leave their birthplace to marry outside their language group (§1.3). This means that many adult women in Belep were born elsewhere and moved to Belep when they married; Belep may be their second or third language. It also means that many women for whom Belep was a first language—but who now normally speak a different Kanak language with their families—live scattered throughout the country, returning to Belep for important cultural events such as weddings and funerals. As a result, Belep children may grow up with a familiarity with both their mother's and their father's language—or perhaps even more languages, since many are raised by adoptive parents or grandparents. Second, Belema children must leave Belep at age 12 to attend school on the Mainland. Most attend the boarding school in Poum, but many are sent elsewhere, and successful students may go on to attend high school in yet another Mainland location. In each of these schools, the Belema child is immersed in a community which speaks a different local language, and he or she may live with a distant relative who does not speak Belep at all. Finally, Belema adults may choose to work in Mainland communities and learn the local language so that they can be friendlier with their coworkers.

The prevalence of Kanak multilingualism does not appear to be a recent innovation. In fact, elderly Belema tend to speak more languages than young people, and oral histories of long voyages, exogamous marriages, and warfare between language areas—as well as archeological evidence (Sand & Sheppard 2000)—suggest that similar patterns of inter-lingual movement existed in Kanak culture prior to European colonization. Multilingualism is thus an important facet of Kanak culture—with the major caveat that one should speak the language appropriate to the particular local context in which one finds oneself. A multilingual person ought to speak Belep in Belep and Balade Nyelâyu in Balade, for example. Language mixing is strongly disfavored.

This attitude towards language use becomes more complex when French is considered as well. French is the national language of New Caledonia[33] and, with such a large amount of linguistic diversity among Kanak people, French's status as the lingua franca is unchallenged (Charpentier 2006). "[French] is needed for participation in the modern political and economic life of the territory, and most school-based education is only available in French" (Gordon & Maddieson 2004:296-297). In Belep, 582 of the 584 people over age 14 who responded to the 1996 census reported speaking French, with only slightly lower numbers for those who could read and write in French (ISEE 1996). In my observation, all adult Belema are fully bilingual in Belep and French.

However, the preferred usage of these two languages is to limit each to its respective sphere: "French is the high and prestige language of government and of upward social movement, while [Kanak languages represent] traditional life. French and the Kanak languages are associated with different semio-cultural worlds" (Cunningham et al. 2006). This diglossia is perpetuated in Northern New Caledonia by the closeness and multiplexity of social networks (Schooling 1990). A similar situation persists in rural Vanuatu, where diglossic speakers reserve the colonial languages for school and government, while a local vernacular or lingua franca is used for social interaction (Crowley 1995).

Though Belep speakers value both French and Belep, they consider code-mixing to be a pollution of both languages. The Belep Language Committee opposes the inclusion of French borrowings in the Belep dictionary; when glossing recorded texts, speakers substitute Belep words for the French ones actually present in the text, and are surprised and disappointed to discover that this is necessary. Belep speakers' chief complaint and worry about the future of their language is its dilution with an influx of French words and code-mixing, a problem perceived primarily in the speech of young people but also present among elders.

This strong bias against code-mixing belies actual linguistic practice in Belep, where skill at code-mixing is necessary for native-like fluency. Many scholars (e.g. Muysken 2004) distinguish code-mixing from code-switching based on whether alternations occur intrasententially (code-mixing) or intersententially (code-switch-

---

33 http://www.ac-noumea.nc/sitevr/spip.php?rubrique48

ing). Though this binary distinction has been challenged (Tay 1989), the speech patterns demonstrated by Belep speakers show a clear bias towards intrasentential and intra-constituent bilingualism, so I refer to it in this work as code-mixing. In current Belep linguistic practice, French words and constituents are 'inserted' into Belep morphosyntax, creating examples of code-mixing like those shown in (4) - (6).

(4) *jename ta ka mae la na grotte-ixeda.*
    jena=me   ta=xa   mae=la   na   [grot]i-xeda
    1TR.INCL.SUBJ=IRR   go.UH=LK   sleep=LOC   interior   cave.LN-DET.UH
    '"We're going to go up and sleep in that cave up there."'

    Yal-19092011-PA_0039

In (4), the French noun *grotte* [gʁɔt] 'cave' is inserted into Belep morphosyntax. The Belep suffix *-xeda* 'UH' is attached to it, and at the morpheme boundary a Belep morphophonemic process occurs whereby an epenthetic [i] is inserted to avoid consonant hiatus (see §3.2.1.4). This usage is not a clear instance of borrowing, since *grotte* violates Belep phonology (§2.9.3). In (5), the French verb *gagner* [gaɲe] 'to win' is inserted into Belep morphosyntax.

(5) *te gagner li wayap.*
    te=   [gaɲe]-li   wayap
    3SG.SUBJ=   win.LN-TR   war
    'He won the war.'

    Yal-20092011-AW3_0088

Here, the verb *gagner* is marked with the Belep subject proclitic *te=* '3SG.SUBJ' and the transitivizing suffix *-li* 'TR'. When code-mixing with French verbs occurs, the verbs are inserted in their infinitive form (the French third person singular inflected form of *gagner* 'to win' is *gagne* [gaɲ(ə)]).

(6) *Et pourtant yo âju to âri yo ô.*
    [e   purtã]   yo=   âju=ro   âri=   yo=   ô
    and.LN   nonetheless.LN 2SG.SUBJ= person=whe NEG= 2SG.SUBJ= good
    'And nevertheless you do not do what is right.'

    Yal-25072010-PT-homily_0064

In (6), the clause-initial linker marking the clause's relationship with the rest of discourse is French *et pourtant* 'and nonetheless', while the clause itself is in Belep. These instances of code-mixing seem to be motivated primarily by a lack of a good correspondence between the French word used and any existing Belep words, although the discourse function of code-mixing in Belep merits further study.

A disconnect between language attitudes and linguistic practice in terms of various types of language mixing is not uncommon cross-linguistically. In one study of language attitudes among Chilean adolescents in Sweden, "participants indicated that code-switching was an integral part of their language use…, but when asked directly to evaluate code-switching, they overwhelmingly rejected it." (King & Ganuza 2005:190-191). Lawson and Sachdev's (2000) study of Tunisian multilingualism found that Tunisians' attitudes towards code-switching were largely negative—a finding not inconsistent with the other negative attitudes they cite in Norwegian (Haugen 1977), "Morocco (Bentahila 1983), India (Pandit 1986), Hong Kong (Gibbons 1987), and the United Kingdom (Romaine 1995)" (Lawson & Sachdev 2000: 1344-1345). In this context, the contrast between Belep attitudes and linguistic practice indicates the multiplicity of identities that Belep speakers negotiate with their choice of language.

1.7.3 Endangerment status and revitalization

According to the typology of language death presented in Fishman (1991), Belep is in stage 6 of 8 (where 8 is moribund). This stage is characterized by "the attainment of intergenerational informal oralcy and its demographic concentration and institutional reinforcement" (Fishman 1991:92). Belep is not immediately endangered; it still has enthusiastic, monolingual child speakers, is used for most types of social interaction among all ages, and its importance and usage is upheld by the Belep school, church, *chefferie*, and *mairie*. Crucially, Belep is still vital for the young: most children speak no French before attending school (unlike in other communes on the Mainland).

The Belep school today plays a particularly important role in the reinforcement of the Belep language variety. Because most children enter the school system as Belep monolinguals,[34] all preschool and kindergarten classes are taught in Belep, with gradual phasing in of French throughout elementary school until students have learned enough to succeed in Mainland secondary school. The majority of educators are Belep native speakers, and they have been following a policy of institutionalizing the Belep language at least since 1999, when the Belep Language Committee was founded and developed its first standardized orthography. The work of BOUEDAOU Thérèse, the school principal, is particularly noteworthy; under her direction, schoolchildren take linguistic field trips to study particular semantic fields (such as shells or trees), and learn to read in Belep before they develop French literacy.

---

34 The few Belep children who speak French or another language at home invariably learn Belep from their teachers and peers at school, since it is necessary for social interaction. I know of at least three families in which this has happened.

However, as Fishman argues, "The family (and even the immediate community) may not be enough for RLS [reversing language shift; that is, language revitalization] to be attained, particularly where outside pressures are both great and hostile" (Fishman 1991: 94). These outside pressures may increase in the coming years as Belep becomes more connected to the rest of the world. Most younger speakers lack the rich cultural vocabulary of the elders, a situation that may deteriorate as traditional folkways are lost. The limited number of economic activities on Belep, combined with the rapidly increasing population, is already contributing to widespread dissatisfaction with life in Belep. These factors may contribute to the decline of the language in the near future. "[T]he number of speakers [of Kanak languages] might well be expected to decline in future years, even as the ethnic population grows" (Gordon and Maddieson 2004:296-297).

The persistence of Kanak languages has occurred largely in spite of colonial efforts to extinguish them. Usage of Kanak languages in Catholic missionary schools—the only schools available for most Kanaks—was forbidden in 1863 by decree of the governor Guillain, and writing in Kanak languages was severely punished until 1970. Elderly Belep speakers describe their school experiences as exceedingly severe, and demonstrate shame towards their largely self-taught level of Belep literacy. Although institutional linguistic prejudice has gradually been withdrawn since 1970 (Moyse-Faurie 2003a), this process is by no means complete. The Nouméa Accords of 1998, which set out the plan for New Caledonian independence in 2013 or 2018, state that "The Kanak languages, together with French, are languages of education and culture in New Caledonia. Their place in school curricula and in the media should therefore be increased" (Australasian Legal Information Institute 2002). However, even today some French secondary school officials in Nouméa view Kanak languages as unworthy of study (V. Fillol, p.c., 2009).

Since 2006, Kanak languages have been taught in nursery schools while bilingual instructors are trained for the higher grades. The Academy of Kanak Languages (ALK), whose goal is "the preservation of the cultural identity of linguistic communities" and to inform people about "the importance of preserving and using vernacular languages", was created in 2007 (Anonymous 2008, September 10). Weniko Ihage, the director of the ALK, personally gave his permission and approval to my project, and Belep had its first official liaison with the ALK in 2011 when BOIGUIVIE Scholastique, the academician in charge of the ALK's Hoot ma Waap branch, visited Belep.

1.8 Methodology

The data collected for this grammar were obtained over the course of three trips to New Caledonia from 2009 to 2011, totaling about seven months in Belep and two months in Nouméa, the capital. I also spent roughly a week each in Koumac, Poum, and Balade.

Belep is fairly remote and travel there is unpredictable. After flying into Nouméa, one must fly to Koumac, and then either take a small propeller plane or a boat to Belep. Flights are scheduled two days a week, but they can be cancelled due to bad weather; a cargo barge and tourist catamaran also make weekly trips, but these are frequently cancelled for long periods if the boat needs repair. Upon reaching Belep, I contacted my host family or the *mairie* so that they could arrange for someone with a car to transport me to my lodgings.

I spent nearly all of my time in Belep in the village of Waala, with short one- or two-day trips to the plantations in Bweo, Âjeeni, Pairoome, and Paave. While Waala has running water, electricity, cellular phone service, and internet access at the *mairie* and the clinic, plantation sites often do not have any of these. About half the time I spent in Belep was in a guest house constructed for Westerners, while the other half was spent in a *case*, a Kanak hut made of coconut leaves. As much as possible, I tried to integrate myself into the community, so that my increased understanding of the culture and the language would reinforce each other. I lived with two 'adoptive' families, eating meals with them when I could and attending social and cultural events such as church, bingo, weddings and funerals.

Early in my field work, my major challenge was in finding Belema speakers who would agree to meet me and answer my questions. Though most of my contacts were pleased that I was doing this work, they did not have much free time to meet with me—most had jobs and families, as well as social responsibilities. Eventually, I assembled a large enough number of consultants that I could cycle through them, not overburdening anyone in particular, and tailoring tasks to consultants with particular skills. I achieved conversational fluency by the beginning of my third field trip, and was able to gather much more data from listening to conversations around me and asking questions in Belep.

My choice of consultants was governed almost entirely by their availability; I also privileged consultants suggested by the Belep Language Committee. My principal consultants were TEANYOUEN Philippe, the church catechist; GUELEME Yasmine, my neighbor; POITTHILI Albert, an adjunct at the *mairie*; and YARIK Darine, a Belep-language instruction kindergarten teacher. I also benefited greatly from the insights of BOUEDAOU Thérèsè, the school principal, and DAYE Alice and MOILOU Ignacia, my two host mothers. Most of the recorded texts from which examples throughout this work are drawn were shared with me by GUELEME Benjamin and Marie-Clothilde, an elderly couple who spend most of their time in Pott; and WAHOULO Amabili, the *grand-chef*. More than twenty other Belema met with me once or twice and allowed me to record them.

The theoretical approach espoused by this grammar is largely functional-typological (Shopen 2007, etc.), and phonetic and phonological analyses are enhanced by the use of Praat (Boersma & Weenik 2007). Explanations for linguistic phenomena are sought in common cross-linguistic patterns of human interaction and cognition, and when possible are placed in a Belep historical and cultural context. In this approach, language is viewed as one interconnected part of a complex web of human social interaction, and instantiations of a particular linguistic phenomenon, recorded in natural discourse, are considered to be evidence for an analysis. Belep is also frequently compared with, when possible, Balade Nyelâyu and Nêlêmwa—closely related languages that are also geographically close—and other languages in the Oceanic family.

Most examples in this grammar consist of four lines. The top line is written in ***bold italics*** in the Belep orthography (§2.6), with rules developed in conjunction with the Belep Language Committee. The second line is written in **bold** using the romanization system developed by the Committee, but with a more phonetic transcription (e.g. words are shown as uttered in incomplete phase; see §2.5.2) and morpheme breaks indicated. Suffixes (§3.2.2.5) are marked with '-'; clitics (§3.2.2.6) are marked with '='; there is no orthographic space between an enclitic and its host, while an orthographic space follows all proclitics (indicating that they have some degree of phonological independence from their host). In a few cases, an IPA transcription in the second line is necessary; IPA transcriptions are surrounded by brackets []. The third line contains English glosses; see the morpheme index in Appendix A. The fourth line contains a free translation into English.

Examples in this grammar come from a variety of sources. Whenever possible, they are drawn from a recorded text—often traditional legends and personal narratives, but also conversations, games, songs, sermons, procedural texts, and public speeches. Each example drawn from natural discourse is marked with a unique marker indicating the text it was drawn from, the speaker, and a time-code so that the reader may listen to the example (see Appendix B for these codes and a description of each text). Examples are also drawn from elicited translations, grammaticality judgments, and wordlists; these are used as little as possible, and are marked with the date and the speaker. Speakers are identified by their initials throughout the text (see Appendix C).

Most recordings were made with an Edirol R-09, recording at 44.1 KHz, 16-bit PCM wav format. A few recordings were conducted with a PC using Audacity[35] after the Edirol's microphone jack broke. Most recordings used Audio-Technica AT831b lavalier microphones. Some data also were video recorded using a Panasonic PV-GS320 Digital Video Camera. Recordings were transcribed, time-aligned, and glossed using primarily Transcriber,[36] Toolbox,[37] and ELAN,[38] and some file conversions used

---

[35] http://audacity.sourceforge.net/
[36] http://trans.sourceforge.net/en/presentation.php
[37] http://www.sil.org/computing/toolbox/
[38] http://www.lat-mpi.eu/tools/elan/

Linguistic Software Converters.³⁹ All of this software is freely downloadable, non-proprietary, and open-source.

I have tried wherever possible to make my corpus and collected data available to the Belema and other Kanaks who wish to benefit from them. I have left copies of my electronic dictionary, scans of Dubois's (1975a-f) and Neyret's (1974a-c) manuscripts, and my recorded corpus with several consultants in Belep who own computers. Copies of my recordings have also been deposited in Nouméa with the Tjibaou Cultural Center and the Académie des langues kanak. I also have plans to archive my data in the CRDO archive administered by CNRS, which is a member of the Open Language Archives Community (OLAC) (Bird & Simons 2003). This archive contains data from several other New Caledonian languages and allows recordings and data to be viewed online.

This grammar is composed of a total of seven chapters. Chapter 2 provides a description of Belep phonology and phonetics. Chapter 3 focuses on morphology. In chapter 4, the word class of nouns and nominal morphology is discussed, while chapter 5 covers verbs and their constituent morphology. Chapter 6 describes basic word order, grammatical relations, and clause structure. Finally, in Chapter 7, speakers' methods of combining clauses are discussed. A sample interlinearized text is provided in Appendix E.

---

39 http://linguisticsoftwareconverters.zong.mine.nu/

2 Phonetics and phonology

2.1 Introduction

In this chapter, I describe the Belep sound system. In comparison with other Northern New Caledonian languages, Belep has a fairly small phonemic inventory. This is largely due to the lack of aspiration contrasts for any consonant—an important feature of other Northern languages.[1] Rather than possessing a phonemic vowel length distinction and diphthongs, Belep treats all sequences of vowels as heterosyllabic instances of hiatus.[2] The segmental inventory of Belep, like that of other languages of Northern New Caledonia (Ozanne-Rivierre et al. 1998, Bril 2000), is characterized by a high degree of phonetic and phonemic nasality in both consonants and vowels. This is a distinguishing characteristic of the New Caledonian languages as a whole that sets them apart from the rest of the Austronesian family (Gordon & Maddieson 2004).

A number of interesting morphophonemic processes occur in Belep, including the obligatory lenition of voiceless stops in word-medial position and an alternation between 'complete' (final) and 'incomplete' (nonfinal) phonetic forms of words.[3] To both native speakers of Belep and speakers of surrounding languages, Belep has a unique and characteristic intonation pattern described as 'songlike'. This intonation pattern is largely the result of the complicated interaction between stress correlates (vowel length, intensity, and pitch). Belep has a prosodic system of fixed stress on the penultimate syllable (with some exceptions), while the final syllable contains the pitch peak.

I discuss the phonemic inventory of Belep in §2.2 and argue for the phonemic status of various sets of phonemes in §2.3. In §2.4 I describe Belep phonemes' acoustic phonetic realizations and discuss patterns of allophony in Belep. In §2.5 the major morphophonemic processes are described, and §2.6 lists the set of correspondences between Belep phones and the orthographic symbols used to write them throughout the rest of this work. Phonotactics (syllable structure) and prosody (stress assignment) are covered in §2.7 and §2.8, respectively, while §2.9 contains a discussion of borrowings and other atypical phonological elements in Belep. All words cited in §2.2 - §2.5 are given in phonemic transcription using the International Phonetic Alphabet

---

[1] Phonemic aspiration contrasts are found in Nixumwak (Bril 2000); Yuanga (Schooling 1992); Balade Nyelâyu (Ozanne-Rivierre 1998); Caaàc (Hollyman 1981); Pije, Nemi, and Jawe (Haudricourt & Ozanne-Rivierre 1982); and the Voh-Koné varieties (Rivierre & Ehrhart 2006).
[2] This characteristic is shared by Leti (Hume 1997).
[3] This phenomenon, called 'phase shift' in this work, is also found in Leti (Hume 1997) and Rotuman (Blevins 1994).

(IPA); in some cases, slash brackets // are added to clarify that a transcription is phonemic. In cases where a phonetic transcription is also provided, square brackets [] are used. The orthographic conventions described in §2.6 are used elsewhere throughout this work.

2.2 Phonemic inventory

Belep has 28 phonemes, including 18 consonants (Table 1) and 10 vowels (Table 2). Table 1 shows the Belep consonant phonemes. In places of articulation where there is a voicing contrast, voiceless consonants are shown on the left, while prenasalized consonants are shown on the right. Minimal pairs illustrating the phonemic contrasts between the consonants are presented in §2.2.1.

Tab. 1: Consonant inventory

	Labiovelar		Bilabial		Alveolar		Palatal		Velar	
Plosive	p^w	$^mb^w$	p	^mb	t	nd	c	$^ɲɟ$	k	^ŋg
Nasal	m^w		m		n		ɲ		ŋ	
Approximant	w				l		j			

Table 2 shows the Belep vowel phonemes. Section §2.2.2 contains examples of minimal pairs which demonstrate the contrasts between the vowels.

Tab. 2: Vowel inventory

	ORAL			NASAL		
	Front	Central	Back	Front	Central	Back
High	i (y)[4]		u	ĩ		ũ
Mid	e		o	ẽ		õ
Low		a			ã	

---

[4] Only one word has been found to contain the vowel /y/: /ã^{m}by/ 'periwinkle'.

2.2.1 Consonants

The consonants of Belep are divided into voiceless stops, prenasalized stops, nasal stops, and approximants at five places of articulation—labiovelar, bilabial, alveolar, palatal, and velar. All consonants may appear syllable-initially (see §2.7 for more on the syllable in Belep), although words beginning with /l/, /ɲ/ and /ŋ/ are unusual. A reduced consonant inventory (which excludes the prenasalized stops and approximants) may occur syllable-finally. Consonant clusters do not occur because coda consonants are only permitted word-finally. Neither labiovelar (§2.3.1.1) nor prenasalized (§2.3.1.3) stops are considered to be clusters.

With only 18 phonemic consonants, Belep has a dramatically smaller consonant inventory than most languages in its subgroup, the Far North subgroup of New Caledonian languages (see §1.5). Other Far North languages contain nearly twice as many consonants: there are 36 in Nêlêmwa (Bril 2002), 32 in Balade Nyelâyu (Ozanne-Rivierre et al. 1998), and 37 in Yuanga (Schooling 1992:100). Even in less-closely related Northern subgroup languages, phoneme inventories are comparably large, as in Pije (37 consonants), Fwai (26 consonants), Nemi (43 consonants), Jawe (35 consonants) (Haudricourt & Ozanne-Rivierre 1982); and Bwatoo, which has 38 consonants (Rivierre & Ehrhart 2006). The reason for this discrepancy is that most Northern languages contain two series each of voiceless stops, approximants, and nasals, which are classified as either 'aspirated' and 'unaspirated'. No comparable aspiration contrast exists in Belep (see §2.3.1.2). In consonant inventory size, Belep is most similar to Paicî, a Northern language which has 17 consonants and also lacks aspiration contrasts (Gordon & Maddieson 2004).

The examples that follow illustrate minimal or near-minimal pairs for the Belep labial (§2.2.1.1), alveolar (§2.2.1.2), palatal (§2.2.1.3), velar (§2.2.1.4), nasal (§2.2.1.5), and approximant (§2.1.1.6) consonants. True minimal pairs are somewhat rare in Belep; this may be attributable to language loss (see §1.7.3).[5]

2.2.1.1 Labial consonants

The labial consonants in Belep include labiovelars[6] /pʷ/, /ᵐbʷ/, and /mʷ/; bilabials /p/, /ᵐb/, and /m/, and approximant /w/. These phonemes are contrastive in word-

---

[5] I hypothesize that the phonemic distinctions in the Belep phoneme inventory served a more robust discriminatory function at some time in the past. The distinctions may have diminished in importance due to such factors as the loss of folkways and thus the words to describe them; universal diglossia and code-switching (removing the necessity of learning the more obscure, high-register Belep words); and the disruption of linguistic transfer to the younger generations.
[6] Labiovelar consonants are phonemically and phonetically distinct from sequences of labial consonant + /u/ (see §2.2.2.1).

initial position before a non-back vowel, as shown in (1). Before back vowels and in word-medial environments, some of these contrasts are neutralized (see §2.3.1.5).

(1) pʷa   'hole'
     ᵐbʷa-   'head'
     mʷa   'house'
     pa   'to take'
     ᵐba   'to kiss'
     ma   'LK4'
     wa   'grandparent'

Sets of contrasting minimal or near-minimal pairs for the labial consonants are shown in (2) - (6). The examples in (2) show the contrasts between the labiovelar stops /pʷ/, /ᵐbʷ/, and /mʷ/.

(2) pʷa   'hole'   ᵐbʷa-   'head'   mʷa   'house'
     pʷac   'habitation'   ᵐbʷac   'dowry'   mʷaak   'rabbitfish'
     pʷaᵑgi-   'to tense'   ᵐbʷaᵑge-   'to return'   mʷaᵑga-   'bend'
     pʷala   'to steer'   ᵐbʷala-   'head'   mʷana-   'house'
     pʷalu   'to be heavy'   -   mʷalu   'Moilou'[7]
     pʷãn   'to push'   ᵐbʷan   'night'   mʷan   'Mwan'[8]
     pʷec   'to be born'   ᵐbʷe-   'top'   mʷek   'to be twisted'
     pʷi   'net'   ᵐbʷi   'to be blind'   mʷiⁿɟa   'thing'

The examples in (3) show the contrasts between the bilabial stops /p/, /ᵐb/, and /m/.

(3) pa   'to take'   ᵐba   'to kiss'   ma   'LK4'
     paⁿdaan   'to fry'   -   maⁿdaan   'weather'
     pe   'stingray'   ᵐbe   'worm'   me   'IRR'
     pia-   'nail'   -   mia   'to be ripe'
     piᵑgi   'to be stuck'   ᵐbiᵑgi-   'to screw'   miᵑgi-   'to hold'
     piin   'thread'   ᵐbiin   'to be skinny'   -

The examples in (4) show minimal or near-minimal pairs for /pʷ/, /p/, and /w/.

(4) pʷa   'hole'   pa   'to take'   wa   'grandparent'
     pʷac   'habitation'   paac   'war'   wac   'to be dishonorable'

---

[7] <Moilou> is the name of one of the clans in Belep.
[8] The toponym <Mwan> is the name of an area in Poc, the islet north of Art.

pʷalu	'to be heavy'	palu	'to be miserly'	wala	'Waala'⁹
pʷaŋ	'bay'	pan	'to go.TV'	wan	'sea turtle'
pʷec	'to be born'	pe	'ray'	we	'water'
pʷiɲit	'to be smallest'	piɲau	'watermelon'	wimawo	'ironwood'

The contrast between /ᵐbʷ/ and /ᵐb/ in word-initial and word-medial position is demonstrated in the examples in (5).

(5)
ᵐbʷa-	'head'	ᵐba	'to kiss'
ᵐbʷaⁿge-	'to return'	ᵐbaⁿge-	'to rub'
ᵐbʷe-	'top'	ᵐbe	'worm'
ᵐbʷi	'to be blind'	ᵐbi	'channel'
ãᵐbʷa	'to raise'	ãᵐba-	'plate'
õᵐbʷac	'to watch'	õᵐba-	'scale'

The examples in (6) show minimal or near-minimal pairs for /mʷ/ and /m/ in word-initial and word-medial position.

(6)
mʷa	'house'	ma	'LK4'
mʷaⁿga-	'bend'	maⁿgao	'air'
mʷek	'to be twisted'	meek	'mango.LN'
mʷiⁿgu	'to play'	miⁿgi-	'to touch'
mʷiⁿɟa	'thing'	miⁿɟa-	'to pinch'
ãmʷa-	'gesture'	ãma=	'DYAD'
cĕmʷe-	'to gut'	cemae	'fatigue'
tamʷa	'woman'	ta-ma	'woman-AC'

Note that, unlike in Nêlêmwa (Bril 2000) and Balade Nyelâyu (Ozanne-Rivierre et al. 1998), Belep labiovelars also contrast with bilabials in syllable-final position. The contrast between /pʷ/ and /p/ syllable-finally is illustrated in (7). The contrast between syllable-final /mʷ/ and /m/ is shown in (8). Note that approximant /w/ and prenasalized stops /ᵐbʷ/ and /ᵐb/ do not occur syllable-finally.

(7)
ăpʷ	'to laugh'	nap	'sail'
noᵐbʷapʷ	'to provoke'	wap	'low tide'
ⁿdepʷ	'deck'	cep	'to build boats'

---

9 The toponym /wala/ <Waala> is the name of the main village in Belep, where the *mairie* and the church are located.

(8) ijam   'tomorrow'   jamʷ   'to marry'
     nam   'to disappear'   na-mʷ   'feces-2SG.POSS'
     ᶮjem   'mangrove crab'   cemʷ   'to sprout'

2.2.1.2 Alveolar consonants

The alveolar consonants in Belep include stops /t/, /ⁿd/, and /n/, as well as approximant /l/. These phonemes are contrastive in word-initial position, as shown in (9).

(9) ta   'to go.UH'
     ⁿda   'blood'
     na-   'interior'
     la   '3PL.INDEP'

Sets of contrasting minimal or near-minimal pairs for the alveolar stop consonants are shown in (10) - (12). The examples in (10) show contrasts between /t/, /ⁿd/, and /n/ in word-initial position.

(10) taac   'bowl.LN'   ⁿdaac   'farm'   nac   'to be surprised'
     tao   'to hurt'   ⁿdao-   'leaf'   nao   'to sing'
     taat   'to flee'   ⁿdaat   'skirt'   naat   'oven'
     te-   'breast'   ⁿde   'fork'   -
     tep   'to click'   ⁿdepʷ   'deck'   nep   'dream'
     ti   'who?'   ⁿdi   'black bean'[10] nic   'shark'
     -                   ⁿdiju   'coins'   niju   'thunder'
     to   'to call'   ⁿdo   'spear'   no   'fish'
     tu   'to go.DH'   ⁿdu   'bone'   nu   'coconut tree'

The examples in (11) show contrasts between syllable-initial /t/, /ⁿd/, and /n/ in word-medial position.

(11) ata-   'underside'   ãⁿda   'alone'   ãna-   'contents'
     pata   'to tell'   paⁿda   'type of seaweed' ⁿgana- 'color'
     tate-   'to escape'   ⁿdaⁿde   'chaste tree'   tãne   'spearhead'
     mati-   'to congratulate'   -   mani   'bird'

---

10 *Castanospermum australe*.

wati-	'to attach'	wã"di-	'to spank'	-	
ãto-	'husband'	ma"do	'emperor bream'	ãno	'child'
utu	'wind'	u"du	'to lower'	kũnu	'to be amputated'

The contrast between /t/ and /n/ in syllable-final position is shown in (12). Neither the prenasalized stop /ⁿd/ nor the approximant /l/ occurs syllable-finally.

(12) ⁿdat   'coral'   ⁿdan   'sky'
      pʷat   'red snapper'¹¹   pʷãn   'to push'
      wat   'type of sardine'¹²   wan   'sea turtle'
      jaat   'to disembark'   jaan   'spangled emperor'¹³
      jet   'pot'   jen   'breadfruit'¹⁴
      ot   'to spill'   õn   'sand'
      koot   'to be soft'   koon   'to be unable'
      tuut   'to fart'   tũũn   'to rub'

The lateral approximant /l/ is very uncommon in word-initial position. Only the Belep words listed in (13) have been identified as beginning with /l/, and, as the glosses show, two are borrowings and three are pronominal.

(13) lãⁿdan   'type of fish'
      lolo   'oarlock'
      laŋen   'eczema'
      loloi   'bougna.LN'¹⁵
      lakau   'papaya.LN'
      le   '3DU.INDEP'
      len   '3PA.INDEP'
      la   '3PL.INDEP'

---

11 *Lutjanus sebae*.
12 Called *sardine prêtre* in French.
13 *Lethrinus nebulosus*.
14 *Artocarpus altilis*.
15 The French term <bougna> is used throughout New Caledonia to refer to a type of traditional Kanak dish which is prepared in coconut leaves inside an earth oven. Typical ingredients are coconut milk, yams, sweet potatoes, taro, potatoes, manioc, and meat (fish, chicken, pork, etc.). Even Kanak groups who did not traditionally prepare *bougna* have adopted the practice in an effort to cater to tourists. According to Dubois (1975c), the Belep word /loloi/ 'bougna' is borrowed from Drehu, the language of Lifou, one of the Loyalty Islands.

The phoneme /l/ is much more common in word-medial position; this is a characteristic shared by the Northern language Paicî (Gordon & Maddieson 2004). The examples in (14) show the contrast between /t/ and /l/.

(14)
ata-	'underside'	ala-	'container'
ᵐbatap	'to exceed'	ᵐbalap	'to move'
keta-	'trace'	kela	'to slide'
ota	'to rain'	ola	'shellfish'
pota	'to massage'	pola	'to pluck'
tata	'to scoop'	tala-	'bed'
ete	'to be different'	ele	'knife'
yate-	'to disembark'	yale	'kudzu'
poto	'to be white'	polo-	'to interrupt'
uto	'to be bald'	ulo	'to be red'
tutu-	'to hide'	tulu	'twine'

See §2.3.1.5 for information on the contrast between /l/ and /n/.

2.2.1.3 Palatal consonants

The palatal consonants in Belep include stops /c/, /ⁿɟ/, and /ɲ/, as well as approximant /j/. These phonemes are contrastive in word-initial position, as shown in (15). In word-medial environments, some of these contrasts are neutralized (see §2.3.1.5).

(15)
ca	'to be how?'
ⁿɟa	'1PL.INCL.INDEP'
ɲa-	'mother'
ja-	'tuber'¹⁶

Sets of contrasting minimal or near-minimal pairs for the palatal stop consonants are shown in (16) - (18). The examples in (16) show contrasts between word-initial /c/, /ⁿɟ/, and /ɲ/.

(16)
caaŋ	'to steal'	ⁿɟaŋ	'to measure'	ɲa-ŋ	'mother-1SG.POSS'
ci	'to sit'	ⁿɟi	'1DU.INCL.INDEP'	ɲi-	'shape'
co	'whale'	ⁿɟo	'chicken'	ɲo-	'tentacle'
cu-	'to overwhelm'	ⁿɟua	'very'	ɲu	'anchor'

---

16 See §4.2.4 on noun classifiers.

The examples in (17) show contrasts between word-initial /c/ and /j/.

(17)　caaŋ　　'to steal'　　　　jaaŋ　　'to search'
　　　cĕĕk　　'swamp harrier'　jeek　　'plant, tree'
　　　cen　　 'salt.LN'　　　　 jen　　 'breadfruit'
　　　cewa-　 'relationship'　　jewa-　 'season'
　　　co　　　'whale'　　　　　 jo　　　'2SG.INDEP'
　　　cu-　　 'to stand'　　　　ju-　　 'to dig'
　　　cuuc　　'councilman'　　 juuc　　'mangrove crab'

The contrast between syllable-final /c/ and /ɲ/ is illustrated in (18). Note that /ⁿɟ/ and /j/ do not occur syllable-finally.

(18)　ãc　　　'man'　　　　　　　　ãɲ　　　'rudder'
　　　caac　　'immature (shellfish)'　cãɲ　　 'to seize'
　　　ⁿdaac　'farm'　　　　　　　　 ⁿdaɲ　　'white-bellied goshawk'[17]
　　　keec　　'to reproduce'　　　　 ⁿgeeɲ　'to regret'
　　　kic　　 'liver'　　　　　　　　kiɲ　　 'type of bird'
　　　poc　　 'Poc'[18]　　　　　　　poɲ　　'beam'
　　　ᵐbuc　　'pawn'　　　　　　　　 ᵐbuɲ　　'great crested tern'[19]

2.2.1.4 Velar consonants

The velar consonants in Belep include stops /k/, /ⁿg/, and /ŋ/. These phonemes are contrastive in word-initial position, as shown in (19).

(19)　ka-　 'leg, foot'
　　　ⁿga-　'sympathy'
　　　ŋa[20]　'to creak'

Sets of contrasting minimal or near-minimal pairs for the velar stop consonants are shown in (20) and (21). The examples in (20) show contrasts between /k/, /ⁿg/, and /ŋ/ in word-initial and word-medial position.

---

17 *Accipiter haplochrous.*
18 Toponym for the islet north of Art.
19 *Sterna bergii.*
20 In some pronunciations. Other speakers say /ⁿgã/.

(20) kaᵐbeat 'jellyfish'   ⁿgaⁿga 'ghost'   ŋaⁿgato 'spider conch'
     kao-   'radius'   ⁿgao   'bamboo'   -
     cake   'to be ashamed' caⁿge- 'to steal.TR' caɲe-   'to switch'

The syllable-final contrast between /k/ and /ŋ/ is shown in (21). Prenasalized /ⁿg/ does not occur syllable-finally.

(21) cak   'to fish with a net'   caaŋ   'to steal'
     mʷaak   'streamlined spinefoot'²¹   mʷaa-ŋ   'house-1SG.POSS'
     waa-k   'DEM.MAN-DET.D.PRX'   waaŋ   'boat'
     jak   'today'   jaaŋ   'to search'
     mʷek   'to be twisted'   mʷeeŋ   'decoration'
     wẽẽk   'tobacco'   wẽẽŋ   'to learn'

2.2.1.5 Nasal consonants

The nasal consonants in Belep include /mʷ/, /m/, /n/, /ɲ/ and /ŋ/. These phonemes are contrastive in syllable-initial position (word-initially and word-medially) as shown in (22), and in syllable-final position (23).

(22) mʷa   'house'
     ma   'LK4'
     na-   'interior'
     ɲa-   'mother'
     ŋa   'to creak'

(23) ã-mʷ   'cutting-2SG.POSS'
     ãm   'plate'
     ã-n   'cutting-3SG.POSS'
     ãɲ   'rudder'
     ã-ŋ   'cutting-1SG.POSS'

Sets of contrasting minimal or near-minimal pairs for the nasal consonants are shown in (24) and (26). The contrast between /mʷ/ and /m/ was demonstrated above in §2.3.1.1. The examples in (24) show contrasts between /n/, /ɲ/, and /ŋ/ in word-initial and word-medial position.

---

21 *Siganus fuscescens*.

(24) nia   'duck'   ɲi-   'shape'   -
      no   'fish'   ɲo-   'tentacle' -
      nu   'coconut tree' ɲu   'anchor'   -
      canan 'to be sour'   cãɲi-   'to faint' caŋe-   'to change'
      mani   'bird'   maɲina- 'CL.yam'   maɲi-   'to be disgusted'

Note that phonemes /ɲ/ and /ŋ/ are considerably rarer than the other nasal consonants, particularly initially and medially. Only three Belep words beginning with /ŋ/ have been identified (25).

(25) ŋaⁿgato 'spider conch'
      ŋa   'to creak'
      ŋini-   'to not see'

The syllable-final contrast between /n/, /ɲ/, and /ŋ/ is shown in (26).

(26) cen   'salt.LN'   cãɲ   'to seize'   caaŋ   'to steal'
      ⁿdan   'sky'   ⁿdaɲ   'goshawk'²²   ⁿʲaŋ   'to measure'
      pʷãn   'to push'   mʷaɲ   'to be bad'   pʷaŋ   'bay'
      paan   'screwpine'   pããɲ   'sow thistle' tããŋ   'to scrape'
      jãn   'ciguatera'²³ -   jããŋ   'to gather'

Unlike most other Northern languages (Ozanne-Rivierre et al. 1998), Belep does not distinguish between so-called "aspirated" nasals (i.e. voiceless nasals) and plain nasals. For example, Balade Nyelâyu contrasts *nu* 'coconut palm' with *nhu* 'hot', while in Belep the words are homophonous: Belep [nu] is 'coconut palm' or 'hot'.

2.2.1.6 Approximants

The Belep approximants are /w/, /j/, and /l/. These phonemes are contrastive in syllable-initial position, as shown in (27). They do not appear in syllable-final position. See §2.2.2.4 for a justification for classifying /w/ and /j/ as consonants in Belep.

---

22 Immature *Accipiter haplochrous*.
23 A type of food poisoning caused by eating fish contaminated with ciguatoxin.

(27) wa   'grandparent'
      ja-   'tuber'
      la   '3PL.INDEP'

As noted above in §2.2.1.2, /l/ is very rare in word-initial position. The examples in (28) show word-initial contrasts between /w/, /j/, and /l/.

(28) waaŋ   'boat'   jaaŋ   'to search'   -
      wala   'Waala'²⁴   jala   'to shake'   -
      wẽẽk   'tobacco'   jeek   'plant'   lee-k   'DEM.DU-DET.D.PRX'
      wo   'to weave'   jo   '2SG.INDEP'   -

Medial [w], [j], and [l] also contrast with one another as shown in the minimal and near-minimal sets in (29). See §2.3.1.5 for more on the neutralizations which make their phonemic forms impossible to reconstruct.

(29) [awaa]   'mat'   [aja-]   'CL.twenty'   [ala-]   'container'
      [tawa]   'to cut'   [tajamõ]   'old woman'   [tala-]   'bed'
      [cawanẽ-]   'mast'   [caja]   'dad'   [calac]   'to brush'
      [kewe-]   'to chase'   [ceje]   'to believe'   [keler]   'coffin'
      [iwi-]   'to file'   [iji]   'louse'   [tili-]   'to knot'
      [puβuⁿdi]   'to be oval' [ᵐbuju]   'sea purslane' [pulu]   'to speak'

Unlike in the other Northern New Caledonian languages, Belep approximants do not contrast in aspiration. For example, Balade Nyelâyu contrasts *wan* 'turtle' and *whan* 'species of sugar cane'; *yen* 'breadfruit' and *yhen* 'to dig, harvest'; and *lhe* '3DU.INDEP' with *-le* '3DU.OBJ' (Ozanne-Rivierre et al. 1998), while in Belep these forms are homophonous.

2.2.2 Vowels

Belep has five²⁵ oral and five nasal vowels: /i/, /e/, /a/, /o/, /u/ and /ĩ/, /ẽ/, /ã/, /õ/, /ũ/. All of these vowels may occur in open or closed syllables (§2.7). Note that Belep does not have a phonemic distinction in vowel length, unlike Balade Nyelâyu (Ozanne-Rivierre et al. 1998).²⁶ Low and mid vowels occur most frequently, while high

---

24 The toponym <Waala> is the name of the main village in Belep.
25 Only the Belep word /ãᵐby/ 'periwinkle' contains the vowel /y/. This word may be a loan from Nêlêmwa /haᵐbʉ/ 'periwinkle' (Bril 2000).
26 See §2.3.2.2 on vowel hiatus.

vowels are less common. The vowel inventory of Belep is largely comparable with that of other Far North New Caledonian languages. Nêlêmwa (Bril 2000) has the same ten vowels, plus two central vowels /ʉ/ and /ø/ which occur in a few words; the same vowel qualities are found in Balade Nyelâyu (Ozanne-Rivierre et al. 1998). Yuanga (Schooling 1992) has ten vowels (five oral and five nasal), plus /ɛ/ and /ɔ/. Other Northern languages have somewhat different vowel inventories; for example, there are ten oral and seven nasal vowels in Paicî (Gordon & Maddieson 2004).

The examples in (30) below show minimal and near-minimal pairs for the five oral vowels in Belep. Minimal pairs for the five nasal vowels are shown in (31). See §2.2.2 and §2.3.2 for more information on the phonological and phonetic characteristics of Belep vowels.

(30)

ti	te-	ta	to	tu
'who'	'breast'	'to go.UH'	'to call'	'to go.DH'
pi-	pe	pa	po	pu-
'to cook'	'ray'	'to take'	'to lie'	'side'
ci	ce	ca	co	cu-
'to sit'	'to settle'	'to be how?'	'whale'	'to stand'
tic	tep	cap	top	tup
'to defecate'	'to click'	'type of dance'	'to melt'	'to dive'
pi-n	-	pan	pon	pu-n
'cook-DA.NSG'		'to go.TV'	'loach'	'pick-DA.NSG'
i-t	e-t	at	ot	-
'skin-3GNR.POSS'	'hand-3GNR.POSS'	'sun'	'2DU.INDEP'	
ᵐbiin	ᵐbeen	paan	-	-
'to be skinny'	'to be wet'	'screwpine'		
-	keec	kaac	koot	kuuc
	'to reproduce'	'to be bitter'	'to be soft'	'few'

(31)

ĩⁿɟi	-	ãⁿɟa	-	ũⁿɟep
'ant'		'to hunt troca'		'sugar cane'
ĩna	ẽna	ãna-	õni	ũⁿdu
'to make'	'to know'	'contents'	'pisonia'	'to drink'
tĩni-	tẽno	tãna	tõnok	pũnu
'to burn'	'type of shell'	'to hear'	'mucus'	'to lower'

kĩɲ		cãɲ	põn	kũɲ
'woodswallow'		'to seize'	'hair'	'to sweat'
nawĭ	pẽ	ciã	õ	pũ
'ironwood'	'bread.LN'	'flea'	'to be good'	'dropseed'
kĩĭt	wĕĕk	kããk	kõõk	kũũt
'to be loud'	'tobacco'	'to yell'	'heron'	'to grunt'

Belep oral and nasal vowels contrast in all positions except for following a prenasalized stop (§2.3.1.3) or a nasal phoneme (a consonant or vowel). In these positions, the contrast between oral and nasal vowels is neutralized (see §2.2.1.5, §2.3.2.3). Some examples of minimal and near-minimal pairs demonstrating the contrast between oral and nasal vowels are shown in (32).

(32) iⁿda-   'lineage'   kĩⁿda   'tropical almond'
      tilie   'to knot'   tĩnie[27]   'to burn'
      wee-ŋ   'food-1SG.POSS'   wẽeŋ   'to organize'
      cen   'salt.LN'   cẽnee   'to swallow'
      pʷaŋ   'bay'   pʷãŋ   'inflorescence of coconut palm'
      apa   '2PL.EXCL.INDEP'   ãpa   'to fish'
      kon   'to cough'   kõnat   'maggot'
      kopa   'to come out'   kõpak   'black heron'
      uⁿdu   'to bend'   ũⁿdu   'to drink'
      pu-   'side'   pũ   'beach dropseed'

Traditionally, Northern New Caledonian grammars draw a distinction between phonemically long and phonemically short vowels (Ozanne-Rivierre et al. 1998, Bril 2000). In this work, I argue that Belep does not contrast phonemically long and short vowels; sequences of identical vowels are heterosyllabic and behave like sequences of unlike vowels (see §2.3.2.2). All vowel sequences may occur, except for those where an oral vowel follows a nasal vowel.

2.3 Description of phonemes

In this section, I describe the phonetic realization of various phonemes in Belep and argue for their phonemic status. Consonants are discussed in §2.3.1 and vowels are discussed in §2.3.2.

---

27 See §2.2.2.5 on neutralizations.

2.3.1 Consonants

In §2.3.1.1, I argue for the phonemic status of labiovelar consonants and provide some acoustic phonetic detail about their realization. In §2.3.1.2, I describe the results of a phonetic study on voice onset time in Belep voiceless stops. I conclude that there is no aspiration contrast for these stops—an unusual characteristic for a Far North language. In §2.3.1.3, I argue for the phonemic status of prenasalized stops and also provide acoustic phonetic evidence for this assertion. In §2.3.1.4, I argue for the phonemic status of approximants /w/ and /j/. In §2.3.1.5, I discuss a number of neutralizations which occur in various phonemic environments in Belep.

2.3.1.1 Labiovelar consonants

The contrast between labiovelars and bilabial consonants is a common feature of Oceanic languages, including many New Caledonian languages (Lynch 2002, Bril 2000).[28]

In Belep, labiovelar stops /pʷ/, /ᵐbʷ/, and /mʷ/ contrast with bilabial stops /p/, /ᵐb/ and /m/ before non-back vowels /i/, /e/, and /a/ in word-initial position (§2.2.1.1) and in a limited number of other environments (see §2.3.1.5). Labiovelar stops do not occur before /u/ or /o/. It is common for "Oceanic languages [to] vary as to the possible combinations of labiovelars with rounded vowels" (Lynch 2002:311); Lynch cites Lewo and Lau as other languages where labiovelars rarely, if ever, occur before /u/ and /o/.

As /w/ is also a phoneme in Belep (§2.2.1.6, §2.3.1.4), one could hypothesize that the Belep labiovelars are, in fact, consonant clusters rather than phonemes. A considerable amount of evidence exists to counter this hypothesis. Labiovelars in Belep contrast with sequences of the form BILABIAL STOP + /u/, as shown in the minimal and near-minimal pairs in (33).

(33)	pʷaka	'to wash'	puaka	'pig'
	pʷec	'to be born'	puet	'to prepare food'
	ᵐbʷa-	'head'	ᵐbua	'to drown'
	ᵐbʷan	'night'	ᵐbuaɲ	'rock'
	mʷa	'house'	mua-	'flower'
	taᵐbʷa	'to attach'	taᵐbua	'to break'

If clusters with /w/ as the second element existed, we would expect a variety of consonants to be able to serve as the first element; however, non-labial consonants in

---

28 Three labiovelar consonants, *bʷ, *pʷ, and *mʷ, have been reconstructed for Proto-Oceanic by Lynch (2002).

Belep cannot be labialized (e.g. there is no */nʷa/ or */ŋgʷa/). No other clusters exist in the language. Finally, there are phonotactic and prosodic differences between sequences of the form LABIOVELAR STOP + VOWEL and sequences of BILABIAL STOP + /u/ + VOWEL—in particular, while the former is monosyllabic, the latter is disyllabic.

For example, monosyllabic /pʷa/ 'hole' contrasts with disyllabic /pua-/ 'side', which is syllabified by speakers as [pu.a]. Spectrograms for these two words are shown in Figure 1 and Figure 2.

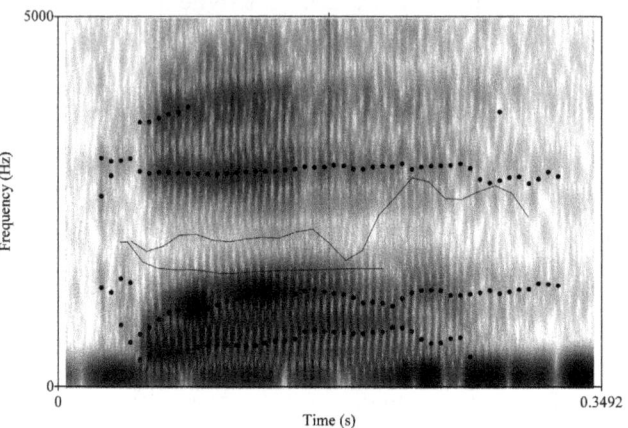

Fig. 1: Labiovelar consonant /pʷ/ in /pʷa/ 'hole'

Figure 1 shows a representative realization of the labiovelar consonant /pʷ/ occurring in the word /pʷa/ 'hole'. The third and fourth formants remain flat through the entire vowel and the pitch curve is flat and roughly parallel to the intensity curve. The total length of the vowel is approximately 210 ms; the initial portion which has the quality of [u] (due to the labialization of the consonant) is extremely short, approximately 17 ms.

By contrast, in the vowel sequence of /pua-/ 'side' (shown in Figure 2), the total length of the vowel sequence is 410 ms (nearly twice as long as the single vowel /a/ in Figure 1). The vowel is divided into two distinct portions, [u] and [a], with changes in all four formants between the two portions. The [u] portion of the vowel is approximately 144 ms, which is much longer than the corresponding [u] portion in Figure 1. As with all disyllabic words in Belep, the first vowel /u/ carries the intensity peak and the second vowel /a/ carries the pitch peak, forming the characteristic overlapping pitch/intensity curves discussed in §2.8.1.

A final piece of evidence for considering Belep labiovelars to be phonemes is that they contrast word-finally with bilabials (§2.2.1.1).

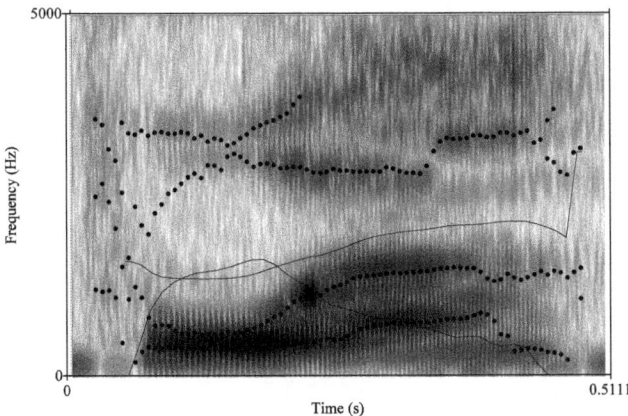

Fig. 2: Consonant + /u/ sequence in /pua-/ 'side'

2.3.1.2 Voiceless stops

The voiceless stop phonemes in Belep are /pʷ/, /p/, /t/, /c/, and /k/. They undergo a considerable amount of allophony based on their position in the phonological word (see §2.4.1.2). According to my measurements of the voice onset time (VOT) of these consonants in word-initial position (based on Cho & Ladefoged 1999, a cross-linguistic study of VOT), they are unaspirated (see the mean VOT values in Table 3).[29]

Tab. 3: Mean VOT by place of articulation

Place of articulation	Mean VOT
Bilabial	19 ms
Alveolar	15 ms
Palatal	39 ms
Velar	29 ms

A VOT of 29 ms for the Belep velar stop is typical of an unaspirated stop (Cho & Ladefoged 1999). The bilabial (19 ms) and alveolar (15 ms) stops have shorter VOT than the velar; they are unaspirated as well. Figure 3 shows a comparison of VOT by place of articulation.

---

29 These values were gathered based on a single speaker; tokens were collected both in isolation and in a carrier phrase. The labiovelar /pʷ/ was excluded from this study.

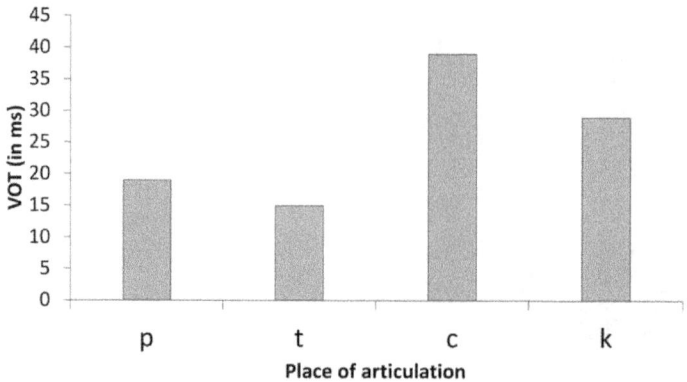

Fig. 3: Mean VOT by place of articulation

The short alveolar VOT and very long palatal VOT (39 ms) observed for Belep (Figure 3) were also noted in other New Caledonian languages such as in Iaai (Maddieson & Anderson 1994) and Ndumbea (Gordon & Maddieson 1999).

Belep is unlike other Northern New Caledonian languages in that it does not contrast aspirated and unaspirated voiceless stops in initial position. For example, Ozanne-Rivierre et al. (1998:19) lists minimal pairs such as *pe* 'ray' vs. *phe* 'file'; *ta* 'to go up' vs. *tha* 'bald'; and *con* 'to cook in an oven' vs. *chon* 'to carry on the shoulder' for Balade Nyelâyu. Belep speakers, though they recognize most of these words, do not acknowledge a difference in pronunciation.

In a case study of voice onset time in Belep, I measured two sets of words: those with reflexes of initial /p/ and those with reflexes of initial /pʰ/.[30] In this study, one speaker was recorded—a male in his 60s who is high-ranking and respected among the Belema. The speaker read from a wordlist written in the locally developed orthography.[31] The VOT for each initial stop was measured on a PC using Praat software (Boersma & Weenink 2010). Boundaries were marked only at zero crossings (Smith 1978).[32]

---

30 Reflexes of Belep words were determined by comparison with cognates in Balade Nyelâyu (Ozanne-Rivierre 1998) and Nêlêmwa (Bril 2000), as well as by notations of aspiration in Dubois's (1975c) Belep dictionary.

31 He was nominated by the Belema Language Committee as one of the best speakers. He was recorded in a quiet room using an Edirol R-09 at 44.1 KHz, 16-bit PCM wav format. Belep words were written beside their French glosses. Each word appeared in at least two wordlists, in a randomized order. Each time a word appeared in a wordlist, the speaker was asked to produce it twice: once in isolation and once in a carrier phrase.

32 For voiceless stops, VOT was measured from the onset of aperiodic noise in the waveform to the onset of periodic voicing; that is, from the beginning of the burst to the beginning of the vowel. Where

The software program PASW was used to conduct statistical analyses. A data instances model (Quene and van den Bergh 2004) with a mixed between- and within-subjects design was used. The between-subjects independent variables were the place of articulation of the stop (bilabial, alveolar, palatal, or velar), the following vowel (either /a/, /e/, /i/, /o/, or /u/), and the reconstructed aspiration class based on dictionary comparison. The within-subjects independent variable was the phonemic environment of the stop (whether it was produced in isolation or in a carrier phrase).[33] The mixed-design ANOVA was conducted on the average across the trials for the corrected VOT.

There was no significant main effect of aspiration class ($F(2, 5) = 1.2, p = .38$), as shown in Figure 4 below.

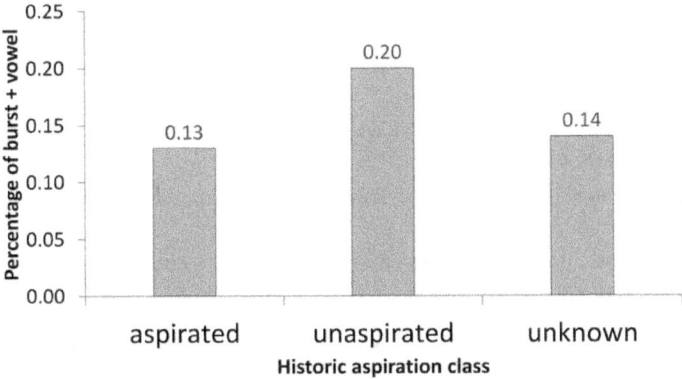

Fig. 4: Mean corrected VOT by aspiration class

Figure 4 shows a lack of significant difference in VOT between consonants which are reconstructed as aspirated and those that are reconstructed as unaspirated. In fact, historically unaspirated stops had a longer mean VOT than historically aspirated ones, though the difference was not found to be statistically significant. This indicates that Belep is not representative of the set of Northern languages which do maintain a contrast between aspirated and unaspirated stops.

The most likely explanation for the loss of an aspiration contrast in Belep initial voiceless stops is that it is simply an extreme extension of an existing trend in the

---

a release burst was not visible on the waveform (notably for /c/), VOT was measured using the beginning point of visible high frequency noise on the spectrogram.

33 After calculating the raw duration values for the VOT, I adjusted the VOT values to control for rate of speech (Boucher 2002). The following formula was used to convert raw VOT values into a percentage of the segment duration: corrected VOT = raw VOT / (raw VOT + duration of following vowel). A correction for vowel duration was also performed.

Northern languages. Table 4 shows that many Northern languages have already lost their contrast for aspiration in oral stops in one or more places of articulation.[34]

Tab. 4: Loss of aspiration contrasts in Northern languages

Language	Notes	Source
Nêlêmwa-Nixumwak	Apirated stops became fricatives in Poum and Tiabet dialects	Bril (2000)
Yuanga	/cʰ/ is rare	Bretteville (1993), Schooling (1992)
Nemi	No /cʰ/	Haudricourt & Ozanne-Rivierre (1982)
Pije	No /cʰ/	Haudricourt & Ozanne-Rivierre (1982)
Fwâi	Voiceless stops are rare and only found in borrowed words	Haudricourt & Ozanne-Rivierre (1982)
Jawe	/cʰ/ found only before nasalized vowels	Haudricourt & Ozanne-Rivierre (1982)
Bwatoo, Haeke, Haveke (Voh-Koné)	Only /tʰ/ is a productive aspirated phoneme; very few lexical items use /pʰ/, /cʰ/, or /kʰ/	Rivierre & Ehrhart (2006)

In some dialects of Nêlêmwa-Nixumwak and the Voh-Koné varieties, aspirated stops have been replaced by fricatives. In Yuanga, Nemi, Pije, and Jawe, the aspirated palatal is rare or only occurs in limited environments. In Fwâi, all voiceless stops are rare. In this context, Belep's lack of aspiration contrasts appears consistent with the other languages in its subfamily.

2.3.1.3 Prenasalized stops

Cross-linguistically, both phonemic and phonetic evidence is used to justify classifying a nasal-consonant (NC) sequence (Riehl 2008), also called a nasal+stop sequence (Ladefoged & Maddieson 2006), as a prenasalized phoneme. In this work, I analyze Belep NC sequences as phonemically prenasalized stops /ᵐbʷ/, /ᵐb/, /ⁿd/, /ᶮɟ/, and /ᵑg/.

There is considerable phonemic evidence for this assertion. First, plain voiced stops do not occur in Belep independently of the nasal portion. NC sequences occur initially and medially, while coda consonants are not permitted except word-finally (34).

---

34 Note that none of these studies includes an acoustic analysis.

(34) /pan/ 'to go.TV'
/paⁿda/ 'type of seaweed'
*/panta/
/pata/ 'to tell'
/ⁿda/ 'what?'
*/nta/
/ta/ 'to go.UH'

Belep speakers sometimes produce French voiced stops with prenasalisation (35).

(35) French *l'eau béni* [lo beni] 'holy water' produced as Belep [loᵐbeni]
Yal-28072010-BGMCG-tahitian_0316

No consonant clusters occur in Belep. In fact, when Herbert (1986) argues that there is no need to consider NC sequences in any language as single phonemic segments, he excludes the set of New Caledonian languages with prenasalized stops from this assertion, claiming that these are simply phonemically voiced stops with phonetic prenasalization.[35] Prenasalized stops have phonemic status in Balade Nyelâyu (Ozanne-Rivierre et al. 1998), Nêlêmwa (Bril 2000), and Paicî (Gordon & Maddieson 2004), among others.[36] In this work, I analyze all Belep NC sequences as phonemic prenasalized stops.

Cross-linguistic phonetic evidence for prenasalization has been somewhat more controversial. Ladefoged & Maddieson (1996) showed that a language can be classified as either containing NC clusters or prenasalized stops, but not both. Riehl (2008) summarizes three types of phonetic evidence that existing studies use to identify prenasalized stops: the duration of the segment; the degree of nasalization in the preceding vowel; and the duration of the preceding vowel (compensatory lengthening). Her study on Tamambo and Erromangan of Vanuatu, and Pamona and Manado Malay of Indonesia, found that the latter two types of evidence were not good predictors. Only segmental duration in comparison with the duration of nasals—where prenasalized stops are comparable in duration to nasals, while NC clusters are longer than nasals—was found to be a significant distinguishing factor (Riehl 2008). However,

---

35 Rivierre (1973) disagrees, arguing that New Caledonian prenasalized stops are in fact phonemic nasals with an allophonic stop release conditioned by a following oral vowel. There is some phonological evidence in Belep for this assertion.

36 Some phonemic evidence exists in Belep to counter the assertion that NC sequences are single phonemes. Inflectional noun and verb stem modifications often correlate prenasalized stops with nasal consonants, e.g. /tolam/ 'basket' vs. /tolaᵐba-/ 'basket', /ãɲ/ 'rudder' vs. /ãⁿɟe-/ 'to steer'. This would seem to indicate that the nasal part of the NC sequence has some degree of phonemic value to speakers. However, in this work I consider this correspondence to be largely the result of historical sound changes, rather than synchronic Belep phonology.

Maddieson (1989) found that prenasalized stops in Fijian have a similar duration to non-nasal segments in that language, namely, /t/, /k/, and /l/.

In the rest of this section, I present an acoustic phonetic analysis of Belep NC sequences. To determine the status of these sequences, I compared the duration of prenasalized stops with that of both voiceless stops (similar to Maddieson 1989) and nasal segments (commensurate with Riehl 2008). I found that Belep NC sequences were shorter in duration than both voiceless stops and nasal consonants—a finding which provides further evidence for the analysis of Belep NC sequences as prenasalized phonemes rather than consonant clusters.

Figure 5 shows a graph of the duration of Belep NC sequences, divided into their nasal and stop portions.[37]

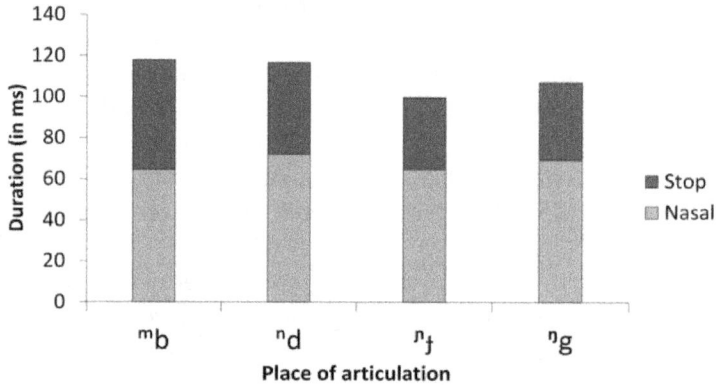

Fig. 5: Mean raw duration of nasal and stop portions by place of articulation

Figure 5 shows that, in general, the overall duration of the segment decreases as the place of articulation moves back, but that this trend is more attributable to the decrease in duration of the stop portion than to the nasal portion. As in Ndumbea (Gordon & Maddieson 1999), the bilabial prenasalized segment is the longest. However, unlike in Ndumbea, where the stop portion makes up on average 29% of the segment, in Belep the stop portion makes up 39% of the segment. This data is also represented in Table 5.

---

37 Prenasalized stops were measured in Praat using the methodology Gordon & Maddieson (1999) used for Ndumbea, a Southern New Caledonian language. The nasal portion was measured from the onset of periodicity in the waveform to the point where the waveform changed shape and decreased in amplitude. The oral portion was measured from here to the burst transient (1999:85). Boundaries were marked only at zero crossings; that is, points where the waveform crossed the x-axis (Smith 1978). The labiovelar /ᵐbʷ/ was excluded from this study.

Tab. 5: Mean duration of nasal and stop portions by place of articulation

Place of Articulation	Nasal portion	Stop portion	Total
Bilabial	64.47 ms	53.53 ms	121 ms
Alveolar	72 ms	44.84 ms	116.84 ms
Palatal	64.58 ms	35.18 ms	99.76 ms
Velar	69.31 ms	38 ms	107.31 ms
Average	**68.34 ms**	**42.89 ms**	**111.23 ms**

Table 5 shows that the mean duration of the nasal portion is 68 ms and the mean duration of the stop portion is 43 ms, for a total segment duration of 111 ms. The mean duration results are consistent with values reported for Fijian, another Oceanic language, where the mean duration across places of articulation is 123 ms (Maddieson 1989), and for Ndumbea, where the mean duration is 116 ms (Gordon & Maddieson 1999).

I compared these segment durations with the duration of voiceless stops. Using only tokens produced in a carrier phrase, I conducted a between-subjects ANOVA on segment duration (averaged across tokens of a word) where the independent variables were place of articulation, following vowel, and whether the segment was a voiceless stop (stop portion + VOT) or a prenasalized stop (nasal portion + stop portion). Figure 6 is a graph showing duration by place of articulation.

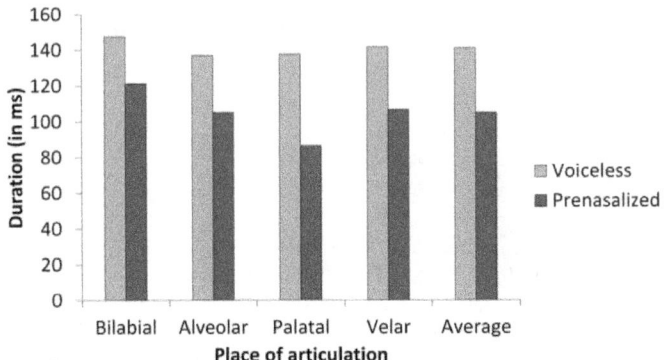

Fig. 6: Mean raw duration of voiceless and prenasalized stops (in a carrier phrase) by place of articulation

The graph in Figure 6 shows that prenasalized stops are shorter than voiceless stops at all places of articulation. This observation was confirmed statistically by the results of the ANOVA, which shows that prenasalized stops are significantly shorter than voiceless stops, $F(1, 18) = 75.26$, $p < .001$. Their means are represented in Table 6.

Tab. 6: Mean raw duration of stops (in a carrier phrase) by place of articulation

Place of Articulation	Voiceless	Prenasalized
Bilabial	147.56 ms	121.23 ms
Alveolar	136.96 ms	105.16 ms
Palatal	137.6 ms	86.5 ms
Velar	141.46 ms	106.53 ms
Average	140.9 ms	104.86 ms

Table 6 shows that the mean duration of voiceless stops is 141 ms while the mean duration of prenasalized stops is 105 ms. This finding differs from Maddieson's (1989) study on Fijian, which found that prenasalized segments were comparable in duration to /t/, /k/, and /l/, which averaged 119 ms. However, it is not surprising, given that several studies have demonstrated that voiced consonants are typically shorter than comparable voiceless consonants (Lehiste 1970, Klatt 1976, Zue and Laferriere 1979). This finding provides further evidence that Belep NC sequences should be considered to be single segments.

Next, I compared the duration of NC sequences with that of nasal consonants. Using only tokens produced in a carrier phrase, I conducted a between-subjects ANOVA on segment duration (averaged across tokens of a word) where the independent variables were place of articulation, following vowel, and whether the segment was a nasal (prestopped portion + nasal portion) or a prenasalized stop (nasal portion + stop portion). Figure 7 is a graph showing duration by place of articulation.

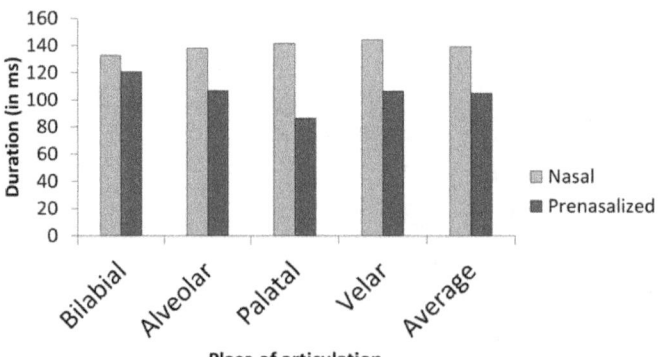

Fig. 7: Mean duration of nasals and prenasalized stops (in a carrier phrase) by place of articulation

The graph in Figure 7 shows that prenasalized stops are shorter than nasals at all places of articulation. This observation was confirmed statistically by the results of the ANOVA, which shows that prenasalized stops are significantly shorter than nasals, $F(1, 13) = 43.72, p < .001$. Their means are represented in Table 7.

Tab. 7: Mean raw duration of nasals and prenasalized stops

Place of Articulation	Nasal	Prenasalized
Bilabial	132.79 ms	120.72 ms
Alveolar	138.08 ms	106.9 ms
Palatal	141.71 ms	86.53 ms
Velar	144.5 ms	106.53 ms
Average	**139.27 ms**	**105.17 ms**

Table 7 shows that the mean duration of nasal segments is 139 ms, while the mean duration of prenasalized segments is 105 ms. Riehl (2008) found that phonemically prenasalized segments were comparable in duration to nasals, while NC clusters were longer; since Belep prenasalized segments are shorter than nasals, this is evidence for their phonemic status as prenasalized segments rather than clusters.

In summary, the duration of prenasalized stops in Belep is comparable to that found in other languages. In a manner consistent with other languages containing prenasalized stops, the stop portion of the prenasalized segment in Belep is longest for bilabials. Unlike in Fijian, prenasalized stops in Belep are shorter than voiceless stops; however, this is not unusual cross-linguistically. A comparison with the duration of nasals shows that prenasalized segments are shorter than nasals, which indicates their status as phonemes rather than clusters.

2.3.1.4 Approximants

Though they are vowel-like, the two central approximants /w/ and /j/ fall into the phonemic category of consonants in Belep. They cannot occur in clusters with other consonants, and sequences of Approximant + Vowel contrast with sequences of vowels, as shown in Table 8.

Tab. 8: Central approximant contrasts with sequences of vowels

wa	'grandparent'	ua-	'portion to suck'
we	'water'	u-e	'remove-SPC'
ⁿdiju	'coins'	ⁿdi-u	'give-DETR'
piji-e	'delouse-3SG.ABS'	pi-e	'cook-3SG.ABS'

The sequences of Approximant + Vowel in the first column of Table 8 are identified by speakers as a single syllable, while the contrasting vowel sequences in the third column are identified as multi-syllabic. Furthermore, both /w/ and /j/ undergo allophonic alternation to more clearly consonantal sounds (§2.4.1.4).

A final piece of evidence that /w/ and /j/ are consonantal in Belep is that their presence blocks the phonetic nasalization of vowels following a nasal segment (§2.5.3). For example, consider the minimal pair /mia/ 'ripe' and /mija/ 'Mass' (a Latin loan from *missa*). The pronunciation of /mia/ as [mĩã] reveals nasal spreading across both vowels of the vowel sequence. By contrast, /mija/ is produced [mĩja]; the consonant /j/ blocks the nasal spreading.

2.3.1.5 Neutralizations

There are a number of consonantal neutralizations which occur in Belep. These include the neutralization of: the labiovelar vs. bilabial contrast before back vowels; the contrast between /pʷ/ vs. /w/, and /c/ vs. /j/, word-medially; and the contrast between /l/ and /n/ in some environments.

The contrast between labiovelars /pʷ/, /ᵐbʷ/, /mʷ/ and bilabials /p/, /ᵐb/, /m/ is neutralized before back vowels /o/ and /u/; no minimal pairs exist in this environment (36).

(36)
	po	'to tell lies'	ᵐbo	'to stink'	mo 'to live'
	pot	'to be boiling'	ᵐbot	'to be shipwrecked'	-
	pu-	'side'	ᵐbu	'fishhook'	mu 'to moor'
	pua	'chinese lantern tree'	ᵐbua	'to drown'	mua- 'flower'
	puc	'to fly'	ᵐbuc	'pawn'	-
	puja	'to uncover'	ᵐbuja	'to agree'	-

It is common for "Oceanic languages [to] vary as to the possible combinations of labiovelars with rounded vowels" (Lynch 2002:311); Lynch cites Lewo and Lau as other languages where labiovelars rarely, if ever, occur before /u/ and /o/. This cross-linguistic evidence, as well as speaker intuitions, indicate that the consonants which occur before /o/ and /u/ are phonemically bilabial.[38]

The contrast between /pʷ/ and /w/ is neutralized word-medially. Only phonetic [w] occurs in this environment. There is morphophonemic evidence that /pʷ/ alternates with [w], as in (37).

---

38 Speakers use bilabial graphemes <p>, <b>, and <m> to write these phonemes (§2.6), despite the fact that they are normally allophonically labialized before back vowels (§2.4.1.1).

(37) ⁿdepʷ   'deck'   [ⁿdewa-]   '(something's) deck'
      noᵐbʷapʷ   'to provoke'   [nõᵐbʷawi-]   'provoke.TR'
      ãpʷ   'to laugh'   [ãwi-]   'laugh.TR'

However, in cases where there is no morphophonological alternation (38), it is impossible to categorize medial [w] as /pʷ/ or /w/.

(38) [awawa-]   'cheek'   /awawa-/ or /apʷapʷa-/
      [ᵐbʷawa]   'to remove'   /ᵐbʷawa/ or /ᵐbʷapʷa/
      [cawi]   'hunger'   /cawi/ or /capʷi/
      [ⁿgawaaɾ]   'day'   /ⁿgawaat/ or /ⁿgapʷaat/
      [nãwe-]   'to leave'   /nawe/ or /napʷe/
      [pawi]   'hibiscus'   /pawi/ or /papʷi/

In words such as those in (38), speakers have chosen to use grapheme <w> (§2.6) for orthographic consistency.

Word-initial /w/ has the allophone [β] before back vowels /o/ and /u/ (§2.4.1). The contrast between word-medial [w] (which is impossible to categorize as either /pʷ/ or /w/) and word-medial /p/ [v] (see §2.4.1.2) is neutralized before back vowels /o/ and /u/. Only phonetic [β] appears word-medially before a back vowel. There is morphophonemic evidence that /pʷ/ and /p/ both alternate with [β], as shown in (39).

(39) ⁿdepʷ   'mat'   [ⁿdeβo-]   '(someone's) mat'
      ⁿdaap   'powder'   [ⁿdaβo-]   '(something's) powder'
                                     [caβõ]   'soap' < Fr. *savon* [savõ]
                                     [caβonẽ]   'Japanese' < Fr. *japonais*
                                                   [ʒapone]

However, in cases where there is no morphophonological alternation (40), it is impossible to categorize medial [β] as /pʷ/, /p/, or /w/.

(40) [aβonõ]   'cemetery'   /apʷono/ or /apono/ or /awono/
      [ãβuɾ]   'wave'   /ãpʷut/ or /ãput/ or /ãwut/
      [kaβu-]   'guardian'   /kapʷu-/ or /kapu-/ or /kawu-/
      [taβo]   'sea cucumber' /tapʷo/ or /tapo/ or /tawo/
      [teβuuɾ]   'to begin'   /tepʷuut/ or /tepuut/ or /tewuut/
      [waβo]   'tide'   /wapʷo/ or /wapo/ or /wawo/

In words such as those in (40), speakers have chosen to use grapheme <w> for consistency.

The contrast between /c/ and /ɟ/ is neutralized word-medially. Only phonetic [j] occurs in this environment. There is morphophonemic evidence that /c/ alternates with [j], as in (41).

(41) kic   'liver'   [kije-]   '(someone's) liver'
      õᵐbʷac   'to watch'   [õᵐbʷaji-]   'watch.TR'
      paac   'smokehouse'   [paja-]   '(something's) smokehouse'
      ãc   'man'   [ãjii-k]   'man-DET.D.PRX'
      capac   'to depart'   [cavaja=ⁿdu]   'depart=DIR.DH'

However, in cases where there is no morphophonological alternation (42), it is impossible to categorize medial [j] as /c/ or /ɟ/.

(42) [ãja]   'to fear'   /ãca/ or /ãja/
      [ᵐbojãm]   'to bathe'   /ᵐbocãm/ or /ᵐbojãm/
      [caja-]   'father'   /caca-/ or /caja-/
      [iju]   'to sell'   /icu/ or /iju/
      [ⁿɟajo]   'milk tree'   /ⁿɟaco/ or /ⁿɟajo/
      [kojap]   'type of lobster' /kocap/ or /kojap/
      [pejeɾe]   'to brawl'   /pecete/ or /pejete/

In words such as those in (42), speakers have chosen to use grapheme <y> (§2.6) for orthographic consistency.

The contrast between /n/ and /l/ is neutralized in some word-medial environments. Only phonetic [l] occurs after an oral vowel, and only phonetic [n] occurs after a nasal vowel, as in (43).[39] Unlike in Balade Nyelâyu, the production of medial [n] as [l] is unacceptable to Belep speakers.

(43) [ala-]   'container'   [ãnã-]   'contents'
      [ᵐbalap]   'to move'   [ãnãp]   'to lie down'
      [cili-]   'to thatch'   [cĩnĩk]   'fifteen'
      [ele]   'knife'   [ẽnẽ-]   'point of reference'
      [kela]   'to slide'   [kẽnãva-]   'tongue'
      [pola]   'to pluck'   [põnã-]   'tail'

---

[39] Ozanne-Rivierre (1998) describes a similar situation in Balade Nyelâyu as the result of a historical process whereby intervocalic *n in the proto-language became intervocalic /l/ in the modern language. "In intervocalic position, a nasal *l* [l̃] developed whose effect is to nasalize the surrounding vowels…This nasal -*l*- derives historically from an older intervocalic *-n-." Then, intervocalic /n/ was reintroduced into Balade Nyelâyu through borrowings from European languages (Ozanne-Rivierre 1998:21-22).

[polo-]	'to interrupt'	[tõnõk]	'snail'
[tala-]	'bed'	[tãnã]	'to hear'
[tulu]	'twine'	[kũnũ]	'to be amputated'

In words containing [l] and [n], speakers have chosen to use grapheme <l> after an oral vowel and grapheme <n> after a nasal or nasalized vowel (see §2.6).

Note that Belep vowels are phonetically nasalized after nasal phonemes and phonetically oral after prenasalized stops (§2.3.2.4). Since the oral vs. nasal contrast for vowels is neutralized in this position, /l/ and /n/ may contrast medially after an open syllable with a nasal or prenasalized stop onset. For example, /ⁿgana-/ 'color' contrasts with /ⁿga-la/ 'sympathy-3PL.POSS'. Some examples of near-minimal pairs are shown in (44).

(44)	ᵐbane-	'companion'	ᵐbala-	'end'
	ᵐbʷena	'type of lizard'	ᵐbela	'to crawl'
	ᵐbonu	'type of cowrie'	ᵐbolao	'banana tree'
	ⁿdana-	'path'	ⁿdalap	'cloth of gold cone snail'
	ᶮɟanu	'spirit'	ᶮɟulã	'fish-poison tree'
	pumʷane-	'whorl'	kumʷala	'sweet potato'
	mʷanok	'moon'	malom	'immaculate'
	mina	'fallow'	nila-	'great-grandparent'

It is likely that medial [n] is in the process of becoming phonemic in these instances. Dubois (1975c) lists [ᶮɟale-] 'ear' and [nõle] 'type of sumac', but I only ever observed the pronunciations [ᶮɟanẽ-] and [nõnẽ].

The contrast between /n/ and /ɲ/ is neutralized at some morpheme boundaries before /i/. For example, the phonemically alveolar nasal in /topen=i cao/ [toveɲĩ c̃c̃ao] 'to finish working' becomes phonetically palatal when followed by genitive enclitic =i (see §6.4.3).

2.3.2 Vowels

In §2.3.2.1, I present acoustic phonetic descriptions of the five canonical oral vowel qualities in Belep. In §2.3.2.2, I describe hiatus in Belep vowel sequences, which may be sequences either of like or unlike vowels. Section §2.3.2.3 presents the phonological and phonetic characteristics of Belep nasal vowels.

2.3.2.1 Vowel quality

There are five basic vowel qualities in Belep: low central vowel /a/, which is by far the most common vowel; close mid vowels /e/ and /o/; and high vowels /i/ and /u/, which are fairly uncommon. Figure 8 and Figure 9 show the respective vowel spaces of a male speaker (age 70) and a female speaker (in her 20s) for vowels in an open syllable.[40] These vowel spaces show that vowel tokens tend to cluster closely together, particularly for the back vowels and /a/. The mid vowels /e/ and /o/ are phonetically fairly high, or 'close'. Also of note is the fact that the female speaker's /u/ vowel is considerably more fronted than the male speaker's, and the /a/ vowel is more dispersed. It is unknown whether these differences are the result of the influence of a sociolinguistic variable.

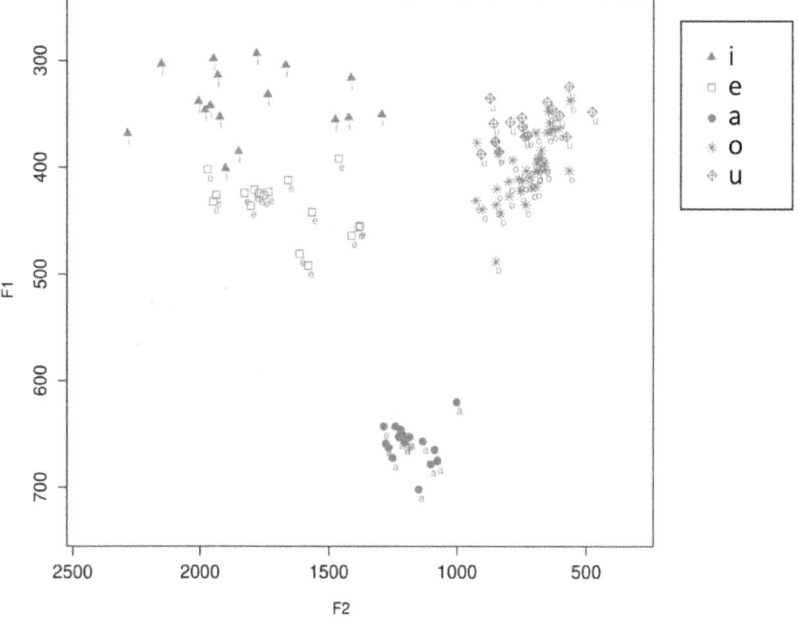

Fig. 8: Vowels before [r], male speaker (age 70), in Hz

---

40 Tokens for the singleton oral vowels averaged here were collected from multisyllabic words where the vowel was taken from the first syllable, which was open and followed by /t/ [r]. This was chosen as the best medial consonant for the vowel to precede, since the other choices were prenasalized stops, [w], [v], [j], [ʁ], and [l]. The tokens represented in Figure 8 and Figure 9 include those produced in isolation, as well as those produced in the carrier phrase /na āti __ āōtaic/ [nā āri __ āōraic] 'I say __ one time'. Formants were measured one-third of the way into the vowel using Praat, unless background noise interfered with the correct measurement at that point.

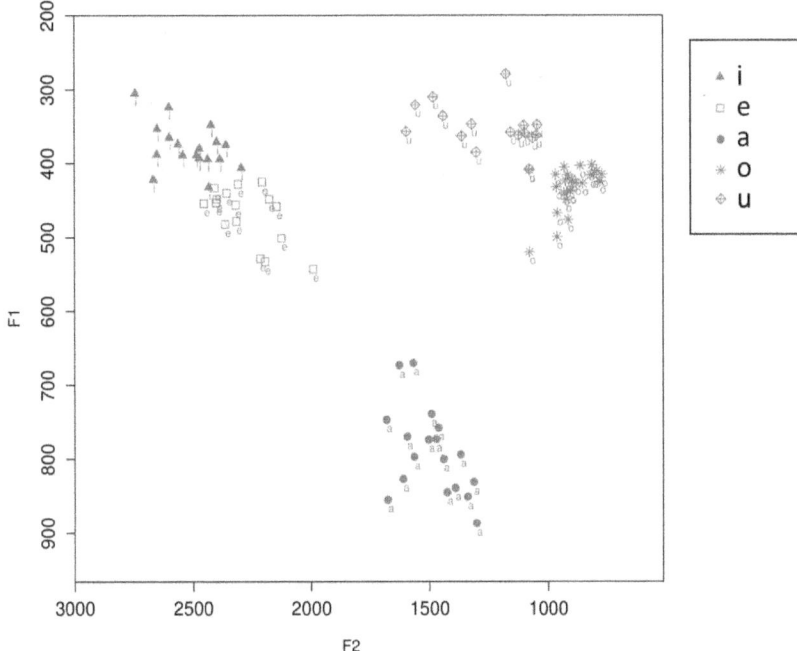

Fig. 9: Vowels before [r], female speaker (age 20s), in Hz

Figure 10 and Figure 11 below, which depict formant values averaged across all instances of the vowel,[41] show that the phonetic quality of a Belep vowel differs depending on whether it occurs in a closed or open syllable. In general in Belep, vowels in a closed syllable tend to be more centralized, as can be seen for a female speaker in her 20s in Figure 10.

---

41 Tokens for the singleton oral vowels averaged here were collected from a) monosyllabic words, where the syllable was closed by a voiceless stop (indicated by a square in the plot); and b) multisyllabic words where the vowel was taken from the first syllable, which was open and followed by /t/~[r] (see §2.4.1.2) (indicated by a circle in the plot). In total, 195 tokens from a male speaker (age 70) and 182 tokens from a female speaker (in her 20s) were collected from 37 words, split between those produced in isolation and those produced in a carrier phrase.

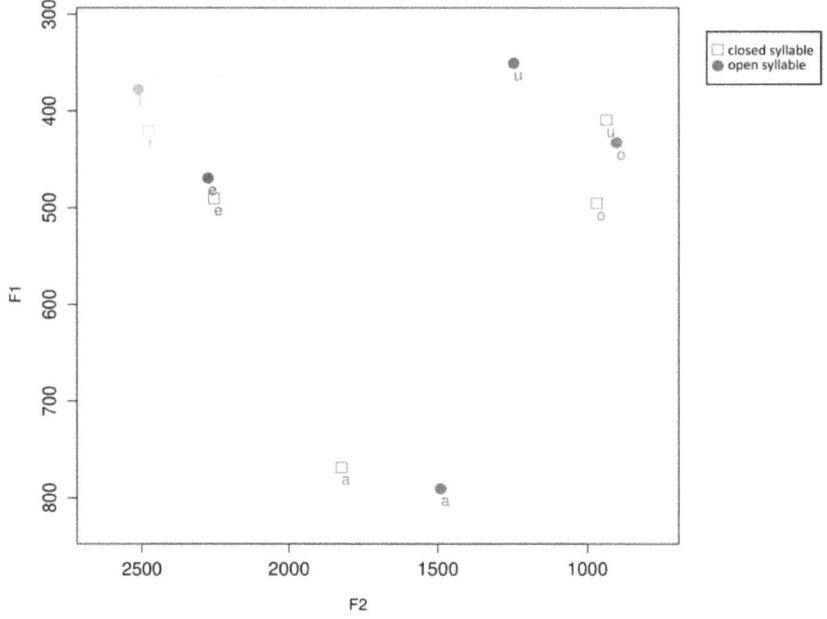

Fig. 10: Average formant values, female speaker (age 20s), in Hz

Figure 11 shows the vowel space of a male speaker (age 70). Curiously, his vowels are more peripheral in closed syllables than in open syllables.

The case of /e/ is of particular note here. For the female speaker (Figure 10), /e/ in a closed syllable is lowered and backed, making its value similar to [ɛ]. For the male Belep speaker (Figure 11), /e/ is higher and fronter in closed syllables, giving it a value of [ɪ]. This variation in the production of /e/ is found throughout the population, though whether it has any correlation with sociolinguistic variables has yet to be determined. Throughout this work, /e/ in a closed syllable will generally be phonetically transcribed as [ɛ].

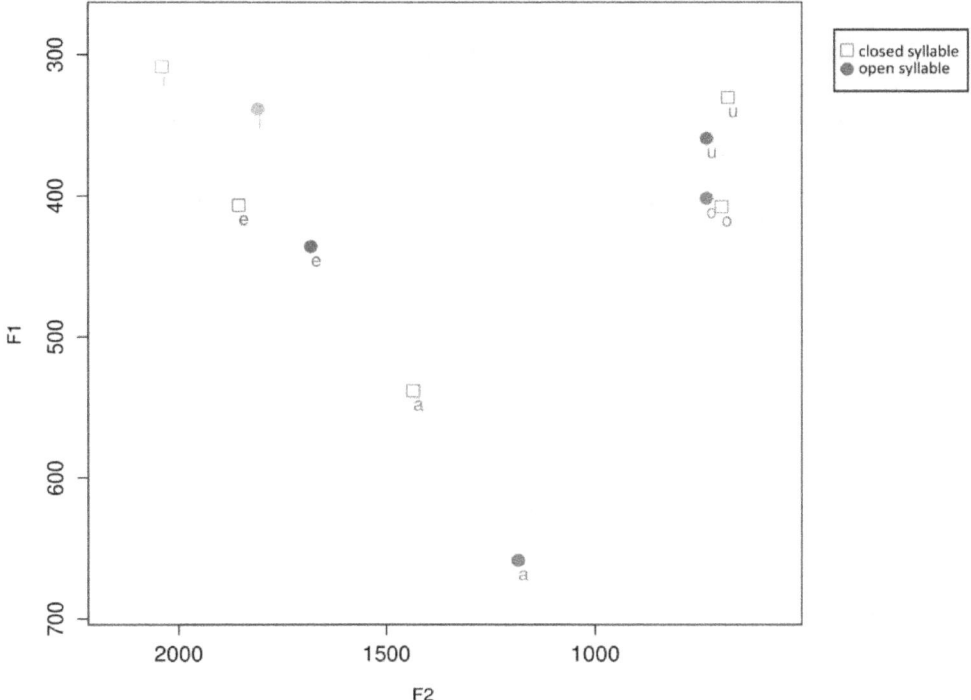

Fig. 11: Average formant values, male speaker (age 70), in Hz

2.3.2.2 Vowel sequences

The phonological status of vowel sequences—that is, sequences of like vowels ('long', 'double', or 'geminate' vowels) and sequences of unlike vowels ('diphthongs', 'clusters' or 'rearticulated vowels')—is a topic of much debate in the literature on Oceanic languages.[42] At least some of this debate hinges on whether vowel sequences should

---

42 In Niuean, some authors (e.g. Sperlich 1997) propose a phonemic distinction between 'short' (V) 'long' (V:) and 'double' (VV) vowels, and between 'diphthongs' (monosyllabic vowel sequences) and 'rearticulated vowels' (multisyllabic vowel sequences); Rolle and Starks (2014) argue that there is no phonemic distinction between 'long' and 'double' vowels. In Fijian, Scott (1948) analyzes so-called 'long vowels' as disyllabic and considers them geminates; Schütz (1999) argues that this analysis confuses the the concepts of syllable and mora. In Samoan, Pawley (1966) states that "short vowels are in phonemic contrast with long vowels" but that a "syllable boundary occurs after every vowel" and that "Long vowels are interpreted as consecutive like vowels" (Pawley 1966:5); Hovdhaugen (1992) argues for a phonological distinction between short and long vowels. In Hawaiian, Elbert and Pukui (1979) distinguish between diphthongs and sequences of unlike vowels, which they term 'clusters'; Rehg (2007) argues that Hawaiian does not have "'true', underlying diphthongs in the form of unit phonemes" (Rehg 2007:129).

be considered monosyllabic (occurring within a single syllable) or heterosyllabic—that is, instances of *hiatus*, defined by Matthews (2007) as "a division between vowels belonging to different...syllables" (see also Maddieson 2011, Ladefoged 1993).

Scholars have traditionally held that New Caledonian languages make a phonemic distinction between short and long vowels,[43] although sequences of unlike vowels are called 'vowel sequences' rather than 'diphthongs' in Nêlêmwa (Bril 2000).

In Belep, there are many contrasting pairs such as those shown in (45).

(45) pi-n   'cook-DA.NSG'   pii-n   'fingernail-3SG.POSS'
      ⁿde   'fork'   ⁿdee   'blacksaddled coral grouper'
      pan   'to go.TV'   paan   'screwpine'
      ka-t   'leg-3GNR.POSS'   kaat   'butterfly fish'
      top   'to melt'   toop   'field'
      puc   'to fly'   puuc   'dust'
      pic   'Alexandrian laurel'   kĩĩt   'to be loud'
      wẽⁿga-   'charity'   wẽẽŋ   'to organize'
      jãn   'ciguatera'   jããŋ   'to gather'
      kõk   'to overflow'   kõõk   'cinnamon night-heron'
      pũmʷ   'smoke'   pũũŋ   'to assemble'

There is evidence to support two possible analyses of the vowel sequences in the right-hand column of (45): (i) in the 'long vowel' hypothesis, instances of monosyllabic long vowels in the right-hand column contrast phonemically with the short vowels in the left-hand column; or (ii) in the 'vowel hiatus' hypothesis, the words in the right-hand column contain heterosyllabic sequences of like vowels. The remainder of this section will provide evidence that the latter analysis is a better fit for my observations—that is, that sequences of like vowels and sequences of unlike vowels are heterosyllabic in Belep.

The first piece of evidence for the 'vowel hiatus' hypothesis is that speakers have no intuition regarding the 'length' of a vowel; however, they can easily split a word into syllables, and they reliably split sequences of like vowels into two separate syllables (§2.7).[44] Some examples of this syllabification are shown in (46), where [.] indicates a syllable break.

---

43 For example, Ozanne-Rivierre et al. (1998) analyze Balade Nyelâyu as having twenty phonemic vowels in total: five short oral vowels, five short nasal vowels, and the long counterparts of each.
44 Speakers' consistent division of vowel sequences into separate units could be interpreted instead as a division into separate moras, which would lend credence to the 'long vowel' hypothesis. This interpretation is countered by the fact that Belep speakers do not assign coda consonants to separate units. Furthermore, some of the sequences of unlike vowels which speakers divide into separate units include an oral vowel followed by a nasal vowel: /ki.ãk/ 'purple swamphen', /ⁿde.ã/ 'type of fly'.

(46) a.wa.a   'mat'
      ᵐbe.en   'to be wet'
      ᵐbi.in   'to be skinny'
      ca.aŋ   'to steal'
      ⁿdo.o   'earth'
      ko.ot   'to be soft'
      mu.u-t   'flower-3GNR.POSS'
      na.ap   'fire'
      pa.ac   'smokehouse'
      pu.up   'to swell'
      te.ec   'to burn'
      wẽ.ẽŋ   'to organize'   Yal-20102011-YG.wav

Speakers also consistently place a syllable boundary in sequences of unlike vowels, as shown in (47). All possible sequences of two unlike vowels occur; examples are given in Table 10 at the end of this section.

(47) mi.a   'to be ripe'
      ca.e   'coral reef'
      ᵐbo.la.o   'banana tree'
      ᶮɟi.tu.a   'bow'

As Table 9 shows, sequences of like vowels (243 ms) have a similar duration to sequences of unlike vowels (252 ms). Sequences of like vowels are significantly longer ($F(1, 29) = 33.36$, $p < .001$) than clearly monosyllabic single vowels which have undergone stress-induced vowel lengthening (see §2.4.2.1).

Tab. 9: Mean duration of vowels

	Mean duration	Example		
Stress-lengthened single vowels	177 ms	/ke.la/	[ˈkeːla]	'to slide'
Sequences of like vowels	243 ms	/ke.ec/	[ˈkeec]	'to have children'
Sequences of unlike vowels	252 ms	/ke.ãp/	[ˈkeãp]	'slab'

Another piece of evidence for the 'vowel hiatus' hypothesis is found in the distribution of sequences of like vowels. If sequences of like vowels were single phonological

---

Nasality spreads across syllable boundaries to the following vowels (§2.5.3); an analysis positing diphthongs with internal variation in nasality seems implausible.

segments, we might expect them to occur in any position where a vowel may occur. However, these sequences have a limited distribution in that they may occur only in the two final syllables of a phonological word (§2.7), a condition which holds for all of the examples in (45). In other words, though there are many Belep words of the form $CV_1.CV(C)$, there are none of the form $CV_1.V_1.CV(C)$. However, those of the form $CV.CV_1.V_1(C)$ are common. A few examples are shown in (48).

(48) ᵐba.tap 'to exceed' ᵐba.ta.ap 'evening'
ca.ke 'to be ashamed' ca.ke.-e 'fish with a net-3SG.ABS'
ã.te- 'gallbladder' ã.te.-e 'dry-3SG.ABS'
a.ti 'sandbar' a.ti.i 'rice.LN'

This evidence could theoretically be interpreted as supporting a 'long vowel' hypothesis for Belep; in many languages with a phonemic vowel-length distinction, the contrast is neutralized in some phonological environments. However, in these languages the neutralization typically occurs at the end of a word.[45] If we ascribed to the 'long vowel' hypothesis in Belep (with the requisite redefinition of the term 'syllable'), the final syllable of a word would be the *only* environment where a vowel length distinction could be said to occur. This is inconsistent with the cross-linguistic pattern.

Sequences of unlike vowels most commonly occur in the last two syllables of a word, although in contrast to sequences of like vowels it is possible for them to occur in other positions. However, in cases where sequences of unlike vowels occur outside the final two syllables, speakers may disagree as to the underlying phonemic form. For example, for some Belep speakers the underlying form of the verb 'to cut' is trisyllabic /tiawa/, while for others it is disyllabic /tawa/. A few other examples are shown in (49).

(49) /ni.a.ɟo/ or /ɲa.ɟo/ 'type of tree'
/pʷa.i.na.ŋgac/ or /pʷe.na.ŋgac/ 'to be beautiful'
/ti.u.ri.en/ or /tu.ri.en/ 'to pray'

Sequences of three vowels are also permitted in Belep (50), though they are fairly uncommon. Note that while sequences of three like vowels are excluded by the constraint that sequences of like vowels are only possible in the last two syllables of a word, sequences of the form $V_1V_2V_2$ do occur as in /ãdeweaa/ 'belligerent rock shell'.

---

[45] "That a vowel length contrast in final position is difficult to maintain is demonstrated by the existence of a number of languages in which vowel length is not contrastive in word-final position, e.g. Kiowa, Wintu, Khmer, Halang, Lao" (Gordon 2006:225). Kuuku Ya'u (Hamilton 1995) and Hungarian (Törkenczy 2004) are other languages where a phonemic vowel length distinction is neutralized in word-final position.

(50) /ⁿdu.a.e-/ 'health'
/ku.a.u/ 'cat'
/ci.a.-e/ 'NEG.LOC-SPC'
/ã.de.we.a.a/ '*Thais armigera*'

Sequences where the first vowel is oral and the second vowel is nasal also occur; for example /ciã/ 'flea', /tuãⁿda/ 'throwing spear'. The converse—where the first vowel is nasal and the second is oral—do not occur (see §2.5.3). It is possible that Belep would support an analysis that sequences of unlike vowels outside the final two syllables are true diphthongs (that is, monosyllabic), while sequences of unlike vowels in the final two syllables are heterosyllabic. This would be a fruitful topic for further research.

Another piece of evidence for the 'vowel hiatus' hypothesis is found in the morphophonemic process of phase shift, discussed in detail in §2.5.2. Briefly, when a word containing a sequence of like vowels is used in the middle of an intonation unit or with some morphosyntactic modification, only the first (stressed) vowel from the vowel sequence is present. For example, though the words /kõk/ 'to overflow' and /kõõk/ 'cinnamon night-heron' contrast in isolation or at the end of an intonation unit, they are homophonous as [kõʁ] in the invented phrases in (51) and (52) (see §2.6 for more information on orthographic conventions in this work). Phase shift has no effect on sequences of unlike vowels.

(51)   **Te kôk xa bwe mar.**
       te=   **kôx=a**   **bwe**   **mar**
       3SG.SUBJ= overflow=LOC top   seashore
       'S/he vomited on the beach.'

(52)   **Tuu kôôk xa bwe mar.**
       tu   **kôx=a**   **bwe**   **mar**
       EX.SPC   heron=LOC   top   seashore
       'There is a cinnamon night-heron on the beach.'

If we ascribed to the 'long vowel' hypothesis, it would be accurate to say that phonemic vowel length distinctions would do very little perceptual work in distinguishing between words in connected speech.

There is also prosodic evidence for the 'vowel hiatus' hypothesis. In unambiguously disyllabic words in Belep, the first syllable carries the intensity peak and the word stress, while the last syllable carries the pitch peak (§2.8.1). An example is shown in Figure 12, which depicts intensity and pitch contours for the disyllabic word /pata/ [paːra] 'to tell' (see §2.4.3.1 on stress-induced vowel lengthening).

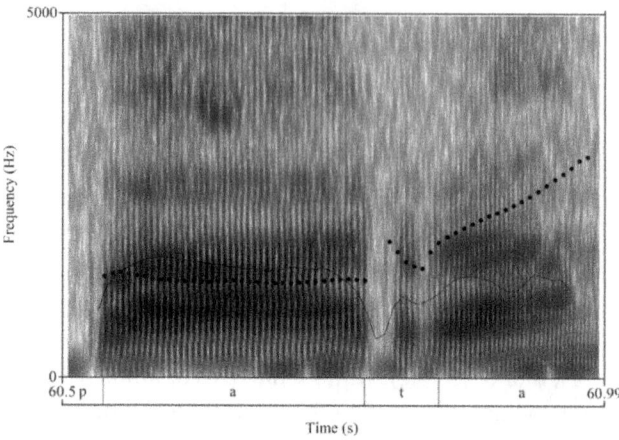

Fig. 12: Intensity and pitch contours for /pata/ 'to tell'

In Figure 12, note that the intensity curve peaks in the first syllable /pa/, while the pitch curve peaks in the second syllable /ta/. In a word containing a sequence of like vowels, a similar intonation pattern occurs. For example, in Figure 13, the spectrogram of the word /kaac/ [kaac] 'to be bitter' shows an intensity peak in the first syllable /ka/ and a pitch peak in the second syllable /ac/.

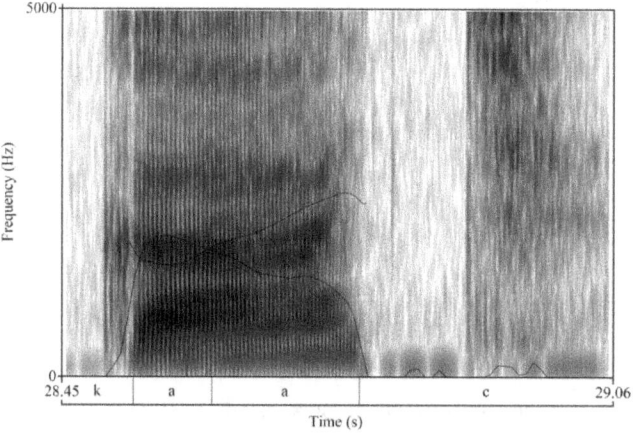

Fig. 13: Intensity and pitch contours for /kaac/ 'bitter'

Unambiguously monosyllabic words such as /kic/ 'liver' do not show this pattern, as shown in Figure 14. This is evidence that vowel sequences should be considered heterosyllabic.

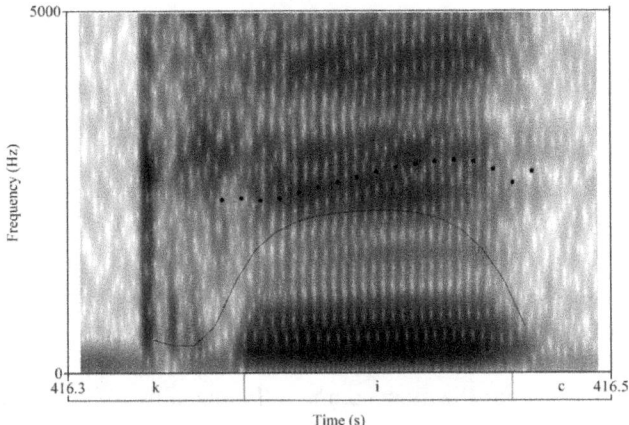

Fig. 14: Intensity and pitch contours for /kic/ 'liver'

Yal-12102011-YG2_416.3-416.5

The evidence presented indicates that the 'vowel hiatus' hypothesis fits the Belep data better than the 'long vowel' hypothesis. As such, the terms 'long vowel' and 'diphthong' will not be used in this work, and sequences of like and unlike vowels will be identified as heterosyllabic instances of hiatus.

Tab. 10: Sequences of unlike vowels

	/i/	/e/	/a/	/o/	/u/
i/	-	/pi-e/	/katia/	/ᵐbʷalawio/	/wiu/
	-	'cook-3SG.ABS'	'to have leprosy'	'Balabio isle'	'to dine'
e/	/walei/	-	/kaᵐbeat/	/ᵐbʷeo/	/toteu/
	'lesser yam'	-	'jellyfish'	'east wind'	'sperm whale'
a/	/caipak/	/cae/	-	/ⁿdao-/	/ⁿdau/
	'rat'	'coral reef'	-	'leaf'	'isle'
o/	/poi/	/po-e/	/ⁿgoa-/	-	/kouloon/
	'pumpkin cake'	'load-3SG.ABS'	'bunch'	-	'to be an albino'
u/	/tu=ic/	/ⁿdue/	/ⁿɟua/	/ⁿɟuo/	-
	'go.DH=CTF'	'to admire'	'to feel'	'petrel'	-

2.3.2.3 Vowel nasality

The languages of Northern New Caledonia are noted for their preponderance of nasal vowels, a feature which is rare in the rest of the Austronesian language family (Gordon & Maddieson 2004) and highly salient to monolingual French speakers (Ozanne-Rivierre et al. 1998). Both phonemically nasal and phonetically nasal vowels occur. Phonemic oral and nasal vowels contrast in a variety of environments, including (a) preceding a consonant, and (b) following a voiceless stop or approximant (§2.2.2). The contrast between oral and nasal phonemic vowels is neutralized after nasal phonemes and prenasalized stops (see §2.3.2.4). Word-final phonemic nasal vowels are unusual; this is commensurate with the findings of Ruhlen (1973) and Schourup (1973) that nasalization is more common cross-linguistically in closed syllables. Of the phonemic nasal vowels, /ã/ is by far the most common, followed by /õ/ and /ẽ/. High vowels /ũ/ and /ĩ/ are quite rare.[46] This is not uncommon; Chen (1975) and Chen and Wang (1975) argue that low nasal vowels are cross-linguistically more common than high nasal vowels.

In general, phonemically nasal vowels in Belep tend to occur in instances of vowel hiatus (§2.3.2.2) rather than singly.[47] Some examples are shown in (53).

(53)
	kãak	'to shout'
	pãaɲ	'sow thistle'
	tãaŋ	'to scrape'
	wẽek	'tobacco'
	pĩik	'static'
	tõon	'to sail with the wind'
	tũun	'to rub'
	kũut	'to grunt'
	kiãk	'purple swamphen'
	ᵐbuãɲ	'stone'
	ão-n	'vine-3SG.POSS'
	kẽap	'slab'

According to Bhat (1975), a nasal vowel in a given language tends to be phonetically higher than its corresponding oral vowel. This pattern is not borne out in the Belep data, shown in Figure 15 and Figure 16.

---

46 A similar pattern holds for oral vowels; see §2.2.2.1.
47 This is unsurprising given that in many languages, nasality and vowel length tend to be linked to one another. For example, in some Eastern Algonquian languages, a nasal vowel developed historically from a long vowel (Whalen & Beddor 1989). See also Hajek (1997) and Beddor (1993).

Description of phonemes — 75

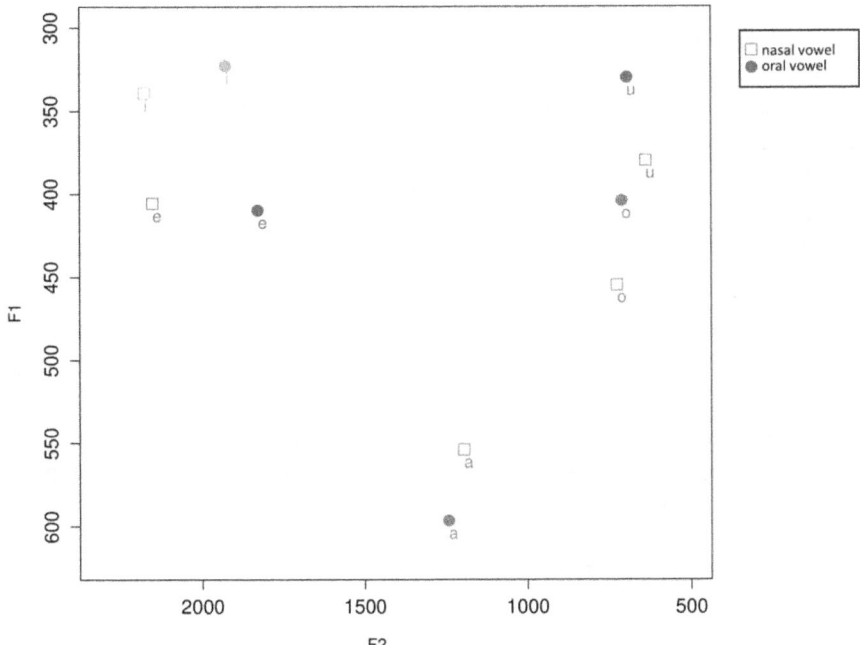

Fig. 15: Oral vs nasal vowels for male speaker (age 70), in Hz

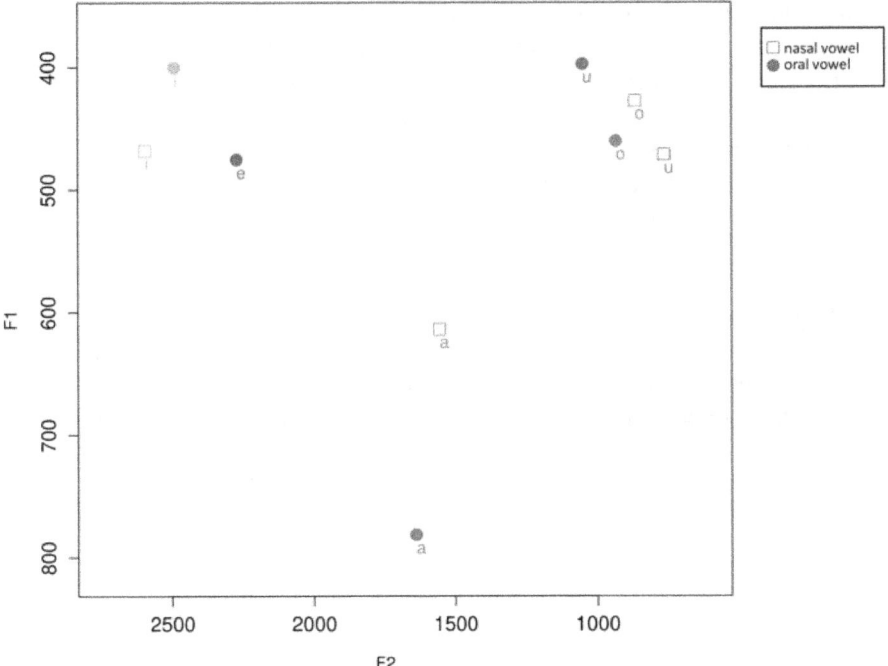

Fig. 16: Oral vs nasal vowels for female speaker (age 20s), in Hz

Figure 15 and Figure 16 show that Belep nasal vowels other than /ã/ tend to be more peripheral (in terms of the second formant) than the corresponding oral vowel. Meanwhile, /a/ and /ã/ contrast primarily in height, with the oral vowel being more peripheral (in terms of the first formant). Note that, for the female speaker whose vowels are shown in Figure 16, no tokens of /ẽ/ and only a few tokens of /ũ/ were included in the analysis; this may account for the fact that /ũ/ was found to be lower than /õ/ for this speaker.

2.3.2.4 Neutralizations

The phonemic contrast between oral and nasal vowels is neutralized after a prenasalized stop (§2.3.1.3). All vowels following prenasalized stops are phonetically oral[48] and there are no minimal pairs in this position. Note that this neutralization only holds within the syllable; a heterosyllabic (§2.3.2.2) nasal vowel may follow a phonetically oral vowel that has been neutralized (54).

(54)   ᵐbu.ãɲ   'stone'
       ⁿde.ã   'type of fly'
       ⁿdu.ãc   'spine'

The phonemic contrast between oral and nasal vowels is also neutralized following a nasal phoneme, either a nasal stop (§2.2.1.5) or a nasal vowel (§2.2.2). All vowels are phonetically nasalized following a nasal phoneme, a phenomenon known as nasal spreading (see §2.5.3). Nasal spreading crosses syllable and morpheme boundaries. There are no minimal pairs for oral and nasal vowels following a nasal phoneme.

A similar neutralization occurs in the Southern New Caledonian language Ndumbea (Rivierre 1973), where "only oral vowels follow prenasalized stops and only nasal vowels occur after nasals" (Gordon & Maddieson 1999:72).

2.4 Allophony

Some variation in the production of consonants (§2.4.1) and vowels (§2.4.2) is phonetic rather than phonemic, and does not contribute to neutralizations (discussed above in §2.3.1.5 and §2.3.2.4). Table 11 shows an inventory of all phonetic consonants which appear in Belep.

---

[48] There may be a few exceptions. For example, some speakers produce /ŋa/ 'to creak' as [ⁿgã]; some speakers may produce /tãnac/ 'ocean' as [ⁿdãnac].

Tab. 11: Phonetic consonant inventory

	Labiovelar	Bilabial	Labiodental	Alveolar	Palatal	Velar	Uvular
Plosive	pʷ ᵐbʷ	p ᵐb		t ⁿd	c ⁿɟ	k ᵑg	q
Nasal	mʷ, ᵇmʷ	m, ᵇm		n, ᵈn	ɲ, ʲɲ	ŋ, ᵍŋ	
Fricative		β	v	s	ʝ	ɣ	χ
Affricate					c͡ç		
Approximant	w			ɹ	j		ʁ
Tap				ɾ			
Trill				r			
Lateral approximant				l			

2.4.1 Consonants

In this section I discuss phonetic labialization (§2.4.1.1), allophony in voiceless stops based largely on word position (§2.4.1.2), allophonic prestopping of nasals (§2.4.1.3), and vowel-conditioned allophony in approximants (§2.4.1.4).

2.4.1.1 Phonetic labialization

When a bilabial consonant /p/, /ᵐb/, or /m/ (§2.2.1.1) precedes a back vowel /o/ or /u/, it is phonetically labialized. Some examples are shown in (55).

(55) /po/   [pʷo]   'to tell lies'
      /ᵐbo/   [ᵐbʷo]   'to smell'
      /mo/   [mʷo]   'to live, stay'
      /mon/   [mʷon]   'side.DH'
      /puu/   [pʷuu]   'to be in heat'
      /ᵐbu/   [ᵐbʷu]   'fishhook'
      /mu/   [mʷu]   'to moor'

Labiovelar approximant /w/ also undergoes allophony before back vowels; see §2.3.1.4 below.

2.4.1.2 Voiceless stops

The Belep voiceless stops /pʷ/, /p/, /t/, /c/ and /k/ undergo a considerable amount of allophony depending on their position in the phonological word. In general, these phonemes are produced as unaspirated stops in word-initial position (§2.3.1.2); as fricatives or approximants in word-medial position (see §2.5.1 for a description of the morphophonemic process of lenition); and as unreleased stops in word-final position. Each phoneme will be discussed in detail in this section.

The phonetic characteristics of the word-initial allophones of labiovelar /pʷ/ and bilabial /p/ (that is, [pʷ] and [p] respectively) were discussed in §2.3.1.1. Word-medially, /pʷ/ has the allophone [w] (see §2.3.1.5), while /p/ has the allophone [v]. The [p] allophone of /p/ does not occur word-medially (56).

(56) /apa-/ [ava-] 'sibling'
/capac/ [cavac] 'to depart'
/papaŋ/ [pavaŋ] 'to prepare'
/topen/ [tovɛn] 'to finish'

Some examples of the morphophonemic correspondence between phonemic /p/ and phonetic [v] are shown in (57).

(57) /naap/ 'fire' /nape-/ [nãve-] '(someone's) fire'
/kĕnap/ 'tongue' /kĕnapa-/ [kĕnãva-] '(someone's) tongue'
/jalap/ 'to rummage' /jalapi-/ [jalavi-] 'rummage.TR'
/te= tup=ⁿdu/ [tetuvaⁿdu] '3SG.SUBJ= dive=DIR.DH' 's/he dove down'
/õ tep=a alaᵐba/ [õtɛvaalaᵐba] 'REAL click=NOM ember' 'an ember popped'

Word-finally (at the end of an intonation unit; see §2.5.2), /pʷ/ and /p/ have the allophones [pʷ̚] and [p̚], respectively. A sample spectrogram of an unreleased final /p/~[p̚] is shown in Figure 17:

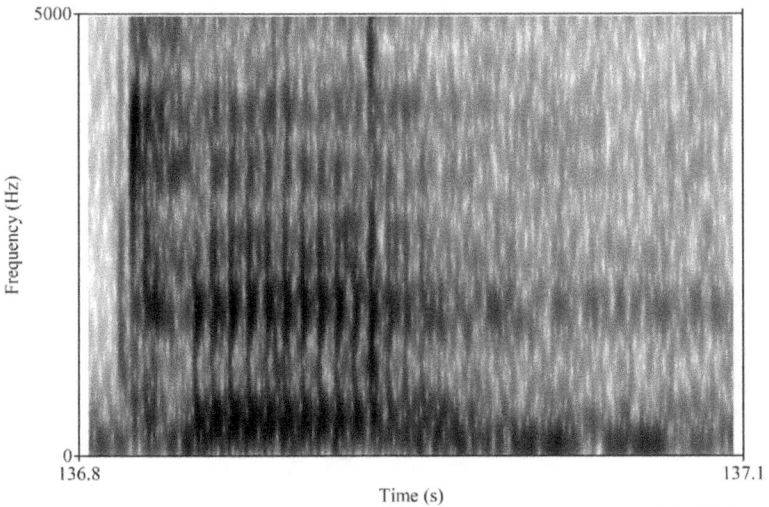

Fig. 17: Spectrogram of final unreleased /p/ in /tep/ 'to click'

Figure 17 shows a spectrogram of the word /tep/ [tɛp̚] 'to click', produced in isolation. No release is visible. Final [pʷ̚] and [p̚] are often phonetically distinguishable solely by a final closure with rounded lips versus a final closure with flat lips.

The only word-initial allophone of /t/ is laminal [t]. Word-medially, [t] does not occur; instead, speakers produce tap [ɾ], trill [r], or approximant [ɹ] as a word-medial allophone of /t/.⁴⁹ The inter- and intra-speaker variation between these two allophones may be conditioned by social factors. Figure 18 shows the production of medial /t/ as [ɾ], a single tap.

---

49 In this work, I use [ɾ] to refer to the most common pronunciation of a medial /t/, in which the tip of the tongue makes a single contact with the alveolar ridge. I use [r] to refer to instances where the tongue tip makes multiple contacts. This is not entirely consistent with Ladefoged's contention that, "In a typical [trill,] even in cases where there is only a single contact with the roof of the mouth, the action is physiologically (but perhaps not auditorily) quite distinct from that of a tap" (Ladefoged 1971:50). It has not been determined whether the Belep single-contact allophone and the multiple-contact allophone use different physiological mechanisms. However, cross-linguistically, trills typically have three contacts with the alveolar ridge (Ladefoged 1971:50), while Belep pronunciations of medial /t/ typically have one. I have thus chosen not to group both Belep [ɾ] and [r] under the category of [r].

80 — Phonetics and phonology

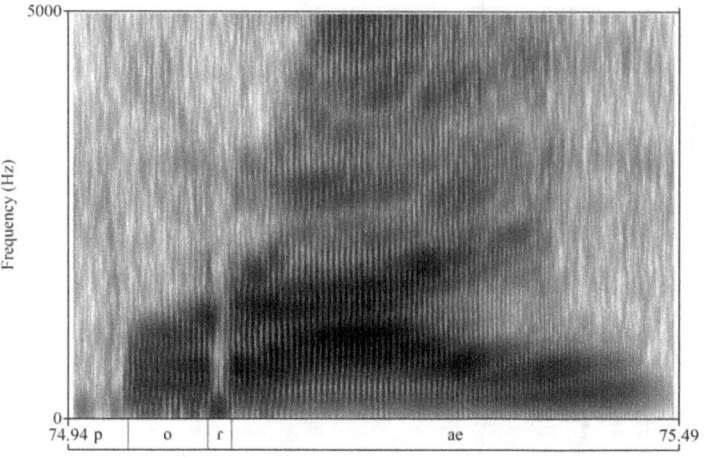

Fig. 18: Spectrogram for /potae/ 'to massage'

Figure 18 shows a spectrogram of the word /pota-e/ [pora-e] 'massage-SPC', as produced in isolation by a female speaker in her twenties. The same speaker also produced medial /t/ as [r], a trill with two (Figure 19) or three (Figure 20) taps.

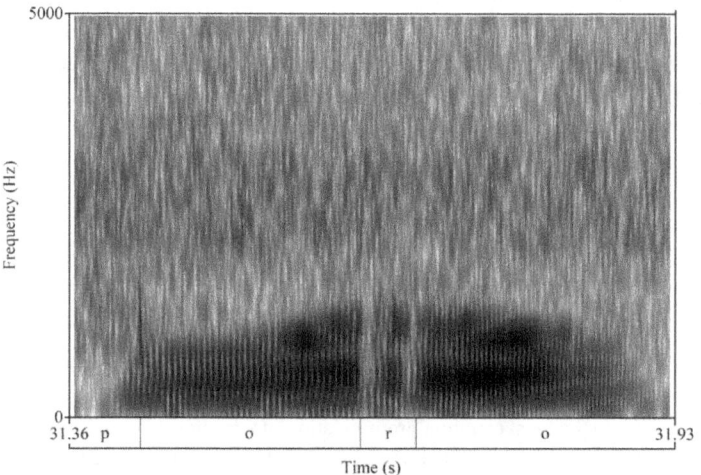

Fig. 19: Spectrogram for /poto/ [poro] 'to be white'

Figure 19 shows a spectrogram of the word /poto/ [poro] 'to be white', as produced in isolation by a speaker in her twenties. This instance of [r] contains two instances where the tongue contacts the alveolar ridge. In the production of the word /puti/

[puri] 'snake' in Figure 20 the speaker's tongue contacts her alveolar ridge three times.

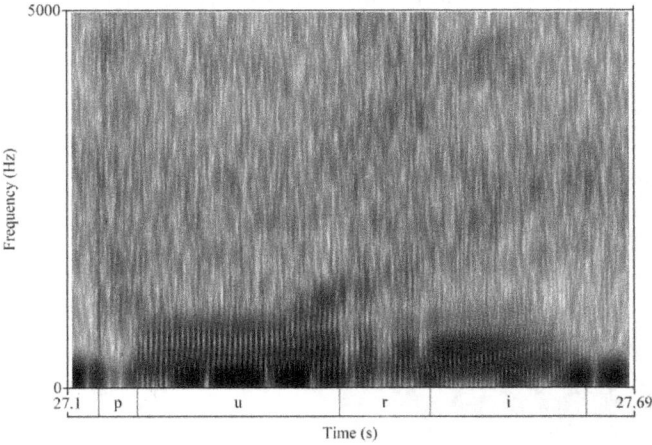

Yal-13102011-YG2_27.1-27.69

Fig. 20: Spectrogram for /puti/ [puri] 'snake'

Another medial allophone of /t/ is [ɹ], an alveolar approximant. An example of this pronunciation is given in Figure 21.

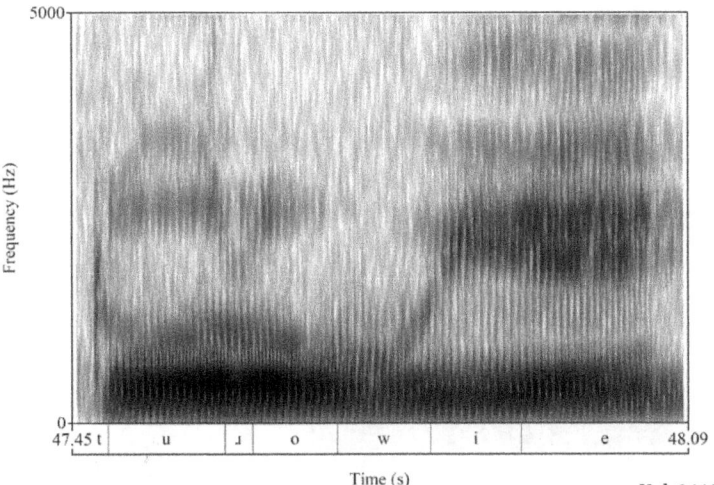

Yal-04102011-PT3_47.45-48.09

Fig. 21: Spectrogram of /tutowie/ [tuɹowie] 'to insult'

Figure 21 shows a spectrogram for the word /tutowi-e/ [tuɹowi-e] 'insult-3SG.ABS', produced in isolation by a male speaker, age 70.

Word-finally, the most common allophone of /t/ is [ɾ] or [r]. An example is given in Figure 22, which shows a spectrogram of the word /cuut/ [c̄çuur] 'to stand' produced by a speaker in her twenties.

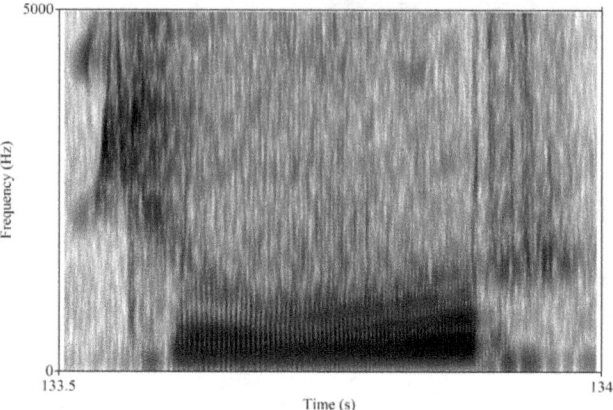

Yal-12102011-YG2_133.5-134

Fig. 22: Spectrogram showing final [r] in the word /cuut/ 'to stand'

Another allophone of final /t/ is apical [ṭ˺], as shown in Figure 23 which shows a spectrogram of the word /cuut/ [c̄çuuṭ˺] 'to stand' produced by an elderly speaker (age 70).

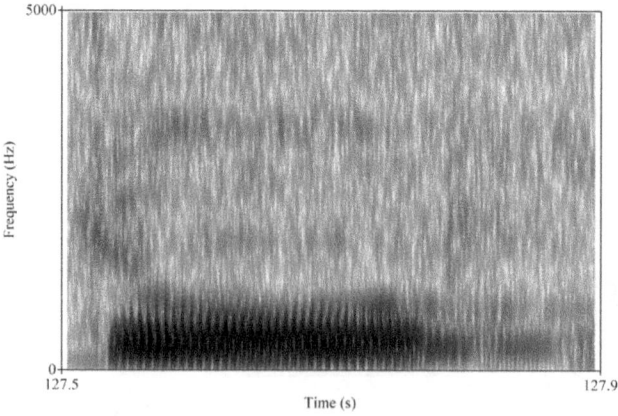

Yal-06102011-PT3_127.5-127.9

Fig. 23: Spectrogram showing final [ṭ˺] in the word /cuut/ 'to stand'

Note that alveolar consonants are normally laminal in Belep. The final apical [t̺] pronunciation is most common among elderly speakers. It is also preserved for most speakers in a few lexical items, namely /jet/ [jɛt̺], a highly productive discourse marker meaning 'that's it, that's all'.

The palatal stop /c/ in word-initial position is usually realized as affricate [c͡ç]; it is typically characterized by a large amount of high-frequency noise, as shown in Figure 24.

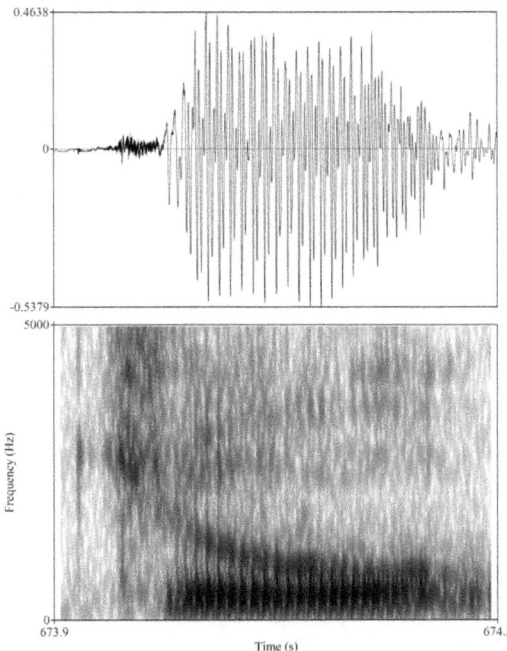

Fig. 24: Spectrogram and waveform for Belep *co* 'whale'

In Figure 24 the lack of a high-amplitude release burst on the waveform, and the high-frequency noise before the periodic voicing of the vowel begins, are indicators of affrication.

In word-medial position, /c/ has the allophone [j] (see §2.3.1.5); [c] does not occur intervocalically. Final /c/ usually has the allophone [c̚]; in these instances, speakers may produce co-articulatory lip movements to indicate the palatal place of articulation (by contrast with the alveolar). These lip movements normally include the drawing down and back of the corners of the mouth to expose the lower teeth.

Another word-final allophone of /c/ which occurs is affricate [c͡ç], as shown in Figure 25.

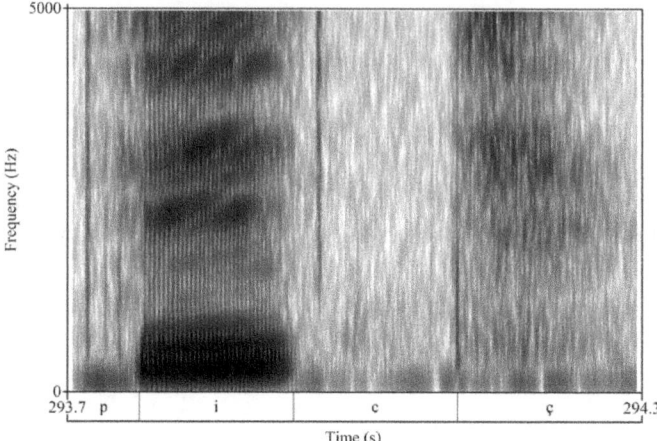

Fig. 25: Spectrogram of final affricate [c͡ç] in /pic/ 'Alexandrian laurel'

Figure 25 shows a spectrogram of the word /pic/ [pic͡ç] 'Alexandrian laurel' produced in isolation.

In a small subset of words, initial and final /c/ may also have the allophone [s], as in the examples shown in Table 12.

Tab. 12: Production of /c/ as [s]

Phonemic form	Phonetic form	Stylized phonetic form	Gloss	Source
/caket/	[c͡çaʁɛr]	[saʁɛr]	'winkle'	
/cekeen/	[c͡çeʁeen]	[seʁeen]	'holy'	
/cãⁿɟeen/	[c͡çãⁿɟeen]	[sãⁿɟeen]	'to believe'	Dubois
/ci/	[c͡çi]	[si]	'to sit'	Dubois
/coⁿɟo/	[c͡çoⁿɟo]	[soⁿɟo]	'to be dirty'	Dubois
/calakina/	[c͡çalaʁinã]	[salaʁinã]	'whistling kite'	Neyret

The forms shown in Table 12 are compiled from my own recordings and from the manuscripts of Dubois (1975c:318) and Neyret (1974a:640). The [s] pronunciation seems to be a sociolinguistically marked one—it originated in religious jargon (the French missionaries could not pronounce [c]), as evidenced by some of the words in Table 12 and it is still the preferred pronunciation in many hymns and prayers. However, it has since expanded in usage to occur in proper names, and it is also used more frequently in discourse by teenagers and young people. More research would be necessary to determine what social factors condition the [s] allophone of /c/.

In initial position, the only allophone of /k/ is [k]. Medially, /k/ has a number of allophones. Its most common medial allophone is uvular approximant/voiced fricative [ʁ], as represented in Figure 26:

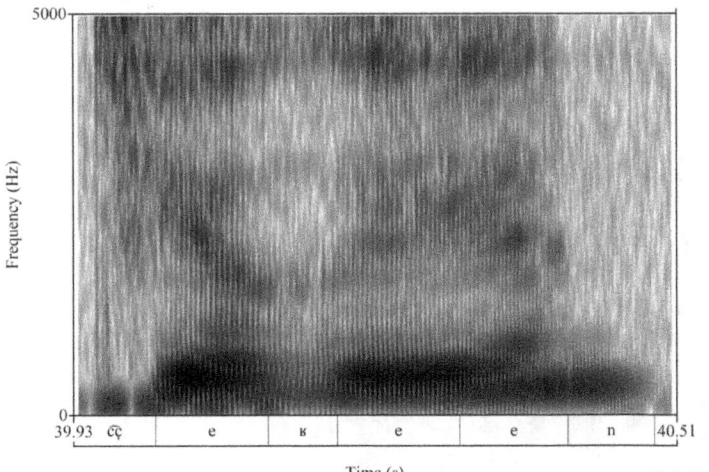

Fig. 26: Spectrogram of /cekeen/ 'sacred'

Figure 26 shows a spectrogram of the word /cekeen/ [c̟çeʁeen] 'sacred', produced by a speaker in her twenties.[50] Another available allophone, used particularly by older speakers, is a voiced velar fricative [ɣ]. An example is given in Figure 27.

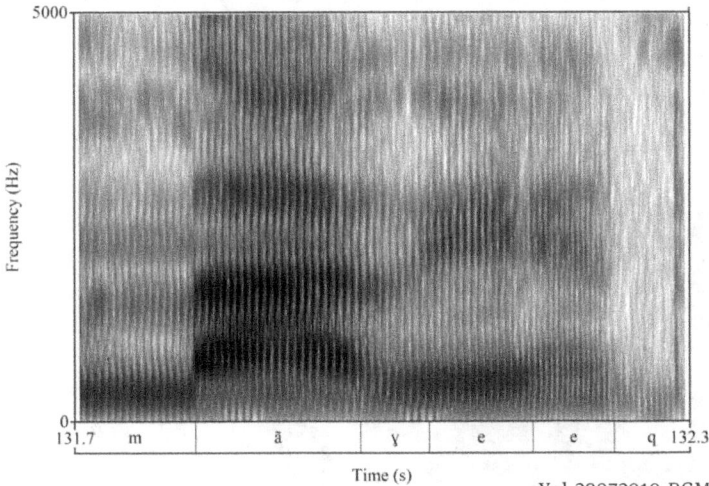

Fig. 27: Spectrogram of /makeek/ (a person's name)

---

50 The availability of the [ʁ] allophone of /k/ occasionally causes some confusion for speakers, especially children, between French and Belep; /ʁ/ is also a phoneme in French, where it is written <r>.

Figure 27 shows a spectrogram of the personal name /makeek/ [mãɣeeq], produced by a male speaker in his 70s. Medial /k/ may also be pronounced as voiceless uvular fricative [χ] by some speakers, particularly younger women, as shown in Figure 28:

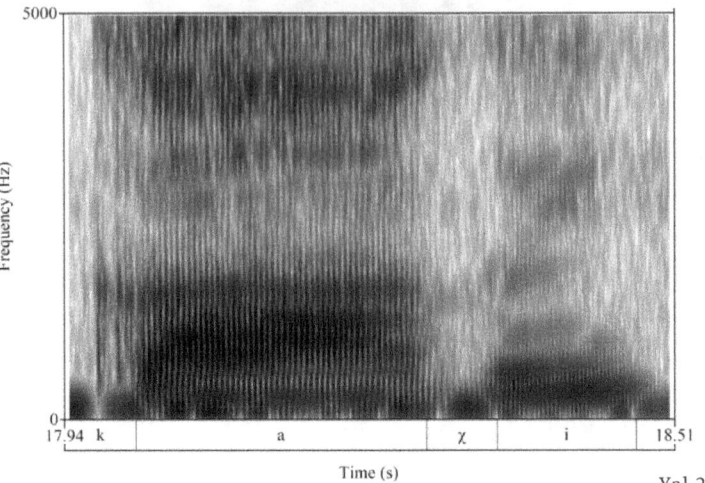

Fig. 28: Spectrogram of /kaki/ 'to look'

Figure 28 shows a spectrogram of the word /kaki/ [kaχi] 'to look', produced by a speaker in her twenties. Some speakers also reportedly produce trilled uvular [ʀ], though I have no examples of this.

Final /k/ normally has the allophone [qˀ] for all speakers. An example in Figure 29 shows a spectrogram of the word /jeek/ [jeeq] 'plant', produced in isolation.

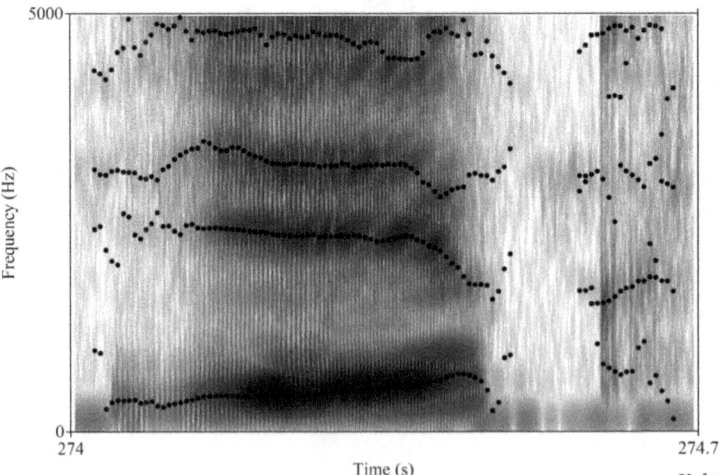

Fig. 29: Spectrogram of uvular place of articulation in /jeek/ 'plant'

Note that there is a slight lowering of F2 before the stop closure; this is noted by Ladefoged and Maddieson (2006) as a pattern characteristic of uvulars, while one might expect a slight convergence of F2 and F3 before a velar (Stevens 1998:367).

2.4.1.3 Prestopped nasals

Prestopped nasals occur in several Australian languages; Ladefoged and Maddieson (2006) cite Diyari, Arabana, Wangganuru, Olgolo, and Arrernte as examples of languages which contain prestopped nasals. In most of these languages, prestopped nasals do not occur word-initially; however, they are permitted in Arrernte.

In Belep, initial nasals are prestopped for some speakers. A sample spectrogram showing prestopping is shown in Figure 30:

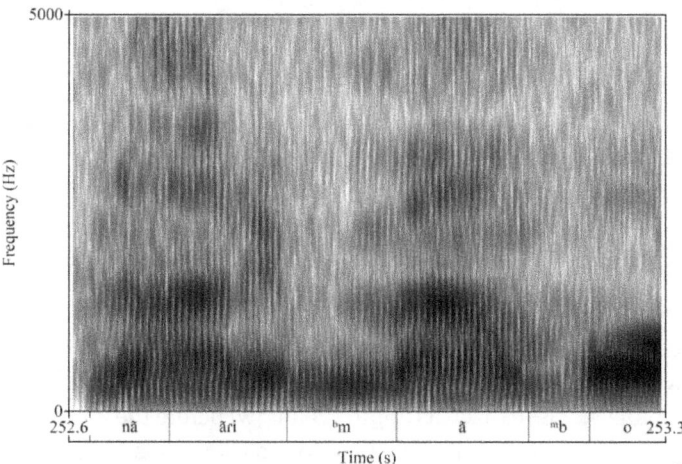

Yal-08112011-PT2_252.6-253.3

Fig. 30: Spectrogram for /ma^{m}bo/ 'honey'

Figure 30 shows a spectrogram of the phrase /na ãti ma^{m}bo/ [nã ãri ^{b}mã^{m}bo] 'I say "honey"', as produced by a male speaker, age 70. The initial /m/ of /ma^{m}bo/ 'honey' is produced as a prestopped [^{b}m], where an approximately 60 ms stop [b] precedes an approximately 70 ms nasal. Nasal formants are visible on the spectrogram only in the second part of the consonant.

Figure 31 shows another example of a prestopped nasal.

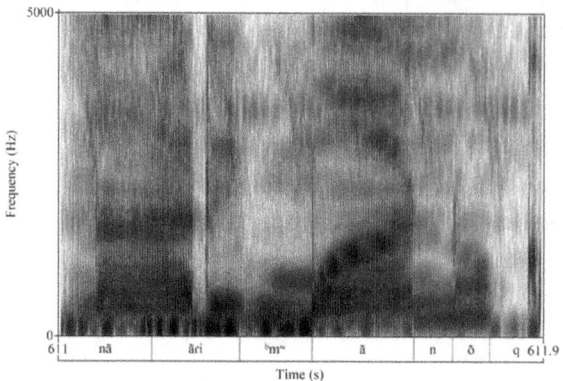

Yal-12102011-YG2_611-611.9

Fig. 31: Spectrogram showing a prestopped nasal in /mʷanok/ 'moon'

Figure 31 shows a spectrogram of the phrase /na ãti mʷanok/ [nã ãɾi ᵇmʷãnõq] 'I say "moon"', as produced by a female speaker in her 20s. The initial /mʷ/ of /mʷanok/ 'moon' is produced as a prestopped [ᵇmʷ], with nasal formants only visible during the second part of the consonant. A more thorough analysis of this phenomenon, including environments in which it occurs and variation among speakers, is a topic for further study.

2.4.1.4 Approximants

Approximants /w/ and /j/ undergo allophony based on the vowel environment. Phonemic /w/ has two allophones; it is realized as approximant [w] before the vowels /i/, /e/, and /a/, but is produced as voiced fricative [β] before back vowels /o/ and /u/. An example of phonemic /w/ realized as phonetic [β] before /o/ is shown in Figure 32. in which the word /woᵐbʷa-n/ 'tomb-3SG.POSS' is produced as [βoᵐbʷan]. Note that this allophony also occurs word-medially, where [β] cannot be identified as /w/, /pʷ/, or /p/ (see §2.3.1.5).

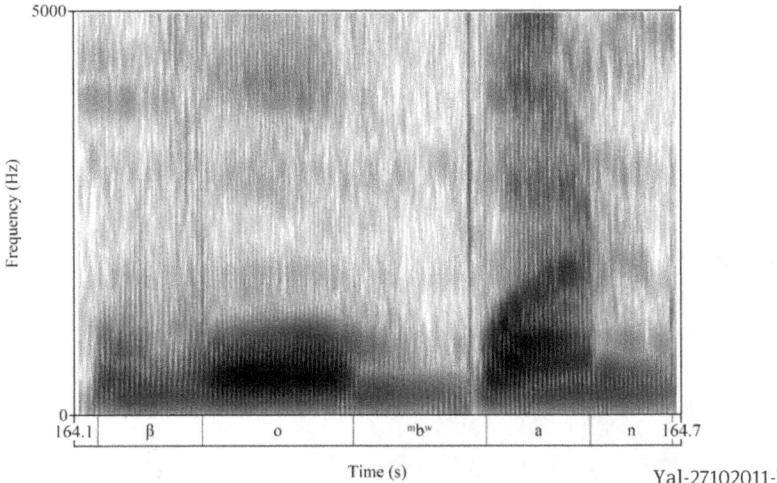

Fig. 32: Pronunciation of /woᵐbʷan/ 'tomb-3SG.POSS' showing fricated initial [β]

Phonemic /j/ also has two allophones; it is realized as approximant [j] before the vowels /e/, /a/, and /o/, while the voiced fricative [ʝ] allophone occurs before high vowels /i/ and /u/. An example of phonemic /j/ realized as phonetic [ʝ] before /u/ is shown in Figure 33:

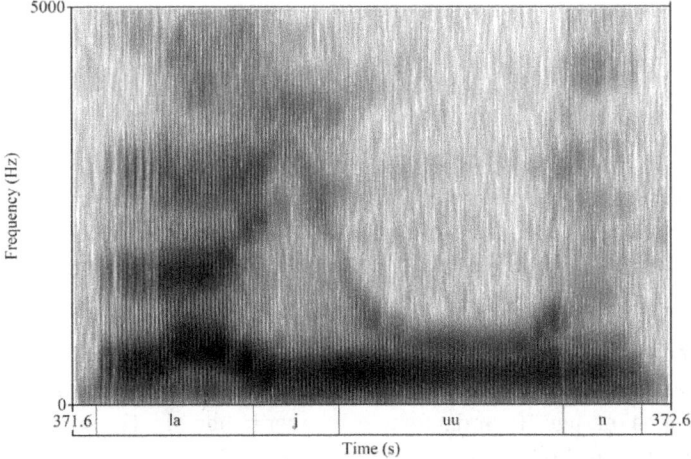

Fig. 33: Spectrogram for /la= juu-n/ [laʝuun] '3PL.SUBJ= dig-DA.NSG'

Figure 33 shows the verb group /la= juu-n/ 'they dug', glossed '3PL.SUBJ= dig-DA.NSG', as produced by a female speaker in her 70s. Phonetic /j/ in /juu/ 'to dig' is produced as fricative [ʝ]; some high frequency vibration is visible on the spectrogram. Note that this allophony also occurs for word medial [j], which cannot be identified as /j/ or /c/ (see §2.3.1.5). An example is shown in Figure 34 where there is a great deal of high frequency noise in the production of voiced fricative [j̝] before /u/.

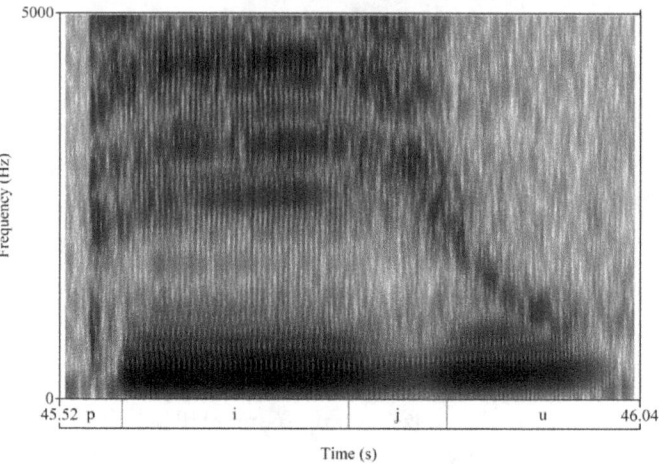

Fig. 34: Spectrogram of /piju/ 'star' showing fricative [j̝]

Figure 34 shows a spectrogram of the word /piju/ [piju] 'star' where the high frequency noise during the production of [j̝] is clearly visible.

2.4.2 Vowels

In §2.3.2.1, I discussed phonetic variation in the quality of vowels depending on whether the syllable is open or closed. The following sections will discuss other allophonic variation in vowels, namely duration (§2.4.2.1) and voice quality (§2.4.2.2)

2.4.2.1 Stress-induced vowel lengthening

I conducted a statistical analysis of Belep vowel duration. Tokens were collected from two speakers—a male speaker, age 70, and a female speaker in her 20s. The speakers read from wordlists written in the locally developed orthography.[51] Vowel duration was measured on a PC using Praat software (Boersma & Weenink 2010). Boundaries

---

[51] They were recorded using an Edirol R-09 at 44.1 KHz, 16-bit PCM wav format. Belep words were written beside their French glosses. Each word appeared in at least three wordlists, in a randomized order. Each time a word appeared in a wordlist, the speaker was asked to produce it twice: once in isolation and once in a carrier phrase.

were marked only at zero crossings where possible (Smith 1978). The software program PASW was used to conduct statistical analyses. A data instances model (Quene and van den Bergh 2004) with a mixed between- and within-subjects design was used. The between-subjects independent variables were the vowel quality (/i/, /e/, /a/, /o/, and /u/) and the syllable type (whether stressed, unstressed, closed, open, etc). The within-subjects independent variables were speaker and whether the token was produced in isolation or in a carrier phrase. The mixed-design ANOVA was conducted on the average across the trials for the duration of the vowel.

Based on my analysis, there is no significant difference in duration between unstressed vowels in an open syllable (109 ms), stressed vowels in a closed syllable (129 ms),[52] and unstressed vowels in a closed syllable (131 ms). However, stressed vowels in an open syllable—that is, vowels which occur in the penultimate syllable of a word (see §2.8.1)—are significantly longer in duration (177 ms).[53] I refer to this pattern as *stress-induced vowel lengthening* and mark it in phonetic transcription with [ː] where it is relevant to the analysis. Table 13 gives some examples of words containing each type of vowel.

Tab. 13: Mean duration of vowels

	Mean duration	Example		
Single vowels	109ms	/ke̲.tae/	[keˈrae]	'to brush'
	129ms	/cep/	[ˈc̣ɛp]	'to build boats'
	131ms	/ta.lep/	[ˈtalɛp]	'to sweep'
Single vowels (stress-lengthened)	177ms	/ke̲.la/	[ˈkeːla]	'to slide'

2.4.2.2 Devoicing and ingressive airstream

In some circumstances, Belep speakers stop all voicing in the middle of an utterance and continue the rest of the utterance with an ingressive airstream mechanism. The sociolinguistic motivation behind this speech style has not yet been determined, though it may be related to the similar South Efate practice of devoicing sensitive topics (Thieberger 2006). It is most commonly practiced by women. For example, Figure 35 shows a spectrogram of ingressive airstream by a female speaker in her 20s.

---

52 Note that stressed closed syllables can only occur in monosyllabic words. See §2.7 and §2.8 for more information.
53 According to the results of statistical contrasts, stressed vowels in an open syllable are significantly longer than unstressed vowels in an open syllable ($F(1, 29) = 32.00$, $p < .001$) and stressed vowels in a closed syllable ($F(1, 29) = 21.70$, $p < .001$).

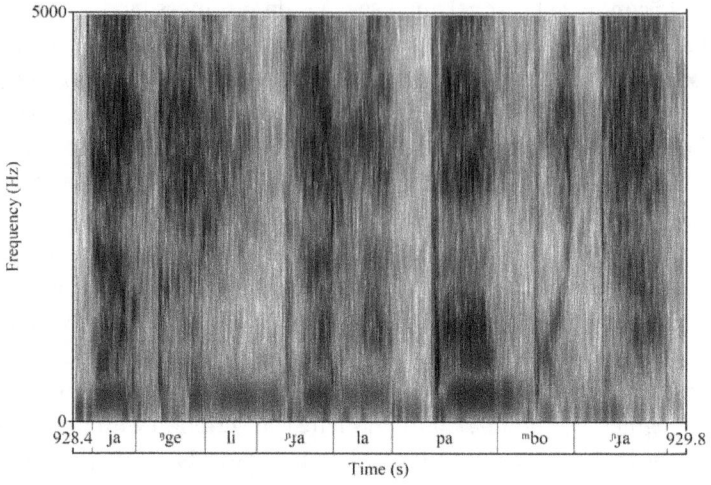

Fig. 35: Spectrogram for ingressive airstream

Yal-27092011-LPLY_928.4-929.8

In Figure 35 the speaker ends an intonation unit with an ingressive airstream mechanism. In the clause shown in (58) (note that orthographic conventions are used here; see §2.6), the sequence /jaⁿge-li-ᶮɟa=la paᵐbo-ᶮɟa/ 'our grandchildren help us' is uttered with an ingressive airstream.

(58) ***Nyami laô besoin de la yagelija la paboja.***
     nya-mi   la=ô   [bəzwɛ̃də]
     DEM.IDF-DET.A.DST   3PL.SUBJ=REAL   need.LN

     la=   yage-li-ja=la   pabo-ja
     3PL.SUBJ= help-TR-1PL.INCL.ABS=NOM   grandchild-1PL.INCL.POSS
     'When our grandchildren will need to help us.' (lit. 'When they will need that our grandchildren help us')

Yal-27092011-LPLY

Another type of vowel allophony that occurs in Belep is that word-initial nasal vowels may be preceded by a nasal fricative burst in careful speech. This is more common when the nasal vowel is a front vowel /ĩ/ or /ẽ/. For example, /ẽna/ 'to know' may be produced [ɦ̃ẽnã], and /ĩᶮɟi/ 'ant' may be produced [ɦ̃ĩᶮɟi].

2.5 Morphophonemic processes

The most significant morphophonemic processes in Belep are the lenition of voiceless stops in word-medial position (§2.5.1), phase shift (§2.5.2), and nasal spreading (§2.5.3).

2.5.1 Lenition

Under some circumstances, Belep phonemic voiceless stops (§2.3.1.2, §2.4.1.2) obligatorily undergo the morphophonemic process of *lenition*. Belep lenition is characterized by the correspondence between voiceless stops /pʷ/, /p/, /t/, /c/ and /k/ and their allophones [w], [v], [ɾ], [j], and [ʁ], respectively, in certain environments.[54] Note that of these lenited phonetic consonants, [w] and [j] are approximants, [v] and [ʁ] are voiced fricatives, and [ɾ] is a tap.[55] All medial allophones of voiceless stops are higher in sonority than their voiceless stop counterparts, where sonority is defined as "the loudness [of a sound] relative to that of other sounds with the same length, stress, and pitch" (Ladefoged 1993:245).

The term 'lenition' is often used in the literature to describe historical processes of sound change; for example, it is defined as "a shift from less sonorous to more sonorous sounds" (Crowley 1997:25). The term may also refer to synchronic processes, "such as initial consonant mutations in the Celtic language[s], but these are called 'lenitions' by an extension of the term from diachrony" (Bauer 1988:381). Belep lenition has both synchronic and diachronic aspects, as I will show.

Synchronically, Belep lenition occurs when a word ending in a voiceless stop is marked with a suffix or enclitic (see §3.2.2.5, §3.2.2.6). As the voiceless stop is now in medial position within the phonological word, it is phonetically realized as one of its medial allophones (§2.4.1.2). Some examples are shown in (59).

---

54 In some cases in South Efate, intervocalic consonants are allophonically lenited; for example, /k/ is realized as [h]. However, this process is optional in South Efate (Thieberger 2006:48), unlike in Belep.
55 As mentioned in §2.4.1.2 and §2.4.1.4, [ɣ] may also be the lenited form of /k/; [r] and [ɹ] may occur as lenited forms of /t/; lenited /pʷ/ and /p/ may be phonetically [β]; and lenited /c/ may be [j].

(59) /pʷ/>[w]   /ⁿdep̲ʷ/ 'deck'   + /-k/ 'DET.D.PRX'   [ⁿdewiiq]
                 /te= ãp̲ʷ=a nae-ŋ/   3SG.SUBJ= laugh=NOM   [te ãwa nãẽŋ]
                                              child-1SG.POSS
     /p/ > [v]   /alap̲/ 'beach'   + /-na/ 'DET.D.MPX'   [alavinã]
                 /ba= talep̲=i-nao/   INSTR= sweep=GEN-1SG.ABS   [ᵐba talɛvinãõ]
                 /te= molep̲=a cama-n/   3SG.SUBJ= be.alive=NOM   [te mõlɛva c̃c̃a-mãn]
                                              father-3SG.POSS
     /t/ > [ɾ]   /mat̲/ 'seashore'   + /-k/ 'DET.D.PRX'   [maɾiiq]
                 /jet̲=i-e/   pot-GEN-3SG.ABS   [jɛɾie]
                 /te= ot̲=a ⁿda-n/   3SG.SUBJ= spill=NOM   [te oɾa ⁿdan]
                                              blood-3SG.POSS
     /c/ > [j]   /capac̲/ 'to depart'   + /=ⁿdu/ 'DIR.DH'   [c̃c̃avajaⁿdu]
                 /ãc̲/ 'man'   + /-mi/ 'DET.A.DST'   [ãjimĩ]
                 /te= ulac̲=a apa-n/   3SG.SUBJ= be.old=NOM sib-   [te ulaja avan]
                                              ling-3SG.POSS
     /k/ > [ʁ]   /mʷanok̲/   + /-k/ 'DET.D.PRX'   [mʷãnõʁiiq]
                 /jeek̲=i-nao/   plant=GEN-1SG.ABS   [jɛʁinãõ]
                 /na= pa= mʷek̲=i-e/   1SG.SUBJ= CAUS=   [nã pa mʷɛʁie]
                                              be.twisted=GEN-3SG.ABS

Lenition also operates during phase shift (see §2.5.2 below), and on code-mixing and words borrowed from French (see §2.6.3). Some examples are shown in (60).

(60) /p/ > [v]   Fr. *papier* [papie]   > B. [pʷavie] 'paper'
     /t/ > [ɾ]   Fr. *couteau* [kuto]   > B. [kuɾo] 'knife'
                  Fr. *pantalon* [pãtalõ]   > B. [paɾanõ] 'pants'
     /c/ > [j]   Fr. *français* [fʁãse]   > B. [prãje] 'French'
                  Fr. *magasin* [magazɛ̃]   > B. [mãⁿgajã] 'store'
     /k/ > [ʁ]   Fr. *tricot* [tʁiko]   > B. [teɾiʁo] 't-shirt'

There is also diachronic evidence for lenition. Many Belep nouns (§4.2.3) and verbs (§5.2.5.1) undergo unpredictable stem modification depending on the morphosyntactic context. These fossilized forms show evidence of lenition having operated at some point in the past. Some examples are shown in (61) and (62).

(61) /pʷ/ > [w]   /ⁿdepʷ/ 'deck'   [ⁿdewa-] '(something's) deck'
      /p/ > [v]   /naap/ 'fire'   [nãve-] '(someone's) fire'
                     /toop/ 'field'   [tova-] '(someone's) field'
      /t/ > [ɾ]   /ⁿɟet/ 'stomach'   [ⁿɟeɾa-] '(someone's) stomach'
      /c/ > [j]   /kic/ 'liver'   [kije-] '(someone's) liver'
                     /teec/ 'burn'   [teja-] '(someone's) burn'
      /k/ > [ʁ]   /pek/ 'flesh'   [peʁa-] '(someone's) flesh'
                     /tõnok/ 'mucus'   [tõnõʁa-] '(someone's) mucus'

(62) /pʷ/ > [w]   /ãpʷ/ 'to laugh'   [ãwi-] 'laugh.TR'
                     /noᵐbʷapʷ/ 'to provoke' [nõᵐbʷawi-] 'provoke.TR'
      /p/ > [v]   /waap/ 'to topple'   [wave-] 'topple.TR'
                     /jaap/ 'to search'   [javi-] 'search.TR'
      /t/ > [ɾ]   /at/ 'to paddle'   [aɾe-] 'paddle.TR'
                     /taat/ 'to flee'   [taɾe-] 'flee.TR'
      /c/ > [j]   /nac/ 'to be surprised' [nãji-] 'be.surprised.TR'
                     /õᵐbʷac/ 'to watch'   [õᵐbʷaji-] 'watch.TR'
      /k/ > [ʁ]   /nook/ 'to solicit'   [nõʁe-] 'solicit.TR'
                     /cak/ 'to fish with a net' [c͡çaʁe-] 'fish.with.net.TR'

In many other New Caledonian languages, lenited consonants have phonemic status (Ozanne-Rivierre et al. 1998, Bril 2000) in that they contrast with voiceless consonants. This is not the case for Belep (§2.3.1.2, §2.4.1.2), although Belep speakers prefer to use different graphemes for voiceless stops and their lenited forms (§2.6).

2.5.2 Phase shift

Many Belep words have two different forms: the 'complete' phase, which occurs in isolation and at the end of an intonation unit, and the 'incomplete' phase, which occurs in most other environments.[56] The phonological correspondence between the complete and incomplete phases of a word relies on its syllabic structure. If the final syllable of the complete phase is open (V or CV), the incomplete phase is identical. Some examples are shown in Table 14.

---

56 This terminology is based on that coined for a similar phenomenon in Rotuman (Churchward 1939). In Rotuman, each word has two forms or 'phases', a longer 'complete' phase and a shorter 'incomplete' phase, which are distributed such that only the complete phase may occur at the end of an intonation unit or word, and all other words occur in the incomplete phase (Blevins 1994).

Tab. 14: Complete and incomplete phases, type 1

Complete		Incomplete		
[õ]	'to be good'	[te= c̃ʒe õ nã=le-ɲɟa-rovɛn]	'it is well with us all' (homily_0092)
[tu]	'to go.DH'	[avena= tu=la awe]	'we went down to Awe' (weekend_0002)
[kova]	'to leave'	[ave= kova=la mãr]	'we left the shore' (tahitien_0184)
[ãva]	'to fish'	[nãᵐbʷa ãva pʷalaic]	'fishing hole' (hamecon_0064)
[cçao]	'to work'	[te= ɲɟua cçao pʷalu]	'it is very hard work' (homily_0067)

If the final syllable of the complete phase is closed (VC or CVC), the incomplete phase adds /a/ to the end of the word. This places the consonant which was previously word-final in a word-medial position, and it is obligatorily lenited (see §2.4.1.2, §2.5.1). Thus, a final closed syllable in the complete phase corresponds to two open syllables in the incomplete phase. In Table 15, some examples of this type of phase shift are shown; the additional /a/ in the incomplete phase is underlined.

Tab. 15: Complete and incomplete phases, type 2

Complete		Incomplete		
[ãc]	'man'	[paᵐbo-ŋã ãja pʷalaic]	'one of my grandsons' weekend_0030
[tɛp]	'to click'	[teva=mẽ=la ᵐbʷe mʷɲ̊ɟa]	'spit (a hot coal) onto it' AP1_0082
[ãβur]	'wave'	[ãβura pʷaⁿdu]	'two waves' sousmarin_0063
[wãnẽm]	'to walk'	[nãra wa wãnẽma=rovɛn]	'in all (our) walking' homily_0007

If there is like-vowel hiatus (§2.3.2.2) in the last two syllables of the word (note that this is the only environment where like-vowel hiatus may occur), like-vowel hiatus in the complete phase corresponds to a single vowel in the incomplete phase. The rules relating to the syllable structure of the final syllable also apply. A few examples are shown in Table 16; the altered vowels are underlined.

Tab. 16: Complete and incomplete phases, type 3

Complete		Incomplete		
[tuu]	'EX.SPC'	[tu ãɲɟu pʷalaic]	'there is one person' AW1_0134
[teãmãã]	'high chief'	[teãma=la kumʷãāk]	'the high chief of Koumac' AW4_0009

Complete		Incomplete	
[toop]	'field'	[la= īnā-ē t<u>o</u>va-māle]	'they made the two fields' AW6_0085
[ᵐbaraap]	'evening'	[ka=ō tu=li ᵐbar<u>a</u>va pʷalaic]	'then, one evening,' lune_0018

Words whose complete form contains a like-vowel hiatus in the last two syllables are thus divided into two categories: those whose final syllable is open, and which therefore 'lose' a syllable in their incomplete form; and those whose final syllable is closed, which therefore contain the same number of syllables in their complete and incomplete forms. For example, Table 16 shows the complete form of /teãmaa/ [teãmãă] 'high chief' (4 syllables) and its incomplete form [teãmã] (3 syllables). In contrast, the complete form of /toop/ [toop] 'field' is two syllables, and its incomplete form [tova][57] is also two syllables. The penultimate syllable, which carries stress (§2.8), is unaffected by phase shift, and it remains the penultimate syllable despite phase shift in all cases.

Note that phase shift may cause words which are not homophonous in complete phase, such as /toop/ 'field' and /top/ 'to melt', to become homophonous in connected speech; the incomplete phase of both words is [tova].

2.5.3 Nasal spreading

Nasal spreading from left to right[58] is the primary cause of phonetic nasalization of vowels in Belep. Nasal consonants (§2.2.1.5) and phonemically nasal vowels (§2.3.2.3) both spread nasality to the following vocalic segments, as the examples in (63) show. Sequences of Nasal consonant + Oral vowel and sequences of Nasal vowel + Oral vowel do not occur in Belep (see §2.3.2.4).

(63) /mʷaⁿde-/ [mʷãⁿde-] 'nose'
      /nu/ [nũ] 'coconut palm'
      /ãota-/ [ãõɾa-] 'instance'
      /tũa-e/ [tũã-ẽ] 'to fool-GNR'

---

57 The process by which [tova] is derived from /toop/ is the following:
1) /toop/ > top like-vowel hiatus rule
2) top > topa since final syllable ends in consonant, final /a/ is added to the end of the word
3) topa > [tova] word-medial consonant undergoes lenition
58 As discussed in Schourup (1972; cited in Cohn 1993).

Nasality spreads through single vowels and both types of vowel hiatus (§2.3.2.2) as shown in (64).

(64) /mia/ [mĩã] 'to be ripe'
      /nao/ [nãõ] 'to sing'
      /teãmaa/ [teãmãã] 'high chief'

Nasality also spreads across morpheme boundaries (65).

(65) /topen=i cao/ [toveŋ=ĩ c͡çao] 'to finish working'
      /cẽne-e/ [c͡çẽnẽ-ẽ] 'to swallow'
      /nanami-u/ [nãnãmĩ-ũ] 'think.TR-DETR'

Nasal spreading is stopped by all consonants, even approximants /w/, /j/ and /l/, as shown in (66).

(66) [ãwu] 'fly'
      [ãja] 'to fear'
      [nõ=la we] 'fish=LOC water'

Some scholars of Northern New Caledonian languages posit different degrees of vowel nasality in contexts where it is not phonemic (Bril 2000). In Balade Nyelâyu, back vowels are more nasalized than non-back vowels; /a/ is more nasalized after the labiovelar nasal than after the bilabial; long vowels are more nasalized than short vowels; and vowels followed by an oral consonant are more nasalized than vowels followed by a nasal consonant (Ozanne-Rivierre et al. 1998:27). Though I have observed similar patterns for Belep, Chen (1997) argues that the degree of vowel nasality can be measured using the amplitude of the nasal formants.[59] The systematic investigation of the degree of nasalization of Belep vowels is a topic for further study.

2.6 Orthographic conventions

The rest of this grammar will eschew phonetic and phonemic transcriptions for most examples, unless it is necessary for explanation. Instead, examples will be written in the official Belep orthography, which was developed by the Belema Language Committee for use in the school in 1999 and presented to the community in 2011. Though

---

[59] She found that the formula A1-P1 (where A1 is the amplitude of the first formant and P1 is the amplitude of the highest peak harmonic around 950 Hz) is a good estimator of the degree of nasality, where a higher difference indicates less nasality and a low or negative difference indicates more nasality (Chen 1997).

many orthographic rules are still under consideration by the Committee, this work will make use of the rules which have been suggested as of this writing.

Table 17 shows equivalent IPA and Belep graphemes. Belep orthographic words and graphemes cited in the text will be in *italics*.

Tab. 17: Orthographic equivalents

IPA	Grapheme	IPA	Grapheme
/i/	i	/pʷ/	**pw** (initial and final), **w** (medial)
/e/	e	/p/	**p** (initial and final), **v** (medial)
/a/	a	/t/	**t** (initial), **r** (medial and final)
/o/	o	/c/	**c** (initial and final), **y** (medial)
/u/	u	/k/	**k** (initial and final), **x** (medial)
/ĩ/	î	/ᵐbʷ/	bw
/ẽ/	ê	/ᵐb/	b
/ã/	â	/ⁿd/	d
/õ/	ô	/ᶮɟ/	j
/ũ/	û	/ᵑg/	g
		/mʷ/	mw
		/m/	m
		/n/	n
		/ɲ/	ny
		/ŋ/	ng
		/l/	l
		/w/	w
		/j/	y

Note that Belep speakers prefer different graphemes for voiceless stops and their lenited (§2.5.1) allophones. Vowel hiatus (§2.3.2.2) will be written with separate graphemes, e.g. *teec* /teec/ [teec] 'to burn'. Nasalization will not be indicated on vowels which are phonetically nasalized due to nasal spreading (§2.5.3), e.g. *mwanok* /mʷanok/ [mʷãnõq] 'moon'. Initial /w/ and medial [w] will always be written *w* before *o* and *u*, even though there is no phonological basis for differentiating medial [w] from [v] in this environment (§2.3.1.5).

Note that there are several digraphs: *pw* /pʷ/, *bw* /ᵐbʷ/, *mw* /mʷ/, *ny* /ɲ/, *ng* /ŋ/. Prenasalization of *bw*, *b*, *d*, *j*, and *g* is not indicated orthographically. Phonemic /ɟ/ is written *y*, while phonemic /ᶮɟ/ is written *j*. Another potential source of confusion is between phonemic *g* /ᵑg/ and *ng* /ŋ/; for example, *cangee* /caŋe-e/ 'to switch' contrasts with *cagee* /caᵑgee/ 'to steal'.

Most example sentences in this reference grammar will make use of a four-line format as in (67), where the first line is orthographic, the second line is morphemic, the third line provides an English gloss, and the fourth line is a free translation into English. A phonetic transcription is also provided here for reference.

(67) [nã ˈmãji ˈc̃çaam]
 Na maac yi caam.
 na=   may=i   caam
 1SG.SUBJ= die=GEN cold
 'I'm cold.' (lit. 'I'm dying of cold.')

At the orthographic level, Belep words will always be written in their complete phases, even when they should be pronounced in their incomplete phases, e.g. *gawaarimi* /ⁿgawaat-mi/ [ⁿgawarimi] 'day-DET.A.DST'. Ditropic clitics (§6.4) will be preceded by an orthographic space, and lenition will not be indicated on the word preceding a ditropic clitic. Instead, ditropic clitics will change orthographic form depending on the preceding phone. For example, (67) uses the ditropic clitic =*li* or =*i* 'GEN', but it is written *yi* in this case because it is preceded by *c*. Proclitics (§3.2.2.6) will always be followed by an orthographic space. Enclitics (other than the locationals in §5.12, which follow the orthographic pattern of ditropic clitics) will not be preceded by an orthographic space, and furthermore consonants preceding an enclitic will be written in their medial form, e.g. *cavac* 'to depart' but *cavayadu* /capac=ⁿdu/ 'to depart=DIR.DH'.

Glosses at the morpheme level will also use Belep graphemes. Here, Belep words will appear in an orthographic representation of their incomplete phase if they do so in the speech event. Lenitions at morpheme boundaries will use graphemes for lenited forms of consonants. For example, in (67), *maac* 'to die' is used in its incomplete form, so only one <a> is used in the morphemic transcription. Furthermore, the addition of ditropic clitic =*i* makes the preceding /c/ consonant word-medial, provoking lenition to [j], which is written <y>.

2.7 Phonotactics

Both open and closed syllables occur in Belep. Only simple onsets are available, and coda consonants are only found word-finally. Table 18 shows the only acceptable syllabic units in Belep.

Tab. 18: Monosyllabic structures in Belep

V	*ô* 'to be good', *i* 'type of crab', *u-* 'to tease', *e-* 'hand'
CV	*no* 'fish', *tu* 'to go.DH'[60]
VC	*uc* 'straw', *ôm* 'to be deaf'
CVC	*pan* 'to go.TV', *top* 'to melt'

Table 18 shows that the maximal syllable in Belep is CVC; it must contain one vowel and may be open or closed. No consonant clusters are permitted in Belep. Sequences of vowels, whether they are like or different, are always heterosyllabic (§2.3.2.2).

Disyllabic words are the most common type of monomorphemic word in Belep. Table 19 shows examples of all possible syllable structures for disyllabic words. Note that in words of two syllables, the first syllable always receives primary stress (§2.8).

Tab. 19: Disyllabic structures in Belep

V.V	*êê* 'yes', *âo-* 'vine', *uo* 'to reminisce'
CV.V	*mia* 'to be ripe', *cae* 'reef', *doo* 'dirt', *Nii* (name of a place)
V.VC	*aom* 'peaceful'
CV.VC	*duup* 'to be dense', *kiâk* 'purple swamphen'
V.CV	*âno* 'aunt', *uya* 'to arrive'
V.CVC	*elac* 'noni tree', *âdap* 'calm'
CV.CV	*taxa* 'to harvest', *piyu* 'star'
CV.CVC	*texec* 'grass', *nibwan* 'type of snake'

Words longer than two syllables in Belep tend to be morphologically complex. However, all trisyllabic combinations may occur (except those with like-vowel hiatus listed in Table 24 as impossible; see §2.8.3.1). Table 20 lists examples of trisyllabic words which are monomorphemic. Note that not all possible combinations are attested in the current corpus; further study is required to determine the reason for this gap.[61]

---

[60] Words of the form CṼ (where the nasalization is phonemic rather than phonetic) are very rare. A few examples are *wâ-* 'root' and *pê* 'bread.LN'.
[61] The unattested structures are attested in multimorphemic words. For example:
VVV *ua-e* 'suck-3SG.ABS'
VVVC *âo-or* 'vine-2DU.POSS'
CVVVC *duae-n* 'health-3SG.POSS'
VVCVC *ua-len* 'suck-3PA.ABS'

Tab. 20: Trisyllabic structures in Belep

V.V.V	–
V.V.VC	–
CV.V.V	*kuau* 'cat', *duae-* 'health', *Weaa* (name of a place)
CV.V.VC	–
V.V.CV	*auva* 'end of mourning', *âora-* 'instance'
V.V.CVC	–
CV.V.CV	*joâye* 'golden-spot hogfish', *Bealo* (clan name)
CV.V.CVC	*caivak* 'rat'
V.CV.V	*awaa* 'mat', *arii* 'rice.LN'
V.CV.VC	*alaar* 'rabbitfish'
V.CV.CV	*ileli* 'snipe'
V.CV.CVC	*ulayar* 'to be big'
CV.CV.V	*waxoe* 'type of lizard', *pinyau* 'watermelon'
CV.CV.VC	*cexeen* 'sacred', *gawaar* 'day'
CV.CV.CV	*kumwala* 'sweet potato'
CV.CV.CVC	*boriric* 'type of bird', *kewowor* 'to snore'

All consonants in the phonemic inventory (§2.2.1) may be syllable onsets. Examples are shown in Table 21.

Tab. 21: Attested consonant onsets

	Word-initial		Word-medial[62]	
pw	pwa	'hole'	-	
p	pa	'to take'	cavac	'to depart'
t	ta	'to go.UH'	uru	'wind'
c	ca	'to be how?'	-	
k	ka-	'foot'	taxa	'to harvest'
bw	bwa-	'head'	nabwa-	'imprint'
b	ba	'to kiss'	coba	'to hide'
d	da	'blood'	muda	'acne'
j	ja	'1pl.incl.indep'	âja	'to hunt troca'
g	ga-	'sympathy'	ôgo	'mountain'

---

[62] Note that the contrast between /pʷ/ and /w/ is neutralized word-medially, as is the contrast between /c/ and /j/; see §2.3.1.5.

	Word-initial		Word-medial[62]	
mw	mwa	'house'	tamwa	'woman'
m	ma	'LK4'	arama-	'face'
n	na-	'interior'	âna-	'contents'
ny	nya-	'mother'	pinye-	'to start a fire'
ng	ngagaro	'spider conch'	cange-	'to choose'
w	wa	'grandparent'	awaa	'mat'
l	la	'3pl.indep'	alap	'beach'
y	ya-	'tuber'	uya	'to arrive'

All vowels in the phonemic inventory (§2.2.2) may serve as syllable onsets, both word-initially and word-medially (Table 22).

Tab. 22: Attested vowel onsets

	Word-initial		Word-medial	
i	ipw	'to be moldy'	caivak	'rat'
e	elac	'noni tree'	cae	'reef'
a	alap	'beach'	pia-	'fingernail'
o	ola	'shellfish'	gao	'bamboo'
u	uru	'wind'	dau	'islet'
î	îji	'ant'	kîîr	'to be loud'
ê	êna	'to know'	wêêk	'tobacco'
â	âno	'aunt'	deâ	'type of fly'
ô	ôgo	'mountain'	yaôva	'rigging'
û	ûdu	'to drink'	kûûr	'to grunt'

A limited consonant inventory is permitted in coda position. Codas only occur word-finally. Some examples are shown in Table 23.

Tab. 23: Attested coda consonants

pw	âpw	'to laugh'
p	nep	'dream'
t	tuur	'to fart'
c	uc	'straw'
k	mwanok	'moon'

mw	pûmw	'smoke'
m	wânem	'to walk'
n	dan	'sky'
ny	geeny	'to regret'
ng	waang	'boat'

Despite the existence of both onset and coda consonants, Belep speakers use a number of strategies to avoid the occurrence of consonant clusters at morpheme and word boundaries. Within a phonological word, roots with a final nasal consonant may be modified by dropping this consonant, e.g. *wânem* 'to walk' + *=da* 'DIR.UH' becomes *wâneda*; *pan* 'to go.TV' + *=me* 'CTP' becomes *pame*. For roots with a final voiceless stop, an epenthetic vowel (usually /i/ or /a/) is inserted between the consonants to avoid a cluster; the voiceless stop is then realized as a lenited allophone (§2.5.1). For example, *cavac* 'to depart + *=du* 'DIR.DH' becomes *cavayadu*; *jec* 'brush' + *-k* 'DET.D.PRX' becomes *jeyiik*. Between phonological words, the first word undergoes phase shift, appearing in its incomplete form (§2.5.2), which always ends with a vowel.

2.8 Prosody

Phonological words in Belep receive stress. According to the typology of stress systems described by Van Zanten & Goedemans (2007), Belep has primarily fixed stress on the penultimate syllable. This is complicated by a large amount of extrametricality of formatives, and by some degree of lexical stress. Furthermore, the traditional cross-linguistic correlates of stress—vowel duration, intensity, and pitch (Lehiste 1970)—behave independently in Belep, making stress difficult to identify in many cases, both instrumentally and to native speaker judgments.

In §2.8.1, I discuss disyllabic words, whose stress patterns are most clearly identifiable both by speaker intuition and by phonetic stress correlates. In §2.8.2, I go into greater phonetic detail about these stress correlates and situations where they do and do not coincide. In §2.8.3, I present evidence that Belep primary stress falls on the penultimate syllable. In §2.8.4 and §2.8.5, exceptions to this pattern (extrametricality and lexical stress, respectively) are discussed.

2.8.1 Disyllabic words

In all Belep disyllabic words (the most common word type), stress falls on the first syllable. Stress in disyllabic words is easier to identify than in other Belep words, since this is the only environment in which the stress correlates of vowel duration and intensity coincide. In disyllabic words, the penultimate syllable is stressed—it contains a vowel of longer duration (§2.4.2.1) and the word's intensity peak—while the final syllable is unstressed and contains the pitch peak. A similar division of stress correlates is observed for other Oceanic languages including Gilbertese, which has primary stress on the penultimate mora[63] and high pitch on the antepenultimate mora; and for Ponapean, which has high pitch on the penultimate mora and primary stress on the final mora (Rehg 1993).

A few examples of the stress pattern for disyllabic words are given in (68). Note that ['] precedes a stressed syllable which is marked as lengthened with [ː], while [´] is marked on vowels to indicate a higher pitch than the surrounding segments.

(68) *alap* [ˈaːlápˀ] 'beach'
 calu [ˈc͡ɕaːlú] 'to unbalance'
 ere [ˈeːɾé] 'to be different'
 mada [ˈmãːⁿdá] 'cloth'
 pulu [ˈpuːlú] 'to speak'
 tolam [ˈtoːlám] 'basket'
 wânem [ˈwãːnẽm] 'to walk'

Figure 36 shows a spectrogram of the characteristic crisscross intensity and pitch curves of a disyllabic Belep word.

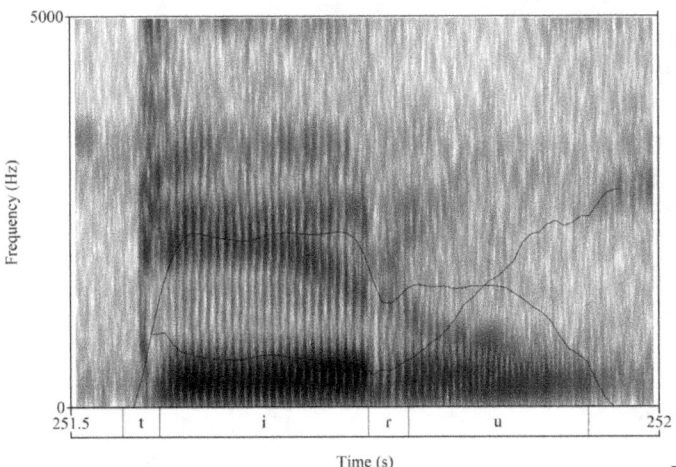

Yal-04102011-PT3_251.5-252

Fig. 36: Spectrogram for /titu/ [tiru] 'stake'

---

[63] Note that in Belep each syllable is assigned one mora.

Figure 36 shows a spectrogram for the word /titu/ [ˈtiˑɾú] 'stake' produced in isolation by a male speaker, age 70. The first syllable /ti/, which is stressed, is of longer duration and higher intensity, while the second syllable /tu/ is unstressed and of higher pitch. Speakers consistently identify the first syllable in disyllabic words as stressed.[64] As discussed in §2.4.2.1, the stressed vowel in a disyllabic word is significantly longer than any other single vowel syllable.

In disyllabic words which contain vowel hiatus (§2.3.2.2), the stress pattern is identical—the first vowel carries the intensity peak while the second vowel carries the pitch peak (69).

(69) ciâ   [ˈc͡çiã] 'flea'
      kaac [ˈkaác] 'to be bitter'
      mae   [ˈmãẽ] 'to sleep'
      puer [ˈpuéɾ] 'to prepare food'
      waup [ˈwaúp̚] 'to be toothless'
      yoor [ˈjoóɾ] 'to wade'

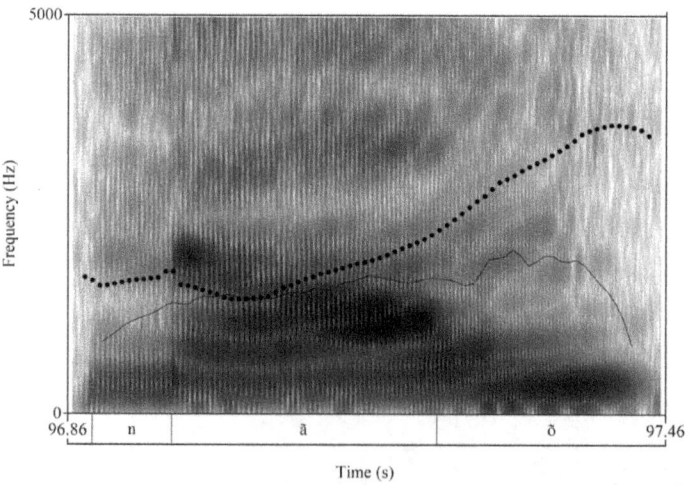

Yal-24102011-YG3_96.86-97.46

Fig. 37: Spectrogram for *nao* 'to sing'

The total duration of the vowel sequence is significantly longer than a single stress-lengthened vowel; however, more research remains to be done to determine whether or not the first vowel in a vowel hiatus undergoes stress-induced lengthening. Figure 37 shows the characteristic crisscrossing intensity and pitch curves of the disyllabic word *nao* [ˈnãṍ] 'to sing', which contains a vowel hiatus.

---

64 To identify speaker intuitions about stress, I asked "Which syllable do you hear the strongest?".

2.8.2 Stress correlates

Despite other evidence for penultimate stress in Belep (§2.8.3), it is not possible to assign stress to words of more than two syllables based on stress correlates alone—in these words, intensity, duration, and pitch all act independently of one another. This is not unknown cross-linguistically; in Hungarian, for example, Fónagy (1958: 51) found that there were no unambiguous cues to stress—there were unstressed syllables that were longer and had greater intensity and higher frequency than a stressed syllable (Lehiste 1970).

In the trisyllabic Belep words represented in (70) and (71), the intensity peaks on the first syllable, while the penultimate syllable is generally of longer duration and the final syllable contains the pitch peak. Here, [ˌ] precedes a syllable to mark it as having the highest intensity, while [ˊ] occurs over a vowel to mark the syllable with the highest pitch. The penultimate syllable is followed by a length marker [ː] which indicates vowel lengthening (§2.4.2.1). An example spectrogram, using the word *baraap* [ˌᵐbaraːáp] 'evening' is shown in Figure 38:

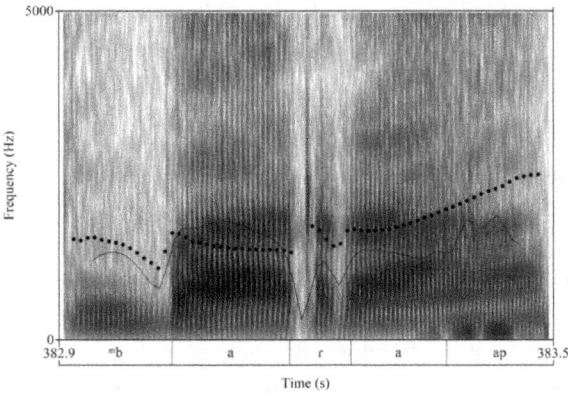

Fig. 38: Spectrogram for *baraap* 'evening'

Speakers do not consistently identify stress in trisyllabic words. The words in (70) were identified by speakers as stressed on the penultimate syllable, while the words in (71) were identified as stressed on the first syllable. Note that the intonation pattern is the same for all words in (70) and (71); at issue is whether the speakers perceive stress on the intensity peak or on the penultimate syllable.

(70) cexeen [ˌc͡çeʁeːén] 'to be sacred'
      baraap [ˌᵐbaɾaːáp] 'evening'
      waxoe [ˌwaʁoːé] 'type of lizard'
      pinyau [ˌpiɲãːṹ] 'watermelon'
      kumwala [ˌkumʷãːlá] 'sweet potato'
      boriric [ˌᵐboɾiːɾíc] 'tern'
      peyere [ˌpeɾeːjé]⁶⁵ 'to brawl'

                                    Yal-18102011-DY1.wav and Yal-18102011-DY2.wav

(71) bolao [ˌᵐbolaːó] 'banana tree'
      tewuur [ˌteβuːúɾ] 'to begin'
      ulayar [ˌulaːjáɾ] 'to be big'
      nyiraic [ˌɲĭɾaːíc] 'midpoint'
      woyino [ˌβojiːnṍ] 'to hang'

                                    Yal-18102011-DY1.wav and Yal-18102011-DY2.wav

For phonological reasons, I will consider the penultimate syllable to be the locus of stress in these trisyllabic words, despite the intensity peak on the first syllable and speaker uncertainty as to the location of stress.⁶⁶

2.8.3 The penultimate stress rule

Several phonological factors influence the choice to consider the penultimate syllable as the carrier of stress. First, the phenomenon of phase shift (§2.5.2) provides evidence that the penultimate syllable receives primary stress. Phase shift, which alters or deletes final syllables, does not affect the onset or nucleus of penultimate syllables. The following sections will discuss two other arguments for penultimate stress: the fact that like-vowel hiatuses are limited in their distribution to occur only in the final two syllables of words (§2.8.3.1) and the fact that penultimate syllables in 'compounded' words still maintain secondary stress despite losing primary stress (§2.8.3.2).

---

65 Note: /pejete/ 'to fight' has undergone metathesis for many speakers, being produced as [pereje].
66 Fontinelle (1976) argues that for Ajië, a Southern New Caledonian language, stress occurs on the first syllable of lexical words, except if the second syllable or mora is long, in which case it may receive lexical stress. This differs from my analysis in that Fontinelle places stress on the first syllable of words (with some exceptions), while I place it on the penultimate syllable (with some exceptions; see §2.8.5).

2.8.3.1 Distribution of like-vowel hiatus

Like-vowel hiatuses—that is, disyllabic sequences of two like vowels (§2.3.2.2)—have a limited distribution in Belep: they are only permitted in the final two syllables of a phonological word.

Disyllabic words with like-vowel hiatus are very common (72).

(72) *kâak* 'to shout'
      naap 'fire'
      neen 'when?'
      koor 'to be soft'
      jiin 'underlayer of a roof'
      duup 'to be dense'

Trisyllabic words with like-vowel hiatus are also quite common (73).

(73) *belooc* 'to be puny'
      kareec 'type of clam'
      biluup 'type of hibiscus'
      madaan 'weather'
      keloop 'hat'
      nodeec 'to daydream'

There are even a few words with four or more syllables which contain a like-vowel hiatus (74).

(74) *karavaa* 'pirogue'
      kaladeen 'to be distracted'
      kawolook 'tout-tout'
      pavadaa 'noise'
      âdeweaa 'belligerent rock shell'

However, there are no Belep words with the syllable structures represented in Table 24.

Tab. 24: Impossible phonotactic structures

V_1V_1CV
V_1V_1CVC
CV_1V_1CV
CV_1V_1CVC
$CV_1V_1V_2$[67]
$CV_1V_1V_2C$

Such word structures, in which a like-vowel hiatus occurs outside of the two final syllables, are impossible in Belep. This limiting of the distribution of like-vowel hiatuses to the final foot of a word is an argument for placing the locus of stress in the final foot as well. And the only available position for stress in the final foot is in penultimate position.

2.8.3.2 'Compounding' stress patterns

There is no formal distinction in Belep between nouns in the dependent possessive construction (§4.2.2.1) and noun compounds (§3.7). However, nouns in the dependent possessive construction differ in their stress pattern depending on whether their possessor is pronominal or nominal. For example, consider the word *tala-* 'bed' in (75).

(75)   *tala-* 'bed'
      tala-n [ˈtaːla-n] 'bed-3SG.POSS' ('his/her bed')
      tala pabo-ng [ˌtala ˈpaːᵐbo-ŋ] 'bed grandchild-1SG.POSS'
                                                                  ('my grandchild's bed')

Example (75) shows that, when *tala-* has a pronominal possessor, it receives primary stress—including stress-induced lengthening—on the penultimate syllable, as with any disyllabic word. However, when it has a nominal possessor, the primary stress in the phonological phase falls on the penultimate syllable of the phrase, leaving both syllables in [tala] without a primary stress and thus without stress-induced lengthening (§2.4.2.1). However, the penultimate syllable of [tala] still carries the intensity peak for the word, marked by [ˌ]. This process is similar to the one found in English compounds, where a rhythmic clash between compounding elements allows "the original primary accent [to shift] to the place of the original secondary accent, and [become] subordinated to the primary accent of the right-hand element of the whole

---

[67] Some speakers contrast [nãõ] '1SG.INDEP' with [nãːõ] 'to sing', though others do not; this may simply be an instance of typical disyllabic stress on the lexical word *nao* 'to sing', while the pronoun is not as strongly stressed.

phrase" (Ewen & Van Der Hulst 2001:214-215).[68] A similar process occurs with finite verb forms (76).

(76) *na coba* [nã= ˈc̦̑oːᵐba] 'I'm hiding'
      na coba-e [nã= c̦̑oˌᵐbaː-e] 'I'm hiding (from him/her)'
      na coba ava-ng [nã= ˌc̦̑oᵐba ˈaːva-ŋ] 'I'm hiding from my brother'

In (76), the intransitive verb *coba* 'to be hiding' receives primary stress [ˈ] on the penultimate syllable, inducing vowel lengthening [ː]. Used transitively but without a nominal absolutive argument, *coba-e* 'to hide from someone' carries both the intensity peak [ˌ] and vowel lengthening in its penultimate syllable, which can thus be unambiguously identified as stressed. However, when a nominal absolutive argument (§6.4.1) is present, that noun receives the primary stress correlates of a disyllabic word (an intensity peak and stress-induced vowel lengthening), while *coba* now receives only an intensity peak and does not undergo vowel lengthening.

The behavior of the stress correlates of intensity and duration in these bound roots provides further evidence for penultimate stress. Even when a penultimate syllable loses its stress-induced vowel lengthening to a superordinate element, it still maintains its intensity peak and thus 'secondary stress'.

2.8.4 Extrametricality

Most Belep suffixes and clitics are extrametrical, as defined by Van Zanten and Goedemans (2007); that is, they are blind to stress assignment based on the penultimate stress rule. These include: noun quantifier suffixes (§4.3), case enclitics (§6.4), aspectual proclitics (§5.5), mood clitics (§5.6), bound absolutive suffixes (§5.7), subject agreement proclitics (§5.8), deictic directional enclitics (§5.12), and the linkers when they are encliticized (§3.3.4). For example, (77) - (79) show morphologically complex phonological words which appear to violate the penultimate stress rule.

(77) *pa-e* [ˈpaː-e] 'take-SPC'
      pa-e=me [ˈpaː-e=mẽ] 'take-SPC=CTP'
      pa-e=me=la [ˈpaː-e=mẽ=la] 'take-SPC=CTP=NOM'

(78) *ava* [ˈaːva] '1PL.EXCL.INDEP'
      avaxa [ˈaːva=ʁa] '1PL.EXCL.SUBJ=ADD'
      avaxaô [ˈaːva=ʁa=õ] '1PL.EXCL.SUBJ=ADD=REAL'

---

[68] One example given by Ewen & Val Der Hulst (2001:215) is: ˌMissisˈsippi *but* ˌMississippi ˈmadrigals.

(79) bwage- [ˈᵐbʷaːⁿge] 'to return'
      bwage-nao [ˈᵐbʷaːⁿge-nãõ] 'return-1SG.ABS'

These examples are not violations of the rule since the lexeme they are derived from maintains its penultimate stress pattern; the suffixes and enclitics which are attached to them simply do not participate in stress assignment.

Not all Belep formatives are extrametrical, however. Formatives which participate in the assignment of stress to the penultimate syllable include: possessive suffixes (§4.2.2.2), nominal determiner suffixes (§4.4.2), and the specific suffix (§5.2.4). Examples (80) and (81) show stress changes provoked by possessive and determiner suffixes, and example (82) shows changes caused by the specific suffix.

(80) mada [ˈmãːⁿda] 'sadness' or 'cloth'
      madaa-n [mãⁿdaːa-n] 'sadness-3SG.POSS'
      mada-or [mãⁿdaː-oɾ] 'sadness-2DU.POSS'
      mada-yeda [mãⁿda-ˈjeːⁿda] 'cloth-DET.DIST.UH'
                                              Yal-12102011-DY.wav

(81) ulac [ˈuːlac] 'old man'
      ulayii-k [ulaˈjiːi-q] 'old man-DET.D.PRX'[69]
      gawaar [ⁿgaˈwaːaɾ] 'day'
      gawaarii-k [ⁿgawaˈriːi-q] 'day-DET.D.PRX'
                                Yal-24102011-YG1.wav – Yal-2410wo11-YG6.wav

(82) êna [ˈẽːnã] 'to know'
      êna-e [ẽˈnãː-ẽ] 'know-SPC'
      coba [ˈc͡çoːᵐba] 'to be hiding'
      coba-e [c͡çoˈᵐbaː-e] 'hide.from-SPC'
                                              Yal-12102011-DY.wav

The existence of such examples reinforces the presence of the penultimate stress rule.

2.8.5 Lexicality

Belep also has some degree of lexical stress, despite its generally applicable penultimate stress rule. It is not cross-linguistically unusual for a language to combine fixed stress and lexical stress (Goedemans & Van der Hulst 2013). In Belep, most words which disobey the fixed stress rule assign stress to the first syllable (83).

---

[69] See §4.4.2.1 on determiner -k and the stem allomorphy it provokes.

(83) *âria* [ˈãːɾia] or [ˈãːɾa] 'NEG.EX'
bwaêdan [ˈᵐbʷaːẽˌⁿdan] 'morning'
cobala [ˈɕoːᵐbala] 'bridge'

Other words with an exceptional stress pattern may be indicative of some form of morphological complexity such as compounding (84), discussed further in §3.7.

(84) *uru* [ˈuɾu] 'wind'
âc [ˈãc] 'man'
uruâny [uɾuˈãɲ] 'hurricane' (lit. 'man-made wind')[70]

Some formatives (as defined in chapter 3) also carry stress.[71] These include: the spatial directional clitics (§5.12), which descend etymologically from lexical verbs; the adverbial clitic =*roven* 'all', which is related to the lexical verb *toven* 'to finish' (§4.3.4); and the derivational proclitics (§3.6). Example (85) illustrates the usage of the stressed spatial directional enclitic =*da* 'DIR.UH'.

[ˈbʷaⁿge-va=ˈⁿda=mẽ=la ˈbʷe ˈwaːla]
(85) **bwagevadame la bwe Waala.**
bwage-va=<u>da</u>=me=la   **bwe**   **Wala**
return-1PL.EXCL.ABS=DIR.UH=CTP=LOC   top   Waala
'[we] went back up to Waala.'
                                                       Yal-17072009-TB-weekend_0042

In example (85), the speaker places =*da* in antepenultimate position within the phonological word; however, =*da* still carries stress, indicating that the stress is lexical in the case of this formative.

2.9 Other phonologies

Prior to this section, I have discussed the phonology of native Belep words; that is, indigenous vocabulary words believed to be in use prior to French colonization. However, adult Belep speakers make use of a variety of other phonologies in their daily interactions (see §1.7.2 on Belep multilingualism). These include sound-symbolic forms; partially-assimilated Latin borrowings; and words of French origin with varying degrees of assimilation. As such, I hypothesize that there is a stratified lexicon in

---

70 In Belep belief, hurricanes are created by a particular ancestral spirit on the northern island of Poc, who sends hurricanes when he is angry.
71 This is similar to the Southern New Caledonian language Ajië, where some suffixes are inherently stressed or provoke stress changes in the word to which they affix (Fontinelle 1976).

Belep (Saciuk 1969), though this grammar will not otherwise engage the framework of Lexical Phonology in which most scholars who posit lexical strata operate (for example, McCawley 1968). I define lexical strata here merely as subsets of the lexicon where different phonological rules apply. The preceding sections have focused on the native BELEP stratum, while the Belep SPECIAL (§2.9.1), LATIN (§2.9.2), and FRENCH (§2.9.3) strata will be discussed below.

2.9.1 Belep SPECIAL stratum

A small subset of words in Belep violate normal phonotactics by allowing phonetically voiceless stops in word-medial position (in BELEP phonology, phonemic voiceless stops in this position are obligatorily lenited; see §2.5.1). These words can be divided into two categories: sound-symbolic forms, and proper names.

2.9.1.1 Sound symbolism

Some sound-symbolic forms are represented in Table 25. Words accompanied by (#) have been observed in both the expected form and the form that preserves the medial voiceless stop.

Tab. 25: Sound symbolic forms

Phonemic form	Expected form	Phonetic form	Gloss
/kūkūūt/#	[kūʁūūr]	[kūkūūr]	'to murmur'
/pipilo/#	[pivilo]	[pipilo]	'swiftlet'
/popot/	[povor]	[popor]	'porcupinefish'
/pupuⁿdi/#	[puβuⁿdi]	[pupuⁿdi]	'symmetrical'
/makajawa/	[māʁajawa]	[māqajawa]	'masked booby'
/watepʷe/	[warewe]	[warepʷe]	'brown booby'
/polipoⁿda/	[poliwoⁿda]	[polipoⁿda]	'butterfly'
/tuci/[72]	[tuji]	[tuci]	'porpoise'

As shown in Table 25, most of the words which violate the medial lenition rule are animal names. The first four words in Table 25 appear to be reduplicated (see §3.8); *makayawa* 'masked booby' and *warepwe* 'brown booby' may be onomatopoetic (it is unknown whether the calls of these birds are similar to their names); and *polipoda*

---

[72] This word is listed in Dubois (1975c) as both /tuci/ and /tuⁿɟi/; the latter form would be in accord with usual Belep phonology.

'butterfly' and *tuci* 'porpoise' are possibly compounds[73] that have maintained their medial stops for sound-symbolism. Some of these words may also be borrowings from other languages of New Caledonia.

2.9.1.2 Proper names

Many proper names in Belep also preserve phonemic medial voiceless stops in their phonetic form. For these names, the expected lenited pronunciation is ungrammatical. Table 26 shows a few examples of Belep names with their corresponding French names (see §1.3.1 for more on proper names in Belep).

Tab. 26: Proper names

Phonemic form	Expected form	Phonetic form	French name	
/pato/	*[paro]	[pato]	Marie-Odile	[maχiodil]
/acia/	*[ajia]	[acia]	Ignacia	[iɲasia]
/iko/	*[iʁo]	[iko]	Rodérick	[ʁodeχik]
/kacaca/	*[kajaja]	[kacaca]	Cassandra	[kasãdχa]
/tete/	*[tere]	[tete]	Thérèse	[teχɛz]
/apo/	*[aβo]	[apʷo]	Apollonie	[apoloni]
/luci/	*[luji]	[luci]	Lucie	[lysi]

It is likely that these SPECIAL stratum words are learned simply as exceptions to the lenition rule.

2.9.2 Religious jargon

When the first Catholic missionaries arrived on Belep, they coined a number of new Belep words to communicate the Catholic faith to the Belema. As the language of the Church was Latin at the time, Belep contains a number of Latinate borrowings which are used in sermons, hymns, prayers, and discussions of religious life. Many of these forms are fully compatible with BELEP phonology (Table 27), and as such hypothesized phonemic forms for each word are indicated in the left column.

---

73 *polipoda* 'butterfly' contains the syllable *da*, which often carries the meaning of 'up', while *tuci* 'porpoise' contains *tu* 'to go.DH'.

Tab. 27: Religious jargon in Belep phonology

Phonemic form	Phonetic form	Latin origin	Gloss
/ājelo/	[ājelo]	angelus (>angelō)	'angel'
/capato/	[c̄çavaro]	sabbatum (>sabbatō)	'sabbath'
/cāto/	[c̄çāro]	sānctus (>sānctō)	'sainted'
/ⁿdemonio/	[ⁿdemōnīō]	daemonium (>daemoniō)	'demon'
/katejita/	[karejira]	catēchista	'catechist'
/kutuje/	[kuruje]	crux (>cruce)	'cross'
/matimonio/	[mārimōnīō]	mātrimōnium (>mātrimōniō)	'wedding'
/mija/	[mīja]	missus (>missa)	'Mass'
/pekato/	[peʁaro]	peccātum (>peccātō)	'sin'

However, many other religious words used in Belep are not compatible with Belep phonology. There are three main differences between Belep phonology and the phonology of this Latin stratum:

(A)   As in the Belep Special stratum, medial voiceless consonants are permitted, and contrast with medial lenited consonants. This results in /r/ and /v/ having phonemic status independent from /t/ and /p/.

(B)   Consonant clusters are permitted, as long as one of the consonants is /r/ or /s/.

(C)   /s/ has phonemic status.

Table 28 shows a few examples of words that fall into this stratum, with their violations of Belep phonology indicated in the left column. Some of these words have undergone a semantic shift.

Tab. 28: Latin stratum

	Phonetic form	Latin origin	Gloss
(A), (B), (C)	[apostolo]	apostolus (>apostolō)	'apostle'
(A)	[karitate]	caritas (>cāritāte)	'charity'
(A), (B), (C)	[kristianō][74]	christiānus (>christiānō)	'Christian'
(A), (B)	[martiir]	martyr	'martyr'
(C)	[paraⁿdiso]	paradīsus (>paradīsō)	'Paradise'

---

[74] An alternate pronunciation, [kirianō], does not violate Belep phonology.

	Phonetic form	Latin origin	Gloss
(A), (B)	[patriaka]	patriarcha	'ancestors' (Latin 'patriarchs')
(A), (B)	[virginẽ]	virgō (>virgine)	'Virgin'
(A), (B)	[virtute]	virtūs (>virtūte)	'to shine' (Latin 'virtue')

In general, speakers are not entirely aware of these words' non-Belep origins.

2.9.3 FRENCH stratum

As all adult Belema are fully bilingual in Belep and French, and children as young as three—who are by no means fluent French speakers—frequently use French words with French phonology (for example, *beurre* [bœʁ] 'butter' or *petit* [pəti] 'little'), it is a nontrivial task to tease apart which words of French origin are truly borrowings and which are instances of code-switching.

Wohlgemuth (2009) distinguishes borrowings, nonce borrowings, and code-switching. Borrowings are "the attempted reproduction in one language of patterns previously found in another" (Haugen 1950). Nonce borrowings occur only once in a corpus, and their "frequency and acceptability criteria are unclear or nonexistent" (Poplack et al. 1988: 52). Instances of code-switching are "instantiations of transfer, but are neither understood nor shared by other speakers of the host language who do not happen to be bilinguals" (Wohlgemuth 2009). Both nonce borrowings and borrowings share the characteristics of "morphological and syntactic integration" (Sankoff et al. 1990:94).

The words represented in Table 29 are the clearest instances of borrowings; they are fully assimilated into BELEP phonology, speakers are not always aware of their French origin, and some of them have undergone semantic shift. All these words occurred frequently in their conventionalized forms over the course of my field work. Hypothesized Belep phonemic forms are listed in the leftmost column.

Tab. 29: French borrowings into BELEP

Phonemic form	Phonetic form	French origin	Gloss
/atii/	[arii]	*ris* [ʁi]	'rice'
/cak/	[c̪ɕaq]	*sac* [sak]	'bag'
/cen/	[c̪ɕɛn]	*sel* [sɛl]	'salt'
/cepeto/	[c̪ɕevero]	*chèvre* [ʃɛvʁ]	'goat'

Phonemic form	Phonetic form	French origin	Gloss
/cimii/	[c͡çimĩĩ]	chemise [ʃəmiz]	'clothes' (French 'shirt')
/cikate/	[c͡çiʁare]	cigarettes [sigaʁɛt]	'cigarettes'
/copan/	[c͡çovan]	cheval [ʃəval]	'horse'
/cuuk/	[c͡çuuq]	sucre [sykχ]	'sugar, sweet'
/ⁿdotot/	[ⁿdoror]	docteur [doktœʁ]	'doctor'
/ⁿgeteec/	[ⁿgereec]	graisse [gʁɛs]	'rich, greasy' (French 'fat')
/kape/	[kave]	café [kafe]	'coffee'
/kilat/	[kilar] or [kular]	culottes [kylot]	'underwear' (French 'trousers')
/kotoje/	[koroje]	crochet [kʁoʃe]	'hook'
/kulieen/	[kulieen]	cuillère [kɥijɛʁ]	'spoon'
/kuto/	[kuro]	couteau [kuto]	'knife'
/kupetu/	[kuveru]	couverture [kuvɛʁtyʁ]	'blanket'
/majin/	[mãjin]	machine [maʃin]	'any motorized device' (French 'machine')
/otoop/	[oroop]	robe [ʁob]	'dress'
/pããc/	[pããc]	pinces [pɛ̃s]	'tongs'
/patano/	[paranõ]	pantalon [pãtalõ]	'pants'
/patin/	[parin]	farine [faʁin]	'flour'
/pẽ/	[pẽ]	pain [pẽ]	'bread'
/pet/	[pɛr]	fête [fɛt]	'party'
/pimaŋ/	[pimãŋ]	piment [pimã]	'hot peppers'
/poc/	[poc]	poche [poʃ]	'pocket'
/pooc/	[pooc]	poste [post]	'post office'
/poliic/	[poliic]	police [polis]	'enforcer' (French 'police')
/putieen/	[purieen]	prière [pʁijɛʁ]	'to pray' (French 'prayer')
/puut/	[puur]	four [fuʁ]	'oven'
/pʷapie/	[pʷavie]	papier [papie]	'paper'
/taac/	[taac]	tasse [tas]	'bowl' (French 'cup')
/taap/	[taap]	table [tabl]	'table'
/te/	[te]	thé [te]	'tea'
/tetiko/	[teriʁo]	tricot [tʁiko]	't-shirt' (French 'knit fabric')

However, the words of French origin in the following sections are less clear instances of borrowing. Though many of them undergo some phonological assimilation into Belep, all violate some rule of BELEP phonology.

2.9.3.1 Phonemic differences

The FRENCH stratum expands on the phonotactic rules of the LATIN stratum.

(D)   Medial voiceless consonants are permitted, and contrast with medial lenited consonants. This results in /r/ and /v/ having phonemic status independent from /t/ and /p/; they may occur word-initially.
(E)   Consonant clusters are permitted, as long as one of the consonants is /r/, /s/, or /l/.
(F)   /s/, /ɛ̃/, /œ/, /ə/, /y/, /z/, and /ʒ/ have phonemic status.

Table 30 shows a number of examples of words in the FRENCH stratum. Many of these words are nonce borrowings (occurring only once in my corpus), while others are more conventionalized borrowings used frequently by all speakers. Their feature(s) which violate BELEP phonology are listed in the left-hand column.

Tab. 30: French stratum

	Phonetic form	French origin	Gloss
(D), (E)	[ᵐbopreer]	beau-frère [bofχɛʁ]	'brother-in-law'
(D), (E)	[klakɛt]	claquettes [klakɛt]	'flip-flops'
(E)	[prãje]	français [fχɑ̃se]	'French'
(E)	[prããc]	France [fχɑ̃s]	'France'
(F)	[pyzi]	fusil [fyzi]	'gun'
(F)	[ʒœn]	jeune [ʒœn]	'youth'
(D)	[loto]	l'auto [loto]	'car'
(F)	[mãⁿgajɛ̃]	magasin [magazɛ̃]	'store'
(E)	[plaji]	place [plas]	'space, area'
(E)	[ploŋ]	plomb [plɔ̃]	'lead weight'
(F)	[ʁaⁿdo]	radeau [ʁado]	'raft'
(D)	[vakãã c]	vacances [vakɑ̃s]	'vacation, holiday'
(F)	[vaji]	vache [vaʃ]	'cow'

If words of French origin were considered to be part of the same phonology as BELEP, it would be necessary to posit a much larger phonemic inventory for Belep. For example, while no minimal pair for [p] and [v] exists in BELEP words, if we include words of French origin we find the following minimal pair:

(86) /paci/ [paji] 'tomahawk'
/vaci/ [vaji] 'cow' < French *vache* [vaʃ]

For these reasons it is best to consider the FRENCH stratum as separate from the BELEP stratum.

2.9.3.2 Phonetic influences

The influence of French also has phonetic effects on Belep. The most salient one of these is the effect on rhotics. French has orthographic <r>, which is realized as [ʁ], [χ], or [ʀ] in Standard dialects. In the French spoken by many adult Belema, orthographic <r> is realized as [ɾ], though people with more exposure to Standard French may produce [ʁ]. Meanwhile, Belep has phonemic /t/ which is medially and finally realized as [ɾ], and phonemic /k/ which is medially realized as [ʁ].

For many Belep children, who are still learning both Belep and French, these rhotics overlap. Some Belep children produce all French <r> as [ʁ], as well as all Belep [ɾ] and [ʁ] as [ʁ]. For example, a three-year-old child might produce Belep /ãti/ [ãɾi] 'to say' as [ãʁi]. By the time they leave elementary school, however, Belep children have generally teased apart their rhotics, producing Belep /t/ and French <r> as [ɾ] and Belep /k/ as [ʁ] as the adults do.

Belep stress patterns are also applied strongly to French borrowings. To use some examples from Table 30 above:

(87) French *claquettes* [klaˈkɛt] 'flip-flops' Belep [ˈklaːkɛt]
French *l'auto* [loˈto] 'car' Belep [ˈloːto]
French *français* [fʁãˈse] 'French' Belep [ˈpɾãːje]

Example (87) shows that French words which are stressed on the final syllable are often borrowed into Belep with the stress on the penultimate syllable, which then undergoes stress-induced lengthening (§2.4.2.1).

2.9.3.3 Morphophonemics

Many words of French origin which occur in Belep maintain the entirety of their French phonology; however, they are distinguished from code-switching by their degree of morphosyntactic integration into the stream of speech. Because of this, they should best be considered borrowings or nonce borrowings. A few examples are given in (88) and (89).

(88) French *grotte* [gʁot] 'cave' +Belep [-ʁeⁿda] 'DET.UH'
> [gʁotiʁeⁿda] 'the cave up there'

(89)   French *jeune* [ʒœn] 'youth' +Belep [-mã] 'AC'
       > [ʒœnãmã] 'teenagers'

In these examples, French and Belep phonology interact at morpheme boundaries. In (88) and (89), word-final consonants in the French word provoke the Belep suffix's allophone for consonant-final Belep words.

2.10 Summary

In this chapter, I have presented the phonemic inventory of Belep (§2.2) with a description of the phonemes (§2.3) and their allophones (§2.4). In §2.5 I described the main morphophonemic processes that occur in Belep, and in §2.6 the orthographic conventions used in the rest of this work were discussed. The following sections described the phonotactics (§2.7) and prosody (§2.8) of Belep. The chapter concluded with a discussion of subsections of the lexicon where different phonological rules apply (§2.9).

3 Architecture of the word

3.1 Introduction

Wordhood in the New Caledonian languages is not comprehensively addressed in the literature. These languages are characterized by a large number of formatives[1] which display some phonological but little morphological independence. Scholars of the area have in most cases chosen not to justify classifying these formatives variously as particles, clitics, or affixes, which has led to a fairly uneven characterization of these languages in terms of Comrie's (1989) indexes of synthesis and fusion.

Most scholars of New Caledonian languages, when they address the question, characterize these languages as highly isolating (e.g. Nêlêmwa, "whose morphology is not very complex, is characterized by the presence of numerous transcategorial and polyfunctional morphemes" (Bril 2002: 18)).[2] This is not an accurate description of Belep, which is very low on the index of fusion (agglutinating) but is somewhere in the middle on the index of synthesis (synthetic).

This chapter will attempt to define the word in Belep (§3.2). I will then enumerate the word classes and their determining features (§3.3), divide the formatives into inflectional and derivational categories (§3.4, §3.5 and §3.6), and discuss other morphological operations (§3.7 and §3.8).

3.2 Definition of the word

In this section I will show that a distinction between the phonological and grammatical word in Belep (as distinguished by Dixon and Aikhenvald (2002)) provides a useful method for characterizing the morphology of the language. I will show that there is an extreme disconnect in Belep between the phonological word and the grammatical word, which, if it were true for other languages of Melanesia, might contribute to the widespread inconsistency in the categorization of formatives.

In fact, the majority of word-forms in Belep can be characterized as either: (a) a grammatical word consisting of more than one phonological word—a phenomenon that also occurs in languages in geographical proximity to Belep including Yidiny

---

1 This work will adopt Bickel and Nichols' (2007) definition of formatives as morphological rather than syntactic entities.
2 "Cette langue, dont la morphologie est peu complexe, se caractérise par la présence de nombreux morphèmes transcatégoriels et polyfonctionnels" (Bril 2002: 18; translation mine).

(Australia), Yimas (Papua New Guinea), and Fijian (Fiji) (Dixon and Aikhenvald 2002: 28); or (b) a phonological word which does not consist of a whole number of grammatical words. This also occurs in Fijian (Dixon and Aikhenvald 2002: 29-31), where a formative associated with one grammatical word is attached to another phonological word, and many examples from other languages are given in Cysouw (2005) under the name *ditropic clitics*. The Belep ditropic clitics are defined in §3.2.2.6 and discussed in detail in §6.4. The Belep *preface* (see §5.3) is another example of a phonological word which does not consist of a whole number of grammatical words.

The wide disconnect in Belep between the phonological and the grammatical word most likely contributes to the lack of a Belep cultural conception of the 'word' as a unit. The Belep lexeme *pulu* has a number of senses: as a verb, it means 'to speak'; as a noun, it may mean 'language' (such as *pulu Belep* 'the language of Belep') or 'speech, utterance' (as in *â pae pulu* 'speech-carrier, spokesman'). The Belema do not have a specific way of referring to a 'word'; if, for instance, a teacher asks a student to repeat what he or she just said, she might use the form *maya pulu* 'section of speech', but this is not a fixed expression or collocation; many speakers would not say or recognize this. The Belep lexeme *nara-* 'name' is commonly used in conversation when defining a word, as in (1), and the term coined for the alphabet is *ba îna naraja* 'thing for making our names'. It is common for languages spoken by small numbers of speakers in Australia, Amazonia, and New Guinea to have a lexeme for 'name' but none for 'word' (Dixon & Aikhenvald 2002:3).

(1) BG: **Wîli yeek, bu lila yeek.**
 wî-li yeek bu=li-la yeek
 DEM.IA-DET.A.PRX wood fishhook=GEN-3PL.ABS wood
 'That wooden thing, their wooden fishhook.'

2 CG: **Iva naran ?**
 iva nara-n
 be.where.GNR name-3SG.POSS
 'What's its name?'

3 BG: **Hein ?**
 ââ
 eh?
 'Eh?'

4   CG: *Ivi naran ?*
          ivi   nara-n
          be.where.SPC   name-3SG.POSS
          'What's its name?'

5   BG: *Na koni nara bu lila,*
          na=   koni   nara   bu=li-la
          1SG.SUBJ= be.unable.TR   name   fishhook=GEN-3PL.ABS

6   *âri na ênae naran.*
          âri=   na=   êna-e   nara-n
          NEG= 1SG.SUBJ= know-SPC   name-3SG.POSS
          'I couldn't say what the name of their fishhook was, I don't know its name.'

          Yal-28072010-BGMCG-hamecon_0092-0096

Example (1) shows several instances of the noun *nara-* 'name' being used to mean 'word'. It is used twice by speaker MCG (in lines 2 and 4) to ask for the word for a type of fishhook, and it is used twice by speaker BG (lines 5 and 6) to disclaim knowledge of the sought-after word.

The Belema also vary widely in their interpretation of the orthographic 'word'. When writing their language, some Belep speakers place spaces between each formative, while others use the character '-'. For example, (2) and (3) show several uses of the genitive enclitic =*li* or =*i* (§6.4.3) written variably attached to the orthographic word preceding it, the word following it, and alone. In example (2), drawn from a word- and phraselist composed by one Belep speaker, the genitive enclitic =*i* is written attached to the following orthographic word.

(2)   < *nâ wa môlep vinâô ka nâ tegelac* >
        Na wa molep vinao, ka na tegelac.
        na   wa=   molev=i-nao   ka na=   tegelac
        interior   RESULT= live=GEN-   LK 1SG.SUBJ= fail
                             1SG.POSS
        'In my life I have failed.'[3]

                                                              PT handout

---

3 « Dans ma vie je suis loupé » (translation mine).

In example (3), which shows a transcription of song lyrics by another Belep speaker, the genitive enclitic =*li* is surrounded by orthographic spaces in line 1, and occurs attached to the preceding orthographic word in line 3.

(3) < *a tamé ka pilou / pilou li gawarick* >
A tame ka pilu / pilu li gawaariik

a=	ta=me	ka	pilu	pilu=li	gawarii-k
2PL.SUBJ=	go.UH=CTP	LK	dance	dance=GEN	day-DET.D.PRX

< *oulé naédjama / ma dja yague lila* >
u le naejama / ma ja yagelila

u=le	nae-ja-ma	ma	ja=	yage-li-la
toward=DAT	child-1PL.INCL.POSS-AC	LK4	1PL.INCL.SUBJ=	help-TR-3PL.ABS

< *bwera tchaolila* >
bweer cao lila

bwe-ra	cao=li-la
top-3SG.POSS	work=GEN-3PL.ABS

'Come and dance / dance for this day / for our children / so that we help them / with their work'

Balade-mariage

Examples (2) and (3) show that native speakers have varied interpretations of the wordhood of formatives such as the genitive enclitic. Speakers also interpret the orthographic wordhood of derivational proclitics (§3.6.2) in various ways. For instance, (4) shows an example (from a speaker-transcribed wordlist) of proclitic *â=* attached to its host with a dash.[4]

(4) < *an-baé-maac* >
â bae maac

â=	bae	maac
AGT=	eat	dead

'cannibal'[5]

PT handout

---

4 Some complex noun phrases in French orthography are joined with dashes.
5 « celui qui mange des morts » (translation mine).

By contrast, example (5) (from speaker-transcribed song lyrics) shows the proclitic *wa=* separated from its host by an orthographic space.

(5) < *mesi li<u>wa</u> djinaô dou la bwedo.*>
    Merci li wa jinaodu la bwe doo.
    [mesi]=li   wa=   ji-nao=du=la   bwe doo
    thank.you.LN=GEN RESULT= give-1SG.ABS=DIR.DH=LOC top earth
    'Thank you for putting me on this earth.'
    Balade-mariage

The following subsections will address inconsistencies related to wordhood and give definitions of the phonological word and the grammatical word in Belep, followed by a discussion of how these categories do (and do not) overlap.

3.2.1 Phonological word

Cross-linguistically, there are many tendencies that can be used to define a phonological word. Aikhenvald (2007: 2) defines a phonological word as "a prosodic unit not smaller than a syllable" and states that "cross-linguistic criteria used to define the phonological word include: (i) stress and other prosodic characteristics; (ii) phonotactics, and phonological rules which apply either word-internally or across word boundaries." Dixon and Aikhenvald (2002) further stipulate that cross-linguistic criteria include internal syllabic structure and phonotactics, pause phenomena, stress and nasalization, and phonological rules applying word-internally or across word boundaries (Dixon & Aikhenvald 2002: 13). Bauer (2003) adds that such criteria as singular, regular word-stress and vowel harmony are also characteristic (Bauer 2003: 58-60).

The following sections will describe how these cross-linguistic criteria correspond to language-specific correlates of the word-form in Belep. The cluster of features which together define the phonological word in Belep include: syllable structure (§3.2.1.1), penultimate stress (§3.2.1.2), allophony conditioned by the phonemic environment (§3.2.1.3), vowel epenthesis (§3.2.1.4), morphophonemic stem alternations (§3.2.1.5), and pause phenomena (§3.2.1.6).

3.2.1.1 Syllable structure

Phonological words in Belep consist of one or more syllables (§2.7). Word-initial and word-medial syllables may have the structure V or CV, while only word final syllables may have the form V, CV, VC, or CVC as shown in example (6).

(6) ô 'to be good' /õ/
pe 'stingray' /pe/
up 'to breathe' /up/
cep 'to build boats' /cep/
pao 'outdoors' /pa.o/
pawi 'hibiscus' /pa.wi/
kiâk 'purple swamphen' /ki.ãk/
talep 'to sweep' /ta.lep/
bolao 'banana tree' /ᵐbo.la.o/
wimawo 'ironwood' /wi.ma.wo/
jabaang 'Spanish mackerel' /ⁿɟa.ᵐba.aŋ/
ulayar 'to be big' /u.la.jat/

In multimorphemic words, processes such as vowel epenthesis and consonant deletion maintain the word-internal syllable structure of Belep (7).

(7) wânem 'to walk' +=da 'DIR.UH' > wâneda
pan 'to go.TV' +=me 'CTP' > pame
jec 'brush' +-k 'DET.D.PRX' > jeyiik
nep 'dream' +-na 'DET.D.MPX' > nevina

3.2.1.2 Penultimate stress

Phonological words in Belep carry primary stress, usually on the penultimate syllable (§2.8). This stress, here marked by ['] preceding the stressed syllable, is often accompanied by vowel lengthening (§2.4.2.1), indicated by [:]. Some examples are shown in (8).

(8) tamwa 'woman' ['ta:mʷã]
komu 'hermit crab' ['ko:mũ]
pulu 'to speak' ['pu:lu]
âvu 'housefly' ['ã:vu]
nara- 'name' ['nã:ra]
jabaang 'Spanish mackerel' [ⁿɟaˡᵐba:aŋ]
cexeen 'to be sacred' [ceˈʁe:en]
bolao 'banana tree' [ᵐboˈla:o]

The addition of some suffixes and enclitics to a phonological word changes the stress pattern (§2.8.4). For example, the stressed vowel /u/ in *ulac* 'old man' is normally lengthened, but if a determiner suffix (§4.4.2) is attached to the word, the stress shifts to the penultimate vowel /i/ and stress-induced lengthening on /u/ is no longer present (9).

(9) *ulac* /ulac/ [ˈuːlac] 'old man'
 ulayiik /ulacii-k/ [ulaˈjiːiq] 'old man-DET.D.PRX'
 Yal-24102011-YG1.wav – Yal-24102011-YG6.wav

Stress changes may also signal other phenomena which operate at the level of the phonological word, such as grammaticalization (10) and compounding (11).

(10) *toven* 'finish' [ˈtoːvɛn]
 =*roven* 'COMPL' [ɾoˈvɛn]

(11) *uru* 'wind' [ˈuːɾu]
 âc 'man' [ˈãc]
 uruâny 'hurricane' (lit. 'man-made wind') [uɾuˈãɲ]

3.2.1.3 Conditioned allophony

Some conditions for allophony in Belep depend on word-level phonology, including /e/ centralization, nasal spreading, and lenition.

The vowel /e/ is frequently centralized to [ɛ] or [ɪ] (§2.3.2.1) when it occurs in a closed syllable; closed syllables only occur word-finally (§2.7). Thus, the addition of some suffixes and enclitics may condition allophonic variation between [e] and [ɛ], as in (12).

(12) *bane-* 'companion' [ˈᵐbaːne]
 bane-mw [companion-2SG.POSS] [ˈᵐbaːnɛmʷ]
 nawe- 'to deposit' [ˈnaːwe]
 nawe-n [deposit-DA.NSG] [ˈnaːwɛn]

Belep nasal spreading (§2.5.3) phonetically nasalizes all vowels following a nasal phoneme. For example, Figure 1 shows a representation of the word *mwanao* 'to approach' with arrows indicating the continuation of nasal formants throughout all the vowels of the word. Here, the nasal consonant /mʷ/ phonetically nasalizes the following /a/, while the nasal consonant /n/ phonetically nasalizes the vowels /a/ and /o/ in the two syllables which follow it.

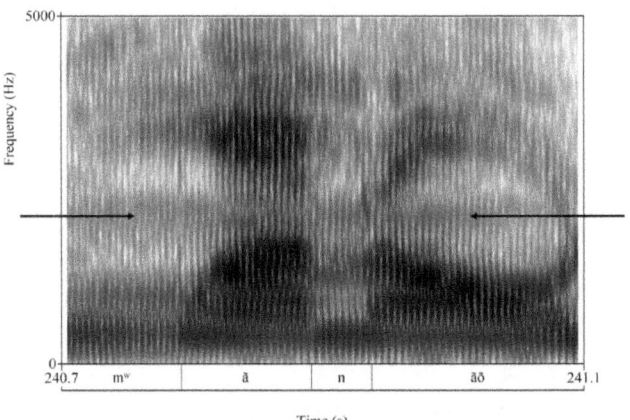

Fig. 1: Spectrogram of *mwanao* 'to approach'

Yal-28072010-BGMCG-tahitian_240.7-241.1

Nasal spreading also crosses suffix and enclitic boundaries. For example, in (13), the locative ditropic clitic =*a* (§6.4.5) is phonetically nasalized because it follows the nasal consonant /m/ in *wânem* 'walk'.

(13) [ka ⁿɟa wãnẽmã ᵐbʷeen]
      Ka ja wânem ma bween,
      ka ja=   wânem=a   bwee-n
      LK 1PL.INCL.SUBJ=   walk=LOC top-3SG.POSS
      'and we walked on it,'

      Yal-28072010-BGMCG-tahitian_0057

Figure 2 shows a spectrogram from the utterance represented in (13), where the nasal formants (marked with an arrow) are visible throughout the enclitic =*a*.

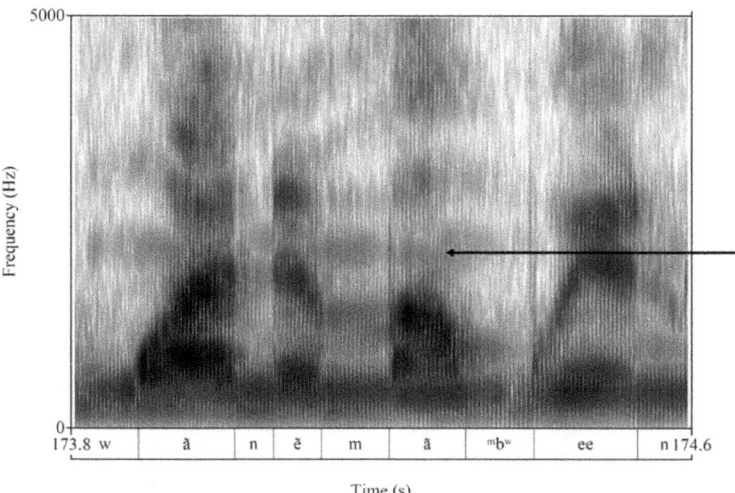

Fig. 2: Spectrogram of nasalized =a after nasal consonant

However, nasal spreading is blocked by a phonological word boundary, as the examples in (14) show. In each of these instances, a phonological word boundary blocks the spreading of phonetic nasality to the first vowel in the second word.

(14) *avena up* [avenã up] 'we smoke'
      teô udu [teõ uⁿdu] 's/he bent down'
      pwaneen alaar [pʷanẽnã alaar] 'how many rabbitfish'

The morphophonemic process of lenition (§2.5.1) provides evidence for the existence of the phonological word in Belep. Lenition—whereby voiceless stops /pʷ/, /p/, /t/, /c/, and /k/ have the intervocalic allophones [w], [v], [ɾ], [j], and [ʁ], respectively—operates only within a phonological word; it does not cross phonological word boundaries. So, for instance, final voiceless stop allophones may become medial, and thus lenited, with the addition of some suffixes and enclitics (15), but initial voiceless stops are never lenited because they are preceded by a phonological word boundary (16).

(15) *koyap* 'lobster sp.' + *-k*   'DET.D.PRX'   > *koyaviik*
      ulac   'old man'   + *-ma* 'AC'   > *ulayama*
      yeek   'plant'   + *=i-e* '=GEN-3SG.ABS'   > *yeexie*

(16) nabwa _ci_ [nã^{m}b^{w}a c͡ɕi] 'seat' (lit. 'imprint of sitting')
 ba _talep_ [^{m}ba= talɛp] 'broom' (lit. 'tool for sweeping')
 te _koor_ [te= koorˌ] 'it is soft'

In connected speech, the presence of a voiceless stop is a signal of a phonological word-boundary.

3.2.1.4 Vowel epenthesis and phase shift

Since consonant clusters are not permitted in Belep (§2.7), speakers use a variety of strategies to avoid them; however, these strategies differ somewhat depending on whether the consonant cluster occurs at a word-boundary or within a phonological word. That is, the difference between epenthesis and phase shift is used here as evidence for the existence of the phonological word in Belep.

Within a phonological word, speakers obligatorily insert an epenthetic vowel between a root and a suffix or enclitic in order to avoid a consonant cluster. Speakers insert the vowel /i/ before determiner suffixes (§4.4.2) and the vowel /a/ before quantifier suffixes (§4.3) and directional enclitics (§5.12). Examples are shown in (17). Note that in these instances, speakers represent the epenthetic vowels orthographically.

(17) ulac 'old man' + -k 'DET.D.PRX' > _ulayiik_[6]
 + -na 'DET.D.MPX' > _ulayina_
 + -xeda 'DET.UH' > _ulayixeda_
 + -li 'DET.A.PRX' > _ulayili_
 + -ma 'AC' > _ulayama_
 cavac 'to depart' + =du 'DIR.DH' > _cavayadu_
 + =van 'DIR.TV' > _cavayavan_

To avoid consonant clusters at phonological word boundaries, speakers use phase shift (§2.5.2), a morphophonemic process which operates at the level of the phonological word. In phase shift, words which ordinarily end in a consonant are converted into vowel-final forms, as shown in (18) where each verb is followed by the adverb _mwa_ 'again' (see §3.3.3). The final vowel of a word's incomplete phase is always /a/. Speakers do not represent phase shift orthographically.

(18) _tûûn_ 'to rub' > [tũnã̱ m^{w}ã] 'rub again'
 top 'to melt' > [tova̱ m^{w}ã] 'melt again'
 _ar_ 'to row' > [ara̱ m^{w}ã] 'row again'
 geek 'to be dirty' > [ᵑgeʁa̱ m^{w}ã] 'be dirty again'

---

[6] See §4.4.2, footnote 22 for an explanation of why this vowel is geminate.

3.2.1.5 Morphophonemic stem alternations

Many possessed nouns (§4.2.2.3) undergo morphophonemic stem alternations depending on whether their possessor is indicated by a pronominal suffix (i.e. part of the same phonological word), or by a full noun phrase (i.e. a separate phonological word). These alternations are thus evidence for the existence of the phonological word in Belep. Some examples are shown in (19). Note that many of the words cited are class 1 nouns (§4.2.1.1) and cannot occur outside the dependent possessive construction (§4.2.2.1).

(19) *bwa-* 'head'   *bwaa-n* 'his/her head'
      âro- 'husband'   *âroo-ng* 'my husband'
      do 'spear'   *doo-mw* 'your spear'
      mua- 'flower'   *muu-r* 'its flower'
      pia- 'fingernail'   *pii-n* 'his/her fingernail'

In these stem alternations, the forms on the left signal the presence of a phonological word-boundary, while those on the right signal the absence of one.

3.2.1.6 Pause phenomena

Pauses in the stream of speech in Belep do not tend to occur within phonological words, but rather between them, a phenomenon noted cross-linguistically by Dixon and Aikhenvald (2002:24). For example, in my corpus, there are no instances of pauses which occur before possessive (§4.2.2.2), quantifier (§4.3), or determiner suffixes (§4.4), before the directional (§5.12) or locational enclitics (§5.13), or before ditropic clitics (§6.4). Pauses do, however, occur between a class 1 noun (§4.2.1.1) and its nominal possessor, as in (20) where the speaker pauses after the class 1 noun *bwe-* 'top' and performs a repair, choosing not to finish the clause she had previously begun.

(20) « *Ava ca ta la bwe – Nyami la ca giva li âjuma la bwe alap,* »

ava=	ca=	ta=la	bwe	nya-mi
1PL.EXCL.SUBJ=	ITER=	go.UH=LOC	top	DEM.IDF-DET.A.DST

la=	ca=	gi-va=li	âju-ma=la
3PL.SUBJ=	ITER=	attack-1PL.EXCL.ABS=GEN	person-AC=LOC

bwe	alap
top	beach

'"We often go onto – When the people kill us on the beach,"'

Yal-01082010-MFD_0041

Though class 1 nouns are particularly tightly bound to their possessors in terms of constituency (see §3.7, §4.2), examples such as (20) show that pauses are a phenomenon associated primarily with the phonological word.

3.2.2 Grammatical word

According to Dixon and Aikhenvald (2002), a grammatical word consists of "a number of grammatical elements which (a) always occur together, rather than scattered through the clause (the criterion of cohesiveness); (b) occur in a fixed order; (c) have a conventionalised coherence and meaning" (Dixon & Aikhenvald 2002:19). Since this definition is not language-specific, I will not enumerate the methods by which grammatical words are distinguished in Belep. Instead I will discuss the major types of grammatical word in Belep.

3.2.2.1 Grammatical words that are also phonological words

Most phonological words in Belep—with the exception of some bound noun stems and bound transitive verb stems (see §3.2.2.3)—are also grammatical words in that they can be listed as a citation form or serve as the answer to a question-word question.

The converse is not true; there are many grammatical words in Belep which do not consist of a single phonological word (see §3.2.2.2). The set of grammatical words that are also single phonological words describes the set of words which can constitute a complete utterance all by themselves (Dixon & Aikhenvald 2002: 24).

Nouns marked with a determiner suffix (described in §4.4.2) are phonological and grammatical words. They can constitute a complete utterance, for instance, as the answer to a question-word question (21).

(21) Q: *Ti li âli îna mwima laak ?*
 ti=li   â-li   îna   mwi-ma
 who=GEN DEM.NEW-DET.A.PRX make.GNR DEM.IA-AC

 laa-k
 DEM.PL-DET.D.PRX
 'Who made these things?'

A: ***Tamwana.***
tamwa-na
woman-DET.D.MPX
'That woman.'
          Yal-05102010-PT1.wav – Yal-05102010-PT3.wav

Nouns marked with a possessive suffix (§4.2.2.2) are also phonological and grammatical words. They may serve as the answer to a question-word question (22).

(22)   Q: ***Yo kiyida ?***
     yo=   **kiyi=da**
     2SG.SUBJ= see.SPC=what
     'What did you see?'

     A: ***Nyang.***
     nya-ng
     mother-1SG.POSS
     'My mother.'
          Yal-05102010-PT1.wav – Yal-05102010-PT3.wav

Nouns participating in the independent possessive construction (§4.2.2.4) with a pronominal possessor also constitute single phonological and grammatical words. For example, in (23), an independently possessed noun with a pronominal possessor constitutes an entire intonation unit.

(23)   ***Euh, bu, bu lila,***
     ââ   **bu**   **bu=li-la**
     um   fishhook   fishhook=GEN-3PL.ABS
     'Um, fishhooks, their fishhooks,'
          Yal-28072010-BGMCG-hamecon_0003

Verbs with valence-changing suffix -*u* 'DETR' (§5.2.5.3), specific suffix -*e* 'SPC' (§5.2.4), differential absolutive suffix -*n* (§5.2.6.1), or an absolutive suffix (§5.7) are both grammatical and phonological words; they are often the citation forms given for verbs and can serve as an intonation unit. For example, in (24), a verb with the detransitive suffix -*u* constitutes an entire intonation unit.

(24)　*Ja âmu kiyau ka, tuya avar ki, .. înau.*
　　　ja=　　　　　âmu=　　kiya-u=xa　　　　tuya
　　　1PL.INCL.SUBJ=　PRF=　see.GNR-DETR=LK　EX.GNR

　　　avari=xi　îna-u
　　　other=REL　make-DETR
　　　'We have seen that, there are others who, make [them].'
　　　　　　　　　　　　　　　　Yal-28072010-BGMCG-hamecon_0051

In (25), the bound transitive verb *gi-* occurs with the absolute suffix *-e*; this form is both a phonological and grammatical word and can constitute an entire intonation unit.

(25)　*Lexa gie, .. gie, gie,*
　　　le=xa　　　　　gi-e　　　　　　gi-e　　　　　　gi-e
　　　3DU.SUBJ=ADD　attack-3SG.ABS　attack-3SG.ABS　attack-3SG.ABS
　　　'And they hit her, hit her, hit her,'
　　　　　　　　　　　　　　　　Yal-28072010-BGMCG-tayamu_0256

3.2.2.2 Grammatical words that are not phonological words

Many grammatical words in Belep consist of greater or less than one phonological word.

Nouns and verbs formed by the addition of a derivational proclitic (§3.2.2.6), such as a nominalizer or causativizer, etc. (§3.6) fit all three of Dixon and Aikhenvald's (2002) criteria for grammatical words though they consist of multiple phonological word-like elements. They always occur together, rather than scattered throughout the clause—the derivational proclitic occurs closer to the root than any other proclitic. For example, in (26) there is a grammatical word *wa= pe= âma= naen* 'way of being a family' with three derivational proclitics, *wa=* 'RESULT', *pe=* 'RECP', and *âma=* 'DYAD'. These proclitics form an instance of layered (hierarchical) morphology (Bickel & Nichols 2007: 214) in which their meaning depends on their ordering, i.e. which derivational morpheme is closer to the root.

(26)　*Toma puur ri wa pe âma naen nile,*
　　　toma　pu-r=i　　　　　　　　　wa=　　　pe=　　　âma=
　　　but　　origin-3GNR.POSS=GEN　RESULT=　RECP=　DYAD=

nae-n=i-le
child-3SG.POSS=GEN-3DU.ABS
'But because of their family ties,' (lit. 'their way of familying themselves')
Yal-25072010-PT-homily_0052

Derivational proclitics also occur in a fixed order in Belep—the proclitic always precedes the root. And each derivational proclitic has a conventionalized meaning (27), though there is some idiosyncrasy in the application of these meanings.

(27) *pa=* V 'cause to V'
      â= V 'agent who does V'
      ba= V 'tool for doing V'

Another instance of a grammatical word that consists of multiple phonological word-like elements is the verb group (§5.3). The elements of the verb group always occur in a fixed order (they are an instance of templatic morphology; c.f. Bickel & Nichols 2007) and cannot undergo any syntactic operations except as a unit. Most elements in a verb group are not obligatory, but when they occur they have a conventionalized meaning and occur in an obligatory order. For example, in (28), the verb group *ava=xa=ô bwage-va* 'and we returned' is a grammatical word.[7]

(28) ***Avaxaô bwagevame la pwemwa,***
      ava=xa=ô   **bwage-va=me=la**   **pwemwa**
      1PL.EXCL.SUBJ=ADD=REAL   return-1PL.EXCL.ABS=CTP=LOC   village
      'And we returned back to the village,'
      Yal-17072009-TB-weekend_0023

Case-marked nouns and pronouns in Belep (§6.4) are grammatical words which consist of a non-whole number of phonological words. The case marker of the noun or pronoun encliticizes to the previous element, as in (29) where the grammatical word *=a Cebaba* '=NOM Cebaba' consists of more than one, but less than two, phonological words.[8]

---

[7] It is in fact a grammatical word that consists of one-and-a-half phonological words. The phonological words in this utterance are *ava=xa=ô* 'and we', *bwage-va=me=la* 'returned back to the', and *pwemwa* 'village'. The grammatical words are *ava=xa=ô bwage-va* 'and we returned', verb phrase enclitic *=me* 'CTP', and the locative noun phrase *=la pwemwa* 'to the village'.

[8] Example (29) consists of two full phonological words: the verb with case enclitic *pan=a*, and the noun phrase *Cebaba*. Proclitic *te=* '3SG.SUBJ' has most of the characteristics of a phonological word except that it does not carry stress; see §3.2.2.6. There are two grammatical words: verb group *te= pan*

(29)   **Te pan na Cebaba,**
　　　te=　　　pan=a　　　Cebaba
　　　3SG.SUBJ= go.TV=NOM Cebaba
　　　'Cebaba went,'

Yal-20092011-AW1_0205

Case markers always immediately precede the noun phrase they mark; nothing can come between the noun phrase and its associated case marker.

The combination of a numeral classifier with a numeric determiner (§4.7.3) is a grammatical word, but it varies as to whether it is one or two phonological words since the numeric determiners have both free and bound forms. For instance, the numerical determiner *tu*, =*ru* 'two' may occur in either of the ways shown in (30).

(30)   **goru**
　　　go=ru
　　　CL:sugar.cane=two
　　　'two packets of (10 pieces of) sugar cane'

　　　âôra tu
　　　âôra　　　**tu**
　　　CL:instance　two
　　　'two times'

Because these forms are used fairly infrequently, the numeric determiners have varying levels of phonological integration with the numeral classifiers.[9] However, this variation seems to be merely phonological; all combinations of numeral classifier and numeric determiner have the same status as grammatical words.

Bound intransitive verbs (§5.2.1.1) are another example of grammatical words which are not full phonological words; they require the presence of a directional enclitic or the suffix -*r* 'NDR'.

---

and subject noun phrase =*a Cebaba*. Note that there is little correspondence between the phonological and grammatical words (§3.2.2.4).

9 The cardinal numeral *pwadu* 'two' is most likely the result of the lexicalization of a former numeral classifier *pwa-* (which occurs in many other cardinal numerals; see §4.7.1) and the numeric determiner *tu*, =*ru*. Though *pwa-* is not a classifier in Belep, it still has this function in Balade Nyelâyu, where it is used to count inanimate objects (Ozanne-Rivierre 1998:45).

3.2.2.3 Intermediate units between grammatical words and syntactic constituents

There are two major classes of elements in Belep which should be considered intermediate forms between a grammatical word and a syntactic constituent: noun phrases (§4.5) consisting of a dependently possessed noun stem (§4.2.2.1) and a nominal possessor; and verb phrases (§5.11) consisting of a bound transitive verb stem (§5.2.3.2) and a nominal absolutive (§6.4.1) argument.

I have already argued that (a) dependently-possessed noun stems (when followed by a nominal possessor) are phonological words; (b) dependently-possessed noun stems with a pronominal suffix are phonological and grammatical words. However, the word-status remains to be determined for complex noun phrases consisting of a dependently-possessed noun and its nominal possessor, both of them independent phonological words (§4.2.2.1). For example, in (31), *ka âju* 'person's foot' has the characteristics of a grammatical word but also resembles a syntactic constituent.

(31)   *ka-n* [foot-3SG.POSS] 'his/her foot'
       ka âju [foot person] 'person's foot'

In (31), *kan* is a phonological word, as are *ka-* and *âju*. Both *kan* and *âju* are grammatical words as well, while *ka-* is not a grammatical word. It remains to be determined whether *ka âju* is a grammatical word or a syntactic constituent.

For one thing, noun phrases such as *ka âju* in this construction should not be considered compounds (I discuss compounding in §3.7). They do not have idiosyncratic meanings and each part can always be used in other possessive constructions (for instance, *ka tavia* 'dog's foot' or *e âju* 'person's hand'). However, the possessed noun cannot ever occur without the possessor; given the form *ka-*, a possessor is obligatory, and nothing can intercede between them. Pause phenomena occur between the possessed noun and its nominal possessor; however, Dixon and Aikhenvald (2002:24) argue that these phenomena occur on the phonological rather than the grammatical word level. There is no way to question a possessed noun (32), though there is a way to question its possessor (33).

(32)   ***Da pawi ?**
       da   pawi
       what hibiscus
       '*The hibiscus's what?'

(33)   **Weeri ?**
       we=ri
       food=who
       'Whose food?'

Yal-05102010-PT1.wav – Yal-05102010-PT3.wav

It seems that dependently-possessed nouns with a noun phrase possessor should best be considered a sort of intermediate form between a grammatical word and a syntactic constituent; that is, they are larger than one grammatical word.

I have already argued that (a) bound transitive verb stems are phonological words; and (b) bound transitive verb stems with valence-changing suffix -*u* 'DETR' (§5.2.5.3), differential absolutive suffix -*n* (§5.2.6.1), or an absolutive suffix (§5.7) are phonological and grammatical words. However, the word-status remains to be determined for bound transitive verb stems followed by a nominal absolutive argument. For example, in (34), *migi buâny* 'hold a stone' has some characteristics both of a grammatical word and a syntactic constituent.

(34) **Te migi buâny,**
te=   migi buâny
3SG.SUBJ= hold stone
'He was holding a stone,'

Yal-20092011-AW1_0254

In (34), *migi-* and *buâny* are both phonological words; the verb's citation form *migi-e* (which has a 3SG.ABS suffix) is also a phonological word. Both *buâny* and *migie* are grammatical words as well, while *migi-* is not a full grammatical word; it cannot be given as a citation form or serve as the answer to a question-word question, nor can it be uttered in isolation. Though pause phenomena can occur between the bound verb stem and its absolutive argument, the only element which can intercede between them is a differential absolutive suffix (§5.2.6). Although noun incorporation is attested in other Far North languages such as Nêlêmwa (Bril 2002:64-65,151-152), and so-called "COMPOSITION BY JUXTAPOSITION [that is, noun incorporation by juxtaposition of two distinct phonological words]...is prevalent in Oceania" (Mithun 1984:849), clauses such as (34) should not be considered instances of noun incorporation for the following reasons: (i) This is the only strategy Belep offers to refer to a verb's effect on a semantic patient, while "all languages which exhibit [noun incorporation] also have syntactic paraphrases" (Mithun 1984:847-848). Calling clauses such as (34) instances of noun incorporation would essentially be arguing that Belep has no transitive verbs. (ii) Semantically, Belep examples such as (34) are used to refer to both general and specific patients; in fact, this particular example is followed in the narrative by another character asking « *yo pae buâny ma da ?* » '"what are you doing with that stone?"', an unexpected question if (34) were an instance of noun incorporation. (iii) Belep examples such as (34) do not have idiosyncratic meanings and their parts are always composable into other verb phrases; both the verb and the absolutive noun phrase can be questioned.[10] The status of *migi buâny* seems to be as an intermediate element between grammatical word and syntactic constituent; that is, it is a unit larger than a grammatical word.

3.2.2.4 Grammatical vs. phonological words

As we have seen, there is little correspondence in Belep between phonological and grammatical words. Example (35) shows the overlap between these two sets.

(35)   *Laxaô kejadu la naerama,*

GR. WORDS   [--------VERB GROUP-----------][VP][-----SUBJECT NP--------]
           la=xa=ô   keja=du=la   nae-ra-ma
           3PL.SUBJ=ADD=REAL run=DIR.DH=NOM child-3GNR.POSS-AC
PH. WORDS   1   2   3
           'And the children ran down,'
                                                  Yal-17072009-TB-weekend_0024

In (35), there are three phonological words: *la=xa=ô* 'and they', *keja=du=la* 'ran down the', and *naerama* 'children'. The elements which may occur elsewhere as full phonological words are *keja* 'run' and *nae-r* 'child'. The grammatical words are the verb group *la=xa=ô keja* 'they ran', the verb phrase enclitic *=du* 'DIR.DH', and the subject noun phrase *=la nae-ra-ma* 'children'.

Most utterances in Belep discourse contain a similar disconnect between the phonological and the grammatical word. This is fairly reminiscent of the situation in Fijian, another Oceanic, non-Polynesian language. Dixon (1988) defines the phonological word in Fijian strictly in terms of stress and diphthong formation, while formatives can "[belong] to the same phonological word as the root; [comprise] the whole of another phonological word; [or be] part of another phonological word" (Dixon 1988: 26).

For this reason it will be necessary to define words and formatives in Belep according to their specific word-properties. This work will use the convention of marking orthographic spaces between phonological words only. Suffixes (§3.2.2.5) will be indicated with '-'. Enclitics (§3.2.2.6) will be written with no space between them and the phonological word they attach to, and will be preceded by '='. Proclitics (§3.2.2.6) will be followed by '=' and an orthographic space, indicating that they have some degree of phonological independence from the phonological word they attach to.

---

[10] The absolutive argument may be questioned by substituting interrogative pronoun *=da* 'what' (§4.6.3). The verb may be questioned with the question verb (§6.6.2) *câmwi* 'do what with', which is also a bound stem.

3.2.2.5 Affixes

Affixes in Belep will be defined as formatives which are neither phonological nor grammatical words. This definition excludes bound lexemes such as *muu-* 'flower', *nya-* 'DEM.IDF', and *tax-* 'distribute', which are neither full phonological nor full grammatical words but have a full lexical meaning. It encompasses only formatives, which "cannot govern or be governed by other words, cannot require or undergo agreement, and cannot head phrases" (Bickel & Nichols 2007: 173).

According to this definition, Belep is an exclusively suffixing language. The suffixes are: possessive suffixes (§4.2.2.2) for dependently-possessed nouns (36); determiner suffixes (§4.4.2) on nouns and demonstrative pronouns (37); quantifier suffixes (§4.3) on nouns (38); various suffixes (§5.2.4, §5.2.5, §5.2.6) on verbs (39); and absolutive pronominal suffixes (§5.7) on verbs (40).

(36) ka-*ng* [foot-1SG.POSS] 'my foot, my leg'
      ka-*la* [foot-3PL.POSS] 'their feet, their legs'

(37) *tamwa* 'woman' *tamwaa-k* [woman-DET.D.PRX] 'this woman'
      nya- 'DEM.IDF' *nya-na* [DEM.IDF-DET.D.MPX] 'that one'

(38) *ulac* 'old man' *ulaya-ma* [old-AC] 'elders'
      nae-r 'child' *nae-ra-ma* [small-3GNR.POSS-AC] 'children'

(39) *îna* 'to make' *îna-e* [make-SPC] *îna-u* [make-DETR]
      ti- 'to write' *ti-n* [write-DA.NSG] *ti-a* [write-DA.IA]
      cu-, cuu- 'to stand' *cuu-r* [stand-NDR]
      kaxi 'to look' *kaxi-li-* [look-TR]

(40) *tâna* 'to hear' *tâna-e-o* [hear-SPC-2SG.ABS] 'hear you'
      migi- 'to hold' *migi-la* [hold-1PL.ABS] 'hold them'

All of these suffixes are categorized as inflectional (see §3.5); however, not all of them are obligatory.

3.2.2.6 Clitics

It will be necessary to use the category of clitics in this work due to the wide disconnect in Belep between the phonological and grammatical word. Linguists have struggled to find a cross-linguistic definition for 'clitic' (e.g. Zwicky 1977, 1985, Haspelmath & Sims 2010); I will define clitics in Belep according to Dixon and Aikhenvald (2002) as "something that is a grammatical word but not a complete phonological word" (Dixon & Aikhenvald 2002:25).

Belep has both simple and special clitics as defined by Zwicky (1977, 1985).[11] Belep simple clitics are primarily linkers (§3.3.4; see also chapter 7) which have both a free form and a bound form. For example, in (41), linker *ka* may appear in either its free form (*ka*) or bound form (=*xa*).

(41) **Leô tu ka âva.**

le=ô	tu	ka	âva
3DU.SUBJ=REAL	go.DH	LK	fish

le=ô	tu=**xa**	âva
3DU.SUBJ=REAL	go.DH=LK	fish

'They went down and fished.'

Yal-01082010-MFD_0006

The majority of Belep clitics, however, are special clitics; their "syntactic distribution differs from that of free forms" (Haspelmath & Sims 2010:200). Both proclitics and enclitics occur, and they behave in quite different ways. Though both proclitics and enclitics are grammatical words in Belep, there is a sharp divide between them in terms of phonological word-like properties.

Enclitics in Belep are very similar to suffixes in terms of their phonological behavior. They trigger in the word to which they are attached many of the phonological word-criteria outlined in §3.2.1, including centralization of /e/, nasal spreading, lenition, and morphophonemic alternations, and in terms of pause phenomena they belong to the phonological word to which they are attached. In other words, phonologically they behave exactly like suffixes. They differ from suffixes only in terms of selectivity: "whether they may attach to anything, or must attach to a particular kind of host" (Aikhenvald 2002:43). That is, enclitics are distinguished from suffixes in that they attach at the constituent level, rather than at the word-class level. The enclitics in Belep are: verb phrase directionals (42) (see §5.12); verb phrase locationals (43) (see §5.13); verbal mood markers (44) (see §5.6); and verb phrase focus markers (45) (see §6.9.2).

---

11 Simple clitics are "Cases where a free morpheme, when unaccented, may be phonologically reduced, the resultant form being phonologically subordinated to a neighboring word" (Zwicky 1977:5); that is, simple clitics have both a bound and a free form which may substitute for one another. Special clitics are "clitics not partaking of the distribution of corresponding full forms" (Zwicky 1985:295); that is, special clitics may not have a free form or may not be able to substitute free/bound forms.

(42)   *Ponaoda la bwe alap.*
      po-nao=da=la   **bwe alap**
      load-1SG.ABS=DIR.UH=LOC top beach
      'Take me up onto the beach.'   =*da* 'DIR.UH'

      Avena panic.
      avena=   **pan=ic**
      1PA.SUBJ= go.TV=CTF
      'We went away.'   =*ic* 'CTF'

(43)   *Le cuur rexeng.*
      le=   **cur=exeng**
      3DU.SUBJ= stand=LOC.DC
      'They stood here.' =*lexeng* or =*exeng* 'LOC.DC'

(44)   *Leô pae wagale,*
      le=ô   **pa-e**   **waga-le**
      3DU.SUBJ=REAL take-SPC boat-3DU.POSS
      'They took their boat,' =*ô* 'REAL'

(45)   *Temere uya,*
      te=me=re   **uya**
      3SG.SUBJ=IRR=ACT arrive
      'It will actually happen,' =*re* 'ACT'

The Belep ditropic clitics (discussed in detail in §6.4) are a special type of enclitic. While phonologically they are bound to the element they follow (e.g. triggering nasal spreading, lenition, morphophonemic alternations, etc.), grammatically they mark the case of the noun phrase they precede. For example, in (46), the ditropic clitic =*la* is phonologically bound to the preceding element *ta=me*, while grammatically it marks the case of *mwaak*. Likewise, in (47), the ditropic clitic =*i* is phonologically bound to the preceding element *pa-er*, though grammatically it marks the case of *Teâ Belep*.

(46)   *Te tame la mwaak,*
      te=   **ta=me=la**   **mwaak**
      3SG.SUBJ= go.UH=CTP=NOM rabbitfish
      'The rabbitfish came up,' =*la* or =*a* 'NOM'

(47) *Te paer ri Teâ Belep.*
 te=   pa-er=i   Teâ Belep
 3SG.SUBJ= take-3SG.ABS=GEN Teâ Belep
 'Teâ Belep took her.'   =*li* or =*i* 'GEN'

In most cases, enclitics in Belep occur further from the stem than suffixes. The two exceptions are when a genitive or dative argument (marked with a case marker =*(l)i* 'GEN' or =*(l)e* 'DAT', respectively; see §6.4) is indexed by a pronominal suffix—an absolutive (§5.7) or possessive (§4.2.2.2) suffix, respectively. Examples are shown in (48) and (49).

(48) *karavaa lie*
 karava=li-e
 pirogue=GEN-3SG.ABS
 'his pirogue'

(49) *Avexa boyu leen.*
 ave=xa   boyu=lee-n
 1PL.EXCL.SUBJ=ADD greet=DAT-3SG.POSS
 'And we greeted him.'

Note that these enclitics cannot occur without a following noun phrase or pronominal element, e.g. *karavaa li teâmaa* 'the chieftain's pirogue' or *boyu le teâmaa* 'greet the chieftain'.

In contrast to Belep enclitics, proclitics show little to no phonological link to the word-form they attach to. They do not trigger lenition (except in a few highly lexicalized cases), /e/ centralization, or phonetic nasalization; they trigger word-boundary vowel epenthesis, and pauses and repairs frequently occur between them and their hosts. In these respects, proclitics behave in most ways like independent phonological words. Belep proclitics include: derivational morphemes (50) (see §3.6); aspectual markers (51) (see §5.5); subject agreement[12] markers (52) (see §5.8); and clausal

---

[12] Note that the 3SG subject agreement marker *te=* may occasionally encliticize to a preceding linker, e.g.
Jie ma te maac.
ji-e   ma=re   maac
give-3SG.ABS   LK4=3SG.SUBJ   die
'Kill him/her.' (lit. 'Give him/her that s/he die.')
This should be considered simple cliticization (Zwicky 1977); *te=* and *=re* appear in the same syntactic position and do not differ in meaning.

negation (53) (see §6.8) and prohibitive markers (54) (see §6.7.2).

(50)   *pa= jajani* [CAUS= be.crazy] 'to make sb. crazy'
       tu= nep [VBLZ= dream] 'to dream'

(51)   **Te tao ta,**
       te=   tao=   ta
       3SG.SUBJ=   HAB=   go.UH
       'He kept going up,'

       La nyi cao,
       la=   nyi=   cao
       3PL.SUBJ=   PUNCT=   work
       'They worked repeatedly,'

(52)   **Te wânem.**
       te=   wânem
       3SG.SUBJ=   walk
       'S/he walks.'

       Na pilu.
       na=   pilu
       1SG.SUBJ=   dance
       'I dance.'

(53)   **Âri na pae,**
       âri=   na=   pa-e
       NEG=   1SG.SUBJ=   take-SPC
       'I'm not taking it,'

(54)   **O wara maduvadu,**
       o=   wara=   maduva=du
       2DU.SUBJ=   NEG.IMPER=   spit=DIR.DH
       'Don't spit,'

The characteristics that distinguish proclitics from independent phonological words are that they do not carry word stress, they require a host for realization, and they always occur in the same position with respect to their host; they are not syntactically free. Furthermore, their meanings are grammatical rather than lexical.

The presence of both proclitics and enclitics in Belep leads to one set of phonological words consisting entirely of clitics. When a subject agreement proclitic is followed by a modal or focus enclitic, they combine into a full phonological word, identified in this work as the *preface* (55). See §5.3 for more information.

(55)   ***Lexaô tume,***
   le=xa=ô   tu=me
   3DU.SUBJ=ADD=REAL go.DH=CTP
   'And they came down,'

This formulation is reminiscent of proclitics in South Efate, a language of Vanuatu, which distinguish realis and irrealis forms (Thieberger 2006:109).

3.3 Word classes

The major classes of phonological words[13] in Belep are nouns and verbs. These are the only open word classes. Many scholars of New Caledonian languages (Bril 2002, Moyse-Faurie 1995, Ozanne-Rivierre et al. 1998, De La Fontinelle 1976) have remarked upon the 'verbo-nominal opposition', or lack thereof, in these languages. That is, a common feature of these languages is that many words may behave as either nouns or verbs without undergoing a derivational process. This work will adopt the position that this feature of New Caledonian languages does not pose a problem for part-of-speech identification; word class will be viewed not as an intrinsic feature of a word, but a result of the manner in which it is used in a given instance. Thus, a word like *cao* 'work' is a verb when it is used as a verb e.g. *na= cao* 'I work', and is a noun when it is used as a noun e.g. *te= pwalu=la cao* 'The work is difficult'. Though many such words seem to pattern equally well as nouns and verbs, most words in Belep clearly behave more frequently as one or the other. In this case it would be best to say that open parts-of-speech classes must be distinguished from one another on the basis of a *cluster* of properties, none of which by itself can be claimed to be a necessary and sufficient condition for assignment to a particular class (Schachter & Shopen 2007:4).

That is, nouns and verbs form a continuum, and while most words seem to gravitate toward one end or the other, many situate themselves somewhere in between.

There are three other closed parts-of-speech classes in Belep. These are adverbs, linkers (or conjunctions), and discourse markers. The properties of each word-class will be discussed in the following sections.

---

[13] See §3.2.2 for the classification of elements which are not phonological words.

3.3.1 Nouns

This section describes the cluster of features which prototypically characterize Belep nouns. See chapter 4 for a more complete description of nominal morphology.

Nouns can be possessed in a possessive construction (§4.2.2), as are for example *tolam* 'basket' and *âpw* 'laugh' in (56).

(56) *tolam* 'basket' *tolaba-ng* [basket-1SG.POSS] 'my basket'
      âpw 'laugh' *âw=i-nao* [laugh=GEN-1SG.ABS] 'my laugh'

Nouns can be marked for case (§6.4) and serve as an argument in a clause, as are *tamwa* 'woman' and *âpw* 'laugh' in (57).

(57) *te= pan=a tamwa* [3SG.SUBJ= go.TV=NOM woman] 'the woman goes'
      te= ô=la âpw [3SG.SUBJ= be.good=NOM laugh] 'laughter is good'

Nouns can be marked with a determiner suffix (§4.4.2) or a quantifier suffix (§4.3), as in (58).

(58) *âc* 'man' *âyi-li* [man-DET.A.PRX] 'this man'
      ulac 'old man' *ulaya-ma* [old.man-AC] 'elders'

Nouns can be replaced with a pronoun (§4.6), as in (59) where the pronoun *yer* '3SG.INDEP' is substituted for the noun *nae-* 'child'.

(59) *te= ta=la nae-r* [3SG.SUBJ= go.UH=NOM child-3GNR.POSS] 'a child goes'
      te= ta=la yer [3SG.SUBJ= go.UH=NOM 3SG.INDEP] 's/he goes'

Nouns can be modified with a numeral (§4.7), another noun, or a demonstrative determiner (§4.4.3), as are *tamwa* 'woman', *we* 'water', and *âju* 'person' in (60).

(60) *tamwa pwadu* [woman two] 'two women'
      we naam [water plain] 'fresh water'
      âju-ma la-mi [person-AC DEM.PL-DET.A.DST] 'those people'

Nouns can be the head of a relative clause (§7.3), as are *âju* 'person' and *pulu* 'speech' in (61).

(61) *âju ki molep* [person REL live] 'people who are alive'
      pulu ki âri-er [speech REL say-3SG.ABS] 'words he said'

Nouns can be conjoined with other nouns (§4.5) using *le* 'LK2', *ka* 'LK', and *ma* 'LK4', as are *Aliic* 'Alice', *nae-* 'child', *uvi* 'yam', *bolao* 'banana', and *cama-* 'father' in (62).

(62) *Aliya le nae-n* [Aliic LK2 child-3SG.POSS] 'Alice and her child'
uvi ka bolao [yam LK banana] 'yam and banana'
le ma cama-ng [1DU.INDEP LK4 father-1SG.POSS] 'They with my father'

Nouns can be topicalized (§6.9.1), as is *caivak* 'rat' in (63).

(63) *caivak te= âva* [rat 3SG.SUBJ= fish] 'the rat, he goes fishing'

Nouns can undergo verbalization (§3.6.4) using *tu=* 'VBLZ' as in (64).

(64) *tu= âmwa-r* [VBLZ= gesture-3GNR.POSS] 'make a gesture'
tu= mweeng [VBLZ= decoration] 'decorate'

Among the subclasses of nouns are pronouns (§4.6) and numerals (§4.7). Pronouns can be marked for case (65) or with a determiner suffix (66), be conjoined with other noun phrases (67), and be topicalized (68).

(65) ***Ka ô ta la la,***
ka=ô   ta=la   la
LK=REAL   go.UH=NOM   3PL.INDEP
'And they went up,'
                                                                          Yal-17092009-TB-weekend_0025

(66) ***« Naok ! »***
nao-k
1SG.INDEP-DET.D.PRX
'"Here I am!"'
                                                                          Yal-20092011-AW1_0303

(67) ***la ma teâmaa***
la   ma   teâmaa
3PL.INDEP LK4 high.chief
'they with the chieftain'
                                                                          Yal-20092011-AW3_0054

(68) ***« Mo ji, ji mewu, »***
mo   ji   ji=   mewu
LK3   1DU.INCL.INDEP 1DU.INCL.SUBJ= category
'"For we, we are the same,"'
                                                                          Yal-20092011-AW4_0033

Numerals can be marked for case (69) or with a quantifier suffix (70) and serve as the head of a relative clause (71).

(69) **Le ta la pwadu.**
  le= ta=la pwadu
  3DU.SUBJ= go.UH=NOM two
  'The two went up.'
  Yal-03102011-NT.wav

(70) **Yo pae pwaduma leek.**
  yo= pa-e pwadu-ma lee-k
  2SG.SUBJ= take-SPC two-AC DEM.DU-DET.D.PRX
  'You take these two.'
  Yal-03102011-NT.wav

(71) **Pwadu ki yo kiyile yemi.**
  pwadu ki yo= kiyi-le yemi
  two REL 2SG.SUBJ= see.SPC-3DU.ABS then
  'The two you saw earlier.'
  Yal-03102011-NT.wav

There is no word class of adjectives in Belep. Property concepts are divided between those expressed as verbs and those expressed as nouns (see also §6.5.3).

3.3.2 Verbs

This section will describe the cluster of features which prototypically characterize Belep verbs. See chapter 5 for a more complete description of verbal morphology.

Some verbs can undergo morphophonological alternations in terms of valency (72) (see §5.2.5), specificity (73) (see §5.2.4), and differential absolutive marking (74) (see §5.2.6).

(72) *wêêng* 'to learn' *wêge-* 'learn.TR'
  kaxi 'to look' *kaxi-li-* 'look-TR'
  ji- 'to give' *ji-u* 'give-DETR'
  pwaxa 'to wash' *pwaxa-u* 'wash-DETR'

(73) *tâna* 'to hear.GNR' *tâna-e* 'hear-SPC'
  pa 'to take.GNR' *pa-e* 'take-SPC'
  kiya 'to see.GNR' *kiyi* 'see.SPC'

(74) *pi-* 'to cook' *pi-n* 'cook-DA.NSG'
      îna 'to make' *îna-e-n* 'make-SPC-DA.NSG'
      yagi- 'search.TR' *yagi-a* 'search.TR-DA.IA'

Verbs can undergo nominalization and other derivational processes (75) (see §3.6).

(75) *â= pilu* [AGT= dance] 'dancer'
      ba= pilu [INSTR= dance] 'thing for dancing'
      wa= pilu [RESULT= dance] 'way of dancing'
      pa= pilu [CAUS= dance] 'cause to dance'
      pe= pilu [RECP= dance] 'dance together'

Verbs can serve as the predicate of a clause. Most basically, this is marked by a subject agreement proclitic (76). See §5.8; for exceptions, see §5.2.2.

(76) *te= pilu* [3SG.SUBJ= dance] 's/he dances'
      la= pilu [3PL.SUBJ= dance] 'they dance'
      na= pilu [1SG.SUBJ= dance] 'I dance'

A verb serving as the predicate of a clause may also be indicated by the presence of one or more nominal case-marked arguments (§6.4). In (77), both *pilu* 'to dance' and *ulayar* 'to be big' are used predicatively.

(77) *te= pilu=la âc* [3SG.SUBJ= dance=NOM man] 'the man dances'
      te= ulayar=a uvi [3SG.SUBJ= be.big=NOM yam] 'the yam is big'

Verbs can be inflected for aspect and mood (78) with a variety of morphemes.

(78) *te=ô ta=me* [3SG.SUBJ=REAL go.UH=CTP] 'he came up'
      te= tao= ta [3SG.SUBJ= HAB= go.UH] 'he kept going up'

Verbs of motion or state can be modified by a verb phrase enclitic of direction or location as in (79).

(79) **Texa jin nyoonadu,**
      te=xa   **ji-na**   **nyo-na=du**
      3SG.SUBJ=ADD   give-DA.NSG   tentacle-3SG.POSS=DIR.DH
      'And he [the octopus] put his tentacles down [into the hole],
      Yal-01082010-MFD_0064

Te ci lexeng,

te=	ci=lexeng
3SG.SUBJ=	sit=LOC.DC

'It sat here,'

Yal-28072010-BGMCG-tahitian_0234

Transitive verbs can take an anaphoric object suffix (80) (see §5.7).

(80)   *yo= taxe-va* [2SG.SUBJ= distribute-1PL.EXCL.ABS] 'you give to us'
         te= pari-nao [3SG.SUBJ= tell.TR-1SG.ABS] 'he told me'

3.3.3 Adverbs

There is a closed set of adverbs in Belep. Some of these are represented in Table 1. The collection and description of the full set of Belep adverbs would be a productive course of future study.

Tab. 1: Adverbs in Belep

Belep	English gloss
âda	'alone'
âyu	'whatever'
jua	'really'
mwa	'again'
pwai	'only'

Adverbs in Belep are distinguished by their ability to appear in a wide variety of positions in the clause. They can appear modifying a noun phrase as in (81) or modifying a verb phrase as in (82).

(81)   *Texa, ka yer âda,*

te=xa	ka	yer	âda
3SG.SUBJ=ADD	LK	3SG.INDEP	alone

'And he- he alone,'

Yal-28072010-BGMCG-tahitian_0280

In (81), adverb *âda* modifies the 3SG.INDEP pronoun *yer*. In (82), *âda* modifies the verb phrase *name cavac* 'I am going to leave'.

(82)   « *Mo nao, name cavac âda.* »
       mo   nao   na=me   cavaya   âda
       LK3   1SG.INDEP   1SG.SUBJ=IRR   leave   alone
       '"While I, I will leave by myself."'
                                                   Yal-20092011-AW1_0106

This definition of adverbs in Belep is somewhat contradictory to Schachter and Shopen's (2007) cross-linguistic definition of adverbs as "modifiers of constituents other than nouns" (Schachter & Shopen 2007:20); however, the term 'adverb' nonetheless seems to be the best fit for the category of unrestricted modifiers in Belep.

Adverbs *âda* 'alone', *âyu* 'whatever', and *mwa* 'again' tend to follow the element they modify. For example, in (83), *âyu* follows the verb phrase it modifies (*jaar* 'want'), and in (84) *âyu* follows the noun phrase it modifies (*buâny* 'stone').

(83)   *Te tume ka jaar âyu,*
       te=   tu=me   ka   jara   âyu
       3SG.SUBJ=   go.DH=CTP   LK   want   whatever
       'He came down and was happy with anything,'
                                              Yal-28072010-BGMCG-tahitian_0329

(84)   *buâny âyu*
       buânya   âyu
       stone   whatever
       'stones wherever'
                                              Yal-28072010-BGMCG-sousmarin_0111

In (85), *mwa* 'again' follows the verb phrase it modifies (*tu* 'go.DH') and in (86) *mwa* follows the noun phrase it modifies (*pwalaic* 'one').

(85)   *Leô tu mwa,*
       le=ô   tu   mwa
       3DU.SUBJ=REAL   go.DH   again
       'They went down again,'
                                              Yal-28072010-BGMCG-tayamu_0115

(86)   *pwalaic mwa*
       pwalaiya   mwa
       one   again
       'one more'
                                              Yal-28072010-BGMCG-tayamu_0179

Adverbs *jua* 'really' and *pwai* 'only', on the other hand, tend to precede the element they modify. In (87), *jua* 'really' precedes the verb phrase *âri te ulac* 'he wasn't old'; in (88) *jua* precedes the noun *bae* 'sardine'.

(87) **Te bwa âno, jua âri te ulac.**
te=   bwa=   âno   jua   âri=   te=   ulac
3SG.SUBJ= CONT= be.young really NEG=   3SG.SUBJ= be.old
'He was still young, he wasn't old at all.'
Yal-20092011-AW3_0006

(88) **jua bae**
jua   bae
really sardine
'true sardine' (e.g. as opposed to other types of sardine)

In (89), pwai 'only' appears in the position of an aspectual proclitic (§5.5),[14] while in (90) pwai modifies the following noun phrase dau ulayar 'the big island'.

(89) **Te pwai ô la enamale.**
te=   pwai ô=la   e-na-male
3SG.SUBJ only be.good=NOM hand-3SG.POSS-ADU
'Only his hands were good.'
Yal-28072010-BGMCG-lune_0016

(90) **Pwai dau ulayar, yali,**
pwai dau   ulayar   ya-li
only islet be.big   DEM.LOC-DET.A.PRX
'Only the big island, that place,'
Yal-20092011-AW6_0117

It is hypothesized that the adverbs which follow the element they modify are etymologically descended from nouns, while those which precede the element they modify come from verbs. These latter adverbs have much in common with the aspectual proclitics, differing only in that they carry word-stress (i.e. they are full phonological words) and can modify nouns in addition to verb phrases.

---

14 Note that this position is also available to *jua* 'really', e.g. *Te= jua yâno=la dan* [3SG.SUBJ= really be.blue=NOM sky] 'The sky is really blue' (Yal-19092011-PA_0059).

Many formatives and words in other classes also serve adverbial functions in Belep; for example, temporal nouns (§6.11), verbs for property concepts (§6.5.3) such as *pôben* 'to be quick' and *cayap* 'to be slow', and aspectual proclitics (§5.5) often serve the function of adverbs, as do the noun suffix *-roven* 'all' (§4.3.4) and the verb suffix *-roven* 'COMPL' (§5.5.11). These forms are not considered to be members of the adverb word class.

3.3.4 Linkers

There is a closed word class of linkers, also called conjunctions (Schachter & Shopen 2007), in Belep. They are shown in Table 2. Note that other words and formatives are used in clause combining as well (see chapter 7), but they do not fall into the word class of linkers.

Tab. 2: Linkers in Belep

Linker	Gloss
ai	'or'
enyi (enyixi)	'if'
ka, =xa	'LK'
ka me	'then'
kara	'well'
ki, =xi	'REL'
le	'LK2'
ma	'LK4'
mo	'LK3'
to, =ro	'when'
toma, =roma	'but'

Linkers *ai* 'or', *ka* 'LK', *le* 'LK2', and *ma* 'LK4' are used to conjoin noun phrases (§4.5). All linkers in Table 2 except for *le* 'LK2' are also used to conjoin clauses (see chapter 7). Belep linkers may be characterized as "prepositive on the second coordinand" (Haspelmath 2007:6); in other words, they precede the element they mark as coordinated, whether that is a clause (91) or a noun phrase (92).

(91) **Ka ô ta la la,**
      ka=ô   ta=la   la
      LK=REAL go.UH=NOM 3PL.INDEP
      'And they went up,'
                                    Yal-17072009-TB-weekend_0025

(92) **Âlalic mo buâny.**
      âlalic   mo buâny
      impossible LK3 stone
      'It was impossible because of the stones.'
                                    Yal-28072010-BGMCG-sousmarin_0111

Many linkers have both a full phonological word form and an enclitic form, making them simple clitics (as defined in Zwicky 1977). At the beginning of an intonation unit the full form tends to be used (93), while the enclitic form often occurs in the middle or at the end of an intonation unit (94).

(93) **Toma yena,**
      toma   yena
      but   today
      'But now[15],'
                                    Yal-28072010-BGMCG-hamecon_0051

(94) **Te pilu toma le gie.**
      te=   pilu=roma le=   gi-e
      3SG.SUBJ= dance=but 3DU.SUBJ= attack-3SG.ABS
      'She was dancing but they attacked her.'
                                    Yal-28072010-BGMCG-tayamu_0253

3.3.5 Interjections and discourse markers

All languages have some sort of discourse particles, also called interjections (Schachter & Shopen 2007:57). These form a closed class. Some of them are represented in Table 3. Several others are mentioned by Dubois (1975c:30).

---

15 The Belep word *yena* 'today, now' temporally references the period from the moment of speaking until the end of the day.

Tab. 3: Interjections and discourse markers in Belep

Belep	English gloss
â	temporizer; 'um'
ai	'no'
ai elo	marker of remembering; 'oh yeah'
bong	response to a criticism; 'yeah right'
ca	exclamation of frustration; 'huh, well!'
e	exclamation to call attention; 'hey!'
êê	'yes'
elo	'okay'
eu	exclamation of exhaustion, regret; 'whew'
ewe	exclamation of pain; 'ow'
jaxa	marker of epistemicity; 'it's like, you could say that'
manya	marker of uncertainty; 'wait a sec'
o	exclamation of surprise; 'hey, what's this?'
o, u	response to a call; 'yes?, what?, here!'
yakor	exclamation of approval; 'good for you!'
yawe	exclamation of fatigue; 'I'm tired'

Members of this word class are characterized by their ability to serve as a single intonation unit, to occur with a large amount of phonetic variation, and not to be able to serve as any other part of speech. They typically express some emotion, stance, or conversational function on the part of the speaker, and often serve to relate parts of the discourse to one another. Some examples are shown in (95) - (97).

In (95), discourse marker *ca* expresses the speaker's disgust or frustration.

(95) *Ca ! Wânevan ma le da pe go la bweelevan,*
     ca   wâne=van   ma   le=   da=   pe=
     ugh   walk=DIR.TV   LK4   3DU.SUBJ=   GNO=   RECP=

   go=la   bwe-le=van
   cry=LOC   top-3DU.POSS=DIR.TV
   'Ugh! [They] just kept walking and crying on each other,'
                                          Yal-19092011-PA_0017

In (96), discourse marker *ai elo* expresses the doubt caused by a lack of knowledge or memory experienced by the animated characters.

(96) *Laxa âri u le teâmaa, « Ai elo ? »*

la=xa	âri	u=le	teâmaa	ai elo
3PL.SUBJ=ADD	say	toward=DAT	high.chief	oh.yeah

'And they said to the chieftain, "Oh yeah?"'

Yal-20092011-AW6_0079

In (97), discourse marker *eu* expresses the animated character's regret and helplessness.

(97) *Texa waak xa tayamoli,*

te=xa	wa-x=a	tayamo-li
3SG.SUBJ=ADD	DEM.MAN-DET.D.PRX=NOM	old.woman-DET.A.PRX

« Eu ! Te bwi la tânema naeng ngi dooyek, »

eu	te=	bwi=la	tânema	nae-ng=i	do-yek
whew	3SG.SUBJ=	be.blind=NOM	eye	child-1SG.POSS=GEN	earth-DET.D.MDS

'And that old woman said, "Woe is me! My child's eyes were blinded by that dirt."'

Yal-28072010-BGMCG-sousmarin_0029-0032

The discourse markers *ai* 'no', *êê* 'yes', and *elo* 'okay', which are used in answering questions, are discussed further in §6.6.3.

3.4 Inflection and derivation

Scholars of New Caledonian languages (Bril 2002, Moyse-Faurie 1995, Ozanne-Rivierre et al. 1998, De La Fontinelle 1976) have traditionally included in their grammars a section on derivational morphology but none on inflectional morphology. Individual morphemes may be identified as inflections or indexes, but in general this is not viewed as a relevant category in New Caledonian languages.

In Belep, the disconnect between the phonological and the morphological word (§3.2) poses some problems for the classification of formatives into inflectional and derivational categories—for example, if proclitics such as the subject agreement markers (§5.8) were analyzed as 'words' (as they commonly are in New Caledonian languages), they could not be said to belong to the domain of morphology and could not thus be categorized as inflectional or derivational. However, this grammar analyzes all formatives in Belep as either suffixes or clitics bound to a host, which provides a possibility of categorizing them in terms of their inflectional or derivational properties.

The notion of unambiguous categorization into two categories, inflectional and derivational, is problematic (Bybee 1985). These two notions will instead be characterized as two ends of a continuum, where a cluster of features tends to define each end but which allows intermediate elements (Haspelmath & Sims 2010, Aikhenvald 2002, Bickel & Nichols 2007). This is particularly helpful since, as we will see, many of the traditional categories of inflection are absent from Belep. Table 4 divides the formatives into clearly inflectional morphemes, those which have both inflectional and derivational characteristics, and those which are purely derivational. For the purposes of this analysis, all of the intermediate elements will be considered inflectional due to their lack of resemblance to canonical derivations in Belep.

Tab. 4: Inflectional and derivational morphology in Belep

Inflectional	Intermediate	Derivational
possessive suffixes (§4.2.2.2)	determiner suffixes (§4.4.2)	ordinal proclitic (§3.6.1.1)
case markers (§6.4)	quantifier suffixes (§4.3)	dyadic proclitic (§3.6.1.2)
specific verb suffix (§5.2.4)	aspect proclitics (§5.5)	nominalizer proclitics (§3.6.2)
patient valence suffixes (§5.2.5)	directional and locational enclitics (§5.12, §5.13)	agent valence proclitics (§5.4)
differential absolutive suffixes (§5.2.6)		verbalizer proclitic (§3.6.4)
anaphoric absolutive suffixes (§5.7)		
mood enclitics (§5.3)		
subject agreement proclitics (§5.8)		

3.5 Inflectional morphology

The features generally characterizing inflectional morphology in the world's languages include: relevance to the syntax, obligatory expression, unlimited applicability, abstract and compositional meaning, and a lack of iterability. Inflectional morphemes induce little base allomorphy, trigger no change of lexeme or word-class, occur at the periphery of words, and have the possibility of cumulative expression (Haspelmath & Sims 2010:90). Inflectional morphology is used to form a complete word and define the characteristics of a word-class; it participates in agreement, does not show paradigm gaps, tends to form smaller systems, and is semantically regular, high frequency, and monosyllabic (Aikhenvald 2002:36). Common categories of inflection include valence, voice, aspect, tense, mood, number, person, and gender (Bybee 1985).

In Belep, there are inflectional categories of valence, aspect, mood, number, and person. Each of these will be examined in the following sections with respect to these common inflectional characteristics.

3.5.1 Nouns

Class 1 nouns (§4.2.1.1) are obligatorily marked with a possessive suffix (§4.2.2.2) if they do not have a nominal possessor (98).

(98)   *ka-ng* [foot-1SG.POSS] 'my foot, my leg'
         yawa-ng [wife-1SG.POSS] 'my wife'
         bwaa-ng [head-1SG.POSS] 'my head'

Nouns in Belep have "declension classes defined by allomorphy of possessive inflection", as do many other languages of the Pacific Rim (Bickel & Nichols 2007:206-207). The inflectional characteristics of these suffixes include obligatoriness, unlimited applicability (to all noun classes which can participate in the dependent possessive construction), lack of iterability, and high frequency. They are monosyllabic, paradigmatic, trigger no change of word-class or lexeme, and are necessary to form a complete word.

Nouns which serve as the argument of a clause are obligatorily marked with a ditropic clitic (§6.4) case marker (99) or are unmarked for the absolutive case.

(99)   ***Te tame la mwaak,***
         te=   ta=me=la   mwaak
         3SG.SUBJ= go.UH=CTP=NOM   rabbitfish
         'The rabbitfish came up,'   =*la* or =*a* 'NOM'

         Te to jier ri Anthony.
         te=   to   ji-er=i   [ãtoni]
         3SG.SUBJ= call give-3SG.ABS=GEN   Anthony
         'Anthony called him.'   =*li* or =*i* 'GEN'

Inflectional characteristics of these case markers include obligatoriness, relevance to the syntax (since case is governed by the verb and the semantic roles of the nouns), unlimited applicability, abstract meaning, lack of iterability, and high frequency.

They trigger no base allomorphy or change of word-class or lexeme, they serve as a defining characteristic of a word-class, and they are monosyllabic.

3.5.2 Verbs

Free transitive verbs (§5.2.3.1) and some intransitive verbs (§5.2.2) are obligatorily marked for the specificity of their absolutive argument (§5.2.4). Some verbs undergo stem-allomorphy to indicate whether their absolutive argument is generic or specific, while others use the regular suffix -*e* 'SPC' (100).

(100)   *kiy-* 'to see' *kiya* [see.GNR] *kiyi* [see.SPC]
         pwaxa 'to wash' *pwaxa* [wash.GNR] *pwaxa-e* [wash-SPC]

The inflectional characteristics of these suffixes include obligatoriness, relevance to the syntax (since the absolutive argument triggers agreement in the verb), unlimited applicability within the class of free transitive verbs, lack of iterability, and high frequency. They do not trigger a change in word-class or lexeme, and they are necessary to form a complete word.

Transitivization of intransitive verbs (§5.2.5.1, §5.2.5.2) and detransitivization of transitives (§5.2.5.3) involves inflectional valence marking. Transitivization is accomplished with stem modification for some intransitive verbs; for the rest, the regular suffix -*li* 'TR' is used (101). Detransitivization with -*u* 'DETR' is available to all transitive verbs (102).

(101)   *câny*   'to seize'   *câje-* [seize.TR]
         mwanao   'to approach'   *mwanao-li-* [approach-TR]

(102)   *pwaxa*   'to wash'   *pwaxa-u* [wash-DETR]
         ti-   'to write'   *ti-u* [write-DETR]

The inflectional characteristics of the valence-changing suffixes include relevance to the syntax (since the presence or absence of an absolutive argument triggers changes in the verb), unlimited applicability—all intransitives may be transitivized using one of the methods, and all transitives may be detransitivized—and high frequency. They do not trigger a change in word-class or lexeme, and they are necessary to form a complete word.

Many transitive verbs may be marked with an inflectional suffix—either -*n* 'DA.NSG' or -*a* 'DA.IA' (103)—which agrees with their absolutive argument in animacy (§5.2.6).

(103)　　pi- 'to cook' *pi-n* [cook-DA.NSG]
　　　　cia- 'NEG.LOC' *cia-n* [NEG.EX-DA.NSG]
　　　　pa 'to take' *pa-e-n* [take-SPC-DA.NSG]
　　　　yaap 'to search' *yavi-a* [search.TR-DA.IA]

The inflectional characteristics of these suffixes include relevance to the syntax (since the absolutive argument triggers agreement in the verb), unlimited applicability within the class of transitive verbs, lack of iterability, and high frequency. They do not trigger a change in word-class or lexeme, and they are necessary to form a complete word.

Pronominal absolutive suffixes on the verb (§5.7), which anaphorically index the absolutive argument, agree with it in person and number (104).

(104)　　*tâna* 'to hear'　　*tâna-e-nao*　　[hear-SPC-1SG.ABS] 'hear me'
　　　　migi- 'to touch'　　*migi-la*　　[touch-3PL.ABS] 'touch them'

The inflectional characteristics of these affixes include relevance to syntax (since they agree with the absolutive argument) and unlimited applicability to the class of transitive verbs. They trigger no change in word-class or lexeme, lack iterability, and are paradigmatic.

Mood (§5.6) is indicated by a preface enclitic within the verb group (§5.3) (105).

(105)　　**Teme uya.**
　　　　te=me　　　　uya
　　　　3SG.SUBJ=IRR　arrive
　　　　'It will happen.'　　=*me* 'IRR'

　　　　Leô pae wagale.
　　　　le=ô　　　　pa-e　　waga-le
　　　　3DU.SUBJ=REAL　take-SPC　boat-3DU.POSS
　　　　'They took their boat.'　　=*ô* 'REAL'

The inflectional characteristics of mood in Belep include its obligatory expression (where zero-marking also has a modal meaning), unlimited applicability, abstract meaning, and high frequency. It triggers no change of word-class or lexeme, is monosyllabic, and serves as a determining characteristic of a word-class.

Subject agreement (§5.8) is indicated on the verb by a proclitic which agrees with the subject in person and number (106).

(106) **Te wânem.**
 te=   wânem
 3SG.SUBJ= walk
 'S/he walks.'

 Na pilu.
 na=   pilu
 1SG.SUBJ= dance
 'I dance.'

The inflectional characteristics of these proclitics include their relevance to syntax (since they agree with the subject), obligatory expression, unlimited applicability (except to absolutive verbs; see §5.2.2), abstract meaning, lack of iterability, and high frequency. They cause no base allomorphy or change in word-class or lexeme, are paradigmatic, and serve as a defining characteristic of a word-class.

3.5.3 Intermediate elements

A number of formatives in Belep are intermediate between inflection and derivation, sharing some properties of both (see §3.5 for characteristics of inflection and §3.6 for characteristics of derivation).

The nominal determiner suffixes (§4.4.2) indicate the proximity and direction of the noun (107).

(107) *tamwa* 'woman' *tamwaa-k* [woman-DET.D-PRX] 'this woman'
 âc 'man' *âyi-na* [man-DET.D.MPX] 'that man'
 gawaar 'day' *gawari-mi* [day-DET.A.DST] 'that day'

Inflectional characteristics of these suffixes include unlimited applicability and lack of word-class or lexeme change. Derivational characteristics include lack of obligatoriness (although speakers think sentences sound odd without them) and irrelevance to the syntax in that they do not trigger agreement.

The noun quantifier suffixes—associative plural *-ma*, associative dual *-male*, general extender *-mene*, and *-roven* 'all'—indicate the quantity of the noun (108).

(108) *ulac*   'old man'   *ulaya-ma*   [old.man-AC] 'elders'
 toop   'field'   *toova-male* [field-ADU] 'two types of fields'
 uruâny 'hurricane' *uruânya-mene* [hurricane-GE] 'bad weather'
 doo   'dirt'   *doo-roven*   [earth-all] 'all the land'

Inflectional characteristics of these nominal suffixes—discussed in further detail in §4.3—include their irregular relevance to syntax (nouns with a number marker sometimes trigger verb agreement and sometimes do not), their expression at the word periphery, and the fact that they trigger no change in word-class. Derivational properties include that they are not obligatory, have limited application (only to certain semantically compatible nouns), have some non-compositional meanings, are infrequent and non-paradigmatic, and may be iterable. Number marking has been categorized as derivational in many Australian and Papuan languages (Aikhenvald 2007:38).

Verbal proclitics (109) are used to indicate aspect (§5.5).

(109)   *Te tao ta,*

        te=   **tao=**   **ta**

        3SG.SUBJ= HAB= go.UH

        'He kept going up,'

        La nyi cao,

        la=   **nyi=**   **cao**

        3PL.SUBJ= PUNCT= work

        'They worked repeatedly,'

These proclitics have the following inflectional characteristics: applicability limited only by semantic compatibility with the verb, no change of word-class or lexeme produced, no base allomorphy, and serving as a defining characteristic of a word-class. The derivational properties of these proclitics are irrelevance to syntax, lack of obligatoriness, occasionally non-compositional meaning, iterability, fairly low frequency, and the fact that they are non-paradigmatic.

The verb phrase directional and locational enclitics (§5.11 and §5.12) indicate the direction or the location of the action or state of the verb (110).

(110)   *Avena panic.*

        avena=   **pan=ic**

        1PA.SUBJ= go.TV=CTF

        'We went away.'   =*ic* 'CTF'

        Le cuur rexeng.

        le=   **cur=exeng**

        3DU.SUBJ= stand=LOC.DC

        'They stood here.' =*lexeng* or =*exeng* 'LOC.DC'

In terms of inflection, these enclitics have unlimited applicability (to verbs of motion and stative verbs), do not change the word-class of their host, are expressed peripherally in the word, and are of fairly high frequency. In some cases, these formatives are obligatory (§5.2.1.1). However, in most cases they are optional, have a concrete meaning, may have a non-compositional meaning, can be iterable, and are not relevant to the syntax in that they do not trigger agreement. In these ways they have derivational properties.

It is unsurprising that it is difficult to draw a clear distinction in Belep between inflection and derivation. "In languages where most grammatical specification is optional it is difficult to draw the line" between them (Aikhenvald 2007:36). For the purposes of this analysis, all of the intermediate elements discussed in this section will be considered inflectional due to their lack of resemblance to canonical derivations in Belep, discussed below.

3.6 Derivational morphology

The features generally characterizing derivational morphology in the world's languages include: irrelevance to syntax, lack of obligatoriness, and limited applicability. Derivational morphology may create a new lexeme, have a concrete or non-compositional meaning, and be possibly iterable. It is expressed close to the base, may trigger base allomorphy or change the word-class, and is not compatible with cumulative expression (Haspelmath & Sims 2010:90). Derivational morphemes may derive a stem which takes inflections, show gaps in their paradigms, form large systems, and do not participate in agreement; they are specific to a word-class, are of low frequency, and are generally longer than monosyllabic (Aikhenvald 2002:36).

All derivational formatives in Belep are proclitics (§3.2.2.6). They differ from class 1 nouns (§4.2.1.1) in that they cannot be possessed and do not carry word stress. They may derive nouns from nouns, nouns from verbs, verbs from verbs, or verbs from nouns. Each of these will be examined in the following sections with respect to the common derivational characteristics.

3.6.1 Denominal nouns

3.6.1.1 Ordinal *ba=*
The ordinal numbers (which fall into the word class of nouns) are derived from cardinal numbers (also nouns) in Belep (§4.7). They are formed by combining the derivational proclitic *ba=* 'ORD' with the cardinal numbers (111). This proclitic is incompatible with the numeral *pwalaic* 'one'.

(111) ba= pwadu [ORD= two] 'second'
       ba= pwajen [ORD= three] 'third'
       ba= toven [ORD= finish] 'last'

The ordinal proclitic is derivational in that it is irrelevant to syntax, not obligatory, creates a new lexeme ("adds some semantic specification to a root without changing its class" (Aikhenvald 2007:36)), and is low frequency.

3.6.1.2 Dyadic *âma=*

The set of dyadic kin terms (Evans 2006) are class 4 nouns derived from class 1 nouns (§4.2.1.1) using the derivational proclitic *âma=* 'DYAD'. This proclitic carries the meaning of 'a group of kin who have reciprocal relationships with one another.' For example, in (112), *âma=* is used to indicate that the relationship of siblinghood is reciprocal between the two participants.

(112) « *Mo ji, ji mewu, ji âma avan.* »

mo	ji	ji=	mewu
LK3	1DU.INCL.INDEP	1DU.INCL.SUBJ=	genus

ji=	âma=	ava-n
1DU.INCL.SUBJ=	DYAD=	sibling-3SG.POSS

"'For we, we are the same, we are brothers.'"

Yal-20092011-AW4_0033

Some speakers disagree on the glosses of dyadic kin terms with *âma=* due to the erosion of the traditional kinship system and accompanying vocabulary loss (see §1.3.1 for a discussion of kinship in Belep). Some examples of nouns formed using *âma=* are shown in (113). Where possible, both an older gloss (from Dubois' (1975c) or Neyret's (1974a) manuscripts) and a modern gloss (from an elderly speaker) are shown.

(113) *âma= ava-n*[16] [DYAD= same.sex.sibling.or.cousin-3SG.POSS]
       'two brothers and sisters' (PT9/2/11beige3)
       'two brothers' (Neyret 1974a:21)

       âma= bega-n [DYAD= cross.cousin-3SG.POSS]
       'two cousins' (PT9/2/11beige3)

---

16 Dubois (1975c:46) also lists *âma= mwana-n* [DYAD= opposite.sex.sibling.or.cousin-3SG.POSS] to mean 'brother and sister, or male and female parallel cousins'; this kin term is not familiar to modern speakers.

'two same-sex cross-cousins' (Neyret 1974a:21)

âma= bee-n [DYAD= sibling.in.law-3SG.POSS]
'a man and his sister's husband, or a woman and her brother's wife' (PT9/2/11beige3)
'two brothers-in-law' (Neyret 1974a:21)

âma= janu [DYAD= spirit]
'people in a clan who share the same totem' (PT9/2/11beige3)
'parent of great-grandparent and/or great-grandparent with great-grandchild' (Dubois 1975c:46)

âma= moo-n [DYAD= parent.in.law-3SG.POSS]
'father and son-in-law, or mother and daughter-in-law' (PT9/2/11beige3)
'maternal uncle and nephew/niece, or paternal aunt and nephew/niece, or parent-in-law and child-in-law' (Dubois 1975c:46)

âma= nae-n [DYAD= child-3SG.POSS]
'family, clan'

âma= nila-n [DYAD= great.grandparent-3SG.POSS]
'great-grandparent and great-grandchild, or two great-grandchildren of the same person' (PT9/2/11beige3)
'great-grandparent and great-grandchild' (Dubois 1975c:46)

âma= pabo-n [DYAD= grandchild-3SG.POSS] or
âma= cêbo-n [DYAD= grandparent-3SG.POSS]
'grandfather and grandson' (PT9/2/11beige3)
'grandparent and grandchild' (Dubois 1975c:46)

âma= yawa-n [DYAD= wife-3SG.POSS]
'married couple'

The *âma=* proclitic is derivational in that it is not relevant to syntax, not obligatory, creates a new lexeme, and adds a semantic specification to a root; *âma naen*, by far the most frequently used of these kin terms, also has a non-compositional meaning.

3.6.2 Deverbal nouns

There are a number of proclitics used to derive nouns from verbs; they generally function at the constituent rather than the word level. They are distinct from dependently possessed class 1 nouns (§4.2.1.1) in that they cannot take possessive suffixes. For example, the class 1 noun *nabwa-* 'imprint'[17] should not be considered a derivational proclitic; despite its participation in constructions such as (114), it can take the generic possessive suffix *-r* (115) (see §4.2.2.2). Note that in (114), *wiu* 'to dine' is zero-derived to act as a nominal possessor of *nabwa-*.

(114)   ***nawba wiu lie***
        nabwa wiu=li-e
        imprint dine=GEN-3SG.ABS
        'his dining areas'
                                                        Yal-20092011-AW1_0009

(115)   ***nabwar***
        nabwa-r
        imprint-3GNR.POSS
        'a scar'
                                            Yal-23082010-IM1.wav – Yal-23082010-IM3.wav

The proclitics to be discussed include agentive *â=*, instrumental *ba=*, and resultative *wa=*. They all change the word-class of their host, create a new lexeme (with a non-compositional meaning), are irrelevant to syntax and not obligatory, occur closer to the base than any inflectional morpheme, and are fairly infrequent and non-paradigmatic.

One interesting characteristic of Belep deverbal nouns is that they often allow inflection to occur closer to the root than derivation, a fairly unusual occurrence cross-linguistically (Haspelmath & Sims 2010:102-105).

3.6.2.1 Agentive *â=*

The agentive proclitic *â=* 'AGT' creates nouns from verbs with the meaning 'person who does V' as in (116), where it derives the noun 'organizer' from the verb *wêêng* 'know how to do something'.

---

[17] A related form in Balade Nyelâyu is classified as a derivational morpheme; Ozanne-Rivierre (1998) lists *ma-V* 'place for V'.

(116)   *â wêêng*
         â=   wêêng
         AGT= organize.GEN
         'organizer (e.g. of the Women's Federation)' (lit. 'someone who knows how')
                                                        Yal-02092010-PT-coutume.wav

The agentive *â=* can also procliticize to an entire verb phrase with a semantic patient included, as in (117) and (118). In both of these examples, the verb is inflected to agree with its absolutive argument in specificity (see §5.2.3.1). This is evidence for a verb phrase as a constituent (see §5.10).

(117)   *â bae maac*
         â=   bae maac
         AGT= bite dead
         'cannibal' (lit. 'someone who eats the dead')
                                                                        PT handout

(118)   *â pae pulu*
         â=   pa-e   pulu
         AGT= take-SPC speech
         'spokesman (of the chief)'[18] (lit. 'someone who carries words')
                                                              Yal-09072009-PT.wav

Other derivational morphemes can intercede between *â=* and the verb. For example, in (119), the derivational causative *pa=* intercedes between *â=* and the transitivized form of *pwec* 'to be born', in this case *pweya-* 'to birth s.b.'. This is an example of layered morphology rather than templatic (Bickel & Nichols 2007:214).

(119)   *â pa pweyau*
         â=   pa=   pweya-u
         AGT= CAUS= be.born.TR-DETR
         'midwife' (lit. 'someone who causes to give birth')
                                                              Yal-09072009-PT.wav

Some instances of *â=* have lexicalized; for example, the tree species name *â= mae* 'Acacia nilotica' literally means 'sleeper' (from *mae* 'to sleep') because it closes its leaves at night.

---

18 In French, *porte-parole du chef*.

3.6.2.2 Instrumental *ba=*

The instrumental proclitic *ba=* 'INSTR' derives nouns from verbs with the meaning 'instrument used to do V', as in (120). The verb group that it procliticizes to may already be inflected, as with the verb *turu-o* [hide-2SG.ABS] 'hide yourself' in (121).

(120) **ba talep**
 ba= talep
 INSTR= sweep
 'broom' (lit. 'tool for sweeping')
 Yal-04072009-BGMCG2.wav

(121) **« Ba turuoda ? »**
 ba= turu-o-da
 INSTR= hide-2SG.ABS-DET.Q2
 '"What [do you use] for a blanket?"' (lit. 'a tool for hiding yourself')
 Yal-05092011-AP1_0078

The proclitic *ba=* can also attach to verb phrase constituents, as in (122) and (123).

(122) **ba îna naraja**
 ba= îna nara-ja
 INSTR= make name-1PL.INCL.POSS
 'alphabet' (lit. 'tool for making our names')
 DY classroom

(123) **ba gi âju**
 ba= gi âju
 INSTR= attack person
 'weapon' (lit. 'tool for attacking people')
 Yal-20092011-AW1_0253

Some instances of *ba=* may have lexicalized. For instance, *bayi* 'chair' may have come from *ba= ci* [INSTR= sit].

3.6.2.3 Resultative *wa=*

The resultative proclitic *wa=* 'RESULT' is used to derive deverbal nouns with the meaning of 'the manner or result of doing V', as in (124) where *wa=* is procliticized to the intransitive verb *molep* 'to be alive' with the resulting meaning 'way or result of being alive; life'.

(124) **wa molep vija**
  wa=   molev=i-ja
  RESULT= be.alive=GEN-1PL.INCL.ABS
  'our lives'
  Yal-25072010-PT-homily_0031

In (124), the noun *wa molep* 'life' which results from the derivation is independently possessed (§4.2.2.4), as is usual for nouns derived with *wa=*. Another example of an independently possessed noun derived with *wa=* occurs in (125), where the intransitive verb is *pe âma naen* 'to be a family'.

(125) **Toma puur ri wa pe âma naen nile,**
  toma   pu-r=i
  but   origin-3GNR.POSS=GEN

  wa=   pe=   âma=   nae-n=i-le
  RESULT= RECP=   DYAD=   child-3SG.POSS=GEN-3DU.ABS
  'But because of their family ties,' (lit. 'their way of familying themselves')
  Yal-25072010-PT-homily_0052

In (125), the deverbal derivational proclitic *pe=* (§3.6.3) intercedes between the denominal *wa=* and the predicate nominal (§6.5.1) *âma= naen* 'family, clan' (see §3.6.1.2 above). This is an example of layered, rather than templatic, morphology (Haspelmath & Sims 2010:214).

Derivational *wa=* may also procliticize to a verb group containing a transitive stem. In many cases, such verbs are inflected before the derivation takes place. For example, in (126), *wa=* procliticizes to the inflected *înaela* 'make them', which contains inflectional specific and absolutive suffixes.

(126) **Êê, tere wa înaela ule.**
  êê   te=re   wa=   îna-e-la   ule
  yes 3SG.SUBJ=ACT RESULT= make-SPC-3PL.ABS   long.ago
  'Yes, that was actually the technique for making them then.'
  Yal-28072010-BGMCG-hamecon_0058

In (126) the derived noun is *wa= îna-e-la* [RESULT= make-SPC-3PL.ABS] 'technique for making them'. Another example occurs in (127), where the derived verb is *înau* 'make', which contains a detransitive inflectional suffix.

(127)   *Âria wa înau ma la terae wayap.*
âria   wa=   îna-u   ma la=   tera-e   wayap
NEG.EX RESULT= make-DETR LK4 3PL.SUBJ= stop-SPC war
'There was no way for them to stop the war.'
                                                Yal-20092011-AW4_0041

In (127), *wa=* procliticizes to the inflected verb *îna-u*, with the resulting meaning of 'way of making something'. Example (128) shows another instance of *wa=* procliticized to an already-inflected word form. Here, the class 1 noun (§4.2.1.1) *cewa-* 'relationship'[19] contains an obligatory possessive suffix, *-la* '3PL.POSS'. It is predicated, then converted to a noun when *wa=* is procliticized to it.

(128)   *Tere wa cewala ule.*
te=re   wa=   cewa-la   ule
3SG.SUBJ=ACT RESULT= relationship-3PL.POSS long.ago
'That's actually how it's related to the ones from back then.'
                                    Yal-28072010-BGMCG-hamecon_0057

Examples (126) - (128) seem to show instances of inflection (e.g. possessive suffixes, absolutive suffixes, detransitive suffixes) occurring closer to the root than derivation (with the resultative proclitic *wa=*).

3.6.3 Deverbal verbs

The valence proclitics discussed in detail in §5.4—causative proclitic *pa=*, reciprocal proclitic *pe=*, and reduced agentive *pu=*—are verbal derivations that create new, non-compositional verb lexemes from verbs (a key characteristic of derivation as distinguished from inflection). Some examples are shown in (129).

(129)   *noor* 'to be awake' > *pa= noor* 'to awaken'
        kôê 'to be tired' > *pa= kôê* 'to annoy'
        ka 'to shatter' > *pe= ka* 'to separate'
        tue 'to find' > *pe= tue* 'to meet'
        kewee 'to chase' > *pu= kewee* 'to follow'

---

[19] The class 1 noun *cewa-* 'relationship' may be related to the verb *ce* 'to settle'; a similar relationship also exists between the intransitive verb *ci* 'to sit' and the noun *ciwa-* 'seat'. I was not able to verify whether this is a productive derivational process.

Other derivational characteristics of these proclitics include that they are not obligatory, they have limited applicability based on their semantic compatibility with the verb stem, they are iterable, and they are limited to the word-class of verbs.

Further evidence of the derivational status of these proclitics is that, in some cases, verbs derived with them have become lexicalized, inducing phonological changes in the stem. Some examples are shown in (130).

(130) *pulu* 'to speak' > *pawulue* 'to engage s.b. in conversation'
kela 'to slide' > *paxela* '*Abelmoschus manihot*'[20]
kewee 'to chase' > *pexewe* 'to race'

The triggering of base allomorphy is another common characteristic of derivational morphology.

3.6.4 Denominal verbs with *tu=*

Most nouns in Belep are capable of serving as verbs with zero derivation. For example, in (131) the noun *tamwa* 'woman' is used as a verb simply by inflecting it for subject agreement with *te=* '3SG.SUBJ'.

(131) **Te tamwa, bébé tamwa.**
te=   tamwa [bebe]   tamwa
3SG.SUBJ= woman baby.LN woman
'It was a girl, a baby girl.'
Yal-28072010-BGMCG-tayamu_0075

However, for a number of nouns, this zero derivation is not possible. Instead, the derivational proclitic *tu=* 'VBLZ' is used to create a denominal verb. Its derivational properties include irrelevance to syntax, lack of obligatoriness, and limited applicability. Its use also creates a new lexeme with a non-compositional meaning and changes the word-class of its host.

One set of denominal verbs which tend to use verbalizer *tu=* are derived from class 1 (§4.2.1.1) or class 2 (§4.2.1.2) nouns; that is, nouns that normally participate in the dependent possessive construction (§4.2.2.1). For example, in (132), *tu=* modifies the class 1 noun *nila-* 'great-grandparent', and in (133) it modifies the class 1 noun

---

[20] An edible plant known as 'Island cabbage'.

tauva- 'replacement'. In these examples, the class 1 noun is still obligatorily possessed, even though it has undergone verbal derivation (another possible case of inflection preceding derivation).

(132) **Te jua tu nilan.**

te=	**jua**	**tu=**	**nila-n**
3SG.SUBJ=	really	VBLZ=	great.grandparent-3SG.POSS

'S/he is very frightened.' (lit. 'S/he really does her great-grandparent.')[21]

Yal-19082010-PT.wav

(133) **Yo tu tauvan.**

yo=	**tu=**	**tauva-n**
2SG.SUBJ=	VBLZ=	replacement-3SG.POSS

'You serve as a replacement for him/her.'

Yal-01092010-AP1.wav – Yal-01092010-AP3.wav

In (134), *tu=* modifies *mweeng* 'decoration', which is a class 2 noun. The noun *do* 'spear' in (135) is also a class 2 noun whose word class is changed by verbalizer *tu=*.

(134) **Te tu mweeng.**

te=	**tu=**	**mweeng**
3SG.SUBJ=	VBLZ=	decoration

'S/he decorates her/himself.' (lit. 'S/he does decorations.')

Yal-04072009-BGMCG2.wav

(135) **« Ji tu do. »**

ji=	**tu=**	**do**
1DU.INCL.SUBJ=	VBLZ=	spear

'"We make peace."' (lit. '"We do our spears [into the ground]."')

Yal-20092011-AW6_0166

The derivational *tu=* is also commonly used when deriving denominal verbs from nouns which have entered the language through borrowing (§1.7.2). For example, in (136), *tu=* converts the noun *covan* 'horse' (from French *cheval* [ʃəval]) to a verb meaning 'to ride'.

---

21 The class 1 noun *nila-* means 'great-grandparent', who is so far back in time that he is approaching the *janu*, the clan totem from which the clan is descended. When you *tu= nila-n*, you have gooseflesh, presumably from a brush with the sacred.

(136) **Mo la tao tu covan na bwe dua noon,**
       mo   la=   tao= tu=   covan=a   bwe dua noo-n
       because 3PL.SUBJ= HAB= VBLZ= horse.LN=LOC top back throat-
                                                                                                                  3SG.POSS
       'Because they[22] were riding on his neck,' (lit. 'they were horsing')
                                                                          Yal-28072010-BGMCG-tahitian_0257

In (137), *tu=* converts the noun *per* 'party' (from French *fête* [fɛt]) to a verb.

(137) BG: **Mo avexaô tu per ra mode ...**
                mo   ave=xa=ô   tu=   per=a   mode
                LK3 1DU.EXCL.SUBJ=ADD=REAL VBLZ= party.LN=LOC together
              BG: 'Because we were partying together with,'

          CG: **âjuma.**
                âju-ma
                person-AC
              CG: 'the people.'
                                                  Yal-28072010-BGMCG-tahitian_0289-0290

In addition to verbing class 1 and class 2 nouns and French loans, *tu=* is also used in Belep in a number of idiomatic expressions. In these instances there is not a clear reason to suppose that *tu=* is not a full lexical verb except that speakers do not feel that this is the case. Though *tu=* appears to carry word stress, speakers do not use a comparable French full verb (such as *faire* 'do, make') to translate *tu=* and do not feel this is appropriate (although it is necessary to use 'do, make' to translate the derived Belep verbs into French or English). Some examples follow in (138) - (141).

(138)   **Te tu komu.**
            te=   tu=   komu
            3SG.SUBJ VBLZ= hermit.crab
            'I have déjà vu.' (lit. 'It did [the same thing all over again] like a hermit crab.')

In (138), the noun *komu* 'hermit crab' is converted with *tu=* to a verb with the meaning 'to have déjà vu'. In (139) below, *yuuc* 'mangrove crab' is converted to a verb with the

---

[22] The *janu*, the ancestral totems, were riding on his neck because he had failed to *faire la coutume* (§1.3.2) to them at Poc.

meaning 'to discuss at length, as mangrove crabs construct elaborate palaces in the sand'.

(139) *Ja nyi tu yuuc ya bween,*

ja=	nyi=	tu=	yuy=a	bwee-n
1PL.INCL.SUBJ=	PUNCT=	VBLZ=	mangrove.crab=LOC	top-3SG.POSS

'We often discuss it,' (lit. 'We make [things] like the mangrove crab,')

Yal-09082010-JMTresponse_0013

In (140), the interrogative pronoun *da* 'what?' (§4.6.3) is converted into a verb using *tu=* in order to pose a question-word question (see §6.6.2).

(140) *« Ma na pan tu da ? »*

ma	na=	pana	tu=	da
LK4	1SG.SUBJ=	go.TV	VBLZ=	what

'Why should I go?' (lit. 'That I go and do what?')

Yal-20092011-AW1_0035

In (141), the noun *pwalu* 'heavy' is converted into a verb with the meaning 'to accord customary respect, as of *la coutume* or the chief' (see §1.3.2 on *la coutume*). This derived verb *tu pwalu* contrasts in meaning with the bound transitive verb *pue* 'to respect someone's person'.

(141) *Na jua tu pwalu liôn.*

na=	jua	tu=	pwalu-li-ôn
1SG.SUBJ=	really	VBLZ=	heavy-TR-2PA.ABS

'I respect you very much.' (lit. 'I make like heavy [things are on my back].')[23]

Yal-09082010-coutume_0117

3.7 Compounding

Scholars of New Caledonian languages remark that noun compounding occurs, but in general do not define its identifying characteristics (Bril 2002, Moyse-Faurie 1995). Noun compounding in Belep would be a fruitful topic for further study. As the dependent possessive construction (§4.2.2.1) involves the simple juxtaposition of two

---

[23] The *grande case*, the ceremonial house of the chief in Kanak culture, has a very low doorjamb and high lintel. To enter, one must normally bend almost double as a symbol of respect.

nouns, there are no morphological criteria which could conceivably distinguish nominal compounding from a possessive construction. If a distinction exists, it would have to be made on phonological, syntactic, or semantic criteria (Aikhenvald 2007:24).

Possible phonological criteria which distinguish a compound include the phonological word-marking criteria discussed in §3.2.1 such as lenition. By this criterion, the example in (142) would be a compound.

(142) *wexaac* 'ocean' < *we* 'water' +*kaac* 'bitter'

A number of other words have been identified which are likely the lexicalized result of previous compounds—a common result of compounding (Aikhenvald 2007). However, not all the parts of these lexicalized compounds are still identifiable, which contradicts the definition of compounds as "the combination of at least two potentially free forms" (Aikhenvald 2007:24). I have attempted to identify their parts in (143), though the phonological reduction and fusion they have undergone makes this difficult.

(143) *uruâny* 'hurricane'   < *uru* 'wind'   + *âc* 'man'[24]
       bwaêdan 'morning'   < *bwa-* 'head'   + *êne-* 'sign' + *taan* 'day'[25]
       kûmedan 'evening'   < ? *kûme*   + *taan* 'day'
       denaar 'daylight'   < *de-* 'light'   + *ar* 'sun'[26]
       mweogo 'mountaintop'   < *bwe-* 'top'   + *ôgo* 'mountain'
       ara kalooc 'shoe'[27]   < *ara-* 'underside' + *ka-* 'foot'/Fr. *galoche* 'clogs'[28]
       câbuk 'very cold'   < *caam* 'cold'   + ? *buk*
       pwairamwa 'girl'   < ? *pwai* 'proud'   + *tamwa* 'woman'
       pwainagac 'beautiful'   < ? *pwai* 'proud'   + *dagac* 'mask'

Many animal and plant names are clearly compounds on semantic criteria, although it is unclear if any other criteria may be used to distinguish them (144).

---

24 This etymology is proposed by several speakers; hurricanes are believed to be the work of a single legendary sorcerer who lives on Poc. It is unknown what conditioned the change from /c/ to /ɲ/, although I speculate it may have occurred by analogy with *mwany* 'bad'.
25 An alternate form is the reduplicated *mwamwaedaan* 'the crack of dawn'.
26 Probably by analogy with *de naap* [light fire] 'firelight'. The word *ar* 'sun' is still used as the name of the main island in Belep, spelled <Art> in French orthography.
27 Note that compounds in Belep should be considered a single grammatical word, although they may consist of multiple phonological words.
28 The etymology *ara-* 'underside' + French *galoche* 'clogs' was suggested in Dubois (1975c).

(144) bwala gom 'moray eel'   < bwala- 'head'[29]   + gom 'sea cucumber'
     cuda âvan 'swamp harrier' < cu=da 'stand=DIR.UH' + âva-n 'wing-3SG'
     nana deâ 'maggot'   < nana- 'feces'   + deâ 'blowfly'[30]
     nu li kiâk 'arrow root'   < nu 'coconut'   +kiâk
                                                      'purple swamphen'[31]
     ulo kan 'silver gull'   < ulo 'red'   + ka-n 'feet-3SG.POSS'
     we modap 'seaweed'   < we 'food'   + modap 'manatee'

A few other words can be characterized as compounds using semantic criteria, though it is unclear if other criteria may be used since in all other ways they are indistinguishable from a possessive construction (145). Verb compounding is discussed in §5.9.

(145) nae dan 'cloud' < nae- 'child' + dan 'sky'
     nae uc 'bastard' < nae- 'child' + uc 'straw'
     waga âno 'cradle' < waga- 'boat' + âno 'child'

3.8 Non-concatenative morphology

There is very little non-concatenative morphology in Belep; the most promising example of non-concatenative morphology is a very limited process of reduplication, which is somewhat surprising given how widespread productive reduplication is in Austronesian languages (Rubino 2013).

Bril (2002) gives two examples of nominal reduplication in Nêlêmwa, where the first syllable is reduplicated with the meaning of 'multiple types of N'. She gives several other examples of verbal reduplication (again of the first syllable) with the meaning 'be very V' or 'do V multiple times'. I have found a few plausible examples of reduplication resembling this in Belep (146).

---

29 Many lexicalized forms in Belep contain *bwala-* 'head' instead of *bwa-*. It is unknown whether there is a productive distinction.
30 *Lucilia caesar*.
31 *Porphyrio porphyrio caledonicus*.

(146)   *kûkûûr*   'to mutter'[32]   <   *kûûr* 'to grunt, growl'
        povoro   'to be daybreak'[33]   <   *poro* 'to be white'
        torop   'to be mushed'   <   *top* 'to be melted'

The other plausible examples of Belep reduplication that I have found, shown in (147) and (148), seem to be onomatopoetic or at least sound-symbolic; in many of these cases, no word form without a reduplicant has been identified.

(147)   *babanu* 'type of lizard'
        jajani 'to be crazy'
        pipilo 'swiftlet'[34]
        tiribic 'to tremble'

(148)   *boriric* 'tern'
        kewowor 'to snore'
        nyomamar 'to whisper'
        palalap 'serpentinite (type of stone)'
        welolop 'type of coconut'[35] < *weloo* 'type of coconut'

In general, there appear to be two types of reduplication: one where the first syllable is reduplicated (147) as in Nêlêmwa, and another where the onset and nucleus of the last syllable are reduplicated (148). More work remains to be done to determine if reduplication is a productive process at all in Belep.

3.9 Summary

In this chapter, I have demonstrated the wide disconnect between the phonological and the grammatical word (§3.2) and described the prototypical characteristics of the five Belep word classes (§3.3). The difference between Belep inflectional (§3.5) and derivational (§3.6) morphology was defined in §3.4. Sections §3.7 and §3.8 have described some less common word-formation processes in Belep.

---

32 Note that some of these sound-symbolic words disobey the normal phonotactics of Belep in allowing medial voiceless stops; see §2.5.1 and §2.9.1.1.
33 This word was found in Dubois (1975c); it was not collected by me.
34 *Collocalia esculenta*, a type of bird.
35 A *weloo* is a green, unripe coconut. A *welolop* is a more mature coconut that makes a hollow sound when you thump it.

4 Nouns and the noun phrase

4.1 Introduction

Nouns in Belep form a word class whose prototypical characteristics were discussed in §3.3.1. They are divided into four noun classes based on their semantic compatibility with inalienable and alienable possession (§4.2). They can be marked with inflectional suffixes for quantity (§4.3) and determination (§4.4). Noun phrases (§4.5) are composed minimally of a head noun, which may be followed by any number of modifying nouns, including numerals (§4.7). Pronouns (§4.6) are defined as full phonological words which are capable of substituting for a noun phrase.

4.2 Nouns and possession

As in many languages of the Pacific Rim, Belep nouns are divided into "declension classes defined by allomorphy of possessive inflection" (Bickel & Nichols 2007: 206). That is, Belep nouns are divided into four classes (§4.2.1) with both a distinction between inherent and optional possession and between inalienable possession (referred to in this work as 'dependent'; see §4.2.2) and alienable ('independent') possession. These classes are defined by the ability of the nouns they contain to appear as free stems and to participate in the two available possessive constructions (§4.2.2). Within these classes, Belep nouns undergo a considerable amount of lexeme-based allomorphy (or 'flexivity' in the terminology of Bickel & Nichols 2007) using stem modification; stems vary phonologically depending on whether they are free or possessed (§4.2.3) and vary further depending on the possessor's position (§4.2.2.3) on the topic-worthiness hierarchy (Payne 1997).

4.2.1 Noun classes

Nouns in Belep are divided into four noun classes based on their compatibility with possessive constructions. Class 1 nouns (§4.2.1.1) are inherently possessed; they do not have free stems and must obligatorily index their possessor using dependent possession (§4.2.2.1). All other noun classes are optionally possessed. Class 2 nouns (§4.2.1.2) have free stems (§4.2.3), but may only be possessed using dependent (inalienable) possession. Class 3 nouns (§4.2.1.3) have free stems and may be dependently or independently (§4.2.2.4) possessed. Class 4 nouns (§4.2.1.4) have free stems and may be independently (alienably) possessed; however, they are incompatible with dependent possession (§4.2.2.1). This classification system is represented in Table 1.

Tab. 1: Compatibility of noun classes with possessive constructions

	Dependent possession	Free	Independent possession
Class 1	✓		
Class 2	✓	✓	
Class 3	✓	✓	✓
Class 4		✓	✓

Nouns are assigned to the various noun classes based on their semantic compatibility with inalienable (dependent) or alienable (independent) possession, as well as with the notion of being free (unpossessed). Class 1 nouns are most likely to be kinship terms and lexical items describing body parts or part/whole relationships; these concepts necessarily have a semantic possessor. Class 2 nouns represent those entities which inalienably belong to their possessor, but nonetheless may be separated from it. Class 3 nouns exist at the semantic margin between alienable and inalienable possession; a class 3 noun's ability to participate in both constructions may or may not be salient for speakers. Class 4 nouns are those which are unequivocally alienable from their possessor—such as features of the natural world—and which lack a phonological form which is compatible with the dependent construction. Lexical nouns which are phonologically identical to corresponding verbs (§3.3) tend to fall into this category, as do all loanwords which are nouns (§2.9, §1.7.2).

4.2.1.1 Noun class 1

Nouns in class 1 are distinguished by the fact that they are semantically inalienably possessed and cannot be separated from their possessor. It is not possible for class 1 nouns to occur outside of the dependent possessive construction (§4.2.2.1); they do not have free (unpossessed) forms (§4.2.3). Class 1 is a very large closed noun class (comprising at least 200 nouns). Some class 1 nouns have invariant stems, while others vary by the animacy or number of the possessor. Some examples of class 1 nouns with invariant stems are shown in Table 2. Note that the stems in Table 2 may be used regardless of whether the possessor is indexed by an animate or inanimate noun phrase or a singular or nonsingular pronominal suffix.

Tab. 2: Examples of class 1 nouns

Class 1 noun	Gloss
âmwa-	'gesture'
âô-	'vine'
ava-	'sibling'

Class 1 noun	Gloss
bane-	'friend, company'
cama-	'father'
e-	'hand'
gana-	'color'
jivi-	'skirt'
ka-	'foot'
mwade-	'nose'
nara-	'name'
nila-	'great-grandparent'
pabo-	'grandchild'
pae-	'importance'
ôga-	'egg'
wêga-	'charity'
yada-	'belongings'

For example, the class 1 noun *nara-* 'name' may occur with either a noun phrase possessor (1) or a pronominal possessive suffix (§4.2.2.2), as in (2), where the possessor is nonsingular, and in (3) where the possessor is singular.

(1) ***nara ulayimi***
nara   ulayi-mi
name   old.man-DET.A.DST
'the name of that old man'
                                                Yal-20092011-AW6_0006

(2) ***narale***
nara-le
name-3DU.POSS
'their names'
                                                Yal-20092011-AW6_0057

(3) ***naran***
nara-n
name-3SG.POSS
'its name'
                                                Yal-20092011-AW6_0117

If the possessor of a class 1 noun is generic/unspecified, the noun occurs with the possessive suffix *-r* '3GNR.POSS' as in (4) and (5).

(4)   **naer**
      nae-r
      small.thing-3GNR.POSS
      'a child'
                                            Yal-28072010-BGMCG-tayamu_0133

(5)   **baner**
      bane-r
      friend-3GNR.POSS
      'a companion' (used here to refer to a side-dish in a meal)
                                            Yal-28072010-BGMCG-tayamu_0020

Many other class 1 nouns undergo stem modification depending on the type of possessor (§4.2.2.3), whether it is indexed by an animate or inanimate noun phrase or a singular or nonsingular possessive suffix. Some examples are shown in Table 3; note that this list is non-exhaustive. Each column shows what stem is required for the type of possessor noted in the column heading; stems carry over to the next column unless a different stem is noted.

Tab. 3: Examples of stem modification in class 1 nouns

Inan. NP	Anim. NP	Nonsg. pron. sfx.	Sg. pron. sfx.	Gloss
ânu-			ânuu-	'beneath'
âro-			âroo-	'husband'
bo-			boo-	'odor'
bwala-	bwa-		bwaa-	'head'
dua-	du-		duu-	'bones'
ga-			gaa-	'sympathy'
mua-		mu-	muu-	'flower'
nyana-	nya-			'mother'
pwâna-	pwa-			'fruit'
wâna-	wâ-		wââ-	'root'

The stem modifications shown in Table 3 are properties of the lexeme and, though they follow several general patterns, are largely irregular and unpredictable.

4.2.1.2 Noun class 2

Like class 1, class 2 contains inalienably possessed nouns, and the only possessive construction with which they are compatible is dependent possession (§4.2.2.1). However, nouns in class 2 are distinguished from nouns in class 1 in that they have free (unpossessed) forms (§4.2.3). Semantically, it is possible to separate class 2 nouns from their possessors. Table 4 shows some examples of class 2 nouns.

Tab. 4: Examples of class 2 nouns

Free stem	Inan. NP	Anim. NP/ Nonsg. poss. sfx.	Sg. poss. sfx.	Gloss
âm	âba-			'plate'
ânaju			ânajuu-	'truth'
bwayu			bwayuu-	'right side'
cawane				'mast'
da			daa-	'blood'
daap	dawo-			'dust'
iyi	iye-			'louse'
jiin	jida-			'story'
mada			madaa-	'sadness'
mwa	mwana-	mwa-		'house'
nep	neve-			'dream'
pa			paa-	'nest'
tolam	tolaba-			'basket'
wa	wale-			'necklace'
waang	waga-			'boat'

As Table 4 shows, every class 2 noun has both a free stem (leftmost column) and at least one possessed stem.[1] Possessed stems in class 2 undergo a large amount of stem modification (§4.2.2.3) depending on whether the possessor is indexed by an inanimate noun phrase, an animate noun phrase or nonsingular possessive suffix, or a singular possessive suffix.

There are two basic patterns for this type of stem modification. In one pattern, the free stem is also used for all types of possessors except for those indexed by a singular pronominal suffix (§4.2.2.2), for which a stem containing a like-vowel hiatus is used. For example, the free stem *da* 'blood' (6) is also used with a noun phrase possessor (7) and a nonsingular pronominal possessive suffix (8). Only a singular possessive suffix requires a different possessed stem, *daa-* 'blood' as in (9).

---

[1] Though it is usual to have phonological alternation between free and possessed stems for class 2 nouns, a few class 2 nouns have phonologically identical free and possessed stems, e.g. *cawane* 'mast'.

(6) « *ma yo tu ma uli da.* »
 ma   yo=   tu   ma   uli   da
 LK4   2SG.SUBJ= go.DH   LK4   pour   blood
 '"that you go and spill blood."'

                                                                               Yal-20092011-AW1_0256

(7) *ka da ulayimi,*
 ka   da   ulayi-mi
 LK   blood   old.man-DET.A.DST
 'and the blood of that old man,'

                                                                               Yal-20092011-AW5_0090

(8) *dala*
 da-la
 blood-3PL.POSS
 'their blood'

(9) *daang*
 daa-ng
 blood-1SG.POSS
 'my blood'

                                                                                    Yal-02092011-PT.wav

In the other pattern, the free stem contrasts with the possessed stem, which is used for all types of possessors. For example, the free stem *waang* 'boat' (10) corresponds to the possessed stem *waga-*, which occurs with both nominal (11) and pronominal (12) possessors.

(10) *Laxa po waang.*
 la=xa   po   waang
 3PL.SUBJ=ADD   load   boat
 'And they loaded the boat.'

                                                                                Yal-20092011-AW3_0077

(11) *Avexa pae waga ulayixedu digi,*
 ave=xa   pa-e   waga   ulayi-xedu   digi
 1DU.EXCL.SUBJ=ADD   take-SPC   boat   old.man-DET.DH   canoe
 'We would take the old man's boat, a canoe,'

                                                         Yal-28072010-BGMCG-tahitian_0013

(12) « *Ka ivi wagaji ?* »
 ka   ivi   waga-ji
 LK   be.where.SPC   boat-1DU.INCL.POSS
 '"And where's our boat?"'
 Yal-01082010-MFD_0016

4.2.1.3 Noun class 3

Class 3 nouns exist at the semantic margin between compatibility with alienable and inalienable possession; they form a fairly small noun class. Nouns in class 3 have free (unpossessed) stems (§4.2.3), and they may be both dependently (§4.2.2.1) and independently (§4.2.2.4) possessed. Dependently possessed class 3 nouns may undergo stem modification for the type of possessor (§4.2.2.3). Some examples of class 3 nouns are shown in Table 5; these were all attested in both possessive constructions in my corpus.

Tab. 5: Examples of class 3 nouns

Free stem	NP/Nonsg. pron. sfx.	Sg. pron. sfx.	Gloss
doo	do-	doo-	'dirt'
gawaar	gaware-		'day'
kayor	kayola-		'barrier'
pulu		puluu-	'speech, language'
pwemwa			'home, village'

Alternation between dependent and independent possession occurs based on a speaker's moment-to-moment conceptualization of a class 3 noun. For example, the free form *pwemwa* 'dwelling' is unpossessed in (13) and dependently possessed in (14), where it is translated as *chez moi* 'home'—a concept which the speaker conceptualizes as inalienable. When *pwemwa* is independently possessed in (15), it is best translated by 'village, inhabited place, locality'—a concept which speakers perceive as alienably possessed.

(13) *Teô ta la pwemwa.*
 te=ô   ta=la   pwemwa
 3SG.SUBJ=REAL   go.UH=LOC   dwelling
 'he had gone home/to the village.'
 Yal-28072010-BGMCG-tahitian_0070

(14)   **pwemwang**
       pwemwa-ng
       dwelling-1SG.POSS
       'my home'

       Yal-28072010-BGMCG-tahitian_0007

(15)   **pwemwa li Ono**
       pwemwa=li   Ono
       dwelling=GEN   Ono
       'the village (named) Ono'

       Yal-28072010-BGMCG-sousmarin_0073

The ability of class 3 nouns to be independently possessed is not generally salient for speakers; that is, when giving an example of a class 3 noun in a possessive construction, speakers will usually choose dependent possession.

4.2.1.4 Noun class 4

Class 4 is a very large, open noun class which contains most animal and plant names, features of the natural world, and all nominal loanwords. Nouns in class 4 have only one stem, which may occur as a free stem (§4.2.3) or be independently possessed (§4.2.2.4). Class 4 nouns are incompatible with dependent possession. Noun classifiers (§4.2.4) are also used to indicate the possessor of a class 4 noun. Some examples of class 4 nouns are shown in Table 6.

Tab. 6: Examples of class 4 nouns

Free stem	Gloss
âju	'person'
âno	'paternal aunt'[2]
bwena	'type of lizard'
câbuk	'cold'
danac	'ocean'
dilic	'mud'
jan	'cord'
jewe	'fairy'
koyap	'type of lobster'

---

[2] A few kinship terms, such as *âno* 'paternal aunt', vocative *wa* 'grandparent', and the derived kin-terms using *âma=* 'DYAD' (§3.6.1.2), including *âma naen* 'family', are class 4 nouns. It is unclear whether there is semantic justification for this or whether it is simply an irregularity.

Free stem	Gloss
kuro	'knife.LN'
maac	'death'
mada	'cloth'
mani	'bird'
nu	'coconut tree'
oroop	'dress.LN'
paan	'screwpine'
pawi	'beach hibiscus'
piyu	'star'
puaxa	'pig.LN'
puri	'snake'
wayap	'war'
yer	'pot'

Examples (16) and (17) show the use of the class 4 noun *âju* 'person' respectively as a free (unpossessed) stem, and as an independently possessed stem.

(16) *Te gi koxo âju,*
te= **gi** **koxo** **âju**
3SG.SUBJ= attack lots person
'He killed many people,'

Yal-20092011-AW3_0087

(17) « *Name pan pan cuuri âju linaoma.* »
na=me **pana** **pana** **curi** **âju=li-nao-ma**
1SG.SUBJ=IRR go.TV go.TV stand.TR person=GEN-1SG.ABS-AC
'"I am going to go and stand before my people."'

Yal-20092011-AW1_0220

Class 4 nouns do not undergo stem modification for the type of possessor (§4.2.2.3).

4.2.2 Possessed nouns

To express nominal possession, Belep speakers use two different possessive constructions, which are termed 'dependent' and 'independent' throughout this work.[3] Abstract representations of these constructions are shown in Table 7; square brackets indicate phonological word boundaries.

Tab. 7: Types of possessive construction in Belep

	NP Possessor	Pronominal Possessor
Dependent	[HEAD NOUN] [NP POSSESSOR]	[HEAD NOUN-POSS. SUFFIX]
Independent	[HEAD NOUN=GEN] [NP POSSESSOR]	[HEAD NOUN=GEN-ABS. SUFFIX]

Table 7 shows that the inflectional morphology used in dependent (§4.2.2.1) and independent (§4.2.2.4) possessive constructions differs depending on whether the possessor is indexed by a full noun phrase or by a pronominal formative. Dependent possession with a full noun phrase possessor is marked by the simple juxtaposition of the noun and its possessor; whereas all independent possession requires the use of the genitive case marker =li or =i 'GEN' (§6.4.3). When the possessor is indexed by a pronominal suffix, nouns in the dependent construction use a possessive suffix (§4.2.2.2), while nouns in the independent construction use an absolutive suffix (§5.7). Speakers use the dependent possessive construction to denote inalienable possession, while they use the independent construction to denote alienable possession; that is, distinguishing between inalienable and alienable possession is the semantic function of the two constructions.

---

3 Scholars of Kanak languages have traditionally used the terms 'dependent' and 'independent' as names for noun classes. Inherently possessed nouns are called 'dependent nouns' by other scholars of New Caledonian languages (Bril 2002), and nouns which are not inherently possessed are called 'independent nouns'. Ozanne-Rivierre (1998) distinguishes a third class for Balade Nyelâyu, 'personal nouns', which includes proper names and certain kinship terms which behave like pronouns in terms of their case-marking. Bril further subdivides 'independent nouns' into several subclasses: those which can be modified by the possessive suffixes used for dependent nouns, and those which cannot; and those whose root undergoes phonological alternation or not when modified by the suffixes. The Belep analysis proposed in this chapter has the benefit of separating the categorization of noun classes from the categorization of possessive constructions, though to provide continuity with previous publications on Kanak languages the terms 'dependent' and 'independent' will continue to be used. In this work they refer to inalienable and alienable possessive constructions, respectively, rather than to particular noun classes.

4.2.2.1 Dependent possession

In the dependent possessive construction, when the possessor is indexed by a noun phrase, the head noun immediately precedes the possessor noun, with no marking to indicate their relationship (other modifying nouns may then follow the possessor). There is no morphological distinction between the dependent possessive construction and nominal compounding (§3.7). Examples of dependent possession are shown in (18) - (21).

(18) **ara   ôgo**
     underside   mountain
     'the bottom of the mountain'

     Yal-20092011-AW6_0139

(19) **tânema   cawone**
     eye   Japanese.LN
     'diving mask' (lit. 'eye of Japanese'; most diving masks are Japanese imports)

     Yal-28072010-BGMCG-tahitian_0041

(20) **ala   karec**
     husk   clam
     'clam shell'

     Yal-05092011-AP1_0096

(21) **pua â mae**
     pua   â=   mae
     trunk   AGT=   sleep
     'mimosa trunk' (lit. 'trunk of sleeper'[4])

     Yal-17072009-TB-weekend_0011

When the possessor is indexed by a pronominal formative, a possessive suffix (§4.2.2.2) is used on the head noun, as in (22) and (23).

(22) **pabong**
     pabo-ng
     grandchild-1SG.POSS
     'my grandchild'

     Yal-17072009-TB-weekend_0030

(23) **oreâva**
     oreâ-va
     breath-1PL.EXCL.POSS
     'our breath'

     Yal-17072009-TB-weekend_0018

---

4 The tree name *â mae* '*Acacia nilotica*' literally means 'sleeper'; it closes its leaves at night.

Nouns of classes 1, 2, and 3 (§4.2.1) may participate in the dependent possessive construction.

4.2.2.2 Possessive suffixes

The possessive suffixes are presented in Table 8. See §4.6.1 for a discussion of personal pronouns in general.

Tab. 8: Possessive suffixes

	Singular	Dual	Paucal	Plural	Generic
1 EXCL	-ng	-ve	-ven	-va	
1 INCL		-ji	-jen	-ja	
2	-mw	-or	-ôn	-ac	
3	-n	-le	-len	-la	-r

The possessive suffixes shown in Table 8 are used primarily on nouns in the dependent possessive construction, as in examples (24) and (25).

(24) *jivive*
jivi-ve
skirt-1DU.EXCL.POSS
'our skirts'

Yal-20092011-AW4_0053

(25) *puluac*
pulu-ac
speech-2PL.POSS
'your language'

Yal-14092011-PT2-avenir_0018

They are also used to index an anaphoric dative argument after the dative case marker =*le* or =*e* 'DAT' (see §6.4.4).

The possessive suffix -*r* '3GNR.POSS' indexes a generic possessor (see §5.2.4 for more on specificity in Belep) of unspecified number, as in examples (26) - (28). It is often used in the citation form of a class 1 noun (§4.2.1.1), as in (26), or with a possessor that is a mass noun (27) or inanimate (28). It occurs with the singular pronominal form of possessed noun stems (§4.2.1).

(26) **mewuur**
mewuu-r
surname-3GNR.POSS
'surname'
Yal-06082010-DY.wav

(27) *Ka naerama, la îbi jawu.*
ka	nae-ra-ma	la=	îbi	jawu
LK	child-3GNR.POSS-AC	3PL.SUBJ=	collect	dead.leaves

'The children, they collected trash.'
Yal-17072009-TB-weekend_0009

(28) *tu ganar*
tu=	gana-r
VBLZ=	color-3GNR.POSS

'to color' (lit. 'to do its/their colors')
Yal-13102010-AP.wav

The usage of generic -*r* contrasts with, for example, the usage of 3SG.POSS suffix -*n*, which occurs when the possessor is singular, specific and directly inferable from context. For example, in (29) and (30), the form -*n* indexes a specific possessor, which can be animate (29) or inanimate (30).

(29) *Teô âyae teeyan.*
te=ô	âya-e	teya-n
3SG.SUBJ=REAL	sense-SPC	burn-3SG.POSS

'He [the Dubageni] felt his burn.'
Yal-05092011-AP1_0085-0086

(30) *La ta la bween.*
la=	ta=la	bwee-n
3PL.SUBJ=	go.UH=LOC	top-3SG.POSS

'They went over the top of it [the reef].'
Yal-20092011-AW2_0037

As affixes (§3.2.2.4), the possessive suffixes condition stem alternations (see §4.2.3, §4.2.2.3) and otherwise act as part of the phonological word (§3.2.1) to which they attach. The possessive suffixes are not clitics (§3.2.2.5); they attach directly to the possessed noun rather than to the noun phrase (§4.6), as in the full noun phrases in (31) and (32).

(31) **nae pabong âc pwalaic**
 nae   pabo-**nga**   âya   pwalaic
 small.thing grandchild-1SG.POSS   man   one
 'my little grandson'

 Yal-17072009-TB-weekend_0030

(32) **weemw wan**
 we-**mwa**   wan
 food-2SG.POSS   sea.turtle
 'your sea turtle (to eat)'

 Yal-20092011-AW5_0026

In (31), the possessed noun is *pabo-* 'grandchild', and in (32) the possessed noun is *we-* 'food'. In both cases, the possessive suffix attaches directly to the possessed noun, rather than to the end of the noun phrase (e.g. to *pwalaic* in (31) or *wan* in (32)).

4.2.2.3 Stem modification for type of possessor

Within the set of dependently possessed noun stems, irregular stem modification frequently occurs based on the position of the possessor on the topic-worthiness hierarchy, as defined in Payne (1997: 150). The conditioning factors include whether the possessor is nominal or pronominal; singular or nonsingular; animate or inanimate.[5]

Many possessed noun stems have multiple phonological forms, depending on whether the possessor is indexed by a full noun phrase, a nonsingular pronominal suffix, or a singular/generic pronominal suffix (see §4.2.2.2). Some examples of possessed stem modification conditioned by animacy are shown in Table 9.

Tab. 9: Stem modification in possessed noun stems depending on what the possessor is indexed by

Noun phrase	Nonsingular pron. sfx.	Singular pron. sfx.	Gloss	Class
mua-	mu-	muu-	'flower'	1
pia-	pi-	pii-	'nails'	1
pua-	pu-	puu-	'trunk'	1
âro-		âroo-	'husband'	1
ga-		gaa-	'sympathy'	1
janu-		januu-	'spirit'	2

---

5 This stem modification occurs in classes 1, 2, and 3 (see §4.2.1 below).

Noun phrase	Nonsingular pron. sfx.	Singular pron. sfx.	Gloss	Class
pulu-		puluu-	'speech, language'	3
we-		wee-	'food'	1

Table 9 shows that some possessed nouns have three forms, depending on whether the possessor is nominal, nonsingular pronominal, or singular pronominal. Examples (33) - (35) show instances of this variation.

(33) *pia kan*
pia   ka-n
nail   foot-3SG.POSS
'his/her toenail(s)'

(34) *pija*
pi-ja
nail-1PL.INCL.POSS
'our nails'

(35) *piin*
pii-n
nail-3SG.POSS
'his nail(s)'

Yal-06092011-PT.wav

Table 9 also shows examples of possessed nouns which have two forms: the stem used with a nominal possessor is identical to that used for a nonsingular pronominal possessor, while the stem used with a singular or generic pronominal possessor has a final like-vowel hiatus (see §2.3.2.2). Examples (36) - (38) show this type of variation.

(36) *Ga Aliic !*
ga   Aliic
sympathy   Alice.LN
'Poor Alice!'

(37) *Gaji !*
ga-ji
sympathy-1DU.INCL.POSS
'Poor us!'

(38)   *Gaamw !*
       gaa-mw
       sympathy-2SG.POSS
       'Poor you!'

A number of possessed noun stems also undergo modification for the animacy of the possessor. In these cases, a suffix (usually -*na* or -*la*[6]) occurs on the possessed stem when its possessor is an inanimate noun phrase, as in Table 10.

Tab. 10: Stem modification depending on what the possessor is indexed by

Inanimate noun phrase	Animate NP or nonsingular pron. sfx.	Singular pron. sfx.	Gloss	Class
bwala-	bwa-	bwaa-	'head'	1
nyoda-	nyo-	nyoo-	'nails'	1
wâna-	wâ-	wââ-	'root'	1
mwana-	mwa-		'house'	2
nana-	na-		'feces'	1
nyana-[7]	nya-		'mother'	1
pwâna-	pwa-		'fruit'	1

As Table 10 shows, sometimes this results in three different possessed stems for the same noun, as in examples (39) - (42).

(39)   ***bwala gom***
       bwala   gom
       head   sea.cucumber
       'moray eel' (lit. 'head of a sea cucumber')[8]

---

6 This suffix is most likely related to the Balade Nyelâyu relator -*la* (Ozanne-Rivierre 1998: 37) or the nasal relator attested in many New Caledonian languages (Ozanne-Rivierre 1991), including Nêlêmwa (Bril 2002: 31-32).
7 When the noun *nyana-* 'mother' has an inanimate possessor, it acts as a classifier meaning 'big thing'. For example, *nyana buâny* literally means 'mother of a stone', but is used to mean 'a big stone'.
8 Note that this is a noun compound based on semantic criteria; however, there is no morphological distinction between compounds and dependent possession (see §4.2.2.1).

(40) ***bwa âju***
 bwa âju
 head person
 'a person's head'

(41) ***bwala***
 bwa-la
 head-3PL.POSS
 'their heads'

(42) ***bwaang***
 bwaa-ng
 head-1SG.POSS
 'my head'

Table 10 also shows some possessed nouns with only two forms: one used with an inanimate noun phrase possessor, and one used with any other possessor. Examples (43) - (46) show this type of variation.

(43) ***mwana purieen***
 mwana purieen
 house prayer
 'church' (lit. 'house of prayer')

(44) ***mwa teâmaa***
 mwa teâmaa
 house high.chief
 'chieftain's house'

(45) ***mwave***
 mwa-ve
 house-1DU.EXCL.POSS
 'our house'

(46) ***mwan***
 mwa-n
 house-3SG.POSS
 'his/her house'

In general, stem modification for the type of possessor cross-cuts the noun classification system, although it is most common for class 1 nouns (§4.2.1.1). It is highly irregular and unpredictable in both its specific forms and in which nouns it applies to.

4.2.2.4 Independent possession

The independent possessive construction is characterized by the presence of the genitive clitic =*li* or =*i* 'GEN' (§6.4.3) in all cases (this alternation is determined by whether the host ends in a vowel or a consonant, respectively). If the possessor is indexed by a full lexical noun phrase, the possessed noun precedes the possessor noun, and the two nouns are separated by the genitive ditropic clitic (§6.4; see also §3.2.2.6). In other words, =*li* or =*i* 'GEN' encliticizes to the possessed noun, marking the possessor noun as in the genitive case. For example, in (47), the possessed noun *kiyooc* 'hut' has the nominal possessor *tayamo Kawo* 'the lady Kawo', which is marked as genitive using =*i* 'GEN'.

(47)   ***kiyooc yi tayamo Kawo***
      kiyoy=i   **tayamo**   **Kawo**
      hut=GEN   old.woman[9]   Kawo
      'the lady Kawo's hut'

                                                                 Yal-20092011-AW1_0263

Other examples of the independent possessive construction with a full noun phrase possessor are shown in (48) - (50). In (48), the possessed noun *pwemwa* 'village' has the nominal possessor *Ono*, which in this case is the name of the village. The genitive clitic =*li* marks the possessor noun phrase.

(48)   ***pwemwa li Ono***
      pwemwa=li   **Ono**
      village=GEN   Ono
      'the village (named) Ono'

                                                        Yal-28072010-BGMCG-sousmarin_0073

In (49), the possessor *bweroo* 'underside' is marked with genitive clitic =*li*.

(49)   ***bweroo li pwemwa***
      bwero=li   **pwemwa**
      underside=GEN   village
      'below the village'

                                                        Yal-28072010-BGMCG-sousmarin_0076

---

[9] The words *tayamo* 'old woman' and *ulac* 'old man' are often used as terms of respect; here, Kawo is a young woman and the wife of the chieftain.

In (50), the possessed noun *per* 'party' (from French *fête* [fɛt] 'party') is possessed by *maac* 'death'. Genitive ditropic clitic =*i* is used to mark the latter noun as in the genitive case.

(50) **per ri maac**
per=i   maac
party.LN=GEN   death
'wake' (lit. 'party of death')

Yal-20092011-AW1_0044

When the possessor is indexed by a pronominal formative, an anaphoric absolutive suffix (§5.7) follows the genitive clitic, as in examples (51) - (53).

(51) **bu lila**
bu=li-la
fishhook=GEN-3PL.ABS
'their fishhooks'

Yal-28072010-BGMCG-hamecon_0092

(52) **tauvar rija**
tauvar=i-ja
punishment=GEN-1PL.EXCL.ABS
'our punishment'

Yal-20092011-AW2_0074

(53) **du liva**
du=li-va
bone=GEN-1PL.EXCL.ABS
'our bones'

Yal-01082010-MFD_0035

Both 3SG.ABS suffixes -*e* and -*er* are used in independent possession; it is not clear what conditions the variation between them (see §5.7.2). Example (54) shows the use of -*e* in independent possession, while (55) shows an example of -*er*.

(54) **karavaa lie**
karava=li-e
pirogue=GEN-3SG.ABS
'his pirogue'

Yal-20092011-AW4_0062

(55) *âju lier pwalaic*
 âju=li-era   **pwalaic**
 person=GEN-3SG.ABS   one
 'one of his people'

                                                                   Yal-20092011-AW1_0174

Nouns of classes 3 and 4 (§4.2.1) may participate in the independent possessive construction.

4.2.3 Free (unpossessed) nouns and stem modification

Many nouns are invariant in that they have the same phonological form whether or not they occur in a possessive construction.[10] For example, the noun *tayamo* 'old woman' appears in (56) without a possessor; it has the same phonological form in (57), where it is independently possessed (§4.2.2.4).

(56) *Mo tayamo ai ?*
 mo   **tayamo**   **ei**
 LK3   old.woman   TAG
 'But rather an old woman, you see?'

                                                    Yal-28072010-BGMCG-tayamu_0134

(57) *tayamo linao*
 tayamo=li-nao
 old.woman=GEN-1SG.ABS
 'my wife' (lit. 'my old woman')

                                                    Yal-20092011-AW1_0183

However, many other nouns undergo stem modification based on whether or not they occur in a possessive construction.[11] Some examples are shown in Table 11.

---

10 Such nouns fall primarily into class 4, discussed below in §4.2.1.4; though some are found in all other classes.
11 These nouns are primarily found in class 2 (see §4.2.1.2), although stem modification does not occur for all class 2 nouns.

Tab. 11: Stem modification of free noun stems

Free stem	Possessed stem[12]	English gloss	
âm	âba-	'plate'	(A), (B)
âny	âje-	'rudder'	(A), (B)
daap	dawo-	'dust'	(A), (C)
depw	dewa-	'deck'	(A)
jiin	jida-	'story'	(A), (B), (C)
kic	kiye-	'liver'	(A)
mweeng	mwega-	'decoration'	(A), (B), (C)
naap	nave-	'fire'	(A), (C)
nep	neve-	'dream'	(A)
pôn	pône-	'hair'	(A)
pûmw	pûmwa-	'smoke'	(A)
teec	teya-	'burn'	(A), (C)
tolam	tolaba-	'basket'	(A), (B)
toop	tova-	'field'	(A), (C)
waang	waga-	'boat'	(A), (B), (C)

The stem modifications shown in Table 11 indicate whether the noun is free or possessed. Though there is no regular rule deriving possessed stems from free stems, they follow several general patterns:

(A) Possessed stems contain a suffixed vowel, usually -*a* or -*e* (see §3.2.1.4 on lenition)
(B) Final nasals in the free stem sometimes correspond to medial prenasalized stops in the possessed stem
(C) Like-vowel hiatuses in the free stem correspond to single vowels in the possessed stem

The fourth column of Table 11 indicates which of these patterns is used in the relevant free-possessed pair.

---

[12] Note that the possessed stems in Table 11 do not vary based on the type of possessor (§4.2.2.3).

4.2.4 Noun classifiers

In Belep, many class 1 nouns (§4.2.1.1) can serve as noun classifiers—that is, classifiers "which are not restricted [to noun phrases including a numeral and a noun], but occur freely in ordinary noun phrases" (Corbett 2007:253). Some examples[13] are given in Table 12. See also §4.4.1 on numeral classifiers.

Tab. 12: Noun classifiers

Classifier	Gloss
â-	'cutting of a plant'
ma-	'thing to chew'
nae-	'small thing'
nyana-	'big thing'
ûdu-, ûduu-	'beverage'
wa-	'thing to suck'
we-, wee-	'food'
ya-, yaa-	'tuber'
yae-	'weapon'
yava-	'catch'
yaya-	'unripe thing'

The classifiers shown in Table 12 are not morphologically distinguishable from class 1 nouns; their status as classifiers is semantic rather than morphosyntactic. As class 1 nouns, classifiers are obligatorily possessed; their possessors may be indexed by a lexical noun (as in (61), (65), and (67) below) or by a pronominal possessive suffix (as in (59), (60), (62)-(64), (66), and (68)-(75) below).

Noun classifier phrases (that is, combinations of a classifier and its obligatorily indexed possessor) are primarily used in Belep as an alternative to independent possession for class 4 nouns. That is, to indicate possession of some class 4 nouns—primarily those related to agriculture—speakers prefer to use a noun classifier phrase rather than the independent possessive construction. For example, rather than use independent possession (58) for the culturally important class 4 noun *uvi* 'yam' (§1.3), speakers prefer to indicate what the yam is to be used for with a noun classifier as in (59) and (60).

---

[13] A similar set occurs in Balade Nyelâyu (Ozanne-Rivierre 1998:39).

(58) **?uvi linao**
 uvi=li-nao
 yam=GEN-1SG.ABS
 '?my yam'

(59) **weeng uvi**
 we-nga   uvi
 food-1SG.POSS   yam
 'my yam (for eating)'

(60) **yaang uvi**
 ya-nga   uvi
 tuber-1SG.POSS   yam
 'my yam (for planting)'

Note that the examples in (59) and (60), and many constructions with noun classifiers, are complex noun phrases (§4.5), each consisting of a head noun (*weeng* and *yaang*, respectively) and a modifying noun (*uvi* 'yam'). They should not be considered compounds (see §3.7). In the rest of this section, I list each classifier and the types of nouns it classifies.

The classifier *â-* indicates a cutting or a seedling of a plant, as used in Belema agriculture. For example, *â nyang uvi* [cutting mother-my yam] in (61) means 'my mother's yam seedlings' (this clause was produced as a translation of the given phrase in French).

(61) *Te ten â nyang uvi yak.*
 te=   te-na   â   nya-nga
 3SG.SUBJ=   plant-DA.NSG   cutting   mother-1SG.POSS

 uvi   yak
 yam   yesterday
 Transl. of *Ma mère a planté ses ignames hier* 'My mother planted her yams yesterday.'

The classifier *ma-* indicates a plant that one intends to chew up, perhaps for the purpose of making medicine, as in (62).

(62) *mang yale, mang pawi*
 ma-nga   yale   ma-nga   pawi
 thing.to.chew-1SG.POSS   kudzu   thing.to.chew-1SG.POSS   hibiscus
 'my kudzu (to chew), my hibiscus (to chew)'

The classifier *nae-*, which is often used to mean 'child' as in (63), also refers to small things which belong to a person, such as a domino tile (64), a fish (65), or shoes (66).

(63)   ***pwadu naen âc,***
        pwadu   nae-na   âc
        two   small.thing-3SG.POSS   man
        'two sons' (lit. 'two small things of men')
                                                           Yal-20092011-AW1_0017

(64)   ***Na nawe naeng.***
        na=   nawe   nae-ng
        1SG.SUBJ=   leave   small.thing-1SG.POSS
        'I'm putting down my domino tile.' (lit. 'my small thing')
                                                  Yal-17092011-IM-dominoes

(65)   ***nae no pwalaic***
        nae   no   pwalaic
        small.thing   fish   one
        'a small fish' (lit. 'one small thing of fish')
                                                   Yal-01082010-MFD_0010

(66)   ***pwadu naeng ara kalooc ulo***
        pwadu   nae-ng   ara kaloya   ulo
        two   small.thing-1SG.POSS   shoe   red
        'my two small red shoes' (lit. 'my two small things of red shoes')
                                                           Yal-29072010-JMT.wav

The classifier *nyana-* refers to a big object, as in (67).

(67)   ***Texa puup va nyana waaga pwalaic,***
        te=xa   puv=a   nyana   waga   pwalaic
        3SG.SUBJ=ADD   swell=NOM   big.thing   boat   one
        'And a big boat popped up,'
                                                        Yal-19092011-PA_0033

The classifier *ûdu-*, which undergoes stem modification to *ûduu-* if the possessor is indexed by a singular pronominal suffix (§4.2.2.3), refers to a beverage which one intends to drink, as in (68).

(68) **ûduung weloo, ûduung we, ûduung lait**
      ûdu-nga   weloo   ûdu-nga   we
      beverage-1SG.POSS   coconut.water   beverage-1SG.POSS   water

      ûdu-nga   [le]
      beverage-1SG.POSS   milk.LN
      'my drink of coconut water, my drink of water, my drink of milk'

The classifier *wa-* refers to a sweet food which one intends to suck, as in (69).

(69) **wang ûjep, wang dowau**
      wa-nga   ûjep
      thing.to.suck-1SG.POSS   sugar.cane

      wa-nga   dowau
      thing.to.suck-1SG.POSS   sweet.coconut
      'my sugar cane (to suck), my sweet coconut[14] (to suck)'

The classifier *we-*, which undergoes stem modification to *wee-* if the possessor is indexed by a singular pronominal suffix (§4.2.2.3), is a general purpose classifier for any food which one intends to eat, as in (70) and (71).

(70) **ô nawen wela uvi,**
      ô   nawe-na   we-la   uvi
      REAL   leave-DA.NSG food-3PL.POSS   yam
      '[they] left their yams intended for eating,'
                                        Yal-28072010-BGMCG-igname_0073

(71) **ka tuvea ween ola,**
      ka   tuve-a   we-na   ola
      LK   dive.TR-DA.IN food-3SG.POSS shellfish
      'and dove for his lobster to eat,'
                                        Yal-28072010-BGMCG-tahitian_0018

---

[14] This is a particular variety of coconut called *coco sucré* 'sugar coco' in French; I have not been able to identify a common English name for it.

The classifier *ya-*, which undergoes stem modification to *yaa-* if the possessor is indexed by a singular pronominal suffix, refers to a starchy tuber. Included in this category are *bolao* 'bananas', *kumwala* 'sweet potatoes', *manyook* 'manioc/cassava', carrots, and yams as in (72).

(72) **La pae yala uvi,**
 la=   pa-e   ya-la   uvi
 3PL.SUBJ= take-SPC   tuber-3PL.POSS   yam
 'They took their tubers of yams,'
 Yal-28072010-BGMCG-igname_0032

The classifier *yava-* refers to one's harvest of food from the ocean, as in (73).

(73) **Ô jua koxo, yavale no,**
 ô   jua   koxo   yava-le   no
 REAL   very   lots   catch-3DU.POSS   fish
 'It was very large, their catch of fish,'
 Yal-20092011-AW1_0068

The classifier *yaya-* refers to unripe fruits which one intends to keep until they ripen, as in (74).

(74) **yayang bolao, yayang papayi, yayang maak**
 yaya-nga   bolao   **yaya-nga**   **papayi**
 unripe.thing-1SG.POSS   banana   unripe.thing-1SG.POSS   papaya.LN

 yaya-nga   **maak**
 unripe.thing-1SG.POSS   mango.LN
 'my unripe banana, my unripe papaya, my unripe mango'

The classifier *yae-* refers to a weapon, as in (75).

(75) **yaeng payi**
 yae-nga   **payi**
 weapon-1SG.POSS   tomahawk
 'my tomahawk'

4.2.5 Locative expressions using possessive constructions

Belep, like most New Caledonian languages (Ozanne-Rivierre 1997), frequently uses an intrinsic system of reference—where objects and events are located with respect to other objects (Levinson 2003:146-168)—in addition to its absolute system of reference for the conceptualization of space (§4.4.1). The possessive locatives which compose this system of reference are possessive noun phrases (§4.2.2) where the possessed noun serves the same function as an adposition—it expresses some kind of a relational or part-whole meaning. There is no distinction in Belep between 'adpositions' and nouns; this is a common cross-linguistic pattern, and is also found in Yagua and Swahili (Payne 1997:88). Some Belep nouns used in possessive locatives are shown in Table 13.

Tab. 13: Locative words

Locative noun	Gloss	Translation	Class
âbur	'uphill side'	'before'	4
ânu-, ânuu-[15]	'shadow, lee'	'beneath'	1
ara-	'base'	'at the bottom of'	1
arama-	'face'	'in front of'	1
bala-	'end, tip'	'at the end of'	1
boda-	'backside'	'at the back of'	1
bwe-, bwee-	'top'	'on'	1
bweroo	'underside'	'under'	4
mana-	'front, tip'	'at the front of'	1
mode-	'accompaniment'	'with'	1
mon	'downhill side'	'after'	4
na-	'interior'	'in'	1
pewo-	'middle'	'between'	1
pu-, puu-	'side'	'beside'	1

Possessive locatives are typically case-marked in discourse with the ditropic clitic =*la*, =*a* 'LOC'; see §6.4.5 for more information.

The most common possessive locatives are those where the possessed noun is *bwe-* 'top' or *na-* 'interior'. For example, in (76) the possessive locative is *bwe alap* 'the top of the beach/on the beach'.

(76) « *Bwa ponaoda la bwe alap.* »
      bwa=   po-nao=da=la   {bwe   alap}
      CONT=   load-1SG.ABS=DIR.UH=LOC   top   beach
      '"Please take me up onto the beach."'
                                              Yal-01082010-MFD_0033

In (77), the possessive locative is *bwe cae* 'the top of the reef/at the reef'.

---

[15] See §4.2.2.3 on stem modification for the type of possessor.

(77) **Ka uya la bwe cae la Bwadalo,**

ka	uya=la	{bwe	cae}=la	Bwadalo
LK	arrive=LOC	top	reef=LOC	Bwadalo

'And [they] arrived at the reef at Bwadalo,'

Yal-19092011-PA_0067

Example (78) uses the possessive locative *na mwa teâmaa* 'the inside of the chieftain's house/in the chieftain's house'.

(78) *ci la na mwa teâmaa.*

ci=la	{na	mwa	teâmaa}
sit=LOC	interior	house	high.chief

'[it] stayed in the chieftain's house.'

Yal-20092011-AW1_0273

Example (79) uses the possessive locative *na puluac* 'the inside of your language/within your language'.

(79) *yamayaap ma a comu la na puluac,*

yamayava	ma	a=	comu=la
concentrate	LK4	2PL.SUBJ=	learn=LOC

{na	pulu-ac}
interior	language-2PL.POSS

'[you must] concentrate on exploring your language,'

Yal-14092011-PT2-avenir_0019

Possessive locatives where the possessor noun is a class 1 noun (§4.2.1.1) differ from those where the possessor noun is a class 4 noun (§4.2.1.4), since the former set requires dependent possession (§4.2.2.1) while the latter set requires independent possession (§4.2.2.4). For example, the possessive locative *boda Poc* 'at the end of Poc' in (80) is a dependent possessive noun phrase, while the possessive locative *mon ni Paixa* 'after Easter' in (81) is an example of independent possession. Note that the locative nouns *âbur* 'uphill side' and *mon* 'downhill side' are most commonly used in discourse to index temporal, rather than spatial, locations, where *âbur* signifies 'before' and *mon* signifies 'after'.

(80) **Le mo la boda Poc.**

le=	mo=la	{boda	Poc}
3DU.SUBJ=	live=LOC	backside	Poc

'They lived at the end of Poc.'

Yal-19092011-PA_0004

(81) **Lame âmu ta la Pouébo la mon ni Paixa.**
    la=me   âmu=   ta=la   Pwewo=la
    3PL.SUBJ=IRR   PRF=   go.UH=LOC   Pouébo=LOC

    {mon=i   Paixa}
    side.DH=GEN   Easter.LN
    'They would go to Pouébo after Easter.'
                                    Yal-20092011-AW2_0069-0070

If the possessor noun phrase in a possessive locative is referred to anaphorically, it follows the same pattern as in other possessive noun phrases. A possessive suffix (§4.2.2.2) is used to index the possessor in dependent possession, and an absolutive suffix (§5.7) is used to index the possessor in independent possession.[16] For example, in (82), the possessive locative is *aran* 'its base/beneath it'; a possessive suffix is used since *ara-* is a class 1 noun (requiring dependent possession).

(82) **Ave nyi tuvadu la aran,**
    ave=   nyi=   tuva=du=la   {ara-n}
    1DU.EXCL.SUBJ= PUNCT=   dive=DIR.DH=LOC   under-3SG.POSS
    'We repeatedly dove under it [a stone],'
                                    Yal-28072010-BGMCG-tahitian_0057

In example (83), the possessive locative is the dependently possessed *nan* 'its interior/in it'; the possessive suffix *-n* is used to index the possessor of the class 1 noun *na-*.

(83) **Texa pan namadu la nan,**
    te=xa   pana   nama=du=la   {na-n}
    3SG.SUBJ=ADD   go.TV   enter=DIR.DH=LOC   interior-3SG.POSS
    'He went and disappeared down into it [a hole],'
                                    Yal-01082010-MFD_0059

4.3 Noun quantifiers

Like most Oceanic languages (Lynch et al. 2002:37), Belep does not have a category of inflectional number marking on nouns; nouns are invariant in form whether they

---

16 There are no examples of this in my corpus, since class 4 locative nouns are few and fairly infrequent.

refer to one or multiple referents. For example, the noun *buâny* 'stone' refers to a singular referent in (84) and multiple referents in (85).

(84) **mu la bwe buâny pwalaic.**
mu=la	bwe	buâny	pwalaic
moor=LOC	top	stone	one

'[we] moored at a stone.'

Yal-28072010-BGMCG-tahitian_0033

(85) **me âlalic mo buâny.**
me	âlalic	mo	buâny
IRR	be.impossible	LK3	stone

'they couldn't because of the stones.'

Yal-28072010-BGMCG-sousmarin_0111

As example (84) shows, if the number of a noun's referent must be specified, speakers can use a numeral (§4.6) or, under certain circumstances, a determiner suffix (§4.4.2). The grammatical number of a subject noun phrase may also be indicated by a subject agreement proclitic (§5.8).

However, there is a small set of inflectional[17] nominal suffixes, called 'noun quantifiers' in this work, which indicate the quantity of the noun to which they attach. These should be considered to mark the number-like category of collectives, as defined in Bickel & Nichols (2007), in that they "imply a number of individuals viewed as a set" (Bickel & Nichols 2007:227). These suffixes are: associative plural *-ma* 'AC', associative dual *-male* 'ADU', general extender *-mene* 'GE', and total *-roven* 'all'. The two former suffixes occasionally trigger stem modification in the noun to which they attach. The two latter suffixes also occur as verb group enclitics. These suffixes are not mutually exclusive and may be combined, as in (86) and (87). In (86), both *-roven* 'all' and *-mene* 'GE' are affixed to the demonstrative pronoun *yak* (§4.6.2).

(86) **Ô yaxarovenamene,**
ô	ya-xa-rovena-mene
REAL	DEM.LOC-DET.D.PRX-all-GE

'It was everywhere and stuff.'

Yal-28072010-BGMCG-tayamu_0228

In (87), both *-ma* 'AC' and *-roven* 'all' are affixed to the noun *âju* 'person'.

---

17 These suffixes are not prototypical examples of inflectional morphology; see §3.5.3.

(87) *Ka âjumaroven.*
 ka âju-ma-roven
 LK person-AC-all
 'And everyone.'
                                                    Yal-20092011-AW1_0053

4.3.1 Associative plural -*ma*

Associative number "is a distinct category of its own in a few languages" (Bickel & Nichols 2007:229). Moravcsik (1994) defines associative plural constructions as those which have the form 'X and X's associated person(s)', where X and X's associates form a semantically related group where the named referent X is the most prominent member of the group. Thus, associative plurals are "more akin to conjoined nominals than to ordinary morphological plurals" (Moravcsik 1994:471).

The noun suffix -*ma* 'AC' marks associative plural in Belep. It indexes a reified group which is semantically related to its host noun—a characteristic which contributes to its use in ethnonyms (§1.3). Example (88) below shows that -*ma* is clearly not a morphological plural; *Teâ Polo* is the chieftain of a village and there are not more than one of him. Instead, -*ma* is used to indicate the group of Teâ Polo and his subjects.

(88) *yamidu la pwemwa Teâ Poloma.*
 ya-midu=la   pwemwa   Teâ Polo-ma
 DEM.LOC-DET.D.DH=LOC village   Teâ Polo-AC
 'down there in the home of Teâ Polo [and his people]'
                                       Yal-28072010-BGMCG-sousmarin_0097

The correspondence between conjoined nominals and associative plurals is especially clear in Belep: associative -*ma* is likely etymologically related to the homophonous dependent linker *ma* (§7.3.2).

Associative plural -*ma* is used most commonly for humans, as in (89) and (90), where it attaches to *âju* 'person' and *ulac* 'old man', respectively.

(89) *Laxa tume la âjuma la mar,*
 la=xa   tu=me=la   âju-ma=la   mar
 3PL.SUBJ=ADD   go.DH=CTP=NOM   person-AC=LOC   seashore
 'And the people from the seashore came,'
                                                    Yal-19092011-PA_0069

(90)　**Ka ulayama, la âva li bu yeek.**
　　　ka　　ulaya-ma　　la=　　　　âva=li　　　bu　　　　yeek
　　　LK　　old.man-AC　3PL.SUBJ=　fish=GEN　fishhook　wood
　　　'And the ancestors, they fished with wooden fishhooks.'
　　　　　　　　　　　　　　　　　　　Yal-28072010-BGMCG-hamecon_0078-0079

Associative plural -*ma* may also be used for animate, nonhuman referents such as *polipoda* 'butterflies' in (91), and even for inanimate referents which are conceptualized as a set, as are the *dau* 'islets' (92) situated to the south of Belep's main island Art.

(91)　**Lame kova la polipodama,**
　　　la=me　　　　　　kova=la　　　　polipoda-ma
　　　3PL.SUBJ=IRR　　leave=NOM　　butterfly-AC
　　　'The butterflies will come out,'
　　　　　　　　　　　　　　　　　　　　　　　　　Yal-20092011-AW5_0054

(92)　**Dauma, la ci la Yade,**
　　　dau-ma　　la=　　　　　ci=la　　　　Yade
　　　islet-AC　　3PL.SUBJ=　sit=LOC　　Yade
　　　'The islets, they are in Yade,'
　　　　　　　　　　　　　　　　　　　　　　　　　Yal-20092011-AW6_0109

A few nouns (93) have irregular associative plural forms.

(93)　*tamwa* 'woman' > *ta-ma* 'woman-AC'
　　　pwairamwa 'girl' > *pwaira-ma* 'girl-AC'
　　　Belep 'Belep'　> *Bele-ma* 'Belep-AC'
　　　Cianup 'Cianup' > *Cianu-ma* 'Cianup-AC'

4.3.2 Associative dual -*male*

In addition to associative plurals (§4.3.2), some languages have associatives indicating other numbers (Corbett & Mithun 1996). Belep has an associative dual nominal suffix, -*male* 'ADU', which indicates that the referent of its host noun is a set of two like objects that are semantically related (i.e. a pair). As with associative plural -*ma*, associative dual -*male* most commonly occurs with a human referent, as in (94) and (95) where the host nouns are *nae-n* 'his children' and *ava-n* 'his sibling', respectively.

(94)   *Texa âri u le naenamale,*
         te=xa   âri   u=le   nae-na-male
         3SG.SUBJ=ADD   say   toward=DAT   child-3SG.POSS-ADU
         'And he said to his two children,'
                                                  Yal-20092011-AW1_0026-0027

(95)   *Le âma avanamale.*
         le=   âma=   ava-na-male
         3DU.SUBJ=   DYAD=   sibling-3SG.POSS-ADU
         'They were brothers.' (lit. 'a pair of siblings')
                                                  Yal-20092011-AW6_0004

Associative dual *-male* also occurs with inanimate nouns. For example, in (96), it marks *kan* 'his feet' and *en* 'his hands' as being members of a pair. Note that the subject agreement proclitic for both nouns is 3SG rather than dual; suffix *-male* is not a grammatical number marker.

(96)   *Te mwany nya kan, kanamale.*
         te=   mwany=a   ka-n   ka-na-male
         3SG.SUBJ=   be.bad=NOM   foot-3SG.POSS   foot-3SG.POSS-ADU

         Te pwai ô la enamale.
         te=   pwai   ô=la   e-na-male
         3SG.SUBJ=   only   be.good=NOM   hand-3SG.POSS-ADU
         'His legs were paralyzed, both his legs. Only his [pair of] hands worked.'
                                                  Yal-28072010-BGMCG-lune_0015-0016

In (97), the inanimate noun *toop* 'field' is marked as part of a pair with *-male*. Here it indicates that the fields are paired because of what is growing in them.

(97)   *La înae toovamale,*
         la=   îna-e   tova-male
         3PL.SUBJ=   make-SPC   field-ADU
         'They made those two types of field [taro and *kowe*, another variety of taro],'
                                                  Yal-20092011-AW6_0085

Nouns which have irregular associative plural forms (93) also have irregular associative dual forms (98).

(98)   *tamwa* 'woman'> *ta-male* 'woman-ADU'
         pwairamwa 'girl' > *pwaira-male* 'girl-ADU'

Another associative dual suffix -*le* exists in Belep as well, although it is not clear how this suffix differs from -*male*, which is much more common. Some examples of -*le* are shown in (99) and (100). In (99), the suffix -*le* is attached to the noun phrase *Teâ Belep* 'the chief of Belep' to indicate 'the chief of Belep and him; the two of them'.

(99)   ***Toma Teâ Belevale, le pe maraic, le pe or.***
       | toma | teâ | beleva-le | le= | pe= | maraic, |
       | but | Teâ | Belep-ADU | 3DU.SUBJ= | RECP= | resemble |

       | le= | pe= | or |
       | 3DU.SUBJ= | RECP= | phratry.Or |

       'But the chief of Belep and him, they are the same, they are both [of phratry] Or.'[18]

                                                                                                                         Yal-20092011-AW3_0026

In (100), the suffix -*le* is attached to the noun phrase *welen uvi* 'their yams to eat' to indicate that there are two members of the set.

(100)   ***ten welen uvile.***
        | te-na | we-lena | uvi-le |
        | plant-DA.NSG | food-3PA.POSS | yam-ADU |

        '[they] planted their two types of yams to eat.'

                                                                                                                          Yal-20092011-AW6_0141

4.3.3 General extender -*mene*

General extenders—that is, pragmatic expressions which are connected to sentence structure and somewhat inflexible in their syntactic distribution (Overstreet 2005:1846)—have been recorded in many languages, including, in the Pacific region, Japanese, Korean, and Hawaiian (Overstreet 1999:8).

In Belep, the nominal suffix -*mene* 'GE' serves as a general extender, identifying a category or set of entities similar to the referent of its host noun, while also serving an interpersonal function between speaker and hearer. In (101), the suffix -*mene* attaches to the host noun *uruâny* 'hurricane', indicating that it is not merely hurricanes, but a set of things related to bad weather that is being referred to.

---

[18] See §1.3 on phratries in New Caledonia.

(101) **Te îna uruânyamene,**
      te=   **îna**   **uruânya-mene**
      3SG.SUBJ=   make.GNR   hurricane-GE
      'He makes hurricanes and stuff,'
                                      Yal-28072010-BGMCG-sousmarin_0048

In (102), general extender *-mene* attaches to the host noun *alcool* 'alcohol', a French borrowing. Here it evokes a set of practices related to youth culture and drugs that are perceived in a negative light.

(102) **Âria kava le alcoolmene,**
      âria   **kava**   **le**   **[alkola]-mene**
      NEG.EX   kava.LN   LK2   alcohol.LN-GE
      'There's no kava or alcohol and stuff [on the Isle of Pines],'
                                                    Yal-27092011-LPLY

The suffix *-mene* is also used in (103), where it references all the parts of a boat that must be constructed before it is finished.

(103) **ka jibuuvamene,**
      ka   **jibuva-mene**
      LK   jib-GE
      'and the jib and stuff like that,'
                                                Yal-29072010-JMT-boats_0020

Note that *-mene* also occurs as a verb group suffix (§5.5.12).

4.3.4 Total *-roven*

The nominal suffix *-roven* 'all'—a grammaticalized form of the full verb *toven* 'to finish'—indicates that its host noun indexes the entire set of its referents. For instance, in (104), *-roven* is affixed to the noun *doo* 'earth', where it evokes the whole set of referents which *doo* indexes.

(104) **Lami kawu doo, kawu dooroven na Pairoome.**
      la-mi   **kawu**   **doo**   **kawu**   **do-roven=a**
      DEM.PL-DET.A.DST   guardian   earth   guardian   earth-all=LOC

> **Pairome**
> Pairoome
> 'Those who are stewards of the land, stewards of all the land in Pairoome.'
>
> Yal-20092011-AW6_0137

In (105), *-roven* is suffixed to *yadan* 'his belongings' to encompass a long list of more specific belongings (t-shirt, cigarettes, sandals) that had been previously mentioned.

(105)   **yadanaroven,**
        yada-na-roven
        belongings-3SG.POSS-all
        'all his belongings,'

Yal-28072010-BGMCG-tahitian_0166

In (106), *-roven* attaches to the host noun *da* 'blood', where it indicates totality of reference.

(106)   *La pan pan ka kiyi daroven,*
        la=   pana   pan   ka   kiyi   da-roven
        3PL.SUBJ= go.TV   go.TV   LK   see.SPC   blood-all
        'They went and saw all the blood,'

Yal-20092011-AW5_0086

Note that *-roven* also occurs as a verb group suffix (§5.5.11).

4.4 Determination and deixis

Nouns in Belep may be modified with a set of inflectional (§3.5.1) suffixes, identified in this work as 'determiners', which express a wide range of semantic distinctions in terms of spatio-temporal reference, including marking distance and direction. The unusual spatial system of Belep, which manifests in the determiner suffixes, is described in detail in §4.4.1. The suffixes themselves are discussed in §4.4.2. These determiners also affix to bound demonstrative pronominal stems (§4.6.2) to produce demonstrative pronouns. Additional types of determination in Belep are discussed in §4.4.3.

Belep determiners can only follow their head noun.[19] When a numeral (§4.7.2) or a demonstrative pronoun (§4.6.2) precedes a lexical noun, the lexical noun acts as a modifier; in a construction such as that shown in (107), the demonstrative pronoun *lami* is the head of the noun phrase (§4.5) and the lexical nouns *kawu doo* 'guardian of the earth' act as modifiers.

(107) **lami kawu doo,**
 la-mi kawu doo
 DEM.PL-DET.A.DST guardian earth
 'those [who are] guardians of the earth,'
 Yal-20092011-AW6_0137

This construction is not readily distinguishable—either syntactically or semantically[20]—from a relative clause headed by a relative pronoun (§7.4.3), as in (108).

(108) **Ka lami mo la bwe alap,**
 ka la-mi mo=la bwe alap
 LK DEM.PL-DET.A.DST live=LOC top beach
 'And those who live on the beach,'
 Yal-20092011-AW1_0052

4.4.1 Conceptualization of space

All New Caledonian languages share a typologically unusual spatial reference system (Ozanne-Rivierre 1997), an absolute system of reference (Levinson 2003:146-168)—where only one set of directional terms ('up' and 'down') is used to describe a variety of axes: inland/seaward, upstream/downstream, toward the coast/toward the seas, and inside/outside. The transverse axis ('across') does not have opposing sides. Cardinal- and speaker-reference spatial orientation is not used; the intrinsic frame of reference was discussed in §4.2.5.

In Belep, the absolute spatial system is realized in verbs of motion (Table 14) and their corresponding verb phrase directional (§5.12) and locational (§5.13) enclitics; and in nominal determiner suffixes (discussed below in §4.4.2).

---

19 This contrasts with both Nêlêmwa (Bril 2002) and Balade Nyelâyu (Ozanne-Rivierre 1998), where there are two sets of determiners: one set precedes the noun and is based on the demonstrative pronouns; the other set consists of nominal suffixes.
20 Relative clauses are most likely to have a lexical verb as in (108), but nouns can easily serve as predicate nominals (§6.5.1) as in (107).

Tab. 14: Spatial system of Belep

Verb	Gloss	Directional	Gloss	Locational	Gloss	Translation
ta	'to go.UH'	=da	'DIR.UH'	=(l)exeda	'LOC.UH'	uphill
				=(l)iyeda	'LOC.DST.UH'	
tu	'to go.DH'	=du	'DIR.DH'	=(l)exedu	'LOC.DH'	downhill
				=(l)imidu	'LOC.DST.DH'	
pan	'to go.TV'	=van	'DIR.TV'			transverse

The prototypical deictic center is located in the village of Waala for a speaker who is facing uphill toward the center of Art island. In this arrangement, they may *ta* 'go.UH' toward the church, *tu* 'go.DH' toward the ocean, or *pan* 'go.TV' to the left or right along the coast.

Figure 1 shows a photograph taken from the church door in Waala looking down toward the harbor. A speaker located at point A could move uphill and inland toward where the photo was taken, *ta* 'go.UH'. They could move downhill towards the water of the harbor, *tu* 'go.DH'. Or they could move to the left or right, *pan* 'go.TV'.

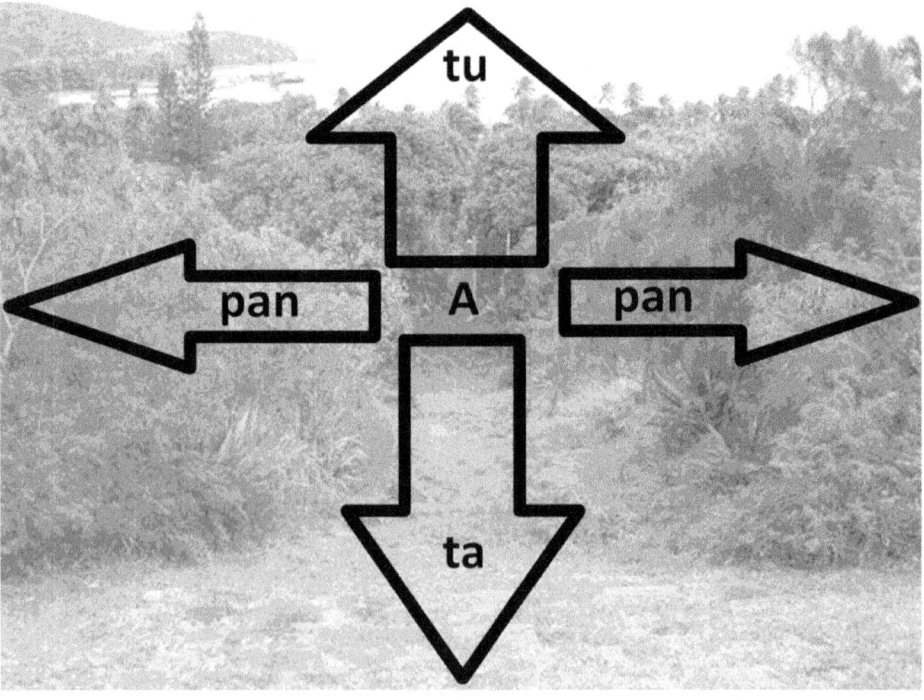

Fig. 1: View from the church in Waala, looking down towards the harbor

If the speaker is conceptualizing space in a larger, more abstract way (perhaps for a trip that will take longer than 20 minutes to walk), they may *ta* 'go.UH' to the southeast, into the prevailing winds, *tu* 'go.DH' to the northwest, away from the prevailing winds, or *pan* 'go.TV' across the islands, perpendicular to the winds (Figure 2).

Fig. 2: Map of Belep showing spatial directions

Figure 2 shows a map of Belep, where, starting in Waala, one would *ta* to travel to Âjeeni in the southeast, *tu* to visit Poc in the northwest, and *pan* to traverse the mountain range and visit Bweo on the northeast coast. In the same vein, if a person is going to leave New Caledonia altogether, they will *tu* 'go.DH' and then *ta* 'go.UH' to return again.

4.4.2 Determiner suffixes

Belep nouns may be modified with a deictic, anaphoric, or interrogative determiner suffix, which marks the proximity and direction of its host noun. These suffixes are shown in Table 15.

Tab. 15: Determiner suffixes

Deictic	Gloss	Anaphoric	Gloss
-k	'DET.D.PRX'	-li	'DET.A.PRX'
-na	'DET.D.MPX'	-mi	'DET.A.DST'
-yek	'DET.D.MDS'		
-xe	'DET.D.DST'		
-xeda	'DET.UH'	**Interrogative**	**Gloss**
-xedu	'DET.DH'	-va	'DET.Q1'
-yeda	'DET.DST.UH'	-da	'DET.Q2'
-midu	'DET.DST.DH'	-ra	'DET.Q3'

Belep determiners are divided into deictic and anaphoric sets. The deictic set (§4.4.2.1), used for spatial deixis, distinguishes the referent's direction and distance from the speaker at the moment of speaking, while the anaphoric set (§4.4.2.2) distinguishes the recentness of identification of the referent in discourse and is used for temporal and discourse deixis. Belep interrogative determiners (§4.4.2.3) are used to question these attributes. Demonstrative pronominal stems (§4.6.2) require an attached determiner suffix.

As affixes (§3.2.2.5), the determiner suffixes trigger stem modifications in their host noun, such as vowel gemination[21] (109) or epenthetic vowel insertion (110).

---

[21] The vowel gemination in the stem provoked by the proximal suffix *-k* is irregular and unpredictable.

(109) | *tamwa* | *tamwaak*
 | **tamwa** | **tamwaa-k**
 | woman | woman-DET.D.PRX
 | 'woman' | 'this woman'

(110) | *ulac* | *ulayixeda*
 | **ulac** | **ulayi-xeda**
 | old.man | old.man-DET.UH
 | 'old man' | 'that old man up there'

The determiner suffixes are not clitics (§3.2.2.6); they attach directly to their host noun rather than to the noun phrase as a whole (§4.6). For example, in the noun phrase *âyili avan* 'that brother of his' (lit. 'that man his brother') in (111), the determiner suffix *-li* is attached to the head noun *âc* 'man' rather than to the end of the noun phrase.

(111) *Teme cao ma teme gier ri âyili avan.*

te=me	cao	ma	te=me	gi-er=i
3SG.SUBJ=IRR	work	LK4	3SG.SUBJ=IRR	attack-3SG.OBJ=GEN

{âyi-li ava-n}
man-DET.A.PRX sibling-3SG.POSS
'That brother of his would try to kill him.'

Yal-20092011-AW6_0035

4.4.2.1 Deictic determiners
The deictic determiners, which are used in spatial deixis, are listed in Table 16.

Tab. 16: Deictic determiners

	Suffix	Gloss	
Positional	-k	'DET.D.PRX'	proximal
	-na	'DET.D.MPX'	medial-proximal
	-yek	'DET.D.MDS'	medial-distal
	-xe	'DET.D.DST'	distal
Dimensional	-xeda	'DET.UH'	uphill
	-xedu	'DET.DH'	downhill
	-yeda	'DET.DST.UH'	distal uphill
	-midu	'DET.DST.DH'	distal downhill

They are divided into positional and dimensional systems of reference, where both indicate the position but only the latter indicates the orientation of the interlocutors.

The first four determiners can be classified as belonging to the positional system of reference, which "localizes areas in space in relation to, and dependent on, the speaker's or the hearer's position" (Senft 1997:2). There is a four-way distinction between proximal -*k*, medial-proximal -*na*, medial-distal -*yek*, and distal -*xe*. A very similar system of positional reference is found in the Mon-Khmer language Jahai (Burenhult 2004). In Belep, proximal suffix -*k* indicates proximity to the speaker, as in (112) where -*k* is suffixed to *mar* 'seashore'.

(112)   « *Yome ta ka ulinao la mariik,* »
   yo=me   ta=xa   uli-nao=la
   2SG.SUBJ=IRR   go.UH=LK   pour-1SG.ABS=LOC

   marii-<u>k</u>
   seashore-DET.D.PRX
   '"You will go up and let me out on this seashore,"'
                                      Yal-28072010-BGMCG-tahitian_0136

Medial-proximal suffix -*na* indicates proximity to the addressee, or to "any location away from the speaker that is not saliently within the system of orientation" (Burenhult 2004:89). An example is shown in (113), where -*na* is suffixed to *tamwa* 'woman' to indicate that its referent is closer to the addressee than to the speaker.

(113)   « *Yome ta ka âri u le tamwana*
       yo=me   ta=xa   âri   u=le   tamwa-<u>na</u>
       2SG.SUBJ=IRR   go.UH=LK   say   toward=DAT   woman-DET.D.MPX

       me âyuang ngi yawang ngie. »
       me   âyua-ng=i   yawa-ng=i-e
       IRR   desire-1SG.POSS=GEN   wife-1SG.POSS=GEN-3SG.ABS
       '"You will go and say to that woman that I want to make her my wife."'
                                                                         Yal-20092011-AW1_0176

Medial-distal suffix *-yek* indicates a location a short distance away from both speaker and addressee, as in (114), where *-yek* is attached to the generically possessed noun *maya-r* 'side, part'.

(114)   *Texa, te nam ma mayariyek,*
       te=xa   te=   nam=a
       3SG.SUBJ=ADD   3SG.SUBJ=   appear=LOC

       maya-ri-<u>yek</u>
       part-3GNR.POSS-DET.D.MDS
       'And he, he appeared on that side [of the rock],'
                                                     Yal-28072010-BGMCG-tahitian_0087

Distal suffix *-xe* indicates a location further away from the speaker and addressee. For example, in (115), the addressee is the daughter of the character animated by the speaker, while the *tawma* 'woman' in question has been spotted in the distance.

(115)   « *Jime to ji tamwaxe.* »
       ji=me   to   ji   tamwa-<u>xe</u>
       1DU.INCL.SUBJ=IRR   call   give   woman-DET.D.DST
       'Let's call to that woman.'
                                                               Yal-20092011-AW1_0143

The last four determiners are part of the dimensional system of reference, which "defines relations in space dependent on the speaker's or hearer's position *and* orientation" (Senft 1997:2). The suffixes *-xeda* and *-xedu* both indicate direction (either 'uphill' or 'downhill') and a position within the "perceived space of speaker and hearer" (Senft 1997:2), while *-yeda* and *-midu* indicate direction and a position outside of the speaker's perceived space. Similar systems are found in some Papuan languages (Kryk-Kastovsky 1996:336) including Eipo (Heeschen 1982:84). Some Belep examples are shown in (116) - (119). In (116), the suffix *-xeda* is attached to the host noun *janeng* 'my ear', here distinguishing the ear which is on top when the speaker lies on his side from the ear on the bottom.

(116) « *Me ala janengixeda*, »
 me   ala   jane-ngi-<u>xeda</u>
 IRR   husk   ear-1SG.POSS-DET.UH
 '[It would be] my top earlobe,'

 Yal-05092011-AP1_0078

In (117), the suffix *-xedu* is attached to *ulac* 'old man', indicating that the old man in question is located within the speaker's perceived space; he lived nearby.

(117) *Avexa pae waga ulayixedu, digi.*
 ave=xa   pa-e   waga   ulayi-<u>xedu</u>   digi
 1DU.EXCL.SUBJ=ADD   take-SPC   boat   old.man-DET.DH   canoe
 'We would take this old man down there's boat, a canoe.'

 Yal-28072010-BGMCG-tahitian_0013

In (118), suffix *-yeda* indicates that its host noun *âju* 'person' is located outside the speaker's perceived space.

(118) « *Yo kiyi âjuyeda, teme perdu.* »
 yo=   kiyi   âju-<u>yeda</u>
 2SG.SUBJ=   see.SPC   person-DET.DST.UH

 te=me   [peʁdy]
 3SG.SUBJ=IRR   lost.LN
 '"You see that person up there, he's going to get lost."'

 Yal-28072010-BGMCG-tahitian_0074

In (119), *-midu* is suffixed to the generically possessed noun *ola-r* 'piece'.

(119) BG: *Texa wali. Ô maac ya,*
 te=xa   wa-li   ô   may=a
 3SG.SUBJ=ADD   DEM.MAN-DET.A.PRX   REAL   die=NOM
 'And it was like that. [They] died,'

CG: **_maac ya olarimidu,_**
may=a   ola-ri-midu
die=NOM   piece-3GNR.POSS-DET.DST.DH
'that part [of the population] down there died,'
                                    Yal-28072010-BGMCG-sousmarin_0103-0104

4.4.2.2 Anaphoric determiners

There are two anaphoric determiner suffixes in Belep which are used for temporal and discourse deixis: proximal *-li* and distal *-mi*. Suffix *-li* indicates that the referent of its host noun has recently been mentioned in discourse, or has just appeared or occurred within the speaker's frame of reference. For example, in (120), the noun *no* 'fish' is first introduced in line 1 in the noun phrase *nae no pwalaic* 'a small fish'. In line 3, *-li* occurs as a suffix on *no* 'fish' to indicate that this is the same fish that has just been mentioned. This is an example of discourse deixis.

(120)   *La âvae nae no pwalaic.*
        la=   âva-e   nae   no   pwalaic
        3PL.SUBJ=   fish-SPC   small.thing   fish   one

2   *Ka mon, ka mon texa maac yi cawi,*
        ka   mon   ka   mon   te=xa
        LK   side.DH   LK   side.DH   3SG.SUBJ=ADD

        may=i   cawi
        die=GEN   hunger

3   *ka bae noli, ka bae wagale,*
        ka   bae   no-li   ka   bae   waga-le
        LK   bite   fish-DET.A.PRX   LK   bite   boat-3DU.POSS
        'A small fish was caught. And then, and then he [the rat] was hungry, and he ate that fish and ate their boat,'
                                              Yal-01082010-MFD_0010-0013

Another example of *-li*, here indicating temporal deixis, is shown in (121). A moment in time is identified in lines 1-2, and then indexed twice in line 3 with the demonstrative pronoun *nyali* (§4.6.2).

(121)   *Ka Nêlêmwa, te to ji Teâ Belep,*
        ka   Nêlêmwa   te=   to   ji   Teâ Belep
        LK   Nêlêmwa   3SG.SUBJ=   call   give   Teâ Belep

2   *ma te tame yagelie ma le wayap.*
ma=re	ta=me	yage-li-e	ma
LK4=3SG.SUBJ	go.UH=CTP	help-TR-3SG.ABS	LK4

le=	wayap
3DU.SUBJ=	war

3   *Toma nyali, nyali te ta la Teâ Belep,*
toma	nya-li	nya-li
but	DEM.IDF-DET.A.PRX	DEM.IDF-DET.A.PRX

te=	ta=la	Teâ Belep
3SG.SUBJ=	go.UH=NOM	Teâ Belep

       'And Nêlêmwa, he called Teâ Belep, so that he would come and help him with the war. But then, when Teâ Belep went up,'

       Yal-20092011-AW3_0038-0039

The anaphoric suffix *-mi* is used for referents that are New or identifiable—that is, textually or situationally evoked, or inferable by logical reasoning (Prince 1981:236). For example, (122) shows a discourse deictic use of *-mi* with the host noun *âc* 'man'. The clause immediately prior to (122) in the narrative stated that the chieftain had five children; the introduction of the oldest son in (122) is thus textually evoked.

(122) *Âyimi ulac, ka naran ni Teâ.*
âyi-**mi**	ulac	ka	nara-n=i	Teâ
man-DET.A.DST	be.old	LK	name-3SG.POSS=GEN	Teâ

       'The oldest son, his name was Teâ.'

       Yal-20092011-AW1_0014-0015

In (123), suffix *-mi* is used to indicate that the referent of its host noun, *âc* 'man', is not the one most recently mentioned but the one mentioned 'formerly'. Prior to the utterance in (123), the speaker has introduced the two characters, Belep and Coigo.

(123) *Le âma avan. Ka Coigo ka teâ.*
le=	âma=	ava-n	ka	Coigo
3DU.SUBJ=	DYAD=	sibling-3SG.POSS	LK	Coigo

ka	teâ
LK	eldest.son

Te ulac, teâ. Toma âyimi, Belep, te mweyau.

te=	ulac	teâ	toma	âyi-**mi**	Belep
3SG.SUBJ=	be.old	eldest.son	but	man-DET.A.DST	Belep

te=	mweyau
3SG.SUBJ=	second.son

'They were brothers. And Coigo, he was the eldest. He was older, the eldest. But that man, Belep, he was the second son.'

Yal-20092011-AW6_0012

An example of the contrast between *-li* and *-mi* is found in (124). Both are attached to the host noun *gawaar* 'day'; *-li* is used as discourse deixis to refer to a day that the speaker has just referenced; then *-mi* is used as temporal deixis to refer to a different day.

(124) *Avenaô mo li gawaarili, ka gawaarimi la mon,*

avena=ô	mo=li	gawari-**li**	ka
1TR.EXCL.SUBJ=REAL	live=GEN	day-DET.A.PRX	LK

gawari-**mi**=la	mon
day-DET.A.DST=LOC	side.DH

'We stayed that day, and the day after,'

Yal-17072009-TB-weekend_0037

In (124), the speaker uses *-li* to refer to a day that she had just been referencing. Then she uses *-mi* to refer to a different day, one that is logically inferable from discourse but has not yet been mentioned. It is thus further away in the speaker's and hearer's consciousness, though it is temporally closer to the moment of speech.

4.4.2.3 Interrogative determiners

There are three interrogative determiners in Belep. Suffix *-va*, glossed 'DET.Q1' with the meaning of 'which', is used to question a distinction between referents in a given set. For example, in (125), suffix *-va* is used in the demonstrative pronoun *nyava* (§4.6.2).

(125) MT: *Bubuc, bwaan.*

bubuc	bwaa-n
unripe	head-3SG.POSS

'Green, its head.'

TM: ***Nyava ?***
   nya-va
   DEM.IDF.DET.Q1
   'Which one?'

MT: ***Nyak.***
   nya-k
   DEM.IDF-DET.D.PRX
   'This one.'

Yal-05102010-MTAD_25:42-25.50

The exchange in (125) occurs in the context of a card game. TM uses *nyava* to ask which of MT's cards she is referring to.

· Suffix *-da* 'DET.Q2' is used to question the attributes of a referent that has not yet been introduced. For example, in (126), *-da* is used to ask what the addressee will use for a *tala-* 'bed', which is a New referent in this context.

(126) « ***Me talamwada?*** »
   me   tala-mwa-da?
   IRR   bed-2SG.POSS-DET.Q2
   '"What will you use for a bed?"'

Yal-05092011-AP1_0076

Suffix *-ra* 'DET.Q3' is used to ask 'what type' and is used primarily to question plant and animal species, e.g. (127).

(127) ***Nora ?***
   no-ra
   fish-DET.Q3
   'What type of fish?'

4.4.3 Other determiners

Determination in Belep is not limited to nominal suffixes. Demonstrative pronouns (§4.6.2) and some nouns can also serve the function of determiners.

In many cases, demonstrative pronouns are used as determiners (in this function, they are identified as 'demonstrative determiners' in this work). They follow the noun they modify as in (128), where the demonstrative determiner *lali* modifies the head noun *âjuma* 'people', and (129) where the demonstrative determiner *leli* modifies the head noun *âwurama* 'waves'.

(128) **Ti li âjuma lali ?**
   ti=li   âju-ma   la-li
   who=GEN   person-AC   DEM.PL-DET.A.PRX
   'Who are those people?'

   Yal-20092011-AW6_0079

(129) **âbur ri âwurama leli**
   âbur=i   âwura-ma   le-li
   side.UH=GEN   wave-AC   DEM.DU-DET.A.PRX
   'before those waves'

   Yal-09082010-JMTresponse_0017

Demonstrative determiners are used primarily, and possibly exclusively, with nouns marked as associative plural (§4.3.1). In my corpus, there are only marginal counter-examples, such as in (130) where, in line 2, the demonstrative pronoun *nyami* follows the noun *pawi* 'hibiscus', which is unmarked for quantity. However, an intonation break occurs between the two words.

(130) « *Name tawae nyana wîna pawi,* »
   na=me   tawa-e   nyana
   1SG.SUBJ=IRR   cut-SPC   big.thing

   wî-na   pawi
   DEM.IA-DET.D.MPX   hibiscus

2   *pawi, nyami cuur ra alap.*
   pawi   nya-mi   cur=a   alap
   hibiscus   DEM.IDF-DET.A.DST   stand=LOC   beach
   '"I'm going to cut down that big hibiscus," hibiscus, the one that stands on the beach.'

   Yal-20092011-AW6_0070-0071

One exceptional use of demonstrative determiners occurs with the inanimate demonstrative pronominal stem *mwi-*, *wî-*, which has other irregularities as well (see §4.6.2). A demonstrative determiner may modify a demonstrative pronoun head if that head contains the stem *mwi-*, *wî-* as in (131). However, the form **mwi-ma*, **wî-ma* cannot occur without a following demonstrative determiner.

(131) **Wîma lami le pa, le pin.**
wî-ma la-mi le= pa
DEM.IA-AC DEM.PL-DET.A.DST 3DU.SUBJ= take.GNR

le= pi-n
3DU.SUBJ= cook-DA.NSG
'What they caught, they cooked.'
Yal-20092011-AW1_0087

In Nêlêmwa (Bril 2002) and Balade Nyelâyu (Ozanne-Rivierre et al. 1998), constructions analogous to the Belep demonstrative determiners are analyzed as determiner suffixes beginning with -*ma*, rather than as demonstrative determiners following an associative plural noun (§4.3.1). If this analysis were posited for Belep, it would necessitate adding the determiner suffixes shown in (132) to the list in §4.4.2. Forms unattested in my corpus are marked with '?').

(132)
	DUAL	PAUCAL	PLURAL
	?-maleek	-malenyiik	-malaak
	?-malena	?-malenyina	-malana
	?-maleyek	?-malenyiyek	-malayek
	?-malexe	?-malenyixe	?-malaxe
	?-malexeda	?-malenyixeda	-malaxeda
	?-malexedu	?-malenyixedu	?-malaxedu
	?-maleyeda	?-malenyiyeda	-malayeda
	?-malemidu	?-malenyimidu	?-malamidu
	-maleli	?-malenyili	-malali
	?-malemi	?-malenyimi	-malami

There is some evidence in Belep for this analysis: I have found no clear examples of demonstrative determiners modifying nouns unmarked for quantity (see (130) above), and speaker intuition is that constructions such as *âjuma lali* 'those people' should be written without an orthographic space. Furthermore, many speakers (particularly younger speakers) are likely to phonetically alter constructions such as *âjuma lali* to [ãⁿɟuᵐblali]. Finally, the demonstrative pronominal stem *mwi-*, *wî-* for inanimates cannot stand alone as associative plural **mwi-ma*, but *mwima lami* is attested and commonly occurs (131).

Despite this evidence, I have chosen to analyze these constructions in Belep as demonstrative pronouns functioning as determiners, which can only follow an associative plural noun. I base this analysis on the fact that most of the hypothetical determiner suffixes in (132) are unattested in my corpus; the infrequency of this collocation (especially compared to the frequency of the determiner suffixes discussed in

§4.4.2) suggests a syntactic rather than a morphological analysis. Furthermore, the demonstrative determiners are able to stand alone as the head of a noun phrase in many other contexts (§4.6.2), while forms beginning with *-ma* cannot serve this function.

In addition to demonstrative determiners, some nouns can serve the function of determiners. The cardinal numeral *pwalaic* 'one' (which falls into the word class of nouns) has grammaticalized into an indefinite article (see §4.7.2). The noun *avar* 'other' (133) can function as a determiner for another noun, as in (134) where its head noun is *ulayili* 'that old man'.

(133) ***Avar, la baela li nic.***
   avar **la**   **bae-la=li**   **nic**
   other 3PL.SUBJ= bite.SPC-3PL.ABS=GEN shark
   'Others, sharks ate them.'
                   Yal-20092011-AW2_0049

(134) ***Te wali la ulayili avar.***
   te=   **wa-li=la**   **ulayi-li**   **avar**
   3SG.SUBJ= DEM.MAN-DET.A.PRX=NOM old.man-DET.A.PRX other
   'That other old man said thusly.'
                   Yal-20092011-AW1_0262

4.5 The noun phrase

A noun phrase in Belep consists minimally of a head noun (or pronoun; see §4.6). The head noun may be a lexical noun, a noun classifier (§4.2.4), a locative noun (§4.2.5), a numeral (§4.7), a demonstrative pronoun (§4.6.2), etc. It may be marked inflectionally to indicate its possessor (§4.2.2), quantity (§4.3), and/or determination (§4.4.2). It may be followed by any number of other nouns, including numerals (§4.7) and determiners (§4.4.3), and/or semantically dependent (§7.3) or relative (§7.4) clauses, which act as modifiers for the head noun. This order of elements is shown in (135). See §6.2 for more on basic word order in Belep.

(135) HEAD NOUN(-POSSESSOR)(-QUANTITY/-DETERMINER) (+ POSSESSOR NP) (+ MODIFYING NP(S)/CLAUSES)

Noun phrase constituency is discussed in §4.5.1. Multiple noun phrases may be conjoined using a reduced set of linkers (§3.3.4), which vary somewhat in their meaning depending on whether they conjoin noun phrases or clauses (see chapter 7). The binomial linker *le* (§4.5.2) can only be used to conjoin noun phrases. Other linkers, such as *ka* (§4.5.3), *ai* (§4.5.4), and *ma* (§4.5.5, §4.5.6), may be used to conjoin both noun phrases and clauses.

4.5.1 Noun phrase constituency

Some examples of noun phrases are shown in (136) - (139). Noun phrases may be nested inside each other, as the brackets {} in these examples show, but there is no strict 'left-branching' or 'right-branching' rule for this nesting. Modifying nouns or noun phrases may occur in a variety of orders following the head noun, which is always initial. In (136), the head noun is *pwemwa* 'village, home'.

(136) **pwemwa ulayili Cebaba.**
{pwemwa   {ulayi-li   Cebaba}}
village   old.man-DET.A.PRX   Cebaba
'the home of that old man Cebaba.'

Yal-20092011-AW1_0231

In (137), the head noun is *ola-* 'piece'.

(137) **ola we teâmaa wan,**
{ola   {{we   teâma}   wan}}
piece   food   high.chief sea.turtle
'the chief's portion of sea turtle to eat,'

Yal-20092011-AW5_0063

In (138), the head noun is *pwemwa* 'village, home'.

(138) **pwemwa la na we la yaxe la bweerada li Poc.**
{{pwemwa=la   {na   we}}=la
village=LOC   interior   water=LOC

{ya-xe=la   {bwe-ra=da=li   Poc}}}
DEM.LOC-DET.D.DST=LOC   top-3GNR.POSS=DIR.UH=GEN   Poc
'a village in the water over there on the upper side of Poc.'

Yal-28072010-BGMCG-hamecon_0067

In (139), the head noun is *gawaar* 'day'.

(139)   ***gawaar ri ci va oreâ naerama li comu,***
       {**gawar=i**   {**ci=va**   {**oreâ**
       day=GEN   sit=INSTR   breath

       nae-ra-ma}=li   **comu}}**
       child-3GNR.POSS-AC=GEN   learn
       'the children's school vacation days,' (lit. 'the days of sitting with the children's breath from learning')[22]
                                           Yal-17072009-TB-weekend_0037-0038

Noun phrase constituents (including relative clauses; see §7.4) typically do not cross intonation unit boundaries, and they can serve alone as an intonation unit. Noun phrases may act as the topic of a clause, as *buâny* 'stone' does in (140).

(140)   « ***Mo buâny, ka banemw,*** »
       mo   {**buâny**}   **ka**   **bane-mw**
       LK3   stone   LK   friend-2SG.POSS
       '"Well, a stone, it's your friend,"'
                                                 Yal-20092011-AW1_0261

They may serve as predicate nominals (as does the independent pronoun *nao* in (141)) or as the answer to a question-word question (as does the demonstrative pronoun *yaxedu* in (142)).

(141)   « ***Êê, tere nao,*** »
       êê   **te=re**   **nao**
       yes   3SG.SUBJ=ACT   1SG.INDEP
       '"Yes, it's actually me,"'
                                                 Yal-20092011-AW1_0283

(142)   MT: ***Teme ci liva ?***
                 te=me   **ci=liva**
                 3SG.SUBJ=IRR   sit=LOC.Q
               'Where does it go?'

---

22 The phrase *ci=va oreâ-* [sit=INSTR breath] 'to sit with one's breath' is used idiomatically to mean 'to rest'. The verb *comu* 'to learn' is sometimes used as a noun to mean 'schooling'.

TM: ***Yaxedu.***
ya-xedu
DEM.LOC-DET.DH
'Down there.'

Yal-05102010-MTAD_31:49-31:52

Noun phrases may also serve as the argument of a clause, where they are marked for case with a ditropic clitic case marker (see §6.4). Only one case marker is used for the entire noun phrase, as shown in example (143), where the nominative case marker =*la* (§6.4.2) introduces the noun phrase *tamwali Kawo* 'that woman Kawo'.

(143) ***Texa ta la tamwali Kawo,***
te=xa	**ta=la**	**tamwa-li**	**Kawo**
3SG.SUBJ=ADD	go.UH=NOM	woman-DET.A.PRX	Kawo

'And that woman Kawo went up,'

Yal-20092011-AW1_0166-0167

Multiple noun phrases may be conjoined with linkers *le* 'LK3', *ka* 'LK', *ai* 'or', and *ma* 'LK4' (see chapter 7 for more information). The following sections discuss these linkers.

4.5.2 Binomial linker *le*

Belep binomial linker *le*, glossed as LK2, is used to conjoin two (and only two) noun phrases which are conceptualized as similar or related, forming a pair. This type of conjunction is identified as "natural conjunction" by Haspelmath (2007:23), and cross-linguistically it is often limited to occurrence with only two coordinands. In Belep, naturally conjoined coordinands are more tightly phonologically linked than in other types of conjunction (though not closely enough to qualify as a coordinative compound (Wälchli 2003)); the first coordinand in natural conjunction always appears in incomplete phase (see §2.5.2), while in other forms of conjunction this phase shift is optional. Some examples are given in (144) - (146).

(144) ***nyale le camale***
nya-le	**le**	**cama-le**
mother-3DU.POSS	LK2	father-3DU.POSS

'their mothers and fathers'

Yal-17072009-TB-weekend_0034

(145) **têno le yâgak**
 têno **le** **yâgak**
 type.of.shell LK2 spider.conch
 'shells and spider conchs'
 Yal-19092011-PA_0010

(146) **teâ le mweau**
 teâ **le** **mweau**
 first.son LK2 second.son
 '[the chief's] first son and second son'
 Yal-20092011-AW6_0007

If speakers conjoin additional noun phrases after the two noun phrases conjoined with *le*, the additive linker *ka* must be used, as in (147).

(147) **Kawo le Ixe ka Jegoloc**
 Kawo **le** **Ixe** **ka** **Jegoloc**
 Kawo LK2 Ixe LK Jegoloc
 'Kawo and Ixe, and Jegoloc'[23]
 Yal-20092011-AW1_0041

Any other linker is ungrammatical, as in (148).

(148) **Le ta la camang le nyang (ka/*ma) avang.**
 le= **ta=la** **cama-nga** **le** **nya-ng**
 3DU.SUBJ= go.UH=NOM father-1SG.POSS LK2 mother-1SG.POSS

 ka (*ma) **ava-ng**
 LK (*LK4) sibling-1SG.POSS
 'My father and my mother, and my sibling, went.'
 Yal-03112011-IM1.wav – Yal-03112011-IM2.wav

4.5.3 Noun phrase coordinator *ka* 'and'

Additive linker *ka* 'LK' (§7.2.1), which is often used to conjoin clauses, is also used to conjoin noun phrases—any number of them—in a list. For example, in (149) two noun phrases (marked with brackets {}) are conjoined with *ka*, while in (150), four noun phrases are conjoined with *ka*.

---

[23] The proper name *Kawo* is traditionally given to the chieftain's eldest daughter. *Ixe* is the name of the chieftain's second daughter. *Jegoloc* is the name given to the youngest child.

(149) ***pwairamwa pwalaic ka nae- pabong âc pwalaic,***

{pwairamwa	pwalaic}	ka	{nae	pabo-nga
girl	one	LK	small.thing	grandchild-1SG.POSS

âya	pwalaic}
male	one

'one daughter and my little grandson,'

Yal-17072009-TB-weekend_0030

(150) ***Na pa claquettes, ka pae terixo ka cixare, ka allumettes, ka yadan.***

na=	pa	claquettes	ka	pa-e	{terixo}
1SG.SUBJ=	take	flipflops.LN	LK	take-SPC	tshirt.LN

ka	{cixare}	ka	{allumettes}	ka	{yada-n}
LK	cigarettes.LN	LK	matches.LN	LK	belongings-3SG.POSS

'I took flip-flops, and took the t-shirt, cigarettes, matches, and his belongings.'

Yal-28072010-BGMCG-tahitian_0142-0145

The use of linker *ka* is not necessary to conjoin noun phrases in a list; noun phrases can be conjoined without any overt marker. In (151), only intonation breaks are used between the coordinands. However, conjunction with *ka* is more common (152).

(151) ***Te bae taro, bolao, uvi.***

te=	bae	{taro}	{bolao}	{uvi}
3SG.SUBJ=	eat	taro	banana	yam

'S/he eats taro, bananas, yams.'

(152) ***Te bae taro ka bolao ka uvi.***

te=	bae	taro	ka	bolao	ka	uvi
3SG.SUBJ=	eat	taro	LK	banana	LK	yam

'S/he eats taro and bananas and yams.'

Yal-03112011-IM1.wav – Yal-03112011-IM2.wav

The functional difference between conjunction with and without the overt linker *ka* requires further study. Linker *ka* is the only linker which may be optionally omitted.

4.5.4 Disjunctive linker *ai* 'or'

The disjunctive linker *ai* (§7.2.2) is used to coordinate both noun phrases and clauses. In noun phrase coordination, *ai* 'or' indicates that the noun phrases it disjoins are possible alternatives for one another. The only example of noun phrase disjunction in my corpus is shown in example (153), where *ai* disjoins the noun phrases *yo* '2SG.INDEP' and *ti* 'who?'.

(153) « *Jua yo ai ti? Kawo?* »
 jua   {yo}   ai   {ti}   Kawo
 truly 2SG.INDEP   or   who?   Kawo
 '"Is it really you or who? Kawo?"'

 Yal-20092011-AW1_0282

4.5.5 Inclusory *ma* 'with'

Linker *ma* 'LK4' is used to conjoin both noun phrases and clauses (§7.3.2). In most cases where *ma* conjoins noun phrases, it is used as an inclusory linker. Inclusory noun phrase conjunction is defined as conjunction where "the result of the conjunction is not the union, but the *unification* of the sets. That is, if some members of the second conjunct set are already included in the first conjunct set, they are not added to the resulting set" (Haspelmath 2007:33). When Belep linker *ma* is used to link noun phrases, the second element (called the 'included conjunct') is subordinated to, and included in, the first element, called the 'inclusory conjunct' (which is typically a nonsingular independent pronoun[24]). This also occurs in Nêlêmwa; Bril (2004a) refers to it as an "asymmetric inclusory construction" such that the second of the conjoined elements is included in the referent of the first. For example, in (154), the *ma*-element—the included conjunct—is included in the pronominal reference of the first element.

(154) *ave ma âroong.*
 {ave}   ma   {âroo-ng}
 1DU.EXCL.INDEP   LK4   husband-1SG.POSS
 'me and my husband.' (lit. 'we with my husband')

 Yal-17072009-TB-weekend_0012

---

[24] In fact, there are no instances in my corpus of inclusory conjuncts which are lexical nouns. When two lexical nouns are conjoined with *ma*, this should be considered an instance of comitative conjunction (see §4.5.6 below) rather than inclusory conjunction.

In (154), *ave ma âroong* 'me and my husband' literally translates as 'we with my husband' or 'the two of us including my husband'. This is an example of a phrasal inclusory construction, where "the inclusory pronominal and the included NP together form a phrase" (Lichtenberk 2000:3). Split inclusory constructions, where the two conjuncts do not form a phrase but rather the inclusory conjunct is marked as a pronominal verbal proclitic (Lichtenberk 2000:3), also occur in Belep. Example (155) shows a split inclusory construction; the inclusory pronominal subject proclitic *ave=* and the included coordinand *tayamook* 'this old woman' (marked with linker *ma*) do not form a phrase.

(155) **Avexa paer yena ma tayamook,**
  {ave=}xa   pa-era   yena ma
  1DU.EXCL.SUBJ=ADD take-3SG.ABS now LK4

  {tayamoo-k}
  old.woman-DET.D.PRX
  'and my wife and I have taken it now,' (lit. 'we have taken it now with this old woman')

  Yal-28072010-BGMCG-lune_0076

Nonetheless, in (155), the *ma*-element *tayamook* 'this old woman' is included in the reference of the proclitic *ave=*.[25] Shown in (156) is another example of a split inclusory construction, where the included conjunct *âjuma la Yade* 'the people of Yade' (marked with linker *ma*) is included in the reference of the plural subject proclitic *la=*, which refers to the entirety of fighters on both sides.

(156) **La peyere ma âjuma la Yade,**
  {la=}   pereye ma   {âju-ma=la   Yade}
  3PL.SUBJ= brawl   LK4   person-AC=LOC   Yade
  'They fought with the people of Yade,'

  Yal-20092011-AW6_0095

In (157) below, the included conjunct (the *ma*-element *naen* 'his child') is included in the dual referent of its controlling element *le* '3DU.INDEP'. However, the subject agreement proclitic *te=* which precedes it is singular.

---

25 The nouns *ulac* 'old man' and *tayamo* 'old woman' are often used as terms of respect for one's family members.

(157) **Te mo li, le ma naen.**
 te= mo=li {le} ma {nae-n}
 3SG.SUBJ= live=LOC.A 3DU.INDEP LK4 child-3SG.POSS
 'He lived there, he and his child.' (lit. 'they two including his child')
 Yal-20092011-AW5_0010

As (157) shows, the *ma*-element may not always trigger subject agreement on the verb.

Linker *ma* cannot be used to conjoin more than two noun phrases (see (148) above). However, example (158) shows that a *ma*-element can itself contain conjoined elements, in this case conjoined with *ka* (see §4.5.3).

(158) **Ava ma naengama pwairama -**
 {ava} ma {nae-nga-ma} pwaira-ma
 1PL.EXCL.INDEP LK4 small.thing-1SG.POSS-AC girl-AC
 'We with the girls – '

 pwairamwa pwalaic, ka nae pabong
 pwairamwa pwalaic} ka {nae pabo-nga
 girl one LK small.thing grandchild-1SG.POSS
 'my daughter, and my little grandson,'

 âc pwalaic, avena mae la pwemwa.
 âya pwalaic} avena= mae=la pwemwa
 male one 1PA.EXCL.SUBJ= sleep=LOC home
 'we slept at home.'
 Yal-17072009-TB-weekend_0029-0031

In (158), we see that the noun phrases conjoined with *ka*—*pwairamwa pwalaic* 'one girl' and *nae pabong âc pwalaic* 'my little grandson'—are included in the reference of the inclusory conjunct, the independent plural pronoun *ava*.

4.5.6 Comitative conjunction

In addition to its use in inclusory conjunction (§4.5.5), where the coordinands are inherently asymmetrical, Belep linker *ma* (§7.3.2) may occasionally be used to conjoin two lexical noun phrases where the coordinands are symmetrical. I will refer to this usage of *ma* as comitative conjunction, defined as conjunction where "the conjunctive coordinator for NPs is identical in shape with the marker for accompaniment" (Haspelmath 2007:29). A similar usage occurs in Nêlêmwa, where inclusory conjunction *ma* is also used for symmetric coordination of "contiguous NPs which must belong to the same category, have the same semantic role and the same syntactic function" (Bril 2004a:5). Two Belep examples of comitative conjunction using *ma* occur in my corpus. In both (159) and (160), the coordinands belong to the same category and are semantically parallel in some way.

(159) **Or ma Waap,**
{or}   ma   {waap}
spill LK4   topple
'Hoot ma Waap,'[26]

Yal-20092011-AW3_0011

(160) **O Keyau ma Kenadu !**
o=   {Keyau}   ma   {Kenadu}
2DU.SUBJ=   Keyau   LK4   Kenadu
'You, Keyau and Kenadu!'[27]

Yal-28072010-BGMCG-tayamu_0151

The use of *ma* to conjoin like members of a set is not very productive in Belep; for example, (161) is ungrammatical.

(161) ***Te bae taro ma bolao.**
te=   bae   {taro}   ma   {bolao}
3SG.SUBJ=   eat   taro   LK4   banana
*'S/he eats taro with banana.'

Yal-03112011-IM1.wav – Yal-03112011-IM2.wav

4.6 Pronouns

Belep pronouns are defined as full phonological words (§3.2.1) which are capable of substituting for a noun phrase in a clause. This definition includes personal pronouns (called 'independent pronouns' in this work; see §4.6.1), demonstrative pronouns (§4.6.2), and interrogative pronouns (§4.6.3). It excludes a variety of other pronominal and anaphoric elements, such as possessive suffixes (§4.2.2.2), subject

---

[26] The two phratries in Northern New Caledonia take their names from two legendary brothers, whose names in Belep are *Or* 'to spill' and *Waap* 'to topple'. The official designation of the tribal region into which Belep falls (according to the indigenous Senate) is <Hoot ma Waap>, named in another Northern language.

[27] *Keyau* and *Kenadu* are proper names of two sisters who are characters in the narrative from which this example is drawn. Throughout this narrative they are portrayed as two of a kind.

agreement proclitics (§5.8), absolutive suffixes (§5.7), and verb phrase locational enclitics (§5.13).

4.6.1 Independent pronouns

The personal pronouns are presented in Table 17. Throughout this work they are referred to as 'independent pronouns', in keeping with the existing literature on New Caledonian languages.[28]

Tab. 17: Independent pronouns

	Singular	Dual	Paucal	Plural
1 exclusive	nao	ave	aven	ava
inclusive		ji	jen	ja
2	yo	or	ôn	ac
3	yer	le	len	la

As Table 17 shows, Belep has a Chechen-type clusivity division (Bickel & Nichols 2005), where an inclusive-exclusive distinction exists in the nonsingular numbers. Belep distinguishes between four numbers in its pronominal system: singular, dual, paucal, and plural. Paucal number is typically used to refer to a small group, or to distinguish a subset from a superset. For example, in (162), the paucal pronoun *aven* '1PA.EXCL.INDEP' refers to a group of at least five people in a self-contained unit—the speaker's family.

(162) ***Aven ma âroong.***
 aven ma âroo-ng
 1PA.EXCL.INDEP LK4 husband-1SG.POSS
 'We with my husband.'
 Yal-17072009-TB-weekend_0031

In (163), the paucal pronoun *len* '3PA.INDEP' refers to Teâ Belep, the legendary founder of the Belep dynasty (§1.3.3), and his two courtiers. It is used first as a topic (§6.9.1)

---

28 This terminology is used by scholars such as Ozanne-Rivierre (1998) and Bril (2002) to differentiate personal pronouns from other pronominal formatives, such as possessive suffixes on nouns and verb agreement morphology. In this work, such formatives are not classified as words, and so do not need to be distinguished from free pronouns which have word-status.

and then as a predicate locative (§6.5) to distinguish this small group from the larger group with whom they are fighting (for whom plural number is used; not shown here).

(163) **Puur ri âmi len, len mode yadalen.**
pu-r=i **â-mi** **len**
origin-3GNR.POSS=GEN DEM.NEW-DET.A.DST 3PA.INDEP

lena **mode** **yada-len**
3PA.INDEP together belongings-3PA.POSS
'Because, as for them, they had their magic.' (lit. 'they were with their belongings')

Yal-20092011-AW6_0160

Independent pronouns are used most commonly in noun phrase coordination, topicalization, for emphasis, and as a response to a question-word question. For example, in (164), the third plural pronoun *la* participates in noun phrase coordination (§4.5).

(164) **la ma teâmaa**
la **ma** **teâmaa**
3PL.INDEP LK4 high.chief
'they with the chieftain'

Yal-20092011-AW3_0054

In (165), the first singular pronoun *nao* acts as the topic (§6.9.1); it is followed by a comment.

(165) « *Toma nao, ka name yaûda la bwe mweogo.* »
toma **nao** **ka** **na=me** **yaûda=la**
but 1SG.INDEP LK 1SG.SUBJ=IRR climb=LOC

bwe **mweogo**
top mountaintop
'"While as for me, I'm going to climb onto the mountaintop."'

Yal-28072010-BGMCG-tahitian_0152

In (166), the third dual pronoun *le* emphatically substitutes for a subject noun phrase (§6.3.1), appearing with a nominative case marker (see §6.4.2).

(166)   *Pan na le,*
       pan=a   le
       go.TV=NOM   3DU.INDEP
       'Went, they did,'

                                                              Yal-20092011-AW6_0114

In (167), the second singular independent pronoun *yo* acts as the response to a question-word question (§6.5.2).

(167)   BG: *Te ta la ti ?*
               te=   ta=la=ri
               3SG.SUBJ=   go.UH=NOM=who
               'Who went up?'

        CG: *Yo.*
               yo
               2SG.INDEP
               'You.'

                                            Yal-28072010-BGMCG-tahitian_0249-0250

4.6.2 Demonstrative pronouns

Demonstrative pronouns in Belep are formed using a bound pronominal stem (Table 18) to which a determiner suffix (§4.5.2) is attached. The functions of each of these stems are further discussed below. See the end of this section for a full chart of the demonstrative pronouns.

Tab. 18: Demonstrative pronominal stems

Stem	Gloss	Definition
â-	DEM.NEW	new
nya-	DEM.IDF	singular identifiable
mwi-, mwii-[29], wî-, wîî-	DEM.IA	singular inanimate
le-, lee-	DEM.DU	dual
lenyi-, lenyii-	DEM.PA	paucal

---

[29] Several demonstrative pronominal stems undergo stem modification (§4.2.2.3) depending on the determiner suffix (§4.5.2). That is, these stems use a like-vowel hiatus when the proximal suffix *-k* is attached; in all other cases, they use a singleton vowel.

Stem	Gloss	Definition
la-, laa-	DEM.PL	plural
ya-	DEM.LOC	locative
wa-, waa-	DEM.MAN	manner
ere-, era-	DEM.PRES	presentative

Demonstrative pronouns are used to replace a full noun phrase as an argument of a clause; to respond to a question word question; as a modifier for the head noun in a noun phrase; and as the head of some relative clauses. For example, in (168), the demonstrative pronoun *leli* acts as the subject (§6.3.1) of a clause; it is marked with the nominative case marker (§6.4.2).

(168) **Mo la leli,**
mo=la   le-li
live=NOM   DEM.DU-DET.A.PRX
'Lived, they did,'

Yal-20092011-AW1_0247

In (169), the demonstrative pronoun *wîmi* acts as the absolute argument of the clause; it is unmarked (§6.4.2).

(169) **Texa pae wîmi la ulayili Cebaba,**
te=xa   pa-e   wî-mi=la
3SG.SUBJ=ADD   take-SPC   DEM.IA-DET.A.DST=NOM

ulayi-li   Cebaba
old.man-DET.A.PRX   Cebaba
'And that old man Cebaba, took that thing,'

Yal-20092011-AW1_0265

In (170), the demonstrative pronoun *yaxedu* serves as the answer to a question-word question (§6.6.2).

(170) MT: **Teme ci liva ?**
           te=me   ci=liva
           3SG.SUBJ=IRR   sit=LOC.Q
           'Where does it go?'

TM: *Yaxedu.*
      ya-xedu
      DEM.LOC-DET.DH
      'Down there.'
                                      Yal-05102010-MTAD_31:49-31.52

In (171), the demonstrative pronoun *lali* acts as a determiner modifying the head noun *âjuma* 'people' (see §4.5.2.5).

(171)   *Ti li âjuma lali ?*
        ti=li   âju-ma   la-li
        who=GEN   person-AC   DEM.PL-DET.A.PRX
        'Who are those people?'
                                      Yal-20092011-AW6_0079

In (172), the dative-marked demonstrative pronoun *lami* acts as a relative pronoun serving as the head of a relative clause (§7.4.3).

(172)   *ka u le lami me tame mwa la mon.*
        ka   u=le   la-mi   me   ta=me
        LK   toward=DAT   DEM.PL-DET.A.DST   IRR   go.UH=CTP

        mwa=la   mon
        again=LOC   side.DH
        'for all of those who will come after you.'
                                      Yal-14092011-PT2-avenir_0022

The demonstrative pronouns are differentiated based on a number of deictic and discourse characteristics, including information status, animacy, and number. The demonstrative pronominal stem *â-* 'DEM.NEW' is used to refer to New information; that is, information which is created by the speaker or which is newly introduced into the conversation (Prince 1981:235). For instance, in (173), the pronoun *âmi* 'the one' is a questioned constituent in a negative question.

(173)   « *Âri yo li âmi ca bae du liva ?* »
        âri=   yo=li   â-mi   ca=
        NEG=   2SG.INDEP=GEN   DEM.NEW-DET.A.DST   ITER=

        bae   du=li-va
        bite   bones=GEN-1PL.EXCL.ABS
        '"Aren't you the one who always eats our bones?"'
                                      Yal-01082010-MFD_0034-0035

In (174), the demonstrative pronoun *âxeda* 'one up there' substitutes for a New noun phrase, *mweogo* 'mountain', that the speaker has not uttered yet.

(174) *uya la bwe âxeda, bwe mweogo na lexeda.*

uya=la	bwe	â-xeda	bwe
arrive=LOC	top	DEM.NEW-DET.UH	top

mweogo	na=lexeda
mountain	interior=LOC.UH

'[I] arrived somewhere up there, on the mountain up there.'

Yal-28072010-BGMCG-tahitian_0160-0161

The pronominal stem *nya-* 'DEM.IDF' indexes a singular, identifiable referent—either one which has previously been textually or situationally evoked, or one which the "speaker assumes the hearer can infer [via logical or plausible] reasoning" (Prince 1981:236). For example, in (175), the noun phrase *buâny* 'stone' is introduced in line 1, so the speaker assumes it is still familiar to the hearer when he refers to it using the demonstrative pronoun *nyaxeda* in line 3. Here the referent has been textually evoked.

(175) *Avexa nyi tuvadu la na buâny waak.*

ave=xa	nyi=	tuva=du=la	na
1DU.EXCL.SUBJ=ADD	PUNCT=	dive=DIR.DH=LOC	interior

buâny	waa-k
stone	DEM.MAN-DET.D.PRX

2 *Ave pe namavan ka namame,*

ave=	pe=	nama=van	ka	nama=me
1DU.EXCL.SUBJ=	RECP=	enter=go.TV	LK	enter=CTP

3 *ka te cuur ka tame, toma bwe nyaxeda,*

ka	te=	cura=xa	ta=me	toma	bwe
LK	3SG.SUBJ=	stand=LK	go.UH=CTP	but	top

nya-xeda
DEM.IDF-DET.UH

'And we kept diving by the rock like this. Together we came and went, and he stood and came up, but on top of that [the rock],'

Yal-28072010-BGMCG-tahitian_0053-0057

The stem *nya-* is also frequently used as the head of a relative clause (§7.4.3) to refer to a moment in time, as in (176). In these instances, the referent is inferable rather than specifically evoked.

(176) **Te nodu, noduxa, koni kiyi Belema, nyami la ta, la ma teâmaa.**

te=	no=du	no=du=xa	koni	kiyi
3SG.SUBJ=	peer=DIR.DH	peer=DIR.DH=LK	never=	see.SPC

Bele-ma	**nya-mi**	**la=**	**ta**	**la**
Belep-AC	DEM.IDF-DET.A.DST	3PL.SUBJ=	go.UH	3PL.INDEP

ma	**teâmaa**
LK4	high.chief

'He looked down, looked down, and couldn't see the Belema, when they were coming, with the chieftain.'

Yal-20092011-AW4_0010-0013

In (176), the speaker uses the demonstrative pronoun *nyami* as a relative pronoun to index a temporal location which is identifiable to the hearer—prior to this point in the narrative, the speaker has already mentioned that the Belema were on their way. The pronominal stem *mwî-* or *wî-* 'DEM.IA'[30] indexes a singular[31] non-human entity. For example, in (177), the demonstrative pronoun *wîîk*[32] substitutes for the noun phrase *kan* 'his feet'[33] as the speaker performs a word search.

(177) **Na tao toda, na pwai kiya nabwa wîîk. Kan. Toma âju, âri na kiyie.**

na=	tao=	to=da	na=	pwai	kiya
1SG.SUBJ=	HAB=	call=DIR.UH	1SG.SUBJ=	only	see.GNR

nabwa	**wîî-k**	**ka-n**	**toma**	**âju**
imprint	DEM.IA-DET.D.PRX	foot-3SG.POSS	but	person

---

30 The phonological form tends to vary by age; older speakers are more likely to use the full form *mwi-* and younger speakers are more likely to use the reduced form *wî-*.

31 That is, one which is unmarked for number; one which is not explicitly marked as dual, paucal, or plural.

32 When the proximal determiner suffix *-k* (§4.5.2) is attached to the stem *mwi-* or *wî-*, the stem is modified (§4.2.2.3) to have a like-vowel hiatus.

33 The noun *ka-* 'foot, feet' is not marked for number.

	âri=	na=	kiyi-e
	NEG=	1SG.SUBJ=	see.SPC-3SG.ABS

'I kept calling and calling but I only saw prints from whatsit. His feet. But the *person* I didn't see.'

Yal-28072010-BGMCG-tahitian_0093-0094

In example (178), the demonstrative pronoun *mwîmi* acts as the head of a relative clause (§7.4.3).

(178) ***Ka temere uya la mwimi te nooxee.***

ka	te=me=re	uya=la	mwi-mi=re
LK	3SG.SUBJ=IRR=ACT	arrive=NOM	DEM.IA-DET.A.DST=3SG.SUBJ

noxe-e
solicit.TR-3SG.ABS
'If s/he asks in my name, what s/he asked for will happen.'

Yal-25072010-PT-homily_0044-0045

Uniquely among the demonstrative pronouns, the bound stems *mwi-, wî-* have the corresponding free stems *mwija, wîja* 'thing',[34] which are full phonological words (§3.2.1) and are not compatible with determiner suffixes (§4.5.2). These forms are used to introduce a New referent into discourse, as in (179) and (180). The stems *mwi-, wî-* also have other irregularities (§4.4.3); it is possible that they are in the process of grammaticalizing from class 1 nouns to pronouns.

(179) ***Enyi te padi mwija pwalaic ki mwany u leen.***

enyi	te=	padi=	mwija	pwalaiyi=xi
if	3SG.SUBJ=	show.SPC	thing	one=REL

mwanya	u=lee-n
bad	toward=DAT-3SG.POSS

'If she is showing something bad to him.'

Yal-20092011-AW4_0058-0059

---

34 These forms are likely related to the Balade Nyelâyu determiner suffix *-ija*, indicating proximity to the speaker (Ozanne-Rivierre 1998: 42).

(180)   *Ô âria wîja leme îna,*
  ô âria wîja le=me   îna
  REAL NEG.EX thing 3DU.SUBJ=IRR make
  'There wasn't anything they would do,'
            Yal-28072010-BGMCG-tayamu_0033

The pronominal stems *le-* 'DEM.DU', *lenyi-* 'DEM.PA', and *la-* 'DEM.PL' index dual, paucal, and plural referents, respectively. There is no stipulation as to whether or not their referents are human. An example of *le-* 'DEM.DU' is shown in (181), where the demonstrative pronoun *leli* is marked as the subject using the nominative case marker (§6.4.2).

(181)   *Mo la leli,*
  mo=la   **le-li**
  live=NOM DEM.DU-DET.A.PRX
  'Lived, did those two,'
            Yal-20092011-AW1_0247

In (182), the stem *lenyii-* 'DEM.PA' is used in the demonstrative pronoun *lenyiik*; the stem contains like-vowel hiatus because the proximal determiner suffix *-k* is attached.

(182)   « *He, âju pwajen ! Lenyiik bwa mo lexeng.* »
  âju   pwajen lenyii-k   bwa= mo=lexeng »
  person three   DEM.PA-DET.D.PRX CONT= live=LOC.DC
  '"Hey, three people! These three are living here."'
            Yal-20092011-AW6_0147

An example of *la-* 'DEM.PL' is shown in (183), where the demonstrative pronoun is *lali*.

(183)   *ma te pa cavac yi lali,*
  ma=re   **pa=**   **cavay=i** **la-li**
  LK4=3SG.SUBJ CAUS= leave=GEN DEM.PL-DET.A.PRX
  'and he made them leave'
            Yal-28072010-BGMCG-tahitian_0256

The pronominal stem *ya-* 'DEM.LOC' is used to index a spatial location. For instance, in (184) the demonstrative pronoun *yamidu*, marked as in the locative case with the case marker *=la* (§6.4.5), substitutes for the toponyms *Weaa* and *Gawe*.

(184) **La mo la Weaa, ka mo la Gawe, yamidu, pwemwala la yamidu,**
   la=   mo=la Weaa ka mo=la   Gawe
   3PL.SUBJ= live=LOC Weaa LK live=LOC Gawe

   ya-midu   **pwemwa-la=la**   **ya-midu**
   DEM.LOC-DET.D.DH village-3PL.POSS=LOC DEM.LOC-DET.D.DH
   'They lived at Weaa, and lived at Gawe, down there, their home down there,'
                    Yal-20092011-AW5_0017-0018

In (185), the demonstrative pronoun *yali* occurs twice, first as a topicalized noun phrase (§6.9.1) and then as the head of a relative clause (§7.4.3).

(185) **Toma yali, yali te uya li,**
   toma **ya-li**   **ya-li**
   but DEM.LOC-DET.A.PRX DEM.LOC-DET.A.PRX

   te=   **uya=li**
   3SG.SUBJ= arrive=DET.A
   'But that place, where she arrived,'
                    Yal-20092011-AW1_0133

The pronominal stem *wa-* 'DEM.MAN' indexes a manner of movement or action and is very productive in discourse and idiom. In (186) and (187), demonstrative pronouns *wali* and *wana* respectively are used adverbially.

(186) **Cexeen ni te tâna ka yo pulu wali.**
   cexen=i **te=**   **tâna** **ka** **yo=**   **pulu**
   sacred=GEN 3SG.SUBJ= hear LK 2SG.SUBJ= speak

   wa-li
   DEM.MAN-DET.A.PRX
   'It is forbidden that he hear you speak like that.'
                    Yal-20092011-AW4_0057

(187) **calayi doo wana,**
   calayi **doo** **wa-na**
   brush.TR earth DEM.MAN-DET.D.MPX
   '[until it] brushed the earth like that,'
                 Yal-28072010-BGMCG-hamecon_0027

Demonstrative pronouns containing *wa-* are commonly predicated to serve as a direct quotative (§6.10.4), as in (188) where the demonstrative pronoun *waak* contains a stem with a like-vowel hiatus due to the presence of the proximal determiner *-k*.

(188) **Texa waak, « Ka ivi wagaji ? »**
 te=xa **waa-k** **ka** **ivi**
 3SG.SUBJ=ADD DEM.MAN-DET.D.PRX LK be.where.SPC

 waga-ji
 boat-1DU.INCL.POSS
 'And he was like, "Well, where's our boat?"'
 Yal-01082010-MFD_0014-0016

Another common usage for the pronominal stem *wa-* is in the construction used to predicate similarity (§6.12.2), as in example (189) where the demonstrative pronoun is *wali*.

(189) **Ka tuu ciraan wali ma bu la Belep.**
 ka **tu** **ciraan** **wa-li** **ma**
 LK EX.SPC barb DEM.MAN-DET.A.PRX similarity

 bu=la **Belep**
 fishhook=LOC Belep
 'And there were barbs like the fishhooks in Belep.'
 Yal-28072010-BGMCG-hamecon_0007-0009

The irregular pronominal stem *ere-*, *era-* 'DEM.PRES'[35] functions as a presentative—that is, a term referring "to an entity which the speaker by means of the associated predication wishes to explicitly introduce into the world of discourse" (Hannay 1985:171, cited in Dik 1997).[36] In its use as a demonstrative pronoun, *ere-*, *era-* is used to index an entity which is being presented by the speaker, either deictically—accompanied by a gesture such as pointing or handing—or anaphorically, to reiterate the relevance of an utterance. For example, in (190), two speakers are playing a card game. When MT asks for a certain card, AD responds by showing her the card (line 3) and using

---

35 This phonological variation depends on the determiner suffix (§4.5.2). The form *era-* is used with *-k*, while the form *ere-* is used with *-na*, *-li*, and *-mi*. The stem *era-*, *ere-* is not compatible with any other determiners.
36 The free stem *era* is also used as a locative verb (§6.4.2). In some cases, it may be difficult to distinguish the demonstrative pronoun from the locative verb: the pronominal stem occurs with only four of the determiners, and the locative verb occurs with only eight of the ten locational verb phrase enclitics (§5.12).

the demonstrative pronoun *erak*. MT affirms that this is the correct card using the demonstrative pronoun *erena* (line 4).

(190) MT: ***Mwija pwalaic te marron, bwaan,***
           mwija   pwalaic   te=   [marõ]   bwaa-n
           thing   one   3SG.SUBJ=   brown.LN   head-3SG.POSS

2   ***ka cuur ra na lunettes bleues.***
           ka   cur=a   na   [lynɛta   blœ]
           LK   stand=LOC   interior   glasses.LN   blue.LN
           'A thing, it's brown, its head, and it's wearing blue glasses.'

3   AD: ***Erak ?***
           era-k
           DEM.PRES-DET.D.PRX
           'Is this it?'

4   MT: ***Erena, êê.***
           ere-na   êê
           DEM.PRES-DET.D.MPX   yes
           'There it is, yeah.'
                                                                      Yal-05102010-MTAD_24:21-24:29

In (191), the speaker has just finished her narrative in response to a request to describe what she did over the weekend. She uses the demonstrative pronoun *ereli* to point out that she has now fully answered the question.

(191)   ***Ô ereli, avenaô mo li gawaarili,***
         ô   ere-li   avena=ô   mo=li
         REAL   DEM.PRES-DET.A.PRX   1TR.EXCL.SUBJ=REAL   live=GEN

         gawari-li
         day-DET.A.PRX
         'There you have it, we stayed that day,'
                                                Yal-17072009-TB-weekend_0036-0037

4.6.2.1 Table of demonstrative pronouns

The demonstrative pronouns (§4.6.2) consist of bound pronominal stems to which determiner suffixes (§4.4.2) must be affixed in order to form a full phonological word (§3.2.1). The table below lists all the demonstrative pronouns which were attested in my fieldwork. Those marked with an asterisk (*) are found in my recorded corpus of naturally-occurring speech. Those marked by (†) and (#) were elicited from speakers using the questions 'Can one say ___?' and 'Does ___ exist?'. Empty spaces in the table indicate demonstrative pronouns which are unattested. In some cases, this is most likely an accidental oversight (e.g. *mwiyeda* is probably used by Belep speakers), though in other cases such as for the bound stem *era-*, *ere-* it is unknown whether the unattested forms are grammatical.

Tab. 19: Demonstrative pronouns

	-k DET.D.PRX	-na DET.D.MPX	-yek DET.D.MDS	-xe DET.D.DST	-xeda DET.UH	-xedu DET.DH	-yeda DET.DST.UH	-midu DET.DST.DH	-li DET.A.PRX	-mi DET.A.DST	-va DET.Q1
â- DEM.NEW	*âk	†âna	#âyek	†âxe	†âxeda	†âxedu	†âyeda	†âmidu	*âli	*âmi	
nya- DEM.IDF	*nyak	*nyana	*nyayek	*nyaxe	*nyaxeda	*nyaxedu	†nyayeda	†nyamidu	*nyali	*nyami	†nyava
mwi- DEM.IA	*mwiik	*mwina	#mwiyek	†mwixe	†mwixeda	†mwixedu		†mwimidu	†mwili	*mwimi	†mwiva
le- DEM.DU	†leek	†lena	#leyek	†lexe	†lexeda	†lexedu	†leyeda	†lemidu	*leli	†lemi	†leva
lenyi- DEM.PA	*lenyiik	†lenyina	#lenyiyek	†lenyixe		†lenyixedu		†lenyimidu	†lenyili	†lenyimi	†lenyiva
la- DEM.PL	*laak	*lana	*layek	†laxe	*laxeda	†laxedu	*layeda	†lamidu	*lali	*lami	†lava
ya- DEMLOC	*yak	†yana	*yayek	*yaxe	*yaxeda	*yaxedu	*yayeda	*yamidu	*yali	*yami	†yava
wa- DEM.MAN	*waak	*wana	†wayek	†waxe	†waxeda			†wamidu	*wali	*wami	†wava
ere- DEM.PRES	*erak	*erena							*ereli		

* attested in my corpus
† IMred76
# DY8-31-2010red51-52

4.6.3 Interrogative pronouns

There are four interrogative pronouns in Belep. They are shown in Table 20. See §6.6 for more information on interrogatives.

Tab. 20: Interrogative pronouns

Pronoun	Gloss
ti, =ri	'who'
da, =da	'what'
neen	'when'
pwaneen	'how many'

Interrogative pronouns *ti* 'who' and *da* 'what' (discussed in depth in §6.6.2) contrast in terms of humanness.[37] Both are simple clitics (as defined by Zwicky 1977); that is, they have full phonological word forms (§3.2.1) as well as enclitic forms (§3.2.2.6). The full forms occur primarily as predicate nominals and in equative constructions (§6.5.1), and in interrogative clefting (§6.6.2). The enclitic forms occur primarily as possessors (§4.2.2) and absolutive arguments (§6.3.3). Other contexts for these interrogative pronouns may vary between the full and encliticized forms.

The interrogative pronouns *neen* 'when' and *pwaneen* 'how many' do not occur in my corpus of natural discourse. Examples of *neen* 'when' from my elicitation and notes are shown in (192) and (193).

(192) ***Yome uya neen ?***
 yo=me uya neen
 2SG.SUBJ=IRR arrive when
 'When will you arrive?'

 overheard

(193) ***Paradiso, yome pe pwemwa, me neen, me neen ?***
 [paɾadiso] yo=me pe= pwemwa me neen
 heaven.LN 2SG.SUBJ=IRR RECP= village IRR when

---

37 While *da* is typically used for animals, *ti* may occasionally refer to an animal.

me neen
IRR when
'Paradise, you will be my home, when, when?'

Paradiso

Examples of *pwaneen* 'how many' are shown in (194) and (195).

(194) **Pwaneen naen ?**
pwanena   nae-n
how.many   small.thing-3SG.POSS
'How many children does s/he have?'

Yal-07112011-TB1.wav – Yal-07112011-TB3.wav

(195) **Yo kiyi pwaneen mani ?**
yo=   kiyi   pwanena   mani
2SG.SUBJ=   see.SPC   how.many   bird
'How many birds do you see?'

Yal-03102011-NT.wav

4.7 Number system and numerals

There is evidence that Proto-Austronesian had a decimal number system, and many Austronesian languages maintain this system today. However, Oceanic languages are more heterogeneous (Bender & Beller 2006:11), with Māori having a vigesimal (base-20) system (Best 1907), and many languages of Vanuatu having quinary (base-5) systems (Lynch et al. 2002:39). The number system in Belep, as in most of the New Caledonian languages (Lavigne 2012), is a combination quinary and vigesimal system, with unique words for 1-5, 10, 15, and 20.

Cardinal and ordinal numerals (§4.7.1) are nouns in Belep (§3.3.1)—they can be marked with a determiner suffix (§4.5.2) and can serve as a case-marked argument of a clause (§6.4) or as the head of a relative clause (§7.4). Belep numerals can serve as both a head noun and as a modifier (§4.7.2) within the noun phrase (§4.6). The numeral *pwalaic* 'one' has grammaticalized as an indefinite article. Belep also uses a variety of numeral classifiers (§4.7.3) to count certain types of objects.

Today, the numerals 1-5 are learned and used by all Belep speakers. For numbers larger than 5, Belema normally use French numerals; the traditional system of Belep numeration is largely unknown to all but the oldest speakers. As such, there is disagreement among speakers as to the proper forms of numerals greater than 5. Numbers greater than 20 are only recorded in Dubois (1975c). I have attempted to reconstruct them based on this manuscript and with the help of speaker THALE Nazaire.

4.7.1 Cardinal and ordinal numerals

Table 21 shows the cardinal numerals from 1-20.

Tab. 21: Belep cardinal numerals, 1-20

Belep	Gloss	Belep	Gloss
pwalaic[38]	1	tûnik nua pwalaic	11 = 10+1
pwadu	2	tûnik nua pwadu	12 = 10+2
pwajen	3	tûnik nua pwajen	13 = 10+3
pwalavaac	4	tûnik nua pwalavaac	14 = 10+4
pwanem	5	cînik	15
(pwanem) nua pwalaic[39]	6 = 5+1	cînik nua pwalaic	16 = 15+1
(pwanem) nua pwadu	7 = 5+2	cînik nua pwadu	17 = 15+2
(pwanem) nua pwajen	8 = 5+3	cînik nua pwajen	18 = 15+3
(pwanem) nua pwalavaac	9 = 5+4	cînik nua pwalavaac	19 = 15+4
tûnik	10	ayaic[40]	20 = 20x1

Yal-03102011-NT.wav

Table 22 shows my hypothesized reconstruction of the cardinal numerals greater than 20 based on Dubois (1975c).

Tab. 22: Belep cardinal numerals, above 20

Belep	Gloss
ayaic nua pwalaic	21 = 20x1+1
ayaic nua pwanem nua pwalaic	26 = 20x1+5+1

---

[38] In Balade Nyelâyu, a quantifier *pwa-* is used for fruit and round things (Ozanne-Rivierre 1998). It is likely that the Belep forms beginning with *pwa-* and *pwala-* are etymologically related to this quantifier; however, Belep *pwa-* is not a quantifier—numerals containing *pwa-* can be used to count any type of object.

[39] The free verb *nua* 'to leave' is used here to indicate addition. Speakers disagree as to whether it is necessary to include *pwanem* 'five' in numerals between 5 and 10. The form *âdenem* (§4.4.3) can also substitute for *pwanem* in these numerals. Some speakers may also use linker *ka* (§7.2.2) before *nua* in the numerals where it appears.

[40] The form *ayaic* 'twenty' is in fact a numeral classifier (§4.7.3), as are other forms beginning with *aya-*.

Belep	Gloss
ayaic bwaar tûnik[41]	30 = 20x1+10
ayaru	40 = 20x2
ayacen	60 = 20x3
ayavaac	80 = 20x4
ayanem	100 = 20x5
ayanem bwaar ayaic	120 = 20x5+20x1
ayanem bwaar ayavaac bwaar tûnik	190 = 20x5+20x4+10
tûnik âjek	200 = 10x20
cînik âjek	300 = 15x20
ayaic âjek	400 = 20x20

These numerals are used to count most types of entities (see §4.7.3 for exceptions).

Ordinal numerals in Belep are formed with the derivational proclitic *ba=* 'ORD' (§3.6.1.1), as shown in Table 23. The ordinal proclitic is incompatible with *pwalaic* 'one' (which is also used to mean 'first'), and it is not usually used with numbers larger than 5.

Tab. 23: Ordinal numerals

Belep	Gloss
ba pwadu	second
ba pwajen	third
ba pwalavaac	fourth
ba pwanem	fifth
ba toven	last (lit. 'ORD= finish')

4.7.2 Numerals in discourse

As nouns, numerals may be used as arguments of a clause, as predicate nominals, and as topicalized noun phrases. For example, in (196), the cardinal numeral *pwalaic* 'one' serves as the absolutive argument (§6.3.3) of the negative existential verb *âria* (§6.5.2).

---

41 If a number greater than 9 is being added, *bwaa-r* 'head-3GNR.POSS' is used to indicate addition instead of *nua* 'to leave'. It is produced as [ᵐbʷara], the incompletive phase of *bwaar* (§2.4.3.2).

(196) *Âria pwalaic ki molep*
       âria   pwalaiyi=xi   molep
       NEG.EX   one=REL   be.alive
       'There wasn't a single one alive.'
                                        Yal-28072010-BGMCG-sousmarin_0106

In (197), the noun phrase headed by ordinal numeral *ba pwadu* 'second' is marked as in the genitive case (§6.4.3).

(197) *Ô tame li ba pwadu gawaar,*
       ô   ta=me=li   ba=   pwadu   gawaar
       REAL   go.UH=CTP=GEN   ORD=   two   day
       'The second day came,'
                                        Yal-28072010-BGMCG-tayamu_0169

In (198), the cardinal numeral *pwanem* 'five' acts as a predicate nominal (§6.5.1).

(198) *Pwanem naen.*
       pwanema   nae-n
       five   small.thing-3SG.POSS
       'He had five children.'
                                                   Yal-20092011-AW1_0013

In (199), the ordinal number *ba pwajen* 'third' acts as the topic of the clause (§6.9.1).

(199) *Ka ba pwajen, ka Jegoloc.*
       ka   ba=   pwajen   ka   Jegoloc
       LK   ORD=   three   LK   Jegoloc
       'And the third one, [she was] Jegoloc.'   Yal-20092011-AW1_0020

Within a noun phrase (§4.6), the first noun always serves as the head. As such, numerals can serve both as the head of a noun phrase with other nominal modifiers, or as modifiers of head nouns. These two constructions differ in meaning. If the numeral acts as the head noun, it has a descriptive function for a Given referent. For example, in (200), the numeral *pwajen* 'three' is the head of the noun phrase *pwajen âju* 'three people' (indicated with {}), which provides a description of a Given referent.

(200) *Mo pwai pwajen nilen ai ? Pwajen nilen. Pwajen âju.*
       mo   pwai   pwajen=i-len   ei   pwajen=i-len
       LK3   only   three=GEN-3TR.ABS   or   three=GEN-3TR.ABS

{pwajena   âju}
three   person
'But there were only three of them, you know? Three of them. Three people.'
                                        Yal-20092011-AW6_0156-0157

In (201), the numeral *pwalaic* 'one' is the head of the noun phrase *pwalaic ola* 'one lobster', which provides a description of the Given referent.

(201)   *Avexa migi pwalaic. Pwalaic ola.*
   ave=xa   migi   pwalaic {pwalaiya ola}
   1DU.EXCL.SUBJ=ADD   catch one   one   shellfish
   'And we caught one. One lobster.'
                                  Yal-28072010-BGMCG-tahitian_0049-0050

More commonly, when the numeral is used as a modifier following the head noun, it indicates that the referent it modifies is New information. For instance, in (202), the noun phrase containing a numeral, *âju pwadu* 'two people', is New information; the numeral follows the head noun as a modifier.

(202)   *Yena, âju lier ka âju pwadu.*
   yena âju=li-er   ka   {âju   pwadu}
   now   person=GEN-3SG.ABS   LK   person   two
   'Now, his courtiers, there were two.'
                                              Yal-20092011-AW6_0056

In (203), the numeral *pwajen* 'three' modifies the head noun *âju* 'person', whose referent is New information.

(203)   « *He, âju pwajen ! Lenyiik bwa mo lexeng.* »
   {âju   pwajen} lenyii-k   bwa=   mo=lexeng »
   person   three   DEM.PA-DET.D.PRX   CONT=   live=LOC.DC
   '"Hey, three people! These three are living here."'
                                              Yal-20092011-AW6_0147

The numeral *pwalaic* 'one' has grammaticalized into an indefinite article when it is used to modify another noun, an unsurprising development since it marks New information when used in this position. For example, in (204), *pwalaic* 'one' is used twice as an indefinite article, first in the noun phrase *gawaar pwalaic* 'one day', and then again in the noun phrase *ulac pwalaic* 'one old man'.

(204) *Gawaar pwalaic, te mo la ulac pwalaic ya Poc.*
{gawara pwalaic} te= mo=la {ulaya
day one 3SG.SUBJ= live=NOM old.man

pwalaiy}=a Poc
one=LOC Poc
'Once upon a time (lit. 'one day'), there lived an old man in Poc.'
Yal-28072010-BGMCG-lune_0003-0004

The Belep numerals are also used in the names for days of the week (Table 24), and may also be used to identify months. See also §6.11.

Tab. 24: Days of the week

Belep	English translation
bwera pwalaic	'Monday' (lit. 'day one')
bwera pwadu	'Tuesday' (lit. 'day two')
bwera pwajen	'Wednesday' (lit. 'day three')
bwera pwalavaac	'Thursday' (lit. 'day four')
bwera pwanem	'Friday' (lit. 'day five')
bwe cavaro	'Saturday' (lit. 'Sabbath day')
bwe cexeen	'Sunday' (lit. 'sacred day')

Not all numerals used in Belep discourse are etymologically numerals. In casual and playful speech environments, speakers tend to use several numerals which have been coined since European colonization. These numerals are somewhat numerological in character and combine both Belep and French elements. They originate from the practice of playing bingo. Some examples are shown in Table 25.

Tab. 25: Bingo numerals

Numeral	Gloss	Origin
apo vingt	20	French *vingt* 'twenty', *trente* 'thirty', etc.
apo trente, etc.	30	
nono	24	
covan	25	*covan* 'horse', from French *cheval*
		25 was the number of a famous racehorse in Belep
ulac	90	*ulac* 'to be old'

Other examples include the use of French *petit* 'small' before French numbers less than 10, as in example (205), and French *coller* for multiples of 11, as in (206).

(205) **petit deux**
[peti ⁿdœ]
little two
'2'

(206) **coller quatre**
[kole katʀ]
glue four
'44'

4.7.3 Numeral classifiers

Not all objects may be counted using the cardinal numbers (§4.7.1). Belep, like many Oceanic languages (Lynch et al. 2002) has several numeral classifiers, which are used for counting specific types of objects. They are shown in Table 26.

Tab. 26: Numeral classifiers

Classifier	Used to count…
âde-	people
âôra-	instances
aya-	sets of 20 objects
go-	sets of 10 pieces of sugar cane
manyina-	sets of 6 yams
puâna-	baskets of yam seedlings
*âdala-[42]	branches
*âvâna-	armlengths
*dabo-	coconuts
*îdana-	rows of yams in a field

---

[42] Many numeral classifiers, marked with (*), have fallen out of use and are only recorded in the manuscripts of Dubois (1975c) and Neyret (1974d); I have attempted to reconstruct them here. Several of the other numeral classifiers are used today only in the formal register of *la coutume* (§1.3.1). Only *âde-* and *âôra-* appear in my corpus.

Classifier	Used to count...
*juna-	strings of fish, clams
*puna-	strings of fish

It seems likely that the numeral classifiers derive etymologically from nouns (§4.2), given their phonological similarity in some cases to nouns with related meanings.[43] However, they are peripheral members at best of the noun word class. Though they are able to serve as an argument or topic of a clause, they are incompatible with all nominal morphology save for the numeric determiner clitics which obligatorily follow them (Table 27).

Tab. 27: Numeric determiners

Determiner	Gloss
ic, =ic	one
tu, =ru	two
cen	three
=vaac	four
nem, =nem	five

The numeric determiners shown in Table 27 are classified as simple clitics (Zwicky 1977), given that they have both free[44] and bound forms, which vary unpredictably depending on the numeral classifier they follow. Numeric determiners do not occur except following a numeral classifier.

Some examples of numeral classifiers in discourse are shown in (207) and (208). In (207), the numeral classifier for people, *âde-*, is followed by the numeric determiner *=ic* 'one'.

---

43 For example, the classifier *âde-* for people bears some similarity to the class 4 noun *âju* 'person'. The class 1 noun *goa-* 'cord (of wood, sugar cane, etc.)' corresponds to the numeral classifier *go-* for cords of sugar cane. The class 1 noun *âda-* 'branch' corresponds to the numeral classifier *âdala-* for branches. The class 1 noun *îda-* 'line, row' corresponds to the numeral classifier *îdana-* for rows of yams.

44 It is likely that these determiners originate from the proto-forms of the cardinal numerals. In Yuanga (a sister language of Belep within the Far North subgroup; see §1.5), the cardinal numerals are *xe* '1', *cu* '2', *kon* '3', *pa* '4', *nim* '5' (Lavigne 2012:39).

(207) **Âdeic, naran ni Keyau.**
âde=ic   nara-n=i   Keyau
CL.person=one   name-3SG.POSS=GEN   Keyau
'One person, her name was Keyau.'
                                      Yal-28072010-BGMCG-tayamu_0057

In (208), the numeral classifier *âôra-*, used for a number of times or instances, is followed by the numeric determiner =*ic* 'one'.

(208) **Laxa keja âôraic ya laxeda,**
la=xa   keja   âôra=iy=a   la-xeda
3PL.SUBJ=ADD   run   CL.instance=one=NOM   DEM.PL-DET.UH
'And the ones up there ran one time.'
                                      Yal-28072010-BGMCG-igname_0068-0069

Table 28 shows a few more examples of noun phrases composed of numeral classifiers plus numeric determiners.

Tab. 28: Numeral classifier NPs

Belep		Belep	Gloss
goic	'one cord'		
goic ûjep	'one cord of sugar cane'	âôraic	'once, one time, first time'
goru ûjep	'two cords of sugar cane'	âôra tu	'twice, two times, second time'
go cen ûjep	'three cords of sugar cane'	âôra cen	'three times, third time'
govaac ûjep	'four cords of sugar cane'	âôravaac	'four times, fourth time'
gonem ûjep	'five cords of sugar cane'	âôranem	'five times, fifth time'

4.8 Summary

In this chapter I have presented the Belep word class of nouns and their associated morphology. Belep nouns are divided into four noun classes (§4.2) based on the allomorphy of the possessive inflections they are compatible with. Though there is no inflectional number marking, quantity of a noun may be indicated by suffixes (§4.3). Nouns may be marked for a variety of discourse-relevant characteristics using determiner suffixes (§4.4). Noun phrases (§4.5) consist of a head noun followed by any modifying nouns, which may include numerals (§4.7). Pronouns (§4.6) may substitute for nouns.

5 Verbs and the verb group

5.1 Introduction

Predicates in unmarked clauses are clause-initial in Belep (§6.2). Prototypically, these predicates are verbal (see §6.5 for exceptions). Verbs may have either a free or bound root and may be intransitive (§5.2.1, §5.2.2)—varying by whether their argument is required to be in the nominative (§6.4.2) or absolutive (§6.4.1) case—or transitive (§5.2.3). The verb word may be modified by a number of inflectional suffixes indicating valency (§5.2.5), the specificity of the absolutive argument (§5.2.4), and the animacy of the absolutive argument (§5.2.5); anaphoric inflectional verbal suffixes also index the person and number of the absolutive argument (§5.7).

The verb word is also prototypically preceded by a host of clitics (§3.2.2.6) which modify its meaning in terms of valence (§5.4; also see §3.4 and §3.6), aspect (§5.5), modality (§5.6),[1] and subject agreement (§5.8), common categories expressed by morphological inflection in many languages (Bybee 1985). As is typical for proclitics in Belep, these verbal modifiers behave as phonological word-like elements separate from the verb word (§3.2.1), though together the verb word and all its modifying suffixes and proclitics form one single grammatical word (§3.2.2) with a number of position classes. Other scholars of New Caledonian languages have not typically used the term 'proclitic' in the description of verbal morphology: Bril (2002) and Ozanne-Rivierre et al. (1998) refer to aspect markers as "morphemes" (Bril 2002: 198) or "particles" (Ozanne-Rivierre et al. 1998: 50). The subject agreement markers are referred to as "indices" (Bril 2002: 88, Ozanne-Rivierre et al. 1998: 50).

In this work, the constituent that consists of the verb word and its various modifying suffixes and proclitics will be called a *verb group* (§5.3), a term which is also used by Ozanne-Rivierre et al. (1998: 40) for Balade Nyelâyu. A larger syntactic constituent *verb phrase* also exists in Belep (§5.11); it minimally contains a verb group and maximally contains this plus an absolutive noun phrase and a number of inflectional enclitics indicating direction (§5.12) and location (§5.13).

5.2 The verb word

'Verb' is a coherent lexical category in Belep with several prototypical characteristics (as discussed in §3.3.2). Belep verbs can be classed into intransitive and transitive

---

[1] Belep has no morphological tense. If necessary, the temporal location of an event may be expressed periphrastically with temporal nouns (§6.10).

types. Intransitive verbs can be further subdivided into those which require a nominative argument (§5.2.1) and those which require an absolutive argument (§5.2.2). This arrangement is typically classified as a split-S system; see §6.3. Transitive verbs have two classes, free (§5.2.3.1) and bound (§5.2.3.2). Free transitive verbs and absolutive-intransitive verbs are inflected to agree with their absolutive argument in specificity (§5.2.4). Most transitives and some intransitives can also be marked inflectionally to agree with their absolutive argument in animacy (§5.2.6). This section will also discuss inflectional valence-changing operations in Belep (§5.2.5).

5.2.1 Intransitive verbs with a nominative argument

Prototypical intransitive verbs in Belep require their argument to be in the nominative case (§6.4.2), thus acting as the subject of the clause (§6.3.1). For example, in (1), the intransitive verb *tu* 'go.DH' has a single argument, *âju* 'person', marked as nominative.[2]

(1)   ***te tume la âju,***
      te=   tu=me=la   âju
      3SG.SUBJ= go.DH=CTP=NOM   person
      'a person came,'
                                              Yal-28072010-BGMCG-lune_0029

In example (2), where the intransitive verb is *ta* 'go.UH', there is no nominal subject; instead, the subject is indexed with a subject agreement marker *ave=* (§5.8).

(2)   ***aveô ta,***
      ave=ô   ta
      1DU.EXCL.SUBJ=REAL   go.UH
      'we went up,'
                                              Yal-28072010-BGMCG-tahitian_0139

Lexically intransitive verbs with a nominative argument include property concepts (3) and stative verbs (4) as well as many dynamic verbs (5). In (3), the intransitive verb is *kop* 'to be white-haired', and the subject *bwaang* 'my head' is marked as nominative with =*a* 'NOM'. The subject agreement marker *te=* '3SG.SUBJ' is the first element in the verb group.

---

[2] The nominative case marker =*la* or =*a* (discussed in §4.7) is a ditropic clitic (§3.2).

(3)   **Teô kop va bwaang.**
        te=ô   kov=a   bwaa-ng
        3SG.SUBJ=REAL be.white.haired=NOM head-1SG.POSS
        'My hair is white.' (lit. 'my head has become white-haired')
                                                                 Yal-28072010-BGMCG-tayamu_0154

In (4), the intransitive verb is *kôê* 'to be tired', and it is modified by the subject agreement marker *te=* '3SG.SUBJ'. The subject *camala* 'their father' is marked as nominative with *=la* 'NOM'.

(4)   **Teô kôê, kôê la camala.**
        te=ô   kôê   kôê=la   cama-la
        3SG.SUBJ=REAL be.tired be.tired=NOM father-3PL.POSS
        'He was tired, tired their father was.'
                                                                  Yal-20092011-AW1_0024

In (5), the intransitive verb is *keja* 'run', modified by the subject agreement marker *ave=* '1DU.EXCL.SUBJ'.

(5)   **ave keja ka najier ra na yali,**
        ave=   keja=xa   naji-er=a   na
        1DU.EXCL.SUBJ   run=LK   let-3SG.ABS=LOC   interior

        ya-li
        DEM.LOC-DET.A.PRX
        'we ran and left[3] him in that place,'
                                                       Yal-28072010-BGMCG-tahitian_0275

Many intransitive verbs can be transitivized with stem modification (§5.2.5.1). Many others can be transitivized with the suffix *-li* (§5.2.5.2).

5.2.1.1 Bound intransitives

Some Belep intransitive verbs lack an uninflected free form. Unlike bound transitives (§5.2.3.2), these verbs must either appear with a spatial directional enclitic (§5.12) or

---

3 Belep distinguishes between *nawee* 'to leave sth., to put sth. down' and *najie* 'to leave sb., to let sb. do sth.' Throughout this text, *nawee* is glossed 'leave' and *najie* is glossed 'let'.

with the suffix -*r* 'NDR'[4] indicating that the verb is unmarked for direction. This situation is reminiscent of Ajië (Fontinelle 1976), where there are a number of verbal 'prefixes' which mark position or manner.

Only a few of these bound intransitives in Belep have been identified. One example is the verb *noo-r* 'to wake up' (6).

(6)   ***Te noor, ai, yer bwa mae.***
       te=   noo-r   ai   yera   bwa=   mae
       3SG.SUBJ= be.awake-NDR no   3SG.INDEP   CONT=   sleep
       'She woke up, no, I mean she was still sleeping.'
                                                      Yal-28072010-BGMCG-tayamu_0104

If *noo-r* is modified with a directional enclitic, its meaning is bleached to 'to peer, look' as in (7) and (8).

(7)   ***Avexa noda, kiyi digi,***
       ave=xa   no=**da**   kiyi   digi
       1DU.EXCL.SUBJ=ADD peer-DIR.UH   see.SPC   canoe
       'And we peered up and saw the canoe,'
                                                      Yal-28072010-BGMCG-tahitian_0186

(8)   ***nodu la wexaac ma leme kiyi mar,***
       no=**du**=la   wexaac ma   le=me   kiyi   mar
       peer=DIR.DH=LOC   ocean   LK4 3DU.SUBJ=IRR see.SPC intertidal.zone
       '[they] looked down to the ocean so they would see when low tide came,'
                                                      Yal-28072010-BGMCG-tayamu_0023

Another example of a bound intransitive verb is *cuu-r* 'to stand' (9).

(9)   ***Teô cuur ra ulayili.***
       te=ô   cuu-r=a   ulayi-li
       3SG.SUBJ=REAL   stand-NDR=NOM   old-DETA.PRX
       'The old man stood up.'
                                                      Yal-28072010-BGMCG-tahitian_0208

---

4 This suffix -*r* 'NDR' bears a resemblance to the 3GNR.POSS nominal suffix -*r* used to indicate a generic possessor (§4.2.2.2). Like some nouns (§4.2.2.3), these bound intransitive verbs undergo stem modification depending on whether they take the NDR suffix or a directional enclitic.

This verb also occurs in *cuda âvan* 'swamp harrier (*Circus approximans*)', the name of a bird whose wings are raised while hunting (10).

(10) **cuda âvan**
 cu=da âva-n
 stand=DIR.UH wing-3SG.POSS
 lit. 'his wings are standing up'

More research is necessary to make a comprehensive list of the bound intransitive verbs in Belep.

5.2.2 Intransitive verbs with an absolutive argument

A few intransitive verbs in Belep require their argument to be in the absolutive case (which is unmarked; see §6.4.1), creating a split-S system (§6.3.2) as defined in Dixon (1994). Some examples of these verbs are shown in Table 1. Note that other such verbs may exist, though they are uncommon.

Tab. 1: Predicates requiring an absolutive S argument

Predicate	Gloss
âria	'NEG.EX'
bwara	'to be missed, hoped for'[5]
ciae, cia[6]	'NEG.LOC'
era	'PRED.LOC'
ivi, iva	'to be where?'
mwanya	'to be many, to be overpowering'[7]
mwanyi	'to be ignorant'[8]
tu-[9], tuya	'EX'

---

5 As in *bwara nabwa mae* [hope place sleep] 'I miss my old bed.'; *bwara wee-ng* [hope food-1SG.POSS] 'I wish I could eat it.'
6 Some of these intransitive verbs are obligatorily inflected for the specificity of their argument; see §5.2.4 below for more information.
7 As in *mwanya câbuk* [lots cold] 'It's really cold.'; *mwanya âju* [lots people] 'There are lots of people.'
8 As in *mwanyi-nao* [ignorant-1SG.ABS] 'I don't know.'
9 *tu* 'EX' is a bound root, used before an absolutive noun phrase. It can occur in a free form as *tu-u*.

Examples (11) - (15) show instances of the use of these absolutive-intransitive verbs. In (11), the nominal S argument *wagaji* 'our boat' is unmarked in the absolutive case.

(11) « *Ka ivi waga-ji ?* »
      ka ivi   waga-ji
      LK be.where.SPC boat-1DU.INCL.POSS
      '"And where is our boat?"'
                                              Yal-01082010-MFD_0016

In (12), the nominal S argument *ûjen* 'his power' is unmarked in the absolutive case.

(12) *Teâ Pûnivaac, mwanya ûjen.*
      Teâ   Pûnivaac mwanya ûje-n
      chief Pûnivaac many   kidney-3SG.POSS
      'Teâ Pûnivaac, his power was strong.'[10]
                                              Yal-20092011-AW5_0005

In (13), the absolutive noun phrases *Or* 'Or phratry' and *Waap* 'Waap phratry' (see §1.3) are the S arguments of the verb *tuya* 'EX.GNR' (see §5.2.4 on specificity).

(13) *Ka tuya Or, ka tuya Waap.*
      ka tuya   or ka tuya   waap
      LK EX.GNR spill LK EX.GNR topple
      'And there is Or [phratry], and there is Waap [phratry].'
                                              Yal-20092011-AW3_0012

When the S argument is indexed by an anaphoric pronominal element, an absolutive suffix (§5.7) is used. In example (14), the suffix *-e* '3SG.ABS' is used on the intransitive verbs *iva* 'to be where?' (inflected for specificity; see §5.2.4) and *cia* 'NEG.LOC'.

(14) « *Ivie ?* » *Ô ciae.*
      ivi-e   ô   cia-e
      be.where.SPC-3SG.ABS REAL NEG.LOC-3SG.ABS
      '"Where is he?" He wasn't there.'
                                              Yal-28072010-BGMCG-tahitian_0178

In (15), the suffix *-len* '3TR.ABS' is used on the intransitive verb *cia* 'NEG.LOC'.

---

10 The word *ûje-* 'kidney' also means 'power, strength' by metaphorical extension.

(15)   **Toma len, cialen,**
       toma   len   cia-len
       but   3PA.INDEP   NEG.LOC-3PA.ABS
       'But they, they weren't there,'

       Yal-20092011-AW6_0161

Intransitive verbs requiring an absolute argument share most prototypical characteristics of verbs (§3.3.2). However, they are incompatible with most deverbal derivational morphology. Derivational proclitics such as *â=* and *wa=* (§3.6.2) are ungrammatical when used with an absolutive-intransitive verb, as in (16) and (17), and these verbs are also incompatible with the valence proclitics (18) (see §5.4).

(16)   ***â ciae**
       â=   cia-e
       AGT=   NEG.LOC-SPC
       '*one who isn't there'

       Yal-22092011-TB.wav

(17)   ***wa tuya**
       wa=   tuya
       RESULT=   EX.GNR
       '*way of existing'

       Yal-22092011-TB.wav

(18)   ***pa âria**
       pa=   âria
       CAUS=   NEG.EX
       '*to cause not to exist'

       Yal-22092011-TB.wav

Absolutive-intransitive verbs are also incompatible with subject agreement proclitics (§5.8). For example, in (19), the negative existential verb *âria* 'NEG.EX' occurs without any subject agreement marker; to use one would be ungrammatical (20).

(19)   **Âria ola.**
       âria   ola
       NEG.EX   lobster
       'There weren't any lobsters.'

       Yal-28072010-BGMCG-tahitian_0032

(20)   *Te âria ola.

   *te=   âria   ola
   3SG.SUBJ= NEG.EX   lobster
   *'There weren't any lobsters'

The absolutive-intransitive verbs can be marked for specificity (§5.2.4) and characteristics of the absolutive argument (§5.2.6), as well as with absolutive suffixes (§5.7), and aspect (§5.5) and mood (§5.8) inflections. Verb phrases using an absolutive-intransitive verb can contain verb phrase enclitic locationals (§5.13).

5.2.3 Transitive verbs

Prototypical transitive verbs in Belep require their semantic agent to be in the nominative (§6.4.2) or genitive (§6.4.3) case (depending on the definiteness of the semantic patient; see §6.3.2) and their semantic patient to be in the absolutive case (§6.4.1); that is, unmarked. Transitive verbs are obligatorily marked to agree with their subject in person and number (with a few exceptions, discussed in §5.8). They can be divided into two classes: 1) free verb roots; and 2) bound verb roots. Free verb roots are obligatorily inflected for the specificity of their absolutive argument (§5.2.4). Both free and bound verb roots can be detransitivized with -*u* (§5.2.5.3). Transitive verbs may be differentially marked to index some of the characteristics of their absolutive argument (§5.2.6).

5.2.3.1 Free transitives

Many transitive verbs in Belep have free roots. Belep speakers may give these forms as citation forms, and they also appear in clauses. A partial list of such verbs is shown in Table 2. Note that most free verbs end in /a/.

Tab. 2: Free transitive verbs

Free verb	Gloss	Free verb	Gloss
âbwa	'to lift'	pajela	'to question'
âva	'to fish'	pera	'to collect'
âya	'to feel, touch'	pora	'to massage'
buya	'to obey'	pua	'to open'
cevera	'to push'	puya	'to uncover'
cibia	'to turn over'	pûnu	'to strike (the sails)'
cibwa	'to throw'	pwaxa	'to wash'
coba	'to hide (from)'	tabwa	'to attach'

cola	'to relax'	tada	'to slap'
êna	'to know'	tâna	'to hear'
îna	'to make'	tawa, tiawa, teawa	'to cut'
karo	'to shave'	taxa	'to unearth'
kera	'to brush'	tera	'to stop'
kiya	'to see'	teva	'to peel'
mija	'to pinch'	tia	'to pierce'
niva	'to lose track of'	tua	'to detach'
nua	'to leave'	waba	'to jiggle'
pa	'to take'	yala	'to shake'

Free transitive verbs are obligatorily inflected for the specificity of their absolutive argument (§5.2.4). The forms in Table 2 are the generic forms of the free verbs, but their specific forms may also be given as citation forms (in which case they are usually marked with the specific suffix -e (§5.2.4).

Some examples of free transitive verbs are shown in (21) - (23). In (21), the generic form of the verb êna 'to know' is used without an overt absolutive argument. It is marked to agree with its 3DU subject.

(21) *Leô, leô êna.*
      le=ô   le=ô   êna
      3DU.SUBJ=REAL 3DU.SUBJ=REAL know.GNR
      'They, they knew.'
                                         Yal-28072010-BGMCG-tayamu_0141

In (22), the generic form of the verb *pa* 'to take' is used with the absolutive nominal *ween nole* 'her meal of fish'. The subject agreement proclitic is omitted (§5.8).

(22) *Ô pa ween nole,*
      ô   pa   wee-na   no-le
      REAL take.GNR food-3SG.POSS fish-ADU
      '[She] took her meal of fish,'
                                         Yal-20092011-AW1_0111

In (23), the verb *tabwa* 'to attach' occurs in its specific form in line 1 with the suffix -*e* 'SPC' (§5.2.4) and the absolutive nominal *kô bolao* 'banana petiole'. In line 2, it appears with the pronominal absolutive suffix -*er* (§5.7.2).

(23) **La tabwae kô bolao la bwe buâny,**
la= tabwa-e kô bolao=la bwe buâny
3PL.SUBJ= attach-SPC petiole banana.tree=LOC top stone

ka tabwaer ra bwe nao,
ka tabwa-er=a bwe nao
LK attach-3SG.ABS=LOC top line

'They attached a banana leaf stalk to a stone, and attached it to the fishing line,'

Yal-28072010-BGMCG-hamecon_0023-0024

See §5.2.4 for the difference between generic and specific free transitives. The differential absolutive suffixes -*n* and -*a* (§5.2.6) attach only to the specific form of free transitives. The detransitivizer -*u* (§5.2.4.3) attaches only to the generic form of free transitives.

5.2.3.2 Bound transitives

A vast number of Belep transitive verbs lack an uninflected free form. Unlike in bound intransitives (§5.2.1.1), the verb root must be followed by a pronominal absolutive suffix (§5.7), a differential absolutive suffix (§5.2.6), or an absolutive noun phrase. In citation form, Belep speakers attach the absolutive suffix -*e* '3SG.ABS' (§5.7.2) to the bound root; this is how these verbs will be cited in this text. A partial list of these bound roots is shown in Table 3. Note that most bound roots end in /i/ or /e/.

Tab. 3: Inherently bound transitive verb roots

Bound root	Gloss	Bound root	Gloss
bage-	'to rub'	padi-	'to show'
be-	'to beat'	paye-	'to set down'
ca-	'to drag'	pi-	'to cook (in a pot)'
cagani-	'to mix'	pinye-	'to kindle (a fire)'
cebe-	'to suspect'	piyi-	'to delouse'
cêbone-	'to moon, expose the buttocks'	po-	'to load'
cêmwe-	'to gut'	pwagi-	'to tense'
cili-	'to throw straw onto a roof'	pwede-	'to turn'
ciwi-	'to bury'	tabo-	'to hit a target'
co-	'to count'	tabua-	'to break'

gi-	'to attack'	tale-	'to cover with a cloth'
îbi-, ôbi-	'to gather'	taxe-	'to distribute'
iwi-	'to scrub'	te-	'to close, plant'
iye-	'to peel'	texe-	'to cradle'
ji-, di-	'to give'	tiwi-	'to push (a car), put on (clothes)'
kâye-	'to keep, guard'	tixi-	'to sew'
kele-	'to scoop'	tu-	'to find'
kewe-	'to chase'	turowi-	'to insult'
maji-	'to send'	turu-	'to hide'
migi-	'to touch, hold'	uli-	'to pour'
mini-	'to braid'	wâdi-	'to whip, beat up'
naji-	'to let'	wi-	'to sharpen'
nawe-	'to leave'	yaxe-	'to expire, wait too long'
ngini-	'to not see, miss'	yaye-	'to ripen'

A few examples of bound verbs are given in (24), where the absolutive argument of the verb *migie* 'to touch, hold' is a full noun phrase; and in (25), where the absolutive argument of the verb *kewee* 'to chase, hunt' is indexed by a pronominal suffix.

(24)   ***te migi buâny,***
      te=   **migi buâny**
      3SG.SUBJ= hold stone
      'he was holding a stone,'
                                                          Yal-20092011-AW1_0254

(25)   ***Naxa kewee.***
      na=xa   **kewe-e**
      1SG.SUBJ=ADD chase-3SG.ABS
      'And I chased him.'
                                            Yal-28072010-BGMCG-tahitian_0075

5.2.3.3 Irregular transitives

Some transitive verbs in Belep do not fit clearly into either the free (§5.2.3.1) or bound (§5.2.3.2) categories. One example is *ue* 'to suck', whose form is *u* before a noun phrase (this behavior resembles a bound verb) and *ua* before an absolutive suffix (this resembles a free verb). Another example is that of *wayule* 'to plow' and *pu* 'to pick [a plant]', which do not inflect for specificity, being invariant before noun phrases and pronominal suffixes (like bound verbs), but which also have free forms. More research remains to be done on identifying and classifying such irregular verbs.

5.2.4 Inflection for specificity

Some Belep verbs are obligatorily marked to indicate the specificity of their absolutive argument; that is, these verbs have both a generic and a specific form. Verbs which undergo this inflectional process include most free transitive verbs (§5.2.3.1) and some intransitive verbs whose argument is absolutive (§5.2.2). In most cases, the addition of the suffix -*e* 'SPC' to the generic form indicates specificity.[11] Other generic/specific verb pairs are irregular. A partial list of generic and specific forms for verbs is shown in Table 4.

Tab. 4: Inflection for specificity

Generic	Specific	Gloss	Transitive/ Intransitive	Irregular?
âbwa	âbwae	'to lift'	TR	
âya	âyae	'to feel, touch'	TR	
ba, bae	bae	'to eat'	TR	irreg.
buya	buyae	'to obey'	TR	
cia	cia, ciae	'NEG.EX'	NTR	irreg.
coba	cobae	'to hide (from)'	TR	
êna	ênae	'to know'	TR	
îna	înae	'to make'	TR	
iva	ivi	'to be where?'	NTR	irreg.
kiya	kiyi	'to see'	TR	irreg.
nua	nuae	'to leave'	TR	
pa	pae	'to take'	TR	
para	pari	'to tell'	TR	irreg.
pûnu	pûnue	'to strike (the sails)'	TR	
pwaxa	pwaxae	'to wash'	TR	
tâna	tânae	'to hear'	TR	

---

11 I hypothesize that the specific marker -*e* originated as the 3SG.ABS pronoun -*e* (§5.7), since it does not ever occur in sequence with this pronoun. It does, however, co-occur with all other pronouns and before absolutive noun phrases, so in these cases it can no longer be said to serve a pronominal function.

| tuya | tu[12] | 'EX' | | NTR | irreg. |
| yala | yalae | 'to shake' | | TR | |

Generic and specific forms of these verbs share most speech environments (Table 5): both can be given as the citation form of a verb and may appear at the end of an intonation unit[13]; both can be used before an absolutive noun phrase. However, only the specific form of these verbs can occur before an absolutive pronominal suffix (§5.7).

Tab. 5: Environments where generic and specific forms may appear

	Free	Before absolutive NP	Before absolutive suffix
Generic	✓	✓	
Specific	✓	✓	✓

The following examples show the distinction between generic- and specific-marked verbs in discourse. In (26) and (27), the verb *îna* 'to make' is used with an absolutive noun phrase. In (26), the absolutive *uruâny* 'hurricane' is marked with the suffix *-mene*, which indicates that it is one in a class of similar objects (see §4.3.3). Since this noun phrase is generic, the verb form that appears is the generic form, *îna*.

(26)   ***Te îna uruânyamene,***

      te=   îna   uruânya-mene

      3SG.SUBJ=   make.GNR   hurricane-accoutrement

      'He makes hurricanes and stuff like that,'

                                                    Yal-28072010-BGMCG-sousmarin_0048

In (27), the absolutive noun phrase is *mwan* 'his house'. The pronominal possessive suffix (§4.2.2.2), and the specific form of the verb, *înae* [make-SPC], together indicate that this absolutive noun phrase is specific.

---

12 The irregular specific forms *kiyi* 'see.SPC', *ivi* 'to be where.SPC', and *tu-* 'EX' are not free; they are bound. The existential verb can occur in a free form as *tu-u*.

13 These occurrences typically serve different functions: the generic form of a verb at the end of an intonation unit is usually being used without an overt absolutive argument; while the specific form of a verb at the end of an intonation unit should be interpreted as an anaphoric pronominal reference to a preceding 3SG argument.

(27)　*Yali la pwemwan, te înae mwan,*
　　　ya-li=la　　　　　　　　　**pwemwa-n**
　　　DEM.LOC-DET.A.PRX=LOC　home-3SG.POSS

　　　te=　　　　**îna-e**　　　**mwa-n**
　　　3SG.SUBJ=　make-SPC　house-3SG.POSS
　　　'There in his home, he made his house,'
　　　　　　　　　　　　　　　　　Yal-20092011-AW1_0006-0007

In (28), the generic form of *âva* 'to fish' is used without an overt absolutive argument, while the specific form *âvae* is used with the absolutive noun phrase *nae no pwalaic* 'a small fish', which is marked as new and indefinite (§2.4.6).

(28)　*Ka mon, caivak te âva, la âvae nae no pwalaic,*
　　　ka　mona　caivak　te=　　　âva　la=　　　âva-e　　nae
　　　LK　side.DH　rat　　3SG.SUBJ=　fish　3PL.SUBJ=　fish-SPC　small.thing

　　　no　pwalaic
　　　fish　one
　　　'And then, the rat, he went fishing, a small fish was caught,'
　　　　　　　　　　　　　　　　　　　Yal-01082010-MFD_0010

If the absolutive argument is anaphorically indexed by a pronominal suffix (§5.7), the specific form of the verb must be used. For example, in (29) the verb *pa* 'to take' is marked with the specific marker *-e*, followed by the pronominal suffix *-le* '3DU.ABS'. The generic form of the verb is ungrammatical before a pronominal suffix.

(29)　*Texaô paele,*
　　　te=xa=ô　　　　　　**pa-e-le**
　　　3SG.SUBJ=ADD=REAL　take-SPC-3DU.ABS
　　　'And he took them,'
　　　　　　　　　　　　　　　　　Yal-28072010-BGMCG-lune_0040

Example (30) shows the use of the specific verb form *pae* 'to take'; used here, the specific marker is reinterpreted as a 3SG.ABS anaphoric reference (§5.7).

(30) **Texaô paeme la Waala.**
   te=xa=ô   pa-e=me=la   Wala
   3SG.SUBJ=ADD=REAL   take-3SG.ABS=CTP=LOC   Waala
   'And he brought him here to Waala.'

   Yal-28072010-BGMCG-tahitian_0221

The difference between the generic and specific forms is clearest in the irregular transitive verb *kiya* 'to see', which has two forms: *kiyi* 'see.SPC' and *kiya* 'see.GNR'. In example (31), *kiyi* is used when its patient is *âju* 'person' (a specific person who had been previously mentioned), while *kiya* is used for the generic *nabwa kan* 'his footprints'.

(31) **Te tao ta, toma âri na kiyi âju.**
   te=   tao=   ta   toma   âri=   na=   kiyi   âju
   3SG.SUBJ=   HAB=   go.UH   but   NEG=   1SG.SUBJ= see.SPC   person

   Na pwai kiya nabwa kan.
   na=   pwai kiya   nabwa ka-n
   1SG.SUBJ=   only see.GNR   imprint foot-3SG.POSS
   "He kept going up, but I didn't see the person. I only saw his footprints.'

   Yal-28072010-BGMCG-tahitian_0096

In example (32), *kiya* and *kiyi* both have the same absolutive argument, *buâny* 'stone'. Both instances of *buâny* 'stone' (32) are definite (marked with determiners (§4.4.2)); however, the use of *kiyi* 'see.SPC' in line 2 references specific stones that the speaker has previously described. In line 3, *kiya* refers to a generic class of such stones, explicitly marked as a class with *-ma* 'AC' (see §4.3.1).

(32) **Ka enyi yome bwa tu yena,**
   ka   enyi   yo=me   bwa=   tu   yena,
   LK   if   2SG.SUBJ=FUT   CONT=   go.DH   now

2 **yome bwa kiyi buânyili.**
   yo=me   bwa=   kiyi   buânyi-li
   2SG.SUBJ=FUT   CONT=   see.SPC   stone-DET.A.PRX

3   *Yome bwa kiya buânyama lali, bwa yena.*

yo=me	bwa=	kiya	buânya-ma	la-li
2SG.SUBJ=FUT	CONT=	see.GNR	stone-AC	3PL.SUBJ-DET.A.PRX

bwa=   yena
CONT= now

'And if you would go down there now, you would see these stones. You would see all these stones if you went now.'

Yal-28072010-BGMCG-sousmarin_0119-0120

5.2.5 Patient valence

This section describes processes for increasing or decreasing the number of semantic patients affected by a verb.

There are two processes for the transitivization of an intransitive verb in Belep: 1) the intransitive stem undergoes unpredictable modification, generally through the addition of a syllable (§5.2.5.1); and 2) the regular suffix *-li* is added to the intransitive verb (§5.2.5.2). In both cases, the transitivized verb falls into the class of bound transitives (§5.2.3.2); it must be followed by a pronominal absolutive suffix (§5.7), a differential absolutive suffix (§5.2.6), or an absolutive noun phrase.

Transitive verbs can also be detransitivized with the suffix *-u* 'DETRANS' (§5.2.5.3), which attaches to the root of bound transitives and to the generic form of free transitives. The use of this suffix precludes the presence of any nominal or pronominal reference to the absolutive argument. The detransitive suffix can be used on verbs which have undergone transitivization.

5.2.5.1 Transitivization with stem modification

A vast number of Belep verbs have both an intransitive and a transitive form (Table 6). Though in many cases the existence of a semantic patient is implied in the intransitive form (e.g. *caang* 'to steal'), the transitive form is used only if the patient is overtly referenced with a pronominal absolutive suffix, differential absolutive marker, absolutive noun phrase, or other word (see §5.10.1).

Tab. 6: Intransitive and transitivized verb stems

Intransitive	Transitive	Gloss	
âny	âje-	'to steer'	(B), (C)
âpw	âwi-	'to laugh, to laugh at'[14]	(A)
ar	are-	'to paddle'	(B)
âya	âyawe-	'to fear'	(B), (E)
bwawa	bwawi-	'to remove'	(A), (E)
caang	cage-	'to steal'	(B), (C), (D)
cak	caxe-	'to fish with a net'	(B)
câny	câje-	'to seize, to press'	(B), (C)
calac	calayi-	'to brush, barely touch'	(A)
câamw	câmwi-	'to do what?, to do what with?'	(A), (D)
côk	côxe-	'to splash, to squirt'	(B)
coon	coni-	'to carry on the shoulder'	(A), (D)
cuu-r[15]	curi-	'to stand, to stand before'	(A), (D)
iru	irue-	'to grate'	(B)
iyu	iyue-	'to buy'	(B)
jang	jage-	'to measure'	(B), (C)
koon	koni-	'to be unable, to be ignorant of'	(A), (D)
nac	nayi-	'to be surprised, to be surprised by'	(A)
nanam	nanami-	'to think, to think about'	(A)
nobwapw	nobwawi-	'to insult'	(A)
nook	noxe-	'to solicit'	(B), (D)
ôbwac	ôbwayi-	'to watch'	(A)
para	pari-	'to tell'	(A), (E)
param	parame-	'to forgive, forget'	(B)
pavang	pavage-	'to prepare'	(B), (C)
payeen	payeni-	'to listen'	(A), (D)
pûmw	pûbwi-	'to smoke (fish)'	(A), (C)
pûnu	pûnue-	'to lower'	(B)
tâang	tâge-	'to scrape'	(B), (C), (D)
taar	tare-	'to flee, to escape from'	(B), (D)
taxaûm	taxaûbe-	'to cover'	(B), (C)
teec	teya-	'to burn'	(D), (E)
toopw	toe-	'to fill'	(B), (D), (E)
tûûn	tûne-	'to rub'	(B), (D)
tup	tuve-	'to dive, to dive for'	(B)

---

14 'to V1, to V2' here means that V1 is the gloss of the intransitive and V2 is the gloss of the transitive.
15 See §5.2.1.1.

up	uve-	'to breathe, smoke (tobacco)'	(B)
waap	wave-	'to topple'	(B), (D)
wêêng	wêge-	'to organize, teach'	(B), (C), (D)
yaang	yagi-	'to search'[16]	(A), (C), (D)
yaap	yavi-	'to search'	(A), (D)
yaar	yare-	'to disembark, to disembark from'	(B), (D)

The stem modifications shown in Table 6 indicate transitivization. Though there is no regular rule deriving transitivized forms from intransitives, they follow several general patterns:

(A)   Transitivized forms may contain a suffixed *-i*; or
(B)   Transitivized forms may contain a suffixed *-e*
(C)   Final nasals in the intransitive form sometimes correspond to prenasalized stops in the transitivized form
(D)   Like-vowel hiatuses in the intransitive form correspond to single vowels in the transitivized form
(E)   Unpredictable segments are added or subtracted

The fourth column of Table 6 indicates which of these patterns is used in the relevant intransitive-transitive pair.

Examples of the usage of these intransitive-transitive pairs are shown below. In (33), intransitive *nook* 'to solicit' is used in line 1, while transitive *noxe* with a pronominal absolutive suffix is used in line 2.

(33) ***Enyi te nook na narang,***
 enyi=re   nook   na   nara-ng
 if=3SG.SUBJ solicit.NTR interior name-1SG.POSS

2   ***Ka temere uya la mwimi te nooxee.***
 ka   te=me=re   uya=la
 LK   3SG.SUBJ=IRR=ACT   arrive=NOM

---

16 It is not clear whether there is any semantic difference between the verbs *yaap* 'to search' and *yaang* 'to search'. They may be alternate phonemic forms for the same meaning, or they may be subtly different.

mwi-mi=re   noxe-e
DEM.INAN-DET.A.DST=3SG.SUBJ solicit.TR-3SG.ABS
'If s/he asks in my name, what s/he asked for will happen.'
                            Yal-25072010-PT-homily_0044-0045

In (34), intransitive *âya* 'to fear' is used with a following semantically dependent clause (see §7.3.7), while transitive *âyawe* is used with the absolutive argument *januun* 'his spirit'.

(34)   « *Na âya li na pan na pu caya puur ri, na âyawe januun.* »
       na=   âya=li   na=   pan=a   pu   caya
       1SG.SUBJ= fear.NTR=GEN   1SG.SUBJ=   go.TV=LOC   side   dad

       pu-r=i   na=   âyawe   januu-n
       origin.3GNR.POSS=GEN   1SG.SUBJ=   fear.TR   spirit-3SG.POSS
           'I am afraid to go near Dad because, I'm afraid of his ghost.'
                                                    Yal-20092011-AW1_0039

In (35), intransitive *param* 'to forget, forgive' is followed by a pseudocoordinate clause (see §7.3.1), while in (36) transitive *parame* is followed by the absolutive noun phrase *narale* 'their names'.

(35)   *te param ka te turowinao,*
       te=   param   ka te=   turowi-nao
       3SG.SUBJ= forget.NTR   LK 3SG.SUBJ= insult-1SG.ABS
           'He forgot he had insulted me,'
                                        Yal-28072010-BGMCG-tahitian_0329

(36)   *na parame narale.*
       na=   parame   nara-le
       1SG.SUBJ= forget.TR name-3DU.POSS
           'I forget their names.'
                                                    Yal-20092011-AW6_0057

Verb forms transitivized through stem modification, like all bound transitives (§5.2.3.2), are eligible to receive the differential absolutive marking suffixes -*n* and -*a* (§5.2.6) and the detransitivizing -*u* suffix (§5.2.4.3). For example, (37) shows the suffixation of -*n* to *yagi*, the transitivized form of *yaang* 'to search'.

(37) *La yuu, yuu, yagin,*

      la=   **yu-u**   **yu-u**   **yagi-n**

      3PL.SUBJ=   dig-DETR   dig-DETR   search.TR-DA.NSG

yuu, yagin, ka koni tun.

yu-u   **yagi-n**   **ka**   **koni**   **tu-n**

dig-DETR   search.TR-DA.NSG   LK   unable.TR   find-DA.NSG

'They dug, dug, searched, dug, searched and never could find anything.'

                                        Yal-28072010-BGMCG-sousmarin_0116

In (38), *-a* is suffixed to the transitivized form *yavi*, from *yaap* 'to search'.

(38) *Ja jua yavia wa înau,*

      ja=   **jua**   **yavi-a**   **wa=**   **îna-u**

      1PL.INCL.SUBJ=   very   search.TR-DA.IN   RESULT=   make.GNR-DETR

      'We truly search for a way,'

                                              Yal-25072010-PT-homily_0055

Example (39) shows the suffixation of detransitive *-u* to *nanami*, the transitivized form of *nanam* 'to think'.

(39) *La nanamiu wali.*

      la=   **nanami-u**   **wa-li**

      3PL.SUBJ=   think.TR-DETR   DEM.MAN-DET.A.PRX

      'They thought thusly.'

                                              Yal-28072010-BGMCG-igname_0062

There is often some degree of semantic bleaching when verbs are transitivized through stem modification. For example, intransitive *câny* 'to seize' generally refers to an epileptic seizure, constipation, or some other involuntary bodily blockage, while its transitive form *câjee* means 'to press on something', usually with the arms or hands.

5.2.5.2 Transitivizer -*li*

Intransitive verbs in Belep which do not have corresponding transitive stems (§5.2.5.1) may be transitivized through the regular addition of the suffix -*li* 'TR'.[17] It is probable that this suffix grammaticalized from the genitive case marker, the ditropic clitic =*li*, =*i* 'GEN', which is used to mark oblique noun phrases (§6.4.3). Some examples of verbs transitivized with -*li* 'TR' are shown in Table 7.

Tab. 7: Verbs transitivized with -*li*

Intransitive	Transitive	Gloss
boyu	boyuli-	'to greet'
cao	caoli-	'to work, mix'
caxe	caxeli-	'to be ashamed, to be ashamed of'
comu	comuli-	'to study'
due	dueli-	'to admire'
ka	kali-	'to break, shatter'
kaxi	kaxili-	'to watch'
mwanao	mwanaoli-	'to approach'
ole	oleli-	'to thank'
to	toli-	'to call aloud, to call sb. sth.'
ûdu	ûduli-	'to drink'
yage	yageli-	'to help'

The transitivized forms of the verbs shown in Table 7 belong to the class of bound transitives (§5.2.3.2); they must be followed by an absolutive suffix (§5.7), a differential absolutive suffix (§5.2.6), or an absolutive noun phrase. For example, in (40) the transitivized verb *dueli* 'admire' is followed by the absolutive suffix -*la*.

(40)   ***Texa duelila, yo kiyie ?***
        te=xa   due-li-la   yoxe
        3SG.SUBJ=ADD admire-TR-3PL.ABS TAG
        'And she admired them, you know?'

                                                                    Yal-20092011-AW1_0169

---

17 It is likely that this morpheme in Belep is etymologically related to one or more of the following morphemes in Nêlêmwa: (i) The verb inflection -*i* used to indicate that the object is human or a given animate (Bril 2002: 42). (ii) The verb suffixes -*le* and -(*i*)*lî*, which indicate an augmentation of valence for an intransitive verb (Bril 2002: 49). (iii) The relators *i* (human) and *o* (non-human) which precede the object of a medio-active verb ('say', 'think', 'know', 'fear', etc.) (Bril 2002: 145-146). They may be reflexes of Proto-Oceanic *i / *aki(ni), which occurs both as a verb suffix and a preposition introducing oblique case nominals (Pawley 1976: 59).

In (41), the transitivized verb *kaxili* 'look' is followed by a differential absolutive marker.

(41)   « *Mo bwa pame ka kaxilin.* »
       mo bwa= pa=me   ka kaxi-li-n
       LK3 CONT= go.TV=CTP LK look-TR-DA.NSG
       '"Well, come and look at them [footprints]."'
       Yal-28072010-BGMCG-tayamu_0176

The transitivized verb *ûduli* 'drink' in (42) is followed by the absolutive noun phrase *we* 'water'.

(42)   *Texa ûduli we,*
       te=xa   ûdu-li   we
       3SG.SUBJ=ADD   drink-TR water
       'And he drank the water,'
       Yal-28072010-BGMCG-tahitian_0313

Some semantic bleaching can occur with *-li* transitivization. For example, the intransitive verb *to* means 'to vocalize, call' and may be used for birds as well as humans (43); however, the absolutive argument of the transitivized form *toli* 'to call sb. sth.' is the recipient of a particular appellation (44).

(43)   *Naxa to, to, to, tovan ka âria.*
       na=xa   to   to   to   to=van   ka   âria
       1SG.SUBJ=ADD call call call call=DIR.TV LK   NEG.EX
       'And I called, and called, and called, and kept calling but there was nothing.'
       Yal-28072010-BGMCG-tahitian_0103-0104

(44)   *Te tao toli tayamook xi nyan.*
       te=   tao=   to-li   tayamoo-x=i   nya-n
       3SG.SUBJ= HAB= call-TR old.woman-DET.D.PRX=GEN mother-3SG.POSS
       'He always called this old woman his mother.'
       Yal-28072010-BGMCG-tahitian_0318

Transitivization of verbs with *-li* has become grammaticalized in Belep code-mixing (§1.7.2) as the method for incorporating verbs from French into Belep morphosyntax.

Any French verb which is used transitively in a Belep clause[18] is marked with the suffix *-li* 'TR', even if the verb is already transitive in French. For example, the transitive verb *soigner* [swaɲe] 'to heal' is inserted into Belep morphosyntax in (45) using *-li*.

(45) **Te soigner-lie ma te ô.**
 te= [swaɲe]-li-e ma=re ô
 3SG.SUBJ= heal.LN-TR-3SG.ABS LK4=3SG.SUBJ be.good
 'She healed him so he was well.'
 Yal-28072010-BGMCG-tahitian_0308

5.2.5.3 Detransitivizer *-u*

All transitive verbs may be marked with the inflectional suffix *-u* 'DETRANS' when they are used without any reference to an absolutive argument—that is, detransitive *-u* is incompatible with inflection for specificity (§5.2.4), with the differential absolutive markers (§5.2.6), with the absolutive suffixes (§5.7), and with a following absolutive noun phrase. The detransitivizer attaches to the generic form of free transitives (§5.2.3.1), and to the root of bound transitives (§5.2.3.2) and transitivized verbs (§5.2.5.1 and §5.2.5.2). A few examples of detransitivized verbs are shown in Table 8.

Tab. 8: Examples of the usage of *-u* 'DETRANS'

Intransitive	Transitive	Detransitive	Gloss
-	êna	ênau	'to know'
-	îna	înau	'to make'
-	pa	pau	'to take'
-	taxa	taxau	'to unearth'
-	gi-	giu	'to attack'
-	ji-	jiu	'to give'
-	kele-	keleu	'to scoop'
-	taxe-	taxu[19]	'to distribute'
bwawa	bwawi-	bwawiu	'to remove'
iyu	iyue-	iyueu	'to buy'
nanam	nanami-	nanamiu	'to think'
wêêng	wêge-	wêgeu	'to organize, teach'

---

18 Note that only the infinitive forms of French verbs are used in Belep code-mixing.
19 *taxe* > *taxu* 'to distribute' is irregular. More research is needed to determine how many other verbs are irregular in this way.

Detransitive -*u* is used when the verb's patient is either obvious or irrelevant. The derivational proclitics to convert verbs to nouns (§3.6.2) often incorporate detransitivized forms of verbs. Speakers might use a detransitivized verb as a response to the question 'What are you doing?', as in (46) where the patient of the detransitivized verb *pwaxa* 'to wash' can only be understood as the speaker's clothing.

(46) **Na pwaxau.**

na=   pwaxa-u

1SG.SUBJ= wash-DETR

'I'm doing the washing [of the laundry].'

Yal-06102010-DY.wav

Speakers might also use a detransitivized verb when its patient is not a simple noun phrase but rather an involved explanation or a set of unrelated things; in these instances, detransitive -*u* serves a sort of 'summing up' function. For example, in (47), detransitivized *pau* 'take' in line 4 refers to all the diverse items the speaker has just enumerated.

(47) « **Jime tu ma, tu la bwe mar.**

ji=me   tu   ma   tu=la   bwe   mar

1DU.INCL.SUBJ=IRR   go.DH   LK4   go.DH=LOC   top   seashore

2   **Tu ma âvae no,**

tu   ma   âva-e   no

go.DH   LK4   fish-SPEC   fish

3   **ai tu ma pae weji ânemar, âna mar.**

ai   tu   ma   pa-e   we-ji

or   go.DH   LK4   take-SPEC   food-1DU.INCL.POSS

ânemar   âna   mar

top.snail   contents   seashore

4   *Jime paudame la pwemwa.* »
    ji=me   pa-u=da=me=la   pwemwa
    1DU.INCL.SUBJ=IRR   take-DETR=DIR.UH=CTP=LOC   village
    '"We're going to go down to the seashore. Go down to catch fish, or go down to get some troca to eat, [and] seafood. We're going to take all that stuff home."'

                                                        Yal-20092011-AW1_0065

5.2.6 Differential absolutive suffixes

Many verbs in Belep may be marked with a suffix—either *-n* 'DA.NSG' or *-a* 'DA.IA'—which identifies some characteristics of the absolutive argument. This is a form of differential object marking (DOM), as defined by Bossong (1985) and described in Comrie (1979, 1980), Bossong (1991), Aissen (2003), etc. Though cross-linguistically DOM is most commonly a form of dependent-marking (as defined by Nichols 1986), in Belep DOM is realized as head-marking.[20] That is, characteristics of the absolutive argument are indicated by verb suffixes. The term 'differential object marking' is not a completely accurate descriptor of the Belep phenomenon because Belep cannot be said to have 'objects'; the Belep suffixes may occur only on verbs which have an absolutive argument (that is, all transitive verbs (§5.2.3) and some intransitive verbs whose argument is in the absolutive case (§5.2.2)). For this reason I have substituted the term 'differential absolutive (DA) marking'.

The inflection for specificity discussed in §5.2.4 is one type of differential absolutive marking in Belep. It is distinct, however, from the two suffixes that will be discussed in this section because it occupies a different position class. These differential absolutive suffixes attach to the root of bound transitives (§5.2.3.2) and transitivized verbs (§5.2.5.1), and to the specific form of free transitives (§5.2.3.1)—free transitives marked with a DA suffix must be obligatorily marked as specific. A few examples are shown in Table 9.[21]

---

20 This also occurs cross-linguistically; Hungarian (Bárány 2015) and Blackfoot (Weber & Matthewson 2014) are two examples of languages with head-marked DOM.
21 Since the differential absolutive suffixes are fairly rare, they lack paradigmatic instantiation in my corpus. It is hypothesized that the forms marked with a question mark are valid, but it has not been confirmed by speakers.

Tab. 9: Examples of differential absolutive suffixes

Intransitive	Transitive	Specific	-n	-a	Gloss
iva	-	ivi	ivin	?ivia	'to be where?'
-	îna	înae	înaen	înaea	'to make'
-	pa	pae	paen	?paea	'to take'
-	pwaxa	pwaxae	pwaxaen	pwaxaea	'to wash'
-	ji	-	jin	jia	'to give'
-	ôbi	-	ôbin	ôbia	'to gather'
-	texe	-	?texen	texea	'to cradle'
kaxi	kaxili	-	kaxilin	?kaxilia	'to look at'
nook	noxe	-	noxen	noxea	'to solicit'
tup	tuve	-	?tuven	tuvea	'to dive, to dive for'
yaap	yavi	-	yavin	yavia	'to search for'

Differential absolutive suffixes are incompatible with pronominal absolutive suffixes (§5.7) and the detransitivizer -*u* (§5.2.5.3). Unlike the absolutive suffixes, DA suffixes can co-occur with absolutive noun phrases.

5.2.6.1 The suffix -*n*

The DA suffix -*n* 'DA.NSG'—also occurring as [-nã] in its incomplete phase (§2.4.3.2)—is used to index inanimate absolutive arguments referring to more than one item. For example, in (48), -*n* 'DA.NSG' occurs with the absolutive noun phrase *tolabava* 'our baskets', a semantically nonsingular, inanimate noun phrase.

(48)   ***Ava nawen tolambava.***
       ava=   nawe-**na**   tolamba-va
       1PL.EXCL.SUBJ= deposit-DA.NSG bag-1PL.EXCL.POSS
       'We put down our baskets.'
                                        Yal-17072009-TB-weekend_0004

In (49), -*n* 'DA.NSG' is suffixed to transitivized *kali* 'to break, shatter' and indexes *nuyan* 'her shroud'.

(49)   ***Pan na Kawo, kalin nuyan,***
       pan=a   Kawo   ka-li-**na**   nuya-n
       go.TV=NOM Kawo   shatter-TR-DA.NSG shroud-3SG.POSS

nyami la nuer,
nya-mi	la=	nu-er
DEM.IDF-DET.A.DST	3PL.SUBJ=	wrap.with.leaves-3SG.ABS

'Kawo went and ripped her shroud, the one they had wrapped her with,'

Yal-20092011-AW1_0301

In (50), *-n* 'DA.NSG' on the bound transitive verb *jie* 'to give' occurs without an absolutive noun phrase; instead it refers anaphorically to the semantically nonsingular, inanimate noun phrase *yadan* 'his clothes'.

(50) **Naxa ta ka pae yadan,**
na=xa	ta=xa	pa-e	yada-n
1SG.SUBJ=ADD	go.UH=LK	take-SPC	belongings-3SG.POSS

2 **ka jin na bwe Ôgaxoe.**
ka ji-<u>n</u>=a	bwe	Ôgaxoe
LK give-DA.NSG=LOC	top	Ôgaxoe

'And I went up and took his clothes, and put them on top of Ôgaxoe [a stone],'

Yal-28072010-BGMCG-tahitian_0165

The DA suffix *-n* is suffixed to the bound transitive verb *pie* 'to cook' in (51); in line 1 it is clause-final, while in line 2 it is followed by the noun phrase *wele nole* 'their fish to eat'.

(51) **Wîma lami le pa, le pin.**
wî-ma	la-mi	le=	pa
DEM.INAN-AC	DEM.PL-DET.A.DST	3DU.SUBJ=	take.GNR

le=	pi-<u>n</u>
3DU.SUBJ=	cook-DA.NSG

2 **Pin wele nole,**
pi-<u>na</u>	we-le	no-le
cook-DA.NSG	food-3DU.POSS	fish-ADU

'The ones they took, they cooked. Cooked their fish,'

Yal-20092011-AW1_0087-0088

Examples (50) and (51) reflect that bound transitive verb stems may become free with the addition of the differential absolutive suffix -*n*, and verbs with this suffix may occur at the end of an intonation unit.[22]

5.2.6.2 The suffix -*a*

The DA suffix -*a* 'DA.IA' indicates that the verb's absolutive argument is inanimate, although more research remains to be done in order to understand its precise meaning and how -*a* differs from -*n* 'DA.NSG'. In (52), -*a* precedes the inanimate noun phrase *wîja* 'something'.

(52) ***Mwaudu li lere înaea wîja ma, ai ?***

mwaudu=li	**le=re**	**îna-e-a**	**wîja**
unknown=GEN	3DU.SUBJ=ACT	make-SPC-DA.IN	DEM.INAN

ma	**ei**
LK4	or

'[She] didn't know that they were actually doing something that, you know?'
Yal-28072010-BGMCG-tayamu_0250

In (53), -*a* references the inanimate noun phrase *ween ola* 'lobster to eat'.

(53) ***ka tuvea ween ola,***

ka	**tuve-a**	**wee-n**	**ola**
LK	dive.TR-DA.IN	food-3SG.POSS	shellfish

'dive for lobster to eat,'
Yal-28072010-BGMCG-tahitian_0018

In (54), both -*n* 'DA.NSG' and -*a* 'DA.IA' occur, each suffixed to an instance of the transitivized verb *noxe* 'solicit'. In line 1, -*n* occurs without an absolutive noun phrase and refers to the previously mentioned banana tree and sugar cane plant. In line 2, -*a* precedes the noun phrase *wîîk* 'this thing'.

---

22 Note that verb forms ending in the DA suffix -*a* are not free; they must be followed by an absolutive noun phrase.

(54) **Laxa pan cuur reen, laxaô nooxen.**
    la=xa   **pana**   **cu-r=ee-n**   **la=xa=ô**
    3PL.SUBJ=ADD go.TV stand-NDR=DAT-3SG.POSS 3PL.SUBJ=ADD=REAL

    noxe-n
    solicit.TR-DA.NSG

    Laô nooxea wîîk,
    la=ô   **noxe-a**   **wîî-k**
    3SG.SUBJ=REAL solicit.TR-DA.IN DEM.INAN-DET.D.PRX
    'And they went and stood before him, and then asked him. They asked for this thing,'
                                                          Yal-28072010-BGMCG-lune_0054-0055

Unlike -*n*, the suffixation of -*a* does not allow a bound verb stem to become free. For example, when -*a* is attached to bound transitive *wêge* (transitivized from *wêêng* 'to learn, organize'), a following absolutive noun phrase is grammatical (55), while an omitted one is not (56).

(55) **Te wêêgea pulu.**
    te=   **wêge-a**   **pulu**
    3SG.SUBJ=   learn.TR-DA.IN   language
    'S/he learns a language.'

(56) ***Te wêêgea.**
    te=   **wêge-a**
    3SG.SUBJ=   learn.TR-DA.IN
    '*S/he learns.'

5.3 The verb group

Verbs in Belep consist generally of the verb word (§5.2) and a number of peripheral inflectional and derivational elements. This combination of suffixes and clitics surrounding the verb word will be termed the *verb group*, a term borrowed from the grammatical sketch of Balade Nyelâyu (Ozanne-Rivierre et al. 1998), which uses a similar morphological unit. This should be differentiated from the Belep *verb phrase* (see §5.11).

The Belep verb group is classified as a clitic group (as defined by Nespor & Vogel 1986, Aikhenvald 2002); the elements around the verb word fall into position classes

(Table 10), are normally unstressed, cannot occur in other clausal positions independently of each other, and have varying levels of phonological integration with the verb and each other.

In most cases, a subject agreement proclitic is the obligatory first element of the verb group (although there are a few exceptions; see for instance §5.6, §5.2.2, §6.8.1 and §7.2.1.1). In many cases throughout this work, subject agreement proclitics will be marked as procliticized to the rest of the verb group, as in (57).

(57) **Te mae.**
      te=   mae
      3SG.SUBJ=   sleep
      'S/he sleeps.'

However, in cases where a subject agreement marker is followed by the additive marker =*xa* 'ADD' (§7.2.1.3), the mood markers =*me* 'IRR' and =*ô* 'REAL' (§5.6), or the focus marker =*re* 'ACT' (§6.9.2.1), these elements will be considered to be encliticized onto the subject agreement marker, forming a phonological word which consists of clitics only.[23] In such cases, the subject agreement proclitic with its attached enclitics will be written as a separate phonological word from the rest of the verb group. The term *preface* will be used for this phonological word, based on the term "prefatory material" used for a similar constituent in Fijian (Dixon 1988). An example is shown in (58).

(58) **Texa mae.**
      te=xa   mae
      3SG.SUBJ=ADD   sleep
      'And s/he sleeps.'

Intonation breaks, pauses, and repairs during the production of the verb group are most likely to occur immediately after the preface; however, these should be considered indicators of a phonological, rather than a grammatical, word boundary (Dixon and Aikhenvald 2002:24). Morphologically, the preface acts as part of the verb group—it cannot occur in any other clausal position or independently of the rest of

---

23 Aikhenvald (2002) identifies phonological words consisting only of clitics as clitic groups.

the verb group, and the individual elements it contains do not have the status of phonological words and cannot be assigned to a word class.[24]

The formatives which compose the verb group (Table 10) fall into the following position classes, from left to right: clausal negation proclitics (§6.8); the preface, including subject agreement proclitics (§5.8), the additive enclitic (§7.2.1.3), the mood enclitics (§5.6), and the focus enclitic (§6.9.2.1); prohibitive proclitics (§6.7.2); aspectual proclitics (§5.5); derivational valence proclitics (§5.4); valence-changing suffixes (§5.2.5) and the specific suffix (§5.2.4) (these two categories are incompatible with one another); differential absolute suffixes (§5.2.6) and anaphoric absolute suffixes (§5.7) (these two categories are incompatible with one another); and miscellaneous verb suffixes (§5.5.11 and §5.5.12). Despite the inflectional status of many verbal elements, most are not obligatory (optional element positions are shown in parentheses in Table 10), and some position classes—marked by (*) in Table 10—allow for the use of multiple formatives from the same category. Note that the order of the mood and focus morphemes is only a tendency, not a rule.

The elements which follow the verb word are exclusively inflectional (§3.5) suffixes (§3.2.2.5), while those that precede it are inflectional and derivational (§3.6) clitics. The ordering of elements with relation to the verb is consistent with Bybee's (1985) generalizations about the categories of inflection. Valence, the inflectional category most closely tied to the verb, is also the closest morphological marking (§5.2). Derivational valence (see §5.4) is closer to the verb than other inflectional categories. Inflectional aspect is marked next-furthest in the position classes (§5.5), followed by mood (§5.6) and subject agreement (§5.8).

5.4 Agent valence

In Belep, the verbal valence proclitics (§3.2.2.6) *pa=* 'CAUS', *pe=* 'RECP', and *pu=* 'RA' are derivational morphemes (see §3.6) used to derive new lexical verbs from other verbs. They can be used to modify the activity level of the agent. The causative and reciprocal are reflexes of Proto-Oceanic prefixes which had the same function (Lynch et al. 2002:83).

---

24 For instance, the preface is not an auxiliary, since it never occurs in the position of a verb (Payne 1997), nor is it a satellite, since it does not overlap any word class (Talmy 2007).

Tab. 10: Verb clitic group position classes

PREFACE		(-6)	(-5)	(-4)	(-3)	(-2*)	(-1*)	0	(+1)		(+2)		(+3*)
(-8)	-7	ADD.	MOOD	FOC.	PROHIBITIVE	ASP.	VAL	VERB	VAL	SPC.	DA	ABS.	MISC.
NEG.	SUBJ. AGR.												
ari= 'NEG'	na= '1SG'	=xa 'ADD'	=me 'IRR'	=re 'ACT'	wara= 'NEG.IMPER'	āga= 'PROG'	pa= 'CAUS'	.	-u 'DETR'	-e 'SPC'	-n 'DA.NSG'	-nao '1SG'	-roven 'COMPL'
kiaxi= 'NEG2'	yo= '2SG'	.	=ô 'REAL'	.	kara= 'NEG.NEC'	âmu= 'PRF'	pe= 'RECP'	.	-ji 'TR'	.	-a 'DA.IN'	-o '2SG'	-mene 'GE'
	te= '3SG'	.	.	.	.	ba= 'SBJ'	pu= 'RA'	.	.	.	.	-e, -er '3SG'	
	ave= '1SG.EXCL'	.	.	.	.	bwa= 'CONT'	.	.	.	.	.	-ve '1SG.EXCL'	
	ji= '1SG.INCL'	.	.	.	.	ca= 'ITER'	.	.	.	.	.	-ji '1SG.INCL'	
	o= '2DL'	.	.	.	.	da= 'GNO'	.	.	.	.	.	-or '2DL'	
	te= '3DL'	.	.	.	.	ma= 'DIM'	.	.	.	.	.	-le '3DL'	
	avena= '1PA.EXCL'	.	.	.	.	nyi= 'PUNCT'	.	.	.	.	.	-ven '1PA.EXCL'	
	jena= '1PA.INCL'	.	.	.	.	tao= 'HAB'	.	.	.	.	.	-jen '1PA.INCL'	
	ôna= '2PA'	.	.	.	.	u= 'DUB'	.	.	.	.	.	-on '2PA'	
	lena= '3PA'	.	.	.	.	.	.	.	.	.	.	-len '3PA'	
	ava= '1PL.EXCL'	.	.	.	.	.	.	.	.	.	.	-va '1PL.EXCL'	
	ja= '1PL.INCL'	.	.	.	.	.	.	.	.	.	.	-ja '1PL.INCL'	
	a= '2PL'	.	.	.	.	.	.	.	.	.	.	-ac '2PL'	
	la= '3PL'	.	.	.	.	.	.	.	.	.	.	-la '3PL'	

5.4.1 Causative *pa=*

The causative proclitic *pa=* 'CAUS' is a derivational morpheme that derives verbs from other verbs. Some examples of attested causatives with *pa=* are shown in Table 11. Those marked with (*) are drawn from Dubois (1975e); all others occur in my corpus and field notes.

Tab. 11: Causativized verbs

Causative	Gloss	Translation
pa abwar	CAUS= rise	'to raise'
pa âya	CAUS= fear	'to scare'
pa bo	CAUS= stink	'to extinguish'
*pa cola	CAUS= be.strong	'to strengthen'
*pa kaxaleva	CAUS= be.flat	'to smooth'
pa kôê	CAUS= be.tired	'to annoy'
pa mae	caus= sleep	'to lull'
pa noor	CAUS= be.awake	'to awaken'
pa pulu > pawulu	CAUS= speak	'to converse'
*pa pwalic	CAUS= be.long	'to lengthen'
pa pweyau	CAUS= give.birth	'to midwife'

Note that in some cases, the morphological causative has become lexicalized to some degree, e.g. *pawulu* 'to converse' from *pa= pulu*. Another example is *pariae* 'to nurse', from *pa= ti* [CAUS= suckle], whose etymology is even more opaque to speakers.

When transitive verbs (§5.2.3) are causativized with *pa=*, the causee may be (un)marked in the absolute case (§6.4.1), as in (59) and (60). In (59) the causee of the causativized transitive verb *bwagee* 'to return [oneself]' is the demonstrative pronoun (§4.6.2) *wîli*, which is unmarked in the absolute case.

(59)   *Te pa bwage wîli,*
       te=   pa=   bwage   wî-li
       3SG.SUBJ= CAUS= return.SPC DEM.INAN-DET.A.PRX
       'He made that thing return [itself],'
                                                    Yal-20092011-AW6_0040

In (60), *pa=* causativizes the transitive verb *tuâgee* 'to tell lies'. Its causee is indexed by the absolutive pronominal suffix *-e* (§5.7).

(60)   *ka pa tuâgee,*
       ka pa=   tuâge-e
       LK CAUS= lie-3SG.ABS
       'and made him tell lies,'
       Yal-28072010-BGMCG-tahitian_0285

The constructed example in (61) was produced as a translation of *Alice a fait fermer la porte à sa soeur* 'Alice made her sister close the door.' Speakers did not translate this clause with causative *pa=*, instead using a transitive construction with *Aliic* 'Alice' as the subject and *pwâna mwa* 'door', the patient of the causativized transitive verb *tee* 'to close', as the absolute argument. The causee, *avan tamwa* 'her sister', is marked as genitive (§6.4.3) with *=li*.

(61)   *Aliic, te te pwâna mwa li avan tamwa.*
       Aliic te=   te   pwâna mwa=li   ava-na   tamwa
       Alice 3SG.SUBJ= close hole house=GEN   sibling-3SG.POSS woman
       'Alice, she made her sister close the door.' (lit. 'Alice, she closed the door by her sister.')

When intransitive verbs (§5.2.1) are causativized with *pa=*, the causee is marked in the genitive (§6.4.3) or instrumental (§6.4.6) case. It is unclear what conditions the choice between the two marking strategies, although it may be related to the animacy of the causee. For example, in (62) and (63), the animate causee is marked with the genitive ditropic clitic *=li* or *=i*.

(62)   *Te pa mwany nyi avan.*
       te=   pa=   mwany=i   ava-n
       3SG.SUBJ=   CAUS= be.bad=GEN   sibling-3SG.POSS
       'He made his brother sick.'
       Yal-20092011-AW6_0023

In (62), the causee *avan* 'his brother' is marked with genitive *=i*, while in (63) the causee *âju* 'person' is marked with genitive *=li*.

(63)   *pa jajani li âju*
       pa=   jajani=li   âju
       CAUS= be.crazy=GEN   person
       'make people irritated'

In examples (64) and (65), the inanimate causee is marked with the instrumental ditropic clitic =va or =vae.

(64)   *Ka ô pa uya va yadava la na mwa,*
      ka   ô   pa=   uya=va   yada-va=la
      LK   REAL CAUS= arrive=INSTR belongings-1PL.EXCL.POSS=LOC

      na   mwa
      interior house
      'And we caused our clothes to come into the house,'
                                                Yal-17072009-TB-weekend_0005

In (64), the causee *yadava* 'our clothes' is marked with instrumental =va. In (65), the causee *naap* 'fire' is marked with instrumental =vae.

(65)   *pa ulo vae naap*
      pa=   ulo=va-e   naap
      CAUS= be.red=INSTR-SPC fire
      'light the fire' (lit. 'cause the fire to be red')

Causative *pa=* is used productively to create morphological causative constructions such as in (66), where the causativized verb is the intransitive *cavac* 'to leave, go far away' in line 2 and the causee is the genitive-marked demonstrative pronoun *lali*.

(66)   BG: *Ma leme soigner lierexeng.*
                    ma   le=me   soigner-li-er=exeng
                    LK4 3SG.SUBJ=IRR heal.LN-TR-3SG.ABS=DET.DC
                    'That they would heal him here.'

2   CG: *Ma te pa cavac yi lali.*
                    ma=re   pa=   cavay=i   la-li
                    LK4=3SG.SUBJ CAUS= leave=GEN DEM.PL-DET.A.PRX
                    'So it would make them [the spirits] leave.'

3   BG: *Ma te pa ca– ji bwage lali,*

            ma   te=   pa=   cavac   ji   bwage
            LK4   3SG.SUBJ=   CAUS=   leave   give   return

            la-li
            DEM.PL-DET.A.PRX
            'So it would make them l- cause them to return,'

4   *ma la pan na Poc.*

            ma   la=   pan=a   Poc
            LK4   3PL.SUBJ=   go.TV=LOC   Poc
            'so that they would go to Poc.'

                                            Yal-28072010-BGMCG-tahitian_0255

Example (66) also demonstrates speakers' sense that morphological causativization with *pa=* implies a semantically more direct causation than the similar periphrastic expression with *ji* 'give' (discussed in §6.10.1). In (66), line 2, speaker MCG expands BG's statement from line 1. BG begins to repeat MCG's morphological causative in line 3, then changes his mind and produces a periphrastic causative. The semantic distinction between morphological and periphrastic causation is also reflected in differing glosses speakers give for them. For example, the glosses in (67) (a morphological causative with *pa=*) and (68) (a periphrastic causative) indicate that speakers perceive the morphological causative as more direct.

(67)   *pa up vi naemw*

        pa=   uv=i   nae-mw
        CAUS=   smoke=GEN   child-2SG.POSS
        'teach your child to smoke'

(68)   *jier ma te up*

        ji-er   ma=re   up
        give-3SG.ABS   LK4=3SG.SUBJ   smoke
        'cause him to smoke [he already knows how]'

5.4.2 Reciprocal *pe=*

The valence proclitic *pe=* 'RECP' is a derivational morpheme that derives new verbs from verbs. Its most basic usage is as a reciprocal marker, as in (69) where it indicates that the participants carried out the action on each other.

(69) **Lexa da pe cebe pwairamale,**
 le=xa da= pe= cebe pwaira-male
 3DU.SUBJ=ADD GNO= RECP= suspect girl-ADU
 'And the two girls just suspected each other,'
 Yal-19092011-PA_0061

More commonly, *pe=* indicates that the action of the verb is distributed or shared among all participants. In (70), *pe=* is used with the transitive verb *tae* 'to encircle'; in (71) *pe=* is used with intransitive *ka* 'to break'. In both examples, *pe=* indicates joint action on the part of the participants.

(70) **La pe taela li Belema.**
 la= pe= tae-la=li Bele-ma
 3PL.SUBJ= RECP= encircle-3PL.ABS=GEN Belep-AC
 'Together, the Belema encircled them.'
 Yal-20092011-AW3_0058

(71) **Avaxaô pe ka.**
 ava=xa=ô pe= ka
 1PL.EXCL.SUBJ=LK=REAL RECP= break
 'We separated.'
 Yal-17072009-TB-weekend_0028

Collective action is an important aspect of Pacific culture in general and Belep society in particular; see Lindstrom (1990) and Giordana (2014). The combination of reciprocal *pe=* with the verb *tue* 'to find' is commonly used to mean 'to assemble, to meet, to be together', as in (72), and the combination of *pe=* with *tâna* 'to hear' means 'to understand; to get along', as in (73).

(72) **ma ja pe pana pe tuja.**

ma	ja=	pe=	pana	pe=	tu-ja
LK4	1PL.INCL.SUBJ=	RECP=	go.TV	RECP=	find-1PL.INCL.ABS

'that we may come together,'

Yal-25072010-PT-homily_0058

(73) **Âbur, la koni pe tâna lile.**

âbur	la=	koni	pe=	tâna=li-le
side.UH	3PL.SUBJ=	never	RECP=	hear.GNR=GEN-3DU.ABS

'Before, they [the Or and Waap phratries] never could get along.'

Yal-20092011-AW3_0017

The various uses of the reflexes of this morpheme in other New Caledonian and Austronesian languages are discussed in Bril (2005).

5.4.3 Reduced agentive *pu=*

There are very few examples of *pu=* (glossed here 'RA'), in my corpus, and it was not possible to gather enough data to fully explain its usage. However, in the examples shown here, *pu=* indicates reduced action of the verb, such that the agent is attributed less agency than normal. For instance, the verb *kewee* 'to chase, to hunt' is shown in its typical usage in (74), where the agent is a frightening demon.

(74) **Teme kewela li Dubageni.**

te=me	kewe-la=li	Dubageni
3SG.SUBJ=IRR	chase-3PL.ABS=GEN	type.of.demon

'The Dubageni will chase them.'

Yal-05092011-AP1_0094

In (75), the modification of *kewee* 'to chase' with the reduced transitive proclitic *pu=* changes the meaning to 'to follow'. The example in (75) occurred several times in conversation with Belema, where the agent was a faithful dog.

(75) **Te pu kewenao.**

te=	pu=	kewe-nao
3SG.SUBJ=	RA=	chase-1SG.ABS

'He's following me.'

Examples (76) and (77) also show the usage of reduced agentive *pu=*. In (76), the normal dynamic meaning of *nginie* 'to miss, to not be able to see' is reduced by *pu=* to mean 'to accidentally not see'.

(76) **La pu ngini cae to bwan.**
    la=   pu= ngini   cae=ro   bwan
    3PL.SUBJ= RA= not.see reef=when night
    'They didn't see the reef in the night.'
                                            Yal-20092011-AW2_0036

In (77), the action of *pa* 'to take' is reduced by *pu=* to indicate that the action was accomplished through magic, rather than through the physical action of the agent.

(77) **Te âri ma, la pu pa dooma lali,**
    te=   âri   ma   la=   pu=   pa
    3SG.SUBJ= say   LK4   3PL.SUBJ= RA=   take.GNR

    do-ma   la-li
    earth-AC   DEM.PL-DET.A.PRX

    ka pu pada la mweogo.
    ka pu= pa=da=la   mweogo
    LK RA= take.GNR=DIR.UH=LOC mountain
    'He commanded that all this earth would be taken, and taken up onto the mountain [using magic].'
                            Yal-28072010-BGMCG-sousmarin_0038-0039

In (78), the action of *wayap* 'to make war' is reduced by *pu=*, signifying that the warriors may have wanted to stop fighting, but could not (in the next clause, the speaker asserts the warriors' inability to stop).

(78) **Ka ô pu wayap, pu wayavavan.**
    ka ô   pu=   wayap   pu=   wayava=van
    LK REAL RA=   make.war RA= make.war=DIR.TV
    'And they kept fighting and fighting.'
                                            Yal-20092011-AW4_0040

Example (79) is from a discussion with a speaker in an attempt to understand the meaning of *pu=*, which is typically glossed by speakers as 'to the side'. In (79), *pu=* decreases the agentivity of the agent of a general motion verb like *pan* 'to go.TV'; however, it is ungrammatical to use it with the more dynamic verb *wânem* 'to walk', which implies a greater amount of agentivity for its agent.

(79) **Na pan.**

    na=   **pan**

    1SG.SUBJ= go.TV

    'I go.'

    Na pu pan.

    na=   **pu=**   **pan**

    1SG.SUBJ= RA= go.TV

    'I go a little; I stop; I do not continue.'

    *****na=**   **pu=**   **wânem**

    1SG.SUBJ= RA= walk

    *'I walk a little.'

5.5 Morphological aspect

Aspect is richly expressed in Belep. It is indicated by a closed set of verbal proclitics (§3.2.2.6), listed in Table 12, which precede the verb in a fixed position. As discussed in §3.5.3, these proclitics are analyzed here as inflectional, though they have some derivational properties—chiefly, that verbs may be unmarked for aspect; aspect marking is not obligatory.[25]

Tab. 12: Aspect clitics

Belep	Gloss	English meaning
âga=	PROG=	progressive (§5.5.1)
âmu=	PRF=	perfect (§5.5.2)

---

[25] It is possible that some of the rarer morphemes classed as aspect markers in this description may in fact belong to the set of derivational proclitics discussed in §5.4. More research is needed in this area.

Belep	Gloss	English meaning
ba=	SBJ=	subjunctive (§5.5.3)
bwa=	CONT=	continuative; 'to still be'; 'to have just' (§5.5.4)
ca=	ITER=	iterative (§5.5.5)
da=	GNO=	gnomic; with its own agency (§5.5.6)
ma=	DIM=	diminished (§5.5.7)
nyi=	PUNCT=	punctual; increased (§5.5.8)
tao=	HAB=	habitual (§5.5.9)
u=	DUB=	dubitative; 'to pretend to'; 'to kind of' (§5.5.10)

Table 13 shows the aspectual morphemes divided into perfective and imperfective groups; there is some language-internal evidence for this division in that some morphemes from one group are incompatible with some morphemes from the other, though this is not always the case and much work remains to be done on this topic. Some aspect clitics can co-occur and some cannot; this will be discussed in-depth here.

Tab. 13: Classes of aspect formatives in Belep

Perfective	Imperfective	Other
ca= 'ITER'	tao= 'HAB'	âmu= 'PRF'
da= 'GNO'	âga= 'PROG'	ba= 'SBJ'
nyi= 'PUNCT'	bwa= 'CONT'	ma= 'DIM'
		u= 'DUB'

Any number of aspectual clitics may be used on a given verb, and their order may vary. For example, in the constructed examples in (80), the aspectual proclitics *nyi=* 'PUNCT' and *tao=* 'HAB' may occur in either order.

(80)   *Te nyi tao tawae yeek.*

te=   nyi=   tao=   tawa-e   yeek
3SG.SUBJ= PUNCT= HAB= cut-SPC plant
'S/he always chops down the trees.'

Te tao nyi tawae yeek.

te=   tao=   nyi=   tawa-e   yeek
3SG.SUBJ= HAB= PUNCT= cut-SPC plant
'S/he always chops down the trees.'

Yal-15092011-TB1.wav – Yal-15092011-TB3.wav

Many aspect clitics are polyfunctional and may occur in other constructions in the language. For example, *âmu=* 'PRF' may also modify nouns (see §5.5.2)); *bwa=* is used in imperatives (§6.7.1) and to form participles (§5.10.2); and *ma=* and *nyi=* are used in comparatives (§6.12).

Two additional morphemes which are not aspect proclitics are discussed in this section. The verb suffixes *-roven* 'COMPL' (§5.5.11) and *-mene* 'GE' (§5.5.12) also serve an aspectual function in Belep. Similar in meaning to the homophonous noun suffixes (§4.3.3, §4.3.4), they occur in the final position class of the verb group, following any absolutive suffixes (§5.3). The verb group directional enclitic *=van* (§5.12) also has an aspectual meaning.

5.5.1 Progressive *âga=*

The progressive aspect clitic *âga=* is used to indicate that the action is an "ongoing, dynamic process" (Payne 1997:240). It is incompatible with *âmu=* 'PRF', *ca=* 'ITER', and *ma=* 'DIM', and with the adverb *mwa* 'again'. For example, in (81), the use of *âga=* implies that it must be possible to describe the action while it is occurring—the action of *tabo* 'fall' must be taking a long time.

(81)   *Te âga tabo.*

te=   âga=   tabo
3SG.SUBJ= PROG= fall
'He is falling (e.g. a parachutist)'

Yal-30092010-PT.wav

In (82), *âga=* is used to represent the continuing action of one participant while other participants perform other actions. In this narrative, an old woman *te âga pilu* 'is still dancing' while two other women stalk her with murderous intent.

(82) *Toma te âga pilu,*
  toma te= âga= pilu
  but 3SG.SUBJ= PROG= dance

  ka âri te ênae, puur ri ma,
  ka âri= re= êna-e pu-r=i ma
  LK NEG= 3SG.SUBJ= know-3SG.ABS origin-3GNR.POSS=GEN LK4

  âri te – ai ? Âri te kiyile ?
  âri= te= ei âri= te= kiyi-le
  NEG= 3SG.SUBJ= or NEG= 3SG.SUBJ= see.SPC-3DU.ABS
  'But she was still dancing, and she didn't know because, she didn't – you see? She didn't see them?'
  Yal-28072010-BGMCG-tayamu_0247-0249

5.5.2 Perfect *âmu=*

Cross-linguistically, the perfect aspect "expresses a relation between two time-points, on the one hand the time of the state resulting from a prior situation, and on the other the time of that prior situation" (Comrie 1976:52). The perfect aspect clitic *âmu=* in Belep may be used to indicate a relation between the past and the present, as in (83) where the use of *âmu=* shows that the action of the verb, *kiya-u* 'see.GNR-DETR' is relevant to the moment of speaking.

(83) *Toma yena, ja âmu kiyau ka,*
  toma yena ja= âmu= kiya-u=xa
  but now 1PL.INCL.SUBJ= PRF= see.GNR-DETR=LK

  tuya avar ki înau.
  tuya avari=xi îna-u
  EX.GNR other=REL make-DETR

Na kiyau la na télé.

na=   kiya-u=la   na   télé
1SG.SUBJ= see.GNR-DETR=LOC interior television.LN

'But now, we have seen that there are others who do it. I saw it on TV.'

Yal-28072010-BGMCG-hamecon_0051-0052

In (83), the fact that the speaker has seen the fishing technique in question on television in the past is relevant to his knowledge of it in the present.

Belep *âmu=* can also be used to express "a relation between a future state and a situation prior to it" (Comrie 1976:53). For example, in (84), *âmu=* is used to indicate that the action it marks, *cavac* 'to leave', is dependent on the event that precedes it, the celebration of Easter. Note that this example occurs within a clause incorporating deontic *te ô ki* (discussed in further detail in §7.3.6) and inceptive *pan* (§5.10.4).

(84)   *Te ô ki ja pan înae Paixa, ka âmu cavac.*

te=   ô=xi   ja=   pana îna-e   Paixa   ka
3SG.SUBJ= good=REL 1PL.INCL.SUBJ= go.TV make-SPC Easter.LN LK

âmu= cavac
PRF= leave

'When we're about to celebrate Easter, we should wait to leave until afterwards.' [as opposed to leaving before Easter]

Yal-20092011-AW2_0075

In (84), the speaker describes a customary rule by which Belema should not travel away from home immediately before Easter (in the context of a story about people who did so and were punished by being shipwrecked and eaten by sharks). Perfect *âmu=* relates the verb it modifies, *cavac* 'to leave', to the prior event upon which it depends, *înae Paixa* 'celebrate Easter'.

Perfect *âmu=* is often translated by Belep speakers as immediate past (85) or present (86), as seen in these constructed examples.

(85)   *Te âmu pae.*

te=   âmu= pa-e
3SG.SUBJ= PRF= take-3SG.ABS

'He has taken it.' (translated by Belep speaker as *il vient de le prendre* 'He just took it')

Yal-13102010-AP.wav

(86)   *Teme âmu pae.*
       te=me   âmu= pa-e
       3SG.SUBJ=FUT PRF= take-3SG.ABS
       'He will have taken it.' (translated by Belep speaker as *il va bientôt le prendre* 'He will take it soon')

       Yal-13102010-AP.wav

In speech, *âmu=* occurs most frequently in a variety of expressions Belep speakers use to say goodbye until the next meeting, thus relating a future state to the present. Here the perfect clitic modifies nouns rather than verbs, as shown in Table 14.

Tab. 14: Belep greetings

Belep greeting	English gloss	English translation
âmu= yena	PRF= now	'see you soon [later today]'
âmu= iyam	PRF= tomorrow	'see you tomorrow' (used to mean 'good night')
âmu= mon	PRF= side.DH	'see you later [our next meeting]'
âmu= jaok iyam	PRF= year-DET.D.PRX tomorrow	'see you next year'

The perfect clitic *âmu=* is incompatible with *âga=* 'PROG' and *ca=* 'ITER'.

5.5.3 Subjunctive *ba=*

The subjunctive mood in Belep may be indicated by the proclitic *ba=*, which falls into the aspect position class (Table 10). This morpheme is used to indicate that the action of the clause in which it occurs is hypothetical, depending on the realization of the clause on which it is semantically dependent (§7.3). The constructed examples in (87) - (89) show this usage.

(87)   *Te wêêng ma te ba comu.*
       te=   wêêng   ma=re   ba= comu
       3SG.SUBJ= organize LK4=3SG.SUBJ SBJ= learn
       'S/he studies so that s/he might learn.'

(88)   *Te pae savon ma te ba boyâm.*
       te=   pa-e   cawô   ma=re   ba=   boyâm
       3SG.SUBJ=   take-SPC   soap.LN   LK4=3SG.SUBJ   SBJ= bathe
       'S/he takes the soap so that s/he might bathe.'
                                          Yal-03112011-IM1.wav – Yal-03112011-IM2.wav

(89)   *Yo yagelinao ma ji ba cavac pôben.*
       yo=   yage-li-nao   ma ji=   ba=   cavaya   pôben
       2SG.SUBJ=   help-TR-1SG.ABS   LK4 1DU.INCL= SBJ= leave   quickly
       'You should help me so that we may leave soon.'

Note that this proclitic is rare and does not occur in my corpus; more research is necessary to understand its usage. It is most likely etymologically related to the instrumental proclitic *ba=* (§3.6.2.2).

5.5.4 Continuative *bwa=*

Though *bwa=* is used as a polite imperative (§6.7.1) and in a complementation strategy (§7.3.9), it also has an aspectual meaning. In this meaning, it is often translated 'just' or 'still'. For example, in the constructed example in (90), it can have either meaning.

(90)   *Na bwa wiu.*
       na=   bwa=   wiu
       1SG.SUBJ=   CONT=   dine
       'I just ate' or 'I'm still eating'[26]

Discourse examples indicate that *bwa=* should be glossed as a continuative, a type of imperfective aspect. In (91), *bwa=* is used to indicate that the action is continuing.

(91)   *te bwa tao ci koon na bwe mar,*
       te=   bwa=   tao=   ci   kon=a   bwe   mar
       3SG.SUBJ=   CONT=   HAB=   sit   unable=LOC   top   seashore
       'he is still nonetheless incapable [of moving the boat] on the seashore,'
                                                            Yal-19092011-PA_0071

---

26 *Je viens de manger* or *Je mange encore.*

In (92), the use of *bwa=* indicates that the verbal state *mo* 'to live' was still continuing.

(92)　**âbur, Pairoome, âjuma lami la bwa mo li.**

âbur	Pairome	âju-ma	la-mi
side.UH	Pairome	person-AC	DEM.PL-DET.A.DST

la=	bwa=	mo=li
3PL.SUBJ=	CONT=	live=DET.LOC

'before, at Pairoome, those people were still living there.'

　　　　　　　　　　　　　　　　　　　　　　Yal-20092011-AW6_0132

In (93), the continuing action marked by *bwa=* is *kela* 'to slide, crawl'.

(93)　**Te wali, te bwa kela.**

te=	wa-li	te=	bwa=	kela
3SG.SUBJ=	DEM.MAN-DET.A.PRX	3SG.SUBJ=	CONT=	slide

'He was like, he was still crawling [he hadn't learned to walk yet].'

　　　　　　　　　　　　　　　　　Yal-28072010-BGMCG-sousmarin_0012

Usages of *bwa=* are incompatible with the gnomic aspect marker *da=* 'GNO' and with *ma=* 'DIM'.

Like all aspect clitics, *bwa=* typically occurs very close to the verb word (see §5.3 and Table 10). However, in some uses of *bwa=* it occurs outside its normal position class. For instance, continuative *bwa=* can mean 'yet' if it occurs in a negated clause (§6.8), as in (94), where *bwa=* occurs before the negative proclitic.

(94)　**Te bwa ânô, bwa âri te – jua âri te ulac.**

te=	bwa=	ânô	bwa=	âri=	te=	jua
3SG.SUBJ=	CONT=	be.young	CONT=	NEG=	3SG.SUBJ=	very

âri=	te=	ulac
NEG=	3SG.SUBJ=	be.old

'He was still young, he wasn't yet – he wasn't old at all.'

　　　　　　　　　　　　　　　　　　　　　　Yal-20092011-AW3_0006

In (94), *bwa=* is used first to indicate that a state is continuing, namely *ânô* 'be young'; then it is used before the negative proclitic *âri=* to mean 'not yet'.

5.5.5 Iterative *ca=*

The iterative aspect clitic *ca=* is used to conceptualize the processual action of the verb as a unit which is repeated multiple times. This iterative aspect is a type of perfective. My corpus includes examples of its use with the verbs *ta* 'go.UH', *mo* 'live, stay', *kiya* 'see', *pae* 'take', *uya* 'arrive'. For example, in (95), *ca=* is used in lines 1 and 2 to indicate that the reified actions of *ta la na toop* 'go up into the fields' and *tu la bwe mar* 'go down to the seashore' were repeated many times throughout the participants' lives.

(95) **Le ca ta la na toop,**
le=   ca=   ta=la   na   toop
3DU.SUBJ= ITER= go.UH=LOC interior field

ka le ca tu la bwe mar.
ka le=   ca=   tu=la   bwe mar
LK 3DU.SUBJ= ITER= go.DH=LOC top seashore
'They would always go up into the fields, and they would always go down to the seashore.'

Yal-19092011-PA_0005

In example (96), *ca=* marks the frequent occurrence of a natural phenomenon.

(96) **Baraap, la ca puc ya kawinama.**
baraap la=   ca=   puy=a   kawina-ma
evening 3PL.SUBJ= ITER= fly=NOM firefly-AC
'In the evening, the fireflies often come out.'

Yal-20092011-AW5_0114

Iterative *ca=* is fairly similar in meaning to habitual *tao=*; Belep speakers translate both of them as *toujours* 'always'. However, *ca=* is incompatible with *âga=* 'PROG' and *âmu=* 'PRF', whereas *tao=* is compatible with both.

5.5.6 Gnomic *da=*

The aspectual clitic *da=* is normally translated *tout seul* 'all by itself' by Belep speakers. While this may describe the etymology of the morpheme—I hypothesize that it derives from the adverb *âda* 'alone' (see §3.3.3)—its modern usage indicates the gnomic aspect, where "the situation described in the proposition is generic; the predicate has held, holds, and will hold for the class of entities named by the subject" (Bybee et al. 1994: 319). Belep *da=* is used to indicate that the action expressed by the verb is expected based on the nature of the participants or is a general truth. For instance, in (97), the use of *da=* shows that the participants, two women, are performing a normal, characteristic activity (in Belep society, collecting edible sea life on the seashore is a task characteristically performed by women and children).

(97) **Lexa da ôbi têno le yâgak,**
 le=xa da= ôbi têno le yâgak
 3DU.SUBJ=ADD STAT= gather type.of.shell LK2 spider.conch
 'They were just gathering *têno* and spider conchs,'
 Yal-19092011-PA_0009

In (98), *da=* expresses that the ancient whitened remains of people killed in a battle are visible to any observer.

(98) **Yo da kiyie, ma la poro, yena, la poro.**
 yo= da= kiyi-e ma la= poro
 2SG.SUBJ= STAT= see.SPC-3SG.ABS LK4 3PL.SUBJ= be.white

 yena la= poro
 now 3PL.SUBJ= be.white
 'You see that they are white, now—they are white.'
 Yal-20092011-AW3_0071-0072

The gnomic aspectual clitic *da=* is incompatible with *bwa=* 'CONT' and *ma=* 'DIM'.

5.5.7 Diminished *ma=*

The aspectual clitic *ma=* is used to indicate a decreased amount of the action of the verb, or that the action of the verb was defective in some way. For example, in (99), *ma=* is used with the verb *ulac* 'be old' to mean that the participant was deficient in performing the action of the verb.

(99)   *ô ma ulac ya naele.*
      ô   ma= ulay=a   nae-le
      REAL DIM= be.old=NOM child-3DU.POSS
      'their child wasn't very old'
                                                Yal-28072010-BGMCG-sousmarin_0011

It is also used in comparative constructions (§6.12.1) to indicate 'less', and is incompatible with *âga=* 'PROG', *bwa=* 'CONT', *da=* 'GNO', and *tao=* 'HAB'.

5.5.8 Punctual *nyi=*

The aspectual clitic *nyi=* is used to indicate that an action is punctual; it occurs at a specific instant in time and has "no internal temporal structure" (Payne 1997: 241). For example, in (100), the action of the verb *tup* 'to dive' is represented as being forceful and occurring at a single moment in time.

(100)   *Avexa nyi tuvadu la na buâny waak.*
      ave=xa   nyi=   tuva=du=la   na   buâny
      1DU.EXCL.SUBJ=ADD   PUNCT= dive=DIR.DH=LOC interior stone

      waa-k
      DEM.MAN-DET.D.PRX
      'And we dove down at the stone like this.'
                                              Yal-28072010-BGMCG-tahitian_0053

In example (101), the use of *nyi=* indicates the manner of *cao* 'to work' and *cibia* 'to turn over'; the participants were planting yam fields, work that requires repeated punctual action of digging a hole, planting a yam, and marking it with a stick.

(101)   *La nyi cao, la nyi cibiae doo,*
      la=   nyi=   cao   la=   nyi=   cibia-e   doo
      3PL.SUBJ= PUNCT= work 3PL.SUBJ= PUNCT= turn-SPC earth
      'They worked, they turned the earth'
                                              Yal-28072010-BGMCG-sousmarin_0016

For Belep speakers, *nyi=* usually implies that the punctual event occurs with a large amount of force or effort exerted by the participants; this is most likely why *nyi=* is also used for comparatives to indicate 'more' (§6.12.1).

5.5.9 Habitual *tao=*

The habitual aspect clitic *tao=* is used to express that "a certain type of event...regularly takes place (i.e. is instantiated by actual events) from time to time" (Payne 1997: 241). It is a type of imperfective aspect in Belep. For example, in (102), the action of the verb is conceptualized as something that is constantly occurring, with no distinct endpoints for iterations.

(102)   *Te tao to li tayamook xi nyan.*
    te=   tao=   to=li   tayamoo-x=i   nya-n
    3SG.SUBJ= HAB=   call-TR old.woman-DET.D.PRX=GEN mother-3SG.POSS
    'He always called this old woman his mother.'
                                         Yal-28072010-BGMCG-tahitian_0318

In example (103), the action of the verb is conceptualized as happening several times, with no distinct endpoints.

(103)   *Na tao toda, na pwai kiya nabwa wiîk.*
    na=   tao=   to=da
    1SG.SUBJ= HAB=   call=DIR.UH

    na=   pwai   kiya   nabwa   wiî-k.
    1SG.SUBJ= only   see.GNR   imprint   DEM.IA-DET.D.PRX
    'I kept calling and calling up, but I only saw prints.'
                                         Yal-28072010-BGMCG-tahitian_0093

Habitual *tao=* is fairly similar in meaning to iterative *ca=*; Belep speakers translate both of them as *toujours* 'always' and feel that one can often substitute for the other. Proclitic *tao=* is incompatible with *ma=* 'DIM'.

5.5.10 Dubitative *u=*

The aspectual clitic *u=* seems to indicate that the action of the verb was performed halfheartedly, and it could be glossed 'kind of'. For example, in (104), *u=* indicates the participant's incomplete performance of the verb *para* 'to tell'.

(104) **Te u parie, toma bwa âri ave âva lie.**

       te=   **u=**   **pari-e**
       3SG.SUBJ=   DUB=   tell.TR-3SG.ABS

       toma bwa=   **âri=**   **ave=**   **âva=li-e**
       but   CONT= NEG= 1DU.EXCL.SUBJ= fish.GNR=GEN-3SG.ABS
       'He kind of talked about it, but we never did fish that way.'
                                                            Yal-28072010-BGMCG-hamecon_0089

The morpheme *u=* is normally incompatible with all other aspectual proclitics.

5.5.11 Completive *-roven*

The completive aspect is accomplished in Belep with the verb suffix *-roven* 'COMPL'[27] rather than with a verb group aspectual proclitic. Cross-linguistically, the completive aspect is associated with several related meanings, including "to do something thoroughly and completely [such that t]he object of the action is totally affected, consumed, or destroyed by the action[, which] may well involve multiple entities" (Bybee et al. 1994: 57).

The Belep suffix *=roven* is compatible with all of these cross-linguistic characteristics of completive aspect. It is used to indicate a thoroughly completed action, as in (105) where the action is described by *ciwie* 'to bury'. Note that a phonologically reduced form of *-roven* is used because the verb group is followed by an absolutive noun phrase, the toponym *Ono*.

(105) **Texa ciwiroven Ono.**

       te=xa   **ciwi-rove**   **Ono**
       3SG.SUBJ=ADD   bury-COMPL   Ono
       'And it [a tsunami] completely buried [the village of] Ono.'
                                                        Yal-28072010-BGMCG-sousmarin_0077

Belep *-roven* also indicates the total affectedness of the patient. For example, in (106), the completive suffix on the transitive verb *bae* 'to eat, bite' is interpreted as meaning that the patient is completely affected—completely eaten.

---

[27] Completive verb suffix *-roven* is clearly a grammaticalized version of the full verb *toven* 'to finish'. It is homophonous with the noun suffix *-roven* 'all' (§4.3.4).

(106) « *Na maac yi cawi, na baeroven.* »
  na=   may=i   cawi   na=   bae=roven
  1SG.SUBJ= die=GEN   hunger   1SG.SUBJ=   bite=COMPL
  '"I was hungry [so] I ate it all up.'
                                              Yal-01082010-MFD_0017

Finally, part of the meaning of the suffix *-roven* is that multiple entities are affected by the action of the verb. For example, in (107), the use of completive *-roven* is intended to mean that all of the agents are affected by the action of the intransitive verb *cavac* 'to leave'.

(107) « *Me âria âju la pwemwajen, enyi ji cavayaroven.* »
  me   âria   âju=la   pwemwa-jen
  IRR   NEG.EX   person=LOC   village-1PA.INCL.POSS

  enyi   ji=   cavaya-roven
  if   1DU.INCL.SUBJ=   leave=COMPL
  '"There won't be anyone in our home, if we *both* leave."'
                                              Yal-20092011-AW1_0083

The difference between the completive aspect verb suffix *-roven* and the total noun quantifier *-roven* is demonstrated in (108) and (109).

(108) *Duaro na mo lexeng, na tânaroven pavadaar pulu.*
  duaro   na=   mo=lexeng
  while   1SG.SUBJ=   live=LOC.DC

  na=   tâna-rovena   pavada-ra   pulu
  1SG.SUBJ=   hear.GNR-COMPL   muttering-3GNR.POSS   speech
  'Living here, I hear everything people grumble about.'
                                              Yal-25072010-PT-homily_0097-0098

(109) *La pan pan ka kiyi daroven,*
  la=   pana   pan   ka   kiyi   da-roven
  3PL.SUBJ=   go.TV   go.TV   LK   see.SPC   blood-all
  'They went along and saw all that blood,'
                                              Yal-20092011-AW5_0086

In (108), the completive verb suffix *-roven* modifies the verb *tâna* 'to hear', indicating that its action is completed thoroughly. In (109), the noun suffix *-roven* modifies the noun *da* 'blood', indicating totality of reference.

5.5.12 General extender *-mene*

General extenders are pragmatic expressions which are connected to sentence structure and somewhat inflexible in their syntactic distribution (Overstreet 2005:1846). The Belep verb suffix *-mene* 'GE' is used as a general extender, identifying a category or set of actions similar to that of its host verb, as in (110).

(110)   *Enyi âmi la oyaavamene, la yava jabaang ngie.*

enyi	â-mi	la=	oyava-mene
if	DEM.NEW-DET.A.DST	3PL.SUBJ=	reel-GE

la=	yava	jabang=i-e
3PL.SUBJ=	catch.GNR	Spanish.mackerel=GEN-3SG.ABS

'Whenever they reeled and stuff, they caught Spanish mackerel with it.'

Yal-28072010-BGMCG-hamecon_0091

Note that *-mene* also occurs as a noun suffix general extender (§4.3.3).

5.6 Morphological mood

In Belep, the mood morphemes =ô 'REAL' and =me 'IRR' form a basic distinction between realis and irrealis modes[28] as defined in Mithun (2001). "The realis portrays situations as actualized, as having occurred or actually occurring, knowable through direct perception. The irrealis portrays situations as purely within the realm of thought, knowable only through imagination" (Mithun 2001: 173).

The morphological mood clitics behave in a manner distinct from the set of aspectual clitics (§5.5). One piece of evidence for the separation of these two categories is that mood markers cluster with the preface (§5.3) rather than with the aspectual proclitics and the rest of the verb group. Some subject agreement proclitics undergo

---

28 The terms *mood*, *mode*, and *modality* are used interchangeably throughout this work.

phonetic reduction when they occur with =ô 'REAL' (see §5.6.1 below), and it is ungrammatical for an aspect proclitic to precede the morpheme =me 'IRR'.[29] These behaviors (i.e. triggering phonemic reduction, strict ordering) are not characteristic of the aspect proclitics.

Another piece of evidence for the existence of a mood category distinct from aspect is that the two categories have different frequencies of occurrence in discourse. The mood markers =ô 'REAL' and =me 'IRR' occur very frequently in natural discourse, while the aspectual proclitics are fairly uncommon. Approximate frequencies from my corpus are represented in Table 15.

Tab. 15: Frequencies of mood and aspect morphemes

Mood morpheme	# of tokens	Aspect morpheme	# of tokens
=ô 'REAL'	429	tao= 'HAB'	57
=me 'IRR'	260	bwa= 'CONT'	49
		nyi= 'PUNCT'	38
		ca= 'ITER'	17
		da= 'GNO'	11
		âmu= 'PRF'	9
		âga= 'PROG'	2

Although it is true that the frequency of semantically transparent elements is dependent on how frequently speakers need to express their meaning in discourse, this marked contrast in the distribution of mood and aspect morphemes provides a further piece of evidence that they should be considered separate grammatical categories in Belep.

Finally, cross-linguistic evidence indicates that a mood category distinct from aspect might exist in Belep. In Nêlêmwa (Bril 2002), there is a 'frame of reference' distinction between 'virtual' clauses (marked with either hypothetical *o* or prospective future *io* preposed to the entire clause) and 'non-virtual' clauses, which are zero-marked. In Boumaa Fijian, 'tense-aspect' markers (indicating 'past', 'future/would/might', and 'contrast with the present') are included in the 'prefatory material' before the verb; they are distinguished from 'stance-aspect' modifiers, which "describe the temporal duration, etc, of the activity or state referred to by the predicate" (Dixon 1988: 76). In South Efate, bound subject pronouns procliticized to the verb complex "distinguish realis and irrealis forms" (Thieberger 2006: 109).

---

29 One speaker stated that it is possible for realis =ô to occur after an aspectual proclitic, though this has never been instantiated in my hearing. She was sure, however, that irrealis =*me* could never occur after an aspectual proclitic.

In Belep, mood is not obligatorily marked in all clauses. Clauses for which the speaker claims actual instantiation of the event described by the verb are marked with the realis marker =ô. Clauses where the instantiation of the verb is hypothetical, conditional, or predicted for the future are marked with the irrealis marker =me. All other clauses are zero-marked. This is reminiscent of the situation in Xârâcùù, where "utterances called 'atemporal', affirmations of a general order...simple statements of a fact or a state, do not necessitate the presence of an aspecto-temporal modal" (Moyse-Faurie 1995: 115). A similar system exists in Nêlêmwa (Bril 2002), where the perfective morpheme can co-occur with both of the 'virtual' morphemes. Bril states that the zero-realization of the perfective morpheme may occur if the action of the verb is "generic, imperfective, or unmarked perfective"[30] when "the situation of the utterance or the discourse context suffices to define the temporal or aspectual reference"[31] (Bril 2002: 198). Speakers assert that the Belep mood morphemes may co-occur, although it is unclear what circumstances might prompt this and how its meaning would be interpreted.

Both mood markers =ô and =me normally occur as enclitics in the preface part of the verb group (§5.3), as in (111) and (112).

(111) **Teô wânem,**
 te=ô   wânem
 3SG.SUBJ=REAL   walk
 'She walked.'
                                                              Yal-20092011-AW1_0113

(112) **Teme cegele,**
 te=me   cege-le
 3SG.SUBJ=IRR   watch-3DU.ABS
 'She would watch them,'
                                                       Yal-28072010-BGMCG-tayamu_0147

However, they should be considered simple clitics according to Zwicky's (1977) definition; they may also appear in a full, uncliticized form when there is no subject agreement proclitic (§5.8) for them to attach to, as in (113) and (114).

---

30 "soit à du générique, soit à de l'inaccompli, soit à de l'accompli non-marqué" (translation mine).
31 "La situation d'énonciation ou le contexte discursif suffisent à définir la référence temporelle ou aspectuelle (accompli)" (translation mine).

(113) *Ô toven.*
ô   toven
REAL finish
'That's it, that's all.'

Yal-20092011-AW1_0306

(114) *« mo me weeng. »*
mo   me   wee-ng
LK3   IRR   food-1SG.POSS
'"as my food."'

Yal-20092011-AW1_0073

5.6.1 Realis =ô

The Belep realis marker =ô (or ô) indicates that the action expressed by the verb is instantiated in an actual event (or something presented by the speaker as an actual event), either within the speaker's memory or his or her knowledge of history and of the world. For example, the beginning of a fable is given in (115). The speaker begins with background, general truths not instantiated by any particular event, which are unmarked for mood (lines 1-2). Then she begins the sequence of events of the story (line 3), which repeatedly uses the =ô realis marker.

(115) *Buny, te tu cage ûjep va pwemwa caivak,*
buny   te=   tu   cage   ûjev=a
great.crested.tern 3SG.SUBJ=   go.DH   steal.TR   sugar.cane=LOC

pwemwa   caivak
village rat
'The tern, he steals sugar cane from the rat's home,'

2   *caivak, texa, te kaac u le buny, ka mon,*
caivak te=xa   te=   kaya   u=le   buny
rat   3SG.SUBJ=LK   3SG.SUBJ=   bitter toward=DAT   great.crested.tern

ka   mon
LK   side.DH
'The rat, he's, he's angry at the tern, and then,'

3 *ka mon, ô bwaêdan, leô– leô– leô pae,*

  ka mon ô bwaêdan le=ô   pa-e
  LK side.DH REAL morning 3DU.SUBJ=REAL take-SPC
  'and then, [one] morning, they- they- they took,'

4 *leô pae, leô pae wagale ûjep,*

  le=ô   pa-e le=ô   pa-e
  3DU.SUBJ=REAL take-SPC 3DU.SUBJ=REAL take-SPC

  waga-le   ûjep
  boat-3DU.POSS sugar.cane
  'they took, they took their sugar cane boat,'

5 *ma leô tu ka âva.*

  ma le=ô   tu=xa âva
  LK4 3DU.SUBJ=REAL go.DH=LK fish.GNR
  'so that they could go down and fish.'

              Yal-01082010-MFD_0003-0006

In example (116), realis =*ô* is used to represent a present state, one of the typical expressions of realis (Chafe 1995). The character animated by the speaker is speaking about a state that is actualized at the moment of speaking.

(116) *Teô kop va bwaang.*

  te=ô   kov=a   bwaa-ng
  3SG.SUBJ=REAL be.white.haired=NOM head-1SG.POSS
  '"my hair is [grown] white."'

              Yal-28072010-BGMCG-tayamu_0154

Realis =*ô* is also used to represent past states, such as in (117).

(117) *Texaô ô, ka ô toven.*

  te=xa=ô   ô ka ô toven
  3SG.SUBJ=LK=REAL good LK REAL finish
  'and he was fine, it was over.'

              Yal-28072010-BGMCG-tahitian_0322

The morpheme =ô can also mark relative future states. In (118), the speaker addresses the hypothetical future readers of this book, speaking to them as if those of his generation are no longer here.

(118) **lami ô cavac ka najiac.**
la-mi   ô   cavay=a naji-ac
DEM.PL-DET.A.DST REAL leave=LK let-2PL.ABS
'those who have gone away and left you.'
Yal-14092011-PT2-avenir_0011

Note that all the instances of le=ô [3DU.SUBJ=REAL] in example (115) are pronounced [lo], and that te=ô [3SG.SUBJ=REAL] in example (116) is pronounced [to]. The reduction of subject agreement markers with enclitic =ô occurs most frequently when the subject agreement marker ends with /e/, as shown in Table 16.

Tab. 16: Reduction of realis =ô

Phonological	Phonetic	Gloss
te=ô	[tõ] or [to]	3SG.SUBJ=REAL
le=ô	[lõ] or [lo]	3DU.SUBJ=REAL
ave=ô	[avõ] or [avo]	1DU.EXCL.SUBJ=REAL

Realis =ô may also precede a temporal noun which acts as a predicate. This construction is used as a sort of 'stage-setting' narrative device. Example (119) shows the use of realis =ô with the predication of *mon gawaar* 'afternoon'.

(119) **ka ô mon gawaar.**
ka   ô   mon   gawaar
LK REAL be.side.DH day
'then it was afternoon.'
Yal-28072010-BGMCG-tahitian_0038

Realis =ô may co-occur with all aspectual clitics, although this is relatively rare: the only such examples in my corpus are of =ô co-occurring with punctual *nyi*= (120).

(120) **Ka teô nyi âri ka, ava keja ka najie.**
ka   te=ô   nyi   âri=xa
LK 3SG.SUBJ=REAL PUNCT= say=LK

ava=   keja=xa najie
1PL.EXCL.SUBJ= run=LK leave-3SG.ABS

'and he kept saying that we had run away and left him.'

Yal-28072010-BGMCG-tahitian_0303

5.6.2 Irrealis =*me*

The irrealis marker =*me* indicates that the action expressed by the verb is hypothetical, prospective, or conditional. For example, in (121), =*me* is used as a marker of immediate future events following the moment of speaking. The speaker begins his story by saying that he is going to tell it.

(121) *Name, na pari para camang,*
       na=**me**   na=   pari para cama-ng
       1SG.SUBJ=IRR 1SG.SUBJ= tell.TR story father-1SG.POSS

'I'm going to- I'm telling a story of my father's.'

Yal-28072010-BGMCG-hamecon_0001

In (122), =*me* clearly has a conditional function. The clause is marked with an initial *enyi* 'if', and both the clause containing the conditional circumstance and the two clauses containing conditional results contain irrealis =*me*.

(122) *Ka enyi yome bwa tu yena,*
       ka enyi yo=**me**   bwa=   tu   yena
       LK if   2SG.SUBJ=IRR CONT= go.DH now

       yome bwa kiyi buânyili.
       yo=**me**   bwa= kiyi   buânyi-li
       2SG.SUBJ=IRR CONT= see.SPC stone-DET.A.PRX

       Yome bwa kiya buânyama lali, bwa yena.
       yo=**me**   bwa=   kiya   buânya-ma lali
       2SG.SUBJ=IRR CONT= see.GNR stone-AC   3PL.SUBJ-DET.A.PRX

bwa=   yena
CONT=   now

'and if you would go down there now, you would see these stones. You would see all these stones, they're there now.'

Yal-28072010-BGMCG-sousmarin_0119-0120

The irrealis clitic =*me* is also commonly used with pseudocoordinate *ma*-clauses (§7.3.2) to indicate that the action is contingent, intended, or desired, but not necessarily accomplished. In the pseudocoordinate *ma*-clause in (123), =*me* indicates a purposive, or an intention of completing the action of the verb *bwawar* 'plant yams' at some point in the future, although the narrated events took place in the past.

(123)   *ka bwagevavan na toop, ma avame bwawar.*

ka bwage-va=van   na   toop ma
LK return-2PL.EXCL.ABS=DIR.TV interior field LK4

ava=**me**   bwawar
1PL.EXCL.SUBJ=IRR   plant.yams

'and [we] returned to the fields, so that we could plant yams.'

Yal-17072009-TB-weekend_0019-0020

The irrealis =*me* is compatible with all aspectual clitics (§5.5). There are examples in my corpus where =*me* occurs with habitual *tao*=, gnomic *da*=, progressive *âga*=, iterative *ca*=, continuative *bwa*=, and punctual *nyi*=.

5.7 Absolutive suffixes

An absolutive noun phrase (§6.3.3, §6.4.1) may be anaphorically referenced by an absolutive suffix, shown in Table 17. For more on the pronominal system in Belep, see §4.6.1.

Tab. 17: Anaphoric absolutive suffixes

	Singular	Dual	Paucal	Plural
1 EXCL		-ve	-ven	-va
INCL	-nao	-ji	-jen	-ja
2	-o	-or	-ôn	-ac

	Singular	Dual	Paucal	Plural
3	-e, -er³²	-le	-len	-la

These suffixes are anaphoric; their referent is Given information. They serve this function in both verbal and nominal morphology. As formatives within the verb group (§5.3), the absolutive suffixes reference the noun phrase serving as the absolutive argument (§6.4.1). Within the noun phrase, absolutive suffixes refer to the possessor in an independent possessive construction (§4.2.2.4), as well as to an argument marked as genitive with the case marker =*li* (§6.4.3).

5.7.1 As verb inflections

The absolutive suffixes are verb inflections that serve as part of the verb group (§5.3). They can refer either to the patient of a transitive verb, as in (124) where *-le* '3DU.ABS' refers to the patient of transitive *migie* 'to touch, catch'; or to the argument of one class of intransitive verb (§5.2.2; see §6.3.3) such as *cia* 'NEG.LOC', as in (125).

(124)   *Jame migile,*
        ja=me   migi-le
        1PL.INCL.SUBJ=IRR hold-3DU.ABS
        '"We will catch them,"'

        Yal-20092011-AW6_0083

(125)   *Toma len, cialen,*
        toma len   cia-len
        but 3PA.INDEP NEG.LOC-3PA.ABS
        'But they, they weren't there,'

        Yal-20092011-AW6_0161

The absolutive suffixes are in complementary distribution with noun phrases, as shown in (126), where the 3PL.ABS pronoun *-la* occurs without a corresponding noun phrase; it refers anaphorically to the noun phrase *avar* 'others', which occurs earlier in the discourse.

---

32 The difference between these 3SG.ABS forms is explained below in §5.7.2.

(126) **La baela li nic.**
　　　la　　　　bae-<u>la</u>=li　　　　　nic
　　　3PL.SUBJ= bite.SPC-3PL.ABS=GEN shark
　　　'Sharks ate them.'
　　　　　　　　　　　　　　　　　　　　　Yal-20092011-AW2_0049

Clauses which contain both an absolutive suffix and an absolutive noun phrase are ungrammatical (127).

(127) ***Te yavie wîmi.**
　　　te=　　　yavi-<u>e</u>　　　　　wî-mi
　　　3SG.SUBJ= search.TR-3SG.ABS DEM.INAN-DET.A.DST
　　　*'S/he searches for it that thing.'

This is in contrast with the DA suffixes -*n* and -*a* (§5.2.3.3, §5.2.3.4), which are often used concurrently with an absolutive noun phrase. For this reason, DA suffixes are not considered to belong to the set of absolutive suffixes, even though the lack of co-occurrence between these two sets makes it impossible to tell whether they belong to the same position class.

The absolutive suffixes are bound to the verb word. They occur immediately after any valence (§5.2.4) or specific[33] (§5.2.3.1) suffixes, and before verb phrase enclitics (§5.12, §5.13), as in (128).

(128) **mo âyuang ngi yo paenaoda,**
　　　mo âyua-ng=i　　　　yo=　　　pa-e-<u>nao</u>=da
　　　LK3 desire-1SG.POSS=GEN 2SG.SUBJ= take-SPC-1SG.ABS=DIR.UH
　　　'but I want you to accompany me up,'
　　　　　　　　　　　　　　　　　　　　　Yal-20092011-AW1_0096

In example (128), the absolutive suffix -*nao* '1SG.ABS' follows the specific suffix -*e* and precedes the verb phrase enclitic =*da* 'DIR.UH'. In (129), the speaker accidentally utters the absolutive suffix after the directional verb phrase enclitic, stops, and makes a repair.

---

[33] Note that the specific suffix -*e* does not co-occur with either 3SG absolutive suffix; the former is most likely a grammaticalized version of the latter.

(129) *Avaxaô bwagedava—*
     ava=xa=ô   bwage=da-<u>va</u>
     1PL.EXCL.SUBJ=LK=REAL   return-DIR.UH-2PL.EXCL.ABS
     'Also we retur-'

     bwagevadame la bwe Waala.
     bwage-<u>va</u>=da=me=la   bwe   Wala
     return-2PL.EXCL.ABS=DIR.UH=CTP=LOC   top   Waala
     'returned back up here to Waala.'
                                                    Yal-17072009-TB-weekend_0042

5.7.2 Suffixes *-e* and *-er*

The variation between the two 3SG.ABS suffixes *-e* and *-er* appears to be conditioned by as-yet-unidentified discourse features.[34] More work remains to be done to fully understand the influencing factors for this variation.[35] The difference in distribution of the two suffixes is the chief evidence for the distinction in meaning. If the clause contains a full, case-marked noun phrase argument—such as a genitive-marked subject (§6.3.2), a locative goal (§6.4.5 and §5.13), a genitive-marked oblique (§6.4.3), etc.—the form *-er* is obligatory and *-e* is ungrammatical. For example, in (130), the suffix *-er* is used because there is a genitive-marked subject, *Belep* 'Chieftain Belep'. The use of *îna-e=li* would be ungrammatical.

(130) *Texa înaer ri Belep ka ô.*
     te=xa   îna-<u>er</u>=i   Belev=a   ô
     3SG.SUBJ=ADD   make-3SG.ABS=GEN   Belep=LK   good
     'And Belep made him better.'
                                                         Yal-20092011-AW6_0055

In (131), the suffix *-er* is used because there is a locative-marked goal noun phrase, *bwe daan* 'on the path'. The use of *nawe-e=la* would be ungrammatical.

---

34 In Nêlêmwa, two 3SG object forms are distinguished by the animacy of their anaphoric referent (Bril 2002: 86).
35 Speakers have difficulty describing the difference between the two morphemes. In a few cases, speakers said that *-er* was 'more specific' than *-e*; one speaker glossed *te= gi-e* as 'he hits him' and *te= gi-er* as 'he hits him (specifically)'. It is unclear how this corresponds to the rest of the evidence.

(131) *ka naweer ra bwe daan.*
 ka nawe-**er**=a   bwe daan
 LK deposit-3SG.ABS=LOC top path
 'and left her on the path.'
 Yal-20092011-AW1_0109

In (132), the suffix *-er* is used because there is a genitive-marked theme noun phrase, *bolao pwâgo* 'poingo banana'.

(132) *Te taxeer ri bolao pwâgo,*
 te=   taxe-**er**=i   bolao   pwâgo
 3SG.SUBJ= distribute-3SG.ABS=GEN banana poingo
 'He gave him poingo bananas,'
 Yal-28072010-BGMCG-lune_0037

In all of these cases, the full noun phrase argument within the clause precludes the use of the suffix *-e*.

By contrast, if the verb group with the absolutive suffix is followed by a verb phrase directional or deictic enclitic (§5.12), the form *-e* is obligatory and *-er* is ungrammatical. For example, in (133) the form *-e* is used; it is followed by verb phrase directional =*du* 'DIR.DH' and deictic =*me* 'CTP'. The form *-er* would be ungrammatical.[36]

(133) *ma le paedume leeng.*
 ma le=   pa-**e**=du=me=lee-ng
 LK4 3DU.SUBJ= take-3SG.ABS=DIR.DH=CTP=DAT-1SG.POSS
 'so they could bring him down to me.'
 Yal-28072010-BGMCG-tahitian_0254

The environments in which *-e* and *-er* occur are not in complementary distribution. Both may be used at the end of an intonation unit. For instance, both *-e* in (134) and *-er* in (135) refer to the patient of the specific form of the verb *kiya* 'to see'. Both occur at the end of an intonation unit and refer to a singular human referent.

---

36 The distinction between *-e* and *-er* may also have a phonological component; *-er* would be phonologically impossible in this environment because it would produce a consonant cluster.

(134) *Toma âju, âri na kiyie.*
      toma   âju   âri=   na=   kiyi-e.
      but   person   NEG=   1SG.SUBJ=   see.SPC-3SG.ABS
      'but the *person* I didn't see.'
                                              Yal-28072010-BGMCG-tahitian_0094

(135) *Le îna ma leô kôk to leô kiyier,*
      le=   îna   ma   le=ô   kôxa=ro
      3DU.SUBJ=   make.GNR   LK4   3DU.SUBJ=REAL   overflow=when

      le=ô   kiyi-er
      3DU.SUBJ=REAL   see.SPC-3SG.ABS
      'They wanted to throw up when they saw her,'
                                                Yal-28072010-BGMCG-tayamu_0233

A similar example occurs in (136) and (137) with the verb *najie* 'to leave, let'; *-e* in (136) and *-er* in (137) both refer to human referents and occur at the end of an intonation unit.

(136) *Lexa pe najie.*
      le=xa   pe=   naji-e
      3DU.SUBJ=ADD   RECP=   let-3SG.ABS
      'and they left [each other].'
                                                Yal-28072010-BGMCG-tahitian_0202

(137) *Ka ave keja ka najier.*
      ka   ave=   keja=xa   naji-er
      LK   1DU.EXCL.SUBJ=   run=LK   let-3SG.ABS
      'and we ran and left him.'
                                                Yal-28072010-BGMCG-tahitian_0274

The distinction between *-e* and *-er* also holds when these absolutive suffixes occur within an independently possessed noun phrase (§4.2.2.4). For example, in (138) and (139), the independently possessed noun *âju* 'person' is modified by an absolutive suffix which refers to the referent *Teâ Belep*. However, the form *-e* is used in (138) while *-er* is used in (139). It is not clear what discourse features might condition this variation.

(138) **La tu la âju lie ma la cao.**

la=	tu=la	âju=li-e	ma
3PL.SUBJ=	go.DH=NOM	person=GEN-3SG.ABS	LK4

la=	cao
3PL.SUBJ=	work

'His people went down to work.'

Yal-20092011-AW6_0062

(139) **Âju lier ka âju pwadu.**

âju=li-er	ka	âju	pwadu
person=GEN-3SG.ABS	LK	person	two

'He had two courtiers.'

Yal-20092011-AW6_0057

5.8 Subject agreement clitics

The subject agreement proclitics are presented in Table 18.

Tab. 18: Subject agreement clitics

	Singular	Dual	Paucal	Plural
1 exclusive	na=	ave=	avena=	ava=
inclusive		ji=	jena=	ja=
2	yo=	o=	ôna=	a=
3	te=	le=	lena=	la=

The subject agreement clitics are verb inflections which typically serve as the first element of the verb group (§5.3). They agree in person and number with the subject of a transitive clause—whether it is marked as nominative (§6.4.2), as in (140), or genitive (§6.4.3; see §6.3.2), as in (141)—and with the subject of most intransitive clauses (§5.2.1), as in (142). Subject agreement proclitics are not present in clauses where the intransitive verb takes an absolutive argument, providing evidence that these arguments should not be considered subjects (§5.2.2; see §6.3.4 on subjecthood in Belep).

In (140), the subject agreement proclitic *te*= '3SG.SUBJ' agrees with the nominative subject *teâmaa* 'high chief'.

(140) **Texa terae wayap va teâmaa,**
    <u>te</u>=xa   tera-e   wayav=a   teâmaa
    3SG.SUBJ=ADD   stop-SPC   war=NOM   high.chief
    'And the chieftain stopped the war,'
                                                        Yal-20092011-AW4_0060

In (141), the subject agreement proclitic *la*= '3PL.SUBJ' agrees with the genitive subject *Âôvaayama* 'the Âôvaac people'.

(141) **La ginao li Âôvaayama.**
    <u>la</u>=   gi-nao=li   Âôvaaya-ma
    3PL.SUBJ= attack-1SG.ABS=GEN Âôvaac-AC
    'The Âôvaac people are attacking me.'
                                                        Yal-20092011-AW3_0029

In (142), the subject agreement proclitic *la*= '3PL.SUBJ' agrees with the intransitive subject *âjuma* 'people'.

(142) **Laxa tame la âjuma,**
    <u>la</u>=xa   ta=me=la   âju-ma,
    3PL.SUBJ=ADD   go.UH=CTP=NOM person-AC
    'and the people came,'
                                                  Yal-28072010-BGMCG-igname_0049

Subject agreement proclitics are not considered to be pronouns; they are not in complementary distribution with noun phrases and are obligatory in most clauses. Examples (140) - (142) show the co-occurrence of a subject agreement proclitic with a full noun phrase subject.

As proclitics, the subject agreement markers do not carry stress. They are often procliticized to the verb group; however, as discussed in §5.3, in the presence of certain morphemes they form a 'clitic-only' phonological word (Aikhenvald 2002: 51) called the 'preface' that can serve as an intonation unit. The morphemes which can trigger the formation of this clitic-only word are the additive enclitic =*xa* 'ADD' (§7.2.1.3); the mood enclitics =*ô* 'REAL' and =*me* 'IRR' (§5.6); and the focus enclitic =*re* 'ACT' (§6.9.2.1). For example, in (143), the speaker uses *texa* '3SG.SUBJ=ADD' as a temporizer, waits 1.21 seconds, and then produces a full clause beginning with *avexa* '1DU.EXCL.SUBJ=ADD'.

(143) **Texa, ...avexa migi pwalaic.**
    te=xa   ave=xa   migi   pwalaic
    3SG.SUBJ=ADD   1DU.EXCL.SUBJ=ADD   catch   one
    'Also it, ...(1.21) also we caught one.'
                                                  Yal-28072010-BGMCG-tahitian_0048-0049

In (144), the speaker uses *lame* '3PL.SUBJ=IRR', pauses for 0.8 seconds, and continues with the rest of the clause.

(144) **ma lame,**
    ma   la=me
    LK4 3PL.SUBJ=IRR

    tu ka âja ka me tame ka,
    tu=xa   âja=xa   me   ta=me=xa
    go.DH=LK dive.for.top.snail=LK IRR go.UH=CTP=LK
    'so that they would, ...(0.8) go down, fish for top snail, and then come back and,'
                                                    Yal-28072010-BGMCG-igname_0052-0053

In (145), the speaker produces *teôre* '3SG.SUBJ=REAL=ACT', pauses for 1.6 seconds, then produces a full clause, repeating the subject proclitic *te=*.

(145) **Teôre, ... te ta,**
    te=ô=re   te=   ta
    33SG.SUBJ=REAL=ACT   3SG.SUBJ= go.UH
    'He actually, ...(1.6) he went up,'
                                                  Yal-28072010-BGMCG-tahitian_0194-0195

The preface—a clitic-only phonological word—is part of the grammatical word formed by the verb group (see §3.2.2).

There are some clauses where use of a subject agreement proclitic is not obligatory. In imperatives where the addressee is singular, subject agreement proclitics are optional (§6.7.1). If the verb is repeated for dramatic effect, the subject agreement marker is not included in the repetition, as in (146), where the verbs *yue* 'to dig' and *yagie* 'to search' are repeated dramatically without the subject agreement marker *la=* '3PL.SUBJ'.

(146) **La yuu, yuu, yagin,**

la=	yu-u	yu-u	yagi-n
3PL.SUBJ=	dig-DETR	dig-DETR	search-VAL

yuu, yagin, ka koni tun.

yu-u	yagi-n	ka	koni	tu-n
dig-DETR	search-VAL	LK	unable	find-VAL

'They dug, dug, searched, dug, searched and never could find anything.'

Yal-28072010-BGMCG-sousmarin_0116

The subject agreement clitic is obligatorily omitted in a clause conjoined with *ka* 'LK' (see §7.2.1.1).

The subject agreement clitics are ubiquitous (there are more than 1000 tokens in my corpus), the majority of clauses begin with one, and they may be ellipted in certain discourse conditions. This may contribute to the maintenance of the basic word order of Belep, which is VOS (see §6.2); since the subject is referred to inflectionally at the beginning of the clause, the fact that the nominal subject is clause-final is not such a detriment to the communicative needs of the speakers (cf. Du Bois 1987).

5.9 Verb compounding

A number of verbal elements which may combine with other verbs have already been examined (Table 19).

Tab. 19: Grammaticalized verb roots

Full verb	Formative
toven 'finish'	-roven 'COMPL'
ta 'go.UH'	=da 'DIR.UH'
tu 'go.DH'	=du 'DIR.DH'
pan 'go.TV'	=van 'DIR.TV'
pa 'take'	=va, =vae 'INSTR'

However, these should be considered fully grammaticalized formatives rather than independent verbs used in compounding, since these meanings are substantially distinct from the corresponding independent verbs and the formatives have a strongly bleached semantic content (Payne 1997: 233). As such, these morphemes will not be further discussed in this section; refer to the various sections in which each is discussed individually (§5.5.11 for =*roven*, §5.12 for =*da*, =*du*, and =*van*, and §6.4.6 for =*vae*). A similar caveat holds for verbs used as the first element in a serial verb construction (§5.10); these should not be considered compounds.

This section will discuss instances of true verb compounding in Belep as defined by Payne (1997): "both roots are recognizable verbs in their own right, but nothing can come in between them, *and* the meaning of the whole structure is 'bleached,' i.e., slightly different from the combination of the lexical meanings of the two roots" (Payne 1997: 233).

There are a few clear examples of this compounding in my data, represented in (147).

(147) *bala koon* 'to be clumsy' (from *balap* 'to move' and *koon* 'to be unable')
       tara koon 'to correspond' (from *tara* 'to scoop' and *koon* 'to be unable')
       to ji 'to call to sb.' (lit. 'call give')

In verb compounding the two verbs behave as one grammatical word—there is only one subject agreement proclitic (§5.8) and absolutive suffix (§5.7) if the verb is transitive, and nothing can intercede between the two verbs. The first element serves as the head of the compound (Nichols 1986). These characteristics are demonstrated in example (148), where the verb is *to ji* 'to call to sb.'

(148) ***Na nyi kewee ka to jie, « Ai ! »***
       na=   nyi=   kewe-e=xa   to   ji-e   ai
       1SG.SUBJ= PUNCT=   run-3SG.ABS=LK   call give-3SG.ABS   no

       Ka me to jie, « Ai ! »
       ka me= to   ji-e   ai
       LK IRR= call give-3SG.ABS   no
       'I immediately chased after him and called to him, "No!" and then called to him, "No!"'

       Yal-28072010-BGMCG-tahitian_0078

More research would be required to determine the productivity of verb compounding in Belep.

5.10 Verb serialization

Many Northern New Caledonian languages have productive serial verb constructions (SVCs). Nêlêmwa and other Northern languages have both same-subject and different-subject SVCs (Bril 2004b). In Belep, same-subject serialization with a limited set of verbs may be used to modify the aspect or modality of the clause. In such cases, the first verb provides modal information and the second verb provides lexical information. Switch-subject SVCs, by contrast, are used as a complementation strategy; in these instances, the first verb is the main verb (see §7.3.9). Belep SVCs are distinguished from compound verbs in that each verb in a SVC can serve independently as the main verb of a clause.

This section describes a number of full verbs which function as modals, occurring in the same position in the verb group as the aspectual (§5.5) proclitics. These modals differ from morphological modals in that they have the capacity to appear in other clauses as the main and only verb. Each full verb presented here—*jaar* 'to be happy' (§5.10.1), *cavie* 'to try' (§5.10.2), *mo* 'to live' (§5.10.3), *pan* 'to go.TV' (§5.10.4), *ci* 'to sit' (§5.10.5), *koon* 'to be unable' (§5.10.6), *toven* 'to finish' (§5.10.7), and others (§5.10.8)— has a semantically shifted meaning when it is used as a modal modifier in a SVC. Intransitive verbs (§5.2.1) used modally in this way occur in their incomplete phase (§2.4.3.2), while transitive (§5.2.3) or transitivized (§5.2.5) verbs occur in their generic (§5.2.4) or bound (§5.2.3.2) forms.

5.10.1 Desiderative *jaar* 'to want to'

When the intransitive verb *jaar* acts as the main verb, its meaning is 'to be happy', as in (149).

(149)   *Ma le jua jaar, jua jaar, jaar.*
       ma   le=   jua   jaar   jua   jaar   jaar
       LK4 3DU.SUBJ= very happy very happy happy
       'So that they were really happy, so happy, happy.'
                                              Yal-28072010-BGMCG-tayamu_0073

When *jaar* is the first element in a SVC, it appears in its incomplete phase (§2.4.3.2) as [ⁿjara], and its meaning is modal; it indicates a desiderative mood for the main verb. In (150) and (151), *jaar* participates in such a SVC and is glossed 'to want.'

(150) **Âri le jaar pulu ma le tao go.**
âri= le= jara pulu ma le= tao= go
NEG= 3DU.SUBJ= want speak LK4 3DU.SUBJ= HAB= cry
'They didn't want to speak because they kept crying.'
Yal-19092011-PA_0021

(151) **Ava jaar bae pê**
ava= jara bae pê
1PL.EXCL.SUBJ= want bite bread
'We want to eat the bread'
Yal-25072010-PT-homily_0030

5.10.2 Conative *cavi* 'to try to'

The bound transitive (§5.2.3.2) verb *cavie* 'to try, to taste' does not occur in my corpus; a constructed example is shown in (152).

(152) **Bwa cavi weemw nook.**
bwa= cavi we-mwa noo-k
CONT= try food-2SG.POSS fish-DET.D.PRX
'Taste this fish.'

The verb *cavie* takes on a conative modal meaning when it is used as the first element in a SVC. Forsyth (1970) uses the term 'conative' to mean "a conscious attempt to perform the action" (Forsyth 1970:71) and "the expression of an action which has not yet taken place, but which is considered as part of a plan or programme arranged to take place" (Forsyth 1970:73).[37] The Belep modal form *cavi* is used with this function as in (153). Note that form *cavi* is the bound form of the verb *cavie*.

(153) **Name cavi pulu.**
na=me cavi pulu
1SG.SUBJ=IRR try speak
'I'm going to try to speak.'
Yal-03112011-IM1.wav – Yal-03112011-IM2.wav

---

37 This is a different sense of the word 'conative' than that used by Jakobson (1960).

5.10.3 Prospective *mo* 'to be about to'

The intransitive verb *mo* 'to live, to stay' is very common in discourse; example (154) is representative.

(154) **La mo la âjuma la yali.**
 la= mo=la âju-ma=la ya-li
 3PL.SUBJ= live=NOM person-AC=LOC DEM.LOC-DET.A.PRX
 'The people lived there.'
 Yal-28072010-BGMCG-igname_0007

When *mo* is used as the first verb in a SVC, by contrast, it takes on the prospective meaning of 'to be about to'. Examples are given in (155) and (156), and in both lines of (157).

(155) **te mo maac ya camala.**
 te= mo may=a cama-la
 3SG.SUBJ= live die=NOM father-3PL.POSS
 'their father was about to die.'
 Yal-20092011-AW1_0030

(156) **Laxa mo tu la bwe mar,**
 la=xa mo tu=la bwe mar
 3PL.SUBJ=ADD live go.DH=LOC top seashore
 'and they were about to go down to the seashore,'
 Yal-28072010-BGMCG-igname_0066

(157) « **Mo mon, yo mo nginie,**
 mo mon yo= mo ngini-e
 LK3 side.DH 2SG.SUBJ= live miss-3SG.ABS

 ***avena mo gio.* »**
 avena= mo gi-o
 1TR.EXCL.SUBJ= live attack-2SG.ABS
 '"For afterwards, you will not see it again; we are about to kill you."'
 Yal-20092011-AW6_0100

These examples show that, as the first element of a SVC, *mo* indicates a modal meaning of incipient intention to commit an action.

5.10.4 Inceptive *pan* 'to be going to'

The intransitive verb *pan* 'to go.TV', which indicates general motion in a transverse direction (see §4.5.1), frequently acts as the main verb of a clause (158).

(158)   ***avena pan na Poc.***
        avena=   **pan=a**   **Poc**
        1TR.EXCL.SUBJ=   go.TV=LOC   Poc
        'we [would] go to Poc.'
                                                  Yal-28072010-BGMCG-tahitian_0012

However, when *pan* is the first element in a SVC (its incomplete phase is [panã]), its meaning shifts to indicate a modal sense of futurity and the initiation of the action of the main verb. "Futurity is never a purely temporal concept; it necessarily includes an element of prediction" (Lyons 1994:677), a characteristic of modality. Some of the "modal characteristics of future time reference" were discussed in Palmer (2001:106).

Examples (159) - (161) show that the meaning of *pan* is modal rather than tense-based. These three examples show the use of modal *pan* with a past (159), present (160), and future (161) event; what these events have in common is the speaker's conceptualization of the event as inceptive or intended. In (159), where the first element is *pan* and the main verb is *nam* 'to disappear', the narrated events take place in the past.

(159)   ***Texa pan namadu la nan,***
        te=xa   **pana**   **nama=du=la**   **na-n**
        3SG.SUBJ=ADD   go.TV   disappear=DIR.DH=LOC   interior-3SG.POSS
        'And he went to disappear into it,'
                                                  Yal-01082010-MFD_0059

Example (160) shows a SVC where the first element is *pan* and the main verb is *balap* 'to move around'.

(160)   ***Texa waak, « Na pan balap. »***
        te=xa   **waa-k**   **na=**   **pana**   **balap**
        3SG.SUBJ=ADD   DEM.MAN-DET.D.PRX   1SG.SUBJ=   go.TV   move
        'And he said, "I'm gonna walk around."'
                                              Yal-19092011-PA_0028-0029

Example (161) shows a SVC where the first element is *pan* and the main verb is *ciwie* 'to bury'.

(161) « *Jename pan ciwi caya.* »
 jena=me pana ciwi caya
 1TR.INCL.SUBJ=IRR go.TV bury dad
 '"We're gonna go and bury Dad."'
 Yal-20092011-AW1_0042

It is worth noting that modal *pan* can also occur in a SVC with the full verb *pan* 'to go.TV', as seen in example (162).

(162) *La pan pan, ka kiyi daroven,*
 la= pana pan ka kiyi da=roven
 3PL.SUBJ= go.TV go.TV LK see.SPC blood=all
 'They were about to continue on when they saw all the blood,'
 Yal-20092011-AW5_0086

5.10.5 Concessive *ci* 'nonetheless'

The full verb *ci* 'to sit, to stay' may act as the main verb of a clause, as in (163).

(163) *Te ci la yaxeda.*
 te= ci=la ya-xeda
 3SG.SUBJ= sit=LOC DEM.LOC-DET.UH
 'It [a boulder] sits up there.'
 Yal-20092011-AW3_0033

However, when it is used as the first element in a SVC, *ci* indicates the accomplishment of the main verb despite resistance. For example, (164) occurs during a story about a shipwreck where, despite the children's best efforts to swim, *la ci maac* 'they died'.

(164) *Naerama, la ci maac.*
 nae-ra-ma la= ci maac
 child-3GNR.POSS-AC 3PL.SUBJ= sit die
 'The children, they died nonetheless.'
 Yal-20092011-AW2_0041

Example (165) occurs during a description of a particular method for fishing. Though this method is also used in Tahiti, *te ci tewuur ra Poc* 'it nonetheless began at Poc', the speaker's ancestral home.

(165) **Te ci tewuur ra Poc.**

te=	ci	tewuu-r=a	Poc
3SG.SUBJ=	sit	beginning-3GNR.POSS=LOC	Poc

'It nonetheless began at Poc.'

Yal-28072010-BGMCG-hamecon_0055

In (166), it is the speaker's reluctance to discourage her interlocutor that provides the resistance inherent in *ci*.

(166) **Na ci âri u lela ka te pwalic ya daan.**

na=	ci	âri	u=le-la
1SG.SUBJ=	sit	say	toward=DAT-1PL.POSS

ka	te=	pwaliy=a	daan
LK	3SG.SUBJ=	long=NOM	path

'I warn them that the road is long.' (lit. 'I reluctantly say to them that the road is long.')

Yal-03112011-IM1.wav – Yal-03112011-IM2.wav

In example (167), the speaker relates a narrative about two sisters fighting over the right to nurse a baby. When one sister succeeds at wresting control of the baby, she (animated by the speaker) says *name ci pariae* 'I will nonetheless nurse it'. An SVC with *ci* is used again in line 2, where she asserts that, despite her resistance, her sister should prepare the food.

(167) « **Name ci pariae,**

na=me	ci	pariae[38]
SG.SUBJ=IRR	sit	nurse.SPC

---

38 The verb *pariae* 'to nurse a child' comes from the causative morpheme *pa=* and the verb *ti* 'to suck, to nurse'.

toma yo, yome ci tînin weji. »

toma	yo	yo=me	ci
but	2SG.INDEP	2SG.SUBJ=IRR	sit

tîni-na	we-ji
burn-DA.NSG	food-1DU.INCL.POSS

"'I will nonetheless nurse it, but you, you should nonetheless cook our food.'"

Yal-28072010-BGMCG-tayamu_0065-0067

5.10.6 *koni* 'to never'

The intransitive verb *koon* 'to be unaware, unable', indicates a sort of powerlessness or a lack of ability on the part of the subject. The phrase *te koon* is sometimes translated as *c'est un idiot* 's/he's an idiot', and example (168) is from a story where the character tries everything possible to move his boat, but fails and turns into a stone in that spot.

(168)   ***Te bwa tao ci koon na bwe mar,***

te=	bwa=	tao=	ci	kon=a	bwe	mar
3SG.SUBJ=	CONT=	HAB=	sit	be.unable=LOC	top	seashore

'He is still nonetheless incapable [of moving the boat] on the seashore,'

Yal-19092011-PA_0071

When it is transitivized through stem modification (§5.2.5.1), its bound transitive form *koni* indicates 'to not know, be ignorant of'; *na koni naran* [1SG.SUBJ= unaware.TR name-3SG.POSS] means 'I don't know his/her name'.

However, *koni* can also be the first element in a serial verb construction, where it may indicate a negative ability or a negative continuative aspect. There is not a clear demarcation between these meanings in Belep; for the sake of simplicity, all modal instances of *koni* will be glossed 'never', although there may be multiple possible translations. For example, in (169), *koni* is used with the verb *ta* 'to go.UH' to indicate primarily a negative continuative, but may be interpreted as a negative ability.

(169)   ***Nanami lami kooni tame li bwe cexeen.***

nanami	la-mi	koni	ta=me=li
think.TR	DEM.PL-DET.A.DST	never	go.UH=CTP=GEN

	bwe	cexeen
	moment	sacred

'Think about those who never come on Sunday.' or 'who can't come'

Yal-25072010-PT-homily_0078

In (170), *koni* largely indicates a negative habitual, though the negative ability is also implied.

(170) ***Âbur, la kooni pe tâna lile. La ca wayap.***

âbur	la=	koni	pe=	tâna=li-le
side.UH	3PL.SUBJ=	never	RECP=	hear.GNR=GEN-3DU.OBJ

la=	ca=	wayap
3PL.SUBJ=	ITER=	war

'Before, they [the Or and Waap phratries] never could get along. They were always at war.'

Yal-20092011-AW3_0017

In (171), *koni* is used with the verb *tue* 'to find' to indicate both an inability and a negative continuative.

(171) ***La yuu, yuu, yagin, yuu, yagin, ka kooni tun.***

la=	yu-u	yu-u	yagi-n
3PL.SUBJ=	dig-DETR	dig-DETR	search.TR-DA.NSG

yu-u	yagi-n	ka	koni	tu-n
dig-DETR	search.TR-DA.NSG	LK	never	find-DA.NSG

'They dug, dug, searched, dug, searched and never could find anything.'

Yal-28072010-BGMCG-sousmarin_0116

In (172), the speaker is narrating a story about chasing after his brother-in-law, who had been turned invisible. Here, *koni* primarily indicates an inability, though the negative continuative is implied for the period of invisibility.

(172) ***Na kooni kiyie,***

na=	koni	kiyi-e
1SG.SUBJ=	never	see.SPC-3SG.ABS

'I couldn't see him' or 'I never saw him'

Yal-28072010-BGMCG-tahitian_0099

Example (173) clearly shows a contrast between the full verb form of *koon* and the modal meaning of *koni*. The speaker's inability (*koon*) to make a certain type of fishhooks is stated as a cause (using *mo* 'LK3'; see §7.2.3) for his never (*koni*) making it.

(173) **Ka ava êna ka kooni înau mo ava koon.**

ka	ava=	êna=xa	koni	îna-u
LK	1PL.EXCL.SUBJ=	know.GNR=LK	never	make-DETR

mo	ava=	koon
LK3	1PL.EXCL.SUBJ=	be.unable

'And we know that [we] never make them, for we cannot.'

Yal-28072010-BGMCG-hamecon_0083

5.10.7 Cessative *toveni* 'to finish'

The intransitive verb *toven* 'to finish' (174) can be transitivized to the bound form *toveni* (not found in my corpus) using stem modification (§5.2.5.1).

(174) **Ka ô toven na para la bween.**

ka	ô	toven=a	para=la	bwee-n
LK	REAL	finish=NOM	story=LOC	top-3SG.POSS

'And the story about that is finished.'

Yal-28072010-BGMCG-lune_0064

This verb has two grammaticalized functions that have already been discussed—use as a verb suffix indicating completive aspect and the total affectedness of the patient (§5.4.11); and as a nominal suffix meaning 'all' (§4.3.4). A further grammaticalized function of *toven* is as the first element of a SVC. Here it appears in its bound form *toveni* and carries the meaning of terminating an ongoing state or action (which is indicated by the second verb). For example, in (175) the second verb is *go* 'to cry'.

(175) **« Toveni go, Ixe, »**

toveni	go	Ixe
finish.TR	cry	Ixe

'"Stop crying, Ixe,"'

Yal-19092011-PA_0016

In (176) and (177), the verbs whose cessation is being predicated are *wayap* 'to make war' and *cao* 'to work', respectively.

(176) ***Teme toveni wayap.***
       te=me   **toveni**   **wayap**
       3SG.SUBJ=IRR   finish.TR   war
       'He will end the war.'
                                                        Yal-20092011-AW4_0050

(177) ***Leô toveni cao,***
       le=ô   **toveni**   **cao**
       3DU.SUBJ=REAL   finish.TR   work
       'They finished working,'
                                     Yal-28072010-BGMCG-sousmarin_0042

5.10.8 Other modal elements

A number of other verbs can serve as the first element in a SVC, where they take on more grammaticalized modal or aspectual meanings. A few of these verbs will be discussed here; however, this is not a complete list.

The verb *ta* 'to go.UH', when serving as the first element in a SVC, seems to indicate that some form of upward motion is necessary in order to complete the action or state predicated by the second verb (this contrasts with the directionals, which indicate the trajectory of the action predicated by the verb). In example (178), the warriors must *ta* 'go.UH' before they *ce* 'settle' on top of the mountain; in (179), soil must first be raised before it can be thrown.

(178) ***La ta ce la bwe mweogo,***
       la=   **ta**   **ce=la**   **bwe**   **mweogo**
       3PL.SUBJ=   go.UH   settle=LOC   top   mountaintop
       'They camped on the mountaintop,'
                                            Yal-20092011-AW3_0044

(179) ***Te ta înae doo la nyan, tayamook.***
       te=   **ta**   **îna-e**   **do=la**
       3SG.SUBJ=   go.UH   make-SPC   earth=NOM

> nya-n tayamoo-k
> mother-3SG.POSS old.woman-DET.D.PRX
> 'His mother, this old woman, flung the soil [into her child's eyes].'
>
> Yal-28072010-BGMCG-sousmarin_0025-0026

A similar situation holds when the verb *tu* 'to go.DH' is the first element in a SVC. In (180), the tern must *tu* 'go.DH' before he can *cage* 'steal' the sugar cane.

(180) **Buny, te tu cage ûjep va pwemwa caivak,**

> buny te= tu cage ûjev=a
> great.crested.tern 3SG.SUBJ= go.DH steal.SPC sugar.cane=LOC
>
> pwemwa caivak
> home rat
> 'The tern, he swooped down and stole sugar cane from the rat's home.'
>
> Yal-01082010-MFD_0003

When the full verb *jie* 'to give' is the first element of a SVC, the meaning of the whole expression is similar to the causative meaning expressed by the periphrastic causative with *jie* (discussed in §6.9.1), as shown in (181).

(181) **« Ma a ji bwagee, »**

> ma a= ji bwage-e
> LK4 2PL.SUBJ= give return-3SG.OBJ
> '"That you give him back,"'
>
> Yal-28072010-BGMCG-tahitian_0168

The verb *îna* 'to make' is used with a similar causative meaning when it occurs as the first verb in a SVC (182).

(182) **te îna bwagee,**

> te= îna bwage-e
> 3SG.SUBJ= make.GNR return-3SG.OBJ
> 'he reversed it,'
>
> Yal-20092011-AW6_0036

The verb *tejoon* 'to plead, to complain' takes on an aspectual meaning of insistence when it is the first element of a SVC, as in (183) where it occurs in its transitivized form *tejoni*.

(183) *Te tejoni âva na ora.*

te=	tejoni	âva	na	ora
3SG.SUBJ=	plead.TR	fish	interior	rain

'He insists on fishing in the rain.'

Yal-03112011-IM1.wav – Yal-03112011-IM2.wav

5.11 The verb phrase

In §5.3 I discussed the *verb group*, the clitic group surrounding the verb word and its accompanying suffixes. There is also a constituent *verb phrase* in Belep, which bears a resemblance to the prototypical verb phrase found in many languages (defined by Van Valin (2004:5) as "the constituent composed of a verb plus following NP"). The Belep verb phrase consists minimally of a verb group and maximally contains an absolutive noun phrase and a number of enclitics (Table 20).

Tab. 20: Verb phrase enclitics

0	(+1)	(+2)	(+3)	(+4)
VERB GROUP	ABS. NP	DIRECTIONAL	DEICTIC	LOCATIONAL
		=da 'DIR.UH'	=me 'CTP'	=(l)exeng 'LOC.DC'
		=du 'DIR.DH'	=ic 'CTF'	=(l)ena 'LOC.MPX'
		=van 'DIR.TV'		=(l)iyek 'LOC.MDS'
				=(l)exe 'LOC.DST'
				=(l)exeda 'LOC.UH'
				=(l)exedu 'LOC.DH'
				=(l)iyeda 'LOC.DST.UH'
				=(l)imidu 'LOC.DST.DH'
				=(l)iva 'LOC.Q'
				=(l)i 'LOC.A'

Verb phrases can occur in both transitive and intransitive clauses. For example, (184) shows a verb phrase with the transitive verb *nawee* 'to deposit', the absolutive noun phrase *pulu* 'speech, language', and the verb phrase enclitic *=me* 'CTP'. Verb phrases are marked with brackets.

(184) *La nawe pulume.*

{la=   nawe   pulu=me}

3PL.SUBJ= deposit language=CTP

'They brought the message here.'

Yal-20092011-AW6_0152

An example of a verb phrase with an absolutive noun phrase in an intransitive clause is shown in (185). The absolutive noun phrase is *wagaji* 'our boat'.

(185) « *Ka ivi wagaji ?* »

ka {ivi   waga-ji}

LK where.SPC boat-1DU.INCL.POSS

'"And where is our boat?"'

Yal-01082010-MFD_0016

5.12 Directionals

Directionals are verb phrase enclitics (§3.2.2.6) in Belep. They are divided into two sets, the spatial directionals—which describe movement with respect to spatial axes (see §4.4.1)—and the deictic directionals, which describe movement with respect to the speaker. A list of the Belep directionals is given in Table 21.

Tab. 21: Belep directionals

	Belep directional	Gloss	Translation
Spatial	=da	'DIR.UH'	uphill; up
	=du	'DIR.DH'	downhill; down
	=van	'DIR.TV'	transverse; persistive 'PER'

	Belep directional	Gloss	Translation
Deictic	=me	'CTP'	centripetal[39]; toward the speaker
	=ic	'CTF'	centrifugal; away from the speaker

The spatial directionals are grammaticalized versions of the corresponding full verbs, as shown in Table 22.

Tab. 22: Spatial directionals and corresponding full verbs

Full verb	Gloss	Directional	Gloss
ta	'to go.UH'	=da	'DIR.UH'
tu	'to go.DH'	=du	'DIR.DH'
pan	'to go.TV'	=van	'DIR.TV'

The deictic directionals are incompatible with spatial directional =van 'TV'; however, they may occur concurrently with =da 'UH' and =du 'DH'. In these cases, the spatial directional always precedes the deictic directional, as in (186).

(186)   *Texa tao migi janenadume,*
       te=xa   tao=   migi jane-na=du=me
       3SG.SUBJ=ADD HAB= hold ear-3SG.POSS=DIR.DH=CTP
       'And he kept clutching his ear,'
                                                                     Yal-05092011-AP1_0092

The spatial directional =van 'DIR.TV' sometimes serves to indicate transverse movement, as in (187).

(187)   *Caivak, te kejavan na na pwa,*
       caivak te=   keja=van=a   na   pwa
       rat   3SG.SUBJ= run=DIR.TV=LOC interior hole
       'The rat, he ran into a hole,'
                                                                     Yal-01082010-MFD_0058

---

[39] The terms *centripetal* and *centrifugal* come from Bril (2002); they are used here rather than the more common terms *venitive* and *andative* for consistency with the rest of the literature on New Caledonian languages.

However, its most common meaning is aspectual (see §5.5 for more information on aspect in Belep). Its use implies that the action of the verb is persistive; it could be translated 'to keep doing' the verb. This aspectual meaning is most clearly demonstrated in instances like (188), where the verb *mo* 'to live, stay' is static rather than dynamic, and (189), where the verb *go* 'to cry' does not indicate movement at all.

(188) ***Lexa movan, movan,***
le=xa   mo=van   mo=van
3DU.SUBJ=ADD   live=DIR.TV   live=DIR.TV
'And they kept living and living,'
                                             Yal-28072010-BGMCG-sousmarin_0010

(189) ***Texa govan na ulac âyili,***
te=xa   go=van=a   ulaya   âyi-li
3SG.SUBJ=ADD   cry=DIR.TV=NOM   old   man-DET.A.PRX
'And that old man kept crying,'
                                               Yal-28072010-BGMCG-tahitian_0244

As enclitics (§3.2.2.6), the directionals trigger phonological changes in their hosts; these include the introduction of epenthetic vowels, as in (190), and the unpredictable loss of final consonants in the host, as in (191). In (190), an epenthetic vowel [a] is inserted between the verb *tup* 'to dive' and the directional =*du* 'DIR.DH'.

(190) ***Avexa nyi tuvadu la na buâny waak,***
ave=xa   nyi=   tuva=du=la   na
1DU.EXCL.SUBJ=ADD   PUNCT=   dive=DIR.DH=LOC   interior

buâny waa-k
stone   DEM.MAN-DET.D.PRX
'And we repeatedly dove down by the stone like this,'
                                               Yal-28072010-BGMCG-tahitian_0053

In example (191), the verb *wânem* 'walk' is reduced to /wâne/ when =*da* 'DIR.UH' is encliticized to it.

(191) *Texa wâneda la bween,*
　　　　te=xa　　　　　wâne=da=la　　　bwee-n
　　　　3SG.SUBJ=ADD　walk=DIR.UH=LOC　top-3SG.POSS
　　　　'And he walked up on it,'
　　　　　　　　　　　　　　　　　Yal-28072010-BGMCG-tahitian_0058

5.13 Locationals

The locationals are verb phrase enclitics which identify the endpoint of motion or the location of the action with respect to the deictic center—this is in contrast with the directionals discussed in §5.12, which primarily describe the direction of motion. The locationals are shown in Table 23. They follow all other verb phrase enclitics.

Tab. 23: Belep locationals

Locational	Gloss
=(l)exeng[40]	'LOC.DC'
=(l)ena	'LOC.MPX'
=(l)iyek	'LOC.MDS'
=(l)exe	'LOC.DST'
=(l)exeda	'LOC.UH'
=(l)exedu	'LOC.DH'
=(l)iyeda	'LOC.DST.UH'
=(l)imidu	'LOC.DST.DH'
=(l)iva	'LOC.Q'
=(l)i	'LOC.A'

The allomorphs containing /l/ are used following a vowel, while those without /l/ are used following a consonant (the same pattern is followed by the ditropic clitics which indicate case; see §6.4). These deictic locative enclitics distinguish among many of the same features as the nominal determiner suffixes (§4.4.2): locational enclitics indicate distance from the speaker and the hearer, as well as direction in relation to the deictic center (uphill or downhill; see §4.4.1). The locationals are pronominal in that they deictically or anaphorically index a locational noun phrase, often one marked as in the locative case (§6.4.5); however, they are not pronouns (§4.6).

---

40 Another locational =*(l)exen* also occurs; it is unknown at this time whether this is a phonological variant of =*(l)exeng* or has a separate meaning.

Locationals =(l)exeng 'LOC.DC', =(l)ena 'LOC.MPX', =(l)iyek 'LOC.MDS' and =(l)exe 'LOC.DST' contrast in terms of distance from the speaker and the hearer. In (192), the use of =lexeng 'LOC.DC' indicates that the event described by the verb occurred at or very near the deictic center.

(192)   *Te ci lexeng nga mwave âbur,*
        te=   ci=<u>lexeng</u>=a   mwa-ve   âbur
        3SG.SUBJ=   sit=LOC.DC=NOM house-1DU.EXCL.POSS   side.UH
        'Our old house sat here before,'
                                                Yal-28072010-BGMCG-tahitian_0234

In (193), =lena 'LOC.MPX' refers to an area near the hearer where the endpoint of the verb's action occurred. At the time of narration, we were fairly near to the beach and I (the hearer) was sitting downhill of the speaker.

(193)   *Toma pwala pwemwa, te tame la pwâna we,*
        toma   pwala   pwemwa te=   ta=me=la   pwâna   we
        but   front   village 3SG.SUBJ=   go.UH=CTP=LOC   hole   water

        pwâna wedame ka uya lena ka pwabo,
        pwâna   we=da=me   ka uya=<u>lena</u>   ka pwabo
        hole   water=DIR.UH=CTP   LK arrive=LOC.MPX   LK reef.well
        'But the tip of the island, the bay moved, moved up here and turned into a reef well right there,'
                                                Yal-28072010-BGMCG-igname_0041-0043

In (194), =(l)iyek 'LOC.MDS' indexes to an area which is a short distance away from both the speaker and the hearer where the action of the verb *âva* 'to go fishing' takes place.

(194)   *Teme âri, teme pan âva liyek,*
        te=me   âri=re=me   pana   âva=<u>liyek</u>
        3SG.SUBJ=IRR   say=3SG.SUBJ=IRR   go.TV   fish=LOC.MDS
        'He would say, he would go fish over there,'
                                                Yal-01082010-MFD_0008

In (195), =(l)exe 'LOC.DST' is used to locate the predicated referent (§5.2.6) far from both the speaker and the hearer, in the deep ocean.

(195) **Era lexe, era la dânac,**
 era=lexe era=la dânac
 3SG.NEW.V=LOC.DST 3SG.V=LOC ocean
 'It was there, it was in the deep ocean,'
 Yal-28072010-BGMCG-igname_0012-0013

Locationals =(l)exeda 'LOC.UH', =(l)exedu 'LOC.DH', =(l)iyeda 'LOC.DST.UH', and =(l)imidu 'LOC.DST.DH' all indicate the location of the predication with respect to both the distance and direction from the deictic center: =(l)exeda and =(l)exedu are used for areas conceptualized as within the boundaries of the speaker's location—areas to which someone could walk in just a few minutes—while =(l)iyeda and =(l)imidu refer to areas conceptualized as outside this boundary, to which someone might travel in hours or multiple days. The enclitics =(l)exeda and =(l)iyeda both refer to the uphill direction, while =(l)exedu and =(l)imidu both refer to the downhill direction (see §4.3). For example, in (196), =lexeda 'LOC.UH' indexes a location which is far from the deictic center, but not conceptualized as being outside of a boundary.

(196) **Texa nyi ce lexeda.**
 te=xa nyi= ce=lexeda
 3SG.SUBJ=ADD PUNCT= settle=LOC.UH
 'And he sat up there [in a tree].'
 Yal-20092011-AW5_0084

By contrast, =liyeda 'LOC.DST.UH' in (197) indexes a location which is far to the southeast of Belep, located on the northwest tip of the Mainland, which might take a day of traveling to reach.

(197) **paeda, uya liyeda.**
 pa-e=da uya=liyeda
 take-3SG.ABS=DIR.UH arrive=LOC.DST.UH
 'brought her up [from Belep], arrived up there [at Pwayili].'
 Yal-20092011-AW1_0230

In (198), =lexedu 'LOC.DH' indexes to a location which is northwest of the speaker, but not conceptualized as being outside of a boundary; on a boat, he might travel there in fifteen minutes.

(198) *Avexa pame, pame, pame, ka mu lexedu.*

ave=xa   pa=me   pa=me
1DU.EXCL.SUBJ=ADD   go.TV=CTP   go.TV=CTP

pa=me   ka   mu=lexedu
go.TV=CTP   LK   moor=LOC.DH

'And we came, came, came and moored down there,'

Yal-28072010-BGMCG-tahitian_0224

By contrast, =*limidu* 'LOC.DST.DH' in (199) refers to a place in Belep which is conceptualized as being outside of a boundary; travel there might take several hours.

(199) *Avaxa uya limidu to bwaêdan,*

ava=xa   uya=limidu=ro   bwaêdan
1PL.EXCL.SUBJ=ADD   arrive=LOC.DIST.DH=when   morning

'And we arrived down there [at Awe] in the morning,'

Yal-17072009-TB-weekend_0003

5.14 Summary

In this chapter, I have presented the Belep word class of verbs and their associated morphology. Intransitive verbs require either a nominative argument (§5.2.1) or an absolutive argument (§5.2.2). Transitive verbs (§5.2.3) are either free or bound. A variety of verb inflections for specificity (§5.2.4), valence (§5.2.5), and differential absolutive marking (§5.2.6) are available for many verbs. The verb group (§5.3) is a constituent including the verb word and its surrounding suffixes and clitics. Included in the verb group are valence proclitics (§5.4), aspectual proclitics (§5.5), modal clitics (§5.6), absolutive suffixes (§5.7), and subject agreement proclitics (§5.8). Some verb compounding exists (§5.9); however, verb serialization (§5.10) is more common. The verb phrase (§5.11) is a constituent which includes a verb group, a nominal absolutive argument, and any accompanying directional (§5.12) or locational (§5.13) enclitics.

6 Basic clause structure

6.1 Introduction

Belep has a fixed word order of VERB + PATIENT + AGENT (§6.2). Its argument structure (§6.3) is unusual in that the Agent of a transitive clause may be marked as nominative or genitive (depending on the definiteness of the Patient) and the argument of an intransitive clause (hereafter S argument) may be marked as nominative or absolutive (depending on the verb; see §5.2.1 and §5.2.2). The Patient of a transitive clause is always (un)marked as absolutive. Belep's system of case-marking ditropic clitics (see §3.2.2.6) is discussed in §6.4. Predicate nominals (§6.5) are used for many pragmatic functions, including some types of questions (§6.6). Imperatives (§6.7) and negation (§6.8) are formed primarily through modifications of verbal morphology. This chapter concludes with a discussion of pragmatically marked clauses (§6.9), periphrastic expressions of voice (§6.10) and temporality (§6.11), and the comparative construction (§6.12).

6.2 Basic word order and typology

The basic word order for transitive clauses with two full noun phrases in Belep is VOS (according to Greenberg's 1963 classification), or VERB GROUP + PATIENT NP + AGENT NP, a fairly rare word-order type found in only about 2% of the world's languages (Dryer 2013). Belep shares this basic constituent order with neighboring Nêlêmwa (Bril 2002); however, Balade Nyelâyu, to which Belep is more closely related, has a different basic word order: VERB + AGENT NP + PATIENT NP (Ozanne-Rivierre 2004).

Examples (1) - (4) demonstrate Belep's basic constituent order, which is invariant in pragmatically unmarked clauses. In (1), the verb group (see §5.3) is clause-initial; it is followed by the patient noun phrase *doo* 'earth' and then the agent noun phrase, *nyan tayamook* 'his mother, this old woman'.

(1) **Te ta înae doo la nyan, tayamook.**

VG			P	A	
[te=	ta	îna-e]	[do]=la	[nya-n	tayamoo-k]
3SG.SUBJ	go.UH	make-SPC	earth=NOM	mother-3SG.POSS	old.woman-DET.D.PRX

'his mother, this old woman, flung dirt.'

Yal-28072010-BGMCG-sousmarin_0025-0026

In example (2), the verb group precedes the patient noun phrase *oyeen* 'his curse' and the agent noun phrase *teâmaa* 'chieftain'.

(2) *ma teme, me âri oyeen na teâmaa.*
           VG   P   A
    ma[=re=me   me âri]   [oye-n]=a   [teâmaa]
    LK4 3SG.SUBJ=IRR IRR say.TR curse-3SG.POSS=NOM high.chief
    'so that the chieftain would, would speak his curse.'
                                                              Yal-20092011-AW6_0038

In (3), the patient noun phrase *wîmi* 'that thing' is followed by the agent noun phrase *ulayili Cebaba* 'that old man Cebaba'.

(3) *Texa pae wîmi la ulayili Cebaba,*
        VG   P   A
   [te=xa   pa-e]   [wî-mi]=la   [ulayi-li   Cebaba]
   3SG.SUBJ=ADD take-SPC DEM.INAN-   old.man-   Cebaba
                                 DET.A.DST=NOM DET.A.PRX
   'And that old man Cebaba took that thing,'
                                                         Yal-20092011-AW1_0265

In example (4), the clause begins with a verb group, followed by the patient noun phrase *wayap* 'war' and the agent noun phrase *teâmaa* 'chieftain'.

(4) *Texa terae wayap va teâmaa,*
      VG   P   A
   [te=xa   tera-e]   [wayav]=a   [teâmaa]
   3SG.SUBJ=ADD   stop-SPC war=NOM   high.chief
   'And the chieftain stopped the war,'
                                                         Yal-20092011-AW4_0060

Transitive clauses like (1) - (4), with a full noun phrase for both agent and patient, are rare in discourse (Du Bois 1987, Thompson & Hopper 2001). Most clauses produced by speakers in natural discourse contain only one full noun phrase argument: either an intransitive S argument, a transitive P argument, or a transitive A argument. In intransitive clauses the order of elements is VERB GROUP + INTRANSITIVE NP, as shown in examples (5) - (7). In (5), the argument of an intransitive verb—hereafter called the S argument—is *mwaak* 'rabbitfish', and it follows the verb group.

(5) *Te tame la mwaak,*
       VG   S
   [te=   ta=me]=la   [mwaak]
   3SG.SUBJ= go.UH=CTP=NOM rabbitfish
   'The rabbitfish came,'
                                                        Yal-01082010-MFD_0033

In (6), the S argument *ulayili* 'that old man' follows the verb group.

(6) *Teô cuur ra ulayili,*
        VG   S
    [te=ô   cur]=a   [ulayi-li]
    3SG.SUBJ=REAL stand=NOM old-DET.A.PRX
    'The old man stood up,'
                                         Yal-28072010-BGMCG-tahitian_0208

In (7), the S argument *ola* 'shellfish' follows the verb group.

(7) *Âria ola.*
        VG   S
    [âria]   [ola]
    NEG.EX shellfish
    'There weren't any lobsters.'
                                         Yal-28072010-BGMCG-tahitian_0032

Examples (8) - (11) show transitive clauses with only one full noun phrase argument. In such clauses, the additional argument is indicated by inflectional morphology within the verb group. In the transitive clauses in (8) and (9), only a noun phrase Patient argument is present. The Agent in both clauses is cross-referenced by a subject agreement proclitic (§5.8) in the verb group. In (8), the subject proclitic *la=* '3PL.SUBJ' refers anaphorically to the Agent, as does the subject proclitic *te=* '3SG.SUBJ' in (9).

(8) *La âvae nae no pwalaic.*
        VG   P
    [la=   âva-e]   [nae   no pwalaic]
    3PL.SUBJ= fish-SPC small.thing fish one
    'They caught one small fish.'
                                                  Yal-01082010-MFD_0010

(9) *te migi buâny,*
        VG   P
    [te=   migi] [buâny]
    3SG.SUBJ= hold   stone
    'he was holding the stone,'
                                                    Yal-20092011-AW1_0254

In the transitive clauses in (10) and (11), only a noun phrase Agent argument is present; the Patient in both clauses is indexed anaphorically by an absolutive pronominal suffix (§5.7) in the verb group. In (10) the Patient is indexed by the 3SG absolutive suffix *-er*, while the 3PL suffix *-la* indexes the Patient in (11).

(10) *Texa înaer ri Belep,*
        VG   A
[te=xa   îna-er]=i   [Belep]
3SG.SUBJ=ADD make-3SG.ABS=GEN Belep
'Belep did it,'
                                            Yal-20092011-AW6_0055

(11) *Teme kewela li Dubageni.*
        VG   A
[te=me   kewe-la]=li   [Dubageni]
3SG.SUBJ=IRR chase-3PL.ABS=GEN type.of.demon
'The Dubageni will chase them.'
                                            Yal-05092011-AP1_0094

These examples have shown that the VERB + PATIENT + AGENT word order in basic Belep clauses does not vary based on the status of the arguments; Belep has a rigid word-order in pragmatically unmarked clauses.

The only variation in word-order is found in a subset of pragmatically-marked clauses; that is, in clauses of the form TOPIC + COMMENT (§6.9.1). In topicalized clauses, the topic noun phrase occurs before the verb, usually with an intonation break between them as in (12).

(12) *ka naerama, la îbi jawu.*
        TOP   VG   P
ka [nae-ra-ma]   [la=   îbi]   [jawu]
LK child-3GNR.POSS-AC 3PL.SUBJ= collect dead.leaves
'and the children, they collected trash.'
                                      Yal-17072009-TB-weekend_0009

According to the typological word-order correlations put forward in Dryer (1992), which adjust linguistic sampling for genetic and areal bias, Belep is a fairly consistent VO language.[1] The rest of this section will elaborate on a few of these correlations.

---

[1] I use Dryer's term 'VO' here to indicate that the order of verb and patient noun phrase in Belep is always VERB + PATIENT. I do not use the term 'object' in this work (see §6.3).

6.2.1 ADPOSITION + NOUN

Belep does not have a class of adpositions (see §3.3). However, the set of locative nouns which serve the function of adpositions (§6.4.5.1) always precede their possessor noun, as in (13) and (14).

(13) **bwe alap**
top beach
'on the beach'

Yal-01082010-MFD_0033

(14) **na buâny**
interior stone
'at the stone'

Yal-28072010-BGMCG-tahitian_0053

This is consistent with the word-order correlate noted by Dryer (1992: 83), that languages with VO order tend overwhelmingly to have prepositions.

6.2.2 NOUN + RELATIVE CLAUSE

Belep also follows the tendency for VO languages to have the relative clause follow the noun, rather than the reverse (Dryer 1992: 86). In all types of relative clauses (§7.4), the relative clause follows the head, as shown in examples (15) and (16).

(15) *Vayimi cuur ra na keloop dadabwa.*
HEAD   RELATIVE CLAUSE
vayi{-mi   cur=a   na   kelova dadabwa}
cow.LN-DET.A.DST   stand=LOC   interior hat   black
'The cow wearing a black hat.'

Yal-05102010-MTAD_45:07-45:11

(16) *Nyana yo migier ri nyoda emwiyek.*
HEAD   RELATIVE CLAUSE
nya{-na   yo=   migi-er=i   nyoda   e-mwi-yek}
DEM.IDF-   2SG.SUBJ= hold-   tenta-   hand-2SG.POSS-
DET.D.MPX   3SG.ABS=GEN   cle   DET.D.MDS
'The one you're holding in your other hand.'

Yal-05102010-MTAD_33:24-33:27

6.2.3 NOUN + GENITIVE

Belep is also consistent with the tendency for VO languages to have the possessor follow the possessed noun, rather than the reverse (Dryer 1992: 91). Section §4.2.2 discussed the possessive constructions in detail; in both the dependent and the independent possessive constructions, the possessed noun always precedes its possessor, as shown in examples (17) and (18).

(17) *oreâ naerama*
 oreâ   nae-ra-ma
 breath child-3GNR.POSS-AC
 'the children's breath'

Yal-17072009-TB-weekend_0038

(18) *pulu li gawaariik*
 pulu=li   gawarii-k
 speech=GEN day-DET.DEICT-PROX
 'the words of this day'

Yal-25072010-PT-homily_0004

6.2.4 ADJECTIVE + STANDARD

Dryer asserts a "clear preference" for adjectives to precede the standard of comparison in VO languages (Dryer 1992: 92). Though Belep does not have a class of adjectives (see §3.3), comparative constructions (§6.12) predicate a property concept (§6.5.3), which is modified by an aspectual proclitic (§5.5) indicating degree. The standard is a dative-marked noun phrase (§6.4.4). As Dryer's generalizations are concerned with conceptual rather than language-specific grammatical categories, Belep fits Dryer's observation that the property concept tends to precede the standard in VO languages, as in example (19).

(19) *Te nyi ulac na le nyak.*

	MARKER	PROPERTY		STANDARD
te=	[nyi=]	[ulay=a]	na=le	[nya-k]
3SG.SUBJ=	PUNCT=	be.old=LOC	interior=DAT	DEM.IDF-DET.D.PRX

'He is older than that one.'

Yal-05102010-PT1.wav – Yal-05102010-PT3.wav

6.2.5 VERB + ADPOSITIONAL PHRASE

There are no adpositions in Belep; their function is served by locative noun phrases headed by a body part noun (§6.4.5.1). Phrases consisting of a body part noun and its nominal possessor—Belep's functional equivalent of adpositional phrases—follow the verb, as in most VO languages (Dryer 1992: 92). An example is given in (20).

(20) « *Ôda la bwe bwaang.* »
      VG   LOC
     [ôda]=la   [bwe bwaa-ng]
     climb=LOC top   head-1SG.POSS
     '"Climb onto my head."'
                                                          Yal-01082010-MFD_0044

6.2.6 VERB + MANNER ADVERB

In Belep, as in most VO languages (Dryer 1992: 93), the manner adverb follows the verb, as in (21) where the manner adverb is the bound demonstrative pronoun *wa-* 'DEM.MAN' (§4.6.2) with the deictic suffix *-na* 'DET.D.MPX' (§4.4.2.1).

(21) *calayi doo wana.*
     calayi   doo wa-na
     brush.TR earth DEM.MAN-DET.D.MPX
     '[until it] brushed the earth like that.'
                                  Yal-28072010-BGMCG-hamecon_0027

6.2.7 WANT + SUBORDINATE VERB

In Belep, as in most VO languages (Dryer 1992: 94), the verb for 'want' precedes the verb describing what is wanted, as in (22). This is further discussed in §5.10.1.

(22) *ava jaar bae pê*
     ava=   jara bae pê
     1PL.EXCL.SUBJ= want bite bread
     'we want to eat the bread'
                                      Yal-25072010-PT-homily_0030

For a discussion of the word order within noun phrases, see §4.4. For the word order within the verb group, see §5.3.

6.3 Argument structure

Grammatical relations in Belep are not easily classifiable into any one alignment system. In transitive clauses, P arguments are always unmarked (§6.4.1), and A arguments can either be marked with =*la* 'NOM' (§6.4.2) or =*li* 'GEN' (§6.4.3) depending on the definiteness of the P argument (see §6.3.2 below). In intransitive clauses, S arguments are either marked with =*la* 'NOM' like some A arguments or are unmarked like P arguments, a distinction governed by the choice of verb (§5.2.1, §5.2.2). This system is depicted in Figure 1.

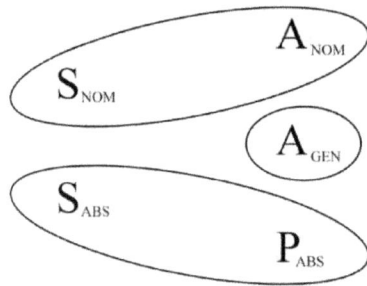

Fig. 1: Argument structure in Belep

As such, Belep demonstrates a pattern of split-intransitivity or split-S (as defined by Andrews 2007a, Dryer 2007) when P is indefinite (A = S_a ≠ S_p = P) and a combination of tripartite and split-intransitive alignment when P is definite (A ≠ S_a ≠ S_p = P). This differs from the majority of New Caledonian languages, which have split-ergative argument structure (Moyse-Faurie 2003b), though they vary as to the conditions of the split.[2] There is no evidence of split-ergativity in Belep.

In the following sections, I will discuss evidence for nominative-accusative alignment (§6.3.1), tripartite alignment (§6.3.2), and absolutive-ergative alignment (§6.3.3), and will then draw together the criteria that lead me to recognize a category of 'subject' in Belep (§6.3.4).

---

[2] Nêlêmwa and Nemi are split according to Silverstein's (1976) empathy/agent-worthiness hierarchy, with a pronoun/noun split and an animate/inanimate split respectively. Drehu's split ergativity is based on different tense/aspects. Ozanne-Rivierre (2004) states that Balade Nyelâyu is split, like Nêlêmwa, based on pronoun/noun.

6.3.1 Nominative-accusative alignment

Belep's argument structure shows a nominative-accusative alignment when P is indefinite if only those intransitive verbs which require a nominative argument (§5.2.1) are considered. These verbs form the majority of intransitives.

Evidence for nominative-accusative alignment is found in nominal case-marking, verb inflection, relativization, and clausal coordination.

Nominal case-marking shows a nominative-accusative alignment. The nominative case marker =*la* or =*a* 'NOM' (§6.4.2) marks A arguments in a transitive clause where the P argument is indefinite (see §6.3.2) and S arguments for a majority of intransitive verbs. For example, in (23), the nominative case marker =*la* 'NOM' marks the transitive A argument *ulayili Cebaba* 'that old man Cebaba'. In (24), the nominative case marker =*a* 'NOM' marks the A argument *teâmaa* 'the chieftain'.[3] In both of these examples, the P argument is unmarked (§6.4.1).

(23) *Texa pae wîmi la ulayili Cebaba,*
      VG[4]   P   A
      [te=xa   pa-e]   [wî-mi]=la   [ulayi-li   Cebaba]
      3SG.SUBJ=ADD take-SPC DEM.INAN-   old.man-   Cebaba
                                  DET.A.DST=NOM   DET.A.PRX
      'And that old man Cebaba, took that thing,'
                                                      Yal-20092011-AW1_0265

(24) *Texa terae wayap va teâmaa,*
      VG   P   A
      [te=xa   tera-e]   [wayav]=a [teâmaa]
      3SG.SUBJ=ADD stop-SPC   war=NOM   high.chief
      'And the chieftain stopped the war,'
                                                      Yal-20092011-AW4_0060

Examples (25) - (28) show the use of the same nominative case marking for the S argument in intransitive clauses. Omission of the case marker—which would make the S argument unmarked (§6.4.1) like a P argument—is ungrammatical. In (25), the S argument *Awuli Cabak* (a personal name) is marked with nominative =*la*.

---

[3] The variation in the form of the nominative case marker is phonological. See §3.2.2.5 on enclitics.
[4] In the examples in this section, 'VG' means 'verb group'; see §5.3.

(25) **Texa ta la Awuli Cabak,**
        VG   S
      [te=xa   ta]=<u>la</u>   [Awuli Cabak]
      3SG.SUBJ=ADD go.UH=NOM Awuli Cabak
      'And Awuli Cabak went up,'
                                                       Yal-19092011-PA_0027

In (26), the intransitive S argument *âju la bween* 'the person on him' is marked with nominative =*la*.

(26) **Texa bwawa la âju la bween.**
        VG   S
      [te=xa   bwawa]=<u>la</u>   [âju=la   bwee-n]
      3SG.SUBJ=ADD   remove.NTR=NOM   person=LOC top-3SG.POSS
      'And the person on him was removed.'
                                                 Yal-28072010-BGMCG-tahitian_0266

In (27), the S argument *Ixe* (a personal name) is marked with nominative =*a*.

(27) **Texa tejoon na Ixe.**
        VG   S
      [te=xa   tejon]=<u>a</u> [Ixe]
      3SG.SUBJ=ADD plead=NOM Ixe
      'And Ixe begged.'
                                                          Yal-20092011-AW1_0100

In (28), the S argument *âju pwalaic* 'a person' is marked with nominative =*a*.

(28) **Texa ovan na âju pwalaic,**
        VG   S
      [te=xa   o=van]=<u>a</u>   [âju   pwalaic]
      3SG.SUBJ=ADD advance=DIR.TV=NOM person one
      'And a person advanced,'
                                                          Yal-20092011-AW5_0076

The argument structure shown here, whereby the A argument of a transitive and the S argument of an intransitive are marked with =*la* or =*a* 'NOM', while the P argument of a transitive is unmarked, can be characterized as a nominative-accusative alignment pattern for case marking.

Cross-referencing of nominal arguments on the verb also demonstrates a nominative-accusative pattern, regardless of the definiteness of the P argument. In transitive clauses, the A argument is obligatorily cross-referenced by a subject agreement proclitic on the verb (§5.8). The P argument may be anaphorically indexed by an absolutive pronominal verb suffix (§5.7). For example, in (29), the verbal proclitic *na*=

'1SG.SUBJ' agrees with the anaphoric A argument. In (30), the verbal suffix *-nao* '1SG.ABS' agrees with the anaphoric P argument.

(29)   *Naô pae tânema cawone,*
              VG   P
              [**na**=ô   pa-e]   [tânema cawone]
              1SG.SUBJ=REAL take-TR eye   Japanese.LN
              'I took my diving mask,' (lit. 'I took my Japanese eye')
                                              Yal-28072010-BGMCG-tahitian_0076

(30)   « *La ginao limidu,* »
              VG
              [la=   gi-**nao**=limidu]
              3PL.SUBJ= attack-1SG.ABS=LOC.DST.DH
              '"They killed me down there,"'
                                               Yal-20092011-AW1_0283

In the intransitive clauses in (31) - (34), verbal proclitics (§5.8) are used to agree with the S argument; use of verbal suffixes (§5.7) is ungrammatical. In (31), the verbal proclitic *na=* '1SG.SUBJ' indexes the S argument of the intransitive verb *puer* 'to cook, prepare food'.

(31)   *Ka nao, na puer,*
                           VG
              ka   nao   [**na**=   puer]
              LK 1SG.INDEP 1SG.SUBJ= cook
              'And as for me, I cooked,'
                                                Yal-17072009-TB-weekend_0014

In (32), *na=* '1SG.SUBJ' occurs on both the intransitive main verb *âya* 'to be afraid' and the intransitive semantically dependent verb *pan* 'to go.TV'.

(32)   *Na âya li na pan na pu caya,*
              VG   VG
              [**na**=   âya]=li   [**na**=   pan]=a   pu   caya
              1SG.SUBJ= be.afraid.NTR=GEN   1SG.SUBJ= go.TV=LOC side dad
              'I am afraid to go near Dad,' (lit. 'I am afraid that I go near Dad'; see §7.3.7)
                                                  Yal-20092011-AW1_0039

In (33), the verbal proclitic *te=* '3SG.SUBJ' indexes the S argument of the intransitive verb *kaac* 'to be angry, bitter'. Note that the 3SG.ABS verb suffixes are *-e* and *-er* (§5.7.2).

(33) **Caivak, texa, te kaac u le buny,**
                                    VG
      caivak   te=xa   [te=   kaya]   u=le   buny
      rat   3SG.SUBJ=ADD 3SG.SUBJ= bitter   toward=DAT great.crested.tern
      'The rat, he, he was angry at the tern,'

                                                                    Yal-01082010-MFD_0004

In (34), the verbal proclitic *yo=* '2SG.SUBJ' indexes the S argument of the intransitive verb *ci* 'to sit, stay'. The corresponding 2SG.ABS verb suffix is *-o* (§5.7).

(34) « *Yome ci la pwemwaji.* »
               VG
      [yo=me   ci]=la   pwemwa-ji
      2SG.SUBJ=IRR sit=LOC village-1DU.INCL.POSS
      '"You will stay in our home."'

                                                              Yal-20092011-AW1_0105

Since a different set of verb agreement markers are used for P arguments in a transitive clause than for intransitive S and transitive A arguments, the system of verb inflections can be said to have a nominative-accusative alignment pattern.

Relativization (§7.4) also shows evidence of a nominative-accusative system. When a third-person singular A argument of a transitive clause is relativized, it is ungrammatical to use a verbal proclitic to index the relativized noun phrase (this is true regardless of the definiteness of the P argument). For example, the A argument *âju* 'person' of the transitive clause with *cage* 'steal.TR' is omitted in (35) (where P is definite) and (36) (where P is indefinite). It is ungrammatical to use the 3SG.SUBJ proclitic *te=* in the location indicated by [0] within the relative clauses (indicated by {}).

(35) **Na ênae âjumi cagele.**
      na=   êna-e   âju{-mi   [0]   cage-le}
      1SG.SUBJ=   know-SPC   person-DET.D.DST   steal.TR-3DU.ABS
      'I know the person who stole them.'

(36) **âjumi jua cagen wîja**
      âju{-mi   [0]   jua   cage-na   wîja}
      person-DET.D.DST   really   steal.TR-DA.NSG thing
      'the person who always steals things'

                                                                  Yal-02112011-DY.wav

In contrast, when the P argument of a transitive clause is relativized, it is obligatorily indexed by a verbal suffix. For example, in (37) the relativized P argument *gawaariik* 'this day' is indexed by the 3SG.ABS verb suffix *-er*.

(37)   *Gawaariik te jier ri kawuja,*
       gawari{-xa=re   ji-er=i
       day-   give-3SG.ABS=GEN
       DET.D.PRX=3SG.SUBJ

   kawu-ja}
   guardian-1PL.INCL.POSS
   'This day that our Lord has given,' (lit. 'This day that our Lord has given it,')
   Yal-25072010-PT-homily_0005

When the third-person singular S argument of a nominative-intransitive clause is relativized, it—like the A argument of a transitive clause—is obligatorily omitted. For instance, in (38), the S argument *âju* 'person' of the intransitive verb *ta* 'to go.UH' is relativized. Use of 3SG.SUBJ proclitic *te=* instead of the indicated gap would be ungrammatical.

(38)   *Âjumi ci ta la na mwanok,*
       âju{-mi   [0]   ci   ta=la   na   mwanok}
       person-DET.A.DST   sit   go.UH=LOC interior moon
       'The person who went to the moon,'
       Yal-28072010-BGMCG-lune_0066-0067

Since S arguments in relativization behave like transitive A arguments rather than transitive P arguments, they are further evidence of a nominative-accusative system.

Finally, nominative-accusative alignment is found in the rules for clausal coordination (§7.2). When transitive clauses with identical A arguments are conjoined with linker *ka* (§7.2.1), the subject agreement proclitic in the non-initial clauses is usually omitted (regardless of the definiteness of the P). By contrast, if the P arguments are identical, the non-initial clauses must all be marked with indexical absolutive pronominal suffixes. For example, in (39), the subject proclitic *te=* '3SG.SUBJ' is used to index the A argument in the first transitive clause (where the verb is *pa* 'to take'), but is omitted in the second transitive clause (where the verb is *nawee* 'to deposit'). The A arguments of the two clauses index the same referent. However, though the P arguments of the clause—*buâny* 'stone' and *-er* '3SG.ABS'—also index the same referent, both must be present.

(39)   *Te pae buâny, ka naweer rexeng,*
       te=   pa-e   buâny   ka   [0] nawe-er=exeng
       3SG.SUBJ=   take-SPC   stone   LK   deposit-3SG.ABS=LOC.DC
       'He took the stoneᵢ, and dropped itᵢ here,'
       Yal-20092011-AW1_0266

When nominative-intransitive clauses with identical S arguments are conjoined using linker *ka*, the subject agreement proclitic in the non-initial clauses is also usually omitted. For example, in (40), intransitive clauses with the verbs *kaac* 'to be angry, bitter' and *go* 'to cry' are conjoined with linker *ka*. In the first clause, subject proclitic *te=* '3SG.SUBJ' is used, but it is obligatorily omitted in the second clause.

(40)   *Teô jua kaac, ka tao go, go.*
        te=ô   jua   kaac   ka   [0]   tao=   go   go
        3SG.SUBJ=REAL   very   bitter   LK   HAB=   cry   cry
        'He was very angry, and kept crying and crying.'
                                                                                  Yal-20092011-AW1_0275

Thus, the S argument of a nominative-intransitive behaves like the A argument of a transitive, and unlike the P argument of a transitive, in terms of clausal conjunction; this is further evidence of nominative-accusative alignment.

6.3.2 Tripartite alignment

There is evidence for Belep tripartite alignment in nominal case-marking. In transitive clauses in Belep, the P argument is always unmarked for case (§6.4.1). The A argument, however, may be marked in one of two ways. If the P is indefinite, the A argument is marked with nominative case marker *=la* or *=a* 'NOM' (§6.4.2). If the P is definite, the A argument is marked with genitive case marker *=li* or *=i* 'GEN' (§6.4.3). This leads to a tripartite system when P is definite and only nominative intransitive verbs (§5.2.1) are considered: the genitive marking of A differs from the nominative marking of S, which differs from the absolutive marking of P.

Example (41), a constructed pair of clauses glossed by a Belep speaker, shows the contrast between nominative- and genitive-marked A arguments in Belep.

(41)   a.   ***Te kiyi Darine na teâmaa.***
                  te=   kiyi   Darin=a   teâmaa
                  3SG.SUBJ= see.SPC Darine=NOM high.chief
                  'The chieftain saw a Darine [I don't think you can identify who I mean].'

       b.   ***Te kiyi Darine ni teâmaa.***
                  te=   kiyi   Darin=i   teâmaa
                  3SG.SUBJ= see.SPC Darine=GEN high.chief
                  'The chieftain saw Darine [and I think you can identify who I mean].'

In (41a), the A argument is marked as nominative; the speaker doesn't think the hearer can identify the indefinite P referent, and the hearer might respond by asking 'Which Darine?'. In (41b), the A argument is marked as genitive; the speaker believes the hearer can identify the referent of the P argument. Note that in both clauses, the verb is marked as specific (§5.2.4). In my corpus of naturally-occurring speech, no examples like (41b) occur—all instances of genitive A arguments in my corpus occur in clauses with pronominal absolutive suffixes (§5.7). From this I infer that transitive clauses with two full noun phrases where the P argument is definite are very unusual in Belep, a finding consistent with Du Bois (1987).

Genitive A arguments are obligatorily cross-referenced on the verb using the same agreement markers as nominative A and S arguments (§5.8). For example, in (42), the A argument *lami bwa molep* 'those still living', marked as genitive with =*i*, is indexed by the 3PL subject agreement marker *la=* in the verb group.

(42) *La kiyier ri lami bwa molep,*
 la=   kiyi-er=i   la-mi   bwa   molep
 3PL.SUBJ= see.SPC-3SG.ABS=GEN DEM.PL-DET.A.DST CONT= alive
 'Those still alive saw it,'
 Yal-20092011-AW2_0073

If, in a transitive clause, the P argument is represented by an anaphoric suffix (§5.7), the A argument is obligatorily marked with the genitive case marker. For example, in (43), the subject *maac* 'death, illness' is marked as genitive with =*li* because the P argument is indexed by the pronominal suffix -*nao* '1SG.ABS'.

(43) « *Te tunao li maac,* »
 te=   tu-nao=li   maac
 3SG.SUBJ= find-1SG.ABS=GEN death
 '"I'm sick,"' (lit. '"death has found me,"')
 Yal-20092011-AW6_0050

In (44), the A argument *ulayama* 'elders, ancestors' is marked as genitive with =*i* since the P argument is referenced by the pronominal suffix -*er* '3SG.ABS' (see §5.7.2).

(44) *Laô paer ri ulayama.*
 la=ô   pa-er=i   ulaya-ma
 3PL.SUBJ=REAL take-3SG.ABS=GEN old.man-AC
 'The ancestors took him.'
 Yal-28072010-BGMCG-tahitian_0113

In (45), the A argument *nic* 'sharks' is marked as genitive with =*li* since the absolutive argument is the pronominal suffix -*la* '3PL.ABS'.

(45) *Avar, la baela li nic.*
 avar la=   bae-la=li   nic
 other 3PL.SUBJ= bite.SPC-3PL.ABS=GEN   shark
 'Others, sharks ate them.'
 Yal-20092011-AW2_0049

Note that clauses of this shape are not morphosyntactically distinguishable from transitive clauses with a genitive oblique representing the semantic theme, instrument, etc., although this does not usually result in ambiguity. For instance, example (46) contains a genitive-marked theme noun phrase, *bolao pwâgo* 'poingo banana' which is morphologically identical to a genitive-marked subject.

(46) *Te taxeer ri bolao pwâgo,*
 te=   taxe-er=i   bolao pwâgo
 3SG.SUBJ=   distribute-3SG.ABS=GEN   banana poingo
 'He gave him poingo bananas,'
 Yal-28072010-BGMCG-lune_0037

The interpretation of *bolao pwâgo* 'poingo banana' as the theme rather than the agent in (46) is based purely on semantic grounds; the clause could also be translated (somewhat nonsensically) as 'A poingo banana gave [it to] him'.

Given this evidence for tripartite alignment, it would be accurate to describe genitive A arguments as 'ergative'—if we limit our scope to core arguments, we observe that there is a marker which occurs only on A arguments and never on P or S arguments (genitive =*li*).[5] However, I have chosen in this work to identify these arguments either as 'genitive A arguments' or as 'subjects' (see §6.3.4 below).

6.3.3 Absolutive-ergative alignment

Belep's argument structure shows an absolutive-ergative alignment when P is indefinite if only those intransitive verbs which require an (unmarked) absolutive argument (§6.4.1) are considered. Some of these verbs (discussed in §5.2.2) are listed in Table 1.[6]

---

[5] Many Australian and Papuan languages have multifunctional 'ergative' markers which are also used to mark possessors (Dixon 1980, Foley 1986, Onishi 2004).
[6] There are most likely several other verbs that fall into this set; however, the total number is still very small.

Tab. 1: Verbs requiring an absolutive S argument

Predicate	Translation
âria	'NEG.EX'
bwara	'to be missed, hoped for'
ciae, cia	'NEG.LOC'
ivi, iva	'to be where?'
mwanya	'to be many, to be overpowering'
mwanyi	'to be ignorant, to dislike'
tu, tuya	'EX'

Evidence for absolutive-ergative alignment for these verbs is found in nominal case-marking and verb inflection.

The case-marking of noun phrases in clauses with the Table 1 verbs shows absolutive-ergative alignment. In transitive clauses, the case marker =*la* or =*a* 'NOM' (§6.4.2) marks transitive A arguments when P is indefinite, while P arguments are unmarked (§6.3.1). For example, in (47), the A argument *teâmaa* 'chieftain' is marked with case marker =*a*, while the P argument *wayap* 'war' is unmarked.

(47)   ***Texa terae wayap va teâmaa,***
              VG   P   A
       [te=xa   tera-e]   [wayav]=a   [teâmaa]
       3SG.SUBJ=ADD stop-SPC   war=NOM   high.chief
       'And the chieftain stopped the war,'
                                              Yal-20092011-AW4_0060

In intransitive clauses using the verbs shown in Table 1, the S argument is unmarked. In (48), the S argument *ola* 'lobster, shrimp' of the negative existential verb *âria* 'NEG.EX' is unmarked.

(48)   ***Âria ola.***
       VG   S
       [âria]   [ola]
       NEG.EX   shellfish
       'There weren't any lobsters.'
                                   Yal-28072010-BGMCG-tahitian_0032

In (49), the S argument *naran* 'its name' of the verb *iva* 'to be where?' is unmarked.

(49) *Iva naran ?*
     VG   S
     [iva]   [nara-n]
     where.GNR   name-3SG.POSS
     'What's it called?' (lit. 'Where is its name?')
                                                          Yal-20092011-AW1_0273

In (50), the S argument *madaan* 'his sadness' of the verb *mwanya* 'to be many' is unmarked.

(50) *Texa mo la Teâ Nenema ka, mwanya madaan, yo kiyie ?*
                                                         VG   S
     te=xa   mo=la   Teâ Nenema   ka [mwanya] [madaa-n]   yoxe
     3SG.SUBJ=ADD live=NOM Teâ Nêlêmwa   LK   many   sadness-   TAG
                                                                                             3SG.POSS
     'And Teâ Nêlêmwa went along and his sadness was great, you see?'
                                                                                Yal-20092011-AW3_0024

The S arguments of the Table 1 verbs behave like transitive P arguments in terms of case-marking rather than like transitive A arguments. This is evidence of absolutive-ergative alignment in Belep.

Verb inflection of the Table 1 verbs also shows evidence of an absolutive-ergative system. In transitive clauses (regardless of the definiteness of the P), the A argument is obligatorily cross-referenced by a subject agreement proclitic on the verb (§5.8). The P argument may be anaphorically indexed by an absolutive pronominal verb suffix (§5.7). If the S argument of a Table 1 verb is referred to anaphorically, an absolutive verb suffix is used. Use of a subject agreement proclitic is ungrammatical. For example, the pronominal verb suffix -*e* '3SG.ABS' in (51) indexes the S argument of *iva* 'to be where?' and *cia* 'NEG.LOC'.

(51) « *Ivie ?* » *Ô ciae.*
     VG   VG
     [ivi-e]   [ô   cia-e]
     where.SPC-3SG.ABS   REAL NEG.LOC-3SG.ABS
     '"Where is he?" He wasn't there.'
                                                     Yal-28072010-BGMCG-tahitian_0178

In the constructed example in (52), the suffix -*er* '3SG.ABS' indexes the S argument of *mwanyi* 'to be ignorant of, dislike'.

(52)   *Mwanyier ri comu.*
       VG
       [mwanyi-er]=i   comu
       dislike-3SG.ABS=GEN   learning
       'He doesn't like school.'

                                                            Yal-22092011-TB.wav

In this respect, S arguments of Table 1 verbs behave like P arguments of transitive verbs, rather than like A arguments of transitive verbs.

Many Belep transitive verbs (§5.2.3.1) obligatorily inflect to agree with their P argument in specificity (§5.2.4). Some of the Table 1 verbs also inflect to agree with their S argument in specificity, as in (49) and (51) above. In these examples, the verb 'to be where?' has two forms, *ivi* when used with a specific S argument and *iva* for a generic S argument. Transitive verbs never agree with their A argument in specificity. This is further evidence of absolutive-ergative alignment in Belep.

6.3.4 Subjecthood in Belep

In Belep, the set containing genitive A arguments, nominative A arguments, and nominative S arguments displays the largest number of subject-like properties, as defined in Keenan (1976). This set of arguments, which together control Belep verb agreement (§5.8)—a subject-like property (Keenan 1976: 316)—are identified in this work as 'subjects'.[7] In addition to controlling verb agreement, these arguments' subject-like properties include their clausal position, their behavior in relativization and causatives, their co-referential deletion across coordination, their restrictions on imperatives, and their semantic roles.

Though Belep nominal subjects obligatorily occur at the end of a clause, verbal proclitics which agree with the subject are normally the first element of a clause. This is consistent with the cross-linguistic tendency of subject-like arguments to be "leftmost" in the clause (Keenan 1976: 319).

Subject relativization is the only type of relativization in Belep which uses the gap strategy (see §7.4.4); this strategy is usually used cross-linguistically for subject-like arguments (Keenan 1976: 320). For relativized 3SG nominative A and S arguments and genitive A arguments, it is ungrammatical to use a verbal proclitic to index the relativized noun phrase. An example of this omitted 3SG subject agreement marker is shown in (53); note that this subject would be marked genitive if it were not relativized since the P argument is definite.

---

[7] Non-nominative subjects, including genitive-marked subjects, are a well-attested cross-linguistic phenomenon. See for example Bhaskararao & Subbarao (2004), Klamer (2000), Kaufman (2011), etc.

(53) **Mo âjumi be pwâna mwa,**
mo   **âju-mi**   **[0] be   pwâna mwa**
LK3   person-DET.A.DST   hit   hole   house
'But the person who knocks at the door,'
Yal-25072010-PT-homily_0046

Another example of an omitted 3SG subject agreement marker is shown in (54); it would be marked as genitive if it were not relativized, as evidenced by the absolutive pronominal suffix -*er* in the second clause.

(54) **lami pae we teâmaa ka jier ra pwemwan.**
la-mi   **[0] pa-e**   **we   teâmaa   ka [0]**
DEM.PL-DET.A.DST   take-SPC   food   high.chief   LK

ji-er=a   **pwemwa-n**
give-3SG.ABS=LOC   village-3SG.POSS
'those who took the chieftain's food and brought it to the village.'
Yal-20092011-AW5_0031

In Belep causatives (§5.4.1), the causer (whether genitive A, nominative A, or nominative S) acts as the subject (consistent with the subject-like properties described by Keenan (1976: 321)); absolutive verbs cannot undergo causativization.

Verbal proclitics which agree with the nominative A or S argument in Belep are usually deleted across the coordinating linker *ka* (§7.2.1), which is a common subject-like property (Keenan 1976: 317). This property is shared by genitive A arguments; for example, in (55), the 2SG argument indexed by the verbal proclitic *yo=* in the first clause is a nominative S argument, while it is a genitive A argument in the second clause conjoined with *ka*, where the agreement proclitic is omitted.

(55) « **Yome ta ka ulinao la mariik.** »
yo=me   **ta=xa**   **[0]   uli-nao=la**   **marii-k**
2SG.SUBJ=IRR   go.UH=LK   pour-1SG.ABS=LOC   seashore-
                                                           DET.D.PRX
'"You go up and let me out on the seashore."'
Yal-28072010-BGMCG-tahitian_0136

However, this subject-like property does not apply to absolutive S and P arguments; co-referential absolutive arguments are both indexed across linker *ka* as in (56).

(56)   *tiae toop ka najie ma te ci.*
tia-e	toop	ka	naji-e	ma=re=	ci
pierce-SPC	field	LK	leave-3SG.ABS	LK4=3SG.SUBJ=	sit

       'dig holes in the field and let it sit' (lit. 'pierce the field and leave it so that it will sit')

Yal-29072010-JMT-igname_0014

In (56), the absolutive argument *toop* 'field' in the first clause is indexed pronominally by *-e* '3SG.ABS' in the second clause conjoined with *ka*.

The addressee of an imperative (§6.7.1) must be the subject (whether genitive A, nominative A, or nominative S) in Belep; absolutive verbs cannot be imperatives. This is common for subject-like arguments cross-linguistically (Keenan 1976: 321).

A wide variety of semantic roles, including Agent, are available to Belep nominative A and S and genitive A arguments; however, absolutive arguments cannot be Agents and are typically Experiencers. This is consistent with Keenan's (1976) contention that subjects "express the agent of the action, if there is one" (Keenan 1976: 321).

In this work, the term 'absolutive' is used for all P arguments and unmarked S arguments. The term 'subject' is used to refer to all A arguments (whether they are marked as nominative or genitive) and S arguments which are marked as nominative.

6.3.4.1 Other candidates for subjecthood

I have argued that Belep genitive A and nominative A and S arguments should be considered subjects. One additional subject-like property displayed by nominative A and S arguments which is not shared by genitive A arguments is that nominative A and S arguments can be indexed by an independent pronoun (§4.6.1) (Keenan 1976: 320), while absolutive S and P arguments, as well as genitive A arguments, cannot.

Though subjecthood in Belep is most clearly aligned with genitive A, nominative A, and nominative S arguments, there are also subject-like properties that absolutive arguments share with these arguments. All core arguments can be topicalized (§6.9.1); cross-linguistically, subjects are "normally the topic" of the clause (Keenan 1976: 318). Further, nominative, genitive, and absolutive arguments can control co-reference in some coordinate clauses.

Belep nominative and genitive A arguments control coreference in some coordinate clauses. The A argument of a transitive clause can be co-referential with the S argument of a *ka*-conjoined intransitive clause (regardless of the definiteness of the P), which is a common characteristic of subjects (Andrews 2007a). For instance, in (57), the A argument of the transitive clause (where the verb is *îna* 'to make') is indexed by the subject agreement proclitic *ja=* '1PL.INCL.SUBJ'; though the subject agreement proclitic is omitted in the conjoined transitive clause (where the verb is *cavac* 'to leave), the referent of the S argument is identical.

(57) **Te ô ki ja pan înae Paixa, ka âmu cavac.**
 te=   ô=xi   ja=   pana îna-e
 3SG.SUBJ= good=REL   1PL.INCL.SUBJ=   go.TV make-SPC

 Paixa   ka [0]   âmu= cavac
 Easter.LN LK   PRF= leave
 'We_i should celebrate Easter, and *then* [we_i] leave.'
                                              Yal-20092011-AW2_0075

Belep absolutive arguments also control coreference in some semantically dependent clauses. The P argument of a transitive clause can be co-referential with the S argument of a following pseudocoordinate clause (see §7.3). For example, in (58), linker *ka* acts as a pseudocoordinator (§7.3.1). The P argument of the transitive clause (where the verb is *îna* 'to make') is indexed by the absolutive 3SG pronominal suffix -*er*. Though the subject agreement proclitic is omitted in the linked pseudocoordinate clause (where the verb is *ô* 'to be good'), the referent of the S argument is identical.

(58) **Texa înaer ri Belep ka ô.**
 te=xa   îna-er=i   Belep   ka   ô
 3SG.SUBJ=ADD   make-3SG.ABS=GEN   Belep   LK   be.good
 'Belep healed him.' (lit. 'Belep made him_i that [he_i] was good.')
                                              Yal-20092011-AW6_0055

6.4 Case and grammatical relations

Noun phrases in Belep are marked to indicate their role in grammatical relations using a set of case-marking formatives which fall under the definition of *ditropic clitics* (see §3.2.2.6), terminology coined by Embick and Noyer (1999:291). Cysouw (2005), who discusses examples of ditropic clitics in a variety of languages, describes them thus: "Functionally, the clitic belongs together with Y [its attractor], yet it is attached morphologically to X [its host, which defies]...all attempts at any unitary structural characterization...The only possible way to describe the surface position of the clitic is by stating that it is attached to whatever element happens to come before its attractor" (Cysouw 2005:2,3-4). Ditropic clitics with noun phrase attractors are attested in Yagua and in some Wakashan languages (Cysouw 2005); in particular, ditropic clitics are used for case marking in Kwakwala (Anderson 1984). In Belep, the formative which marks the grammatical role of a noun phrase is realized as an enclitic (§3.2.2.6) on whatever element immediately precedes that noun phrase.

The Belep case-marking ditropic clitics are shown in Table 2. Absolutive arguments are unmarked for case. Nominative, genitive, dative, and locative case markers vary phonologically depending on whether they are preceded by a vowel or consonant. The instrumental case marker varies based on whether its noun phrase attractor is specific or generic (§5.2.4).

Tab. 2: Ditropic clitic case markers

Clitic	Case
=(l)a	nominative
=(l)i	genitive
=(l)e	dative
=(l)a	locative
=va(-e)	instrumental

These case markers pose a bracketing paradox for Belep (cf. Sproat 1988). Morphologically, they belong with their host, the element that precedes them, while syntactically and semantically they belong with their attractor, a noun phrase whose case they mark. For example, in (59), the noun phrase attractor *teâmaa* 'chieftain' is the subject of the clause; this is indicated by the nominative ditropic enclitic =*a* which is attached to the host verb *kaac* 'to be bitter'.

(59)   *Ka kaac, kaac ya teâmaa.*
      ka   kaac   kay=a   teâmaa
      LK   be.bitter   be.bitter=NOM   high.chief
      'And [he was] angry, the chieftain was angry.'
                                                     Yal-20092011-AW1_0233

In this work, case markers are not considered to be part of the noun phrase constituent (§4.5) since they do not act as part of that unit. Case markers are used only when a noun phrase appears in situ as an argument of a clause; in all other noun phrases, such as topicalized noun phrases, answers to question-word questions, appositive noun phrases, etc., use of a case marker is ungrammatical. For example, in noun phrase topicalization (§6.9.1), the topicalized noun phrase is not marked for case (60).

(60)   *Naerama, la ci maac. Maac ya naerama,*
      [0]   nae-ra-ma   la=   ci   maac   may=a
          child-3GNR.POSS-AC   3PL.SUBJ=   sit   die   die=NOM

      nae-ra-ma
      child-3GNR.POSS-AC
      'The children, they died nonetheless. The children died,'
                                               Yal-20092011-AW2_0041-0042

Example (60) shows a clause with the topicalized noun phrase *naerama* 'the children', which is used without a case marker (indicated here with [0]). This contrasts with the subsequent clause, where *naerama* acts as the subject and is marked with the nominative case marker =*a*. Also, in noun phrase responses to question-word questions (§6.6.2), use of case-markers is ungrammatical (61).

(61a) *Âyuamw mwi ti ?*
âyua-mw=i=ri
desire-2SG.POSS=GEN=who
'Who do you love?' (lit. 'Who is your desire?')

(61b) *Âyuang ngi Kacaca.*
âyua-ng=i   Kacaca
desire-1SG.POSS=GEN   Kacaca
'I love Kacaca.' (lit. 'Kacaca is my desire.')

(61c) *Kacaca.*
Kacaca
Kacaca
'Kacaca.'

(61d) **Li Kacaca.*
=li   Kacaca
=GEN   Kacaca
*'Of Kacaca.'

Yal-05102010-PT1.wav – Yal-05102010-PT3.wav

The answer to the questioned genitive argument in (61a) can be either a full clause as in (61b) or an unmarked noun phrase as in (61c), but it cannot be a noun phrase marked for case as in (61d). In addition, appositive noun phrases, set apart by intonation breaks, are not marked for case (62).

(62) *Ta la Nic, Nic, yami na âri li, yaxe.*
ta=la   Nic   Nic   ya-mi
go.UH=LOC   Nic   Nic   DEM.LOC-DET.A.DST

na=   âri=li   ya-xe
1SG.SUBJ=   say=LOC.A.DST   DEM.LOC-DET.D.DST
'[They] went up to Nic, Nic, that place I mentioned, over there.'

Yal-20092011-AW1_0193

In (62), only the first mention of *Nic*, a toponym, is marked for case with the locative case marker =*la*. The appositive noun phrases that follow it—a repetition of the toponym *Nic*, the relative pronoun-headed (§7.4.3) relative clause *yami na âri li* 'the place I mentioned', and the demonstrative pronoun *yaxe* (§4.6.2)—are not marked for case.

Furthermore, in my corpus, pauses, word-searches, and intonation breaks do not occur in discourse before a case marker (that is, between a ditropic clitic and its host); however, they frequently occur between a case marker and its noun phrase attractor, as shown in (63).[8]

(63) **Texa tame la, texa pame la, buny,**
te=xa   ta-me=la:::   te=xa
3SG.SUBJ=ADD   go.UH=CTP=NOM   3SG.SUBJ=ADD

pa-me=la:::   buny
go.TV=CTP=NOM   great.crested.tern
'Came the=, ...(.9) came the=, ...(.8) tern,'
                                         Yal-01082010-MFD_0015

In (63), pauses and repairs occur after the nominative case marker =*la* but before the noun it modifies (*buny* 'great crested tern'). This example provides evidence that case markers do not pattern with their noun phrase attractor, and should best be considered part of the syntax of Belep rather than part of the noun phrase constituent.

6.4.1 Absolutive case

Noun phrases in the absolutive case—all P arguments of a transitive clause, and some S arguments of an intransitive clause (see §6.3.3, §5.2.2)—are unmarked in Belep. For example, in (64), the absolutive noun phrases *uvi* 'yam', *bolao* 'banana tree', and *ûjep* 'sugar cane', which are all P arguments of the transitive (§5.2.3.2) verb *tee* 'to plant', are unmarked.

(64) **Le te uvi, te bolao, ka te ûjep,**
le=   te   {uvi}   te   {bolao}   ka
3DU.SUBJ=   plant   yam   plant   banana.tree   LK

---

8 Note that I use here the discourse transcription conventions recommended by Du Bois et al. (1993), where [:::] indicates a lengthened vowel. The duration of the pauses is indicated in parentheses in the free translation.

        te   {ûjep}
        plant sugar.cane
        'They planted yams, planted bananas, and planted sugar cane,'
                                            Yal-28072010-BGMCG-tayamu_0015-0018

In (65), the unmarked absolutive noun phrase is *waga ulayixedu digi* 'that old man's boat, a canoe'. It serves as the P argument of the transitive (§5.2.3.1) verb *pa* 'to take'.

(65)   ***Avexa pae waga ulayixedu digi,***
           ave=xa   pa-e   {waga   ulayi-xedu   digi}
           1DU.EXCL.SUBJ=ADD   take-SPC boat   old.man-DET.DH canoe
           'And we took that old man's boat, a canoe,'
                                             Yal-28072010-BGMCG-tahitian_0013

In (66), the absolutive S argument *âju* 'person' of the negative existential verb (§5.2.2, §6.3.3) *âria* is unmarked for case.

(66)   *Ô âria âju.*
           ô   âria   {âju}
           REAL   NEG.EX   person
           'There were no people.'
                                                 Yal-20092011-AW5_0070

In (67), the noun phrase *mwadeng* 'my nose' is not modified by a case marker; it acts as the S argument of the negative locative verb *cia*.

(67)   « *Cia mwadeng.* »
           cia   {mwade-ng}
           NEG.LOC nose-1SG.POSS
           '"I don't have a nose."' (in context 'without a nose')
                                                 Yal-20092011-AW5_0107

An absolutive suffix (§5.7) may substitute for an unmarked absolutive argument, as in (68) where the first singular absolutive suffix *-nao* anaphorically indexes an absolutive argument.

(68)   « *Ka nawe<u>nao</u> la bwe daan* ».
           ka   nawe-<u>nao</u>=la   bwe   daan
           LK   deposit-1SG.OBJ=LOC top   path
           'And leave me on the path.'
                                                 Yal-20092011-AW1_0097

6.4.2 Nominative case

Noun phrases in the nominative case—that is, most S arguments of an intransitive clause (§6.3.1) and some A arguments of a transitive clause (§6.3.2)—are case-marked with the ditropic enclitic =la or =a 'NOM' on the preceding element. The =la form occurs when its host ends in a vowel (69); the =a form occurs when its host ends in a consonant (70).

(69) **Laxaô kejadu la naerama,**
    la=xa=ô   keja=du=<u>la</u>   {nae-ra-ma}
    3PL.SUBJ=ADD=REAL   run=DIR.DH=NOM child-3GNR.POSS-AC
    'And the children ran down,'
                                                    Yal-17072009-TB-weekend_0024

(70) **Te nam ma denaar.**
    te=   nam=<u>a</u>   {denaar}
    3SG.SUBJ= disappear=NOM sun
    'The sun was setting.'
                                                    Yal-17072009-TB-weekend_0005

In (69) and (70), the S argument of an intransitive clause—indicated with {}—is marked as in the nominative case. The nominative ditropic clitic case marker is also used to mark the A argument of a transitive clause when the P argument is indefinite, as in (71) and (72).

(71) **Texa pae wîmi la ulayili Cebaba,**
    te=xa   pa-e   wî-mi=<u>la</u>
    3SG.SUBJ=ADD take-SPC DEM.INAN-DET.A.DST=NOM

    {ulayi-li   Cebaba}
    old.man-DET.A.PRX Cebaba
    'And that old man Cebaba took that thing,'
                                                   Yal-20092011-AW1_0265

In (71), nominative-marked *ulayili Cebaba* 'that old man Cebaba' is the A argument of a transitive clause. In (72), the A argument *teâmaa* 'chieftain' of a transitive clause is marked as nominative.

(72) **ma teme, me âri oyeen na teâmaa.**
    ma=re=me   me   âri   oye-n=<u>a</u>   {teâmaa}
    LK4=3SG.SUBJ=IRR IRR say.TR curse-   high.chief
                                               3SG.POSS=NOM
    'so that the chieftain would, would speak his curse.'
                                                   Yal-20092011-AW6_0038

Note that the variation in the phonological form of the nominative marker in (71) and (72) is triggered by the final phoneme of its host.

A pronoun may substitute for a nominative-marked noun phrase, as in (73) where the independent pronoun *le* (§4.6.1) is marked as nominative, or in (74) where the demonstrative pronoun *leli* (§4.6.2) is marked as nominative. Such a substitution is pragmatically marked.

(73) **Ka ô tuic ya le,**
ka   ô   tu=iy=a   {le}
LK   REAL   go.DH=CTF=NOM   3DU.INDEP
'And went down they did,'
                            Yal-28072010-BGMCG-tayamu_0164

(74) **Mo la leli,**
mo=la   {le-li}
live=NOM   DEM.DU-DET.A.PRX
'Lived those two did,'
                            Yal-20092011-AW1_0247

6.4.3 Genitive case

Noun phrases in the genitive case—that is, some A arguments of a transitive clause (§6.3.2), all independent possessors (§4.2.2.4), some obliques, and various other arguments—are case-marked with the ditropic enclitic =*li* or =*i* 'GEN' on the preceding element. The form =*li* occurs if the host ends in a vowel (75), while the form =*i* occurs if the host ends in a consonant (76).

(75) **« La ginao li Âôvaayama. »**
la=   gi-nao=li   {Âôvaya-ma}
3PL.SUBJ=   attack-1SG.ABS=GEN   Âôvaac-AC
'"The Âôvaac people are attacking me."'
                            Yal-20092011-AW3_0029

In (75), the genitive case-marking ditropic clitic =*li* marks the A argument of a transitive clause, *Âôvaayama* 'the Âôvaac people'. In (76), the form =*i* marks the A argument *Anthony* of a transitive clause.

(76) **To jier ri Anthony.**
to   ji-er=i   {[ãtoni]}
call   give-3SG.ABS=GEN   Anthony.LN
'Anthony called him.'
                            Yal-05092011-AP1_0040

In both (75) and (76), the A argument of a transitive clause is marked as genitive because the P argument is definite (§6.3.2).

The term 'genitive' is used for the case marker =*li*, =*i* because its prototypical use is to mark the possessor noun phrase in the independent possessive construction (§4.2.2.4). For example, in (77), the genitive ditropic clitic marks *teâmaa* 'chieftain' as the possessor of *âju* 'person', and in (78) it marks *Awucili*, a clan name, as the possessor of *âma naen* 'clan, family'. The phonological variation is due to the final phoneme of its host.

(77)   *âju li teâmaa,*
        âju=li   **{teâmaa}**
        person=GEN   high.chief
        'the chieftain's vassal' (lit. 'the chieftain's person')
                                                                             Yal-20092011-AW5_0076

(78)   *Pwai âma naen ni Awucili,*
        pwai   **âma=**   **nae-n=i**   **{Awucili}**
        only   DYAD=   child-3SG.POSS=GEN   Awucili
        'Only the clan of Awucili,'
                                                                             Yal-20092011-AW6_0134

Another use of the genitive case marker is as a marker for oblique arguments. In (79) and (80), genitive =*li*, =*i* is used to mark the semantic theme.

(79)   *Te tao toli tayamook xi nyan.*
        te=   **tao=**   **to-li**   **tayamoo-x=i**
        3SG.SUBJ=   HAB=   call-TR   old.woman-DET.D.PRX=GEN

        {nya-n}
        mother-
        3SG.POSS
        'He always called this old woman his mother.'
                                                    Yal-28072010-BGMCG-tahitian_0318

In (79), genitive =*i* marks the oblique noun phrase *nyan* 'his mother' as the theme. In (80), the noun phrase *pê koba gawaar* 'daily bread' is marked as genitive with =*li*.

(80)   *Yo taxeva li pê kôba gawaar.*
        yo=   **taxe-va=li**
        2SG.SUBJ=   distribute-2PL.EXCL.ABS=GEN

{pê   kôba   gawaar}
bread.LN   entirety   day
'You give us our daily bread.'

Yal-25072010-PT-homily_0028

Present/future temporal deixis is also accomplished with the genitive marker (this contrasts with past temporal deixis, for which the adverbial linker *to* 'when' is used; see §7.3.3.2). For example, in (81) the noun phrase *bwe cexeeniik* 'this Sunday' is marked as genitive with =*li*.

(81)   *yena li bwe cexeeniik,*
       yena=li   {bwe   cexenii-k}
       now=GEN   moment   sacred-DET.D.PRX
       'today this Sunday,'

Yal-25072010-PT-homily_0054

In (82), the noun phrase *bwaêdan* 'morning' is marked as genitive with =*i*.

(82)   *noor iyam mi bwaêdan,*
       no-ra   **iyam=i**   {bwaêdan}
       awake-NDR   tomorrow=GEN   morning
       '[he] woke up the next morning,'

Yal-05092011-AP1_0024

Both genitive-marked noun phrases in (81) and (82) refer to present or future temporal locations.

The S argument of an equative construction (§6.5.1) is also typically marked as in the genitive case, as in (83) and (84). In (83), genitive =*li* marks the noun phrase *âjuma lali* 'those people' as the S argument of a predicate nominal (see §6.6.2).

(83)   « *Ti li âjuma lali ?* »
       ti=li   {âju-ma   la-li}
       who=GEN   person-AC   DEM.PL-DET.A.PRX
       '"Who are those people?"' (lit. '"Those people are who?"')[9]

Yal-20092011-AW6_0079

In (84), genitive =*i* marks the proper noun *Tayema* as the S argument of a predicate nominal.

---

9 To translate *Ces gens sont qui ?* 'Those people are who?', Belep speakers use a topicalization construction (§6.9.1) such as *âjuma lali, (mo) ti lila ?* 'those people, (well) who are they?'.

(84) *Naran ni Tayema, tahitien.*
nara-n=i {Tayema} [taisjẽ]
name-3SG.POSS=GEN Tayema Tahitian.LN
'Tayema was his name, a Tahitian.'
Yal-28072010-BGMCG-tahitian_0003

Genitive-marked noun phrases can be replaced by an absolutive suffix (§5.7) while the genitive marker remains. An example is shown in (85) where the third plural absolutive suffix *-la*, marked with the genitive marker =*li*, anaphorically indexes a noun phrase.

(85) *Toma bu lila yeek,*
toma bu=li{-la} yeek
but fishhook=GEN-3PL.ABS wood
'While their wooden hooks,'
Yal-28072010-BGMCG-hamecon_0034

In (86), the third paucal absolutive suffix *-len* substitutes for a genitive-marked noun phrase.

(86) *Pwajen nilen.*
pwajen=i{-len}
three=GEN-3PA.ABS
'There were three of them.'
Yal-20092011-AW6_0156-0157

The Belep genitive marker may be etymologically related to the Nêlêmwa relator *i*, which is used for human obliques. Bril (2002:146) remarks that this relator is most likely the reflex of Proto-Oceanic preposition *i/*aki(ni), which "introduc[es] oblique case nominals" (Pawley & Reid 1976:59).

6.4.4 Dative case

Noun phrases in the dative case—that is, primarily semantic recipients—are case-marked with the ditropic clitic =*le* or =*e* 'DAT' on the preceding element. The form =*le* occurs if the host ends with a vowel (87), while the form =*e* occurs if the host ends in a consonant (88).

(87) *Ka cavac ya Ciaup, ka pan mo le âju liema,*
ka cavay=a Ciaup ka pana
LK leave=NOM Ciaup LK go.TV

        mo=le   {âju=li-e-ma}
        live=DAT person=GEN-3SG.ABS-AC
        'And Ciaup left, and went to be with his people,'
                                                      Yal-20092011-AW1_0222-0223

In (87), the dative marker =*le* marks the noun phrase *âju liema* 'his people' as a semantic recipient. In (88), the dative-marked argument *teâmaa* 'chieftain' is indicated by the ditropic clitic =*e*.

(88)   « *Jame pan ne teâmaa.* »
        ja=me   **pan=e**   {teâmaa}
        1PL.INCL.SUBJ=IRR go.TV=DAT high.chief
        '"We will go to the chieftain."'
                                                      Yal-20092011-AW5_0037

The dative case marker occurs most commonly following the class 1 nouns *na-* 'interior' and *u-* 'toward'[10]. A dative-marked noun phrase following *na-* 'interior' typically indexes the experiencer of a predicated emotional affect, such as difficulty (89), pain, preference, etc. In (89), the noun phrase *naerama lami* 'those children' is marked as the experiencer using the dative case marker =*le*.

(89)   *Me cao pwalu na le naerama lami,*
        me   cao   pwalu   **na=le**
        IRR   work   heavy   interior=DAT

        {nae-ra-ma}   la-mi}
        child-3GNR.POSS-AC DEM.PL-DET.A.DST
        'It is difficult for those children,'
                                                    Yal-25072010-PT-homily_0089

A dative-marked noun phrase following *u-* 'toward' indexes the recipient of the action of the predicate. For example, in (90), the dative-marked noun phrase *âju lieramale* 'his two courtiers' is the recipient of the action of the transitive verb *ârie* 'to say'.

(90)   *Te âri u le âju lieramale,*
        te=   âri   **u=le**   {âju=li-era-male}
        3SG.SUBJ= say   toward=DAT person=GEN-3SG.ABS-ADU
        'He said to his two courtiers,'
                                                    Yal-20092011-AW6_0111

---

10 The morpheme *u-* 'toward' is not attested in my corpus in any position except followed by the dative case marker; I have classed it as a noun due to its parallelism with *na-* 'interior', which displays a number of nounlike characteristics.

In (91), the noun phrase *buny* 'tern' is marked as the recipient of the action of the intransitive verb *kaac* 'to be bitter, angry' using the dative marker =*le*.

(91)   ***Te kaac u le buny,***
        te=   kaya   u=<u>le</u>   {buny}
        3SG.SUBJ= be.bitter toward=DAT great.crested.tern
        'He was angry at the tern,'
                                                            Yal-01082010-MFD_0004

A possessive suffix (§4.2.2.2) may substitute for a dative-marked noun phrase. The dative case marker—unlike the other case markers—undergoes vowel gemination if a singular possessive suffix follows it (see §4.2.2.3). For example, in (92), the plural possessive suffix -*ac*, marked with the genitive case marker =*le*, indexes a noun phrase.

(92)   ***Ma yena to name tiu u leac,***
        ma   yena=ro   na=me   ti-u
        LK4   now=when   1SG.SUBJ=IRR prick-DETR

        u=<u>le</u>{-ac}
        toward=DAT-2PL.POSS
        'But now, as I am writing to you,'
                                                       Yal-14092011-PT2-avenir_0016

In (93), the third singular possessive suffix -*n* anaphorically indexes a noun phrase; since it is singular, the dative case marker that precedes it contains a like-vowel hiatus.

(93)   ***Avexa boyu leen.***
        ave=xa   boyu=<u>lee</u>{-n}
        1DU.EXCL.SUBJ=ADD   greet=DAT-3SG.POSS
        'We greeted him.'
                                              Yal-28072010-BGMCG-tahitian_0236

Examples (94) and (95) also show instances of vowel gemination in the dative case marker when the noun phrase indexed by its pronominal suffix is singular. In (94), the case marker follows the noun *na*- 'interior', indexing the experiencer of an emotion or affect.

(94)   ***« Te mwany na leeng, »***
        te=   mwany   na=<u>lee</u>{-ng}
        3SG.SUBJ= bad   interior=DAT-1SG.POSS
        '"I'm sick,"'
                                                  Yal-20092011-AW6_0050

In (95), the dative case marker marks the noun phrase it modifies as the recipient of the action of the intransitive verb *cuur* 'to stand'.

(95) ***Te kuarive ki ave cuur reen.***
    te=   **kuar-i-ve**   **ki**
    3SG.SUBJ=   refuse-TR-1DU.EXCL.ABS   REL

    ave=   **cur=ee{-n}**
    1DU.EXCL.SUBJ=   stand=DAT-3SG.POSS
    'He didn't want us to stand before him.'
                                                    Yal-28072010-BGMCG-tahitian_0271

6.4.5 Locative case

Noun phrases in the locative case—that is, which index a semantic location, source, or goal—are case-marked with the ditropic clitic *=la* or *=a* 'LOC' on the preceding element.[11] The form *=la* occurs if the host ends in a vowel (96), while the form *=a* is used if the host ends in a consonant (97). In (96), the semantic goal noun phrases *Cager* and *Âmwany*, both toponyms, are marked with the case-marker *=la*.

(96) ***uya la Cager ka uya la Âmwany.***
    uya=la   **{Cager}**   **ka**   **uya=la**   **{Âmwany}**
    arrive=LOC   Cager   LK   arrive=LOC   Âmwany
    '[we] arrived at Cager and arrived at Âmwany.'
                                        Yal-28072010-BGMCG-tahitian_0028-0030

In (97), the toponym *Poc*, a semantic goal, is marked with the case-marker *=a*.

(97) ***Avena pan na Poc.***
    avena=   **pan=a**   **{Poc}**
    1TR.EXCL.SUBJ=   go.TV=LOC   Poc
    'We would go to Poc.'
                                              Yal-28072010-BGMCG-tahitian_0012

Example (98) shows the ditropic clitic *=la* being used to mark a semantic source noun phrase, the toponym *Ono*.

---

[11] The locative case marker is homophonous with the nominative case marker (§6.4.2); however, in practice, this homophony does not pose any problems for comprehension—very few semantic locations could serve as the subject of a clause. These should be considered separate case markers because nominative case-marked arguments require a subject clitic (§5.8) that agrees with them in person and number, while locative case-marked arguments do not.

(98) *Te cavac ci la Ono.*
 te=   cavaya   ci=<u>la</u>   {Ono}
 3SG.SUBJ=   leave   sit=LOC   Ono
 'He came from Ono.'
 Yal-05092011-AP1_0006

The locative case marker can also indicate that the noun phrase it marks is the location of the action of the predicate, as in (99) and (100). In (99), the locative case-marked location is *pwemwa* 'home, village'.

(99) *Bwa tuu per ra pwemwa.*
 bwa=   tu   per=<u>a</u>   {pwemwa}
 CONT=   EX.SPC   party.LN=LOC   village
 'There was still a party in the village.'
 Yal-28072010-BGMCG-tahitian_0293

In (100), the attractor of locative case-marker =*la* is the demonstrative pronoun *yaxeda* (§4.6.2).

(100) *Te ci la yaxeda.*
 te=   ci=<u>la</u>   {ya-xeda}
 3SG.SUBJ=   sit=LOC   DEM.LOC-DET.UH
 'It sits up there.'
 Yal-20092011-AW3_0033

Demonstrative pronouns are the only pronouns in Belep which can substitute for a locative-marked noun phrase. The verb phrase locational enclitics (§5.12) can also be used to indicate the location of the action of a predicate.

The locative case marker is also used to mark possessive noun phrases which function as locative expressions (§4.2.5). For example, in (101), the locative ditropic clitic marks the noun phrase *na kiyooc* 'in the hut' (lit. 'the interior of the hut').

(101) *Le tu ka ta la na kiyooc,*
 le=   tu   ka   ta=<u>la</u>   {na   kiyooc}
 3DU.SUBJ=   go.DH   LK   go.UH=LOC   interior   hut
 'They went down and went into the hut,'
 Yal-20092011-AW1_0263

In (102), the locative case marker's attractor is the noun phrase *bwe janen* 'on his ear' (lit. 'the top of his ear').

(102)   **Ka ce la bwe janen.**
      ka   ce=la   {bwe   jane-n}
      LK   settle=LOC top   ear-3SG.POSS
      'And landed on his ear.'
                                                                Yal-05092011-AP1_0083

For possessive locatives of this type, a possessive suffix (§4.2.2.2) may be used on the possessed noun to anaphorically index the frame of reference for the location (103).

(103)   **La ta la bween.**
      la=   ta=la   {bwee-n}
      3PL.SUBJ= go.UH=LOC top-3SG.POSS
      'They went onto it [a reef].'
                                                         Yal-20092011-AW2_0037

6.4.6 Instrumental case

Noun phrases in the instrumental case—those which index a semantic instrument—are case-marked with the ditropic clitic =*va* 'INSTR.GNR' or =*va-e* 'INSTR.SPC' on the preceding element. The generic and specific forms of the instrumental case marker contrast based on the specificity of the case-marked noun phrase (§5.2.4). For example, in (104), the instrumental noun phrase *oreâva* 'our breath' is marked as generic with the case-marker =*va*.

(104)   **Ka ci va oreâva,**
      ka   ci=va   {oreâ-va}
      LK   sit=INSTR.GNR breath-1PL.EXCL.POSS
      'and [we] rested,' (lit. 'and [we] sat with our breath')[12]
                                            Yal-17072009-TB-weekend_0017-0020

In (105), the noun phrase *yadan* 'his belongings' is marked as generic with the instrumental case-marker =*va*.

(105)   **yaûda va yadan,**
      yaûda=va   {yada-n}
      climb=INSTR.GNR belongings-3SG.POSS
      'climbed with his belongings,'
                                            Yal-28072010-BGMCG-tahitian_0158

---

12 'To sit with one's breath' is an idiomatic expression meaning 'to rest'.

Example (106) shows the instrumental noun phrase *digi* 'canoe' marked as specific with =*vae*.

(106)   ***Ka teô tame la Maxeek vae digi.***
        ka=re=ô   ta=me=la   Maxexa=<u>va</u>-e   {digi}
        LK=3SG.SUBJ=REAL   go.UH=CTP=NOM   Maxeek=INSTR-SPC canoe
        'And Maxeek came with the canoe.'
                                                                 Yal-28072010-BGMCG-tahitian_0105

In example (107), the specific instrumental case-marker is used to mark the noun phrase *karavaali* 'that pirogue'.

(107)   ***Pan na teâmaa vae karavaali,***
        pan=a   teâma=<u>va</u>-e   {karava-li}
        go.TV=NOM   high.chief=INSTR-SPC pirogue-DET.A.PRX
        'The chieftain went with that pirogue,'
                                                                 Yal-20092011-AW5_0042

An absolutive suffix (§5.7) may substitute for an instrumental-marked noun phrase, as in (108), where the absolutive suffix *-er* is case-marked with instrumental =*va*.

(108)   ***Laô wânem vaer ri janu,***
        la=ô   wâne=<u>va</u>{-er}=i   janu
        3PL.SUBJ=REAL   walk=INSTR-3SG.ABS=GEN spirit
        'The spirits were walking with him,'
                                                      Yal-28072010-BGMCG-tahitian_0299-0300

The instrumental case-marker is a grammaticalized form of the transitive (§5.2.3.1) verb *pa* 'to take', whose specific form is *pa-e*.

6.5 Non-prototypical clause types

Cross-linguistically, clauses which express equation, location, attribution, existence, and possession tend to "lack a semantically rich lexical verb" (Payne 1997: 112) and to share other morphosyntactic characteristics (Lyons 1967, Clark 1978). In Belep, these functions are divided into roughly three types of clauses: predicate nominals (§6.5.1); clauses typified by existentials (§6.5.2); and attributive clauses (§6.5.3). Only predicate nominals and some predicate possessives lack a verb altogether; in these clauses, the predicate is a demonstrative pronoun (§4.6.2), locative pronoun, or a noun phrase (§4.5) which may be marked to indicate aspect (§5.5), mood (§5.6), or negation (§6.8). Belep predicates existence, location, and sometimes possession using non-prototypical absolutive verbs (§5.2.2). Property concepts are either expressed as prototypical nominative verbs (§5.2.1), or they fall into one of the other categories. There is no copula in Belep.

6.5.1 Predicate nominals and the equative construction

Belep predicate nominals are nouns (see §3.5.1) or nominal elements which serve as the predicate of a clause. As predicates, predicate nominals appear clause-initially (§6.1) and can be marked to indicate aspect (§5.5), mood (§5.6), or negation (§6.8).

Predicate nominals often occur without a nominal argument. Temporal nouns (§6.11) are one class of such predicate nominals; they are typically used to predicate the time of day, as in (109).

(109)   *ka mon, ô bwaêdan,*
                      PRED
       ka mon   [ô   bwaêdan]
       LK side.DH REAL morning
       'and then, it was morning,'

Yal-01082010-MFD_0005

Another class of predicate nominals which are used without a nominal argument is the set of pronouns which are used to predicate location (Table 3).

Tab. 3: Pronominal predicate locatives

	Singular	Dual	Trial	Plural
1 exclusive	nao	ave	aven	ava
inclusive		ji	jen	ja
2	yo	or	ôn	ac
3	yer, era	le	len	la

The only difference between these pronouns and the independent pronouns (§4.6.1) is that *era* '3SG.PRED' is present in this set. The difference between *yer* '3SG.PRED' and *era* '3SG.PRED' has not yet been determined. Examples of the use of predicate locative pronouns are shown in (110) and (111). In these examples, deictic verb phrase enclitics (§5.12) index the locative S argument.

(110) *Ô era lexeng*
  PRED
  [ô=   era=lexeng]
  REAL= 3SG.PRED=LOC.DC
  'S/he was here.'

  Yal-22092011-TB.wav

(111) *Bwa la lexeng.*
  PRED
  [bwa=   la=lexeng]
  CONT= 3PL.PRED=LOC.DC
  'They're still here.'

  Yal-28072010-BGMCG-sousmarin_0121

These predicate locative pronouns can also occur with a nominal argument, which is marked as in the locative case (§6.4.5). In (112), the predicate locative pronoun *era* '3SG.PRED' is used with the locative-marked argument *Poc* '[the islet of] Poc'.

(112) *Toma olan, ka era- bwa era la Poc.*
                             PRED
  toma ola-n   ka era   [bwa= era]=la   Poc
  but piece-3SG.POSS LK 3SG.PRED CONT= 3SG.PRED=LOC Poc
  'But his portion, it's- it's still at Poc.'

  Yal-20092011-AW5_0026

The predication of locative noun phrases is discussed below in §6.5.2.

Predicate nominals can also act as the first clause in a complex construction whereby the semantically dependent clause is marked by genitive =*li* or =*i* (§7.3.7), as in (113) and (114).

(113) « *âyua teâma li teme paeo ma yawan.* »
  PRED
  [âyua teâma]=li   te=me   pa-e-o
  desire high.chief=GEN 3SG.SUBJ=IRR take-SPC-2SG.ABS

  ma   yawa-n
  LK4   wife-3SG.POSS
  '"The chieftain wants to take you as his wife."' (lit. '"The chieftain's desire is that he takes you as his wife."')

  Yal-20092011-AW1_0178

(114)   *ka jagar ri te jie ma ja nginie.*
        PRED
        ka   [jaga-r]=i   te=   ji-e
        LK   capacity-3GNR.POSS=GEN   3SG.SUBJ= give-3SG.ABS

        ma   **ja=**   **ngini-e**
        LK4   1PL.INCL.SUBJ= miss-3SG.ABS
        'He could make himself invisible.' (lit. 'It was possible that he would make himself such that we did not see him.')
                                                                           Yal-20092011-AW6_0091

Most commonly, predicate nominals occur in an equative construction, where they are used to predicate either the equation[13] of two noun phrases or, in some cases, the possession of an inherently possessed noun phrase. In typical intransitive clauses, the S argument is marked either as nominative (§6.4.2, §5.2.1) or as absolutive (§6.4.1, §5.2.2). However, in the predicate nominal construction, the S argument is marked as genitive with =*i* or =*li* 'GEN' (§6.4.3). Pronominal S arguments in an equative construction are indexed by the absolutive pronominal suffixes (§5.7).

The primary use of the equative construction is to predicate the equation of two nominals. Examples (115) - (117) show this function of the predicate nominal construction. In (115), the predicate nominal is *talang* 'my bed' and the intransitive argument is *ala janengexedu* 'my lower earlobe', which is marked as genitive with =*i*.

(115)   *Talang ngi ala janengexedu,*
        PRED   **S**
        [tala-ng]=i   [ala jane-ng-exedu]
        bed-1SG.POSS=GEN   husk ear-1SG.POSS-DET.DH
        '"My lower earlobe is my bed,"'[14]
                                                                            Yal-05092011-AP1_0077

In (116), the predicate nominal is *naran* 'his name' and the intransitive argument is *Teâ*, a personal name which also means 'chief', which is marked as genitive with =*i*.

---

[13] In discourse, a Topic-Comment structure using the linker *ka* (§7.2.2.3) is also used frequently to indicate equation. In some speech situations this usage is not easily distinguishable from a copular usage.
[14] This utterance is drawn from a narrative about the Dubageni, a demon who has very large ears. It is uttered in response to the question 'What is your bed?'.

(116)   **ka naran ni Teâ.**
       PRED   S
       ka [nara-n]=i   **[Teâ]**
       LK name-3SG.POSS=GEN Teâ
       'and Teâ is his name.'
                                                                      Yal-20092011-AW1_0015

In (117), the predicate nominal is the interrogative pronoun *ti* 'who?' (§4.6.3) and the S argument is indexed by the absolutive pronominal suffix *-o* '2SG.ABS' (§5.7) marked as genitive with *=li*.

(117)   **« Ti lio ? »**
       PRED
       [ti]=li-o
       who?=GEN-2SG.ABS
       '"Who are you?"' (lit. 'You are who?')
                                                                    Yal-20092011-AW1_0299

In (118) - (120), the S argument is also indexed by an absolutive pronominal suffix. In (118), the predicate nominal is *koxo* 'a lot'. In (119) the predicate nominal is *mwauju* 'no idea'. Example (120) shows the use of a numeral (§4.7) as a predicate nominal.

(118)   **Jua koxo lila.**
       jua koxo=li-la
       very a.lot=GEN-3PL.ABS
       'There were a lot of them.' (lit. 'They were many.')
                                                                 Yal-20092011-AW2_0042

(119)   **Mwauju lile,**
       mwauju=li-le
       no.idea=GEN-3DU.ABS
       'They had no idea.'
                                             Yal-28072010-BGMCG-tayamu_0250

(120)   **Pwajen nilen.**
       pwajen=i-len
       three=GEN-3TR.ABS
       'There were three of them.' (lit. 'They were three.')
                                                      Yal-20092011-AW6_0156

In (121), the predicate nominal is the independent pronoun *yo* '2SG.INDEP' (§4.6.1), and the S argument is the genitive-marked relative clause (§7.4.3) *âmi ca bae du liva* 'the one who always eats our bones'.

(121) « Âri yo li âmi ca bae du liva ? »
      PRED   S
      [âri=   yo]=li   [â-mi
      NEG=   2SG.INDEP=GEN   DEM.NEW-DET.A.DST

      ca=   bae   du=li-va]
      ITER=   bite   bones=GEN-1PL.EXCL.ABS
      '"Aren't you the one who always eats our bones?"'
                                                                 Yal-01082010-MFD_0034-0035

The equative construction is also used to predicate the possession of a Given element, which is typically dependently possessed (§4.2.2.1). In this usage, the predicate nominal is normally *îna-* 'possession'. Examples (122) - (125) show instances of this usage.

(122) **înaang ngi tolamiik**
      îna-ng=i   **tolamii-k**
      possession-1SG.POSS=GEN   basket-DET.D.PRX
      'This basket is mine [I made it].'
                                       Yal-07112011-TB1.wav – Yal07112011-TB3.wav

(123) *âri înaang ngi tolamiik*
      âri=   îna-ng=i   **tolamii-k**
      NEG=   possession-1SG.POSS=GEN   basket-DET.D.PRX
      'This basket is not mine [I didn't make it].'
                                     Yal-07112011-TB1.wav – Yal07112011-TB3.wav

(124) *âri tolabang ngi âk*
      âri=   tolaba-ng=i   â-k
      NEG=   basket-1SG.POSS=GEN   DEM.NEW-DET.D.PRX
      'This thing is not my basket [it's something else].'
                                     Yal-07112011-TB1.wav – Yal07112011-TB3.wav

(125) *înaamw mwi jia ti ?*
      îna-mw=i   jia ti
      possession-2SG.POSS=GEN gift who?
      'Who gave you that?' (lit. 'Your possession is a gift from whom?')
                                                                       overheard

Under some conditions, S arguments in a predicate nominal equative construction may be marked as nominative (§6.4.2) with =*la* or =*a* 'NOM'; however, the conditions under which this may occur are unclear. For instance, compare the usual genitive-marked S argument in (126) with the nominative-marked S argument in (127).

(126) *Nyang ngi tamwa la Poum ai tamwa la Koumac ?*
 nya-ng=i tamwa=la pûmw ai tamwa=la kumwaak
 mother-1SG.POSS=GEN woman=LOC Poum or woman=LOC Koumac
 'Is the woman from Poum or the woman from Koumac my mother?'
 Yal-07112011-TB1.wav – Yal07112011-TB3.wav

(127) *Nyang nga tamwa la Poum.*
 nya-ng=a tamwa=la pûmw
 mother-1SG.POSS=NOM woman=LOC Poum
 'My mother is from Poum.' (transl. by speaker)
 Yal-07112011-TB1.wav – Yal07112011-TB3.wav

Some nominative-marked S arguments also seem to occur when a numeral is used as a predicate nominal, as in (128).

(128) *Pwajen na âju.*
 pwajen=a âju
 three=NOM person
 'There were three people.' (lit. 'People were three.')
 Yal-20092011-AW6_0157

More research is needed to determine the discourse conditions under which this alternation occurs.

6.5.2 Existence and location

Existence in Belep is predicated using verbs which require an absolutive argument (§5.2.2). Location of a noun phrase and some forms of possession are also predicated using absolutive verbs. The relevant verbs are shown in Table 4.

Tab. 4: Predicate existential and locative verbs

	Affirmative	Negative
Existential	tu-, tuya	âria
Locative	era	cia, ciae

There are two predicate existential verbs in Belep. The verb *tuya* 'EX.GNR'—which inflects obligatorily for the specificity of its argument (§5.2.4)—is used to predicate the existence of an absolutive argument (that is, an unmarked one; see §6.4.1), while the verb *âria* 'NEG.EX'¹⁵ is used to predicate the non-existence of an absolutive-marked noun phrase. For example, in (129), the existence of the absolutive noun phrases *Or* 'Or phratry' and *Waap* 'Waap phratry' (see §1.3) is predicated using generic *tuya* 'EX.GNR'.

(129)   **Ka tuya Or, ka tuya Waap.**
        ka tuya   or ka tuya   waap
        LK EX.GNR spill LK EX.GNR topple
        'And there is Or [phratry], and there is Waap [phratry].'
        Yal-20092011-AW3_0012

In (130), the existence of the absolutive noun phrase *âju* 'people' is predicated by the bound specific form of the existential verb, *tu* 'EX.SPC'.

(130)   **La êna, la la Belep, ka tuu âju la bwe dau.**
        la=   êna   la=la   Belep ka tu
        3PL.SUBJ= know.GNR   3PL.INDEP=LOC Belep LK EX.SPC

        âju=la   bwe dau
        person=LOC   top islet
        'They knew, those on Belep, that there were people on the islet.'
        Yal-20092011-AW2_0056

To predicate the non-existence of a noun phrase, speakers use the negative existential verb *âria* 'NEG.EX'. For instance, in (131), *âria* predicates the non-existence of *mwa pwalaic* 'one house', followed by the non-existence of any *âju* 'people'.

(131)   **Âria mwa pwalaic ki la tue. Âria âju.**
        âria   mwa   pwalaiyi=xi la=   tu-e   âria   âju
        NEG.EX   house one=REL   3PL.SUBJ= find-3SG.ABS NEG.EX person
        'There was not a single house that they found. There were no people.'
        Yal-28072010-BGMCG-sousmarin_0117

In (132), the non-existence of *ûjela* 'their power' is predicated using *âria* 'NEG.EX'.

(132)   **Âria ûjela.**
        âria   ûje-la
        NEG.EX kidney-3PL.POSS
        'They had no power.' (lit. 'Their power did not exist.')
        Yal-20092011-AW5_0068

---

15 The negative existential verb *âria* is etymologically related to the proclitic used for sentential negation, *âri=* 'NEG' (§6.8).

In addition to predicating non-existence, the main discourse function of the negative existential verb *âria* is in the adjacency pair for expressing gratitude (133).

(133) P1: ***Olelio !***
 ole-li-o
 thank-TR-2SG.ABS
 'Thank you!'

 P2: ***(Bwa) Âria !***
 bwa=   âria
 CONT= NEG.EX
 'You're welcome!' (lit. 'It's nothing.')

Existential verbs *tuya* 'EX.GNR' and *âria* 'NEG.EX' do not occur with pronominal arguments.

There are two predicate locative verbs in Belep: locative *era* 'PRED.LOC' and negative locative *cia* 'NEG.LOC'. To predicate the location of a full noun phrase,[16] Belep speakers use the predicate locative verb *era* 'PRED.LOC'.[17] For example, in (134), the location of *cae pwalaic* 'a reef' is predicated using *era*. Note that the English translation does not capture the Belep distinction between existential and locative predication.

(134) ***Era cae, cae pwalaic, te ci liyeda.***
 PRED   S
 [era]   cae [cae pwalaic] te=   ci=liyeda
 PRED.LOC   reef reef   one 3SG.SUBJ=   sit=LOC.DST.UH
 'There's a reef, a reef, it sits up there.'
 Yal-20092011-AW2_0034

In (135), the noun phrase whose location is predicated with *era* 'PRED.LOC' is the participial (§7.3.9) *âju bwa tu covan* 'a person riding'.

---

16 The location of a pronominal referent is predicated using predicate nominals, discussed above (§6.5.1).
17 This verb was most likely formed as an etymological extension of the locative pronoun *era* '3SG.PRED' (discussed in §6.5.1 above). The related bound form *era-* 'DEM.PRES' is a presentative demonstrative pronoun (§4.3.2).

(135) **Te be duun, yami**
       te=   be   duu-n   ya-mi
       3SG.SUBJ= beat back-3SG.POSS DEM.LOC-DET.A.DST

       era âju bwa tu covan nexen.
       PRED   **S**
       [era]   [âju   bwa=   tu=   covan]=exen
       PRED.LOC   person   CONT=   VBLZ= horse.LN=LOC.A
       'He hit his back, the place where there was a person riding.'
                                                    Yal-28072010-BGMCG-tahitian_0262

To predicate the non-location of a full noun phrase or a pronominal referent, Belep speakers use the absolutive verb *cia* 'NEG.LOC', which may inflect to agree with the specificity of its absolutive argument (its specific form may be either *cia* or *ciae*; see §5.2.4). In example (136), the nonexistence of *Kawo*, a personal name, is predicated in a location understood from context.

(136) **Ô cia Kawo.**
       PRED   **S**
       [ô   cia]   [Kawo]
       REAL NEG.LOC Kawo
       'Kawo wasn't there.'
                                                                 Yal-20092011-AW1_0235

In (137), the non-existence of the absolutive argument *mwadeng* 'my nose' is predicated with *cia* 'NEG.LOC' in a location understood from context.

(137) **« Cia mwadeng. »**
       cia   mwade-ng
       NEG.LOC nose-1SG.POSS
       'I don't have a nose.' (lit. 'My nose isn't there.')
                                                                 Yal-20092011-AW5_0107

In (138) and (139), the referent whose non-location is predicated is represented by an anaphoric absolutive pronoun (§5.7). In (138) the pronominal verb suffix is *-e* '3SG.ABS'; in (139) the pronominal verb suffix is *-er* '3SG.ABS' (see §5.7.2 for a discussion of the difference between these two suffixes).

(138) **Te cuur rexeng, ka mon ciae.**
       te=   cur=exeng   ka   mona   cia-e
       3SG.SUBJ= stand=LOCDC LK side.DH NEG.LOC-3SG.ABS
       'He would be standing here, and then not be here.'
                                                                 Yal-20092011-AW6_0092

(139)   « *Ah, mo âria, mo ciaer,* » *wali la teâmaa, Teâ Pûnivaac.*
         mo âria   mo cia-er   wa-li=la
         LK3 NEG.EX   LK3 NEG.LOC-3SG.ABS   DEM.MAN-DET.A.PRX=NOM

         teâmaa   Teâ Pûnivaac
         high.chief   Teâ Pûnivaac
         '"Ah, well, there isn't any, it's not here," said the chieftain, Teâ Pûnivaac.'
                                                                Yal-20092011-AW5_0064

The existential and locative verbs discussed in this section may also be used to predicate some types of possession. For instance, some expressions which might use a predicate possessive in English, such as the one in (140), normally use a predicate existential or locative in Belep. The question in (140) is commonly used to make small talk with a newly introduced person.

(140)   *Tuu avamw ?*
         tu   ava-mw
         EX.SPC   sibling-2SG.POSS
         'Do you have any siblings?' (lit. 'Do your siblings exist?')

6.5.3 Attribution

There is no word class of adjectives in Belep (see §3.3). Most property concepts are expressed as intransitive verbs which take a nominative argument (§5.2.1); a few are expressed as nouns. Consequently, the predication of a property concept takes the form either of a regular intransitive clause or of a predicate nominal (§6.5.1).

The property concepts most commonly expressed cross-linguistically by adjectives—age, dimension, value, and color (Dixon 1977)—are all expressed by nominative verbs in Belep. For example, in (141), the nominative verb *ulac* 'to be old' expresses the predicated attribute. Its anaphoric S argument is indexed by the verbal proclitic *te=* '3SG.SUBJ'.

(141)   *Teô ulac. Te mwanaoli maac.*
                 PRED
         [te=ô   ulac] te=   mwanao-li   maac
         3SG.SUBJ=REAL   be.old 3SG.SUBJ=   approach-TR death
         'He was old. He was approaching death.'
                                                                Yal-20092011-AW1_0023

In (142), the predicated attribute is expressed by the verb *ulayar* 'to be big'. The S argument *uvi* 'yams' is marked by the nominative case marker *=a* (§6.4.2).

(142) *Ka ô ulayar ra uvi,*
            PRED   S
      ka [ô   ulayar]=a [uvi]
      LK REAL be.big=NOM yam
      'and the yams were big,'

                                        Yal-28072010-BGMCG-igname_0086

In (143), the verb *ô* 'to be (morally) good, to be (physically) well' expresses the predicated attributive. The S argument *âju* 'person' is marked by the nominative case marker =*la*.

(143) *Toma teô ô la âju.*
                 PRED   S
      toma [te=ô   ô]=la   [âju]
      but   3SG.SUBJ=REAL be.good=NOM person
      'But that person was healed.' (lit. 'But the person was good.')

                                        Yal-28072010-BGMCG-lune_0042

Example (144) shows a predicate attributive using the verb *yâno* 'to be blue'. The S argument is *dan* 'sky'.

(144) « *Eh, te jua yâno la dan !* »
              PRED   S
      [te=   jua yâno]=la [dan]
      3SG.SUBJ= very be.blue=NOM sky
      '"Hey, the sky is really blue!"'

                                                Yal-19092011-PA_0059

Only a few property concepts are expressed as nouns in Belep. One example is the class 1 noun *ga-* 'sympathy, poverty' (§4.2.1). This attributive is predicated as a predicate nominal (§6.5.1), as in example (145), which shows a common expression of sympathy in discourse.

(145) *Gaan !*
      gaa-n
      poverty-3SG.POSS
      'Poor him/her!' or 'S/he is poor.'

6.6 Question formation

Belep uses a wide variety of question-formation strategies. There are interrogative pronouns (§4.6.3), interrogative determiners (§4.4.2.3), interrogative verbs, intonational patterns, tags, and word-order patterns that will be further discussed in this section.

6.6.1 Yes-no questions

In Belep, rising intonation is normally the only indication of a yes-no question. Example (146) shows a statement *te dadabwa* 'he is black' in line 1, which is repeated in line 2.

(146)   ***Toma te dadabwa, te wa-***
         toma=re   **dadabwa**   **te=**   **wa-**
         but=3SG.SUBJ   black   3SG.SUBJ=   DEM.MAN

         Êê, te wali maar ri te dadabwa.
         êê   **te=**   **wa-li**   **ma-r=i**
         yes   3SG.SUBJ=   DEM.MAN-DET.A.PRX   similarity-3GNR.POSS=GEN

         te=   **dadabwa**
         3SG.SUBJ=   black
         'But he was black, he was l- Yeah, he was, like, black.'
                                                             Yal-28072010-BGMCG-tahitian_0205

The intonation curves for the two statements of *te dadabwa* 'he is black' are represented in Figure 2 (continuing intonation) and Figure 3 (final intonation).

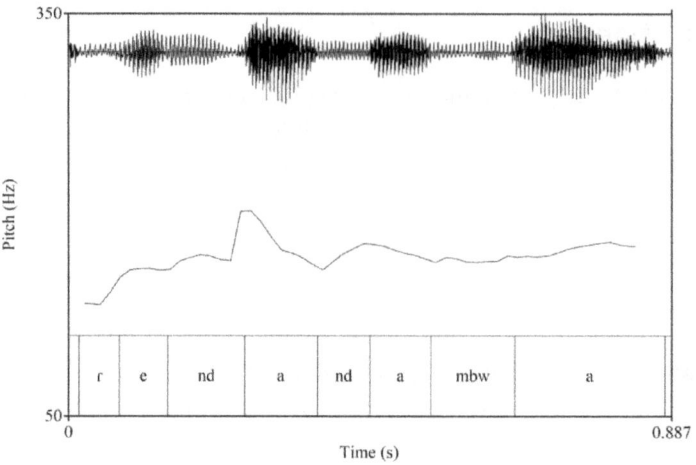

Fig. 2: Intonation curve for *te dadabwa*, continuing intonation

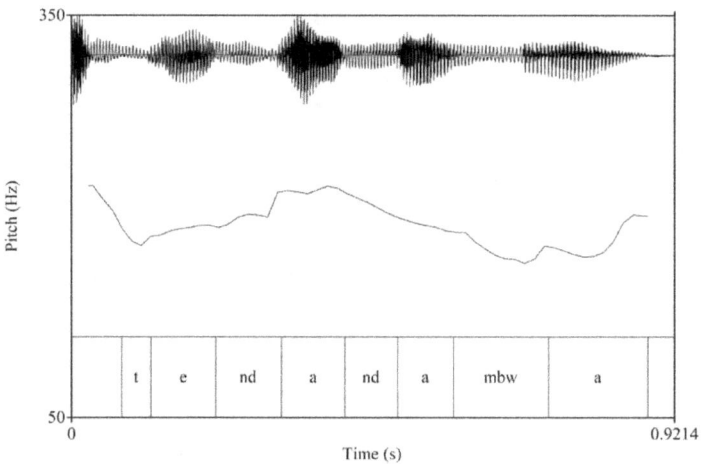

Fig. 3: Intonation curve for *te dadabwa*, final intonation

We see that these statement intonations are characterized by, in the case of continuing intonation, a fairly flat and even pitch, and in the case of final intonation, a gradual pitch fall throughout the utterance. In contrast, example (147), shows the yes-no question *te ulo* 'is it red?'.

(147)   **Ganan, te ulo ?**
         gana-n   te=   ulo
         color-3SG.POSS   3SG.SUBJ=   be.red
         'His color, is it red?'

                                        05102010-MTAD-jeu 3:33-3:38.2

Figure 4 shows an intonation curve for the question in (147). The intonation pattern is characterized by a sharp rise in pitch in the last syllable of the clause.[18]

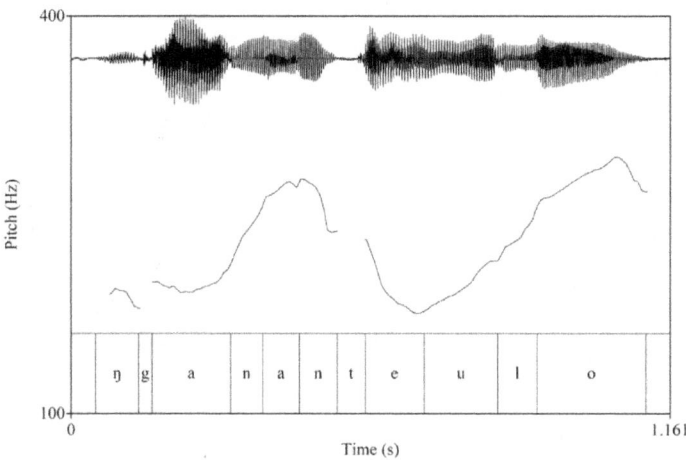

Fig. 4: Intonation curve for *te ulo?*, a yes-no question

Negative (§6.8) yes-no questions are formed in the same way as affirmative ones; that is, with a sharp rise in pitch in the last syllable of the clause. In (148), there is a small rise in pitch in line 3 in the final syllable of *du liva* 'our bones', followed by a sharp pitch rise in the last syllable of *âjuma* 'people' in line 4.

(148)   **Texa waak xa mwaak,**
         te=xa   wa-x=a   mwaak
         3SG.SUBJ=ADD   DEM.MAN-DET.D.PRX=NOM   rabbitfish
         'The rabbitfish was like,'

---

18 There is a difference in frequency range between the statement and question examples because the speaker for example (146) *te dadabwa* 'he is black' is male while the speaker for example (147) *te ulo?* 'is it red?' is female. The male speaker's pitch range is from 50 to 350 Hz, while the female speaker's pitch range is from 100 to 400 Hz. The pitch windows are the same size.

« *Âri yo li âmi ca bae-*
âri= yo=li â-mi ca= bae
NEG= 2SG.INDEP=GEN DEM.NEW-DET.A.DST ITER= bite
'"Aren't you the one who always eats-"'

bae du liva ? Nyami ava-
bae du=li-va nya-mi ava=
bite bones=GEN- DEM.IDF- 1PL.EXCL.SUBJ=
     1PL.EXCL.ABS DET.A.DST
'"eats our bones? When we-"'

ca giva li âju-ma ? »
ca= gi-va=li âju-ma
ITER= attack-1PL.EXCL.POSS=GEN person-AC
'"[when] the people always kill us?"'

Yal-01082010-MFD_0034-0035

Yes-no questions may also be formed with a tag. Two common ones are *yo kiyie* 'you see?', normally produced in the highly reduced form [jəʁe]; and *ai* 'right?', which is phonologically related to the discourse marker *ai* 'no' (§6.6.3) and the linker *ai* 'or' (§7.2.2), but which is produced in the reduced form [əɪ] when used as a tag.[19] An example of the tag *yo kiyie* 'you see?' (produced in its reduced form [jəʁe]) is found in (149).

(149) *Texa duelila, yo kiyie ?*
te=xa due-li-la [jəʁe]
3SG.SUBJ=ADD admire-TR-3PL.ABS TAG
'And she admired them, you know?'

Yal-20092011-AW1_0169

In (149), speaker AW uses the tag *yo kiyie* 'you see?' and rising intonation to make sure his listener is tracking with him. A similar function is served by his use of the tag *ai* 'right?' in (150); the listener's expected response is in the affirmative.

(150) *Mo pwai pwajen nilen, ai ?*
mo pwai pwajen=i-len [əɪ]
LK3 only three=GEN-3TR.ABS TAG
'But there were only three of them, you know?'

Yal-20092011-AW6_0156

---

19 In Nêlêmwa, the alternation linker *ai* 'or' also serves the function of a question tag.

6.6.2 Question-word questions

Question-word questions are formed in a variety of ways, though they tend strongly to favor predication of the questioned element.

To question an argument of a clause, Belep speakers may use an interrogative determiner suffix on a noun (§4.4.2); a verb phrase enclitic; or an interrogative pronoun (§4.6.3).

The interrogative determiner suffix is -*va* 'DET.Q', meaning 'which?', as in (151).

(151)   *Tamwava ?*
   tamwa-va
   woman-DET.Q
   'Which woman?'

It can also be affixed to any demonstrative pronoun (§4.6.2) and predicated. For example, in (152) -*va* 'DET.Q' is suffixed to the demonstrative pronoun *wa-* 'DEM.MAN' to act as a nominative verb (§5.2.1) meaning 'how; in what manner?'.

(152)   *Yo wava ma yo uya ?*
   yo=   wa-va   ma   yo=   uya
   2SG.SUBJ= DEM.MAN-DET.Q LK4   2SG.SUBJ= arrive
   'How did you arrive?' (lit. 'You did which manner such that you arrived?')
   Yal-05102010-PT1.wav – Yal-05102010-PT3.wav

Other interrogative pronouns formed in this manner include *yava?* 'where?, in what place?' and *nyava?* 'which one?'. As the -*va* determiner is unusual in my corpus, more data is needed to further examine its use.

To question the location of an action, the verb phrase enclitic =*(l)iva* 'LOC.Q' (§5.12) is used as in (153) and (154).

(153)   *Yo cayi liva ?*
   yo=   cayi=liva?
   2SG.SUBJ= be.from=LOC.Q
   'Where are you from?' or 'Where did you come from?'[20]
   Yal-05102010-PT1.wav – Yal-05102010-PT3.wav

---

20 The verb *cayi* 'to be from' has likely lexicalized from the verb group *ca= ci* [ITER= sit]; a remnant of this structure is still found in the typical response to the question in (153): *na= tu=me ci=la* ... [1SG.SUBJ= go.DH=CTP sit=LOC] 'I come from...'.

(154)   « *Awuli Cabak, yo liva ?* »
Awuli Cabak   yo=liva?
Awuli Cabak   2SG.INDEP=LOC.Q
'Awuli Cabak, where are you?'

Yal-19092011-PA_0031

There are four interrogative pronouns, *ti* 'who?', *da* 'what?', *neen* 'when?' and *pwaneen* 'how many?' which may either occur *in situ*—that is, in the same location in the clause that the questioned argument would; be predicated as predicate nominals (§6.5.1); or occur in a cleft construction. The pronouns *ti* 'who?' and *da* 'what?' are simple clitics (as defined by Zwicky 1977) and are invariant in terms of case (§4.6.3), save for a morphophonemic alternation whereby *ti* is realized as [ri] if it occurs in its encliticized form (§3.2.2.6). The usage of pronouns *neen* 'when?' and *pwaneen* 'how many?' is not well understood at this time and requires further study.

In example (155), nominative-marked *ti* 'who?' occurs *in situ* in the same clausal location as *Maxeek*, a personal name, in example (156).

(155)   *Te ta la ti ?*
te=   ta=la=ri
3SG.SUBJ=   go.UH=NOM=who?
'Who went up?'

Yal-28072010-BGMCG-tahitian_0249

(156)   *Te tame la Maxeek,*
te=   ta=me=la   Maxeek
3SG.SUBJ=   go.UH=CTP=NOM   Maxeek
'Maxeek came up,'

Yal-28072010-BGMCG-tahitian_0107

The interrogative pronouns may also appear in place of a questioned absolutive argument as in (157), or in place of a questioned possessor as in (158).

(157)   « *Ho, tuya da lexen ?* »
tuya   da=lexen
EX.GNR   what?=LOC.A
'"Ho, what do we have here?"' (lit. '"What exists here?"')

Yal-19092011-PA_0020

(158)   « *Naveri ?* »
nave=ri
fire-who?
'"Whose fire is this?"'

Yal-20092011-AW6_0052

Interrogative pronouns in Belep are also used as predicate nominals (§6.5.1), as in (159).

(159) *« Jua yo ai ti ? Kawo ? »*
jua yo ai ti Kawo
very 2SG.INDEP or who? Kawo
'Is it really you or who? Kawo?'

Yal-20092011-AW1_0282

Predicated interrogative pronouns are often used in equative constructions (§6.5.1), with the genitive (§6.4.3) S argument being indexed either by a full noun phrase, as in (160), or by an anaphoric pronominal suffix (§5.7), as shown in example (161).

(160) *« Ti li âjuma lali ? »*
ti=li âju-ma la-li
who?=GEN person-AC DEM.PL-DET.A.PRX
'"Who are those people?"' (lit. '"Those people are who?"')

Yal-20092011-AW6_0079

(161) *« Ti lio ? »*
ti=li-o
who?=GEN-2SG.ABS
'"Who are you?"' (lit. '"You are who?"')

Yal-20092011-AW1_0299

Interrogative pronouns in Belep also participate in a construction which I will call *interrogative clefting*.[21] Interrogative clefting in Belep is a type of focus construction (§6.9.2) which places the question word at the beginning of the clause—a common position for the question word in VO languages like Belep (Greenberg 1966). In Belep interrogative clefting, the S argument of the predicated interrogative pronoun is a relative clause headed by a relative pronoun (§7.4.3). This structure is represented schematically in (162).

(162) **PRED**   **S**
       [interr. pron.]=GEN   [DEM.PRON.-DET verb group]
                              relative clause

Example (163) shows an instance of interrogative clefting. The interrogative pronoun *ti* 'who?' is predicated, while the genitive-marked S argument *âmi âyuan na pewola* 'the one she liked among them' is a relative clause headed by a relative pronoun, as discussed in §7.4.3.

---

[21] The term *interrogative clefting* is based on terminology from Payne (1997).

(163) *Me ti li âmi âyuan na pewola ?*

	PRED		S	
	[me ti]=li	[â-mi	âyua-n=a	pewo-la]
	IRR who?=GEN	DEM.NEW-DET.A.DST	desire-3SG.POSS=LOC	middle-3PL.POSS

'Who among them did she like?' (lit. 'The one she liked among them was who?')

Yal-20092011-AW1_0173

Another example of interrogative clefting is shown in (164), where the relative clause is *âli îna mwima laak* 'the one who made these things'.

(164) *Ti li âli îna mwima laak ?*

	PRED		S		
	[ti]=li	[â-li	îna	mwi-ma	laa-k]
	who?=GEN	DEM.NEW-DET.A.PRX	make.GNR	DET.INAN-AC	DEM.PL-DET.D.PRX

'Who made these things?' (lit. 'The one who made these things is who?')

Yal-05102010-PT1.wav – Yal-05102010-PT3.wav

To question a noun phrase whose grammatical role is unknown, Belep speakers generally use interrogative verbs. A list of some of these is given in Table 5, though there may be others.

Tab. 5: Interrogative verbs

Interrogative verb	English translation	Notes
ca	'to be in what state?'	nominative verb; §5.2.1
câamw, câmwi	'to do what with something?'	nominative intr., bound tr.; §5.2.5.1
iva, ivi	'to be where?'	absolutive verb, infl. for spc.; §5.2.2, §5.2.4
wa	'to go where?'	nominative verb; §5.2.1

To inquire about a state, Belep speakers use the nominative intransitive (§5.2.1) verb *ca* 'be in what state?, be how?'. The verb *ca* is usually used to inquire after someone's health, and its usage implies that the speaker believes something is wrong—Belema often respond to the question *Te ca ?* 'How are you?' by saying *Âria* 'It's nothing'. A similar usage of *ca* 'to be how?' is shown in (165).

(165) « *Âyina, yo ca ? Avang, yo ca ?* »
      âyi-na   **yo=**   **ca**   **ava-ng**   **yo=**   **ca?**
      man-DET.D.MPX   2SG.SUBJ= be.how? sibling-1SG.POSS 2SG.SUBJ= how
      'Hey man, are you okay? Brother, how are you?'

      « *Ah, mo te mwany na leeng, teme tunao li maac,* »
      mo   **te=**   **mwany**   **na=lee-ng**
      LK3   3SG.SUBJ=   bad   interior=DAT-1SG.POSS

      te=me   **tu-nao=li**   **maac**
      3SG.SUBJ=IRR   find-1SG.ABS=GEN   death
      'Ah, well I feel horrible, I might die,'
                                                                 Yal-20092011-AW6_0050

The nominative intransitive verb (§5.2.1) *cââmw* 'to do what with something?' is used to inquire about an action completed using an instrument. Its bound lexically transitivized form (§5.2.5.1) is *câmwi* 'to do what with?', as in example (166).

(166) « *Yome pae wîna ma yome câmwie ?* »
      yo=me   **pa-e**   **wî-na**   **ma**
      2SG.SUBJ=IRR   take-SPC DEM.INAN-DET.D.MPX LK4

      yo=me   **câmwi-e**
      2SG.SUBJ=IRR do.what.TR-3SG.ABS
      '"What are you going to do with it if you take it?"' (lit. '"You would take this thing so that you would do what with it?"')
                                                                 Yal-20092011-AW1_0292

The verb *iva* 'to be where?' is an intransitive absolutive verb (§5.2.2) which inflects to agree with its argument in specificity (§5.2.4). In (167), the specific form *ivi* questions the location of the absolutive argument *wagaji* 'our boat'.

(167) « *Ka ivi wagaji ?* »
      ka   **ivi**   **waga-ji**
      LK   where.SPC boat-1DU.INCL.POSS
      '"And where is our boat?"'
                                                                   Yal-01082010-MFD_0016

This verb is also commonly used to inquire about a name—one literally asks 'where is his/her/its name?' rather than 'what is his/her/its name?'. In example (168), *iva* is used to question a name.

(168) BG: **Wîli yeek, bu lila yeek.**
wî-li yeek
DEM.INAN-DET.A.PRX plant

bu=li-la yeek
fishhook=GEN-3PL.POSS plant
'That wooden thing, their wooden fishhook.'

CG: **Iva naran?**
iva nara-n
where.GNR name-3SG.POSS
'What's its name?'

Yal-28072010-BGMCG-hamecon_0093-0094

The customary greeting in Belep is to inquire where someone is going (rather than e.g. how they are feeling, etc.). This is accomplished with the nominative intransitive (§5.2.1) verb *wa* 'to go where?'. For example, in (169), the speaker animates a character's greeting to the Dubageni, a type of demon.

(169) « **Wa Dubageni, yo wa ?** »
wa Dubageni yo= wa
grandparent type.of.demon 2SG.SUBJ= go.where?
'"Grandfather Dubageni, where are you going?"'

Yal-05092011-AP1_0012-0013

Example (170) shows a more general use of the verb *wa* 'to go where?'.

(170) **Texa waak xa Maxeek, « Ji wa ? »**
te=xa wa-x=a Maxeek ji= wa?
3SG.SUBJ=ADD DEM.MAN- Maxeek 1DU.INCL.SUBJ= go.where?
DET.D.PRX=NOM
'And Maxeek was like, "Where are we going?"'

Yal-28072010-BGMCG-tahitian_0121

To question a verb, Belep speakers generally use the derived verb *tu da* 'to do what?', which attaches the denominal verbalizer proclitic *tu=* 'VBLZ' (§3.6.4) to the interrogative pronoun *da* 'what?'. An example is shown in (171).

(171) « **Ma na pan tu da ?** »
ma na= pana tu= da
LK4 1SG.SUBJ= go.TV VBLZ= what?
'"What am I going to do?"'

Yal-20092011-AW1_0032

To question a reason, Belep speakers use an equative construction (§6.5.1) with the predicate nominal *puu-r* 'origin-3GNR.POSS' (§7.3.8) and the interrogative pronoun *da* 'what?', as in (172).

(172)   « *Caivak, puur ri da yo go ?* »
        caivak   pu-r=i   da   yo=   go
        rat   origin-3GNR.POSS=GEN   what?   2SG.SUBJ=   cry
        '"Rat, why are you crying?"' (lit. 'because of what')
                                                                    Yal-01082010-MFD_0025

6.6.3 Answering, agreeing, and disagreeing

To respond to yes-no questions like the constructed example shown in (173), Belep speakers may say *êê* 'yes' (as in response (a)) or *ai* 'no' (as in response (b)).

(173)   **Bwa tuu no ?**
        bwa=   tu   no
        CONT=   EX.SPC   fish
        'Are there still fish?'

(a)   **Êê, bwa tuu.**
        êê   bwa=   tuu
        yes   CONT=   EX.SPC
        'Yes, there are.'

(b)   **Ai, mo âria.**
        ai   mo   âria
        no   LK3   NEG.EX
        'No, there aren't.'
                                                                    Yal-05102010-PT

Speakers may also use *êê* and *ai* to respond to a negative question, as in (174). Some speakers do not find *êê* to be an acceptable response to a negative question and may substitute French *si* 'yes (in response to a negative question)'.

(174)   **Âri yo kiyi naeng ?**
        âri=   yo=   kiyi   nae-ng
        NEG=   2SG.SUBJ=   see.SPC   child-1SG.POSS
        'Didn't you see my child?'

(a) ***Êê.***
êê
yes
'Yes (I saw her).'

(b) ***Ai.***
ai
no
'No (I didn't see her).'

Belep speakers may also use *elo* 'okay' to respond to a yes-no question under certain circumstances, as in (175).

(175) ***Yo me îna yagelinao ?***
yo=me   îna   yage-li-nao
2SG.SUBJ=IRR   make.GNR   help-TR-1SG.ABS
'Will you please help me?'

Elo.
elo
okay
'Yes.'

These three discourse markers (§3.3.5) also have a number of other discourse functions which will be explained in the rest of this section.

The discourse marker *êê* 'yes' has the characteristic intonation pattern of disyllabic words (§2.8.1). An intonation curve for this word is shown in Figure 5. Speakers may also produce this discourse marker as [m̩m̩] with the same intonation.

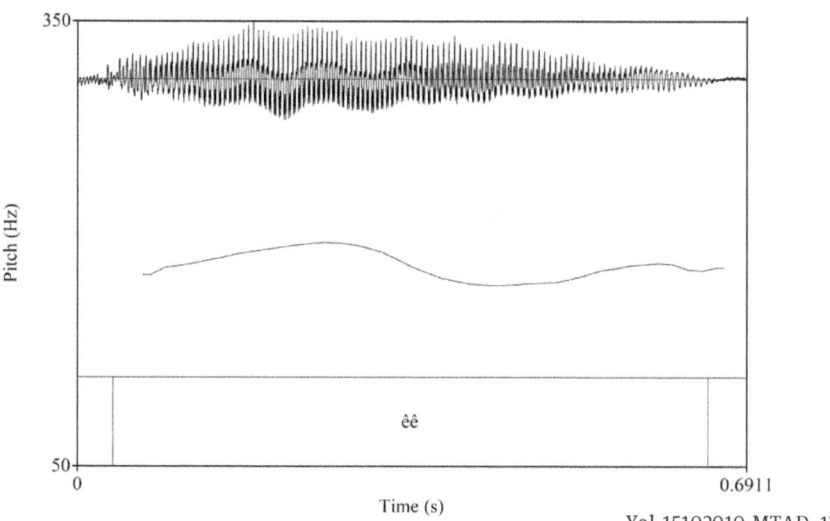

Fig. 5: Intonation curve for *êê* 'yes'

Belep speakers use *êê* 'yes' to agree with their interlocutor. For example, in (176), speaker BG pauses to perform a word search in line 1, eventually producing *janu* 'spirits' as the genitive-marked subject (§6.3.2). Meanwhile, his interlocutor CG produces another possible word to fill the blank in line 2: *ulayama* 'the ancestors, the elders'. Speaker BG then agrees with the validity of this word in line 3, using the discourse marker *êê* 'yes'.

(176)   BG: ***laô wanem vaer ri …janu,***
                     la=ô   wane=va-er=i   janu
                     3PL.SUBJ=REAL   walk=INSTR-3SG.ABS=GEN   spirit
                '[they] were walking with him, …the spirits,'

          CG: ***ulayama,***
                    ulaya-ma
                    old.man-AC
                    'ancestors,'

          BG: ***Êê, ulayama.***
                    êê   ulaya-ma
                    yes   old.man-AC
                    'Yes, the ancestors.'

To acknowledge the receipt of new information, to accept the premise of an interlocutor's speech, or to agree to do something, Belep speakers use *elo* 'okay'. For instance, in (177), MT explains a game rule to AD, who acknowledges receipt of this information with *elo*.

(177) MT: **Leô pwai ci êê ou ai.**
le=ô   pwai ci êê ou   ai
3DU.SUBJ=REAL only sit yes or.LN no
'They can only be yes or no.'

AD: **Elo.**
elo
okay
'Okay.'

Yal-15102010-MTAD_3:44.989-3:47.757

If *elo* is used with the sharply rising intonation of a yes-no question (§6.6.1), its meaning is 'really?'. For example, in (178), MT responds to AD's statement with *elo*, indicating both that she is accepting the new information and requesting confirmation.

(178) AD: **Naô tue.**
na=ô   tu-e
1SG.SUBJ=REAL   find-3SG.ABS
'I found it.'

MT: **Elo ? Bwa kaxi ?**
elo   bwa=   kaxi
okay   CONT= look
'Oh, really? Let me see?'

AD: **Nyak ?**
nya-k
DEM.IDF-DET.D.PRX
'This one?'

Yal-15102010-MTAD_18:12.603-18:16.1

Example (179) illustrates more clearly the difference between *êê* 'yes' and *elo* 'okay'. In line 3 *elo* is used to acknowledge receipt of information, while BG's *êê* in line 5 is used to provide agreement with what CG said in line 4.

(179) BG: *Te ta la ti ?*
te=   ta=la=ri?
3SG.SUBJ=   go.UH=NOM=who?
'Who went up?'

CG: *Yo.*
yo
2SG.INDEP
'You.'

BG: *Elo, nao.*
elo   nao
okay   1SG.INDEP
'Okay, me.'

CG: *Ai, ave ma ulayiik.*
ai   ave   ma   ulayii-k
no   1DU.EXCL.INDEP   LK4   old-DET.D.PRX
'No, we two with that old man.'

BG: *Êê, or ma Orilô.*
êê   or   ma   Orilô
yes   2DU.INDEP   LK4   Orilô
'Yeah, you two with Orilô.'

Yal-28072010-BGMCG-tahitian_0249-0250

Speakers can also use the independent pronoun *yo* '2SG.INDEP' as an agreement token; it is generally used to indicate that permission has been granted or approval offered, as in (180), a constructed example that is representative of discourse I have overheard.

(180) S1: *Na pan nawe tolabang.*
na=   pana   nawe   tolaba-ng
1SG.SUBJ= go.TV   leave   basket-1SG.POSS
'I'm going to go put my purse down.'

S2: *Yo.*
yo
2SG.INDEP
'Go ahead.'

It is unknown whether other second person independent pronouns can also serve this function.

The discourse marker *ai* 'no' has many functions in Belep; its use as a disjunctive coordinator is discussed in §4.5.4 and its use as a question tag is discussed in §6.6.1. It is also used in answering and disagreeing. To respond negatively to a question, speakers of Belep use *ai* 'no', as in line 2 in (181).

(181) MT: ***Nyami yudu ? Ai ? Tere***
nya-mi yudu ai te=re
DEM.IDF-DET.A.DST red.mullet no 3SG.SUBJ=ACT
'That one, a red mullet? No? Is it even-'

AD: ***Ai.***
ai
no
'No.'

MT: ***no pwalaic ?***
no pwalaic
fish one
'a fish?'

Yal-15102010-MTAD_4:46.75-4:52.107

The discourse marker *ai* 'no' is also used to disagree, as in (182), where the speaker animates a negotiation between two characters, Ixe and Kawo, who repeatedly use *ai* 'no' to indicate that they disagree with their interlocutor.

(182) « ***Ai. Enyi yome cavac, na cavac ya modemw.***
ai enyi yo=me cavac na= cavay=a
no if 2SG.SUBJ=IRR leave 1SG.SUBJ= leave=LOC

mode-mw
together-2SG.POSS

***Na kuar ri na ci la pwemwa.* »**
na= kuar=i na= ci=la pwemwa
1SG.SUBJ= refuse=GEN 1SG.SUBJ= sit=LOC village
'[Ixe:] "No. If you leave, I'm going with you. I don't want to stay at home."'

« ***Ai,* »** *te âri u leen ni Kawo.* « ***Ai.***
ai te= âri u=lee-n=i Kawo ai
no 3SG.SUBJ= say toward=DAT-3SG.POSS.SPC=GEN Kawo no

Yo ci. Yome ci la pwemwaji. »
yo=   ci   yo=me   ci=la   pwemwa-ji
2SG.SUBJ= sit   2SG.SUBJ=IRR sit=LOC village-1DU.INCL.POSS
'"No," Kawo said to her. "No. You stay. You should stay at home."'
Yal-20092011-AW1_0102-0105

Finally, discourse marker *ai* 'no' can be used as in example (183), where it functions as a negative imperative to mean 'Don't!'

(183) *Na nyi kewee ka to jie, « Ai ! »*
      na=   nyi=   kewe-e=xa   to   ji-e   ai
      1SG.SUBJ= PUNCT= run-3SG.ABS=LK   call   give-3SG.ABS   no

      Ka me to ji-e, « Ai ! »
      ka   me=   to   ji-e   ai
      LK   IRR= call   give-3SG.ABS   no
      'I immediately chased after him and called to him, "No!" and then called to him, "No!"'
Yal-28072010-BGMCG-tahitian_0078

6.7 Imperatives and prohibitives

There is no morphology that is unique to imperatives in Belep; they are indicated primarily by the omission of the subject agreement proclitic (§5.8) or by context. Prohibitives are formed using a set of verb group proclitics (§5.3) which fall into a position class between the subject agreement proclitics and the aspectual proclitics.

6.7.1 Imperatives

The simplest imperatives in Belep are formed in the same way as declarative clauses, except that the subject agreement proclitic (§5.8) is omitted. For example, (184) shows a constructed example of a declarative clause with a subject agreement proclitic, while (185) shows a parallel imperative clause where the subject proclitic is omitted.

(184) *Te pame.*
      te=   pa=me
      3SG.SUBJ= go.TV=CTP
      'S/he comes.'

(185)　**Pame !**
　　　　pa=me
　　　　go.TV=CTP
　　　　'Come!'

A discourse example of an imperative is found in (186), where CG directs BG to speak Belep (rather than French) and does not use a subject agreement proclitic.

(186)　**Mo tao pulu Belep !**
　　　　mo　　tao=　pulu　　Belep
　　　　LK3　HAB=　speak　Belep
　　　　'Hey, speak Belep!'
　　　　　　　　　　　　　　　　　　　　　　Yal-28072010-BGMCG-tahitian_0114

Speakers can produce a more polite imperative by using the aspectual proclitic *bwa=* 'CONT' (§5.5.4). The cognate of this formative in Nêlêmwa has been described as emphatic, producing increased surety of the predication (Bril 2002). However, in Belep imperatives, it seems to have the opposite effect, decreasing a speaker's epistemic attachment to the predication and rendering the imperative more polite. For example, in (187), the character animated by the speaker is requesting help, so he uses the more polite *bwa=*.

(187)　**« Iya, bwa ponaoda ? »**
　　　　iya　　　　bwa=　　po-nao=da
　　　　octopus　CONT=　load-1SG.ABS=DIR.UH
　　　　'"Octopus, would you take me up [to the beach]?"'
　　　　　　　　　　　　　　　　　　　　　　Yal-01082010-MFD_0043

In some cases, speakers may use a subject agreement proclitic in an imperative, as in (188) - (190). In these cases, imperatives are morphosyntactically identical to declaratives and their pragmatic force is understood from context. Prosodic cues may also indicate an imperative, but this is not obligatory. For example, in (188), the imperative is not distinguishable from the declarative 'You come home' except through context.

(188)　**« Yo pame la pwemwa, »**
　　　　yo=　　　　pa=me=la　　　　pwemwa
　　　　2SG.SUBJ=　go.TV=CTP=LOC　village
　　　　'"Come home,"'
　　　　　　　　　　　　　　　　　　　　　　Yal-20092011-AW1_0030

In (189), the imperative pragmatic force is also understood through context, since subject agreement proclitics are used.

(189) *« Yome jua îna ôe, yome nue, »*
     yo=me   jua   îna   ô-e   yo=me
     2SG.SUBJ=IRR very make.GNR be.good-3SG.ABS 2SG.SUBJ=IRR

     nu-e
     wrap.with.leaves-
     3SG.ABS
     '"Prepare it well, wrap it with leaves,"'   Yal-20092011-AW1_0072

In (190), the speaker quotes his own earlier production of imperatives using subject agreement proclitics.

(190) *Naxa waak, « Yome bwageo.*
     na=xa   waa-k   yo=me   bwage-o
     1SG.SUBJ=ADD DEM.MAN-   2SG.SUBJ=IRR return-
                              DET.D.PRX   2SG.ABS

     Yome bwageo, Maxeek.
     yo=me   bwage-o   Maxeek
     2SG.SUBJ=IRR return-2SG.ABS Maxeek

     Yoxame tu mwa la yamidu Âmwany. »
     yo=xa=me   tu   mwa=la   ya-midu   Âmwany
     2SG.SUBJ=ADD=IRR go.DH again=LOC DEM.LOC-DET.D.DH Âmwany
     'And I was like, "You go back. You go back, Maxeek. And you go down there to Âmwany again."'
                                        Yal-28072010-BGMCG-tahitian_0148-0150

Note that in (189) and (190), the irrealis modal *=me* 'IRR' (§5.6.2) is used to make the imperative more polite. Inclusion of the subject agreement proclitic in imperatives is more common for nonsingular and first person addressees and may be obligatory in these cases. For example, the paucal subject agreement proclitic is used in the imperative in (191), and the first person dual proclitic is used in (192).

(191) *Ôna paramenao.*
     ôna=   parame-nao
     2TR.SUBJ= forgive.TR-1SG.ABS
     'Forgive me.'
                                        Yal-09082010-JBM-coutume_0003

(192) *Te âri u le Ixe, « Jime cavac. »*
     te=   âri   u=le   Ixe   ji=me   cavac
     3SG.SUBJ= say toward=DAT Ixe 1DU.INCL.SUBJ=IRR leave
     'She said to Ixe, "Let's leave."'   Yal-20092011-AW1_0063-0064

Other clauses with an imperative pragmatic force include those using the deontic linker *ki* (§7.3.6).

6.7.2 Prohibitives

There are two prohibitive proclitics in Belep, *wara=* 'NEG.IMPER' and *kara=* 'NEG.NEC'. Their position class in the verb group (§5.3) immediately precedes any aspectual proclitics. Like imperatives, prohibitives may omit the subject agreement proclitic (§5.8), though this is unusual if the addressee is not second person singular. The pattern whereby prohibitives use the same construction as imperatives with a non-declarative sentential negation strategy is fairly common among Oceanic languages (van der Auwera et al. 2011).

The prohibitive proclitic *wara=* is used to form a negative imperative, as in the overheard examples in (193) and (194).

(193)   *Wara migie !*
         wara=   migi-e
         NEG.IMPER= touch-3SG.ABS
         'Don't touch it!'

(194)   *Wara pa kôêlinao.*
         wara=   pa=   kôê-li-nao
         NEG.IMPER= CAUS= tired-TR-1SG.ABS
         'Don't make me tired.'

In some uses of the prohibitive, the subject proclitic may be omitted, as in line 1 of (195), or it may be included as in line 2. Note that line 2 also contains an imperative without a subject proclitic (§6.7.1).

(195)   « *Wara, wara maac,* » *te âri u le naen,*
         wara=   wara=   maac   te=   âri   u=le
         NEG.IMPER= NEG.IMPER= die   3SG.SUBJ= say toward=DAT

         Teâ Pûnivaac. « *Yo wara maac, mo ci.* »
         nae-n   Teâ Pûnivaac yo=   wara=   maac mo ci
         child-3SG.POSS Teâ Pûnivaac 2SG.SUBJ= NEG.IMPER= die   LK3 sit
         '"Don't, don't die," she said to her child, Teâ Pûnivaac. "Don't die, but stay."'
                                                                                                      Yal-20092011-AW5_0102

Example (196), a young woman's motherly advice to her present and future children, also shows the alternation between the omission and inclusion of the second person singular subject proclitic in prohibitives. The prohitibitives are indicated by square brackets.

(196) **Name âri u le naeng ma**
na=me   âri   u=le   nae-ng   ma
1SG.SUBJ=IRR say   toward=DAT   child-1SG.POSS   LK4

2 **te wara wânem mi bwan.**
[te=   wara=   wânem=i   bwan]
3SG.SUBJ=   NEG.IMPER=   walk=GEN   night

3 **Name âri u le ânomale, « Wara wânem mi bwan.**
na=me   âri   u=le   âno-male
1SG.SUBJ=IRR say   toward=DAT   child-pair

[wara=   wânem=i bwan]
NEG.IMPER=   walk=GEN night

4 **O wara tu jaar. Wara up, wara ûdu.**
[o=   wara=   tu=   jaar]   [wara=   up]
2DU.SUBJ=   NEG.IMPER=   VBLZ=   be.happy NEG.IMPER=   smoke

[wara=   ûdu]
NEG.IM-   drink
PER=

5 **Surtout wânem mi bwan, te jua mwany nya nyali.**
surtout   wânem=i bwan   te=   jua
above.all.LN   walk=GEN night 3SG.SUBJ=   very

mwany=a   nya-li
be.bad=NOM   DEM.IDF-DET.A.PRX

6 **Wara pae daana nyanya, mo te nyana mwany nya daana nyanya. »**
[wara=   pa-e   dana nyanya] mo   te=   nyana
NEG.IMPER=   take-TR   road Mom   LK3   3SG.SUBJ=   big.thing

mwany=a   dana   nyanya
be.bad=NOM   road   Mom

'I would say to my child that he mustn't walk at night. I would say to my kids, "Don't walk at night. Don't party. Don't smoke, don't drink. Above all don't walk at night, that's really bad. Don't follow Mom's example, because Mom's example is really bad."'   Yal-27092011-LPLY

In (196), prohibitives in lines 3, 4, and 6 omit subject proclitics, while those in lines 2 and 4 include them. The prohibitive in line 2 has a 3SG addressee while the others all have a 2DU addressee. Example (197) shows the inclusion of a subject proclitic with a prohibitive where the addressee is 1SG.

(197)   *Na wara pulu mwany.*
        na=   wara=   pulu   mwany
        1SG.SUBJ=   NEG.IMPER=   speak   be.bad
        'I will not curse.' (lit. 'Don't curse.')

                                                                                                DY classroom

In general, the proclitics seem to be included with a prohibitive when the addressee is not clear from context.

The prohibitive proclitic *kara=* 'NEG.NEC' indicates a negative necessity, as in (198). It can occur with or without a subject proclitic, as in (199).

(198)   *Kara migie !*
        kara=   migi-e
        NEG.NEC=   touch-3SG.ABS
        'You mustn't touch it.'

(199)   *(Yo) Kara tu.*
        (yo=)   kara=   tu
        2SG.SUBJ=   NEG.NEC   go.DH
        'You mustn't go down.'

                                                                          Yal-22092011-TB.wav

According to speakers, the meaning of *kara=* is similar to that of the sentential negative proclitic *kiaxi=* (§6.8.1); however, there are not enough examples of its use in discourse to distinguish it from other similar morphemes. More research is needed to understand the function of prohibitive *kara=*.

6.8 Negation

Most negation of predicates—including that of predicate nominals (§6.5.1)—is accomplished in Belep using the verb group proclitic *âri=* 'NEG'; another verb group proclitic *kiaxi=* 'NEG.NEC' is also used (§6.8.1). There are also a number of inherently negative verbs (§6.8.2) and some inherently negative nouns used in predicate nominals. A number of other negation strategies are discussed elsewhere: negative existentials and locatives in §6.5.2; negative interrogatives in §6.6; negative imperatives in §6.7.2. There is no constituent negation in Belep.

6.8.1 Regular predicate negation

In predicate negation, negative proclitics *âri=* 'NEG' and *kiaxi=* 'NEG.NEC' are attached to the verb group (§5.3) or predicate nominal, typically appearing clause-initially and always preceding the subject agreement proclitic. Most predicate negation uses *âri=* 'NEG', as in examples (200) - (202), where a verbal predicate is negated.

(200) *Âri te baele,*
 âri=re=   bae-le
 NEG=3SG.SUBJ= bite-3DU.ABS
 'He didn't eat them,'
 Yal-28072010-BGMCG-lune_0047

(201) *Toma âri te wânem mo te paralysé.*
 toma   âri=re=   wânem mo=re   [paralize]
 but   NEG=3SG.SUBJ=   walk   LK3=3SG.SUBJ= paralyzed.LN
 'But he didn't walk, because he was paralyzed.'
 Yal-28072010-BGMCG-lune_0014

(202) *Toma âju, âri na kiyie.*
 toma   âju   âri=   na=   kiyi-e
 but   person   NEG=   1SG.SUBJ=   see.SPC-3SG.ABS
 'But the *person* I didn't see.'
 Yal-28072010-BGMCG-tahitian_0094

Proclitic *âri=* 'NEG' is also used to negate predicate nominals, as in (203).

(203) *Mo âri Dau Ar, naran ni Dau Belep.*
 mo âri= dau ar   nara-n=i   dau Belep
 LK3 NEG= islet sun name-3SG.POSS=GEN   islet Belep
 'And it was not Dau Ar [the Isle of the Sun], but rather Dau Belep [the Isle of Belep].'
 Yal-20092011-AW6_0190

When a modal morpheme is present (§5.6, §5.5.4), it typically precedes the negative proclitic.[22] For example, modal *me* 'IRR' precedes *âri=* 'NEG' in (204).

---

22 When the modal precedes the negative proclitic as in these examples, the modal meaning has scope over the negation.

(204) « mo me âri na uli da. »
mo me âri= na= uli da
LK3 IRR NEG= 1SG.SUBJ= pour blood
'But I'm not going to commit bloodshed.'
Yal-20092011-AW1_0259

In (205), realis modal ô 'REAL' precedes âri= 'NEG', which modifies the predicate nominal koxo 'many'.

(205) Ô âri koxo li lami pwai ci.
ô âri= koxo=li la-mi pwai ci
REAL NEG= many=GEN DEM.PL-DET.A.DST only sit
'Those who only stayed were not many.'
Yal-28072010-BGMCG-sousmarin_0107

In (206), bwa= is used before the negative proclitic âri= to mean 'not yet'.

(206) Te bwa âno, bwa âri te – jua âri te ulac.
te= bwa= ânô bwa= âri= te= jua
3SG.SUBJ= CONT= be.young CONT= NEG= 3SG.SUBJ= very

âri= te= ulac
NEG= 3SG.SUBJ= be.old
'He was still young, he wasn't yet – he wasn't old at all.'
Yal-20092011-AW3_0006

The other negative proclitic kiaxi= 'NEG.NEC' is rare in my corpus and more work remains to be done to understand its function. Examples are shown in (207) and (208), where it appears to indicate a negative necessity. In both of these examples, kiaxi= negates a pseudocoordinate clause marked with ma 'LK4' (§7.3.2).

(207) le cobae âjuma la Yade, ma kiaxi la kiyile,
le= coba-e âju-ma=la Yade ma
3DU.SUBJ= hide.from-SPC person-AC=LOC Yade LK4

kiaxi= la= kiyi-le
NEG.NEC= 3PL.SUBJ= see.SPC-3DU.ABS
'they hid from the people of Yade, so that they wouldn't see them,'
Yal-20092011-AW6_0063-0064

(208) « Jime cavac yena, ma kiaxi la kiyiji. »
ji=me cavaya yena ma
1DU.INCL.SUBJ=IRR leave now LK4

kiaxi=   la=   kiyi-ji
NEG.NEC=   3PL.SUBJ= see.SPC-1DU.INCL.ABS
'Let's leave now, so that they don't see us.'

Yal-20092011-AW1_0190

6.8.2 Inherently negative predicates

A number of Belep verbs and predicate nominals are inherently semantically marked as negative. These include the absolutive verbs *âria* 'NEG.EX', *cia* 'NEG.LOC' (discussed in §6.5.2), and *mwanyi* 'to not know' (§5.2.2), as well as those shown in Table 6.

Tab. 6: Inherently negative predicates

Belep predicate	English translation	Notes
âlalic	'to be impossible'	pred. nom. (§6.5.1) w/genitive =*li* (§7.3.7)
koon, koni	'to not be able to, to not know'	nom. intr. (§5.2.1); bound tr. w/stem mod. (§5.2.5.1); see also §5.10.6
kuar, kuari	'to refuse, to not want'	nom. intr. (§5.2.1); bound tr. w/stem mod. (§5.2.5.1); see also §7.3.7.1
mwauju	'to have no idea'	pred. nom. (§6.5.1) w/genitive =*li* (§7.3.7)
niva	'to lose track of, to not notice'	free tr. (§5.2.3.1)
ngini	'to not be able to see'	bound tr. (§5.2.3.2)

See the indicated sections for further information on each of these predicates; only the predicate nominal *âlalic* 'to be impossible' will be further discussed here.

Example (209) shows the use of predicate nominal *âlalic* 'to be impossible' without an S argument.

(209)   **me âlalic mo buâny.**
        me âlalic   mo buâny
        IRR be.impossible LK3 stone
        'they couldn't because of the stones.' (lit. 'it was impossible')

Yal-28072010-BGMCG-sousmarin_0111

Predicate *âlalic* can also be used in an equative construction (§6.5.1) with a marker of semantic dependency (§7.3) such as *ki* 'REL' (210) or *ma* 'LK4' (211) marking the dependent clause.

(210) *Âlalic ki yome kuar.*
   âlaliyi=xi   yo=me   kuar
   be.impossible=REL 2SG.SUBJ=IRR refuse
   'It is impossible for you to refuse.'

   Yal-25072010-PT-homily_0062

(211) *Âlalic ma la gilen.*
   âlalic   ma   la=   gi-len
   be.impossible LK4 3PL.SUBJ= attack-3TR.ABS
   'They couldn't kill them.' (lit. 'It was impossible')

   Yal-20092011-AW6_0095

6.9 Topicalization and focalization

Pragmatically marked clauses with topicalized or focused referents are primarily formed in Belep using deviations from the standard word order and predication of the marked elements. There is no unique morphology to indicate topicalization, while focalization involves a closed set of enclitics (§3.2.2.6) and some focus constructions.

6.9.1 Topicalization

Topicalized arguments in Belep are unmarked for case and appear at the beginning of the clause as exceptions to the normal verb-initial pattern (§6.2), creating a Topic-Comment structure with an intonation break between the two parts. This structure is consistent with the three-part referent-foregrounding sequence observed for topicalization in English (Geluykeans 1988, Keenan & Schieffelin 1976), whereby the intonation break between the topic and the comment is often filled by backchanneling from the interlocutor. For example, in (212) the clause-initial topic *naerama* 'children' is set apart from the clause that modifies it by an intonation break.

(212) *Ka naerama, la îbi jawu.*
   ka   nae-ra-ma   la=   îbi   jawu
   LK   child-3GNR.POSS-AC   3PL.SUBJ= gather   dead.leaves
   'And the children, they collected trash [to burn].'

   Yal-17072009-TB-weekend_0009-0011

In (213) the topic is *caivak* 'rat'.

(213)   *Ka caivak, te âva la bwe radeau.*
        ka   caivak   te=   âva=la   bwe   [ʁaⁿdo]
        LK   rat   3SG.SUBJ=   fish.GNR=LOC   top   raft.LN
        'And the rat, he fished on the raft.'
                                                    Yal-01082010-MFD_0009

In (214) the topicalized noun phrase is *pwairamale* 'the pair of girls'.

(214)   *Pwairamale, le tao tu,*
        pwaira-male   le=   tao=   tu
        girl-pair   3DU.SUBJ=   HAB=   go.DH
        'The two girls, they often went down,'
                                                    Yal-19092011-PA_0069

In (215), the topic is Teâ Nêlêmwa, a proper name which means 'the chieftain of the Nenema people [in Poum]'.

(215)   *Teâ Nêlêmwa, te cuur,*
        Teâ Nêlêmwa   te=   cuur
        Teâ Nêlêmwa   3SG.SUBJ=   stand
        'Teâ Nêlêmwa, he stood up,'
                                                    Yal-20092011-AW1_0175

Arguments other than nominative-marked ones may be topicalized as well. Example (216) shows the topicalization of a genitive subject. The noun phrase *âjuma la Yade*, marked with genitive =*i* in line 1, acts as the topic of the clause in line 2.

(216)   *Laô kiyilen ni âjuma la Yade.*
        la=ô   kiyi-len=i   âju-ma=la   Yade
        3PL.SUBJ=REAL   see.SPC-3TR.ABS=GEN   person-AC=LOC   Yade

        Âjuma la Yade, la kiyilen.
        âju-ma=la   Yade   la=   kiyi-len
        person-AC=LOC   Yade   3PL.SUBJ=   see.SPC-3TR.ABS
        'The people of Yade saw them. The people of Yade, they saw them.'
                                                    Yal-20092011-AW6_0078

Example (217) shows the topicalization of an absolutive argument, in this case the 3PA independent pronoun *len*.

(217)   *Toma len, cialen,*
        toma   len   cia-len
        but   3PA.INDEP   NEG.LOC-3PA.ABS
        'But they, they weren't there,'
                                                    Yal-20092011-AW6_0161

A variety of linkers can also be used to topicalize a noun phrase. For example, linker *ka* 'LK' (§7.2.1.2) can serve as a topicalizer as in (218).

(218) **Ka puluac ka jia,**
   ka pulu-aya=xa   jia
   LK language-2PL.POSS=LK gift

   tere jia ulayama lami cêboac,
   te=re   jia ulaya-ma   la-mi   cêbo-ac
   3SG.SUBJ=ACT gift old.man-AC DEM.PL-DET.A.DST grandparent-
                                                       2PL.POSS
   'And your language, it's a gift, it's actually a gift from your ancestors,'
   Yal-14092011-PT2-avenir_0008-0009

Causal linker *mo* 'LK3' (§7.2.3) and evidential linker *kara* 'well' (§7.2.5) can also be used in topicalization, as in example (219) where the sequence *kara mo* is used to introduce a comment after a topicalized noun phrase.

(219) ***Ka nyami la mayaravan, kara mo tuu keloop vier bleu.***
   ka nya-mi=la   maya-ra=van
   LK DEM.IDF-DET.A.DST=LOC   side-3GNR.POSS=DIR.TV

   kara mo   tu   kelov=i-era   [blœ]
   well LK3 EX.SPC hat=GEN-3SG.ABS   blue.LN
   'And the one next to it, well he has a blue hat.'
   Yal-15102010-MTAD_24:30-24:40

6.9.2 Focalization

The function of marked or contrastive focus (Chafe 1976, Givón 2001, König 1991) in Belep is served mainly by two focus enclitics, actual =*re* 'ACT' and additive =*xa* 'ADD'. Enclitic =*re* 'ACT', which occupies the FOCUS position class within the verb group (§5.3), attaches to the preface, the phonological word which includes the subject agreement proclitic. Its meaning may be translated as 'actually'; it "counters the assumed presupposition [on the part of the hearer] that the truth value of the entire clause is in question" (Payne 1997: 268). Enclitic =*xa* 'ADD' attaches to a clause or noun phrase, indicating that the entity they index, counter to the hearer's perceived expectations, has a role in some state of affairs. Noun phrases can also be focused by being predicated (§6.5.1), and interrogative pronouns can be focused in an interrogative cleft construction (§6.6.2). No focalization pattern for declarative clauses (Givón 2001) that directly parallels this cleft structure has been observed in Belep.

6.9.2.1 Actual =re

The enclitic =*re* 'ACT', which can be translated 'actually', is used within the verb group (§5.3) to indicate that the truth value of the clause is contrary to the hearer's perceived expectations. Enclitic =*re* 'ACT' attaches to the end of the preface, the phonological word which includes the subject agreement proclitic, any modal enclitics (§5.6), and the clause-chaining enclitic =*xa* 'ADD' (§7.2.1.3).

Examples (220) - (222) show instances of actual =*re* 'ACT' within a clause. In (220), the character animated by the speaker is lying about his murderous intent, claiming that he is not going to use his weapon to kill, he just enjoys carrying it.

(220) « *Enyi na cavac, na wânem, nare pae.* »
 enyi na= cavac na= wânem na=re pa-e
 if 1SG.SUBJ= leave 1SG.SUBJ= walk 1SG.SUBJ=ACT take-3SG.ABS
 '"Whenever I leave or walk, I actually take it."'
 Yal-20092011-AW1_0262

The character animated by the speaker in (220) uses =*re* to counter the perceived suspicions of his interlocutor that he is not being truthful. In example (221), which is drawn from a religious text, the speaker uses =*re* to counter the perceived doubts of his congregation.

(221) *Ka temere uya la mwimi te nooxee.*
 ka te=me=re uya=la
 LK 3SG.SUBJ=IRR=ACT arrive=NOM

 mwi-mi=re noxe-e
 DEM.INAN-DET.A.DST=3SG.SUBJ solicit.SPC-3SG.ABS
 'And what s/he asked for will actually happen.'
 Yal-25072010-PT-homily_0045

In example (222), speaker BG is contrasting his actions with the beliefs of another character in the narrative. He narrates that his brother-in-law accused him of abandonment, but uses =*re* 'ACT' to indicate that real events were counter to his brother-in-law's beliefs.

(222) *Mo âri ave keja, mo avere tao ci lexeng.*
 mo âri= ave= keja mo ave=re
 LK3 NEG= 1DU.EXCL.SUBJ= run LK3 1DU.EXCL.SUBJ=ACT

 tao= ci=lexeng
 HAB= sit=LOC.DC
 'But we didn't run away, because we actually were here the whole time.'
 Yal-28072010-BGMCG-tahitian_0278

6.9.2.2 Additive =xa

Enclitic =*xa* 'also', glossed 'ADD', is used at the end of an intonation unit—a clause, or a focused noun phrase—as an additive focus marker meaning 'also, too'. It indicates that some entity is involved in the relevant event, counter to the hearer's perceived expectations. Its scope is determined based on the context; a sentence such as constructed example (223) may focus either the agent or the patient, depending on the speaker's intent.

(223) **Te pae waangaxa.**
te= **pa-e** **wanga=xa**
3SG.SUBJ= take-SPC boat=ADD
'S/he takes the boat too.'
'S/he also takes the boat.'
Yal-03112011-IM1.wav – Yal-03112011-IM2.wav

In example (224) from discourse, the noun phrase *tamwa Puma* 'a woman from Balade' is focused using =*xa* 'ADD' to indicate that she participated in the relevant state of affairs, despite the hearer's perceived expectations.

(224) **Nyan ka tamwa Pumaxa.**
nya-n **ka** **tamwa** **Puma=xa**
mother-3SG.POSS LK woman Balade=ADD
'His mother, she was *also* from Balade.'
Yal-20092011-AW4_0030

In (225), =*xa* 'ADD' focuses *keloop vier* 'his hat', whose non-existence is counter to the hearer's perceived expectations.

(225) **Âria keloop vieraxa.**
âria **kelov=i-era=xa**
NEG.EX hat=GEN-3SG.ABS=ADD
'Also, he doesn't have a *hat*.'
Yal-05102010-MTAD_22:15-22:20

Enclitic =*xa* 'ADD' is clearly etymologically related to additive linker *ka* 'LK' (§7.2.1); however, its distribution is different from that of *ka*. In addition to being used as a focus morpheme, enclitic =*xa* 'ADD' is used in clause-chaining (§6.9.2). See §7.2.1.3 for a discussion of this clause-chaining function.

6.10 Voice and valency

The morphological expression of valence was described in §5.2.5 and §5.4. This section will analyze other ways that the functions of voice and valency are performed in

Belep, including periphrastic causatives, reflexive and passive meanings, and quotatives.

6.10.1 Periphrastic causatives

In addition to the morphological causative using proclitic *pa=* 'CAUS' (§5.4.1), Belep speakers also make use of a periphrastic causative using pseudocoordinator *ma* 'LK4' (§7.3.2). This causative construction involves less direct causation than the morphological causative; it is represented in Table 7.

Tab. 7: Structure of periphrastic causatives

CAUSE		CAUSED EVENT
[CAUSER ji-CAUSEE]	ma	[CLAUSE]
SUBJ= give-ABS	LK4	

In this periphrastic causative construction, the main clause verb is the bound transitive (§5.2.3.2) *jie* 'to give' with the causer as the main clause subject and the causee as the absolutive argument of the main clause. The subject of the pseudocoordinate caused-event *ma*-clause is co-referential with the causee. For example, in (226), the causer is indexed by the subject agreement proclitic *la=* '3PL.SUBJ' (§5.8) in the main clause. The causee is indexed by the absolutive suffix *-la* '3PL.ABS' (§5.7) in the main clause, and by the subject agreement proclitic *la=* '3PL.SUBJ' in the pseudocoordinate clause.

(226) **La jila ma la ci.**
la=   ji-la   ma la=   ci
3PL.SUBJ= give-3PL.ABS LK4 3PL.SUBJ= sit
'They made them stay.' (lit. 'they₁ gave them₁ that they₁ would sit')
Yal-20092011-AW3_0066

In (227), the causer is indexed by the subject proclitic *le=* '3DU.SUBJ' in the main clause, while the causee is indexed by the absolutive suffix *-e* '3SG.ABS' in the first clause and the subject proclitic *te=* '3SG.SUBJ' in the pseudocoordinate clause.

(227) **Lexa ta jie ma te cuur ri,**
le=xa   ta   ji-e   ma=re   cur=i
3DU.SUBJ=ADD   go.UH   give-3SG.ABS   LK4=3SG.SUBJ   stand=LOC
'They went up and made him stand there,' (lit. 'gave him that he stand there')
Yal-20092011-AW6_0098

In example (228), the unstated causer 'they' causes the caused event *te mae* 'she sleeps'.

(228)   *ka ô jie ma te mae.*
        ka ô   ji-e   ma=re   mae
        LK REAL give-3SG.ABS LK4=3SG.SUBJ sleep
        'and [they] put it to sleep' (lit. '[they] gave it$_i$ that it$_i$ would sleep')
                                                                             Yal-28072010-BGMCG-tayamu_0096

Main clause verbs other than *jie* 'to give' may also be used in periphrastic causatives. For example, the verb *nawee* 'to leave' is used in example (229) in a similar construction to that shown in Table 7.

(229)   « *Nawenao ma na maac.* »
        nawe-nao   **ma na=**   **maac**
        deposit-1SG.ABS LK4 1SG.SUBJ= die
        'Let me die.' (lit. 'Leave me that I die.')
                                                                          Yal-20092011-AW5_0109

6.10.2 Reflexives

Belep has no distinct morpheme with a reflexive meaning. Instead, the function of reflexivity is accomplished using a clause in which the nominative-marked (§6.4.2) or genitive-marked (§6.4.3) and absolutive arguments (§6.4.1) are co-referential. This means that there is systematic ambiguity between disjoint reference (clauses such as 'he$_1$ saw him$_2$') and coreference (clauses such as 'he$_1$ saw him$_1$'). Many Austronesian and Papuan languages also share this feature.[23]

For example, the bound transitive verb (§5.2.3.2) *bwagee* 'to return (oneself)' is normally used reflexively, as in (230), where the clause *teme bwagee* contains the co-referential subject proclitic (§5.8) *te=* '3SG.SUBJ' and absolutive suffix (§5.7) -*e* '3SG.ABS'.

(230)   *Teme bwagee ai teme,*
        te=me   **bwage-e**   **ai**   **te=me**
        3SG.SUBJ=IRR   return-3SG.ABS   or   3SG.SUBJ=IRR

---

[23] Examples include Nêlêmwa (Bril 2002), Xârâgurè (Moyse-Faurie 2008), Tolai (Mosel 1991), Loniu (Hamel 1994), and Harway (Heine & Miyashita 2008).

teme toveni wayap.

te=me	toveni	wayap
3SG.SUBJ=IRR	finish	war

'He must turn [himself] around or he must, he must end the war.'

Yal-20092011-AW4_0050

In example (231), the free transitive verb (§5.2.3.1) *yala* 'to shake' is used reflexively; the 3PL subject of the second clause (indexed by the 3PL.INDEP pronoun in the first clause) is co-referential with the absolutive suffix *-la* '3PL.ABS'.

(231) ***Ka ô ta la la, ka yalaela la na gawe.***

ka	ô	ta=la	la	ka
LK	REAL	go.UH=NOM	3PL.INDEP	LK

yala-e-<u>la</u>=la	na	gawe
shake-TR-3PL.ABS=LOC	interior	stream

'And they went up and rinsed themselves off in the stream.'

Yal-17072009-TB-weekend_0025

Most transitive verbs can be used reflexively. Table 8 lists some of these verbs which are attested to occur in a reflexive construction, with co-referential subject and absolutive argument.

Tab. 8: Reflexive verbs

Belep	Transitive meaning	Reflexive meaning
pwedee	'to turn sth.'	'to turn oneself'
pwaxa	'to wash sth.'	'to wash oneself'
karo	'to shave sth.'	'to shave oneself'
tawa	'to cut sth.'	'to cut oneself'

Yal-23082010-IM1.wav – Yal-23082010-IM3.wav

Reciprocity uses a different construction; see §5.4.2.

6.10.3 Passives

There is no unique morphological or syntactic passive construction in Belep. An ordinary transitive agent's importance can be downplayed by using a 3PL subject. For example, in (232), the speaker wishes to downplay the subject of the clause, marked with subject proclitic *la=* '3PL.SUBJ'.

(232) *Avar, la tolila li jewe.*
avar   la=   to-li-la=li   jewe
other 3PL.SUBJ=   call-TR-3PL.ABS=GEN   goblin
'The others, they are called *jewe*.' (lit. 'they call them *jewe*')
Yal-11082010-ET2-jewe_0006

If the speaker in (232) had not been trying to downplay the subject, he might have used the subject proclitic *ja=* '1PL.INCL.SUBJ' instead (i.e. to say 'we call them *jewe*'). Another example of the passive meaning is found in (233), where the subject is unimportant; what is important is the woman's marital status.

(233) *La tu buac yinao.*
la=   tu=   buay=i-nao
3PL.SUBJ=   VBLZ=   bride.price=GEN-1SG.ABS
'I am reserved [for marriage].' (lit. 'They have done a *buac* for me'; see §1.3.2)

6.10.4 Quotatives

Belep speakers do not use the verb *âri* 'to say' to quote direct speech. Instead it is used to provide a summary of what was said. In this usage it is followed by a pseudocoordinate clause marked with the linker *ka* (§7.3.1). Examples of this construction are shown in (234) and (235).

(234) *Ka teme âri ka, âlalic ki te, me puae pwâna mwa,*
ka=re=me   âri=xa   âlaliyi=xi=re=   me
LK=3SG.SUBJ=REAL   say=LK   be.impossible=REL=3SG.SUBJ=   IRR

pua-e   pwâna   mwa
open-SPC   hole   house
'And He will say that, He can't open the door,'
Yal-25072010-PT-homily_0051

(235) *te âri ka ave, ka ave keja ka najier,*
te=   âri ka ave=   keja ka naji-er
3SG.SUBJ=   say LK 1DU.EXCL.SUBJ=   run   LK leave-3SG.ABS
'He said that we had, that we had run away and left him,'
Yal-28072010-BGMCG-tahitian_0273-0274

For direct quotatives, Belep speakers predicate a form of the demonstrative pronoun *wa-* 'DEM.MAN' (§4.6.2) with an attached determiner suffix (§4.4.2). This intransitive predicate acts as a nominative verb (§5.2.1) whose S argument indexes the quoted referent. This predication may precede (236) or follow (237) the quoted speech, from which it is separated by an intonation break.

(236) **Texa waak xa Awuli Cabak, « Ho, tuya da lexen ? »**
      te=xa   wa-x=a   Awuli Cabak
      3SG.SUBJ=ADD DEM.MAN-DET.D.PRX=NOM Awuli Cabak

      o   tuya   da=lexen
      hey   EX.GNR what?=DC.A
      'And Awuli Cabak was like, "Hey, what have we here?"'

      Yal-19092011-PA_0022

In (236), the quotative predicate is *waak* 'to be like' (formed from proximal deictic suffix *-k*); while in (237) the quotative predicate is *wali* 'to be like' (with proximal anaphoric suffix *-li*).

(237) **« Name ta ma yavi Kawo, » te wali la teâmaa.**
      na=me   ta   ma yavi   Kawo
      1SG.SUBJ=IRR   go.UH LK4 search.TR   Kawo

      te=   wa-li=la   teâmaa
      3SG.SUBJ=   DEM.MAN-DET.A.PRX=NOM   high.chief
      '"I'm going to go up and search for Kawo," said the chieftain.'

      Yal-20092011-AW1_0276

6.11 Expression of temporal location

The temporal location of an event is not expressed morphologically in Belep; only mood (§5.6) and aspect (§5.5) are valid inflectional categories. If the expression of temporal location is necessary, Belep speakers use a variety of other strategies involving the temporal nouns represented in Table 9.

Tab. 9: Temporal nouns

Belep	English translation	Belep	English translation
âbur	'before'[24]	bwaêdan	'morning'[25]
mon	'after'	taan	'daytime'

---

24 See §4.5.1.
25 Probably from *bwa* 'head' + *êne-* 'reference' + *taan* 'day'.

Belep	English translation	Belep	English translation
naemi	'back in the day'	baraap	'evening'
ule	'long ago'	bwan	'nighttime, darkness'
yak[26]	'yesterday, a few days ago'	bwera pwalaic	'Monday' (lit. 'day one')
yemi	'earlier today'	bwera pwadu	'Tuesday' (lit. 'day two')
yena	'today, now, later'	bwera pwajen	'Wednesday' (lit. 'day three')
iyam	'tomorrow'	bwera pwalavaac	'Thursday' (lit. 'day four')
êne denaar	'hour' (lit. 'sun's reference')	bwera pwanem	'Friday' (lit. 'day five')
gawaar	'(calendar) day'	bwe cavaro	'Saturday' (lit. 'Sabbath day')
mwanok	'moon, month'	bwe cexeen	'Sunday' (lit. 'sacred day')
jao	'year'		

These nouns can serve as predicate nominals, as discussed in (§6.5.1); they can be marked as arguments of a clause with genitive =*li*; they can be marked with adverbial linker *to* 'when' (§7.3.3); or they can be unmarked adverbial modifiers.

In some cases, temporal nouns are used as arguments of a clause, where they are marked with the genitive case marker =*li* or =*i* (§6.4.3). For example, in (238) the temporal noun phrase *gawaarimi la mon* 'the next day' is marked as genitive with =*li*, indicating that it is serving as an oblique argument of the main verb *pa* 'to take'.

(238) ***ava mo pae comu li gawaarimi la mon.***
 ava= mo pa-e comu=li gawari-mi=la mon
 1PL.EXCL.SUBJ= live take-SPC school=GEN day-DET.A.DST=LOC side.DH
 'we had school the next day.'
 Yal-17072009-TB-weekend_0041

In (239), the temporal noun *bwan* 'night' is marked with genitive =*i* and acts as an oblique argument of the verb *puc* 'to fly'.

(239) ***la puc yi bwan,***
 la= puy=i bwan
 3PL.SUBJ= fly=GEN night
 'they fly at night,'
 Yal-20092011-AW5_0116

---

26 *yak* 'yesterday' is homophonous with *ya-k* [DEM.LOC-DET.D.PRX] 'here; this place' (§4.3.2).

When *to* introduces a temporal noun phrase, it adverbially describes the temporal location of the action of the clause.²⁷ For example, in (240), *to* precedes the temporal noun *bwan* 'night', which describes when the action of the clause took place.

(240) **la nginie, la pu ngini cae to bwan.**
la=	**nginie,**	**la=**	**pu=**	**ngini**
3PL.SUBJ=	miss.GNR	3PL.SUBJ=	VOX=	miss.SPC

cae=ro	**bwan**
reef=when	night

'they didn't see it, they just didn't see the reef in the night.'
Yal-20092011-AW2_0036

In (241), the temporal noun is the reduplicated *bwabwaêdan* 'early morning', describing when the action took place.

(241) **Texa noor ra Awuli Cabak to bwabwaêdan,**
te=xa	**nor=a**	**Awuli**	**Cabax=o**
3SG.SUBJ=ADD	awake=NOM	Awuli	Cabak=when

bwa-bwaêdan
REDUP-morning
'And Awuli Cabak woke up early in the morning,'
Yal-19092011-PA_0056-0057

In (242), the temporal noun introduced by *to* is *baraap* 'evening', and in (243) the temporal noun is the dependent possessive noun phrase *bwe cavaro* 'Saturday' (see §4.7).

(242) « **Ai elo, » kaô mae, mae to baraap.**
ai	**elo=xa=ô**	**mae**	**mae=ro**	**baraap**
no	yes=LK=REAL	sleep	sleep=when	evening

'[He said] "Oh, okay," and slept, slept in the evening.'
Yal-05092011-AP1_0071

(243) **Yak to bwe cavaro, avena tu la Awe.**
yaxa=ro	**bwe**	**cavaro**	**avena=**
yesterday=when	moment	sabbath.LN	1TR.EXCL.SUBJ=

---

27 *to* may have originated as a temporal case marker and been extended to use as a linker.

        tu=la   Awe
        go.DH=LOC Awe
        'The other day, Saturday, we went down to Awe.'
Yal-17072009-TB-weekend_0001-0002

Note that *to* cannot be used to introduce a temporal noun referring to a future time (244).

(244)   ***yena=ro**   **baraap**
          now=when   evening
          *'this evening'

          yena=li   **baraap**
          now=GEN   evening
          'this evening, tonight'

Temporal nouns are also used in Belep in adverbial noun phrases which are separated from the main clause by intonation breaks or which are unmarked for case. For example, in (245) the temporal noun phrase *iyam* 'tomorrow' precedes the clause it modifies and is separated from it by an intonation break. In (246) *iyam* follows the clause it modifies; it is unmarked for case.

(245)   « *Iyam, jename tu la Yade.* »
          iyam   jena=me   tu=la   Yade
          tomorrow 1TR.INCL.SUBJ=IRR go.DH=LOC Yade
          '"Tomorrow, we're going to Yade."'
Yal-20092011-AW6_0058

(246)   « *Jena mo pan na Belep iyam.* »
          jena=   mo   pan=a   Beleva iyam.
          1TR.INCL.SUBJ= stay go.TV=LOC Belep   tomorrow
          '"We're going to Belep tomorrow."'
Yal-20092011-AW6_0127

6.12 Comparison

6.12.1 Comparative construction

There are no morphemes used exclusively for comparative constructions in Belep. Instead, two aspectual proclitics (§5.5), *nyi=* 'PUNCT' and *ma=* 'DIM' are used in comparative constructions to mean, respectively, 'more' and 'less'. The Belep comparative construction is represented schematically in Table 10.

Tab. 10: Comparative construction

	MARKER	QUALITY		STANDARD
SUBJ=	[nyi= / ma=]	[VERB]	na=le	[NP]
	more / less		interior=DAT	

As shown in Table 10, the property concept being compared is normally a verb (§6.5.3) which serves as the main verb of the clause. The marker of comparison is an aspectual verb group proclitic. The entity being compared is the subject or topic of the clause, and the standard of comparison is marked in the dative case (§6.4.4) after the noun *na-* 'interior'.

An example of this construction is found in the constructed example in (247). The topic is *tolamiik* 'this basket'. The aspectual proclitic *ma=* 'DIM' attached to the verb *mama* 'to be light' marks it as 'less than' the standard of comparison *nyak* 'this one', marked as dative.

(247) **Tolamiik, ka te ma mama na le nyak.**
tolami-x=a=re=   **ma=**   **mama**   **na=le**
basket-DET.D.PRX=LK=3SG.SUBJ=   DIM=   be.light   interior=DAT

nya-k
DEM.IDF-DET.D.PRX
'This basket, it's less light than that one.'
                           Yal-05102010-PT1.wav – Yal-05102010-PT3.wav

In the constructed example in (248), the subject *wêgan* 'her mercy' is compared to the standard, indexed by the dative-marked 3PL pronoun. The aspectual proclitic *nyi=* 'PUNCT' marks the verb *ô* 'to be good' as 'more than' the standard of comparison.

(248) **Ba pwadu, ka te nyi ô la wêgan na lela.**
ba=   **pwadu**   **ka=re=**   **nyi=**   **ô=la**   **wêga-n**
ORD=   two   LK=3SG.SUBJ=   PUNCT=   be.good=NOM   mercy-3SG.POSS

na=le-la
interior=DAT-3PL.POSS
'The second one, she's nicer than the others.' (lit. 'Her mercy is more good than them.')
                           Yal-05102010-PT1.wav – Yal-05102010-PT3.wav

Comparative constructions are very rare in my corpus. Example (249) shows the use of *nyi=* 'PUNCT' to indicate a comparison in line 2.

(249) *Ô âri koxo li lami pwai ci,*
ô âri= koxo=li la-mi pwai ci
REAL NEG= many=GEN DEM.PL-DET.A.DST only sit

lami molep, toma nyi koxo li lami maac.
la-mi molep *toma nyi=* *koxo=li*
DEM.PL-DET.A.DST alive but PUNCT= many=GEN

la-mi maac
DEM.PL-DET.A.DST die
'Those still alive were not many, while those who were dead were much more numerous.'
Yal-28072010-BGMCG-sousmarin_0107-0108

6.12.2 Expression of similarity

Expression of similarity in Belep is a highly productive and idiomatic discourse phenomenon using mostly the two morphemes *wa-* 'DEM.MAN' (4.2.2) and *ma-*, a class 1 noun (§4.2.1.1) meaning 'similarity'.[28]

As mentioned in §4.6.2, *wa-* 'DEM.MAN' can be used adverbially, as in (250). It can also serve as a nominative predicate (§5.2.1), as in (251), and a subset of these uses are quotative (see §6.10.4).

(250) *calayi doo wana,*
calayi doo **wa-na**
brush.TR earth DEM.MAN-DET.D.MPX
'[until it] brushed the earth like that,'
Yal-28072010-BGMCG-hamecon_0027

(251) *Texa waak xie.*
te=xa **wa-x=i-e**
3SG.SUBJ=ADD DEM.MAN-DET.D.PRX=GEN-3SG.ABS
'And he did like that to him.'
Yal-28072010-BGMCG-tahitian_0263

In usages such as in line 3 of (252), *wa-* has an epistemic meaning, indicating that the events recounted by the speaker are merely his understanding.

---

28 The class 1 noun *ma-* 'similarity' is most likely the origin of the linker *ma* (§7.3.1).

(252) BG: *laô wanem vaer ri ...janu,*
 la=ô wane=va-er=i janu
 3PL.SUBJ=REAL walk=INSTR-3SG.ABS=GEN spirit
 '[they] were walking with him, ...the spirits,'

 CG: *ulayama,*
 ulaya-ma
 old.man-AC
 'ancestors,'

 BG: *Êê, ulayama. Texa wali.*
 êê ulaya-ma te=xa wa-li
 yes old.man-AC 3SG.SUBJ=ADD DEM.MAN-DET.A.PRX
 'Yes, the ancestors. That's what it was like.'
 Yal-28072010-BGMCG-tahitian_0299-0301

The predicated form of *wa-* is also used transitively to express similarity, as in (253) - (255). In these examples, the noun phrase headed by the class 1 noun *ma-* 'similarity' acts as the P argument of the transitive clause. For example, in (253), the P argument is *ma Teâ Belep* 'like Teâ Belep'.

(253) *Te wali ma Teâ Belep.*
 te= wa-li ma Teâ Belep
 3SG.SUBJ= DEM.MAN-DET.A.PRX similarity Teâ Belep
 'He was like Teâ Belep.'
 Yal-20092011-AW4_0030

If the standard of comparison is pronominal, a possessive suffix (§4.2.2.2) is used, as in (254).

(254) *Te wali maamw.*
 te= wa-li maa-mw
 3SG.SUBJ= DEM.MAN-DET.A.PRX similarity-2SG.POSS
 'S/he is like you.' or 'S/he looks like you.'

Most commonly, the generic 3SG possessive suffix is used, e.g. in (255), where it is followed by the morpheme *=li* 'GEN' and a semantically dependent clause (§7.3.7). This construction is used to decrease the speaker's epistemic attachment to a clause.

(255) *Êê, te wali maar ri te dadabwa.*
 êê te= wa-li ma-r=i
 yes 3SG.SUBJ= DEM.MAN-DET.A.PRX similarity-3GNR.POSS=GEN

te=	dadabwa
3SG.SUBJ=	be.black
'Yeah, he was, like, black.'	Yal-28072010-BGMCG-tahitian_0205

Note that for some speakers, expressions of similarity have lexicalized. Some younger speakers argue that *walima* is a transitive verb meaning 'to resemble'; it may also be produced [wanĩmã]. The root *ma-* 'similarity' can also be found in the nominative intransitive verb *maraic* 'to be the same', as in (256).

(256) ***Toma Teâ Belevale, le pe maraic, le pe Or.***
 toma Teâ Beleva-le le= pe= maraic le= pe= Or
 but Teâ Belep-pair 3DU.SUBJ= RECP= be.same 3DU.SUBJ= RECP= spill
 'But he and Teâ Belep, they were the same, they were both Or [phratry].'
 Yal-20092011-AW3_0026

6.13 Summary

In this chapter, I have discussed basic Belep VOS word order (§6.2) and Belep's argument structure (§6.3), which is split-intransitive where P is indefinite and a combination of split-intransitive and tripartite where P is definite. Case (including nominative, genitive, dative, locative, and instrumental) is marked in Belep with ditropic clitics (§6.4); absolutive case is unmarked. Some non-prototypical clauses (§6.5) use a predicate nominal, while others use an intransitive verb which requires an absolutive argument. In terms of question formation (§6.6), yes-no questions are formed using rising intonation, while question-word questions use a variety of strategies which strongly favor predication of the questioned element, including some interrogative verbs. There is no morphology that is unique to imperatives, while prohibitives are formed using a set of verb group proclitics (§6.7). Regular predicate negation is accomplished using a verb group proclitic; there are also some inherently negative verbs (§6.8). Topicalized noun phrases occur at the beginning of a clause and are usually followed by an intonation break; focalization is indicated by a clitic within the verb group (§6.9). Discussions of periphrastic constructions to indicate voice (§6.10) and tense (§6.11), as well as a discussion of comparatives (§6.12) concluded the chapter.

7 Clause combining

7.1 Introduction

Cross-linguistically, there are a number of ways that clauses can be combined with one another to form more complex constructions. These combinations of clauses can be arranged on a continuum of dependency, where the most independent clauses are identified as coordinate[1] and the most dependent clauses are identified as subordinate. Complement clauses[2] and relative clauses[3] are typically categorized as types of subordinate clauses, while adverbial clauses[4] are characterized as being somewhat more independent (Lehmann 1988, Dixon 2006, Thompson et al. 2007).

In Belep, both coordinate (§7.2) and relative clause (§7.4) constructions are present. The question of the existence of complement clause constructions in Belep is much more problematic. Dixon (1995) argues that complementation is not a linguistic universal, being "common among the languages of Europe, Oceania and Africa but rare in those of Australia and South America" (Dixon 1995:183). Languages which lack complementation, however, "still do have some grammatical mechanism for stating what a proposition is which is seen, heard, believed, known, liked, etc. These mechanisms are called complementation strategies" (Dixon 2006:1). In Belep, there are no clear instances of complementation where a clause acts as an argument of a predicate. Instead, there are a number of complementation strategies, which indicate a semantic relationship without any markers of morphosyntactic dependency. Belep complementation strategies, and evidence for a lack of a true complement clause construction, will be discussed in §7.3. Belep adverbial clauses are typically accomplished with complementation strategies as well; see especially the sections on purpose clauses (§7.3.2.1), reason clauses (§7.3.8), conditional clauses (§7.3.4), and general adverbials (§7.3.3).

---

[1] Coordinate constructions are defined as those where two or more clauses "are combined into a larger unit and still have the same semantic relations with other surrounding elements" (Haspelmath 2007:1).
[2] Complement clauses are defined by "the syntactic situation that arises when a notional sentence or predication is an argument of a predicate" (Noonan 2007:52).
[3] Relativization is defined as a construction whereby a clause becomes part of a noun phrase (Keenan & Comrie 1977:67).
[4] Adverbial clauses are defined as clauses "which function as modifiers of verb phrases or entire clauses" (Thompson et al. 2007: 238). They may include clauses of time, manner, purpose, reason, condition, etc.

Some combinations of clauses in Belep use case markers (§6.4) or determiner suffixes (§4.4.2) as morphosyntactic indicators.[5] However, most coordinate constructions, complementation strategies, and relative clause constructions in Belep are accomplished by means of linkers, a Belep word class (§3.3.4). Belep linkers precede the constituent that they mark as coordinated or semantically dependent. Most linkers are capable of marking either a clause or a noun phrase (in the latter case, they function as discourse markers); this chapter gives many examples of both uses. Many linkers are simple clitics (Zwicky 1977), such that they have both a full and an encliticized form. The linkers used in clause-combining are represented in Table 1. Note that disjunctive linker *ai*, additive linker *ka*, and purpose clause marker *ma* also have roles in noun phrase conjunction (§4.5).

Tab. 1: Linkers used in combining clauses and noun phrases

Form	Gloss	Functions related to combining clauses and noun phrases
ai	'or'	disjunctive linker
enyi (enyixi)	'if'	conditional linker
ka, =xa	'LK'	conjunctive linker, topicalizer, pseudocoordinator
ka me	'then'	sequential linker
kara	'well'	evidential linker
ki, =xi	'REL'	deontic linker, relativizer
ma	'LK4'	purpose clause pseudocoordinator, correlational linker
mo	'LK3'	causal linker
to, =ro	'when'	adverbial linker
toma, =roma	'but'	adversative linker

7.2 Clausal coordination

Clausal coordinate constructions are described as those constructions where one clause "is linked to a second clause...each of which can stand by itself" (Dixon 2006:2), with the "optional omission of some material that would have been repeated. The non-identical material in the two original sentences [is] called the **coordinands**" (Drellishak 2004:17, emphasis in original). Conjunction, disjunction, causal coordination, and adversative coordination are the four basic types of clausal coordination

---

[5] Belep makes no distinction between finite and non-finite clauses in clause combining because there are no non-finite verbs in Belep (with the possible exception of those marked with *ba=*; see §5.5.3).

which are normally distinguished cross-linguistically (Haspelmath 2004:5-6). Coordination strategies can be grouped into asyndetic—lacking an overt coordinating morpheme—or syndetic, where the coordinating morpheme is called a coordinator (Haspelmath 2007:6).

In Belep, both asyndetic and syndetic coordination occur. Example (1) shows an instance of asyndetic coordination, also called juxtaposition (Drellishak 2004).

(1) *Te ta la teâmaa la Yade, te tu la tamwa pwalaic.*
te=	ta=la	teâma=la	Yade
3SG.SUBJ=	go.UH=NOM	high.chief=LOC	Yade

te=	tu=la	tamwa	pwalaic
3SG.SUBJ=	go.DH=LOC	woman	one

   'The chieftain of Yade went up, a woman went down.'
   Yal-20092011-AW6_0080-0081

In Belep, syndetic coordination is vastly more common than juxtaposition and can be characterized as monosyndetic—using only one coordinator which is prepositive on the second coordinand (as defined by Haspelmath 2007:6). For example, in (2), the first coordinand *le ca ta la na toop* 'they would go up to the fields' is not marked with a coordinator, while coordinator *ka* is prepositive on the second coordinand, *le ca tu la bwe mar* 'they would go down to the seashore'.

(2) *Le ca ta la na toop, ka le ca tu la bwe mar.*
le=	ca=	ta=la	na	toop
3DU.SUBJ=	ITER=	go.UH=LOC	interior	field

ka	le=	ca=	tu=la	bwe	mar
LK	3DU.SUBJ=	ITER=	go.DH=LOC	top	seashore

   'They would go up to the fields, and they would go down to the seashore.'
   Yal-19092011-PA_0005

The Belep coordinators all fall into the word class of linkers (§3.3.4). The most common coordinator is the conjunctive linker *ka* 'and', which has many functions (§7.2.1). Other coordinating linkers include disjunctive linker *ai* 'or' (§7.2.2), causal linker *mo* 'for' (§7.2.3), adversative linker *toma* 'but' (§7.2.4), and evidential linker *kara* 'well' (§7.2.5). See §4.5 for a description of noun phrase coordination.

7.2.1 Conjunctive linker *ka*

Conjunctive linker *ka*, glossed 'LK', is the most common and most versatile linker in Belep, where it primarily indicates "'And'-coordination" as described by Haspelmath (2007:1)—that is, coordination in which both of the coordinands are conceptualized as true. It is used in noun phrase coordination (see §4.5.3) and clausal pseudocoordination (§7.3.1), as well as clausal coordination where it conjoins events (§7.2.1.1) and topic-comment coordinands (§7.2.1.2). In these uses, *ka* is a simple clitic (Zwicky 1977), having both a free form *ka* and an encliticized form *=xa*;[6] speakers say that these forms are interchangeable. For example, both the free form *ka* in (3) and the encliticized form *=xa* in (4) may be used without a noticeable difference in meaning.

(3)   *Texa ta ka mu la mayariik xi pwemwa.*
       te=xa   ta   ka   mu=la
       3SG.SUBJ=ADD   go.UH   LK   moor=LOC

       maya-ri-x=i   pwemwa
       part-3GNR.POSS-DET.D.PRX=GEN   village
       'And he went up and moored on this side of the country.'
                                                                  Yal-20092011-AW3_0047

(4)   *Teô tu ka înae yadan,*
       te=ô   tu=xa   îna-e   yada-n
       3SG.SUBJ=REAL   go.DH=LK   make-SPC   belongings-3SG.POSS
       'He went down and did his magic,'
                                         Yal-28072010-BGMCG-sousmarin_0052-0053

Another clearly related form is the verb group (§5.3) additive clitic *=xa*, always glossed 'ADD', which is used in clausal coordination but which can never be interchanged with *ka*. Its use in coordination will be discussed in (§7.2.1.3).

7.2.1.1 Event coordinator *ka* 'and'
The most common use for *ka* is to conjoin predicates and clauses. This can occur conjoining several verbs, as in (5) - (7). In (5) below, *ka* conjoins the two verbs *cao* 'to work' and *pa=me* 'to come'.

---

[6] Note that, though the encliticized form *=xa* is phonologically bound to the element that precedes it, it is syntactically bound to the clause that follows it and still qualifies as prepositive on the second coordinand, according to Haspelmath's (2007:6) definition. This is not uncommon elsewhere in Belep; see §6.4.

(5) **Te cao, ka pame,**
 te= cao ka pa=me
 3PL.SUBJ= work LK go.TV=CTP
 'She worked, and came,'
 Yal-28072010-BGMCG-tayamu_0091

In (6), *ka* conjoins the verbs *wiu* 'to dine' and *wânem* 'to walk'.

(6) **Teô wiu, kaô wânem.**
 te=ô wiu ka=ô wânem
 3SG.SUBJ=REAL dine LK=REAL walk
 'He dined, and walked.'
 Yal-05092011-AP1_0038

In (7), *ka* conjoins the verbs *ci* 'to sit' and *no=du=me* 'to peer'.

(7) **La ci ka nodume,**
 la= ci ka no=du=me
 3PL.SUBJ= sit LK peer=DIR.DH=CTP
 'They sat and peered down here,'
 Yal-20092011-AW3_0045

Examples (8) and (9) below show the use of *ka* to conjoin multiple verb phrases. In (8), the verb phrases *texa maac yi cawi* 'he was hungry', *bae noli* 'ate that fish', and *bae wagale* 'ate their boat' (indicated by brackets) are conjoined with *ka*.

(8) **Ka mon, texa maac yi cawi**
 ka mon {te=xa may=i cawi}
 LK side.DH 3SG.SUBJ=ADD die=GEN hunger

 ka bae noli, ka bae wagale,
 ka {bae no-li} ka {bae waga-le}
 LK bite fish-DET.A.PRX LK bite boat-3DU.POSS
 'And then, he was hungry and ate[7] that fish, and ate their boat,'
 Yal-01082010-MFD_0012-0013

In (9), the verb phrases *uya la na mwa* 'leave the house', *tu la pao* 'go outdoors', *tu* 'go down', *mae* 'sleep', and *tale talan* 'make his bed' are all conjoined with *ka*.

---

[7] Belep verb *wiu* 'to dine' is intransitive (§5.2.1), while verb *bae* 'to bite' is transitive (§5.2.3.1). Both may be translated into English as 'to eat'.

(9) **Texa, teme uya la na mwa,**
      te=xa   te=me   uya=la   na   mwa
      3SG.SUBJ=ADD   3SG.SUBJ=IRR   appear=LOC   interior   house

      ka tu la pao.
      ka   tu=la   pao
      LK   go.DH=LOC   outdoors

      Ka me tu ka mae, tale talan ka mae.
      ka me   tu   ka   mae   tale   tala-n   ka   mae
      then   go.DH   LK   sleep   cover   bed-3SG.POSS   LK   sleep
      'And he, he would leave[8] the house, and go outdoors. And would go down and sleep, prepare his bed and sleep.'
                                                            Yal-28072010-BGMCG-lune_0011-0013

When *ka* is used to conjoin two or more predicates or clauses, it is unusual to use a subject agreement proclitic on any clause but the initial one;[9] this holds for both same-subject and different-subject coordination.

In same-subject coordination with *ka*, the subject proclitic is usually either omitted from the second clause (10), or the additive clause-chaining enclitic =*xa* (§7.2.1.3) is used (11) instead of *ka*. Example (12), where the second of the clauses conjoined with *ka* contains a subject agreement proclitic, was judged ungrammatical by one speaker, although as noted above such constructions are (occasionally) found in naturally-occurring discourse.

(10) **Na ta ka wiu.**
       na=   ta   ka   wiu
       1SG.SUBJ=   go.UH   LK   dine
       'I go up and dine.'
                                                 Yal-03112011-IM1.wav – Yal-03112011-IM2.wav

---

8 The Belep word *uya* is usually glossed 'to arrive' in deference to speakers' typical French gloss *arriver* 'to arrive, to happen'; however a more accurate gloss would be 'to cross a boundary into the speaker's view; appear'. Its opposite, *nam* 'to disappear', is more accurately glossed 'to cross a boundary and leave the speaker's view'. In example (9), the speaker makes his bed outside so that he can watch the moon.

9 See examples (2), (15), (23), and (44) in this chapter for examples of subject agreement proclitics on coordinands other than the first coordinand.

(11)   **Na ta, naxa wiu.**
       na=   ta   na=xa   wiu
       1SG.SUBJ= go.UH   1SG.SUBJ=ADD   dine
       'I go up, and I dine.'[10]

(12)   *****na=**   ta   ka   na=   wiu
       1SG.SUBJ= go.UH   LK   1SG.SUBJ= dine
       *'I go up and I dine'
                                      Yal-03112011-IM1.wav – Yal-03112011-IM2.wav

In different-subject coordination, speakers typically use the additive clause-chaining enclitic =xa (§7.2.1.3) as shown in (13); the use of ka 'LK' was judged ungrammatical by one speaker in example (14), although again note that this does occasionally occur in natural discourse (15).

(13)   **Na ta, texa wiu.**
       na=   ta   te=xa   wiu
       1SG.SUBJ= go.UH   3SG.SUBJ=ADD   dine
       'I go up, and s/he dines.'[11]
                                      Yal-03112011-IM1.wav – Yal-03112011-IM2.wav

(14)   *****na=**   ta   ka   te=   wiu
       1SG.SUBJ= go.UH   LK   3SG.SUBJ= dine
       *'I go up and s/he dines'
                                      Yal-03112011-IM1.wav – Yal-03112011-IM2.wav

---

10 This clause was not checked for grammaticality with a native speaker; however, similar clauses appear in my corpus. For example:
Na taic, naxa waak, na= ta=ic na=xa waa-k
1SG.SUBJ=go.UH=CTF 1SG.SUBJ=ADD DEM.MAN-DET.D.PRX
'I went up, and I said,'
                                      Yal-28072010-BGMCG-tahitian_0073

11 This clause was not checked for grammaticality with a native speaker; however, similar clauses appear in my corpus. In the example below, the 3SG subject proclitic te= occurs twice; the first time, it indexes a pirogue, while the second time it indexes the chieftain. In the second instance, additive enclitic =xa is used rather than conjunctive linker ka.
Nyami teme cavac, texa kuar ra teâmaa.
nya-mi te=me cavac te=xa kuar=a teâmaa
DEM.IDF-DET.A.DST 3SG.SUBJ=IRR depart 3SG.SUBJ=ADD not.want=NOM high.chief
'When it₁ [the pirogue] left, the chieftainⱼ didn't want it to.'
                                      Yal-20092011-AW2_0019

(15) **Lexa ta ka la to ji âjuma.**
   le=xa   ta=xa   la=   to ji âju-ma
   3DU.SUBJ=ADD go.UH=LK 3PL.SUBJ= call give person-AC
   'They [2] went up and they [pl.] called the people.'
                         Yal-20092011-AW1_0050

7.2.1.2 *ka* in topicalization

Linker *ka* also serves the function of linking a topic and a comment. In (16), the Topic + *ka* + Comment structure is used twice: *ka* follows the topic *âyimi ulac* 'the oldest boy' to introduce the comment *naran ni Teâ* 'his name was Teâ'; then *ka* follows the topic *ba pwadu* 'the second [boy]' to introduce the comment *mweyau* '[it was] Mweyau.'

(16) **Âyimi ulac, ka naran ni Teâ.**
   âyi-mi   ulac ka nara-n=i   Teâ
   man-DET.A.DST be.old LK name-3SG.POSS=GEN Teâ

   Ka ba pwadu, ka Mweyau.
   ka ba= pwadu ka Mweyau
   LK ORD= two   LK Mweyau
   'The oldest boy, his name was Teâ. And the second, it was Mweyau.'
                    Yal-20092011-AW1_0014-0016

In (17), *ka* links the topic *uvi* 'yams' with the comment *te tao ci lexeda* 'they were still sitting up there'.

(17) **Toma uvi, ka te tao ci lexeda.**
   toma uvi ka=re   tao= ci=lexeda
   but   yam LK=3SG.SUBJ HAB= sit=UH
   'But the yams, they[12] were still sitting up there.'
                  Yal-28072010-BGMCG-igname_0077

In (18), *ka* links the topic *âju* 'people' with the comment *jago la Ono* 'there were many at Ono.'

---

12 Nouns are not marked for number in Belep (§4.3); *uvi* 'yam' in example (17) refers back to *wela uvi* 'their yams (to eat)' (see §4.2.4), which is translated into English as a plural noun.

(18)   *Toma âju, ka jago la Ono.*
         toma   âju   ka   jago=la   Ono
         but   person   LK   many=LOC   Ono
         'But the people, there were a lot of them at Ono.'
                                    Yal-28072010-BGMCG-sousmarin_0072

In (19), *ka* appears twice: in line 1, it appears in its encliticized form linking the topic *na bwe Grande-Terre* 'on the Mainland' with the comment *Belep* 'it's Belep'; in line 2, *ka* appears in its full form linking the topic *na lexeng* 'here' with the comment *Bewa* 'it's Bewa'.

(19)   *Toma, na bwe Grande-Terre ka Belep.*
         toma   na   bwe   [grandtɛr]=xa   Belep
         but   interior top   Mainland.LN=LK   Belep
         'But, on the Mainland, it [the name of the yam species] is Belep.'

2   *Toma na lexeng ka Bewa.*
         toma   na=lexeng   ka   Bewa
         but   interior=DC   LK   Bewa
         'But here, it's Bewa.'
                                    Yal-28072010-BGMCG-igname_0089-0092

7.2.1.3 Additive =*xa* 'ADD' in clause chaining

As discussed above in §7.2.1.1 and §7.2.1.2, the conjunctive linker *ka* 'LK', which serves as a prepositive coordinator on the second coordinand in clausal conjunction, is a simple clitic with free and bound forms. The additive verb group clitic =*xa* 'ADD', though clearly etymologically related to the conjunctive linker, has a separate use and function. Occurring only bound within the verb group preface (§5.3), additive =*xa* 'ADD' is not interchangeable with the form *ka*, which is ungrammatical in this position.[13] In these instances, =*xa* is encliticized to the subject agreement proclitic, creating a phonological word completely made up of clitics (§3.2.2.6). It is not uncommon for a coordinator of this sort to come in second position.[14]

The primary use of the verb group additive clitic =*xa* 'ADD' is in clause-chaining, the creation of a sequencing link with the clause that preceded it. Unlike coordination with *ka* (§7.2.1.1), clauses chained with additive =*xa* may alternate or recycle the subject agreement proclitic. For example, in (20), two clauses with different subject

---

13 Additive =*xa* also occurs as a focus enclitic (see §6.9.2.2).
14 This may occur in OV languages such as Latin (Gildersleeve & Lodge 2003:300) and Turkish (Kornfilt 1997:120) as well as in VO languages such as Yoruba (Payne 1997:338).

agreement proclitics are chained using enclitic =*xa* after the second subject agreement proclitic; no *ka* is used to conjoin them.

(20) **Te pae fusil sous-marin nie, avenaxa pan.**
    te=   pa-e   [pyzisumarɪn]=i-e
    3SG.SUBJ= take-SPC underwater.speargun.LN=GEN-3SG.ABS

    avena=xa   pan
    3TRI.SUBJ=ADD go.TV
    'He took his underwater speargun; and we went on.'
                                        Yal-28072010-BGMCG-tahitian_0020-0021

In example (21), the subject and topic of lines 1-3 is one character (Coigo), but in line 4 the speaker changes the subject of the narration to a different character (Belep). As this switch in topic occurs, the speaker uses =*xa* on the new subject agreement proclitic, signaling a new chaining element.

(21) **te înae yadan,**
    te=   îna-e   yada-n
    3SG.SUBJ= make-SPEC belongings-3SG.POSS

2   **panang, panang ngie, te înae.**
    panang   panang=i-e   te=   îna-e
    sorcery   sorcery=GEN-3SG.ABS 3SG.SUBJ= make-SPC

3   **Te înae ma teme maac ya Belep.**
    te=   îna-e   ma=re=me   may=a   Belep
    3SG.SUBJ= make-SPC LK4=3SG.SUBJ=IRR die=NOM Belep

4   **Texa, Belep, âri te êna,**
    te=xa   Belep   âri=   te=   êna
    3SG.SUBJ=ADD Belep   NEG=   3SG.SUBJ= know.GNR
    'he [Coigo] did his thing, sorcery, his sorcery—he did it. He did it so that Belep would die. And he, Belep, he didn't know.'
                                        Yal-20092011-AW6_0026-0028

In example (22), =*xa* is used to chain multiple clauses with the same subject.

(22)   *Avaxaô wiu baraap,*
       ava=xa=ô   **wiu**   **baraap**
       1PL.EXCL.SUBJ=ADD=REAL   dine   evening

       avaxaô pe ka,
       ava=xa=ô   **pe=**   **ka**
       1PL.EXCL.SUBJ=ADD=REAL   RECP=   shatter
       'And we had dinner, and we separated,'
                                 Yal-17072009-TB-weekend_0027-0028

In (22), the same subject agreement proclitic is repeated twice with *=xa* encliticized to it, though it always refers to the same referent. Example (23) below shows the differing uses of the additive linker and enclitic in clausal conjunction and chaining. It illustrates a point of possible confusion for the listener and immediate clarification by the speaker.

(23)   *To jier ka tame ka lexa wiu. Le puer ka lena wiu.*
       to   **ji-er**   **ka**   **ta=me**   **ka**   **le=xa**   **wiu**
       call   give-3SG.ABS   LK   go.UH=CTP   LK   3DU.SUBJ=ADD   dine

       le=   **puer**   **ka**   **lena=**   **wiu**
       3DU.SUBJ=   cook   LK   3PA.SUBJ=   dine
       '[Cebaba] called her [Kawo] and [she] came and they [2] dined. They [2] cooked and they [3] dined.'
                                                   Yal-20092011-AW1_0145

In (23), the speaker is telling a story about a man named Cebaba who is living with his grown daughter. As Cebaba woos a new wife, Kawo, the speaker narrates that *to jier* '[he] called her [Kawo]' and *tame* '[she] came'—these two clauses are conjoined with *ka*. Then the speaker adds that *lexa wiu* 'they [2] dined'. In this part of the story, enclitic *=xa* is used to indicate that the subject has changed, while events are still occurring sequentially. The next line *le puer ka lena wiu* 'they [2] cooked and they [3] dined' is a clarification: it is unclear which two of the three active participants (Cebaba, his daughter, and Kawo) did the dining, and the speaker clarifies that it was Kawo and the daughter who prepared food and the three of them who ate it. This instance is an exception to the observation that two clauses with different subject agreement proclitics are not generally conjoined with *ka*; it is likely allowed in this instance because the participants to which the two pronominals refer significantly overlap.

While it is clear that *=xa* 'ADD' has an important role in clausal coordination, the difference in meaning between use of *=xa* and use of conjunctive linker *ka*—as demonstrated by the availability of both (10) and (11) above—is unknown.

7.2.2 Disjunctive linker *ai* 'or'

The disjunctive linker *ai* 'or' is used in disjunctive clausal coordination—that is, coordination where only one of the coordinands is conceptualized as true—as well as in disjunctive noun phrase coordination (see §4.5.4). In example (24), *ai* conjoins the noun phrases *yo* '2SG.INDEP' and *ti* 'who?'.

(24)   ***Jua yo ai ti? Kawo?***
        jua   yo   ai   ti   Kawo
        truly   2SG.INDEP   or   who?   Kawo
        'Is it really you or who? Kawo?'
                                                                            Yal-20092011-AW1_0282

In example (25), *ai* conjoins the clauses *tu ma âvae no* 'go down and catch fish' and *tu ma pae weji ânemar* 'go down and get some troca to eat'.

(25)   ***Tu ma âvae no,***
        tu   ma   âva-e   no
        go.DH   LK4   fish.for-SPC   fish

        ai tu ma pae weji ânemar.
        ai   tu   ma   pa-e   we-ji   ânemar
        or   go.DH   LK4   take-SPC   food-1DU.INCL.POSS   top.snail
        'Go down to catch fish, or go down to get some troca[15] to eat.'
                                                                           Yal-20092011-AW1_0065

In example (26), *ai* coordinates the clauses *teme bwagee* 'he must turn around' and *teme toveni wayap* 'he must end the war'.

(26)   ***Teme bwagee ai teme,***
        te=me   bwage-e   ai   te=me
        3SG.SUBJ=IRR   return-3SG.ABS   or   3SG.SUBJ=IRR

        teme toveni wayap.
        te=me   toveni   wayap
        3SG.SUBJ=IRR   finish   war
        'He must turn around or he must, he must end the war.'
                                                                   Yal-20092011-AW4_0050

---

15   See §4.2.4 on noun classifiers.

A phonologically reduced form of disjunctive linker *ai, ei*, is used as a final tag for yes-no questions, or to elicit feedback from the listener (§6.5.1). Note that the disjunctive linker *ai* 'or' is segmentally indistinguishable from the discourse marker *ai* 'no'; however, the discourse marker receives stress and undergoes stress-induced lengthening, while the linker is unstressed.

7.2.3 Causal linker *mo* 'for'

Causal linker *mo*, glossed 'LK3', is used most basically in clausal coordination. As a prepositive coordinator on the second coordinand (according to Haspelmath's (2007:6) definition), *mo* links two predications which bear some causal or correlative relationship. Neither clause is grammatically subordinate to the other—both are fully independent clauses. The clause introduced by *mo* may provide a purpose, a reason, an excuse, or an alternative. For example, in (27), the *mo*-clause *te mwany nya doo* 'the earth is bad' is provided as an explanation for why it is *âlalic* 'impossible' to plant crops there.

(27) **Âlalic, mo te, te mwany nya doo.**
âlalic   mo=re   te=   mwany=a   doo
impossible   LK3=3SG.SUBJ   3SG.SUBJ=   be.bad=NOM   earth
'It's impossible, for the, the earth is bad.'
                                                Yal-20092011-AW6_0116

In (28), the clause introduced by *mo* provides an explanation for the listener's expected question.

(28) **Âri te baele mo te tele.**
âri=   te=   bae-le   mo=re   te-le
NEG=   3SG.SUBJ=   bite-3DU.ABS   LK3=3SG.SUBJ   plant-3DU.ABS
'He didn't eat them for he planted them.'
                                            Yal-28072010-BGMCG-lune_0047

In (28), the *mo*-clause *te tele* 'he planted them' is provided as an explanation for *âri te baele* 'he didn't eat them'. In (29), *mo* introduces only a noun phrase, *buâny* 'stones', which provides the explanation for *âlalic* 'it's impossible'.

(29) **Yuu, mais âlalic, mo buâny.**
yu-u   mais   âlalic   mo   buâny
dig-DETR   but.LN   impossible   LK3   stone
'[They] dug up everything, but it was impossible because of the stones.'
                                        Yal-28072010-BGMCG-sousmarin_0111

In example (30), the *mo*-clause *ji âma avan* 'we are brothers' provides an explanation for *na kuar ri ji wayap* 'I don't want us to make war'.

(30) « *Ai, na kuar ri ji wayap, mo ji, ji mewu, ji âma avan.* »

ai   na=   kuar=i   ji=   wayap   mo
no   1SG.SUBJ= not.want=GEN   1DU.INCL.SUBJ=   make.war   LK3

ji   ji=   mewu
1DU.INCL.INDEP   1DU.INCL.SUBJ=   genus

ji=   âma=   ava-n
1DU.INCL.SUBJ=   DYAD=   sibling-3SG.POSS

'"No, I don't want us to make war, for we, we are the same, we are brothers."'

Yal-20092011-AW4_0033

In addition to the clausal coordination function of *mo*, it also serves to introduce clauses or noun phrases which provide an explanation. At the beginning of an intonation unit, *mo* serves as a discourse marker indicating that the purpose of what follows is to answer a potential question of the listener's. In (31), it occurs twice, in lines 2 and 4.

(31) BG: *Era bwa mo la,*

         era   bwa=   mo=la
         DEM.PRES   CONT=   live=LOC
         'He was still living at –'

2 CG: *Ai, mo bwa tuu lexedu la na yewarili.*

         ai   mo   bwa=   tu=lexedu=la
         no   LK3   CONT=   EX.SPC=LOC.DH=LOC

3   na   yewa-ri-li
         interior   time-3GNR.POSS-DET.A.PRX
         'No, for there still were some down there back then.'

4   BG: *Êê, mo puur ri âmi la bwa modame la yak xa Wayibole.*

                êê   mo   pu-r=i   â-mi
                yes   LK3   origin-3GNR.POSS=GEN   DEM.NEW-DET.A.DST

                la=   bwa=   mo=da=me=la
                3PL.SUBJ= CONT=   live=DIR.UH=CTP=LOC

                ya-x=a   Wayibole
                DEM.LOC-DET.D.PRX=LOC Wayibole
                'Yeah but, because they were still living up here at Wayibole.'

                                        Yal-28072010-BGMCG-sousmarin_0102

In (31), *mo* is used at the beginning of an intonation unit in lines 2 and 4, where it introduces a clause which explains the reason for the speaker's disagreement. In (32), *mo* is used to introduce the noun phrase answer to a question-word question.

(32)   *Ti li âmi kawu Fédération ?*
         ti=li   â-mi   kawu   fédération
         who=GEN   DEM.NEW-DET.A.DST guardian   Federation.LN
         'Who is the president of the [Women's] Federation?'

         Mo Larisa.
         mo   Larisa
         LK3   Larisa
         'It's Larisa.'
                                  Yal-05102010-PT1.wav – Yal-05102010-PT3.wav

In (33), after a digression to explain the habits and appearance of *kawina* 'firefly', the speaker returns to the topic of his story with a clause prefaced by *mo*.

(33)   *Kara mo yer, te câye, nyan, ka kawina.*
         kara   mo   yer   te=   câye
         well   LK3   3SG.INDEP   3SG.SUBJ= change

         nya-n   ka   kawina
         mother-3SG.POSS.SPC LK   firefly
         'Well, so she, she changed, his mother did, into a firefly.'
                                               Yal-20092011-AW5_0116

In general, in both its clausal coordination and its discourse marking functions, *mo* is characterized as introducing an explanatory or clarifying predication. Its likely etymological origin is the full verb *mo* 'to live, to stay' and it is likely also related to the modal use of *mo* in a serial verb construction (§5.10.3).

7.2.4 Adversative linker *toma* 'but'

Adversative linker *toma* 'but' is used to introduce a contrasting or unexpected element, whether a noun phrase or a clause. In (34), the clause introduced by *toma* contrasts with the preceding clause.

(34)　**Tamwali, tamwa la Belep, toma te yamw mwa Pwewo.**
　　　tamwa-li　　　　　　**tamwa=la**　　**Belep**
　　　woman-DET.A.PRX　　woman=LOC　　Belep

　　　toma　**te=**　　　　　**yamw=a**　　　　**Pwewo**
　　　but　　3SG.SUBJ=　　marry=LOC　　Pouébo
　　　'This woman was from Belep, but she married in Pouébo.'
　　　　　　　　　　　　　　　　　　　　　　Yal-20092011-AW2_0016

In (35), the clause introduced by *toma* contrasts with the preceding clause.

(35)　**Te u parie toma bwa âri ave âva lie.**
　　　te=　　　　　**u=**　　　**pari-e**　　　　　　**toma**
　　　3SG.SUBJ=　　DUB=　　tell.TR-3SG.ABS　　but

　　　bwa=　　**âri=**　　**ave=**　　　　　　　　**âva=li-e**
　　　CONT=　　NEG=　　1DU.EXCL.SUBJ=　　fish.for.GNR=GEN-3SG.ABS
　　　'He sort of told about it, but we never did fish with it.'
　　　　　　　　　　　　　　　　　　　　Yal-28072010-BGMCG-hamecon_0089

In (36), *toma* (line 3) introduces a noun phrase *tayamo* 'old woman', which is an unexpected element in this story—the two women in the story were expecting to see a baby.

(36)　**Le nodame ka kiyi mwija pwalaic**
　　　le　　　　**no=da=me**　　　　　　**ka**　　**kiyi**　　　**mwija**　　**pwalaic**
　　　3DU.SUBJ=　peer=DIR.UH=CTP　　LK　　see.SPC　　thing　　one

2   ***to te uya, uya la na mwa,***
to=re	uya	uya=la	na	mwa
when=3SG.SUBJ	appear	appear=LOC	interior	house

3   ***ma te tu, toma tayamo !***
ma=re	tu	toma	tayamo
LK4=3SG.SUBJ	go.DH	but	old.woman

    'They looked up and saw something appearing, coming out of the house to come down, but it was an old woman!'

    Yal-28072010-BGMCG-tayamu_0220-0222

7.2.5 Linker *kara* 'well'

The Belep linker *kara* 'well', like its English counterpart, is used to negotiate common ground (Jucker 1993). It normally occurs when speakers try to establish a shared frame of reference, as in example (37). Here *kara* (line 3) is used between a digression and a return to the topic at hand, where the purpose of the digression is to make sure the speaker and listener share the same point of reference.

(37) CG: ***Pwemwale naran ni Pwac.***
pwemwa-le	nara-n=i	pwac
village-3DU.POSS	name-3SG.POSS=GEN	Pwac

    'Their home was named Pwac.'

2   BG: ***Bwayayo ai ?***
Bwayayo	ei
Bwayayo	TAG

    'Wasn't it Bwayayo?'

3   CG: ***Manya, kara, toma na pwayili ka le mo li, naran ni Bwayayo.***
manya	kara	toma	na	pwayi-li
wait	well	but	interior	inhabited-DET.A.PRX

4   ka   le=   mo=li   nara-n=i
    LK   3DU.SUBJ=   live=LOC.A   name-3SG.POSS=GEN

Bwayayo
Bwayayo
'Wait, well, but in the place where they lived, it was called Bwayayo.'
                                    Yal-28072010-BGMCG-tayamu_0007-0009

Though the function of establishing shared reference is not normally included in types of coordination, *kara* seems to have some uses similar to other coordinators and it often occurs concurrently with *mo* 'LK3' (§7.2.3). For example, in (38), two characters in a narrative—Ciaup, the chief of Nic, and his wife Kawo—are animated by the speaker. Ciaup uses *kara* twice (in lines 1 and 3) while trying to establish common ground with Kawo, who has just come back from the dead. The first usage includes *mo* while the second usage does not.

(38) « *Naok.* » « *Kara mo na tame paeo.* »
      nao-k   kara   mo   na=   ta=me
      1SG.INDEP-DET.D.PRX   well   LK3   1SG.SUBJ=   go.UH=CTP

      pa-e-o
      take-SPC-2SG.ABS
      '[Kawo:] "Here I am." [Ciaup:] "Well then, I've come to take you."'

2   *Te wali u le teâmaa,* « *Naok!* »
      te=   wa-li   u=le   teâmaa
      3SG.SUBJ=   DEM.MAN-DET.A.PRX   toward=DAT   high.chief

      nao-k
      1SG.INDEP-DET.D.PRX
      'She said to the chief, "Here I am!"'

3   « *Kara na tame paeo*
      kara   na=   ta=me   pa-e-o
      well   1SG.SUBJ=   go.UH=CTP   take-SPC-2SG.ABS
      '[Ciaup:] "Well I've come to take you"'

4   *ma ji tu la pwemwaji. »*
        ma   ji=   tu=la   pwemwa-ji
        LK4   1DU.INCL.SUBJ=   go.DH=LOC   village-1DU.INCL.POSS
        'so that we go back home.'"
                                                        Yal-20092011-AW1_0303-0304

In (38), the speaker's use of *kara* 'well' indicates the character's surprise and acceptance of the news that Kawo has come back to life. In example (39), *kara mo* acts as a linker between a topic *nyali, premier vayi* 'that one, the first cow' and a comment, *âria yadan* 'he doesn't have any clothes on'.

(39)   *Bwa kaxi ! Nyali, premier vayi, kara mo âria yadan.*
        bwa=   kaxi   nya-li   [prɛmie]   vayi
        CONT=   look   DEM.IDF-DET.A.PRX   first.LN   cow.LN

        kara   mo   âria   yada-n
        well   LK3   NEG.EX   belongings-3SG.POSS
        'Hey! That one, the first cow, well he doesn't have any clothes on.'
                                                        Yal-05102010-MTAD_16:51-16:55

The use of *kara* in the topic-comment construction in (39) indicates that the speaker is directing her interlocutor's attention to a shared referent before she continues.

Although *kara* occurs most often with *mo*, the fact that it does not always do so indicates that it should be considered a linker in its own right.

7.3 Complementation strategies

In many languages, the function of "stating what a proposition is which is seen, heard, believed, known, liked, etc." (Dixon 2006:1) is served by complementation, where "certain verbs...can take a clause, instead of [a noun phrase] as a core argument" (Dixon 2006:1). In Belep, there is no evidence of clauses which act as arguments of other clauses. For example, in (40)—which requires a complement clause to translate it into English—there are two independent clauses, *texa noxeve* 'he asked us' and *avena pan* 'we go'.

(40)   *Texa noxeve ma avena pan,*
        {te=xa   noxe-ve}   ma
        3SG.SUBJ=ADD   solicit.TR-1DU.EXCL.ABS   LK4

{avena=	pan}
1PA.EXCL.SUBJ=	go.TV

'And he asked us to go,' (lit. 'And he asked us [2] and we [3] go,')

Yal-28072010-BGMCG-tahitian_0011

The second clause *avena pan* is not an argument of the first clause; that position is filled by the absolutive pronominal suffix *-ve* (see §5.7, §5.2.3). There are no restrictions on aspect or modality in the second clause. The order of the clauses can also be reversed without a significant change in meaning, as in (41) and (42) below.

(41) *Âri na ênae puur ma na tume.*

{âri=	na=	êna-e	puu-r}
NEG=	1SG.SUBJ=	know-SPC	origin-3GNR.POSS

ma	{na=	tu=me}
LK4	1SG.SUBJ=	go.DH=CTP

'I don't know why I came down here.' (lit. 'I don't know the reason that[16] I came down here.')

Yal-03112011-IM1.wav – Yal-03112011-IM2.wav

(42) *Ma te cavac, ka âri na ênae puur.*

ma{=re=	cavac}	ka
LK4=3SG.SUBJ=	depart	LK

{âri=	na=	êna-e	puu-r}
NEG=	1SG.SUBJ=	know-SPC	origin-3GNR.POSS

'The reason that she left is not evident.' (lit. 'That she left, I don't know the reason.')

In (41) and (42), the absolutive argument slot of the verb *êna* 'to know' is filled by the noun *puur* 'origin';[17] the clauses marked by *ma* in both examples are independent and do not act as arguments of *âri na ênae puur* 'I don't know the reason'. There is, in fact, no morphosyntactic basis for distinguishing clauses such as (40) - (42) from instances of clausal coordination (§7.2). A similar situation holds for South Efate (a language of Vanuatu), where "in general subordinate clauses display no features that distinguish

---

16 In English this clause must be translated as a relative clause; however, it is not one in Belep. See §7.4 on relative clauses.
17 The noun *puu-r* 'origin' can refer both to a cause or purpose and to an ancestor.

them from other clauses, apart from the subordinators that link them to the preceding main clause" (Thieberger 2006:303).[18]

Languages such as Dyirbal (Dixon 1995) and colloquial Indonesian (Englebretson 2003) also lack complementation, instead employing alternative grammatical means dubbed *complementation strategies* by Dixon (1995, 2006). Though Belep lacks complementation, it makes use of a variety of complementation strategies. The primary complementation strategy in Belep is best described as a type of *pseudocoordination* (as defined in Ross 2016)—a construction that resembles clausal coordination (§7.2) but which nonetheless indicates a semantic relationship of dependency. Morphemes used to indicate semantic dependency include linkers *ka* (§7.3.1), *ma* (§7.3.2), *to* (§7.3.3), *enyi* (§7.3.4), *ka me* (§7.3.5), and *ki* (§7.3.6), as well as the genitive case marker =*li* (§7.3.7). Most of these morphemes may introduce either a clause or a noun phrase. Other complementation strategies used in Belep include relative clauses and other constructions using *puur* (§7.3.8), serial verb constructions (§7.3.9), and nominalizations (discussed in §3.6.2).

Both Nêlêmwa (Bril 2002) and Fijian (Dixon 1995) distinguish actual and virtual complementizers. Though there is no complementation in Belep, morphemes which indicate semantic dependency can generally be characterized as realis or irrealis, as in Table 2.

Tab. 2: Modality of morphemes indicating semantic dependency

Realis	Irrealis
ka 'LK'	enyi 'if'
ka me 'then'	ki 'REL'
to 'when'	=li/=i 'GEN'
	ma 'LK4'

In general, noun phrases and clauses marked with a realis morpheme reference instances of perception, logical progression, and the knowledge of past events—predications speakers might wish to mark as instantiated in reality. Clauses marked with an irrealis morpheme tend to incorporate hypotheticals, deontic or conditional modalities, and future events—predications which do not necessarily have instantiation in reality. Examples of the use of these morphemes are given in the following sections.

---

18 Note, however, that Thieberger (2006) analyzes these subordinate clauses in South Efate as complements.

7.3.1 Linker *ka* in pseudocoordination

Conjunctive linker *ka* 'LK' is used in noun phrase coordination (§4.5.3) and clausal coordination, as discussed above in §7.2.1. Another function of *ka* is as a realis pseudocoordinating morpheme for discursive verbs and verbs of perception, as for example in (43) where linker *ka* acts as a pseudocoordinator after *kiya* 'to see'.

(43)   ***Toma yena ja âmu kiyau ka tuya avar ki înau.***

toma	yena	{ja=	âmu=	kiya-u}
but	now	1PL.INCL.SUBJ=	PRF=	see-DETR

ka	{tuya	avari=xi	îna-u}
LK	EX.GNR	other=REL	make-DETR

'But now we have seen that there are others who make them.' (lit. 'But now we have seen it and there are others who make them.')

Yal-28072010-BGMCG-hamecon_0051

In (43), the first clause *ja âmu kiyau* 'we have seen' is a full independent clause; the detransitive suffix *-u* on the verb *kiya* 'to see' precludes the presence of an absolutive argument. The second clause *tuya avar ki înau* 'there are others who make them', though introduced by pseudocoordinator *ka*, is also a fully independent clause and does not act as the absolutive argument of the first clause. Note that morphosyntactically there is no basis for distinguishing pseudocoordination with *ka* from coordination; the semantic relationship is only parsed from context.

Another example of *ka* acting as a pseudocoordinator is found in (44), where the first verb is the intransitive *param* 'to forget'. Note that when *ka* is used as a pseudocoordinator here, coreferential subject proclitics appear in both the first and second clauses, which is unusual in coordination with *ka* (§7.2.1.1).

(44)   ***Te param ka te turowinao,***

{te=	param}	ka	{te=	turowi-nao}
3SG.SUBJ=	forget.NTR	LK	3SG.SUBJ=	insult-1SG.ABS

'He forgot that he had insulted me,' (lit. 'He forgot and he insulted me,')

Yal-28072010-BGMCG-tahitian_0329

In (45), *ka* is used as a pseudocoordinator after *êna* 'to know'. Here its cliticized form *=xa* is used rather than its full form (see §3.2.2.6, §3.3.4).

(45)   *na êna ka âbur la âva li yeek,*
      {na=   êna}=<u>xa</u>
      1SG.SUBJ= know.GNR=LK

      {âbura   la=   âva=li   yeek}
      side.UH   3PL.SUBJ= go.fishing=GEN plant
      'I know that, before, they fished with wooden [ones].' (lit. 'I know and before they fished with wooden [ones].')
                                           Yal-28072010-BGMCG-hamecon_0075-0076

In (46), *ka* is used as a pseudocoordinator after *câyi* 'to change'. Here the second clause is the predicate nominal *buâny* 'stone'.

(46)   *texa câyi ka buâny.*
      {te=xa   câyi}   ka   {buâny}
      3SG.SUBJ=ADD change LK   stone
      'and he turned into a stone.' (lit. 'and he changed and a stone.')
                                                     Yal-19092011-PA_0071

Linker *ka* is frequently used as a quotative for indirect speech, where it acts as a pseudocoordinator after the intransitive verb *âri* 'to say', as in (47) and (48).

(47)   *Toma yer, te âri ka cexeen.*
      toma   yer   {te=   âri}   ka   {cexeen}
      but   3SG.INDEP 3SG.SUBJ= say LK   sacred
      'But him, he says that it's forbidden.'
                                                   Yal-20092011-AW4_0048

(48)   *Avexa âri ka, ai.*
      {ave=xa   âri} ka {ai}
      1DU.EXCL.SUBJ=ADD say   LK   no
      'And we said no.'
                                           Yal-28072010-BGMCG-tahitian_0277

7.3.2 Linker *ma* in pseudocoordination

Linker *ma*, glossed 'LK4', is polyfunctional. It is used in inclusory (§4.5.5) and comitative (§4.5.6) noun phrase coordination, and it functions as a pseudocoordinator in periphrastic causative constructions (§6.10.1) and clauses (§7.3.2.1) and predicate nominals (§7.3.2.2) which express an intention or goal.

7.3.2.1 Purpose clauses with *ma* 'so that'

One function of linker *ma* in Belep is to serve as a pseudocoordinator for purpose clauses—clauses which are optative, desiderative, or express an intended result. In most instances Belep purpose clauses are best translated into English with an infinitive verb. For instance, example (49) shows the clause *temere puae pwâna mwa*, literally 'he will truly open the door', which is marked with purpose clause marker *ma*. In coordination with the preceding clause *teme yamayaap* 'he will try his best', the semantic content of the *ma*-clause is interpreted as dependent on that of the prior clause, necessitating the translation 'He will try his best to truly open the door'.

(49) **Teme yamayaap ma temere puae pwâna mwa.**
      {te=me   yamayava}   ma{=re=me=re
      3SG.SUBJ=IRR   concentrate   LK4=3SG.SUBJ=IRR=ACT

      pua-e   **pwâna**   **mwa}**
      open-SPC   hole   house
      'He will try his best to truly open the door.' (lit. 'He will concentrate and he will truly open the door.')
                                                             Yal-25072010-PT-homily_0053

Another example of a purpose clause with *ma* is shown in (50). Here the predicate of the first clause is the verb phrase *leô pae wagale ûjep* 'they took their sugar cane boat', and the purpose clause is *leô tu ka âva* 'they went down and fished'. The implication is that the first clause was performed with the intention to perform the second clause.

(50) **Leô pae wagale ûjep, ma leô tu ka âva.**
      {le=ô   pa-e   waga-le   ûjep}
      3DU.SUBJ=REAL   take-SPC boat-3DU.POSS sugar.cane

      ma   {le=ô   tu=xa   âva}
      LK4   3DU.SUBJ=REAL go.DH=LK   go.fishing
      'They took their sugar cane boat to go down and fish.' (lit. 'They took their sugar cane boat and went down and fished.')
                                                             Yal-01082010-MFD_0006

Note that the clauses coordinated with *ma* may have different subjects. For example, in (51), the first clause and the purpose *ma*-clause do not have co-referential subject agreement proclitics.

(51) *Lami maac, la nawela ma la ci la bwe mweogo,*

la-mi	maac	{la=	nawe-la}
DEM.PL-DET.A.DST	die	3PL.SUBJ=	deposit-3PL.ABS

ma	{la=	ci=la	bwe	mweogo}
LK4	3PL.SUBJ=	sit=LOC	top	mountaintop

'The dead, they left them to lie on the mountaintop,'

Yal-20092011-AW3_0069

Though both clauses contain the subject proclitic *la=* '3PL.SUBJ', they refer to different groups ('the surviving Belema warriors' and 'the dead' respectively). In (52), multiple purpose *ma*-clauses occur. In line 2, the purpose *ma*-clause *yo wânem* 'you walk' provides an intention for the performance of the first clause, *bae weemw pida wiu lexeng* 'have some of this food here'. An alternate purpose clause is begun in line 2 and continued in line 3, and is further explicated by another purpose clause in line 3.

(52) « *Pana tame ka bae weemw pida wiu lexeng.*

pana=	ta=me=xa	{bae	wee-mwa	pida	wiu=lexeng}
go.TV=	go.UH=CTP=LK	bite	food-2SG.POSS	tip	meal=LOC.DC

2 *Ma yo wânem, ma yo - tuu ûjemw ma yo wânem.* »

ma	{yo=	wânem}	ma	yo=
LK4	2SG.SUBJ=	walk	LK4	2SG.SUBJ=

3

{tu=	ûje-mw}	ma	{yo=	wânem}}
EX.SPC=	kidney-2SG.POSS	LK4	2SG.SUBJ=	walk

'"Come on up here and have some of this food here. So that you can walk, so that you- you have the strength to walk."'

Yal-05092011-AP1_0035-0036

In lines 2 and 3 of (52), two coordinated *ma*-clauses provide an intention for the first clause *bae weemw pida wiu lexeng* 'have some of this food here'. The *ma*-clause in line 3, *yo wânem* 'you walk' is semantically dependent on the *ma*-clause in lines 2-3, *tuu ûjemw* 'you have strength', with the resulting meaning of 'you have the strength to walk'. In fact the semantic dependency here is nested, with the meaning of one *ma*-clause dependent upon another (marked with {}); however, morphosyntactically, the clauses are merely coordinated. Another example of nested pseudocoordination is shown in (53), where a number of semantically related *ma*-clauses are chained together in morphosyntactic coordination. A separate *ma*-clause occurs in lines 2, 3, 4, 5, and 6. Note the considerable alternation of subjects from one clause to the next.

(53) BG: **Lexa ta ka pae.**
le=xa   ta=xa   pa-e
3DU.SUBJ=ADD   go.UH=LK   take-SPC
'And they [Kloin and Orilô] went up and got him$_j$.'

2   **Pae camang ma le paedume leeng.**
{pa-e   cama-ng}   ma
take-SPC   father-1SG.POSS   LK4

{le=   pa-e=du=me=lee-ng}
3DU.SUBJ=   take-SPC=DIR.DH=CTP=DAT-1SG.POSS
'Got my father$_j$ so they could bring him$_j$ down here.'

3   **Ma leme soigner lier rexeng.**
ma   {le=me   soigner=li-er=exeng}
LK4   3DU.SUBJ=IRR   heal.LN=GEN-3SG.ABS=LOC.DC
'So they could heal him$_i$ [Tayema] here.'

4   CG: **Ma te pa cavac yi lali.**
ma{=re   pa=   cavay=i   la-li}
LK4=3SG.SUBJ   CAUS=   depart=GEN   DEM.PL-DET.A.PRX
'So he$_j$ could make them[19] depart.'

5   BG: **Ma te pa ca - ji bwage lali,**
ma{=re   pa=   ca -   ji   bwage   la-li}
LK4=3SG.SUBJ   CAUS=   give   return   DEM.PL-DET.A.PRX
'So he$_j$ could make them l- have them return,'

6   **ma la pan na Poc.**
ma   {la=   pan=a   Poc}
LK4   3PL.SUBJ=   go.TV=LOC   Poc
'so they would go to Poc.'

                                                           Yal-28072010-BGMCG-tahitian_0253-0256

Example (53) shows successive nesting of semantic relationships. The *ma*-clause in line 6 is provided as the intention of the *ma*-clauses in lines 4 and 5 (which are largely synonymous with each other); the *ma*-clause in line 4 is semantically dependent on

---

[19] 'them' refers to the spirits of the ancestors which are possessing Tayema, making him sick. They dwell near Poc, the island to the north of Belep.

the *ma*-clause in line 3, which is semantically dependent on the *ma*-clause in line 2. This clause is in turn semantically dependent on the first clause, *pae camang* 'took my father' in line 2. None of this dependency is morphosyntactic; each *ma*-clause is indistinguishable from a coordinate clause construction.

7.3.2.2 Correlational *ma* 'as'

Belep linker *ma* may also be used as a pseudocoordinator for predicate nominals, where it carries the meaning of 'as' or 'like'.[20] Here I use the term 'correlational' to mean that *ma* implies a semantic correlation between the predicate nominal it marks and the absolutive argument of the preceding clause. Some examples of this usage are shown in (54) - (57).

(54) « *Hé, âyua teâmaa li teme paeo ma yawan.* »
      e   âyua   teâma=li   {te=me   pa-e-o}
      hey! desire high.chief=GEN 3SG.SUBJ=IRR take-SPC-2SG.ABS

      ma   {yawa-n}
      LK4   wife-3SG.POSS
      '"Hey! The chief would like to take you as his wife."' (lit. 'The chief's desire is that he takes you as his wife.')
                                                                    Yal-20092011-AW1_0178

In (54), the predicate nominal marked with *ma* is *yawan* 'his wife'; it is correlated with the absolutive argument of the preceding clause, indexed by the second person pronominal suffix -*o*. In (55), *ma* marks the predicate nominal *jivimw* 'your skirt', which is correlated with the absolutive noun phrase *jivive* 'our skirts' in the preceding clause.

(55) « *Yome pa jivive ma jivimw,* »
      {yo=me   pa   jivi-ve}   ma   {jivi-mw}
      2SG.SUBJ=IRR take.GNR skirt-1DU.EXCL.POSS LK4 skirt-2SG.POSS
      '"You take our skirts as your skirt,"'
                                                                        Yal-20092011-AW4_0054

---

20 This *ma* may derive diachronically from the class 1 noun *ma-* 'likeness, similarity'; however, this analysis is not valid synchronically—if *ma* in these examples were acting as a noun, we would expect it to be case-marked (§6.4).

In (56), the predicate nominal *naer* 'child' is marked with *ma*; it is correlated with the third singular absolutive argument of the preceding clause, indexed by the pronominal suffix *-er*.

(56) **Te turuer ma naer.**
    {te=   turu-er}   ma   {nae-r}
    3SG.SUBJ=   hide-3SG.ABS LK4 child-3GNR.POSS
    'She was hiding herself in the form of a child.'
                                          Yal-28072010-BGMCG-tayamu_0136

In (57), *ma* marks predicate nominal *baner* 'friend, accompaniment', which is correlated with the absolutive noun phrase *mwija* 'thing' in the preceding clause.

(57) **me âria mwija ma baner,**
    {me   âria   mwija}   ma   {bane-r}
    IRR=   NEG.EX   thing   LK4   friend-3GNR.POSS
    '[they] wouldn't have anything as an accompaniment,'
                              Yal-28072010-BGMCG-tayamu_0019-0020

7.3.3 Adverbial linker *to* 'when'

Linker *to*, glossed 'when', is used as a pseudocoordinator to introduce either a clause (§7.3.3.1) or a noun phrase (§7.3.3.2) that gives some sort of adverbial information related to the preceding clause. Adverbial *to* is a simple clitic (Zwicky 1977) which has both a full form *to* and an enclitic form =*ro*. An adverbial *to*-clause must follow the clause whose meaning it modifies (see the ungrammaticality of (58)); however, because an intonation break may occur between the two clauses, *to* may occasionally occur at the beginning of an intonation unit as in (59). Usually, *to* occurs in medial position in its encliticized form =*ro* (60).

(58) *****To   na   bae   no,   na   ca   teec.**
    when   1SG.SUBJ= eat   fish   1SG.SUBJ= ITER=   burn
    *'Whenever I eat fish, I repeatedly burn myself.'

(59) **?to   na   bae   no**
    when   1SG.SUBJ= eat   fish
    ?'whenever I eat fish'

(60)   *Na ca teec to na bae no.*
       na=   ca=   teya=ro   na=   bae   no
       1SG.SUBJ= ITER= burn=when   1SG.SUBJ=   eat   fish
       'I repeatedly burn myself when I eat fish.'
                           Yal-03112011-IM1.wav – Yal-03112011-IM2.wav

7.3.3.1 Adverbial *to* 'as'

When *to* precedes a clause, it marks that clause as adverbial—as modifying, but not serving as an argument of, the preceding clause or verb phrase (Payne 1997:316-317). Belep adverbial *to*-clauses are a form of pseudocoordination which would often best be translated by a participle[21] in languages which have them. Belep *to*-clauses act as modifiers of the clause, verb phrase, or noun phrase that they follow.

In example (61), *to* introduces the clause *laô êna*, literally 'they knew' (followed by a pseudocoordinate clause with *ka*; see §7.3.1). Here the first clause is *la mo*, literally 'they lived'; the *to*-clause acts as an adverbial modifier of this main idea.

(61)   *La mo to laô êna, ka Nenemwa, te to ji Teâ Belep,*
       {la=   mo}=<u>ro</u>   {la=ô   êna}
       3PL.SUBJ=   live=when   3PL.SUBJ=REAL   know.GNR

       ka   Nenemwa   te=   to   ji   Teâ Belep
       LK   Nêlêmwa   3SG.SUBJ=   call   give   Teâ Belep
       'They came to realize that Nêlêmwa, he had called for Teâ Belep,' (lit. 'They lived when they knew and Nenemwa, he had called for Teâ Belep,')
                                                    Yal-20092011-AW3_0037-0038

More commonly, *to*-clauses act as modifiers of verb phrases. In example (62), *to* introduces a full clause *te uya*, literally 'it appears', which modifies the preceding verb phrase *kiyi mwija pwalaic* 'saw something'. Note that this is not a relative clause (§7.4).

(62)   *Le nodame ka kiyi mwija pwalaic to te uya,*
       le=   no=da=me
       3DU.SUBJ=   peer=DIR.UH=CTP

---

21 Noonan (2007:72) defines participles as verb forms which "are not the heads of constructions, but rather modify some noun which functions as the head".

	ka	{kiyi	mwija	pwalaic}	to{=re	uya}
	LK	see.SPC	thing	one	when=3SG.SUBJ	appear

'They looked up and saw something appearing,' (lit. 'saw something as it was appearing' or 'saw something when it was appearing')

Yal-28072010-BGMCG-tayamu_0220

In example (63), *to* introduces the clause *ciae* 'she wasn't there' which modifies the verb phrase *tu Kawo* 'find Kawo'.

(63) *mo la leli ka tu Kawo to ciae,*

mo=la	le-li	ka	{tu
live=NOM	DEM.DU-DET.A.PRX	LK	find

Kawo}=ro	{cia-e}
Kawo=when	NEG.LOC-3SG.ABS

'those two did go along and find Kawo had disappeared,' (lit. 'find Kawo when she wasn't there,')

Yal-20092011-AW1_0247

Noun phrases may also be modified by adverbial *to*-clauses. In (64), the *to*-clause *le yabwar riyek*, literally 'they rose in the distance', modifies the noun phrase *âwur pwadu* 'two waves'.

(64) *Âwur pwadu to le yabwar riyek, lexa pame.*

{âwura	pwadu}=ro	{le=	yabwar=i-yek}
wave	two=when	3DU.SUBJ=	rise=DEM.LOC-DET.D.DST

le=xa	pa=me
3DU.SUBJ=ADD	go.TV=CTP

'Two waves rising in the distance, they came.' (lit. 'two waves when they rose in the distance, and they came')

Yal-28072010-BGMCG-sousmarin_0064

Example (65) shows the *to*-clause *name tiu u leac*, literally 'I will write to you', which modifies the noun phrase *yena* 'now'.

(65) *Ma yena to name tiu u leac,*

ma	{yena}=ro	{na=me	ti-u	u=le-ac}
LK4	now=when	1SG.SUBJ=IRR	prick-DETR	toward=DAT-2PL.POSS

'That now, as I am writing to you,'

Yal-14092011-PT2-avenir_0016

7.3.3.2 Temporal *to* 'at the time of'

Adverbial linker *to*, =*ro* may also be used to mark a predicate nominal as modifying a preceding clause, verb phrase, or noun phrase; in this usage, it may be translated as 'at the time of' because such predicate nominals are almost always temporal nouns (§6.11). These pseudocoordinate clauses describe the temporal location of the action of the preceding clause.[22] For example, in (66), *to* marks the predicate nominal temporal noun *bwan* 'night', which describes when the action of the preceding clause took place.

(66) *la nginie, la pu ngini cae to bwan.*
      la=   ngini-e
      3PL.SUBJ= miss-3SG.ABS

      {la=   pu=   ngini   cae}=<u>ro</u>   {bwan}
      3PL.SUBJ= RA=   miss.   reef=when night
      'they didn't see it, they just didn't see the reef in the night.' (lit. 'they just didn't see the reef when it was night')
                                                                Yal-20092011-AW2_0036

In (67), the temporal noun introduced by *to* is *baraap* 'evening', and in (68) the temporal noun phrase introduced by *to* is *bwe cavaro* 'Saturday'.

(67) *« Ai elo, » kaô mae, mae to baraap.*
      ai   elo=xa=ô   mae   {mae}=<u>ro</u>   {baraap}
      no   yes=LK=REAL sleep sleep=when evening
      '[He said] "Oh, okay," and slept, slept in the evening.' (lit. 'slept when it was evening')
                                                                Yal-05092011-AP1_0071

---

[22] *to* may have originated as a temporal case marker and been extended to use as a linker and pseudo-coordinator.

(68) **Yak to bwe cavaro, avena tu la Awe.**
  {yaxa}=<u>ro</u>   {bwe   cavaro}   avena=
  yesterday=when   moment   sabbath.LN   1TR.EXCL.SUBJ=

  tu=la   Awe
  go.DH=LOC   Awe
  'The other day, Saturday, we went down to Awe.' (lit. 'yesterday when it-was Saturday')
  Yal-17072009-TB-weekend_0001-0002

In (68), *to* marks a temporal noun phrase referring to a moment in the past. Note that *to* cannot be used to introduce a temporal noun referring to a future time (69) since in this construction *to* has a semantically realis meaning.

(69) *****yena to baraap**
  yena=ro   baraap
  now=when   evening
  *'this evening'

Instead, the irrealis morpheme *=li* is used (§7.3.7) to refer to future temporal locations, as in example (70).

(70) **yena li baraap**
  yena=li   baraap
  now=GEN   evening
  'this evening, tonight'

7.3.4 Conditional linker *enyi* 'if'

A clause is introduced by *enyi* 'if'[23] to mark it as a protasis; that is, as the clause in an 'if-then' construction which expresses the condition. The conditional *enyi*-clause

---

[23] There are two possibilities for the form of this lexeme: 1) *enyi* and *enyixi* are alternative forms of the same lexeme; and 2) *enyi* is the lexeme and *enyixi* is a linker combination (see §7.5) of *enyi* and relativizer *ki*. Speaker intuitions indicate that variation between *enyi* and *enyixi* is sociolinguistic; the *enyixi* pronunciation tends to be used more by older speakers. Dubois (1975e) lists <eni>, <ehni>, and <ênixii> in his dictionary. Neyret (1974a) lists <eki>. The first possibility, that *enyi* and *enyixi* are alternative forms of the same lexeme, seems most likely—*enyixi* could plausibly have been reduced to *enyi*, since the negative marker *âri=* 'NEG' underwent a similar process. Dubois (1975e) lists <hââriki,

may precede (71) or follow (72) the clause it modifies (the apodosis, which expresses the consequence).

(71) **Enyi ja tânae baro ja cuginy.**
  enyi {ja= tâna-e baro} {ja= cuginy}
  if 1PL.INCL.SUBJ= hear-SPC bell 1PL.INCL.SUBJ= strive
  'If we hear the bell[24] we exert ourselves.' (lit. 'If we hear the bell we strive.')
  Yal-25072010-PT-homily_0009

(72) *« Me âria âju la pwemwajen. Enyi ji cavayaroven. »*
  {me âria âju=la pwemwa-jen}
  IRR NEG.EX person=LOC village-1TR.INCL.POSS

  enyi {ji= cavaya-roven}
  if 1DU.INCL.SUBJ= depart-COMPL
  '"There won't be anyone at home. If we both leave."'
  Yal-20092011-AW1_0083

In (71), the *enyi*-clause *ja tânae baro* 'we hear the bell' precedes the clause *ja cuginy*, literally 'we strive', which it modifies. In contrast, in (72) the *enyi*-clause *ji cavayaroven* 'we both leave' follows the main clause *me âria âju la pwemwajen* 'there won't be anyone at home'.

Conditional clauses are not limited to occurrence in such predictive, cause-and-effect statements. Clauses introduced by *enyi* can also describe hypothetical or generic events, as in (73) and (74).

(73) **Cexeen ni te kiyi tamwa.**
  cexen=i te= kiyi tamwa
  sacred=GEN 3SG.SUBJ= see.SPC woman

  Enyi te padi mwija pwalaic ki mwany u leen.
  enyi {te= padi mwija pwalaiyi=xi
  if 3SG.SUBJ= show thing one=REL

---

hâârixi, hârixi> as the only acceptable forms of the negative marker, while Neyret (1974a) lists <anriki>. Older speakers still occasionally use the form *ârixi=*, but the morpheme has almost entirely decayed to *âri=*.
24 *baro* 'bell' is derived from *ba= to* [INSTR= call] 'thing for calling'.

	mwanya	u=lee-n}
	bad	toward=DAT-3SG.POSS

'It is forbidden that he see a woman if she is showing something bad to him.'

Yal-20092011-AW4_0058-0059

(74) *Toma nyali, teme cegele, enyi le cego ma leô tu.*

toma	nya-li	te=me	cege-le
but	DEM.GIV-DET.A.PRX	3SG.SUBJ=IRR	watch-3DU.ABS

enyi	{le=	cego	ma	le=ô	tu}
if	3DU.SUBJ=	descend	LK4	3DU.SUBJ=REAL	go.DH

'But she, she will watch for the two of them to go down [to the beach].' (lit. 'she will watch them if they descend to go down.')

Yal-28072010-BGMCG-tayamu_0147

In (73), the conditional *enyi*-clause *te padi mwija pwalaic ki mwany u leen* 'she is showing something bad to him' is a hypothetical condition, as is the *enyi*-clause in (74), *le cego ma leô tu* 'they descend to go down'.

In addition to introducing clauses, linker *enyi* is also used as a discourse marker to introduce a noun phrase.[25] In these instances, *enyi* marks the following noun as the topic, as in the question in (75).

(75) *Enyi ti ?*

if	who

'Who are you talking about?'

Examples such as (75) are found frequently in discourse. For example, in (76), the speaker marks *ulayili* 'that old man' as the topic with *enyi* in line 3.

(76) *Na tuvavan ka bwagenao, ka ta ka uc,*

na=	tuva=van	ka	bwage-nao	ka	ta
1SG.SUBJ=	dive=DIR.TV	LK	return-1SG.ABS	LK	go.UH

ka	uc
LK	surface

---

[25] According to Haiman (1978), conditional markers and topic markers are identical in many of the world's languages, indicating that they serve the same function.

2   *ka oyâno, ka noda lier to teô ta,*
ka	oyâno	ka	no=da=li-era=ro
LK	look	LK	peer=DIR.UH=GEN-3SG.ABS=when

te=ô	ta
3SG.SUBJ=REAL	go.UH

3   *teô ta la pwemwa, enyi*
te=ô	ta=la	pwemwa	enyi
3SG.SUBJ=REAL	go.UH=LOC	village	if

4   *ulayili, texaô ta,*
{ulayi-li}	te=xa=ô	ta
old.man-DET.A.PRX	3SG.SUBJ=ADD=REAL	go.UH

    'I continued to dive and returned, and went up and surfaced, and looked around, and peered up at him as he was going, he was going home, that old man, he was going,'

    Yal-28072010-BGMCG-tahitian_0066-0072

Conditional linker *enyi* 'if' can also precede a relative clause (see §7.4.3), as in (77) and (78).

(77) *Enyi âmi na ca bae no, na ca teec.*
enyi	{â-mi	na=	ca=	bae	no}
if	DEM.NEW-DET.A.DST	1SG.SUBJ=	ITER=	bite	fish

na=	ca=	teec
1SG.SUBJ=	ITER=	burn

'Whenever I eat fish, I burn myself.'

Yal-03112011-IM1.wav – Yal-03112011-IM2.wav

(78) *Enyi âmi te tunao li maac, la ca tiaenao.*
enyi	{â-mi	te=	tu-nao=li	maac}
if	DEM.NEW-DET.A.DST	3SG.SUBJ=	find-1SG.ABS=GEN	death

la=	ca=	tiae-nao
3PL.SUBJ=	ITER=	pierce-1SG.ABS

'Whenever I am sick, I have myself pricked [by a healer].'

Yal-03112011-IM1.wav – Yal-03112011-IM2.wav

7.3.5 Sequential linker *ka me* 'then'

In many 'if-then' statements in Belep, the conditional clause (protasis) is marked with *enyi* while the resultative clause (the apodosis; the clause that expresses the consequence) is marked by linker *ka me*, glossed as 'then', as in (79).

(79) *Ka enyi leô mo wiu, ka me, me âria mwija ma baner,*

ka	enyi	{le=ô		mo	wiu}	ka me
LK	if	3DU.SUBJ=REAL		live	dine	then

{me	âria	mwija	ma	bane-r}
IRR	NEG.EX	thing	LK4	friend-3SGNR.POSS

'And if they were about to eat, then they wouldn't have anything to eat as an accompaniment,'

Yal-28072010-BGMCG-tayamu_0019-0020

The function of *ka me* is broader than simply marking the consequence of a conditional clause. It is used primarily to indicate a sequential clause, a predication conceptualized as being ordered sequentially after what came before it. Linker *ka me* is often used to temporally order clauses, such as in (80).

(80) *Na nyi kewee ka to jie, « Ai ! »*

na=	nyi=	kewe-e	ka	to	ji-e	ai
1SG.SUBJ=	PUNCT=	chase-3SG.ABS	LK	call	give-3SG.ABS	no

2 *Ka me to jie, « Ai ! »*

ka me	{to	ji-e}	ai
then	call	give-3SG.ABS	no

3 *Ka me to mwa, to jie : « Ai ! »*

ka me	{to	mwa}	to	ji-e	ai
then	call	again	call	give-3SG.ABS	no

'I ran after him and called, "No!", then called "No!", then called again, called to him, "No!"'

Yal-28072010-BGMCG-tahitian_0077-0080

In (80), *ka me* is used twice, in lines 2 and 3, to indicate that each time the speaker called to his brother-in-law it was located temporally after the previous time. On the other hand, *ka me* is also used to sequence elements non-temporally; for example, in (81), *ka me* is used to sequence the introductions of two sisters, with the older one first, followed by *ka me* and then the name of the younger one (a repair occurs immediately after *ka me* in line 2, so is it unknown what sequential clause the speaker originally had in mind).

(81) **Âde ic, naran ni Keyau,**
      âde=   **ic**   **nara-n=i**   **Keyau**
      QT.entity=   one   name-3SG.POSS=GEN   Keyau

2   *ka me – nyami tayamo, naran ni Keyau,*
    ka me   **nya-mi**   **tayamo**
    then   DEM.GIV-DET.A.DST   old.woman

    nara-n=i   **Keyau**
    name-3SG.POSS=GEN   Keyau

3   *ka nyami âno, Kenadu.*
    ka   **nya-mi**   **âno**   **Kenadu**
    LK   DEM.GIV-DET.A.DST   young   Kenadu
    'One of them was named Keyau, and then—the older one was Keyau and the younger, Kenadu.'
                                        Yal-28072010-BGMCG-tayamu_0057-0059

Linker *ka me* is also used to introduce a sequential and contrasting element, as in (82) where it introduces the new topic *jivimw* 'your skirt'.

(82) **« Yome pa jivive ma jivimw, ka me jivimw, jivimw yome jie ma jivive. »**
      yo=me   **pa**   **jivi-ve**   **ma**   **jivi-mw**
      2SG.SUBJ=IRR   take.GNR   skirt-1DU.EXCL.POSS   LK4   skirt-2SG.POSS

      ka me   **{jivi-mw}**   **jivi-mw**   **yo=me**   **jie**
      then   skirt-2SG.POSS   skirt-2SG.POSS   2SG.SUBJ=IRR   give

      ma   **jivi-ve**
      LK4   skirt-1DU.EXCL.POSS
      '"You take our skirts as your skirt, while your skirt, you give it to us to wear."'
                                              Yal-20092011-AW4_0054

The morphological parse for *ka me* is unknown. Clearly *ka* is from linker *ka* (§7.2.1), which is also used to mark the apodosis of an 'if-then' statement, as in (83). This construction is indistinguishable from topicalization with *ka* (§7.2.1.2).

(83) « *Enyi yo cavac, ka na cavac ya modemw.* »
enyi   {yo=   cavac}   ka   {na=   cavay=a
if   2SG.SUBJ=   depart   LK   1SG.SUBJ=   depart=LOC

mode-mw}
together-2SG.POSS

"'If you leave, then I'm leaving with you.'"

Yal-20092011-AW1_0080

However, the origins of *me* are unclear, as is the question of whether *me* can occur independently. It may be etymologically related to the irrealis marker =*me* (§5.6.2), though its distribution is different; the irrealis marker always occurs after the subject proclitic if there is one, while linker *ka me* always occurs before the subject proclitic. For example, in (84), *ka me* precedes the subject proclitic *ji=*.

(84) *Yo yagelinao, ka me ji mo cavac pôben.*
yo=   yage-li-nao   ka me   {ji=   mo
2SG.SUBJ=   help-TR-1SG.OBJ   then   1DU.INCL.SUBJ=   live

cavaya   pôben}
leave   quickly

'You helped me, therefore we will leave sooner.'

Yal-03112011-IM1.wav – Yal-03112011-IM2.wav

It is unknown whether *me* can appear independently of *ka* because all of my corpus examples are ambiguous; they appear with non-prototypical clauses which would not normally have subject proclitics. In these cases, *me* is glossed as 'LK2'. For example, an independent *me* occurs before the predicate nominal *ti* 'who' in (85).

(85) *Toma te koni êna li ti, me ti li âmi âyuan na pewola.*
toma   te=   koni   êna=li   ti
but   3SG.SUBJ=   never   know.GNR=GEN   who

me   {ti}=li   â-mi
LK2   who=GEN   DEM.NEW-DET.A.DST

âyua-n=a   pewo-la
desire-3SG.POSS=LOC   middle-3PL.POSS

'But she didn't know who, who was the one she preferred among them.'

Yal-20092011-AW1_0173

In (86), an independent *me* precedes the predicate nominal *cao pwalu* 'hard work'.

(86) **Me cao pwalu na le naerama lami confirmation,**
     me   **cao**   **pwalu**   **na=le**
     LK2   work   heavy   interior=DAT

     nae-ra-ma   **la-mi**   [kõfiʁmasjõ]
     child-3GNR.POSS-AC   DEM.PL-DET.A.DST   Confirmation.LN
     'It is hard work for the children in Confirmation,'
                                                            Yal-25072010-PT-homily_0089

7.3.6 Linker *ki* as a complementation strategy

Linker (§3.3.4) *ki*, a simple clitic with free form *ki* and bound form =*xi*, is glossed 'REL' throughout this work based on its role in relativization (§7.4.1). However, its primary use in Belep is as a marker for semantically dependent clauses (see §7.3 above) which indicate deontic modality, defined as "concerned with moral obligation or permission" (Noonan 2007:138). For example, in (87), *ki* marks the following clause *ave cuur reen* 'we visit him' as a semantically dependent clause which is concerned with permission.

(87) **Te kuarive ki ave cuur reen.**
     te=   **kuar-i-ve**   **ki**
     3SG.SUBJ=   refuse-TR-1DU.EXCL.ABS   REL

     {**ave=**   **cur=ee-n**}
     1DU.EXCL.SUBJ=   stand=DAT-3SG.POSS
     'He didn't want us to visit him.' (lit. 'He didn't want us that we visit him.')
                                                            Yal-28072010-BGMCG-tahitian_0271

Linker *ki* occurs most frequently in discourse in a grammaticalized construction which indicates moral obligation: a construction of the form *te ô ki* + CLAUSE. Here, full clause *te ô* 'it is good' is followed by deontic linker *ki* and a semantically dependent clause, which is construed to have deontic modality.[26] *Te ô ki* (IPA: /te= õ ki/), which translates literally as 'it is good that...', is usually pronounced in a phonetically

---

[26] Deontic modality may also be expressed using the construction *te ô li* + CLAUSE, where =*li* introduces a semantically dependent clause (§7.3.7). There are not enough examples of this usage in my corpus to determine the difference in meaning between *te ô ki* and *te ô li*.

reduced form as [tõʁi].[27] An example of the use of *te ô ki* to express moral obligation is found in (88) below.

(88) ***Ka te ô ki a tao kâye pulu,***
     ka   {te=   ô}=xi   {a=   tao=   kâye   pulu}
     LK   3SG.SUBJ= be.good=REL   2PL.SUBJ= HAB=   keep   language
     'And you all must always keep your language,' (lit. 'And it is good that you always keep your language.')
                                                                   Yal-14092011-PT2-avenir_0013-0014

In (88), the clause *te ô* 'it is good' precedes the *ki*-clause *a tao kâye pulu* 'you always keep your language'. This construction creates a modality of obligation in the *ki*-clause, leading to a free translation of 'And you all must always keep your language'. A similar modality of obligation is created by *te ô ki...* in examples (89) and (90).

(89) « ***Te ô ki yo ci.*** »
     {te=   ô}=xi   {yo   ci}
     3SG.SUBJ= be.good=REL   2SG.SUBJ= sit
     '"You must stay."' (lit. '"It is good that you stay."')
                                                                        Yal-20092011-AW1_0082

(90) ***Ka te ô ki te ce.***
     ka   {te=   ô}=xi{=re   ce}
     LK   3SG.SUBJ= be.good=REL=3SG.SUBJ settle
     'And may it be so.'
                                                                      Yal-25072010-PT-homily_0020

7.3.7 Genitive =*li* as a complementation strategy

As a case marker, =*li* or =*i* 'GEN' has a variety of uses, including being used to mark some genitive noun phrases (§4.2.2.4), some oblique noun phrases (§6.4.3), and the argument of some predicate nominals (§6.5.1). In this section, a further use of =*li* will be discussed: it occurs after a verb describing an emotion or a mental state, and it introduces an irrealis clause which is relevant to that mental state. For example, in (91), =*li* follows the verb *êna* 'to know', marking the following clause *te mo la St. Joseph ai Teôgo* 's/he lives in St. Joseph or Teôgo' as semantically dependent.

---

[27] This pronunciation is used in examples (88) through (90) below, though it is not indicated in the word-by-word gloss, which only marks morphosyntactic boundaries.

(91)   *Na yaang ma na êna li te mo la St. Joseph ai Teôgo.*
      na=   yaang   ma   na=   êna=li
      1SG.SUBJ= search.NTR LK4   1SG.SUBJ= know.GNR=GEN

      {te=   mo=la   [cĕjojɛp]   ai   Teôgo}
      3SG.SUBJ= live=LOC St. Joseph   or   Teôgo
      'I seek to know whether s/he lives in St. Joseph or Teôgo.'
                                      Yal-03112011-IM1.wav – Yal-03112011-IM2.wav

In (92), the semantically dependent clause *na pan na pu caya*, literally 'I go near Dad', is marked by =*li* and follows the intransitive verb *âya* 'to fear'.

(92)   « *Na âya li na pan na pu caya,* »
      na=   âya=li   {na=   pan=a   pu   caya}
      1SG.SUBJ= fear.NTR=GEN 1SG.SUBJ= go.TV=LOC side   dad
      '"I'm afraid to go near Dad,"' (lit. 'I fear that I go near Dad,')
                                                Yal-20092011-AW1_0039

Note that the semantically dependent clause in (92) does not act as an argument of the preceding clause, where the verb *âya* 'to fear' is intransitive. It would be required to have the transitivized form *âyawe* if it had an absolutive argument (§5.2.5.1).

A clause marked as semantically dependent with =*li* or =*i* can also follow a predicate nominal. For example, in (93), a clause marked with =*i* follows the predicate nominal *weeng* 'my food'.

(93)   *me weeng ngi name cavac.*
      me   wee-ng=i   {na=me   cavac}
      IRR   food-1SG.POSS=GEN 1SG.SUBJ=IRR depart
      'as food for my trip.' (lit. 'as my food that I will depart.')
                                                Yal-20092011-AW1_0074

In (94), a clause marked with =*i* follows the predicate nominal *jaga-r* 'to be possible' (literally 'capacity-3GNR.POSS').

(94)   *Ka jagar ri te jie ma ja nginie.*
      ka   jaga-r=i   {te=   ji-e}
      LK   capacity-3GNR.POSS=GEN 3SG.SUBJ= give-3SG.ABS

ma	ja=		ngini-e
LK4	1PL.INCL.SUBJ=		miss-3SG.ABS

'He could make himself invisible.' (lit. 'It was enough that he could make it that we don't see him.')

Yal-20092011-AW6_0091

In (95), a clause marked with =*li* follows the predicate nominal *âyuale* 'they wanted' (literally 'their desire').

(95) *Âyuale li me tuu naele.*

âyua-le=<u>li</u>	{me	tu	nae-le}
desire-3DU.POSS=GEN	IRR	EX.SPC	child-3DU.POSS

'They wanted to have children.' (lit. 'Their desire was that their children exist.')

Yal-28072010-BGMCG-tayamu_0028

7.3.7.1 Negative desiderative *kuar* 'to not want'

The most common use for the semantically dependent clause marker =*li*, =*i* in discourse is following the negative desiderative verb *kuar* 'to not want'. When this verb is used without a semantically dependent clause, its meaning overlaps with a range of English expressions. Its intransitive form *kuar* may sometimes be best translated by 'to refuse', as in (96), while its transitive form *kuari-* is best translated by 'to dislike' (97).

(96) *Ka âlalic ki yome kuar,*

ka	âlaliyi=xi	yo=me	kuar
LK	impossible=REL	2SG.SUBJ=IRR	not.want.NTR

'And, it's impossible that you could refuse,'

Yal-25072010-PT-homily_0062

(97) « *Na kuari Ixe, mo âyuang ngi Kawo.* »

na=	kuari	Ixe	mo	âyua-ng=i	Kawo
1SG.SUBJ=	not.want.TR	Ixe	LK3	desire-1SG.POSS=GEN	Kawo

'"I dislike Ixe, for I love Kawo."'

Yal-20092011-AW1_0294

When followed by genitive =*li* and a semantically dependent clause, *kuar* is best translated by 'to not want'. For example, in (98) and (99), =*i* is used after *kuar* to mark a clause as semantically dependent.

(98) *Te kuar ri te pan.*
      te=   kuar=i̱   {te=   pan}
      3SG.SUBJ=   not.want=GEN   3SG.SUBJ=   go.TV
      'He didn't want to go.' (lit. 'He didn't want that he goes.')
                                                      Yal-20092011-AW1_0048

(99) *La kuar ri la payeeni teâmaa.*
      la=   kuar=i̱   la=   payeni   teâmaa
      3PL.SUBJ=   not.want=GEN   3PL.SUBJ=   listen.TR   high.chief
      'They didn't want to listen to the chief.' (lit. 'They didn't want that they listen to the chief.')
                                                      Yal-20092011-AW2_0026

Note that, in these two examples, the subject of the first clause and the subject of the second clause clause are co-referential. In (98), the subject is referenced by a third singular *te=* in both clauses; in (99), the co-referential subject is third plural *la=*. Examples (100) and (101) show the use of *kuar* + *=li* as a complementation strategy where the two clauses have non-co-referential subjects.

(100) « *Na kuar ri yo cavac ka najinao.* »
      na=   kuar=i̱   {yo=   cavaya}=xa   naji-nao
      1SG.SUBJ=   not.want=GEN   2SG.SUBJ=   depart=LK   let-1SG.ABS
      "'I don't want you to leave me.'" (lit. "'I don't want that you depart and leave me.'")
                                                      Yal-20092011-AW1_0079

(101) « *na kuar ri ji wayap,* »
      na=   kuar=i̱   {ji=   wayap}
      1SG.SUBJ=   not.want=GEN   1DU.INCL.SUBJ=   war
      "'I don't want us to be at war.'" (lit. "'I don't want that we make war.'")
                                                      Yal-20092011-AW4_0033

7.3.8 Reason clause marker *puu-r* 'origin'

Several constructions which are used as complementation strategies in Belep, including some predicate nominals (see §7.3.7) and relative clauses (discussed in detail in §7.4), may incorporate the form *puu-r*, which is associated with adverbial predications of reason or purpose. *Puu-r* falls into the word class of nouns (§3.3.1), being the generically possessed form of the class 1 (§4.2.1.1) noun *pu-* 'origin, reason, ancestor'. Examples (102) and (103) show the use of this noun as the argument of a clause; such usages are uncommon in Belep, as *puu-r* is more frequently used in a variety of complementation strategies.[28]

(102) **Mari, yo ki âda jua âria puumw mo pu âjuroven.**
      Mari   **yo**   **ki**   **âda**
      Mary   2SG.INDEP   REL   alone

      jua   **âria**   **<u>puu</u>-mw**   **mo**   **pu**   **âju-roven**
      truly   NEG.EX   origin-2SG.POSS   LK3   origin   person-all
      'Mary, you who alone truly have no ancestors but are the ancestor of all.'
                                                                                                                                                  Paradiso

(103) **Ma te cavac, ka âri na ênae puur.**
      ma=re   **cavac**   **ka**
      LK4=3SG.SUBJ   depart   LK

      âri=   **na=**   **êna-e**   **puu-r**
      NEG=   1SG.SUBJ= know-SPC   origin-3GNR.POSS
      'The reason she left is not obvious.' (lit. 'That she left, I don't know the reason.')
                                                      Yal-11112011-PT1.wav – Yal-11112011-PT2.wav

In one Belep complementation strategy, *puu-r* acts as a predicate nominal (§6.5.1) and is followed by the morpheme =*li*, =*i* (§7.3.7) and a semantically dependent clause. For example, in (104), *puu-r* is followed by =*i* and a reason clause *na âyawe januun* 'I fear his spirit'.

(104) « **Na âya li na pan na pu caya puur ri, na âyawe januun.** »
      na=   **âya=li**   **na=**   **pan=a**   **pu**   **caya**
      1SG.SUBJ= fear.GNR=GEN   1SG.SUBJ= go.TV=LOC   side   dad

      {pu-r}=<u>i</u>   **{na=**   **âyawe**   **januu-n}**
      origin-3GNR.POSS=GEN   1SG.SUBJ= fear.SPC   spirit-3SG.POSS
      'I am afraid to go near Dad because, I fear his spirit.' (lit. 'I am afraid to go near Dad, the reason is, I fear his spirit.')
                                                                       Yal-20092011-AW1_0039

---

[28] Note that *puu-r* rarely occurs in its complete phase in discourse (see §2.5.2).

Another example is found in (105), where reason clause *kîîr ra denaar* 'the sun was bright' (marked by =*i*) follows *puu-r*. This clause modifies the earlier proposition (not shown here) that *te koni kiyi Belema* 'he didn't see the Belema'.

(105)   *Puur ri kîîr ra denaar.*
      {pu-r}=i̱   {kîr=a   denaar}
      origin-3GNR.POSS=GEN   be.loud=NOM   daylight
      'Because the sun was so bright.' (lit. 'The reason was that the sun was bright.')
                                                                                     Yal-20092011-AW4_0014

In many cases, predicate nominal *puu-r* may participate in an equative construction (§6.5.1), where its genitive-marked argument is a noun phrase which functions to provide a reason or cause, as in examples (106) - (108).

(106)   *Puur ri wa pe âma naen nile.*
      {pu-r}=i̱
      origin-3GNR.POSS=GEN

      {wa=   pe=   âma=   nae-n=i-le}
      NMLZ=   RECP= DYAD=   child-3SG.POSS=GEN-3DU.ABS
      'Because of their family ties.' (lit. 'Their way of being a family is the reason.')
                                                        Yal-25072010-PT-homily_0052

In (106), the argument of the predicate nominal *puu-r* is the genitive-marked noun phrase *wa pe âma naen nile* 'their way of being a family'. In (107), the argument of *puu-r* is *ûjen* 'his power'.

(107)   *Tere êna. Puur ri ûjen.*
      te=re   êna   {pu-r}=i̱
      3SG.SUBJ=ACT   know.GNR   origin-3GNR.POSS=GEN

      {ûje-n}
      power-3SG.POSS
      'He will actually know. Because of his power.' (lit. 'He will actually know. His power is the reason.')
                                                           Yal-20092011-AW5_0051

In (108), the argument of predicate nominal *puu-r* is *camang* 'my father'.

(108) **Toma naoxa na pwai ênau to puur ri camang.**
       toma   nao=xa   na=   pwai
       but   1SG.INDEP=ADD   1SG.SUBJ=   only

       êna-u=ro   {pu-r}=i̱   {cama-ng}
       know-DETR=when   origin-3GNR.POSS=GEN   father-1SG.POSS
       'But me too, I only know because of my father.'
                                                    Yal-28072010-BGMCG-hamecon_0084

Belep speakers use a similar predicate nominal construction *puur ri da ?* 'why?' (lit. 'the reason is what?') to question a reason, as in (109).

(109) **« Caivak, puur ri da yo âpw ? »**
       caivak   {pu-r}=i̱   {da}   yo=   âpw
       rat   origin-3GNR.POSS=GEN   what   2SG.SUBJ= laugh
       '"Rat, why are you laughing?"' (lit. '"What is the reason that you are laughing?"')
                                                               Yal-01082010-MFD_0050

The argument of predicate nominal *puu-r* may also be a demonstrative pronoun (§4.3.2). For example, in (110), the argument of *puu-r* is the demonstrative pronoun *â-li* 'DEM.NEW-DET.A.PRX'; the use of the proximal anaphoric determiner suffix implies that the reason was evident in the entirety of the preceding explanation.

(110) **Laxa âmu êna ka, tuu ûje teâmaa to puur ri âli.**
       la=xa   âmu=   êna   ka
       3PL.SUBJ=ADD   PRF=   know.GNR   LK

       tu   ûje   teâma=ro   {pu-r}=i̱
       EX.SPC   power   high.chief=when   origin-3GNR.POSS=GEN

       {â-li}
       DEM.NEW-DET.A.PRX
       'And they knew that the chief was powerful because of this.'
                                                          Yal-20092011-AW2_0071

When the argument of predicate nominal *puu-r* is a demonstrative pronoun, it may function in turn as the head of a relative clause (§7.4.3) which predicates a reason or purpose. For example, (111) and (112) both demonstrate this structure.

(111)   *Puur ri âmi ava mo pae comu li gawaarimi la mon.*
        {pu-r}=i̱   {â-mi   ava=
        origin-3GNR.POSS=GEN   DEM.NEW-DET.A.DST   1PL.EXCL.SUBJ=

        mo   pa-e   comu=li   gawari-mi=la   mon}
        live   take-SPC   school=GEN   day-DET.A.DST=LOC   side.DH
        'Because we had school the next day.' (lit. 'The fact that we had school the next day was the reason.')
                                                Yal-17072009-TB-weekend_0041

In (111), predicate nominal *puu-r* has as its argument the relative clause *âmi ava mo pae comu li gawaarimi la mon* 'the fact that we had school the next day', which is headed by the demonstrative pronoun *â-mi*. In (112), the relative clause *âmi laô wanem vaer ri janu* 'the fact that the spirits were walking with him' serves as the argument for predicate nominal *puu-r*.

(112)   *Puur ri âmi laô wanem vaer ri janu.*
        {pu-r}=i̱   {â-mi
        origin-3GNR.POSS=GEN   DEM.NEW-DET.A.DST

        la=ô   wane=va-er=i   janu}
        3PL.SUBJ=REAL   walk=INSTR-3SG.ABS=GEN   spirit
        'Because the spirits were walking with him.' (lit. 'The fact that the spirits were walking with him was the reason.')
                                                Yal-28072010-BGMCG-tahitian_0299-0300

7.3.8.1 Linkers and *puu-r*

Combinations of linkers with *puu-r* also occur in Belep. There are examples of *puu-r* preceding *to* 'when' (§7.3.3), as in (113) and (114).

(113)   *Te wiu puur to te maac yi cawi.*
        te=   wiu   pu-ra=ro
        3SG.SUBJ=   dine   origin-3GNR.POSS=when

        te=   may=i   cawi
        3SG.SUBJ=   die=GEN   hunger
        'He eats because he is hungry.'
                                                Yal-03112011-IM1.wav – Yal-03112011-IM2.wav

(114) **_puur to te para,_**
 pu-ra=ro te= para
 origin-3GNR.POSS=when 3SG.SUBJ= tell.GNR
 'because he told me,'
 Yal-28072010-BGMCG-hamecon_0086

There are also instances of *to* 'when' preceding *puu-r*, as shown in example (115).

(115) **_Toma nao, ka na pwai ênau to puur ri camang._**
 toma nao=xa na= pwai
 but 1SG.INDEP=LK 1SG.SUBJ= only

 êna-u=ro pu-r=i cama-ng
 know-DTR=when origin-3GNR.POSS=GEN father-1SG.POSS
 'But me too, I only know because of my father.'
 Yal-28072010-BGMCG-hamecon_0084

Puu-r may also occur with *ma* 'LK4' (§7.3.2.1), as shown in example (116).

(116) **_Âri na ênae puur ma na tume._**
 âri= na= êna-e puu-r
 NEG= 1SG.SUBJ= know-SPC origin-3GNR.POSS

 ma na= tu=me
 LK4 1SG.SUBJ= go.DH=CTP
 'I don't know why I came down here.'
 Yal-03112011-IM1.wav – Yal-03112011-IM2.wav

7.3.9 Serialization as a complementation strategy

The modal function of same-subject serial verb constructions (SVCs) in Belep was discussed in §5.10. Switch-subject SVCs,[29] by contrast, are used as a complementation strategy.[30]

In Belep, when an SVC is used as a complementation strategy, it conforms to the pattern shown in (117), where two verb phrases (§5.11) occur in series with no linking morphology.

---

[29] That is, serialized clauses with different subjects.
[30] The similarity between the use of paratactic complements and verb serialization in complementation is described in Noonan (2007:65).

	VP1	VP2
(117)	{VERB ABS.}	{bwa= VERB (ABS.)}

Here, the first verb phrase obligatorily contains an absolutive (§6.4.1) argument (whether it is indexed by a full noun phrase or by a pronominal suffix) which serves as the subject of the second verb phrase. The second verb phrase obligatorily contains the continuative aspectual proclitic *bwa=* (§5.5.4), and no other verbal modifiers, such as mood or subject agreement, may occur within it. In SVCs which can be schematized as in (117), the first verb phrase contains a verb of perception; in my corpus, only *kiya* 'to see' and *tue* 'to find' are represented. The verb in the second verb phrase tends to be semantically stative and intransitive.

For example, in (118), the absolutive argument of the first verb phrase, indexed by the pronominal suffix *-e*, serves as the subject for the second verb phrase *bwa mae* 'sleeping'. The shared argument is underlined.

(118)   ***Lexa tue bwa mae.***
        {le=xa   tu-<u>e</u>}   {bwa=   mae}
        3DU.SUBJ=ADD   find-3SG.ABS   CONT=   sleep
        'And they found her sleeping.'
                                                                                    Yal-20092011-AW1_0263

Note that there is no morphosyntactic link between the two verb phrases, and that the second verb phrase does not contain a subject agreement proclitic (§5.8)—to do so would be ungrammatical. The same situation holds in (119), where the absolutive argument of *kiyi* 'see.SPC' is indexed by *-e* and also serves as the subject of *bwa maac* 'dead'.

(119)   ***Pame la teâmaa ka kiyie bwa maac.***
        pa=me=la   **teâmaa**   **ka**   **{kiyi-<u>e</u>}**
        go.TV=CTP=NOM   high.chief   LK   see.SPC-3SG.ABS

        {bwa=   maac}
        CONT=   die
        'The chief came and saw her dead.'
                                                                                    Yal-20092011-AW1_0274

In examples (120) - (122), the absolutive argument of the first verb phrase is indexed by a full noun phrase, which also acts as the subject of the second verb phrase. In (120), the first verb is *tue* 'to find'; its absolutive argument is *Kawo* 'Kawo [a person's name]'. *Kawo* is also understood as the subject of the verb phrase *bwa mo la mwa* 'living in the house'.

(120) *Cebaba le ulayimi banen, ka, tu Kawo bwa mo la mwa.*
      Cebaba   le   ulayi-mi   bane-n   ka
      Cebaba   LK2 old.man-DET.A.DST friend-3SG.POSS LK

      {tu   Kawo}   {bwa=   mo=la   mwa}
      find   Kawo   CONT=   live=LOC house
      'Cebaba and his old friend, they found Kawo living in the house.'
                                                            Yal-20092011-AW1_0225-0226

In (121), the first verb is *kiyi* 'see.SPC'; its absolutive argument *naer pwalaic* 'a child' also serves as the subject of the second verb phrase *bwa go* 'crying'.

(121) *kiyi naer pwalaic bwa go.*
      {kiyi   nae-ra   pwalaic} {bwa=   go}
      see.SPC   child-3SG.POSS one   CONT=   cry
      '[they] saw a child crying.'
                                                  Yal-28072010-BGMCG-tayamu_0045

In (122), the first verb is *era* (§5.2.2); its absolutive argument is *âju* 'person', which also serves as the subject of the second verb phrase *bwa tu covan nexeng* 'riding here'.

(122) *era âju bwa tu covan nexeng.*
      {era   âju}   {bwa=   tu=   covan=exeng}
      DEM.PRES   person   CONT=   VBLZ=   horse=LOC.DC
      'there was a person riding here [on his back].'
                                                  Yal-28072010-BGMCG-tahitian_0262

In example (123), though the absolutive argument of the first verb phrase *kiya* 'see.GNR' is not explicitly stated within the clause, it is understood from context to be the *daan* 'blood' that was just mentioned. This noun phrase also functions as the subject of the second verb phrase in the serial construction, *bwa ce la bwe yeek* 'sitting on a branch'.

(123) *La noda, te tu la daan, kiya bwa ce la bwe yeek.*
      la=   no=da   te=   tu=la
      3PL.SUBJ=   peer=DIR.UH   3SG.SUBJ=   go.DH=NOM

daa-n	**{kiya}**	**{bwa=**	**ce=la**		**bwe**	**yeek}**
blood-3SG.POSS	see.GNR	CONT=	settle=LOC		top	tree

'They looked up, his blood was flowing, [they] saw [some] sitting on a branch.'

Yal-20092011-AW5_0091

7.4 Relative clauses

Most languages have some construction whereby the subject of a clause is relativized such that the clause becomes part of a noun phrase (Keenan & Comrie 1977: 67). Many languages are also capable of relativizing other noun phrases, and Keenan and Comrie's (1977) accessibility hierarchy (Figure 1), revised in Comrie and Keenan (1979), explores what roles these noun phrases are likely to have within the relative clause. Namely, "If a language can relativize any position on the A[ccessibility] H[ierarchy], then it can relativize all higher positions" (Comrie & Keenan 1979: 651); that is, all positions to the left.[31]

SU > DO > IO > OBL > GEN > OCOMP

Fig. 1: Keenan and Comrie's (1977: 66) accessibility hierarchy

Belep speakers are able to relativize most corresponding positions on the Accessibility Hierarchy, including subjects (see §6.3), absolutive arguments (§6.4.1), datives (§6.4.4), and locatives (§6.4.5). Temporal obliques, which do not receive case-marking in simple clauses, can also be relativized.

There are three types of relative clause construction in Belep, which will be discussed in detail in the sections that follow. In the first type (§7.4.1), the relative clause is marked with the linker *ki*, =*xi* 'REL' (see §7.3.6) and the head noun phrase is New information. The second type (§7.4.2), which uses a noun phrase-suffixed determiner as the relativizer, is used when the head noun phrase is Identifiable information. The third type (§7.4.3) uses relative pronouns[32] which agree in number and animacy with the head noun phrase. This type of relative can best be characterized as 'empty head' (Fox & Thompson 2007) or 'free' (Andrews 2007b).

There are two main grammatical strategies in Belep by which the relativized noun phrase's role in the relative clause can be understood by the hearer: pronominal elements, where an appropriate pronoun appears in the position of the NP_{rel}; and the gap strategy, where the normal position of the NP_{rel} is empty. Both of these strategies

---

31 Subject, direct object, indirect object, oblique, genitive, and object of comparison.
32 These relative pronouns are drawn from the set of demonstrative pronouns (§4.6.2).

are commonly found cross-linguistically (Keenan & Comrie 1977, Comrie & Keenan 1979, Keenan 1985, Payne 1997). In Belep, the three types of relatives differ in terms of the strategies they employ to identify the role of the NP$_{rel}$. These differences are discussed in §7.4.4.

In the examples that follow, relative clauses will be surrounded by {...} and the noun phrase head will be underlined. Omitted reference to the relativized noun phrase will be indicated by [0].

7.4.1 Relative clauses with relativizer *ki* 'REL'

Relativizer *ki* is used when the head noun phrase of the relative clause is New information.[33] This relative clause construction can be used to relativize subjects, as in (124), or absolute arguments as in (125) and (126). It is unknown whether *ki*-relativization, which is fairly uncommon, can be used to relativize other types of arguments.

(124)   *Tere tuya âju avar ki ce.*
       te=re   tuya   âju   avari{=xi   [0]   ce}
       3SG.SUBJ=ACT EX.GNR person other=REL   settle

       Âri jaroven.
       âri=   ja-roven
       NEG=   1PL.INCL.INDEP-all
       'There are actually other people who stay [on the good path]. It's not all of us.'
                                                Yal-25072010-PT-homily_0073

Note that the relativized subject argument in (124) is omitted, while the relativized absolutive in (125) is indicated by the pronominal verb suffix *-e*.

(125)   *Âria mwa pwalaic ki la tue.*
       âria   mwa   pwalaiyi{=xi   la=   tu-e}
       NEG.EX house   one=REL   3PL.SUBJ= find-3SG.ABS
       'There was not a single house that they found.'
                                      Yal-28072010-BGMCG-sousmarin_0117

---

33 A similar system is found in Nêlêmwa (Bril 2002), where the invariant relativizer is *xe*, and Balade Nyelâyu (Ozanne-Rivierre 1998), where the relativizer is of the form *ka*.

(126)   *Toma âria coutume ki avena îna.*
        toma   âria   coutume   {ki   avena=   îna}
        but   NEG.EX   ritual.gift.LN REL   1TR.EXCL.SUBJ=   make.GNR
        'But there was no ritual gift that we performed.'
                                            Yal-28072010-BGMCG-tahitian_0026

As these examples show, relativization with *ki* is most common with an existential or negative existential predicate in the main clause; the relativized noun phrase is being introduced as New. Interestingly, *ki*-relativization can also occur without a noun phrase head, as in (127).

(127)   *Ka âria ki tame la Weaa.*
        ka   âria{=xi   ta=me=la   Weaa}
        LK   NEG.EX=REL   go.UH=CTP=LOC   Weaa
        'And there was nothing that made it up to Weaa.'
                                            Yal-28072010-BGMCG-sousmarin_0094

7.4.2 Relative clauses with a determiner

In some relative clauses in Belep, a determiner suffix (§4.5.2) attaches to the lexical head noun phrase, where it acts as a relativizer. This construction is used in Belep when the head noun phrase is Identifiable information—that is, information which has previously been textually or situationally evoked, or which the "speaker assumes the hearer can infer [via logical or plausible] reasoning" (Prince 1981:236). Such determiner-relatives are fairly uncommon in my corpus.

If the relativized noun phrase acts as the relative clause subject, the NP$_{rel}$ reference on the verb (the subject agreement proclitic) is omitted, as in (128) and (129), where it is indicated by **[0]**.

(128)   *Âjumi ci ta la na mwanok,*
        âju{-mi   [0]   ci   ta=la   na   mwanok}
        person-DET.A.DST   sit   go.UH=LOC   interior   moon
        'The person who nonetheless went to the moon,'
                                            Yal-28072010-BGMCG-lune_0066-0067

(129)   *Na ênae âjumi cagele.*
        na=   êna-e   âju{-mi   [0]   cage-le}
        1SG.SUBJ=   know-SPC   person-DET.D.DST   steal.TR-3DU.ABS
        'I know the person who stole them.'
                                            Yal-02112011-DY.wav

In other types of determiner-relatives, the NP$_{rel}$ is indicated by a pronominal element. In (130) and (131), the relativized absolute argument is indicated by the pronominal verb inflection *-er*.

(130) ***tayamomi yo kiyier yak***
tayamo{-mi   yo=   **kiyi-era**   **yak}**
old.woman-DET.D.DST 2SG.SUBJ=   see.SPC-3SG.ABS   yesterday
'the woman you saw yesterday'

Yal-02112011-DY.wav

(131) ***Gawaariik te jier ri kawuja,***
gawari{-xa=re   **ji-er=i**
day-DET.D.PRX=3SG.SUBJ   give.SPC-3SG.ABS=GEN

kawu-ja}
guardian-1PL.INCL.POSS
'This day that our Lord has given,'

Yal-25072010-PT-homily_0005

In (132), the relativized noun phrase is a dative argument, referenced by the possessive pronominal suffix *-n*.

(132) ***âma naenimi na pana oyer reen***
âma=   **nae-ni{-mi**   na=
DYAD=   child-3SG.POSS-DET.D.DST   1SG.SUBJ=

pana=   **oyer=ee-n}**
go.TV   visit=DAT-3SG.POSS
'the family I visited'

Yal-02112011-DY.wav

In (133), the relativized noun phrase is a locative argument, referred to by the possessive pronominal suffix *-n*.

(133) ***yerimi na ji ariidu la nan***
yeri{-mi   na=   ji
pot-DET.D.DST   1SG.SUBJ=   give

```
ari=du=la              na-n}
rice=DIR.DH=LOC        interior-3SG.POSS
'the pot I put rice in'
```

Yal-02112011-DY.wav

7.4.3 Relative clauses with a relative pronoun

The most common type of relative clause in Belep is demonstrative-relatives; that is, relative clauses which employ a demonstrative pronoun (§4.6.2) as a relative pronoun.[34] These relative pronouns are composed of bound pronominal stems to which a determiner suffix (§4.5.2) is attached. As with determiner-relatives (discussed above in §7.4.2), the determiner suffix in demonstrative-relatives acts as a relativizer. The role of the head noun phrase, on the other hand, is filled by the bound pronominal stem, which is marked for number, animacy, and information structure (though not grammatical function). As this head noun phrase is semantically empty rather than lexical, these Belep demonstrative-relatives are best characterized as 'empty head' relatives. Fox and Thompson (2007) define "Empty Head NPs to be those which are not lexically specific and/or which index generic groups or sets of individuals or objects" (Fox & Thompson 2007:297). Comparable relative clauses in other languages have also been termed 'free relatives' (Andrews 2007b:213), although there is some disagreement among scholars as to whether 'empty heads' should be considered outside of or part of the relative clause (Bresnan & Grimshaw 1978).

Belep demonstrative-relatives may occur with both New and Identifiable information as the head noun phrase. As with determiner-relatives, a relativized subject argument is not marked within the relative clause; the subject reference on the verb is omitted, as shown in (134) and (135).

```
(134)   Âri yo li âmi ca bae - bae du liva,
        âri=    yo=li           â{-mi
        NEG=    2SG.INDEP=GEN   DEM.NEW-DET.A.DST
```

---

34 The term 'relative pronoun' is overused cross-linguistically and relative pronouns should in general be considered an areal feature of European languages (Comrie 1998). Nonetheless, a Belep demonstrative pronoun which acts as the head of a relative clause should be considered a relative pronoun because it "reflects some properties of the NP$_{rel}$ within the restricting clause" (Payne 1997:326); namely, Belep relative pronouns are marked for the number, animacy, and information structure of the NP$_{rel}$.

    [0]   ca=   bae   bae   du=li-va}
            ITER   bite   bite   bones=GEN-1PL.EXCL.ABS
    '"Aren't you the one who always eats- eats our bones,"'
                                             Yal-01082010-MFD_0034-0035

(135)   *Pawi, nyami cuur ra alap.*
        pawi   nya{-mi   [0]   cur=a   alap}
        beach.hibiscus   DEM.IDF-DET.A.DST   stand=LOC beach
        'The hibiscus, the one that stands on the beach."
                                             Yal-20092011-AW6_0071

If an absolutive argument is relativized, the NP$_{rel}$ is referenced by a pronominal element. In the absolutive relatives in (136) and (137), the NP$_{rel}$ is marked by the third singular absolutive suffix -*e* on the verb.

(136)   *nyami na, na bwawie,*
        nya{-mi   na=   na=   bwawi-e}
        DEM.IDF-DET.A.DST   1SG.SUBJ=   1SG.SUBJ=   remove.TR-3SG.ABS
        'the one I adopted,' (lit. 'the one I removed,')
                                             Yal-17072009-TB-weekend_0033

(137)   *Ka temere uya la mwimi te nooxee.*
        ka   te=me=re   uya=la
        LK   3SG.SUBJ=IRR=ACT   arrive=NOM

        mwi{-mi=re   noxe-e}
        DEM.IA-DET.A.DST=3SG.SUBJ   solicit.TR-3SG.ABS
        'And what s/he asked for will happen.'
                                             Yal-25072010-PT-homily_0045

In (138), the relativized noun phrase is a locative, and is marked within the relative clause by the anaphoric locational enclitic =*i* 'there' (§5.13).

(138)   *Yami teô pwec yi.*
        ya{-mi=re=ô   pwey=i}
        DEM.LOC-DET.A.DST=3SG.SUBJ=REAL   be.born=LOC.A
        'Where she was born.'
                                             Yal-20092011-AW1_0271

In (139) and (140), the relativized noun phrase is a temporal oblique and is not referenced within the relative clause.

(139) **nyami le uya la Nic,**
 nya{-mi le= uya=la Nic}
 DEM.GIV-DET.A.DST 3DU.SUBJ= arrive=LOC Nic
 '[the time] when they arrived at Nic,'
 Yal-20092011-AW1_0217

(140) **nyali te ta la Teâ Belep,**
 nya{-li te= ta=la Teâ Belep}
 DEM.GIV-DET.A.PRX 3SG.SUBJ= go.UH=NOM Teâ Belep
 '[the time] when Teâ Belep came up,'
 Yal-20092011-AW3_0039

7.4.4 Identification of the relativized noun phrase

As I have already mentioned, the three types of relative clause constructions may also be distinguished from one another on the basis of the strategies they employ to mark the grammatical role of the relativized noun phrase.

Though both *ki*-relatives and headless relatives employ the gap strategy for some types of subject-relativization and pronominal elements for most other types (except for relativized temporal obliques), they differ in the exact point on the Accessibility Hierarchy where they draw the line between these two strategies. Briefly, for *ki*-relatives, only third person singular subject relatives are omitted; other subject relatives use pronominal elements. For example, (141) contains a subject relative with a second person singular subject; the pronominal element *yo=* is used.

(141) **Enyi ki, enyi ki yo âju ki âri yo ce ô,**
 enyixi enyixi yo
 if[35] if 2SG.SUBJ=

 âju{=xi **âri=** **yo=** **ce** **ô}**
 person=REL NEG= 2SG.SUBJ= settle good
 'If, if you are a person who does not stay well [on the good path],'
 Yal-25072010-PT-homily_0060

---

35 Note that the form *enyixi* is most likely an older form of *enyi* (§7.3.4).

In (142), the subject relative has a third person plural subject; again, a pronominal element (*la=*) is used.

(142) **Lame migila ki la ta.**
 la=me migi-la{=xi la= ta}
 3PL.SUBJ=IRR catch-3PL.ABS=REL 3PL.SUBJ= go.UH
 'They would catch the ones that were going up.'
 Yal-28072010-BGMCG-igname_0038

In contrast, demonstrative-relatives use the gap strategy for all subject relatives. Example (143) shows an omitted subject reference for a third person plural subject relative.

(143) **La kiyier ri lami bwa molep,**
 la= kiyi-er=i la{-mi
 3PL.SUBJ= see.SPC-3SG.ABS=GEN DEM.PL-DET.A.DST

 [0] bwa= molep}
 CONT= be.alive
 'Those who were still alive saw them,'
 Yal-20092011-AW2_0073

Determiner-relatives behave more like headless relatives in that all subject markers are omitted; example (144) shows that the use of a third person plural verb agreement proclitic is ungrammatical, while omitting the clitic makes it grammatical.

(144) *__âjuli la bwa molep__
 âju{-li la= bwa= molep}
 person-DET.A.PRX 3PL.SUBJ= CONT= be.alive
 *'people who are still alive'

 âjumi bwa molep
 âju{-mi [0] bwa= molep}
 person-DET.A.DST CONT= be.alive
 'people who are still alive'
 Yal-02112011-DY.wav

7.5 Summary

In this chapter, I have presented the set of clausal combinations that exist in Belep. Clausal coordination, in which linkers *ka* 'LK', *ai* 'or', *mo* 'LK3', *toma* 'but', and *kara* 'well' are used, was discussed in §7.2. A variety of Belep complementation strategies (as defined by Dixon 1995, 2006) were discussed in §7.3; most of them involve semantically dependent pseudocoordinate clauses (as described in Ross 2016) which are morphosyntactically indistinguishable from coordinate clauses. Here, linkers such as *ka* 'LK', *ma* 'LK4', *to* 'when', *enyi* 'if', and *ka me* 'then', act as pseudocoordinators. Other complementation strategies include predicate nominals (see §7.3.7 and §7.3.8), serialization (§7.3.9), and nominalization using derivational morphology (discussed in §3.6.2). Note that no true complementation, where a clause acts as an argument of another clause (Noonan 2007), exists in Belep—this contrasts with related languages such as Nêlêmwa (Bril 2002), South Efate (Thieberger 2006), and Fijian (Dixon 1995), which do have complementation. Belep relative clauses were discussed in §7.4; they play a role in various other constructions in Belep, including question-word questions (§6.6.2) and complementation strategies (see §7.3.6 and §7.3.8).

Appendix A: Glossing conventions

1DU.EXCL.ABS	-ve	first dual exclusive absolutive verb suffix; §5.7
1DU.EXCL.INDEP	ave	first dual exclusive independent pronoun; §4.6.1
1DU.EXCL.POSS	-ve	first dual exclusive possessive nominal suffix; §4.2.2.2
1DU.EXCL.SUBJ	ave=	first dual exclusive subject proclitic in the verb group; §5.8
1DU.INCL.ABS	-ji	first dual inclusive absolutive verb suffix; §5.7
1DU.INCL.INDEP	ji	first dual inclusive independent pronoun; §4.6.1
1DU.INCL.POSS	-ji	first dual inclusive possessive nominal suffix; §4.2.2.2
1DU.INCL.SUBJ	ji=	first dual inclusive subject proclitic in the verb group; §5.8
1PA.EXCL.ABS	-ven	first paucal exclusive absolutive verb suffix; §5.7
1PA.EXCL.INDEP	aven	first paucal exclusive independent pronoun; §4.6.1
1PA.EXCL.POSS	-ven	first paucal exclusive possessive nominal suffix; §4.2.2.2
1PA.EXCL.SUBJ	avena=	first paucal exclusive subject proclitic in the verb group; §5.8
1PA.INCL.ABS	-jen	first paucal inclusive absolutive verb suffix; §5.7
1PA.INCL.INDEP	jen	first paucal inclusive independent pronoun; §4.6.1
1PA.INCL.POSS	-jen	first paucal inclusive possessive nominal suffix; §4.2.2.2
1PA.INCL.SUBJ	jena=	first paucal inclusive subject proclitic in the verb group; §5.8
1PL.EXCL.ABS	-va	first plural exclusive absolutive verb suffix; §5.7
1PL.EXCL.INDEP	ava	first plural exclusive independent pronoun; §4.6.1
1PL.EXCL.POSS	-va	first plural exclusive possessive nominal suffix; §4.2.2.2
1PL.EXCL.SUBJ	ava=	first plural exclusive subject proclitic in the verb group; §5.8
1PL.INCL.ABS	-ja	first plural inclusive absolutive verb suffix; §5.7
1PL.INCL.INDEP	ja	first plural inclusive independent pronoun; §4.6.1
1PL.INCL.POSS	-ja	first plural inclusive possessive nominal suffix; §4.2.2.2
1PL.INCL.SUBJ	ja=	first plural inclusive subject proclitic in the verb group; §5.8
1SG.ABS	-nao	first singular absolutive verb suffix; §5.7
1SG.INDEP	nao	first singular independent pronoun; §4.6.1
1SG.POSS	-ng	first singular possessive nominal suffix; §4.2.2.2
1SG.SUBJ	na=	first singular subject proclitic in the verb group; §5.8
2DU.ABS	-or	second dual absolutive verb suffix; §5.7
2DU.INDEP	or	second dual independent pronoun; §4.6.1
2DU.POSS	-or	second dual possessive nominal suffix; §4.2.2.2
2DU.SUBJ	o=	second dual subject proclitic in the verb group; §5.8
2PA.ABS	-ôn	second paucal absolutive verb suffix; §5.7
2PA.INDEP	ôn	second paucal independent pronoun; §4.6.1
2PA.POSS	-ôn	second paucal possessive nominal suffix; §4.2.2.2
2PA.SUBJ	ôna=	second paucal subject proclitic in the verb group; §5.8
2PL.ABS	-ac	second plural absolutive verb suffix; §5.7
2PL.INDEP	ac	second plural independent pronoun; §4.6.1
2PL.POSS	-ac	second plural possessive nominal suffix; §4.2.2.2
2PL.SUBJ	a=	second plural subject proclitic in the verb group; §5.8
2SG.ABS	-o	second singular absolutive verb suffix; §5.7
2SG.INDEP	yo	second singular independent pronoun; §4.6.1
2SG.POSS	-mw	second singular possessive nominal suffix; §4.2.2.2
2SG.SUBJ	yo=	second singular subject proclitic in the verb group; §5.8
3DU.ABS	-le	third dual absolutive verb suffix; §5.7

3DU.INDEP	le	third dual independent pronoun; §4.6.1
3DU.POSS	-le	third dual possessive nominal suffix; §4.2.2.2
3DU.SUBJ	le=	third dual subject proclitic in the verb group; §5.8
3GNR.POSS	-r	third generic possessive nominal suffix; §4.2.2.2
3PA.ABS	-len	third paucal absolutive verb suffix; §5.7
3PA.INDEP	len	third paucal independent pronoun; §4.6.1
3PA.POSS	-len	third paucal possessive nominal suffix; §4.2.2.2
3PA.SUBJ	lena=	third paucal subject proclitic in the verb group; §5.8
3PL.ABS	-la	third plural absolutive verb suffix; §5.7
3PL.INDEP	la	third plural independent pronoun; §4.6.1
3PL.POSS	-la	third plural possessive nominal suffix; §4.2.2.2
3PL.SUBJ	la=	third plural subject proclitic in the verb group; §5.8
3SG.ABS	-er, -e	third singular absolutive verb suffix; §5.7
3SG.INDEP	yer	third singular independent pronoun; §4.6.1
3SG.POSS (3SG.POSS.SPC)	-n	third specific singular possessive nominal suffix; §4.2.2.2
3SG.SUBJ	te=	third singular subject proclitic in the verb group; §5.8
ABS		absolutive suffix; §5.7, §6.4.1
AC	-ma	associative plural nominal suffix; §4.3.1
ACT	=re	actual verb group enclitic; §6.9.2.2
ADD	=xa	additive verb group enclitic; §6.9.2.1
ADU	-male	associative dual nominal suffix; §4.3.2
AGT	â=	agentive derivational proclitic; §3.6.2.1
CAUS	pa=	causative verb group proclitic; §5.4
CL		numeral classifier; §4.7.3
COMPL	-roven	total nominal (§4.3.4) or completive verb group suffix (§5.5.11)
CONT	bwa=	continuative aspect verb group proclitic; §5.5.4
CTF	=ic	centrifugal (away from the speaker) verb phrase enclitic; §5.12
CTP	=me	centripetal (toward the speaker) verb phrase enclitic; §5.12
D		deictic
DA.IA	-a	inanimate differential absolutive verb suffix; §5.2.6
DA.NSG	-n	nonsingular differential absolutive verb suffix; §5.2.6
DAT	=(l)e	dative case ditropic clitic; §6.4.4
		ALTERNATE FORM =(l)ee
DEM		demonstrative pronoun; §4.6.2
DEM.DU	le-	dual demonstrative pronoun; §4.6.2
		ALTERNATE FORM lee-
DEM.IA	mwi-	singular inanimate demonstrative pronoun; §4.6.2
		ALTERNATE FORMS mwii-, wî-, wîi-
DEM.IDF	nya-	singular identifiable demonstrative pronoun; §4.6.2
DEM.LOC	ya-	locative demonstrative pronoun; §4.6.2
DEM.MAN	wa-	manner demonstrative pronoun; §4.6.2
		ALTERNATE FORM waa-
DEM.NEW	â-	new demonstrative pronoun; §4.6.2
DEM.PA	lenyi-	paucal demonstrative pronoun; §4.6.2
		ALTERNATE FORM lenyii-
DEM.PL	la-	plural demonstrative pronoun; §4.6.2
		ALTERNATE FORM laa-

DEM.PRES	ere-	presentational demonstrative pronoun; §4.6.2
		ALTERNATE FORM era-
DET		determiner suffix ; §4.4.2
DET.A.DST	-mi	distal anaphoric determiner nominal suffix; §4.4.2.2
DET.A.PRX	-li	proximal anaphoric determiner nominal suffix; §4.4.2.2
DET.D.DST	-xe	distal deictic determiner nominal suffix; §4.4.2.1
DET.D.MDS	-yek	medial-distal deictic determiner nominal suffix; §4.4.2.1
DET.D.MPX	-na	medial-proximal deictic determiner nominal suffix; §4.4.2.1
DET.D.PRX	-k	proximal deictic determiner nominal suffix; §4.4.2.1
DET.DH	-xedu	downhill deictic determiner nominal suffix; §4.4.2.1
DET.DST.DH	-midu	distal downhill deictic determiner nominal suffix; §4.4.2.1
DET.DST.UH	-yeda	distal uphill deictic determiner nominal suffix; §4.4.2.1
DET.Q1	-va	interrogative determiner nominal suffix; §4.4.2.3
DET.Q2	-da	interrogative determiner nominal suffix; §4.4.2.3
DET.Q3	-ra	interrogative determiner nominal suffix; §4.4.2.3
DET.UH	-xeda	uphill deictic determiner nominal suffix; §4.4.2.1
DETR	-u	detransitive verb suffix; §5.2.5
DIM	ma=	diminished aspect verb group proclitic; §5.5.7
DIR.DH	=du	downhill directional verb phrase enclitic; §5.12
DIR.TV	=van	transverse directional verb phrase enclitic; §5.12
DIR.UH	=da	uphill directional verb phrase enclitic; §5.12
DST		distal
DU		dual number
DUB	u=	dubitative aspect verb group proclitic; §5.5.10
DYAD	âma=	dyadic derivational proclitic; §3.6.1.2
EX	tuya	existential absolute intransitive verb; §5.2.2
		ALTERNATE FORMS tuu, tu
EXCL		exclusive
GE	-mene	general extender nominal (§4.3.3) or verb group suffix (§5.5.12)
GEN	=(l)i	genitive case ditropic clitic; §6.4.3
GNO	da=	gnomic aspect verb group proclitic; §5.5.6
GNR		generic; §5.2.4
HAB	tao=	habitual aspect verb group proclitic; §5.5.9
INCL		inclusive
INDEP		independent pronoun; §4.6.1
INSTR	ba=	instrumental derivational proclitic; §3.6.2.2
INSTR	=va	instrumental case ditropic clitic; §6.4.6
		ALTERNATE FORM =vae
IRR	=me	irrealis verb group enclitic; §5.6.2
ITER	ca=	iterative aspect verb group proclitic; §5.4.5
LK	ka	NP coordinator (§4.5.1) and clausal additive linker (§7.2.2)
LK2	le	binomial linker; §4.5.2
LK3	mo	causal linker; §7.2.3
LK4	ma	inclusory (§4.5.5) or comitative (§4.5.6) NP linker; purpose clause and correlational clausal linker (§7.3.2)
LN		loanword or instance of code-mixing; §1.7.2
LOC	=(l)a	locative case ditropic clitic; §6.4.5
LOC.A	=(l)i	anaphoric locational verb phrase enclitic; §5.13
LOC.DC	=(l)exeng	deictic center locational verb phrase enclitic; §5.13

LOC.DH	=(l)exedu	downhill locational verb phrase enclitic; §5.13
LOC.DST	=(l)exe	distal locational verb phrase enclitic; §5.13
LOC.DST.DH	=(l)imidu	distal downhill locational verb phrase enclitic; §5.13
LOC.DST.UH	=(l)iyeda	distal uphill locational verb phrase enclitic; §5.13
LOC.MDS	=(l)iyek	medial-distal locational verb phrase enclitic; §5.13
LOC.MPX	=(l)ena	medial-proximal locational verb phrase enclitic; §5.13
LOC.Q	=(l)iva	interrogative locational verb phrase enclitic; §5.13
LOC.UH	=(l)exeda	uphill locational verb phrase enclitic; §5.13
MDS		medial-distal
MPX		medial-proximal
NDR	-r	verb suffix indicating bound intransitive verb is unmarked for direction; §5.2.1.1
NEG	âri=	negative verb group proclitic; §6.8
NEG.EX	âria	negative existential absolute intransitive verb; §5.2.2
NEG.IMPER	wara=	prohibitive verb group proclitic; §6.7.2
NEG.LOC	cia	negative locative absolutive intransitive verb; §5.2.2 ALTERNATE FORM **ciae**
NEG.NEC	kara=	prohibitive verb group proclitic; §6.7.2
NEG.NEC	kiaxi=	negative verb group proclitic; §6.8
NOM	=(l)a	nominative case ditropic clitic; §6.4.2
NTR		intransitive; §5.2
ORD	ba=	ordinal derivational proclitic; §3.6.1.1
PA		paucal number
PL		plural number
POSS		possessive suffix; §4.2.2.2
PRF	âmu=	perfect aspect verb group proclitic; §5.5.2
PROG	âga=	progressive aspect verb group proclitic; §5.5.1
PRX		proximal
PUNCT	nyi=	punctual aspect verb group proclitic; §5.5.8
RA	pu=	reduced agentive verb group proclitic; §5.4
REAL	=ô	realis verb group enclitic; §5.6.1
RECP	pe=	reciprocal verb group proclitic; §5.4
REL	ki	relativizer (§7.4.1) and deontic clause marker (§7.3.6)
RESULT	wa=	resultative derivational proclitic; §3.6.2.3
SBJ	ba=	subjunctive aspect verb group proclitic; §5.5.3
SG		singular number
SPC	-e	specific verb suffix; §5.2.4
SUBJ		subject agreement; §5.8
TR		transitive; §5.2.5
TR	-li	transitive verb suffix; §5.2.5
UH		uphill; §4.4
VBLZ	tu=	verbalizer derivational proclitic; §3.6.4

Appendix B: Cited texts

Where possible, all examples in this book are drawn from texts—recorded and transcribed instances of language use by Belep speakers. These texts are normally cited using a unique code which contains the date (in the format DDMMYYYY), the speaker's initials, and a timecode. For example, 'Yal-17072009-TB-weekend_0036-0037' is a reference to the text entitled 'Yal-17072009-TB-weekend', at the timecode 0036-0037 (this identifier refers to a unique entry in a Toolbox database). Other texts, which do not yet have an associated Toolbox database, are cited with a timecode in a different format, e.g. 'Yal-05102010-MTAD_24:21-24:29'.

The following is a list of texts from which citations are drawn, as well as short descriptions of each text.

Yal-17072009-TB-weekend
BOUEDAOU Thérèse discusses what she and her family did last weekend.
Yal-25072010-PT-homily
TEANYOUEN Philippe gives a sermon at the church in Waala; he deconstructs the Lord's Prayer.
Yal-28072010-BGCG-lune
GUELEME Benjamin and Marie-Clothilde tell the legend of a paralyzed man from Poc who was the first person to visit the moon.
Yal-28072010-BGCG-hamecon
GUELEME Benjamin and Marie-Clothilde describe a particular technique for fishing.
Yal-28072010-BGCG-tahitian
GUELEME Benjamin and Marie-Clothilde tell a story about Benjamin's brother-in-law, a Tahitian, who offended the spirits at Poc and was punished.
Yal-28072010-BGCG-tayamu
GUELEME Marie-Clothilde and Benjamin tell a legend about two sisters who adopt a baby, but the baby turns out to be an old woman in disguise.
Yal-28072010-BGCG-sousmarin
GUELEME Benjamin and Marie-Clothilde tell a legend about a tsunami that wiped out the village of Ono.
Yal-28072010-BGCG-igname
GUELEME Benjamin and Marie-Clothilde discuss the religious significance of a particular site.
Yal-29072010-JMT-igname
THALE Jean-Marie describes the procedure for planting and harvesting yams.
Yal-01082010-MFD
TEAMBOUEON Marie-France tells a legend about the octopus and the rat.
Yal-09082010-coutume
MOILOU Jean-Baptiste performs a *coutume* before the *Conseil des anciens*.
Yal-09082010-JMTresponse
THALE Jean-Marie performs a *yayila*, a response to Jean-Baptiste.
Yal-11082010-ET2-jewe
THALE Elie tells a story about his father, who got lost because of *jewe*, mischievous spirits.
Yal-05092011-AP1
POITHILI Albert tells the legend of the Dubageni, a frightening demon.
Yal-05102010-MTAD
DAYE Alice and TEAMBOUEON Marjorie play card games.
Yal-14092011-PT2-avenir

TEANYOUEN Philippe gives his advice for future generations of Belema.

Yal-17092011-IM-dominoes
A group of women, including MOILOU Ignacia, play dominoes.

Yal-19092011-PA
POITHILI Allen tells the legend of the rock formation called Kawo and Ixe.

Yal-20092011-AW1
WAHOULO Amabili tells the story of Kawo, the daughter of Teâ Ciaup, being raised from the dead.

Yal-20092011-AW2
WAHOULO Amabili tells the story of a shipwreck at Easter where many members of clan THALE were killed.

Yal-20092011-AW3
WAHOULO Amabili tells the story of the battle of Koumac.

Yal-20092011-AW4
WAHOULO Amabili tells the story of the chief's daughters Kawo and Ixe halting a battle.

Yal-20092011-AW5
WAHOULO Amabili tells the story of Teâ Pûnivaac and his defeat by Teâ Belep.

Yal-20092011-AW6
WAHOULO Amabili tells the story of Teâ Belep's arrival on the island.

Yal-27092011-LPLY
PIDYO Lalita and YARIK Lisianne answer interview questions about their experience of being young people in Belep.

Balade-mariage
A collection of handwritten lyrics for traditional wedding songs.

DY classroom
A collection of handwritten signs posted in YARIK Darine's primary school classroom.

Paradiso
Song lyrics for a traditional mourning song.

PT handout
A set of typed and typewritten lists of vocabulary and grammar composed by TEANYOUEN Philippe.

Where examples could not be found in recorded texts, I have drawn them from elicitation or naturally-occurring speech that I overheard. In these cases, where possible, I have indicated the filename(s) of the recording where the example occurred. In these instances, .wav is always included in the citation code, e.g. 'Yal-07112011-TB1.wav – Yal-07112011-TB3.wav' indicates that the example was drawn from a recording session encompassed by three .wav files. These files are currently available in the archives of the ALK and of the Tjibaou Cultural Center.

Appendix C: Speakers

The following is a list of all Belep speakers whose speech was recorded for this work. Note that many, many other Belema assisted with the project, defined words, provided translations, wrote texts, engaged me in conversation, etc., allowing me to form a more complete understanding of the language. Some speakers are referred to by initials in the text; their names are indicated here.

	BOUEDAOU Edwin
TB	BOUEDAOU Thérèse
AD	DAYE Alice
	DAYE Laurente
BG	GUELEME Benjamin
CG	GUELEME Marie-Clothilde
	GUELEME Siméon
YG	GUELEME Yasmine
IM	MOILOU Ignacia
JBM	MOILOU Jean-Baptiste
AP	POITHILI Albert
PA	POITHILI Allen
	POITHILI Alexandrine
PP	POITHILI Pierre
	PIDJO Bruno
LP	PIDYO Lalita
	TEAMBOUEON Eulalie
	TEAMBOUEON François
MFD	TEAMBOUEON Marie-France
MT	TEAMBOUEON Marjorie
JT	TEANYOUEN Madeleine
PT	TEANYOUEN Philippe
ET	THALE Elie
JMT	THALE Jean-Marie
NT	THALE Nazaire
AW	WAHOULO Amabili
CW	WAHOULO Christine
DY	YARIK Darine
LY	YARIK Lisianne

Appendix D: Sample interlinearized text

The following is a narrative by GUELEME Benjamin (called Korowi in Belep) and his wife GUELEME Marie-Clothilde (who goes by Clothilde or Kloin). It is a description of an experience Benjamin had as a young man. The text is presented first in Belep, then in a free English translation, then in the four-line interlinearization used in the rest of this work.

GUELEME Benjamin and GUELEME Marie-Clothilde, 28 July 2010
Waala, Belep

BG:Elo, name pari l'histoire ra bweeng. Nao ka ulayixedu, Maxeek. Te uya la beau-frère rive pwalaic, naran ni Tayema, tahitien. Te tu ka tame ka pae avave tamwa. Texa wali, te- leme tume, toma te ca nobwawinao, ka nobwawi pwemwang, nyayek, te ca nobwawiva.

Texa tume, ô tume li vacances pwalaic, ka înae vacances yier rexeng, yak xeve.

Texa nooxeve ma avena pan, avena pan na Poc, ave ma ulayina. Avexa pae waga ulayixedu digi, avenaô pan. Ave ma tiaea ween no, ka tuve -- cawone ka tuvea ween ola. Avenaxa pan, te pae fusil sous-marin nie, avenaxa pan, avena panic, pan aven, pan aven, ka tabo la mayarixeda, yaxeda li Poc. Avena tewuur ra Iniwan. Avenaxa tu.

Toma âria coutume ki avena îna. Avenaô wana.

Avenaôxa tu, cawoneduic, tuic, tuic, tuic ka uya la Cager ka uya la Âmwany. Âria. Âria ola. Avenaxa pan. Avena ci -- mu la bwe buâny pwalaic. Mana buâny. Toma yali, ka naran ni Pwaraweli. Avena nawe nyu, ka ô ânap. Ka ô mon ni gawaar, avenaô wiu gawaar, ka ô toven.

Avexa, ave ma Maxeek, ave pa tânema cawone ka tu ka tuve ola. Na buânyili. Avexa tu la na buâny, toma yer, Tayema, tahitien, ka te ci la bwe digi. Toma ave, aveô plonger, aveô ta ka cawone, avexa cawonevan, cawonevan. Texa, avexa migi pwalaic. Pwalaic ola. Ka naxa paedu ka jida leen. Avexa ta ma naxa ta, avexa nyi tuvadu la na buâny waak. Ave pe namavan ka namame.

Ka te cuur ka tame, toma bwe nyaxeda (ka ja wânem ma bween, wali maan, te plat ra nyana buânyili). Ave nyi tuvadu la aran. Texa wâneda la bween, wânedaic, wânedaic, avexa, ave nyi tao nyi înae ola, ave koni pau. Pwai pwalaic pa ave. Avexa nyi înau, înau ka koni pau. Texa taic, naxa, ave cawonevan, naxa, na tuvavan, naxa bwagenao, ka ta ka uc, ka oyâno, ka noda lier to teô ta, teô ta la pwemwa. Enyi ulayili. Texaô ta.

Naô taic, naxa waak : « Hé ! Yo kiyi âjuyeda, teme perdu ! » Naxa kewee. Nao, naô pae tânema cawone, payee, ka kewee. Na nyi kewee ka to jie : « Ai ! » Ka me to jie, « Ai ! » Ka me to mwa, « Ai ! » Ka tabodu ka kewee. To na êna ka te perdu. Naxa kewee. Avexa taic, taic. Na koni mwanaolie. Ave ta, pewove li maan pwalaic, maana buâny to waak xa maan. Texa, te nam ma mayariyek, toma bwa nao lexeng. Te wadivan, toma bwa nao la mayariik. Naxa, na kovavan, ka naô yaagie, ciae. Te wali maar ri te disparu na yali. Ô ciae.

Naxa, na tao toda, na pwai kiya nabwa wîîk, kan. Toma âju, âri na kiyie. To na pwai kiya nabwa kan to te been na bwe buâny. Te tao ta, toma âri na kiyi âju, na pwai kiya nabwa kan. Tayi ave, yaûda la bwe mweogo. Nare yaûda la moden. Tere cegon ni buâny, toma na koni kiyie. Te nyi tabo buâny nya bwe nabwa kan. Texa ta. Tayi ave, ka naô cuur ra bwe wîmi, ma na kaxi, te cegodu la na gawe, cegodu la na gawe ma teme ta. Naxa to, to, to, tovan ka âria.

Ka teô tame la Maxeek vae digi. Toma teô jua disparu, ô jua ciae. Te tame la Maxeek, ka waaxadame : « Ivie ? »

Naxa waak, « Ô ciae. Teô perdu. »

Texa waak, « Ca ! »

Naxa -- laô paer ri ulayama. « Maxeek, laô pae. Ô ciae. Yo âya. » Âya la Maxeek. Ka ô tuic, tu la nao ka ôda la bwe, bwe digi.

Texa waak xa Maxeek, « Ji wa ? »

Na waak, « Ji ta. Yo ta. Ji ta la Panan. » Avexa tame, aveô tuic ka ô ta le mayin. Jua âya la Maxeek. Avexaô tame.

Toma te naji terixo, ka cixare, ka claquettes. Te wânem âria claquettes. Avexa tame, naxa waak, « Yome ta ka ulinao la mariik, naran ni Bwadalo. » Aveô ta, ta la ave ka mu la yali, ave mu la Bwadalo. Naxa, na pa claquettes, ka pae terixo ka cixare, ka allumettes, na pae yadanada, ka uya la bwe mweogo Nyi Pwiya. Na Poc, naran ni We Tânema Kiliik.

Naxa waak, « Yome bwageo, yome bwageo Maxeek, yoxame tu mwa la yamidu Âmwany. Mo te perdu la Âmwany. Teme bwagedu la Âmwany. Toma nao, ka name yaûda la bwe mweogo, ka me tuic, me tu la Âmwany. »

Naxaô ta, ka ô nawe Maxeek, teô bwage Maxeek. Toma nao, naô yaûda la bwe ôgo. Na yaûda va wîîk, yadan. Paroven. Pada, pada, ka uya la bwe âxeda, bwe mweogo na lexeda, ka uya la bwe nyana buâny pwalaic, to Ôgaxoe. Te ci la bwe daan. Naxa ta ka pae yadan, ka jin na bwe Ôgaxoe. Na pojenin wana. Mo yadanaroven.

Naxa waak, « Na nook ma a ji bwage tahitien-mi a pae. » Naxa, na nawen yadan, naxaô tu la Âmwany, bwagenaodu, ô tu ka tu Maxeek, avexaô tame. Na pae bwe ôgo, toma Maxeek te pae we. Naxare wali. Toma cao la bweeng, cao nanamiu linao.

Ka ô tu la ave, ka tu la nao, ô tu Maxeek, ka ôdu la bwe waang. Texa waak, « Ka ivie ? » « Ô ciae. Toma lame jier ri ulayama ma te kova. » Avexaô tame. Avexaô pae digi ka ô tame. Tame la ave, ka kova la yamidu la Aliân. Ave kova la mariik xa Aliân, ka pame la Ima. Ave pame ce la Ima. Avexa noda, kiyi digi, pwalaic to te cavac ya na Panan, texa kejadu ka kova. Texa nome la ulayimi pae, ka kiyive. Te ta ma nawe bwagee. Texa kuar. Te kuar ra tahitien-li, mo âyuan ni texaô pame la Belep.

CG : Toma te waak, « Or riva ? »

BG : La tuer ra Panan, teôre, te ta, ka pae bwe ôgoda, ka wâneda. La paer ri ulayama, paeda, paedaic, wâneda, te bwageer ra mana pwemwa, ma na -- te bwageer ri coutume. Te îna ka te bwageer ri ka tume, ka tume cego la Panan.

Na cegodu la Panan, ka tuu ulac pwalaic, na Panan. Le ma yawan, lexa pe nayie, lexa âri ka ulac cavane, toma ulayili, tahitien (Toma te dadabwa, êê, te wali maar ri te dadabwa), ka go. Go u le ulayili ma te paeme la Belep. Teô cuur ra ulayili ka ô pae, paeme, toma ave tame, ka mwa tamwa, ka cuur ra pwemwa, yami la Panan. Ave ma ulayina, Maxeek, avexa ta pajer.

Texa âri (la vieille, yer, la vieille li ulayili, mo avave ma Maxeek), texa âri ka, ô erak ma leô tue teô godume ci la yayeda. Toma te da yagier ri, na yeexamene, te da, da la pegaon, ma te âri ka tuu âju ki ce lexeng. Te îniae wîîk. Te wali maar ri te tu covan na bwe dua noon. Te tao pae. Texaô paeme la Waala.

Avexa ta la ave, ka mu, texa âri la tayamoli avexa bwagevedu ka pame la moden, avexa pame, pame, pame, ka mu lexedu, toma teô, avena pe co ma digi to teô bwagee. (Ulayili, naran ni Edouard.) Teô bwageevan na Poc, toma aveô tame ka mu lena.

Ô baraap. Teô nam ma denaar. Avexa tame, pe tuve ma Maxeek. Avexaô tame, ta ma yagi ulayili. Avexa tame ka tuer rexeng, yak, na mwami âbur. (Te ci lexeng nga mwave âbur, tere yak xa playi.) Avexa, avexa boyu leen. Te kuarive. Te jua kuarive. Ka kâyee la tayamook. Te kâyeer ri tayamook xa na baraap, bwanili. Texa, tayamook, te taxeer ri we cexeen, ma te ûdu. Texa govan na ulac -- âyili, te govan na tahitien-li, ka pajeri âju wîmi me soigner-lie. Toma camang, camang te mo lexeda. Yaxeda le Joel. Texa, tume. Te to jie. Te ta la ti ?

CG : Yo.
BG : Elo, nao.
CG : Ai, ave ma ulayiik.

BG: Êê, or ma Orilô. Le ta ma âyimi avang, lexa ta, naran ni Orilô. Lexa ta ka pae. Pae camang ma le paedume leeng. Ma te me soigner-lier rexeng.

CG: Ma te pa cavac yi lali.

BG: Ma te pa ca- ji bwage lali, ma la pan na Poc. Mo la tao tu covan na bwe dua noon.

Tume la camang, ka pulu mwany u leen, texa, te tabodu ka te ca mwiik, te bee. Te be duun, yami era âju bwa tu covan nexeng. Texa waak xie. Te be waak xie, ka porae. Texa bwawa la âju la bween. Êê, te wali maar ri te bwawa. Toma tao tuu ûjen. Texa, ave nyi tao cuur, toma te jua kuarive. Te kuarive ki ave cuur reen. Puur ri âmi te âri ka,

CG: Or, o keja cibwae.

BG: Te âri ka ave, ka ave keja ka najier, ave keja ka najier ra na yali, ma ave pan na bwe dau, dau pwadu. Avexa âri ka, ai. Mo âri ave keja, mo avere tao ci lexeng. Toma yer, ka te kiyive to aveô cavac. Ka yer âda. La pa jajani bwaan, layek, ka pa tuâgee.

Toma te âri ka te ta, nyami te or ra bwe digi ma te ta, ta leve, ka ô âri ave, mo avexaô tu per ra mode âjuma, âjuma la Poc. Ka najie. Êê, wali maar ri ave najie. (Ava âga nyi jaar, ava, bwa tuu per ra pwemwa.) Ka ôda la yer, ka pae daan to wîîk, coaltar, la coaltar-er ri daan, ka ci la Âmwany, ka uya la Mwaan. Texa pae, toma âria, puur ri âmi laô wâne vaer ri janu, ulayama. Texa wali. Ka yali, teô raconter-moi lexeng, ka teô nyi âri ka, ave keja ka najie.

Ka înauvan, ka soigner-lier ri camang, soigner-lier ri tayamook, soigner-lie. Te yer, te soigner-lie ma te ô. Tayamook. Soigner-lie, taxeer ri we cexeen. Taxeer ri we cexeen ma te ûdu. Te jie ma te ûduli we. Texa ûduli we, texa tue ka te ô. Teô nyi bwawa la âju la bween. Te guéri-lier ri l'eau béni, na yali. Ka tao, te tao toli tayamook xi nyan. Avexaô walivan ka ô mae. Ô mae ka ô taan.

Texaô ô, ka ô toven. Ô âria, ô âria para mwa, mo teô ô na leen. Ka ô molep, ka ô bwageda la Numia to teô ô na leen. Toma histoire ra bwe wîna, bwe tahitien, to puur ri âmi te tume, ka nyana, te tume ka jaar âyu, toma te param ka te turowinao, turowivenadume. Ka histoire ra bwe nyali, yet, toven.

Yal-28072010-BGCG-tahitian

'BG: Okay, I'm going to tell a story about myself, me and that old man Maxeek down there. One of our brothers-in-law arrived, Tayema was his name, a Tahitian. He went down [left Tahiti] and came up [to New Caledonia] and married our sister. He was like, he --[1] they would come down [to Belep], but he would always provoke me, and provoke the whole household, in that place, he always provoked us.

And he came down, during one vacation he came down, and took his vacation here, with us. And he asked to go to Poc with us, the two of us with that old man [Maxeek]. We took that old man's boat, a canoe, and went. We shot a few fish for him to eat, and dove -- snorkeled and caught some shellfish for him to eat. And we kept going, he had his underwater speargun, and we kept going, we went away, went and went, and ended up on the other side, up above Poc. We started at Iniwan. And we went down.

But we didn't give any ritual gift. We just went.

We went down and snorkeled, down, down, down and arrived at Cager and arrived at Âmwany. There weren't any, not any shellfish. And we kept going. We stopped -- moored on a rock, in front of the stone. But that place, Pwaraweli is its name. We let down the anchor and struck the sails. And it was afternoon, and we had lunch, and finished.

---

[1] I use here the discourse transcription conventions recommended by Du Bois et al. (1993), where a truncated intonation unit is indicated by two hyphens (--) and a truncated word is indicated by one hyphen (-).

And we, me and Maxeek, we took our diving masks and went down to dive for shellfish by the stone. We went down by the stone. But Tayema, the Tahitian, he stayed in the canoe. But we two, we dove, we went up and snorkeled, and kept snorkeling and snorkeling, and he, we caught one. One shellfish. And I took it down and handed it up to him. We went up so that I could go up. And we repeatedly dove down at the stone like that. Together we kept disappearing and coming back.

And he [Tayema] rose and came up on top of that thing [Pwaraweli]. (We walk on it, like that, that big stone is flat.) We kept diving underneath it, and he walked up on it, walked away up, walked away up. And we, we repeatedly kept trying to get shellfish, we never got any. Only one did we get. And we kept trying and trying but never got any. And he went away up, we two kept snorkeling, and I, I kept diving, I returned, and went up and surfaced and looked around, and peered up at him as he was ascending. He was going up onto the land. That old man. He was ascending.

I went up there, and I was like, "Hey! You see that person up there, he's going to get lost!" I chased him. I, I took my snorkel off, put it down, and chased him. I sprinted and called to him, "No!" And called, "No!" And called again, "No!" And fell and kept chasing him, because I knew he would be lost. And I chased him. The two of us went away up, away up. I never got close to him. We went up, there was a promontory between us, a stone promontory like this. And he, he disappeared on the other side, but I was still here. He went around, but I was still on this side. And I, I went around, and I looked for him, and he wasn't there. It's like he disappeared in that place. He wasn't there.

And I, I kept calling up, I only saw some imprints of whatsit, his feet. But the person I didn't see. When I saw his footprints, they were wet on top of the stone. He kept ascending, but I never saw the person, I only saw his footprints. Together, we climbed to the mountaintop. I actually climbed right with him. Stones were actually falling, but I never saw him. He kept hitting stones on his footprints. And he ascended. We were together, and I stood on top of that thing, so that I could watch as he dropped down into the stream, dropped down into the stream so he could go up. I called, and called, and called, and kept calling but there wasn't anything.

Maxeek came up with the canoe. But he had truly disappeared, he really wasn't there. Maxeek came up, and said up at me, "Where is he?"

I was like, "He's not here. He's lost."

He was like, "Ugh!"

And I -- the [spirits of] the elders took him. "Maxeek, they took him. He's not there. You're afraid." Maxeek was afraid. And I went down, went down I did and climbed into the canoe.

Maxeek was like, "Where are we going?"

I was like, "Let's go up. You go up. Let's go up to Panan." And we came up, we went away and came back with the motor running. Maxeek was really scared. And we came up.

But he [Tayema] had left his t-shirt, and cigarettes, and flip-flops. He had been walking without his shoes. And we came up, and I was like, "Go up and leave me on this seashore, Bwadalo is its name." We went up, went up we did and moored in that place. We moored at Bwadalo, and I, I took flip-flops, and took the t-shirt and cigarettes, and matches, I took his belongings up, and arrived on top of the mountaintop Nyi Pwiya. On Poc. It's called We Tânema Kiliik.

And I said, "You go back, you go back, Maxeek, you go down again to that place Âmwany. Because he got lost at Âmwany. He'll return at Âmwany. While as for me, I'm going to climb onto the mountaintop, and then go down, go down to Âmwany."

I went up and left Maxeek, Maxeek went back. While as for me, I climbed up the mountain. I climbed with whatsit, his belongings. Took it all, took it up, took it up, and arrived on top of a thing up there, on top of the mountaintop up there, and arrived on top of a big stone, Ôgaxoe. It sits on the path. And I went up and took his belongings, and put them on top of Ôgaxoe. I placed them like that. That is, all his stuff.

And I was like, "I ask that you return the Tahitian that you took." And I, I left his belongings, and I went down to Âmwany, returned down, went down and found Maxeek, and we came up. I took the mountain [path], while Maxeek took the water [path]. I actually did that. But I was working, my thoughts were working.

And we went down, and I went down, found Maxeek, and [he] got out of the boat. He was like, "Well, where is he?"

[I said,] "He's not there. But the [spirits of] the elders are going to give him back." And we came up. We took the canoe and came up. Came up we did, and came out at Aliân. We left this shore of Aliân, and came to Ima. We came and settled at Ima.

We looked up and saw a canoe, as it was leaving Panan. It ran down and left. And that old man who was paddling it [Edouard] looked over and saw us. He [Edouard] was going up [in his canoe] to let him [Tayema] return [to Belep]. And he was really unhappy. That Tahitian was really unhappy, because he wanted to go to Belep.

CG: But he was like, "Where were you?"

BG: He was found at Panan, he had actually, he went up, and took the mountain up, and walked up. The [spirits of the] elders took him, took him up, took him up and away, walked up, he returned at the front of the island, that I- the coutume brought him back. It made him return there and come down, and come drop down at Panan.

I got out at Panan, and there's this one old man [Edouard], at Panan. He and his wife, they had been surprised to see him. They said that the Javanese, I mean the Tahitian (but, he was dark-skinned, yeah, he was like, black), that he had cried. Cried to this old man to take him to Belep. That old man got up and took him, brought him here, but we came up, and the woman's house, it stands at their home, there at Panan. We with that old man Maxeek, we went up to question her.

She said (the old woman, her, the wife of that old man, Maxeek's and my sister), she said that, there he was, they found him, he was crying and sitting up there. But he was all scratched there, in the trees and stuff, his body was bloody, bloody, and he said that, there was a person sitting here, he [Tayema] was doing like this. It was like, he [the person] was riding on the back of his [Tayema's] neck. It kept overwhelming him. And he [Edouard] brought him [Tayema] to Waala.

And went up we did, and moored, that old woman said we should return and go with him [Tayema]. We came and came and came, and moored down there, but he, we met the canoe as it was coming back. (That old man's name was Edouard.) He went back to Poc, but we two came up [to Belep] and moored over there [in the bay of Waala].

It was evening. The sun was setting. And the two of us came up, me and Maxeek together, and we came up, came up to look for that old man [Tayema]. And we came up and found him here, in this place, in the old house (our old house sat here, its place was here). And we, and we greeted him [Tayema]. He refused us. He really hated us. And this old woman [Clothilde] was looking after him, this old woman was looking after him in the evening, that night. And she, this old woman, gave him some sacred water [seawater], to drink. And that old man -- that man kept crying, that Tahitian kept crying, and asking people for something to heal him. But my father, my father, he lived up there. That place up there with Joel. And, he came down, she called him. Who went up?

CG: You.

BG: Okay, me.

CG: No, me and that old man.

BG: Yeah, you and Orilô. She and my brother, they went up (his name is Orilô), and they went up and got him. Got my father so they could bring him down to me. So that he could heal him here.

CG: So that he could make them [the spirits] leave.

BG: So that he could make them l- cause them to return, so that they would go to Poc. Because they kept riding on the back of his neck.

My father came down and cursed at him, and he, he fell on him and kept doing like this to him, he beat him. He beat his back, the place where the person was riding. And he did like this to him. He beat him like this, and massaged him. And the person on him was removed. Yeah, it was like it was removed. But it still had power. And he, we kept going to him, but he really didn't want us. He really didn't want to see us.

CG: Because he said that you two, you had run away and abandoned him.

BG: He said that we had, that we had run away and left him, we had run away and left him in that place, so that they could go to the islets, the two islets. And we said, no. We didn't run away, we actually were here the whole time. But as for him, he saw us leaving. He [believed that he] was alone. They made him crazy in the head, those [spirits] over there, they made him tell untruths.

But he said that he went up, when he came out in his canoe to go up [to Belep], go up with us, that we didn't, that we were partying with people, the people of Poc. And left him. Yeah, it was like we had left him. (We often party, us, there's still parties at home [on Poc].) And climbed up he did, and took the path they had, whatsit, paved, they paved the road, at Âmwany, and it goes to Mwan. And he took it, but there wasn't anything there, because the spirits, the elders, were walking with him. And it was like that. In that place, he told that to me here, and he kept insisting that we had run away and left him.

And he kept doing it, and my father healed him, this old woman [Clothilde] healed him, healed him. It was her, she healed him so he was well. This old woman. Healed him, gave him holy water. Gave him holy water to drink. She had him drink water. And he drank water, and he found that he was well. The person on him was suddenly gone. She healed him with holy water, in that place. And he kept, he kept calling this old woman his mother. And we kept doing like that and then we slept. Slept and then it was day.

He was well, and it was finished. There's no more, there's no more to the story, for he was well. And he lived, and he returned to Nouméa when he was well. But the story on that topic, the Tahitian, because he came down, and that one, he came down and was pleased with everything, but he forgot that he had insulted me, insulted us down here. And the story about that topic, that's all, it's done.'

(1)   *Elo, name pari l'histoire ra bweeng*.
        elo   na=me   pari   [listwar]=a   bwee-ng
        yes   1SG.SUBJ=IRR   tell.SPC   story.LN=LOC   top-1SG.POSS
        'Okay, I'm going to tell a story about myself.'

(2)   *Nao ka ulayixedu, Maxeek.*
        nao   ka ulayi-xedu   Maxeek
        1SG.INDEP   LK old.man-DET.DH   Maxeek
        'Me and that old man Maxeek down there.'

(3)   *Te uya la beau-frère rive pwalaic,*
        te=   uya=la   [boprer]=i-ve   pwalaic
        3SG.SUBJ=   arrive=NOM   brother.in.law.LN=GEN-1DU.EXCL.ABS one
        'One of our brothers-in-law arrived,'

(4)   *naran ni Tayema, tahitien.*
        nara-n=i   Tayema [taisjẽ]
        name-3SG.POSS=GEN   Tayema Tahitian.LN
        'Tayema was his name, a Tahitian.'

(5) *Te tu ka tame ka pae avave tamwa.*
te=   tu   ka   ta=me   ka   pa-e
3SG.SUBJ= go.DH   LK   go.UH=CTP   LK   take-SPC

ava-ve   tamwa
sibling-1DU.EXCL.POSS   woman
'He went down and came up and married our sister.'

(6) *Texa wali:*
te=xa   wa-li
3SG.SUBJ=ADD   DEM.MAN-DET.A.PRX
'He was like:'

(7) *Te- leme tume, toma te ca nobwawinao,*
te=   le=me   tu=me   toma
3SG.SUBJ=   3DU.SUBJ=IRR go.DH=CTP   but

te=   ca=   nobwawi-nao
3SG.SUBJ=   ITER=   provoke.TR-1SG.ABS
'He- They would come down, but he would always provoke me,'

(8) *ka nobwawi pwemwang, nyayek,*
ka   nobwawi   pwemwa-ng   nya-yek
LK   provoke.TR   village-1SG.POSS   DEM.IDF-DET.D.MDS
'and provoke the whole household, in that place,'

(9) *te ca nobwawiva.*
te=   ca=   nobwawi-va
3SG.SUBJ=   ITER=   provoke-1PL.EXCL.ABS
'he always provoked us.'

(10) *Texa tume, ô tume li vacances pwalaic,*
te=xa   tu=me   ô   tu=me=li   [vakãja]   pwalaic
3SG.SUBJ=ADD   go.DH=CTP   REAL   go.DH=CTP=GEN   vacation.LN   one
'And he came down, during one vacation he came down,'

(11) *ka înae vacances yier rexeng, yak xeve.*
ka   îna-e   [vakãj]=i-er=exeng
LK   make-SPC   vacation.LN=GEN-3SG.ABS=LOC.DC

ya-k=e-ve
DEM.LOC-DET.D.PRX=DAT-1DU.EXCL.POSS
'and took his vacation here, with us.'

(12) *Texa nooxeve ma avena pan,*
te=xa   noxe-ve   ma   avena=   pan
3SG.SUBJ=ADD   ask.TR-1DU.EXCL.ABS   LK4   1PA.EXCL.SUBJ=   go.TV
'And he asked us [2] that we [3] go,'

(13) *avena pan na Poc, ave ma ulayina.*
avena=   pan=a   Poc ave   ma   ulayi-na
1PA.EXCL.SUBJ= go.TV=LOC Poc 1DU.EXCL.INDEP   LK4   old.man-DET.D.MPX
'that we go to Poc, the two of us with that old man [Maxeek].'

(14) *Avexa pae waga ulayixedu digi, avenaô pan.*
ave=xa   pa-e   waga   ulayi-xedu   canoe
1DU.EXCL.SUBJ=ADD   take-SPC   boat   old.man-DET.DH   canoe

avena=ô   pan
1PA.EXCL.SUBJ=REAL   go.TV
'We took that old man's boat, a canoe, and went.'

(15) *Ave ma tiaea ween no, ka tuve-*
ave=   ma=   tia-e-a   we-na   no   ka tuve
1DU.EXCL.SUBJ= DIM=   pierce-SPC-DA.NSG   food-3SG.POSS   fish LK dive.TR
'We shot a few fish for him to eat, and dove-'

(16) *cawone ka tuvea ween ola.*
cawone   ka tuve-a   we-na   ola
snorkel.LN   LK dive.TR-DA.NSG   food-3SG.POSS   shellfish
'snorkeled[2] and caught some shellfish for him to eat.'

(17) *Avenaxa pan, te pae fusil sous-marin nie,*
avena=xa   pan   te=   pa-e
1PA.EXCL.SUBJ=ADD   go.TV   3SG.SUBJ= take-SPC

[pyzisumarın]=i-e
underwater.speargun.LN=GEN-3SG.ABS
'And we kept going, he had his underwater speargun,'

(18) *avenaxa pan, avena panic, pan aven, pan aven,*
avena=xa   pan   avena=   pan=ic   pan   aven
1PA.EXCL.SUBJ=ADD   go.TV   1PA.EXCL.SUBJ=   go.TV=CTF   go.TV   1PA.EXCL.INDEP
'And we kept going, we went away, went and went,'

(19) *ka tabo la mayarixeda, yaxeda li Poc.*
ka   tabo=la   maya-ri-xeda   ya-xeda=li   Poc
LK   fall=LOC   part-3GNR.POSS-DET.UH   DEM.LOC-DET.UH=GEN   Poc
'and ended up on the other side, up above Poc.'

---

2 The Belep word *cawone* may either be a noun meaning 'Japanese person' (from Fr. *japonais* [ʒapɔnɛ]) or a verb meaning 'to snorkel, dive with a mask'. The latter meaning comes from a particular type of snorkel, common in Belep, which is made in Japan.

(20) *Avena tewuur ra Iniwan. Avenaxa tu.*
avena=   tewur=a   Iniwan
1PA.EXCL.SUBJ=   begin=LOC Iniwan

avena=xa   tu
1PA.EXCL.SUBJ=ADD   go.DH
'We started at Iniwan. And we went down.'

(21) *Toma âria coutume ki avena îna.*
toma âria   [kutym]   ki   avena=   îna
but   NEG.EX ritual.gift.LN   REL   1PA.EXCL.SUBJ=   make.GNR
'But we didn't give any ritual gift.'

(22) *Avenaô wana.*
avena=ô   wa-na
1PA.EXCL.SUBJ=REAL   DEM.MAN-DET.D.MPX
'We just went.'

(23) *Avenaôxa tu, cawoneduic,*
avena=ô=xa   tu   cawone=du=ic
1PA.EXCL.SUBJ=REAL=ADD   go.DH   snorkel.LN=DIR.DH=CTF
'We went down and snorkeled,'

(24) *Tuic, tuic, tuic ka uya la Cager ka uya la Âmwany,*
tu=ic   ka   uya=la   Cager   ka   uya=la
go.DH=CTF   LK   arrive=LOC   Cager   LK   arrive=LOC

Âmwany
Âmwany
'Down, down, down and arrived at Cager and arrived at Âmwany.'

(25) *Âria. Âria ola. Avenaxa pan.*
âria   âria   ola   avena=xa   pan
NEG.EX   NEG.EX   shellfish   1PA.EXCL.SUBJ=ADD   go.TV
'There weren't any. Not any shellfish. And we kept going.'

(26) *Avena ci- mu la bwe buâny pwalaic.*
avena=   ci   mu=la   bwe   buâny   pwalaic
1PA.EXCL.SUBJ=   sit   moor=LOC   top   stone   one
'We stopped- moored on a rock.'

(27) *Maana buâny. Toma yali, ka naran ni Pwaraweli*
mana   buâny   toma   ya-li   ka   nara-n=i   Pwaraweli
front   stone   but   DEM.LOC-DET.A.PRX   LK   name-3SG.POSS=GEN   Pwaraweli
'In front of the stone. But that place, Pwaraweli is its name.'

(28) *Avena nawe nyu, ka ô ânap.*
avena=   nawe   nyu   ka ô   ânap
1PA.EXCL.SUBJ= leave anchor   LK REAL strike.sail
'We let down the anchor and struck the sails.'

(29) *Ka ô mon ni gawaar, avenaô wiu gawaar,*
ka   ô   mon=i   gawaar avena=ô   wiu   gawaar
LK   REAL side.DH=GEN   day   1PA.EXCL.SUBJ=REAL   dine   day
'And it was afternoon, and we had lunch.'

(30) *Ka ô toven. Avexa, ave ma Maxeek,*
ka   ô   toven   ave=xa   ave   ma   Maxeek
LK   REAL finish   1DU.EXCL.SUBJ=ADD   1DU.EXCL.INDEP   LK4   Maxeek
'And finished. And we, me and Maxeek,'

(31) *ave pa tânema cawone ka tu ka tuve ola.*
ave=   pa   tânema   cawone   ka tu   ka tuve   ola
1DU.EXCL.SUBJ=   take.GNR   eye   Japanese.LN   LK go.DH   LK dive.TR shellfish
'we took our diving masks and went down to dive for shellfish.'

(32) *Na buânyili. Avexa tu la na buâny,*
na   buânyi-li   ave=xa   tu=la   na   buâny
interior   stone-DET.A.PRX   1DU.EXCL.SUBJ=ADD   go.DH=LOC   interior   stone
'In the stone. We went down in the stone.'

(33) *toma yer, Tayema, tahitien, ka te ci la bwe digi.*
toma   yer   Tayema   [taisjẽ]   ka   te=   ci=la   bwe   digi
but   3SG.INDEP   Tayema   Tahitian.LN   LK   3SG.SUBJ=   sit=LOC   top   canoe
'but Tayema, the Tahitian, he stayed in the canoe.'

(34) *Toma ave, aveô plonger,*
toma   ave   ave=ô   [plõʒe]
but   1DU.EXCL.INDEP   1DU.EXCL.SUBJ=REAL   dive.LN
'But we two, we dove,'

(35) *aveô ta ka cawone, avexa cawonevan, cawonevan,*
ave=ô   ta   ka   cawone   ave=xa   cawone=van
1DU.EXCL.SUBJ=REAL   go.UH   LK   snorkel.LN   1DU.EXCL.SUBJ=ADD   snorkel.LN=DIR.TV
'We went up and snorkeled, and kept snorkeling and snorkeling,'

(36) *Texa, avexa migi pwalaic. Pwalaic ola.*
te=xa   ave=xa   migi   pwalaic   pwalaiya   ola
3SG.SUBJ=ADD   1DU.EXCL.SUBJ=ADD   hold   one   one   shellfish
'And he, we caught one. One shellfish.'

(37) *Ka naxa paedu ka jida leen.*
ka   na=xa   pa-e=du   ka   ji=da=lee-n
LK   1SG.SUBJ=ADD   take-3SG.ABS=DIR.DH   LK   give=DIR.UH=DAT-3SG.POSS
'And I took it down and handed it up to him.'

(38) *Avexa ta ma naxa ta,*
ave=xa　　　　　ta　　ma　na=xa　　　　　ta
1DU.EXCL.SUBJ=ADD　go.UH　LK4　1SG.SUBJ=ADD　go.UH
'We went up so that I could go up.'

(39) *Avexa nyi tuvadu la na buâny waak.*
ave=xa　　　　　nyi=　　tuva=du=la　　　　na
1DU.EXCL.SUBJ=ADD　PUNCT=　dive=DIR.DH=LOC　interior

buâny　　waa-k
stone　　DEM.MAN-DET.D.PRX
'And we repeatedly dove down at the stone like that.'

(40) *Ave pe namavan ka namame,*
ave=　　　　　pe=　　nama=van　　　　ka　nama=me
1DU.EXCL.SUBJ=　RECP=　disappear=DIR.TV　LK　disappear=CTP
'Together we kept disappearing and coming back,'

(41) *Ka te cuur ka tame, toma bwe nyaxeda,*
ka　te=　　　　cura=xa　ta=me　　　toma　bwe　nya-xeda
LK　3SG.SUBJ=　stand=LK　go.UH=CTP　but　top　DEM.IDF-DET.UH
'And he rose and came up, but on top of that thing,'

(42) *Ka ja wânem ma bween, wali maan,*
ka　　　　ja=　　　　　　　wânem=a　　　bwee-n
LK　　　　1PL.INCL.SUBJ=　walk=LOC　　　top-3SG.POSS

wa-li　　　　　　　　maa-n
DEM.MAN-DET.A.PRX　similarity-3SG.POSS
'We walk on it, like that,'

(43) *te plat ra nyana buânyili,*
te=　　　　[plar]=a　　　　nyana　　　buânyi-li
3SG.SUBJ=　flat.LN=NOM　big.thing　stone-DET.A.PRX
'That big stone is flat,'

(44) *ave nyi tuvadu la aran.*
ave=　　　　　nyi=　　tuva=du=la　　　　ara-n
1DU.EXCL.SUBJ=　PUNCT=　dive=DIR.DH=LOC　underside-3SG.POSS
'we kept diving underneath it.'

(45) *Texa wâneda la bween, wânedaic, wânedaic,*
te=xa　　　　　wâne=da=la　　　　bwee-n　　　　wâne=da=ic
3SG.SUBJ=ADD　walk=DIR.DH=LOC　top-3SG.POSS　walk=DIR.UH=CTF
'And he walked up on it, walked away up, walked away up'

(46) *Avexa, ave nyi tao nyi înae ola,*
 ave=xa ave= nyi= tao= nyi= îna-e ola
 1DU.EXCL.SUBJ=ADD 1DU.EXCL.SUBJ= PUNCT= HAB= PUNCT= make-SPC shellfish
 'And we, we repeatedly kept trying to get shellfish,'

(47) *ave koni pau. Pwai pwalaic pa ave.*
 ave= koni pa-u pwai pwalaiya pa ave
 1DU.EXCL.SUBJ= never take-DETR only one take.GNR 1DU.EXCL.INDEP
 'we never got any. Only one did we get.'

(48) *Avexa nyi înau, înau ka koni pau.*
 ave=xa nyi= îna-u îna-u ka koni pa-u
 1DU.EXCL.SUBJ=ADD PUNCT= make-DETR make-DETR LK never take-DETR
 'And we kept trying and trying but never got any.'

(49) *Texa taic, naxa, ave cawonevan,*
 te=xa ta=ic na=xa ave= cawone=van
 3SG.SUBJ=ADD go.UH=CTF 1SG.SUBJ=ADD 1DU.EXCL.SUBJ= snorkel.LN=DIR.TV
 'And he went away up, we two kept snorkeling,'

(50) *naxa, na tuvavan, naxa bwagenao,*
 na=xa na= tuva=van na=xa bwage-nao
 1SG.SUBJ=ADD 1SG.SUBJ= dive=DIR.TV 1SG.SUBJ=ADD return-1SG.ABS
 'and I, I kept diving, I returned,'

(51) *ka ta ka uc, ka oyâno*
 ka ta ka uc ka oyâno
 LK go.UH LK surface LK look
 'and went up and surfaced and looked around,'

(52) *ka noda lier to teô ta,*
 ka no=da=li-era=ro te=ô ta
 LK peer=DIR.UH=GEN-3SG.ABS=when 3SG.SUBJ=REAL go.UH
 'and peered up at him as he was ascending,'

(53) *teô ta la pwemwa. Enyi ulayili.*
 te=ô ta=la pwemwa enyi ulayi-li
 3SG.SUBJ=REAL go.UH=LOC home if old.man-DET.A.PRX
 'he was going up onto the land. That old man.'

(54) *Texaô ta. Naô taic,*
 te=xa=ô ta na=ô ta=ic
 3SG.SUBJ=ADD=REAL go.UH 1SG.SUBJ=REAL go.UH=CTF
 'He was ascending. I went up there,'

(55) *naxa waak : « Hé ! »*
 na=xa waa-k e
 1SG.SUBJ=ADD DEM.MAN-DET.D.PRX hey
 'and I was like, "Hey!"'

(56) *« Yo kiyi âjuyeda, teme perdu ! »*
yo=   kiyi   âju-yeda   te=me   [peʁdy]
2SG.SUBJ= see.SPC person-DET.UH 3SG.SUBJ=IRR lost.LN
'"You see that person up there, he's going to get lost!"'

(57) *Naxa kewee.*
na=xa   kewe-e
1SG.SUBJ=ADD chase-3SG.ABS
'I chased him.'

(58) *Nao, naô pae tânema cawone, payee, ka kewee.*
nao   na=ô   pa-e   tânema cawone
1SG.INDEP 1SG.SUBJ=REAL   take-SPC   eye   Japanese.LN

paye-e   kewe-e
put-3SG.ABS   chase-3SG.ABS
'I, I took my snorkel off, put it down, and chased him.'

(59) *Na nyi kewee ka to jie : « Ai ! »*
na=   nyi=   kewe-e   ka to ji-e   ai
1SG.SUBJ= PUNCT=   chase-3SG.ABS   LK call give-3SG.ABS   no
'I sprinted and called to him, "No!"'

(60) *Ka me to jie, « Ai ! » Ka me to mwa, « Ai ! »*
Ka me to ji-e   ai ka me to   mwa   ai
LK IRR call give-3SG.ABS no LK IRR call again no
'And called, "No!" And called again, "No!"'

(61) *Ka tabodu ka kewee. To na êna ka te perdu.*
ka tabo=du   ka kewe-e   to   na=   êna   ka te=   [peʁdy]
LK fall=DIR.DH   LK chase-3SG.ABS   when   1SG.SUBJ= know   LK 3SG.SUBJ= lost.LN
'And fell and kept chasing him, because I knew he would be lost.'

(62) *Naxa kewee. Avexa taic, taic.*
na=xa   kewe-e   ave=xa   ta=ic   ta=ic
1SG.SUBJ=ADD   chase-3SG.ABS 1DU.EXCL.SUBJ=ADD   go.UH=CTF   go.UH=CTF
'And I chased him. The two of us went away up, away up.'

(63) *Na koni mwanaolie.*
na=   koni   mwanao-li-e
1SG.SUBJ= never approach-TR-3SG.ABS
'I never got close to him.'

(64) *Ave ta, pewove li maan pwalaic,*
ave=   ta   pewo-ve=li   mana pwalaic
1DU.EXCL.SUBJ=   go.UH   middle-1DU.EXCL.POSS=GEN   point one
'We went up, there was a promontory between us,'

(65) *mana buâny to waak xa maan.*
    mana   buânya=ro   wa-x=a   maa-n
    point   stone=when   DEM.MAN-DET.D.PRX=NOM   similarity-3SG.POSS
    'a stone promontory like this.'

(66) *Texa, te nam ma mayariyek,*
    te=xa   te=   nam=a   maya-ri-yek
    3SG.SUBJ=ADD   3SG.SUBJ=   disappear=LOC   part-3GNR.POSS-DET.D.MDS
    'And he, he disappeared on the other side,'

(67) *toma bwa nao lexeng.*
    toma   bwa=   nao=lexeng
    but   CONT=   1SG.PRED=LOC.DC
    'but I was still here.'

(68) *Te wadivan, toma bwa nao la mayariik.*
    te=   wadi=van   toma   bwa=   nao=la
    3SG.SUBJ=   go.around=DIR.TV   but   CONT=   1SG.PRED=LOC

    maya-rii-k
    part-3GNR.POSS-DET.D.PRX
    'He went around, but I was still on this side.'

(69) *Naxa, na kovavan, ka naô yagie,*
    na=xa   na=   kova=van   ka   na=ô   yagi-e
    1SG.SUBJ=ADD   1SG.SUBJ   leave=DIR.TV   LK   1SG.SUBJ=REAL   search.TR-3SG.ABS
    'And I, I went around, and I looked for him,'

(70) *ciae. Te wali maar ri*
    cia-e   te=   wa-li
    NEG.LOC-3SG.ABS   3SG.SUBJ=   DEM.MAN-DET.A.PRX

    ma-r=i
    similarity-3GNR.POSS=GEN
    'and he wasn't there. It's like'

(71) *te disparu na yali.*
    te=   [dispary]   na   ya-li
    3SG.SUBJ=   disappeared.LN   interior   DEM.LOC-DET.A.PRX
    'he disappeared in that place.'

(72) *Ô ciae. Naxa, na tao toda,*
    ô   cia-e   na=xa   na=   tao=   to=da
    REAL   NEG.LOC-3SG.ABS   1SG.SUBJ=ADD   1SG.SUBJ=   HAB=   call-DIR.UH
    'He wasn't there. And I, I kept calling up,'

(73) *na pwai kiya nabwa wîîk, kan.*
na=   pwai kiya   nabwa   wîî-k   ka-n
1SG.SUBJ= only see.GNR imprint DEM.IA-DET.D.PRX foot-3SG.POSS
'I only saw some imprints of whatsit, his feet.'

(74) *Toma âju, âri na kiyie.*
toma âju   âri= na=   kiyi-e
but   person NEG= 1SG.SUBJ= see.SPC-3SG.ABS
'But the person I didn't see.'

(75) *To na pwai kiya nabwa kan to te been na bwe buâny.*
to   na=   pwai kiya   nabwa   ka-na=ro   te=
when 1SG.SUBJ= only see.GNR imprint foot-3SG.POSS=when 3SG.SUBJ=

ben=a   bwe buâny
be.wet=LOC   top stone
'When I saw his footprints, they were wet on top of the stone.'

(76) *Te tao ta, toma âri na kiyi âju,*
te=   tao= ta   toma âri= na=   kiyi   âju
3SG.SUBJ= HAB= go.UH   but NEG= 1SG.SUBJ= see.SPC   person
'He kept ascending, but I never saw the person,'

(77) *na pwai kiya nabwa kan.*
na=   pwai kiya   nabwa   ka-n
1SG.SUBJ= only see.GNR imprint foot-3SG.POSS
'I only saw his footprints.'[3]

(78) *Tayi ave, yaûda la bwe mweogo.*
tayi   ave   yaûda=la   bwe mweogo
scoop 1DU.EXCL.INDEP   climb=LOC   top mountaintop
'Together, we climbed to the mountaintop.'

(79) *Nare yaûda la moden.*
na=re   yaûda=la   mode-n
1SG.SUBJ=ACT   climb=LOC   together-3SG.POSS
'I actually climbed right with him.'

(80) *Tere cegon ni buâny, toma na koni kiyie.*
te=re   cego-n=i   buânya=roma   na=   koni
3SG.SUBJ=ACT drop-DA.NSG=GEN   stone=but   1SG.SUBJ= never

kiyi-e
see.SPC-3SG.ABS
'Stones were actually falling, but I never saw him.'

---

3 That is, Tayema is invisible at this point in the narrative.

(81) **Te nyi tabo buâny nya bwe nabwa kan.**
te=   nyi=   tabo buâny=a   bwe nabwa   ka-n
3SG.SUBJ= PUNCT= hit   stone=LOC top   imprint   foot-3SG.POSS
'Stones kept falling on his footprints.'

(82) **Texa ta. Tayi ave,**
te=xa   ta   tayi   ave
3SG.SUBJ=ADD   go.UH   scoop   1DU.EXCL.INDEP
'And he ascended. We were together,'

(83) **ka naô cuur ra bwe wîmi,**
ka   na=ô   cur=a   bwe   wî-mi
LK   1SG.SUBJ=REAL   stand=LOC   top   DEM.IA-DET.A.DST
'and I stood on top of that thing,'

(84) **ma na kaxi, te cegodu la na gawe,**
ma   na=   kaxi=re=   cego=du=la   na   gawe
LK4   1SG.SUBJ=   look=3SG.SUBJ=   drop=DIR.DH=LOC   interior torrent
'so that I could watch as he dropped down into the stream,'

(85) **cegodu la na gawe ma teme ta.**
cego=du=la   na   gawe   ma=re=me   ta
drop=DIR.DH=LOC   interior   torrent   LK4=3SG.SUBJ=IRR   go.UH
'dropped down into the stream so he could go up.'

(86) **Naxa to, to, to, tovan ka âria.**
na=xa   to   to=van   ka   âria
1SG.SUBJ=ADD   call   call=DIR.TV   LK   NEG.EX
'I called, and called, and called, and kept calling but there wasn't anything.'

(87) **Ka teô tame la Maxeek vae digi.**
ka   te=ô   ta=me=la   Maxexa=va-e   digi
LK   3SG.SUBJ=REAL   go.UH=CTP=NOM   Maxeek=INSTR-SPC   canoe
'Maxeek came up with the canoe.'

(88) **Toma teô jua disparu, ô jua ciae.**
toma   te=ô   jua   [dispary]   ô   jua
but   3SG.SUBJ=REAL   really   disappeared.LN   REAL   really

cia-e
NEG.LOC-3SG.ABS
'But he had truly disappeared, he really wasn't there.'

(89) **Te tame la Maxeek, ka waaxadame : « Ivie ? »**
te=   ta=me=la   Maxeex=a
3SG.SUBJ=   go.UH=CTP=NOM   Maxeek=LK

```
              wa-xa=da=me                     ivi-e
              DEM.MAN-DET.D.PRX=DIR.UH=CTP    be.where-SPC
              'Maxeek came up, and said up at me, "Where is he?"'
```

(90)   *Naxa waak, « Ô ciae. Teô perdu. »*
```
       na=xa           waa-k                  ô        cia-e
       1SG.SUBJ=ADD    DEM.MAN-DET.D.PRX      REAL     NEG.LOC-3SG.ABS

       te=ô            [peʁdy]
       3SG.SUBJ=REAL   lost.LN
       'I was like, "He's not here. He's lost."'
```

(91)   *Texa waak, « Ca ! »*
```
       te=xa           waa-k                  ca
       3SG.SUBJ=ADD    DEM.MAN-DET.D.PRX      ugh
       'He was like, "Ugh!" [laughter]'
```

(92)   *Naxa- laô paer ri ulayama,*
```
       na=xa           la=ô           pa-er=i           ulaya-ma
       1SG.SUBJ=ADD    3PL.SUBJ=REAL  take-3SG.ABS=GEN  old.man-AC
       'And I- the [spirits of] the elders took him.'
```

(93)   *« Maxeek, laô pae. Ô ciae. »*
```
       la=ô            pa-e           ô        cia-e
       3PLSUBJ=REAL    take-3SG.ABS   REAL     NEG.LOC-3SG.ABS
       '"Maxeek, they took him. He's not there."'
```

(94)   *« Yo âya. » Âya la Maxeek.*
```
       yo=        âya           âya=la        Maxeek
       2SG.SUBJ=  be.afraid     be.afraid=NOM Maxeek
       '"You're afraid." Maxeek was afraid.'
```

(95)   *Ka ô tuic, tu la nao ka ôda la bwe bwe digi.*
```
       ka  ô     tu=ic         tu=la       nao          ka  ôda=la    bwe     digi
       LK  REAL  go.DH=CTF     go.DH=NOM   1SG.INDEP    LK  climb=LOC top     canoe
       'And I went down, went down I did and climbed into the canoe.'
```

(96)   *Texa waak xa Maxeek, « Ji wa ? »*
```
       te=xa           wa-x=a                     Maxeek  ji=              wa
       3SG.SUBJ=ADD    DEM.MAN-DET.D.PRX=NOM      Maxeek  1DU.INCL.SUBJ=   go.where
       'Maxeek was like, "Where are we going?"'
```

(97)   *Na waak, « Ji ta. »*
```
       na=        waa-k                 ji=              ta
       1SG.SUBJ=  DEM.MAN-DET.D.PRX     1DU.INCL.SUBJ=   go.UH
       'I was like, "Let's go up."'
```

(98) *« Yo ta. Ji ta la Panan. »*
yo= ta ji= ta=la Panan
2SG.SUBJ= go.UH 1DU.INCL.SUBJ= go.UH=LOC Panan
'"You go up. Let's go up to Panan."'

(99) *Avexa tame, aveô tuic*
ave=xa ta=me ave=ô tu=ic
1DU.EXCL.SUBJ=ADD go.UH=CTP 1DU.EXCL.SUBJ=REAL go.DH=CTF
'And we came up, we went away'

(100) *ka ô ta le mayin.*
ka ô ta=le mayin
LK REAL go.UH=DAT motor.LN
'and came back with the motor running.'

(101) *Jua âya la Maxeek. Avexaô tame,*
jua âya=la Maxeek ave=xa=ô
really be.afraid=NOM Maxeek 1DU.EXCL.SUBJ=ADD=REAL

ta=me
go.UH=CTP
'Maxeek was really scared. And we came up,'

(102) *Toma te naji terixo, ka cixare, ka claquettes.*
toma te= naji terixo ka cixare ka [klaket]
but 3SG.SUBJ= leave tshirt.LN LK cigarettes.LN LK flipflops.LN
'But he [Tayema] had left his t-shirt, and cigarettes, and flip-flops.'

(103) *Te wânem âria claquettes.*
te= wânem âria [klaket]
3SG.SUBJ= walk NEG.EX flipflops.LN
'He had been walking without his shoes.'

(104) *Avexa tame, naxa waak,*
ave=xa ta=me na=xa waa-k
1DU.EXCL.SUBJ=ADD go.UH=CTP 1SG.SUBJ=ADD DEM.MAN-DET.D.PRX
'And we came up, and I was like,'

(105) *« Yome ta ka ulinao la mariik,*
yo=me ta ka uli-nao=la marii-k
2SG.SUBJ=IRR go.UH LK pour-1SG.ABS=LOC seashore-DET.D.PRX
'"Go up and leave me on this seashore,'

(106) *naran ni Bwadalo. »*
nara-n=i Bwadalo
name-3SG.POSS=GEN Bwadalo
'Bwadalo is its name."'

(107) *Aveô ta, ta la ave*
      ave=ô   ta   ta=la   ave
      1DU.EXCL.SUBJ=REAL   go.UH go.UH=NOM   1DU.EXCL.INDEP
      'We went up, went up we did'

(108) *ka mu la yali,*
      ka   mu=la   ya-li
      LK   moor=LOC   DEM.LOC-DET.A.PRX
      'and moored in that place,'

(109) *Ave mu la Bwadalo, naxa,*
      ave=   mu=la   Bwadalo   na=xa
      1DU.EXCL.SUBJ= moor=LOC   Bwadalo   1SG.SUBJ=ADD
      'We moored at Bwadalo, and I,'

(110) *na pa claquettes, ka pae terixo ka cixare, ka allumettes,*
      na=   pa   [klaket]   ka   pa-e   terixo   ka   cixare
      1SG.SUBJ= take.GNR flipflops.LN LK take-SPC tshirt.LN LK cigarettes.LN

      ka   [alumet]
      LK   matches.LN
      'I took flip-flops, and took the t-shirt and cigarettes, and matches,'

(111) *na pae yadanada, ka uya la bwe mweogo Nyi Pwiya.*
      na=   pa-e   yada-na=da   ka   uya=la   bwe
      1SG.SUBJ= take-SPC   belongings-3SG.POSS=DIR.UH   LK arrive=LOC   top

      mweogo   Nyi Pwiya
      mountaintop Nyi Pwiya
      'I took his belongings up, and arrived on top of the mountaintop Nyi Pwiya.'

(112) *Na Poc, naran ni We Tânema Kiliik.*
      na   Poc   nara-n=i   We Tânema Kiliik
      interior Poc name-3SG.POSS=GEN We Tânema Kiliik
      'On Poc. It's called We Tânema Kiliik.'

(113) *Naxa waak, « Yome bwageo,*
      na=xa   waa-k   yo=me   bwage-o
      1SG.SUBJ=ADD DEM.MAN-DET.D.PRX 2SG.SUBJ=IRR return-2SG.ABS
      'And I said, "You go back,'

(114) *yome bwageo Maxeek,*
      yo=me   bwage-o   Maxeek
      2SG.SUBJ=IRR   return-2SG.ABS   Maxeek
      'you go back, Maxeek,'

(115) *yoxame tu mwa la yamidu Âmwany.*
      yo=xa=me   tu   mwa=la   ya-midu   Âmwany
      2SG.SUBJ=ADD=IRR go.DH again-LOC DEM.LOC-DET.DST.DH Âmwany
      'you go down again to that place Âmwany.'

(116) *Mo te perdu la Âmwany. Teme bwagedu la Âmwany.*
      mo=re=   [peʁdy]=la   Âmwany   te=me
      LK3=3SG.SUBJ= lost.LN=LOC   Âmwany   3SG.SUBJ=IRR

      bwage=du=la   Âmwany
      return=DIR.DH=LOC Âmwany
      'Because he got lost at Âmwany. He'll return at Âmwany.'

(117) *Toma nao, ka name yaûda la bwe mweogo, ka me tuic,*
      toma   nao   ka   na=me   yaûda=la   bwe   mweogo
      but   1SG.INDEP LK   1SG.SUBJ=IRR climb=LOC   top   mountaintop

      ka   me   tu=ic
      LK   IRR   go.DH=CTF
      'While as for me, I'm going to climb onto the mountaintop, and then go down,'

(118) *me tu la Âmwany. »*
      me   tu=la   Âmwany
      IRR go.DH=LOC Âmwany
      'go down to Âmwany.'"

(119) *Naxaô ta, ka ô nawe Maxeek, teô bwage Maxeek.*
      na=xa=ô   ta   ka ô   nawe Maxeek te=ô
      1SG.SUBJ=ADD=REAL   go.UH LK REAL leave Maxeek 3SG.SUBJ=REAL

      bwage   Maxeek
      return   Maxeek
      'I went up and left Maxeek, Maxeek went back.'

(120) *Toma nao, naô yaûda la bwe ôgo.*
      toma nao   na=ô   yaûda=la   bwe   ôgo
      but   1SG.INDEP 1SG.SUBJ=REAL climb=LOC top   mountain
      'While as for me, I climbed up the mountain.'

(121) *Na yaûda va wîîk, yadan.*
      na=   yaûda=va   wîî-k   yada-n
      1SG.SUBJ= climb=INSTR   DEM.IA-DET.D.PRX belongings-3SG.POSS
      'I climbed with whatsit, his belongings.'

(122) *Paroven. Pada, pada, ka uya la bwe âxeda,*
      pa-roven   pa=da   pa=da   ka   uya=la
      take-COMPL   take=DIR.UH take=DIR.UH   LK   arrive=LOC

bwe â-xeda
top DEM.NEW-DET.UH
'Took it all, took it up, took it up, and arrived on top of a thing up there,'

(123) bwe mweogo na lexeda, ka uya la bwe nyana buâny pwalaic, to Ôgaxoe.
bwe mweogo na=lexeda ka uya=la bwe nyana
top mountaintop interior=LOC.UH LK arrive=LOC top big.thing

buânya pwalaic to Ôgaxoe
stone one when Ôgaxoe
'on top of the mountaintop up there, and arrived on top of a big stone, Ôgaxoe.'

(124) Te ci la bwe daan. Naxa ta ka pae yadan,
te= ci=la bwe daan na=xa ta=xa
3SG.SUBJ= sit=LOC top path 1SG.SUBJ=ADD go.UH=LK

pa-e yada-n
take-SPC belongings-3SG.POSS
'It sits on the path. And I went up and took his belongings,'

(125) ka jin na bwe Ôgaxoe. Na pojenin wana.
ka ji-n=a bwe Ôgaxoe na= pojeni-na wa-na
LK give-DA.NSG=LOC top Ôgaxoe 1SG.SUBJ= place-DA.NSG DEM.MAN-DET.D.MPX
'and put them on top of Ôgaxoe. I placed them like that.'

(126) Mo yadanaroven, naxa waak,
mo yada-na-roven na=xa waa-k
LK3 belongings-3SG.POSS-all 1SG.SUBJ=ADD DEM.MAN-DET.D.PRX
'That is, all his stuff. And I was like,'

(127) « Na nook ma a ji bwage tahitien-mi a pae. »
na= nook ma a= ji bwage
1SG.SUBJ= solicit LK4 2PL= give return

[taisjɛ̃]-mi a= pa-e
Tahitian.LN-DET.A.DST 2PL= take-3SG.ABS
'"I ask that you return the Tahitian that you took."'

(128) Naxa, na nawen yadan,
na=xa na= nawe-na yada-n
1SG.SUBJ=ADD 1SG.SUBJ= leave-DA.NSG belongings-3SG.POSS
'And I, I left his belongings,'

(129) naxaô tu la Âmwany, bwagenaodu,
na=xa=ô tu=la Âmwany bwage-nao=du
1SG.SUBJ=ADD=REAL go.DH=LOC Âmwany return-1SG.ABS=DIR.DH
'and I went down to Âmwany, returned down,'

(130) *ô tu ka tu Maxeek, avexaô tame.*
ô   tu   ka tu   Maxeek   ave=xa=ô   ta=me
REAL go.DH LK find Maxeek 1DU.EXCL.SUBJ=ADD=REAL go.UH=CTP
'went down and found Maxeek, and we came up.'

(131) *Na pae bwe ôgo, toma Maxeek te pae we.*
na=   pa-e   bwe ôgo=roma   Maxeek te=   pa-e   we
1SG.SUBJ= take-SPC top mountain=but Maxeek 3SG.SUBJ= take-SPC water
'I took the mountain [path], while Maxeek took the water [path].'

(132) *Naxare wali. Toma cao la bweeng,*
na=xa=re   wa-li   toma   cao=la
1SG.SUBJ=ADD=ACT DEM.MAN-DET.A.PRX but   work=LOC

bwee-ng
top-1SG.POSS
'I actually did that. But I was working,'

(133) *cao nanamiu linao.*
cao   nanami-u=li-nao
work think-DETR=GEN-1SG.ABS
'my thoughts were working.'

(134) *Ka ô tu la ave, ka tu la nao,*
ka ô   tu=la   ave   ka tu=la   nao
LK REAL go.DH=NOM 1DU.EXCL.INDEP LK go.DH=NOM 1SG.INDEP
'And we went down, and I went down,'

(135) *ô tu Maxeek, ka ôdu la bwe waang. Texa waak,*
ô   tu   Maxeek   ka   ôdu=la   bwe   waang
REAL find Maxeek LK descend=LOC top boat

te=xa   waa-k
3SG.SUBJ=ADD DEM.MAN-DET.D.PRX
'found Maxeek, and [he] got out of the boat. He was like,'

(136) *« Ka ivie ? » « Ô ciae.*
ka ivi-e   ô   cia-e
LK be.where-3SG.ABS REAL NEG.LOC-3SG.ABS
'"Well, where is he?" [I said,] "He's not there.'

(137) *Toma lame jier ri ulayama ma te kova. »*
toma la=me   ji-er=i   ulaya-ma ma=re=   kova
but 3PL.SUBJ=IRR give-3SG.ABS=GEN old.man-AC LK4=3SG.SUBJ= leave
'But the [spirits of] the elders are going to give him back."'

(138) *Avexaô tame. Avexaô pae digi*
 ave=xa=ô   ta=me   ave=xa=ô
 1DU.EXCL.SUBJ=ADD=REAL   go.UH=CTP   1DU.EXCL.SUBJ=ADD=REAL

 pa-e   digi
 take-SPC canoe
 'And we came up. We took the canoe'

(139) *ka ô tame. Tame la ave,*
 ka ô   ta=me   ta=me=la   ave
 LK REAL   go.UH=CTP   go.UH=CTP=NOM   1DU.EXCL.INDEP
 'and came up. Came up we did,'

(140) *ka kova la yamidu la Aliân.*
 ka kova=la   ya-midu=la   Aliân
 LK leave=LOC   DEM.LOC-DET.DH=LOC   Aliân
 'and came out at Aliân.'

(141) *Ave kova la mariik xa Aliân,*
 ave=   kova=la   marii-k=a   Aliân
 1DU.EXCL.SUBJ=   leave=LOC   seashore-DET.D.PRX=LOC   Aliân
 'We left this shore of Aliân,'

(142) *ka pame la Ima.*
 ka pa=me=la   Ima
 LK go.TV=CTP=LOC   Ima
 'and came to Ima.'

(143) *Ave pame ce la Ima.*
 ave=   pa=me   ce=la   Ima
 1DU.EXCL.SUBJ=   go.TV=CTP   settle=LOC   Ima
 'We came and settled at Ima.'

(144) *Avexa noda, kiyi digi, pwalaic to te cavac ya na Panan,*
 ave=xa   no=da   kiyi digi   pwalaiya=ro=re=
 1DU.EXCL.SUBJ=ADD   peer=DIR.UH   see canoe   one=when=3SG.SUBJ=

 cavay=a   na   Panan
 leave=LOC   interior   Panan
 'We looked up and saw a canoe, as it was leaving Panan,'

(145) *texa kejadu ka kova.*
 te=xa   keja=du   ka kova
 3SG.SUBJ=ADD   run=DIR.DH   LK leave
 'It ran down and left.'

(146) *Texa nome la ulayimi pae, ka kiyive.*
 te=xa   no=me=la   ulayi-mi   pa-e
 3SG.SUBJ=ADD   peer=CTP=NOM   old.man-DET.A.DST   take-3SG.ABS

```
                    ka  kiyi-ve
                    LK  see.SPC-1DU.EXCL.ABS
                    'And that old man who was paddling it [Edouard] looked over and saw us.'
                    [Tayema was with him.]

(147)    Te ta ma nawe bwagee. Texa kuar.
         te=           ta       ma      nawe    bwage-e
         3SG.SUBJ=     go.UH    LK4     leave   return-3SG.ABS

         te=xa               kuar
         3SG.SUBJ=ADD        not.want
         'He [Edouard] was going up [in his canoe] to let him [Tayema] return [to Belep]. And he
         was really unhappy.'

(148)    Te kuar ra tahitien-li, mo âyuan ni
         te=         kuar=a         [taisjɛ̃]-li            mo     âyua-n=i
         3SG.SUBJ=   not.want=NOM   Tahitian-DET.A.PRX    LK3    desire-3SG.POSS=GEN
         'That Tahitian was really unhappy, because he wanted'

(149)    texaô pame la Belep.
         te=xa=ô                    pa=me=la           Belep
         3SG.SUBJ=ADD=REAL          go.TV=CTP=LOC      Belep
         'to go to Belep.'

(150)         CG:   Toma te waak, « Or riva ? »
                    toma       te=         waa-k                  or=iva
                    but        3SG.SUBJ=   DEM.MAN-DET.D.PRX      2DU.PRED=LOC.Q
                    'But he was like, "Where were you?"'

(151)         BG :  La tuer ra Panan, teôre, te ta,
                    la=           tu-er=a              Panan   te=ô=re              te=           ta
                    3PL.SUBJ=     find-3SG.ABS=LOC     Panan   3SG.SUBJ=REAL=ACT    3SG.SUBJ=     go.UH
                    'He was found at Panan, he had actually, he went up,'

(152)    ka pae bwe ôgoda, ka wâneda.
         ka  pa-e      bwe  ôgo=da            ka  wâne=da
         LK  take-SPC  top  mountain=DIR.DH   LK  walk=DIR.UH
         'and took the mountain up, and walked up.'

(153)    La paer ri ulayama,
         la=          pa-er=i              ulaya-ma
         3PL.SUBJ=    take-3SG.ABS=GEN     old.man-AC
         'The [spirits of the] elders took him,'

(154)    paeda, paedaic,
         pa-e=da                   pa-e=da=ic
         take-3SG.ABS=DIR.UH       take-3SG.ABS=DIR.UH=CTF
         'took him up, took him up and away,'
```

(155) **wâneda, te bwageer ra mana pwemwa,**
wâne=da te= bwage-er=a mana pwemwa
walk=DIR.UH 3SG.SUBJ= return-3SG.ABS=LOC point country
'walked up, he returned at the front of the island,'

(156) **ma na- te bwageer ri coutume.**
ma na= te= bwage-er=i [kutym]
LK4 1SG.SUBJ= 3SG.SUBJ= return-3SG.ABS=GEN ritual.gift.LN
'that I- the coutume brought him back.'

(157) **Te îna ka te bwageer ri ka tume,**
te= îna ka te= bwage-er=i
3SG.SUBJ= make.GNR LK 3SG.SUBJ= return-3SG.ABS=LOC.A

ka tu=me
LK go.DH=CTP
'It made him return there and come down,'

(158) **ka tume cego la Panan.**
ka tu=me cego=la Panan
LK go.DH=CTP drop=LOC Panan
'and come drop down at Panan.'

(159) **Na cegodu la Panan, ka tuu ulac pwalaic, na Panan.**
na= cego=du=la Panan ka tu ulaya pwalaic
1SG.SUBJ= drop=DIR.DH=LOC Panan LK EX.SPC old.man one

na Panan
interior Panan
'I got out at Panan, and there's this one old man [Edouard], at Panan.'

(160) **Le ma yawan, lexa pe nayie,**
le ma yawa-n le=xa
3DU.INDEP LK4 wife-3SG.POSS 3DU.SUBJ=ADD

pe= nayi-e
RECP= be.surprised.TR-3SG.ABS
'He and his wife, they had been surprised to see him.'

(161) **lexa âri ka ulac cavane, toma ulayili, tahitien,**
le=xa âri ka ulaya cavane toma
3DU.SUBJ=ADD say LK old.man Javanese.LN but

ulayi-li [taisjẽ]
old.man-DET.A.PRX Tahitian.LN
'they said that the Javanese, I mean the Tahitian,'

(162) *(Toma te dadabwa,*
    toma   te=   dadabwa
    but   3SG.SUBJ=   be.black
    '(But, he was dark-skinned,'

(163) *êê, te wali maar ri te dadabwa.)*
    êê   te=   wa-li   ma-r=i
    yes   3SG.SUBJ=   DEM.MAN-DET.A.PRX   similarity-3GNR.POSS=GEN

    te=   dadabwa
    3SG.SUBJ=   be.black
    'yeah, he was like, black.)'[4]

(164) *Ka go. Go u le ulayili*
    ka   go   go   u=le   ulayi-li
    LK   cry   cry   toward=DAT   old.man-DET.A.PRX
    'that he had cried. Cried to this old man'

(165) *ma te paeme la Belep.*
    ma   te=   pa-e=me=la   Belep
    LK4   3SG.SUBJ=   take-3SG.ABS=CTP=LOC   Belep
    'to take him to Belep.'

(166) *Teô cuur ra ulayili ka ô pae, paeme,*
    te=ô   cur=a   ulayi-li   ka   ô
    3SG.SUBJ=REAL   stand=NOM   old.man-DET.A.PRX   LK   REAL

    pa-e   pa-e=me
    take-3SG.ABS   take-3SG.ABS=CTP
    'That old man got up and took him, brought him here,'

(167) *toma ave tame, ka mwa tamwa, ka cuur ra pwemwa,*
    toma   ave=   ta=me   ka   mwa   tamwa   ka   cur=a   pwemwa
    but   1DU.EXCL.SUBJ=   go.UH=CTP   LK   house   woman   LK   stand=LOC   home
    'but we came up, and the woman's house, it stands at their home,'

(168) *yami la Panan. Ave ma ulayina, Maxeek,*
    ya-mi=la   Panan   ave   ma
    DEM.LOC-DET.A.DST=LOC   Panan   1DU.EXCL.INDEP   LK4

    ulayi-na   Maxeek
    old.man-DET.D.MPX   Maxeek
    'there at Panan. We with that old man Maxeek,'

---

4 This is the speaker's explanation for why he had momentarily forgotten that Tayema was Tahitian rather than Javanese.

(169) *avexa ta pajer.*
      ave=xa   ta   pajer
      1DU.EXCL.SUBJ=ADD   go.UH   question
      'we went up to question her.'

(170) *Texa âri (la vieille, yer, la vieille li ulayili,*
      te=xa   âri   [laviej]   yer
      3SG.SUBJ=ADD say old.woman.LN 3SG.INDEP

      [laviej]=li   ulayi-li
      old.woman.LN=GEN old.man-DET.A.PRX
      'She said (the old woman, her, the wife of that old man,'

(171) *mo avave ma Maxeek),*
      mo   ava-ve   ma   Maxeek
      LK3   sibling-1DU.EXCL.POSS LK4   Maxeek
      'Maxeek's and my sister),'[5]

(172) *texa âri ka, ô erak ma leô tue*
      te=xa   âri   ka   ô   era-k
      3SG.SUBJ=ADD say LK   REAL DEM.PRES-DET.D.PRX

      ma   le=ô   tu-e
      LK4 3DU.SUBJ=REAL find-3SG.ABS
      'she said that, there he was, they found him,'

(173) *teô godume ci la yayeda.*
      te=ô   go=du=me   ci=la   ya-yeda
      3SG.SUBJ=REAL cry=DIR.DH=CTP sit=LOC DEM.LOC-DET.DST.UH
      'he was crying and sitting up there.'

(174) *Toma te da yagier ri, na yeexamene,*
      toma   te=   da=   yagi-er=i   na   yeexa-mene
      but   3SG.SUBJ= GNO= scratch-3SG.ABS=LOC.A interior plant-GE
      'But he was all scratched there, in the trees and stuff,'

(175) *te da, da la pegaon, ma te âri ka*
      te=   da   da=la   pegao-n   ma   te=   âri ka
      3SG.SUBJ= be.bloody be.bloody=NOM body-3SG.POSS LK4 3SG.SUBJ= say LK
      'his body was bloody, bloody, and he said that,'

(176) *tuu âju ki ce lexeng. Te înae wîîk.*
      tu   âju   ki   ce=lexeng
      EX.SPC   person   REL   settle=LOC.DC

---

[5] Here the speaker avoids saying the woman's name because she is his sister.

	te= îna-e wîî-k

        te= îna-e wîî-k
        3SG.SUBJ= make-SPC DEM.IA-DET.D.PRX
        'there was a person sitting here, he [Tayema] was doing like this.'

(177) ***Te wali maar ri***
    te= wa-li   ma-r=i
    3SG.SUBJ= DEM.MAN-DET.A.PRX similarity-3GNR.POSS=GEN
    'It was like,'

(178) ***te tu covan na bwe dua noon.***
    te= tu= covan=a bwe dua noo-n
    3SG.SUBJ= VBLZ= horse.LN=LOC top back neck-3SG.POSS
    'he [the person] was riding on the back of his [Tayema's] neck.'

(179) ***Te tao pae. Texaô paeme la Wala.***
    te= tao= pa-e   te=xa=ô
    3SG.SUBJ= HAB= take-3SG.ABS 3SG.SUBJ=ADD=REAL

    pa-e=me=la   Wala
    take-3SG.ABS=CTP=LOC Waala
    'It kept overwhelming him. And he [Edouard] brought him [Tayema] to Waala.'

(180) ***Avexa ta la ave, ka mu,***
    ave=xa   ta=la ave   ka mu
    1DU.EXCL.SUBJ=ADD go.UH=NOM 1DU.EXCL.INDEP LK moor
    'And went up we did, and moored,'

(181) ***texa âri la tayamoli***
    te=xa   âri=la tayamo-li
    3SG.SUBJ=ADD say=NOM old.woman-DET.A.PRX
    'that old woman said'

(182) ***avexa bwagevedu***
    ave=xa   bwage-ve=du
    1DU.EXCL.SUBJ=ADD return-1DU.EXCL.ABS=DIR.DH
    'we should return'

(183) ***ka pame la moden,***
    ka pa=me=la mode-n
    LK go.TV=CTP=LOC with-3SG.POSS
    'and go with him [Tayema],'

(184) ***avexa pame, pame, pame, ka mu lexedu, toma teô,***
    ave=xa   pa=me ka mu=lexedu toma te=ô
    1DU.EXCL.SUBJ=ADD go.TV=CTP LK moor=LOC.DH but 3SG.SUBJ=REAL
    'we came and came and came, and moored down there, but he,'

(185) *avena pe co ma digi to teô bwagee.*
avena= pe= co ma digi=ro te=ô bwage-e
1PA.EXCL.SUBJ= RECP= meet LK4 canoe=when 3SG.SUBJ=REAL return-3SG.ABS
'we met the canoe as it was coming back.'

(186) *(Ulayili, naran ni Edouard.)*
ulayi-li nara-n=i Edouard
old.man-DET.A.PRX name-3SG.POSS=GEN Edouard
'(That old man's name was Edouard.)'

(187) *Teô bwageevan na Poc,*
te=ô bwage-e=van=a Poc
3SG.SUBJ=REAL return-3SG.ABS=DIR.TV=LOC Poc
'He went back to Poc,'

(188) *toma aveô tame ka mu lena,*
toma ave=ô ta=me ka mu=lena
but 1DU.EXCL.SUBJ=REAL go.UH=CTP LK moor=LOC.MPX
'but we two came up [to Belep] and moored over there [in the bay of Waala],'

(189) *ô baraap. Teô nam ma denaar.*
ô baraap te=ô nam=a denaar
REAL evening 3SG.SUBJ=REAL disappear=NOM sun
'it was evening. The sun was setting.'

(190) *Avexa tame, pe tuve ma Maxeek,*
ave=xa ta=me pe= tu-ve ma Maxeek
1DU.EXCL.SUBJ=ADD go.UH=CTP RECP= find-1DU.EXCL.ABS LK4 Maxeek
'And the two of us came up, me and Maxeek together,'

(191) *avexaô tame, ta ma yagi ulayili.*
ave=xa=ô ta=me ta ma yagi ulayi-li
1DU.EXCL.SUBJ=ADD=REAL go.UH=CTP go.UH LK4 search.TR old.man-DET.A.PRX
'and we came up, came up to look for that old man [Tayema].'

(192) *Avexa tame ka tuer rexeng, yak,*
ave=xa ta=me ka tu-er=exeng ya-k
1DU.EXCL.SUBJ=ADD go.UH=CTP LK find-3SG.ABS=LOC.DC DEM.LOC-DET.D.PRX
'And we came up and found him here, in this place,'

(193) *na mwami âbur,*
na mwa-mi âbur
interior house-DET.A.DST side.UH
'in the old house,'

(194) *te ci lexeng nga mwave âbur,*
te= ci=lexeng=a mwa-ve âbur
3SG.SUBJ= sit=LOC.DC=NOM house-1DU.EXCL.POSS side.UH
'our old house sat here,'

(195) *tere yak xa playi. Avexa,*
 te=re ya-x=a playi
 3SG.SUBJ=ACT DEM.LOC-DET.D.PRX=NOM place.LN

 ave=xa
 1DU.EXCL.SUBJ=ADD
 'its place was here. And we,'

(196) *avexa boyu leen. Te kuarive.*
 ave=xa boyu=lee-n te= kuar-i-ve
 1DU.EXCL.SUBJ=ADD greet=DAT-3SG.POSS 3SG.SUBJ= not.want-TR-1DU.EXCL.ABS
 'and we greeted him [Tayema]. He refused us.'

(197) *Te jua kuarive.*
 te= jua kuar-i-ve
 3SG.SUBJ= really not.want-TR-1DU.EXCL.ABS
 'He really hated us.'

(198) *Ka kâyee la tayamook.*
 ka kâye-e=la tayamoo-k
 LK keep-3SG.ABS=NOM old.woman-DET.D.PRX
 'And this old woman [Clothilde] was looking after him,'

(199) *Te kâyeer ri tayamook xa na baraap, bwanili.*
 te= kâye-er=i tayamo-x=a na
 3SG.SUBJ= keep-3SG.ABS=GEN old.woman-DET.D.PRX=LOC interior

 baraap bwani-li
 evening night-DET.A.PR
 'This old woman was looking after him in the evening, that night.'

(200) *Texa, tayamook, te taxeer ri we cexeen,*
 te=xa tayamoo-k te= taxe-er=i
 3SG.SUBJ=ADD old.woman-DET.D.PRX 3SG.SUBJ= distribute-3SG.ABS=GEN

 we cexeen
 water sacred
 'And she, this old woman, gave him some sacred water [seawater],'

(201) *ma te ûdu. Texa govan na ulac- âyili,*
 ma te= ûdu te=xa go=van=a
 LK4 3SG.SUBJ= drink 3SG.SUBJ=ADD cry=DIR.TV=NOM

 ulac âyi-li
 old.man man-DET.A.PRX
 'to drink. And that old man- that man kept crying,'

(202) *te govan na tahitien-li,*
 te= go=van=a [taisjẽ]-li
 3SG.SUBJ= cry=DIR.TV=NOM Tahitian.LN-DET.A.PRX
 'that Tahitian kept crying,'

(203) *ka pajeri âju wîmi me soigner-lie.*
 ka pajeri âju wî-mi me [swaɲe]-li-e
 LK question.TR person DEM.IA-DET.A.DST IRR heal.LN-TR-3SG.ABS
 'and asking people for something to heal him.'

(204) *Toma camang, camang te mo lexeda.*
 toma cama-ng cama-ng te= mo=lexeda
 but father-1SG.POSS father-1SG.POSS 3SG.SUBJ= live=LOC.UH
 'But my father, my father, he lived up there.'

(205) *Yaxeda le Joel. Texa, tume.*
 ya-xeda=le Joel te=xa tu=me
 DEM.LOC-DET.UH=DAT Joel 3SG.SUBJ=ADD go.DH=CTP
 'That place up there with Joel. And, he came down,'

(206) *Te to jie. Te ta la ti ?*
 te= to ji-e te= ta=la=ri?
 3SG.SUBJ call give-3SG.ABS 3SG.SUBJ= go.UH=NOM=who?
 'She called him. Who went up?'

(207) CG: *Yo.*
 yo
 2SG.INDEP
 'You.'

(208) BG: *Elo, nao.*
 elo nao
 okay 1SG.INDEP
 'Okay, me.'

(209) CG: *Ai, ave ma ulayiik.*
 ai ave ma ulayii-k
 no 1DU.EXCL.INDEP LK4 old-DET.D.PRX
 'No, me and that old man.'

(210) BG: *Êê, or ma Orilô.*
 êê or ma Orilô
 yes 2DU.INDEP LK4 Orilô
 'Yeah, you and Orilô.'

(211) **Le ta ma âyimi avang, lexa ta,**
le=   ta   ma   âyi-mi   ava-ng   le=xa   ta
3DU.SUBJ=   go.UH   LK4 man-DET.A.DST   sibling-1SG.POSS   3DU.SUBJ=ADD   go.UH
'She and my brother, they went up,'

(212) **naran ni Orilô. Lexa ta ka pae.**
nara-n=i   Orilô   le=xa   ta=xa   pa-e
name-3SG.POSS=GEN   Orilô   3DU.SUBJ=ADD   go.UH=LK   take-3SG.ABS
'his name is Orilô. And they went up and got him.'

(213) **Pae camang ma le paedume leeng.**
pa-e   cama-ng   ma
take-SPC   father-1SG.POSS   LK4

le=   pa-e=du=me=lee-ng
3DU.SUBJ=   take-3SG.ABS=DIR.DH=CTP=DAT-1SG.POSS
'Got my father so they could bring him down to me.'

(214) **Ma te me soigner-lier rexeng,**
ma=re=me   [swaɲe]-li-er=exeng
LK4=3SG.SUBJ=IRR   heal.LN-TR-3SG.ABS=LOC.DC
'So that he could heal him here,'

(215) CG: **Ma te pa cavac yi lali.**
ma=re=   pa=   cavay=i   la-li
LK4=3SG.SUBJ=   CAUS=   depart=GEN   DEM.PL-DET.A.PRX
'So that he could make them leave.'

(216) BG: **Ma te pa ca- ji bwage lali,**
ma=re=   pa=   ça   ji   bwage   la-li
LK4=3SG.SUBJ=   CAUS=   depart   give   return   DEM.PL-DET.A.PRX
'So that he could make them l- cause them to return,'

(217) **ma la pan na Poc.**
ma   la=   pan=a   Poc
LK4   3PL.SUBJ=   go.TV=LOC   Poc
'so that they would go to Poc.'

(218) **Mo la tao tu covan na bwe dua noon.**
mo   la=   tao=   tu=   covan=a   bwe   dua   noo-n
LK3   3PL.SUBJ= HAB=   VBLZ=   horse.LN=LOC   top   back   neck-3SG.POSS
'Because they kept riding on the back of his neck.'

(219) **Tume la camang, ka pulu mwany u leen,**
tu=me=la   cama-ng   ka pulu   mwanya   u=lee-n
go.DH=CTP=NOM   father-1SG.POSS   LK speak   be.bad   toward=DAT-3SG.POS
'My father came down and cursed at him,'

(220) *texa, te tabodu*
te=xa te= tabo=du
3SG.SUBJ=ADD 3SG.SUBJ= fall=DIR.DH
'and he, he fell on him'

(221) *ka te ca mwiik, te bee.*
ka te= ca= mwii-k te= be-e
LK 3SG.SUBJ= ITER= DEM.IA-DET.D.PRX 3SG.SUBJ= beat-3SG.ABS
'and kept doing like this to him, he beat him.'

(222) *Te be duun,*
te= be duu-n
3SG.SUBJ= beat back-3SG.POSS
'He beat his back,'

(223) *yami era âju bwa tu covan nexeng.*
ya-mi era âju bwa= tu= covan=exeng
DEM.LOC-DET.A.DST PRED.LOC person CONT= VBLZ= horse.LN=LOC.DC
'the place where the person was riding.'

(224) *Texa waak xie.*
te=xa waa-x=i-e
3SG.SUBJ=ADD DEM.MAN-DET.D.PRX=GEN-3SG.ABS
'And he did like this to him.'

(225) *Te be waak xie, ka porae.*
te= be waa-x=i-e ka pora-e
3SG.SUBJ= beat DEM.MAN-DET.D.PRX=GEN-3SG.ABS LK massage-3SG.ABS
'He beat him like this, and massaged him.'

(226) *Texa bwawa la âju la bween.*
te=xa bwawa=la âju=la bwee-n
3SG.SUBJ=ADD remove=NOM person=LOC top-3SG.POSS
'And the person on him was removed.'

(227) *Êê, te wali maar ri te bwawa.*
êê te= wa-li ma-r=i
yes 3SG.SUBJ= DEM.MAN-DET.A.PRX similarity-3GNR.POSS=GEN

te= bwawa
3SG.SUBJ= remove
'Yeah, it was like it was removed.'

(228) *Toma tao tuu ûjen. Texa,*
toma tao= tu ûje-n te=xa
but HAB= EX.SPC power-3SG.POSS 3SG.SUBJ=ADD
'But it still had power. And he,'

(229) *ave nyi tao cuur, toma te jua kuarive.*
 ave=   nyi=   tao=   cuu-r   toma
 1DU.EXCL.SUBJ= PUNCT= HAB=   stand-NDR   but

 te=   jua   kuar-i-ve
 3SG.SUBJ= really   not.want-TR-1DU.EXCL.ABS
 'we kept going to him, but he really didn't want us.'

(230) *Te kuarive ki ave cuur reen.*
 te=   kuar-i-ve   ki
 3SG.SUBJ=   not.want-TR-1DU.EXCL.ABS   REL

 ave=   cur=ee-n
 1DU.EXCL.SUBJ=   stand=DAT-3SG.POSS
 'He really didn't want to see us.'

(231) *Puur ri âmi te âri ka,*
 pu-r=i   â-mi   te=   âri   ka
 origin-3GNR.POSS=GEN   DEM.NEW-DET.A.DST   3SG.SUBJ=   say   LK
 'Because he said that,'

(232) CG: *Or, o keja cibwae.*
           or   o=   keja   cibwa-e
           2DU.INDEP   2DU.SUBJ=   run   throw-3SG.ABS
           'You two, you had run away and abandoned him.'

(233) BG: *te âri ka ave, ka ave keja ka najier,*
           te=   âri ka ave=   keja ka naji-er
           3SG.SUBJ= say LK 1DU.EXCL.SUBJ= run   LK leave-3SG.ABS
           'He said that we had, that we had run away and left him,'

(234) *ave keja ka najier ra na yali,*
 ave=   keja ka naji-er=a   na   ya-li
 1DU.EXCL.SUBJ=   run LK leave-3SG.ABS=LOC   interior   DEM.LOC-DET.A.PR
 'we had run away and left him in that place,'

(235) *ma ave pan na bwe dau, dau pwadu.*
 ma   ave=   pan=a   bwe dau   pwadu
 LK4   1DU.EXCL.SUBJ=   go.TV=LOC   top islet   two
 'so that we could go to the islets, the two islets.'

(236) *Avexa âri ka, ai.*
 ave=xa   âri ka ai
 1DU.EXCL.SUBJ=ADD   say LK no
 'And we said, no.'

(237) *Mo âri ave keja, mo avere tao ci lexeng.*
mo âri= ave= keja mo ave=re tao= ci=lexeng
LK3 NEG= 1DU.EXCL.SUBJ= run LK3 1DU.EXCL.SUBJ=ACT HAB= sit=LOC.DC
'We didn't run away, we actually were here the whole time.'

(238) *Toma yer, ka te kiyive to*
toma yer ka=re= kiyi-ve=ro
but 3SG.INDEP LK=3SG.SUBJ= see.SPC-1DU.EXCL.ABS=when
'But as for him, he saw us'

(239) *aveô cavac. Ka yer âda.*
ave=ô cavac ka yer âda
1DU.EXCL.SUBJ=REAL depart LK 3SG.INDEP alone
'leaving. He [believed that he] was alone.'

(240) *La pa jajani bwaan,*
la= pa= jajani bwaa-n
3PL.SUBJ= CAUS= be.crazy head-3SG.POSS
'They made him crazy in the head,'

(241) *layek, ka pa tuâgee.*
la-yek ka pa= tuâge-e
DEM.PL-DET.D.MDS LK CAUS= tell.untruths-3SG.ABS
'those [spirits] over there, they made him tell untruths.'

(242) *Toma te âri ka te ta,*
toma te= âri ka te= ta
but 3SG.SUBJ= say LK 3SG.SUBJ= go.UH
'But he said that he went up,'

(243) *nyami te or ra bwe digi ma te ta,*
nya-mi te= or=a bwe digi ma=re= ta
DEM.IDF-DET.A.DST 3SG.SUBJ= spill=LOC top canoe LK4=3SG.SUBJ= go.UH
'when he came out in his canoe to go up [to Belep],'

(244) *ta leve, ka ô âri ave,*
ta=le-ve ka ô âri= ave=
go.UH=DAT-1DU.EXCL.POSS LK REAL NEG= 1DU.EXCL.SUBJ=
'go up with us, that we didn't,'

(245) *mo avexaô tu per ra mode âjuma,*
mo ave=xa=ô tu= per=a mode âju-ma
LK3 1DU.EXCL.SUBJ=ADD=REAL VBLZ= party.LN=LOC together person-AC
'that we were partying with people,'

(246) *âjuma la Poc. Ka najie.*
âju-ma=la Poc ka naji-e
person-AC=LOC Poc LK leave-3SG.ABS
'the people of Poc. And left him.'

(247) *Êê, wali maar ri ave najie.*
êê wa-li ma-r=i
yes DEM.MAN-DET.A.PRX similarity-3GNR.POSS=GEN

ave= naji-e
1DU.EXCL.SUBJ= leave-3SG.ABS
'Yeah, it was like we had left him.'

(248) *(Ava âga nyi jaar, ava,*
ava= âga= nyi= jaar ava
1PL.EXCL.SUBJ= PROG= PUNCT= be.happy 1PL.EXCL.INDEP
'(We often party, us,'

(249) *bwa tuu per ra pwemwa.)*
bwa= tu per=a pwemwa
CONT= EX.SPC party=LOC village
'there's still parties at home [on Poc].)'

(250) *Ka ôda la yer, ka pae daan to wîîk,*
ka ôda=la yer ka pa-e dana=ro wîî-k
LK mount=NOM 3SG.INDEP LK take-SPC path=when DEM.IA-DET.D.PRX
'And climbed up he did, and took the path they had, whatsit,'

(251) *coaltar, la coaltar-er ri daan,*
[koltar] la= [koltar]-er=i daan
asphalt.LN 3PL.SUBJ= asphalt.LN-3SG.ABS=GEN path
'paved, they paved the road,'

(252) *ka ci la Âmwany, ka uya la mwaan.*
ka ci=la Âmwany ka uya=la Mwan.
LK sit=LOC Âmwany LK arrive=LOC Mwan
'at Âmwany, and it goes to Mwan.'

(253) *Texa pae, toma âria, puur ri âmi*
te=xa pa-e toma âria pu-r=i
3SG.SUBJ=ADD take-3SG.ABS but NEG.EX origin-3GNR.POSS=GEN

â-mi
DEM.NEW-DET.A.DST
'And he took it, but there wasn't anything there, because'

(254) *laô wâne vaer ri janu, ulayama.*
la=ô wâne=va-er=i janu ulaya-ma
3PL.SUBJ=REAL walk=INSTR-3SG.ABS=GEN spirit old.man-AC
'the spirits, the elders, were walking with him.'

(255) **Texa wali. Ka yali**
te=xa wa-li ka ya-li
3SG.SUBJ=ADD DEM.MAN-DET.A.PRX LK DEM.LOC-DET.A.PRX
'And it was like that. In that place,'

(256) **teô raconter-moi lexeng,**
te=ô [rakõtemwa]=lexeng
3SG.SUBJ=REAL tell.me.LN=LOC.DC
'he told that to me here,'

(257) **ka teô nyi âri ka, ave keja ka najie.**
ka te=ô nyi= âri ka ave= keja
LK 3SG.SUBJ=REAL PUNCT= say LK 1DU.EXCL.SUBJ= run

ka naji-e
LK leave-3SG.ABS
'and he kept insisting that we had run away and left him.'

(258) **Ka înauvan, ka soigner-lier ri camang,**
ka îna-u=van ka [swaɲe]-li-er=i cama-ng
LK make-DETR=DIR.TV LK heal.LN-TR-3SG.ABS=GEN father-1SG.POSS
'And he kept doing it, and my father healed him,'

(259) **soigner-lier ri tayamook, soigner-lie.**
[swaɲe]-li-er=i tayamoo-k [swaɲe]-li-e
heal.LN-TR-3SG.ABS=GEN old.woman-DET.D.PRX heal.LN-TR-3SG.ABS
'this old woman [Clothilde] healed him, healed him.'

(260) **Te yer, te soigner-lie**
te= yer te= [swaɲe]-li-e
3SG.SUBJ= 3SG.INDEP 3SG.SUBJ= heal.LN-TR-3SG.ABS
'It was her, she healed him'

(261) **ma te ô. Tayamook.**
ma=re= ô tayamoo-k
LK4=3SG.SUBJ= be.good old.woman-DET.D.PRX
'so he was well. This old woman.'

(262) **Soigner-lie, taxeer ri we cexeen.**
[swaɲe]-li-e taxe-er=i we cexeen
heal.LN-TR-3SG.ABS distribute-3SG.ABS=GEN water sacred
'Healed him, gave him holy water.'

(263) **Taxeer ri we cexeen ma te ûdu.**
taxe-er=i we cexeen ma=re= ûdu
distribute-3SG.ABS=GEN water sacred LK4=3SG.SUBJ= drink
'Gave him holy water to drink.'

(264) *Te jie ma te ûduli we.*
 te= ji-e ma=re= ûdu-li we
 3SG.SUBJ= give-3SG.ABS LK4=3SG.SUBJ= drink-TR water
 'She had him drink water.'

(265) *Texa ûduli we, texa tue ka te ô.*
 te=xa ûdu-li we te=xa tu-e
 3SG.SUBJ=ADD drink-TR water 3SG.SUBJ=ADD find-3SG.ABS

 ka te= ô
 LK 3SG.SUBJ= be.good
 'And he drank water, and he found that he was well.'

(266) *Teô nyi bwawa la âju la bween.*
 te=ô nyi= bwawa=la âju=la bwee-n
 3SG.SUBJ=REAL PUNCT= remove=NOM person=LOC top-3SG.POSS
 'The person on him was suddenly gone.'

(267) *Te guéri-lier ri l'eau béni, na yali.*
 te= [geri]-li-er=i [lombeni] na ya-li
 3SG.SUBJ= heal.LN-TR-3SG.ABS=GEN holy.water.LN interior DEM.LOC-DET.A.PRX
 'She healed him with holy water, in that place.'

(268) *Ka tao, te tao toli tayamook xi nyan.*
 ka tao= te= tao to-li tayamoo-x=i nya-n
 LK HAB= 3SG.SUBJ= HAB= call-TR old.woman-DET.D.PRX=GEN mother-3SG.POSS
 'And he kept, he kept calling this old woman his mother.'

(269) *Avexaô walivan ka ô mae.*
 ave=xa=ô wa-li=van ka ô mae
 1DU.EXCL.SUBJ=ADD=REAL DEM.MAN-DET.A.PRX=DIR.TV LK REAL sleep
 'And we kept doing like that and then we slept.'

(270) *Ô mae ka ô taan.*
 ô mae ka ô taan
 REAL sleep LK REAL day
 'Slept and then it was day.'

(271) *Texaô ô, ka ô toven.*
 te=xa=ô ô ka ô toven
 3SG.SUBJ=ADD=REAL be.good LK REAL finish
 'He was well, and it was finished.'

(272) *Ô âria, ô âria para mwa,*
 ô âria ô âria para mwa
 REAL NEG.EX REAL NEG.EX story again
 'There's no more, there's no more to the story,'

(273) *mo teô ô na leen.*
mo=re=ô   ô   na=lee-n
LK3=3SG.SUBJ=REAL be.good interior=DAT-3SG.POSS
'for he was well.'

(274) *Ka ô molep,*
ka ô   molep
LK REAL be.alive
'And he lived,'

(275) *ka ô bwageda la Numia to*
ka ô   bwage=da=la   Numia=ro
LK REAL return=DIR.UH=LOC   Nouméa=when
'and he returned to Nouméa'

(276) *teô ô na leen.*
te=ô   ô   na=lee-n
3SG.SUBJ=REAL be.good interior=DAT-3SG.POSS
'when he was well.'

(277) *Toma histoire ra bwe wîna, bwe tahitien,*
toma [istwar]=a   bwe wî-na   bwe [taisjɛ̃]
but story.LN=LOC   top DEM.MAN-DET.D.MPX top Tahitian.LN
'But the story on that topic, the Tahitian,'

(278) *to puur ri âmi te tume,*
to   pu-r=i   â-mi   te=   tu=me
when origin-3GNR.POSS=GEN DEM.NEW-DET.A.DST 3SG.SUBJ= go.DH=CTP
'because he came down,'

(279) *ka nyana, te tume ka jaar âyu,*
ka nya-na   te=   tu=me   ka jara   âyu
LK DEM.IDF-DET.D.MPX 3SG.SUBJ= go.DH=CTP LK be.happy any
'and that one, he came down and was pleased with everything,'

(280) *toma te param ka te turowinao,*
toma=re=   param   ka te=   turowi-nao
but=3SG.SUBJ=   forget   LK 3SG.SUBJ=   insult-1SG.ABS
'but he forgot that he had insulted me,'

(281) *turowivenadume. Ka histoire ra bwe nyali,*
turowi-vena=du=me   ka [istwar]=a   bwe nya-li
insult-1PA.EXCL.ABS=DIR.DH=CTP   LK story.LN=LOC top DEM.IDF-DET.A.PRX
'insulted us down here. And the story about that topic,'

(282) *yet, toven.*
yet   toven
done finish
'That's all, it's done.'

References

AIKHENVALD, ALEXANDRA Y. 2002. Typological parameters for the study of clitics, with special reference to Tariana. *Word: A cross-linguistic typology*, ed. by R.M.W. Dixon and Alexandra Y. Aikhenvald, 42–78. New York: Cambridge University Press.

AIKHENVALD, ALEXANDRA Y. 2003. Language contact and language change in Amazonia. *Historical linguistics 2001: Selected papers from the 15th International Conference on Historical Linguistics, Melbourne, 13–17 August 2001*, ed. by Barry J. Blake and Kate Burridge, 1–20. Philadelphia: John Benjamins.

AIKHENVALD, ALEXANDRA Y. 2007. Typological distinctions in word-formation. *Language typology and syntactic description, Second Edition, Volume III: Grammatical categories and the lexicon*, ed. by Timothy Shopen, 1–65. New York: Cambridge University Press.

AISSEN, JUDITH. 2003. Differential object marking: Iconicity vs. economy. *Natural Language & Linguistic Theory 21* (3). 435–483.

AMMANN, RAYMOND (Recorder). 1994. Belep dance. Nouméa. Tjibaou Cultural Center DAT 92.03.

AMMANN, RAYMOND. 1997. *Kanak dance and music: Ceremonial and intimate performance of the Melanesians of New Caledonia, historical and actual.* New York: Kegan Paul International.

ANDERSON, STEPHEN R. 1984. Kwakwala syntax and the government-binding theory. *Syntax and semantics, Vol. 16: The syntax of Native American languages*, ed. by Eung-Do Cook and Donna B. Gerdts, 21–75. London: Academic Press, Inc.

ANDREWS, AVERY D. 2007a. The major functions of the noun phrase. *Language typology and syntactic description, Second Edition, Volume I: Clause structure*, ed. by Timothy Shopen, 132–223. New York: Cambridge University Press.

ANDREWS, AVERY D. 2007b. Relative clauses. *Language typology and syntactic description, Second Edition, Volume II: Complex constructions*, ed. by Timothy Shopen, 206–236. New York: Cambridge University Press.

ANONYMOUS. 2008. Weniko Ihage: « Nos langues kanak sont en danger. » *Les Nouvelles Calédoniennes*, 10 September 2008. Online: http://www.info.lnc.nc/articles/article_69749_225981_70389.htm.

ANONYMOUS. 2012. Belep. *Tourisme Province nord*. Skazy, 15 May 2012. Online: http://www.tourismeprovincenord.nc/fr/les-communes/belep.

Australasian Legal Information Institute. 2002. Noumea Accord.

Australian Indigenous Law Reporter. Online: http://www.austlii.edu.au/au/journals/AILR/2002/17.html.

BÁRÁNY, ANDRÁS. 2015. *Differential object marking in Hungarian and the morphosyntax of case and agreement*. Ph.D. dissertation, Downing College, University of Cambridge.

BAUER, LAURIE. 1988. What is lenition? *Journal of Linguistics 24* (2). 381–392.

BAUER, LAURIE. 2003. *Introducing linguistic morphology, Second Edition*. Edinburgh: Edinburgh University Press.

BEDDOR, PATRICE SPEETER. 1993. The perception of nasal vowels. *Nasals, nasalization and the velum*, ed. by Marie K. Huffman and Rena A. Krakow, 171–196. San Diego: Academic Press.

BENDER, ANDREA AND SIEGHARD BELLER. 2006. "Fanciful" or genuine?: Bases and high numerals in Polynesian number systems. *The Journal of the Polynesian Society 115* (1). 7–46.

BENSA, ALBAN. 1988. Colonialisme, racisme et ethnologie en Nouvelle-Calédonie. *Ethnologie française 18* (2). 188–197.

BENSA, ALBAN AND ANTOINE GOROMIDO. 1997. The political order and corporal coercion in Kanak societies of the Past (New Caledonia). *Oceania 68* (2). 84–106.

BENTAHILA, ABDELÂLI. 1983. *Language attitudes among Arabic-French bilinguals in Morocco*. Clevedon: Multilingual Matters.
BEST, ELSDON. 1907. Maori numeration: The vigesimal system. *The Journal of the Polynesian Society* 16 (2). 94–98.
BHASKARARAO, PERI AND KARUMURI VENKATA SUBBARAO (eds.). 2004. *Non-nominative subjects: Vol. 1. Typological Studies in Language 60*. Philadelphia: John Benjamins.
BHAT, D.N.S. 1975. Two studies on nasalization. *Nasálfest: Papers from a symposium on nasals and nasalization*, ed. by Charles A. Ferguson, Larry M. Hyman, and John J. Ohala, 27–47. Stanford: Stanford University.
BICKEL, BALTHASAR AND JOHANNA NICHOLS. 2005. Inclusive-exclusive as person vs. number categories worldwide. *Clusivity: Typology and case studies of the inclusive-exclusive distinction*, ed. by Elena Filimonova, 49–72. Philadelphia: John Benjamins Publishing Company.
BICKEL, BALTHASAR AND JOHANNA NICHOLS. 2007. Inflectional morphology. *Language typology and syntactic description, Second Edition, Volume III: Grammatical categories and the lexicon*, ed. by Timothy Shopen, 169–240. New York: Cambridge University Press.
BIRD, STEVEN AND GARY SIMONS. 2003. Seven dimensions of portability for language documentation and description. *Language 79*. 557–82.
BLEVINS, JULIETTE. 1994. The bimoraic foot in Rotuman phonology and morphology. *Oceanic Linguistics 33* (2). 491–516.
BLUST, ROBERT. 2013. *The Austronesian languages, Revised Edition*. Asia-Pacific Linguistics Open Access Monographs, A-PL 008. Canberra, Australia: Asia-Pacific Linguistics. Online: http://hdl.handle.net/1885/10191.
BOERSMA, PAUL AND DAVID WEENINK. 2010. Praat: Doing phonetics by computer [Computer program]. Version 5.1.31, retrieved 4 April 2010 from http://www.praat.org/.
BOSSONG, GEORG. 1985. *Empirische Universalienforschung: Differentielle Objektmarkierung in den neuiranishen Sprachen*. Tübingen: Narr.
BOSSONG, GEORG. 1991. Differential object marking in Romance and beyond. *New analyses in Romance linguistics*, ed. by Dieter Wanner and Douglas A. Kibbee, 143–170. Current Issues in Linguistic Theory 69. Amsterdam: John Benjamins.
BOUCHER, VICTOR J. 2002. Timing relations in speech and the identification of voice-onset times: A stable perceptual boundary for voicing categories across speaking rates. *Perception & Psychophysics 64*(1). 121–130.
BRESNAN, JOAN AND JANE GRIMSHAW. 1978. The syntax of free relatives in English. *Linguistic Inquiry 9* (3). 331–391.
BRETTEVILLE, DOMINQUE. 1993. *700 mots yuanga: Esquisse d'un lexique thématique français yuanga accompagné d'un texte traduit*. In collaboration with la Chefferie Malouma. Nouvelle Calédonie: CTROP.
BRIL, ISABELLE. 2000. *Dictionnaire nêlêmwa-nixumwak français-anglais (Nouvelle-Calédonie)*. Selaf 383. Paris: Peeters.
BRIL, ISABELLE. 2002. *Le nêlêmwa: Analyse syntaxique et sémantique*. Selaf 403. Paris: Peeters.
BRIL, ISABELLE. 2004a. Coordination strategies and inclusory constructions in New Caledonian and other Oceanic languages. *Coordinating constructions*, ed. by Martin Haspelmath, 499-536. Typological Studies in Language 58. Philadelphia: John Benjamins.
BRIL, ISABELLE. 2004b. Complex verbs and dependency strategies in Nêlêmwa (New Caledonia). *Complex predicates in Oceanic languages: Studies in the dynamics of binding and boundedness*, ed. by Isabelle Bril and Françoise Ozanne-Rivierre. New York: Mouton de Gruyter.
BRIL, ISABELLE. 2005. Semantic and functional diversification of reciprocal and middle prefixes in New Caledonian and other Austronesian languages. *Linguistic Typology 9*. 25–76.
BRUNTON, RON. 1971. Cargo cults and systems of exchange in Melanesia. *Mankind 8*. 115–128.

BURENHULT, NICLAS. 2004. Spatial deixis in Jahai. *Papers from the Eleventh Annual Meeting of the Southeast Asian Linguistics Society 2001*, ed. by Somsonge Burusphat, 87–100. Arizona State University: Program for Southeast Asian Studies.
BYBEE, JOAN L. 1985. *Morphology*. Philadelphia: John Benjamins.
BYBEE, JOAN, REVERE PERKINS, AND WILLIAM PAGLIUCA. 1994. *The Evolution of Grammar: Tense, aspect, and modality in the languages of the world*. Chicago: The University of Chicago Press.
CAPELL, ARTHUR. 1962. Oceanic linguistics today. *Current Anthropology 3*(4). 371–428.
CHAFE, WALLACE L. 1976. Givenness, contrastiveness, definiteness, subjects, topics, and point of view. *Subject and topic*, ed. by C.N. Li, 25–55. New York: Academic Press.
CHAFE, WALLACE. 1995. The realis-irrealis distinction in Caddo, the Northern Iroquoian languages, and English. *Modality in grammar and discourse*, ed. by Joan L. Bybee and Suzanne Fleischman, 349–365. Typological Studies in Language 32. Philadelphia: John Benjamins.
CHARPENTIER, JEAN-MICHEL. 2006. The future of the languages of Vanuatu and New Caledonia. *Language diversity in the Pacific: Endangerment and survival*, ed. by Denis Cunningham, D.E. Ingram, and Kenneth Sumbuk, 131–136. Buffalo, NY: Multilingual Matters Ltd.
CHEN, MARILYN Y. 1997. Acoustic correlates of English and French nasalized vowels. *Journal of the Acoustical Society of America 102* (4). 2360–2370.
CHEN, MATTHEW Y. 1975. An areal study of nasalization in Chinese. *Nasálfest: Papers from a symposium on nasals and nasalization*, ed. by Charles A. Ferguson, Larry M. Hyman, and John J. Ohala, 81–123. Stanford: Stanford University.
CHEN, MATTHEW Y. AND WILLIAM S-Y. WANG. 1975. Sound change: Actuation and implementation. *Language 51* (2).255–281
CHO, TAEHONG AND PETER LADEFOGED. 1999. Variation and universals in VOT: Evidence from 18 languages. *Journal of Phonetics 27*. 207–229.
CHURCHWARD, C.M. 1939. *Tales of a lonely island*. Oceanic Monograph no. 4. Sydney.
CLARK, EVE. 1978. Locationals: Existential, locative, and possessive constructions. *Universals of human language, Volume IV: Syntax*, ed. by Joseph H. Greenberg, 85–126. Stanford: Stanford University Press.
CLARK, GEOFFREY. 2003. Shards of meaning: Archaeology and the Melanesia-Polynesia divide. *The Journal of Pacific History 38* (2). 197–215.
COHN, ABIGAIL. 1993. The status of nasalized continuants. *Nasals, nasalization, and the velum*, ed. by Marie K. Huffman and Rena Krakow, 329–367. Phonetics and phonology 5. San Diego: Academic Press.
COMRIE, BERNARD. 1976. *Aspect*. Cambridge Textbooks in Linguistics. Cambridge: Cambridge University Press.
COMRIE, BERNARD. 1979. Definite and animate direct objects: A natural class. *Linguistica Silesiana 3*. 13–21.
COMRIE, BERNARD. 1980. Agreement, animacy, and voice. *Wege Zur Universalienforschung: Sprachwissenschaftliche Beiträge zum 60, Geburstag von Hansjakob Seiler*, ed. by G. Brettschneider and C. Lehmann, 229–234. Tübingen: Narr.
COMRIE, BERNARD. 1989. *Language universals and linguistic typology*, 2nd edn. Chicago: University of Chicago Press.
COMRIE, BERNARD. 1998. Rethinking the typology of relative clauses. *Language Design 1*(1). 59–86.
COMRIE, BERNARD AND EDWARD L. KEENAN. 1979. Noun phrase accessibility revisited. *Language 55* (3). 649–664.
CORBETT, GREVILLE G. 2007. Gender and noun classes. *Language typology and syntactic description, Second Edition, Volume III: Grammatical categories and the lexicon*, ed. by Timothy Shopen, 241–279. New York: Cambridge University Press.

CORBETT, GREVILLE G. AND MARIANNE MITHUN. 1996. Associative forms in a typology of number systems: Evidence from Yup'ik. *Journal of Linguistics 32*(1). 1–17.

CROWLEY, TERRY. 1995. Melanesian languages: Do they have a future? *Oceanic Linguistics 34*(2). 327–344.

CROWLEY, TERRY. 1997. *An introduction to historical linguistics,* 3rd edn. Oxford: Oxford University Press.

CYSOUW, MICHAEL. 2005. Morphology in the wrong place: A survey of preposed enclitics. *Morphology and its demarcations: Selected papers from the 11th Morphology Meeting, Vienna, February 2004*, ed. by Wolfgang U. Dressler, Dieter Kastovsky, Oskar E. Pfeiffer, and Franz Rainer, 17–38. Current Issues in Linguistic Theory 264. Philadelphia: Benjamins.

DAHL, MARTINE (Recorder). 1984. Belep festival. Belep. Tjibaou Cultural Center DAT 84.11.

DAHL, ÖSTEN. 1985. *Tense and aspect systems*. New York: Basil Blackwell Inc.

DE LA FONTINELLE, JACQUELINE. 1976. *La langue de Houaïlou (Nouvelle-Calédonie): Description phonologique et description syntaxique*. Langues et civilisations à tradition orale 17. Centre national de la recherche scientifique. Paris: SELAF.

DIK, SIMON C. 1997. *The theory of functional grammar,* 2nd edn. Berlin: Mouton de Gruyter.

DIXON, R. M. W. 1977. Where have all the adjectives gone?. *Studies in Language 1*. 19–80.

DIXON, R.M.W. 1980. *The languages of Australia*. New York: Cambridge University Press.

DIXON, R.M.W. 1988. *A grammar of Boumaa Fijian*. Chicago: University of Chicago Press.

DIXON, R.M.W. 1994. *Ergativity*. Cambridge Studies in Linguistics 69. Cambridge University Press.

DIXON, R.M.W. 1995. Complement clauses and complementation strategies. *Grammar and meaning: Essays in honour of Sir John Lyons*, ed. by Frank R. Palmer, 175–220. New York: Cambridge University Press.

DIXON, R.M.W. 2006. Complement clauses and complementation strategies in typological perspective. *Complementation*, ed. by R.M.W. Dixon and Alexandra Y. Aikhenvald, 1–48. Explorations in Linguistic Typology. New York: Oxford University Press.

DIXON, R.M.W. AND ALEXANDRA Y. AIKHENVALD. 2002. Word: A typological framework. *Word: A cross-linguistic typology*, ed. by R.M.W. Dixon and Alexandra Y. Aikhenvald, 1–41. New York: Cambridge University Press.

DOUGLAS, BRONWEN. 1982. "Written on the ground": Spatial symbolism, cultural categories and historical process in New Caledonia. *The Journal of the Polynesian Society 91* (3). 383–415.

DOUGLAS, BRONWEN. 1990. 'Almost constantly at war'?: An ethnographic perspective on fighting in New Caledonia. *The Journal of Pacific History 25* (1). 22–46.

DOUGLAS, BRONWEN. 1992. Doing ethnographic history: The case of fighting in New Caledonia. *History and tradition in Melanesian anthropology*, ed. by James G. Carrier, 86–115. Berkeley: University of California Press.

DRELLISHAK, SCOTT. 2004. A survey of coordination strategies in the world's languages. Unpublished master's thesis. University of Washington, Seattle, WA.

DRYER, MATTHEW S. 1992. The Greenbergian word order correlations. *Language 68* (1). 81–138.

DRYER, MATTHEW S. 2007. Clause types. *Language typology and syntactic description, Second Edition, Volume I: Clause structure*, ed. by Timothy Shopen, 224–275. New York: Cambridge University Press.

DRYER, MATTHEW S. 2013. Order of subject, object, and verb. *The world atlas of language structures online*, ed. by Matthew S. Dryer and Martin Haspelmath. Leipzig: Max Planck Institute for Evolutionary Anthropology. Online:http://wals.info/chapter/81.

DU BOIS, JOHN W. 1987. The discourse basis of ergativity. *Language 63* (4). 805–855.

DU BOIS, JOHN W., STEPHAN SCHUETZE-COBURN, SUSANNA CUMMING, AND DANAE PAOLINO. 1993. Outline of discourse transcription. *Talking Data: Transcription and coding in discourse research*, ed. by Jane A. Edwards and Martin D. Lampert, 45–90. New York: Psychology Press.

DUBOIS, MARIE-JOSEPH. 1975a. Bélèp, synthèse historique d'après les traditions. Unpublished manuscript. Paris: Institut d'ethnologie.
DUBOIS, MARIE-JOSEPH. 1975b. Corpus de textes de Bélèp. Unpublished manuscript. Paris: Institut d'ethnologie.
DUBOIS, MARIE-JOSEPH. 1975c. Dictionnaire Belep-Français. Unpublished manuscript. Paris: Institut d'ethnologie.
DUBOIS, MARIE-JOSEPH. 1975d. Dictionnaire des noms propres de Bélèp: Noms de personnes, de clans, de lieux. Unpublished manuscript. Paris: Institut d'ethnologie.
DUBOIS, MARIE-JOSEPH. 1975e. Dictionnaire Belep-Français. Unpublished manuscript. Paris: Institut d'ethnologie.
DUBOIS, MARIE-JOSEPH. 1975f. Les généalogies de Bélèp. Unpublished manuscript. Paris: Institut d'ethnologie.
DUBOIS, MARIE-JOSEPH. 1975g. Bélèp, synthese historique d'après les traditions. Unpublished manuscript. Paris: Institut d'ethnologie.
DUBOIS, MARIE-JOSEPH. 1985. *Histoire résumée de Belep*. Nouméa: Société d'études historiques de la Nouvelle Calédonie.
DYEN, ISIDORE. 1965. *A lexicostatistical classification of the Austronesian languages*. Baltimore: Waverly Press.
ELBERT, SAMUEL H. AND MARY KAWENA PUKUI. 1979. *Hawaiian grammar*. Honolulu: University Press of Hawaii.
EMBICK, DAVID AND ROLF NOYER. 1999. Locality in post-syntactic operations. *Papers in morphology and syntax, Cycle Two,* ed. by David Embick and Rolf Noyer, 265–317. MIT Working Papers in Linguistics 34. Cambridge, Mass.: MIT.
ENGLEBRETSON, ROBERT. 2003. *Searching for structure: The problem of complementation in colloquial Indonesian conversation*. Philadelphia: John Benjamins.
EVANS, NICHOLAS. 2006. Dyad constructions. *Encyclopedia of language and linguistics* vol. 4, 2nd edn., ed. by Keith Brown, 24-27. Oxford: Elsevier.
EWEN, COLIN AND HARRY VAN DER HULST. 2001. *The phonological structure of words*. Cambridge: Cambridge University Press.
FISHMAN, JOSHUA. 1991. *Reversing language shift: Theoretical and empirical foundations of assistance to threatened languages*. Avon, England: Multilingual Matters Ltd.
FOLEY, WILLIAM A. 1986. *The Papuan languages of New Guinea*. Cambridge Language Surveys. New York: Cambridge University Press.
FÓNAGY, IVAN. 1958. Elektrophysiologische Beiträge zur Akzentfrage. *Phonetica 2.* 12–58.
FORSYTH, J. 1970. *A grammar of aspect: Usage and meaning in the Russian verb*. Studies in the Modern Russian Language. New York: Cambridge University Press.
FOX, BARBARA A. AND SANDRA A. THOMPSON. 2007. Relative clauses in English conversation: Relativizers, frequency, and the notion of construction. *Studies in Language 31* (2). 293–326.
GELL, ALFRED. 1992. Inter-tribal commodity barter and reproductive gift-exchange in old Melanesia. *Exchange and value: An anthropological approach*, ed. by Caroline Humphrey and Stephen Hugh-Jones, 142–168. New York: Cambridge University Press.
GELUYKENS, RONALD. 1988. The interactional nature of referent-introduction. *Chicago Linguistic Society 24* (1). 141–154. Chicago: Chicago Linguistic Society.
GERAGHTY, PAUL. 1988. The reconstruction of Proto-Southern Oceanic. *VICAL 1: Oceanic Languages: Papers from the Fifth International Conference on Austronesian Linguistics*, ed. by R. Harlow & R. Hooper, 141–156. Auckland, New Zealand: Linguistic Society of New Zealand.
GERAGHTY, PAUL. 1994. Linguistic evidence for the Tongan Empire. *Trends in Linguistics, Studies and Mongraphs 77: Language contact and change in the Austronesian world*, ed. by Tom Dutton and Darrell T. Tryon, 233–250. Berlin: Mouton de Gruyter.

GIBBONS, JOHN. 1987. *Code-mixing and code choice: A Hong Kong case study*. Clevedon: Multilingual Matters.
GILDERSLEEVE, BASIL L. AND G. LODGE. 2003. *Gildersleeve's Latin grammar*. Wauconda, IL: Bolchazy-Carducci Publishers, Inc.
GIORDANA, LARA. 2014. Waala, l'anomalia di un villaggio kanak (Nuova Caledonia). *L'uomo : società, tradizione, sviluppo 39* (2). 25–44.
GIVÓN, TALMY. 2001. *Syntax: An introduction*. 2 vols. Philadelphia: John Benjamins.
GOEDEMANS, ROB AND HARRY VAN DER HULST. 2013. Fixed stress locations. *The world atlas of language structures online*, ed. by Matthew S. Dryer and Martin Haspelmath. Leipzig: Max Planck Institute for Evolutionary Anthropology. Online:http://wals.info/chapter/14.
GORDON, MATTHEW. 2006. *Syllable weight: Phonetics, phonology, typology*. New York: Routledge.
GORDON, MATTHEW AND IAN MADDIESON. 1999. The phonetics of Ndumbea. *Oceanic Linguistics 38*. 66–90.
GORDON, MATTHEW, AND IAN MADDIESON. 2004. The phonetics of Paicî vowels. *Oceanic Linguistics 43*(2). 296–310.
GRACE, GEORGE W. 1985. Oceanic subgrouping: Retrospect and prospect. *Austronesian linguistics at the 15th Pacific Science Congress, Pacific Linguistics C*, vol. 88, ed. by Andrew Pawley and Lois Carrington, 1-18. Dunedin, NEw Zealand: Linguistic Circle of Canberra.
GRACE, GEORGE W. 1991. The "aberrant" (vs. "exemplary") Melanesian languages. *Patterns of change, change of patterns: Linguistic change and reconstruction methodology*, ed. by Philip Baldi, 109–128. New York: Mouton de Gruyter.
GRACE, GEORGE W. 1992. How do languages change? (More on "aberrant" languages). *Oceanic Linguistics 31* (1). 115–130.
GRACE, GEORGE W. 1995. Regularity of change in what?. *The comparative method reviewed: Regularity and irregularity in language change,* ed. by Mark Durie and Malcolm Ross, 157-179. New York: Oxford University Press.
GREENBERG, JOSEPH H. 1963. Some universals of grammar with particular reference to the order of meaningful elements. *Universals of language*, ed. by Joseph H. Greenberg. Cambridge, MA: MIT Press.
GREENBERG, JOSEPH H. 1966. *Language universals: With special reference to feature hierarchies*. Janua Linguarum Series Minor 59. The Hague: Mouton.
GUIART, JEAN. 1957. Les modalités de l'organisation dualiste et le système matrimonial en Nouvelle-Calédonie. *Cahiers Internationaux de Sociologie 22*. 21–39.
HAIMAN, JOHN. 1978. Conditionals are topics. *Language 54* (3). 564–589.
HAJEK, JOHN. 1997. *Universals of sound change in nasalization*. Oxford: Blackwell.
HAMELIN, CHRISTINE, CHRISTINE SALOMON, RÉMI SITTA, ALICE GUÉGUEN, AND DIANE CYR. 2009. Childhood sexual abuse and adult binge drinking among Kanak women in New Caledonia. *Social Science & Medicine 68* (7). 1247–1253.
HAMILTON, PHILIP. 1995. Vowel phonotactic positions in Australian Aboriginal languages. Proceedings of the 21st Annual Meeting of the Berkeley Linguistics Society: General Session and Parasession on Historical Issues in Sociolinguistics/Social Issues in Historical Linguistics. 129–140.
HANNAY, MICHAEL. 1985. *English existentials in functional grammar*. Dordrecht: Foris.
HASPELMATH, MARTIN. 2004. Coordinating constructions: An overview. *Coordinating constructions*, ed. by Martin Haspelmath, 3-40. Typological Studies in Language 58. Philadelphia: John Benjamins.
HASPELMATH, MARTIN. 2007. Coordination. *Language typology and syntactic description, Second Edition, Volume II: Complex constructions*, ed. by Timothy Shopen, 1–51. New York: Cambridge University Press.

HASPELMATH, MARTIN AND ANDREA SIMS. 2010. *Understanding morphology, 2nd edn*. Understanding Language. London: Hachette.
HAUDRICOURT, ANDRE-GEORGES. 1964. Nature et culture dans la civilisation de l'igname: L'Origine des clones et des clans. *L'Homme 4* (1). 93–104.
HAUDRICOURT, ANDRE-GEORGES. 1971. New Caledonia and the Loyalty Islands. *Current Trends in Linguistics, Vol. 8: Linguistics in Oceania*, ed. by Thomas A. Sebeok, 359–396. The Hague: Mouton.
HAUDRICOURT, ANDRE-GEORGES, JEAN-CLAUDE RIVIERRE, FRANÇOISE RIVIERRE, CLAIRE MOYSE-FAURIE, AND JACQUELINE DE LA FONTINELLE. 1979. *Les langues mélanésiennes de Nouvelle-Calédonie*. Collection Eveil. Nouméa: Bureau psychopédagogique.
HAUDRICOURT, ANDRE-GEORGES, AND FRANÇOISE OZANNE-RIVIERRE. 1982. *Dictionnaire thématique des langues de la région de Hienghène (Nouvelle-Calédonie): Pije, fwâi, nemi, jawe*. Paris: SELAF.
HAUGEN, EINAR. 1950. The analysis of linguistic borrowing. *Language 26*. 210–231.
HAUGEN, EINAR. 1977. Norm and deviation in bilingual communities. *Bilingualism: Psychological, social and educational implications*, ed. by Peter A. Hornby, 91-102. New York: Academic Press.
HEESCHEN, VOLKER. 1982. Some systems of spatial deixis in Papuan languages. *Here and there: Cross-linguistic studies on deixis and demonstration*, ed. by Jürgen Weissenborn and Wolfgang Klein, 81-110. Philadelphia: John Benjamins.
HEINE, BERND AND HIROYUKI MIYASHITA. 2008. The intersection between reflexives and reciprocals: A grammaticalization perspective. *Reciprocals and reflexives: Theoretical and typological explorations*, ed. by Ekkehard König and Volker Gast. Trends in Linguistics 192. Berlin: Walter de Gruyter. 169–224.
HERBERT, ROBERT K. 1986. *Language universals, markedness theory and natural phonetic processes*. Berlin: Mouton de Gruyter.
HISCOCK, PETER. 2008. *Archaeology of ancient Australia*. New York: Routledge.
HOLLYMAN, K.J. WITH MAURICE MOUÉAOU AND MARIE-LOUISE GALAOUI. 1981. *La buse et l'hirondelle: un conte en caaàc d'il y a 120 ans*. Auckland: Linguistic Society of New Zealand.
HOLLYMAN, K.J. 1999. *Etudes sur les langues du Nord de la Nouvelle-Calédonie*. Selaf 377. Paris: Peeters.
HOVDHAUGEN, EVEN. 1992. Phonetic vowel length in Samoan. *Oceanic Linguistics 31* (2). 281–285.
HUME, ELIZABETH V. 1997. Vowel preservation in Leti. *Oceanic Linguistics 36* (1). 65-101.
IEOM (Institut d'emission d'Outre-mer). 2011. *Nouvelle-Calédonie: Rapport annuel 2010*. Paris: Siège Social. Online: http://www.ieom.fr/IMG/pdf/ra2010_nouvelle-caledonie.pdf.
ISEE (Institut de la statistique et des études économiques). 1996. Portrait de votre commune - Belep. Online: http://www.isee.nc/portraitcommune/belep.html.
ISEE (Institut de la statistique et des études économiques). 2004. Portrait de votre commune – Belep. Online: http://www.isee.nc/portraitcommune/belep.html.
JAKOBSON, ROMAN. 1960. Linguistics and poetics. *Style in Language*, ed. by Thomas Sebeok, 350–377. Cambridge: MIT Press.
JUCKER, ANDREAS H. 1993. The discourse marker *well*: A relevance-theoretical account. *Journal of Pragmatics 19*. 435-452.
KASARHÉROU, EMMANUEL, GÉRARD DEL RIO, AND EMMANUEL TJIBAOU. 2007. Le pays Béléma: Une histoire pleine d'avenir. *Mwà Véé: Revue culturelle kanak 56*. Nouméa: ADCK-Tjibaou Cultural Center.
KAUFMAN, DANIEL. 2011. Exclamatives and temporal nominalizations in Austronesian. *Nominalization in Asian languages: Diachronic and typological perspectives*, ed. by Foong Ha Yap, Karen Grunow-Hårsta, and Janick Wrona, 721–756. Typological Studies in Language 96. Philadelphia: John Benjamins.
KEEN, IAN. 2002. Seven aboriginal marriage systems and their correlates. *Anthropology Forum 12*. 145-157.

KEENAN, EDWARD L. 1976. Towards a universal definition of "subject". *Subject and topic*, ed. by C. Li, 305–333. New York: Academic Press.
KEENAN, EDWARD L. 1985. Relative clauses. *Language typology and syntactic description, Volume II: Complex Constructions*, ed. by Timothy Shopen, 141-170. Cambridge: Cambridge University Press.
KEENAN, EDWARD L. AND BERNARD COMRIE. 1977. NP accessibility and universal grammar. *Linguistic Inquiry 8*. 63-100.
KEENAN, ELINOR OCHS AND BAMBI SCHIEFFELIN. 1976. Foregrounding referents: a reconsideration of left dislocation in discourse. *Proceedings of the 2nd Annual Meeting of the Berkeley Linguistics Society*. 240-257.
KEESING, ROGER M. 1982. Kastom in Melanesia: An overview. *Mankind 13* (4). 297–301.
KING, KENDALL AND NATALIA GANUZA. 2005. Language, identity, education, and transmigration: Chilean adolescents in Sweden. *Journal of Language, Identity, and Education* 4(3). 179–199.
KIRCH, PATRICK V. 1991. Prehistoric exchange in Western Melanesia. *Annual Review of Anthropology 20*. 141–165.
KLAMER, MARIAN. 2000. How report verbs become quote markers and complementisers. *Lingua 110*. 69–98.
KLATT, DENNIS H. 1976. Linguistic uses of segmental duration in English: Acoustic and perceptual evidence. *Journal of the Acoustical Society of America 59*. 1208–1221.
KÖNIG, EKKEHARD. 1991. *The meaning of focus particles: A comparative perspective*. New York: Routledge.
KORNFILT, JAKLIN. 1997. *Turkish*. Descriptive Grammars. London: Routledge.
KRYK-KASTOVSKY, BARBARA. 1996. The linguistic, cognitive and cultural variables of the conceptualization of space. *The construal of space in language and thought*, ed. by Martin Pütz and René Dirven, 329-344. Cognitive Linguistics Research. New York: Mouton de Gruyter.
LABOV, WILLIAM, MARK KAREN, AND COREY MILLER. 1991. Near-mergers and the suspension of phonemic contrast. *Language Variation and Change 3*. 33–74.
LADEFOGED, PETER. 1971. *Preliminaries to linguistic phonetics*. Chicago: University of Chicago Press.
LADEFOGED, PETER. 1993. *A course in phonetics, 3rd edn*. Fort Worth: Harcourt Brace College Publishers.
LADEFOGED, PETER AND IAN MADDIESON. 2006. *The sounds of the world's languages*. Oxford; Cambridge: Wiley-Blackwell.
LAGARDE, LOUIS AND ANDRÉ-JOHN OUETCHO. 2015. Rocks, pottery and bird bones: New evidence on the material culture of Isle of Pines (New Caledonia) during its 3000-year-long chronology. *The Lapita Cultural Complex in time and space: Expansion routes, chronologies and typologies*, ed. by Christophe Sand, Scarlett Chiu, and Nicholas Hogg. Archeologia Pasifika 4. Institut d'archéologie de la Nouvelle-Calédonie et du Pacifique. 103–123.
LAMBERT, PIERRE. 1855–1859. Petit journal de France à Bélèp, 1855-1859. Manuscript typed by P. Laurenge. Archevêché de Nouméa.
LAMBERT, PIERRE. 1860–1875. Petit journal de 1860-1875. Manuscript typed by P. Laurenge. Archevêché de Nouméa.
LAMBERT, PIERRE. 1900. *Mœurs et superstitions des Néo-Calédoniens*. Nouméa: Nouvelle Imprimerie Nouméenne.
LANGEWEG, S.J. 1988. *The stress system of Dutch*. Ph.D. dissertation, Leiden University.
LAVIGNE, GERARD. 2012. Compter dans sa langue pour mieux compter dans l'autre: Pour une approche ethnomathématique du nombre à l'école de Nouvelle-Calédonie. *The Plurilingual School in the Communities of the Pacific, 18-21 October 2010, Nouméa, New Caledonia*, ed. by Jacques Vernaudon and Stéphanie Geneix-Rabault, 30–43. Nouméa: Académie des langues kanak.

LAWSON, SARAH AND ITESH SACHDEV. 2000. Codeswitching in Tunisia: Attitudinal and behavioural dimensions. *Journal of Pragmatics 32*. 1343–1361.
LEENHARDT, MAURICE. 1946. *Langues et dialectes de l'Austro-Mélanésie*. Travaux et mémoires de l'Institut d'ethnologie, vol. 46. Paris: Institut d'ethnologie, Université de Paris.
LEENHARDT, RAYMOND (Recorder). 1958. Linguistic survey. Various locations. Tjibaou Cultural Center DAT 98.11.
LEHISTE, ILSE. 1970. *Suprasegmentals*. Cambridge, MA: MIT Press.
LEHMANN, CHRISTIAN. 1988. Towards a typology of clause linkage. *Clause combining in grammar and discourse*, ed. by John Haiman and Sandra Thompson, 181-225. Amsterdam and Philadelphia: John Benjamins.
LEVINSON, STEPHEN C. 2003. *Space in language and cognition: Explorations in cognitive diversity*. Cambridge: Cambridge University Press.
LEWIS, M. PAUL, GARY F. SIMONS, AND CHARLES D. FENNIG (eds.). 2016. *Ethnologue: Languages of the world, Nineteenth Edition*. Dallas, Tex.: SIL International. Online version: http://www.ethnologue.com/.
LICHTENBERK, FRANTISEK. 2000. Inclusory pronominals. *Oceanic Linguistics 39* (1). 1–32.
LINDSTROM, LAMONT. 1990. Straight talk on Tanna. *Disentangling: Conflict discourse in Pacific societies*, ed. by Karen Ann Watson-Gegeo and Geoffrey M. White. Stanford: Stanford University Press. 373–411.
LYNCH, JOHN. 2002. The Proto-Oceanic labiovelars: some new observations. *Oceanic Linguistics 41* (2).
LYNCH, JOHN AND FRANÇOISE OZANNE-RIVIERRE. 2001. Some shared developments in pronouns in languages of Southern Oceania. *Oceanic Linguistics 40*(1). 33–66.
LYNCH, JOHN, MALCOLM ROSS AND TERRY CROWLEY. 2002. *The Oceanic Languages*. Richmond, Surrey: Curzon.
LYNCH, JOHN, AND DARRELL T. TRYON. 1985. Central-Eastern Oceanic: A subgrouping hypothesis. *Austronesian Linguistics at the 15th Pacific Science Congress, Pacific Linguistics C, Vol. 88*, ed. by Andrew Pawley and Lois Carrington, 31-52. Dunedin, New Zealand: Linguistic Circle of Canberra.
LYONS, JOHN. 1967. A note on possessive, existential and locative sentences. *Foundations of Language 3* (4). 390–396.
LYONS, JOHN. 1994. *Semantics: Vol. 2*. New York: Cambridge University Press.
MADDIESON, IAN. 1989. Prenasalized stops and speech timing. *Journal of the International Phonetic Association 19*(2). 57–66.
MADDIESON, IAN. 2011. Vowel quality inventories. *The world atlas of language structures online*, ed. by Matthew S. Dryer and Martin Haspelmath. Munich: Max Planck Digital Library, chapter 1. Online: http://wals.info/chapter/2.
MADDIESON, IAN AND VICTORIA B. ANDERSON. 1994. Phonetic structures of Iaai. *UCLA Working Papers in Phonetics 87*. 163–182.
MADDIESON, IAN AND PETER LADEFOGED. 1993. Partially nasal consonants. *Nasals, nasalization, and the velum*, ed. by M. Huffman and R. Krakow, 329–367. Phonetics and Phonology 5. San Diego: Academic Press.
MATTHEWS, P.H. 2007. *The concise Oxford dictionary of linguistics*. Oxford: Oxford University Press.
MCCAWLEY, JAMES. 1968. *The phonological component of a grammar of Japanese*. The Hague: Mouton.
MENU, SVEN, JEAN-BRICE HERRENSCHMIDT, AND PASCAL HÉBERT. 2007–2008. Gestion participative des récifs coralliens et des écosystèmes associés du Grand Lagon Nord: Site inscrit au Patrimoine Mondial de l'UNESCO, Province Nord, Juillet 2007-Juillet 2008. Nouméa: Gestion Intégrée de l'Environnement en l'Océanie.
MITHUN, MARIANNE. 1984. The evolution of noun incorporation. *Language 60* (4). 847–894.

MITHUN, MARIANNE. 2001. *The languages of Native North America*. Cambridge Language Surveys. New York: Cambridge University Press.

MORAVCSIK, EDITH. 1994. A semantic analysis of associative plurals. *Studies in Language 27* (3). 469–503.

MOSEL, ULRIKE. 1991. Transitivity and reflexivity in Samoan. *Australian Journal of Linguistics 11* (2). 175–194.

MOYSE-FAURIE, CLAIRE. 1995. *Le xârâcùù: langue de Thio-Canala, Nouvelle-Calédonie, éléments de syntaxe*. Paris: Peeters.

MOYSE-FAURIE, CLAIRE. 1998. Constructions expressing middle, reflexive and reciprocal situations in some Oceanic languages. *Reciprocals and reflexives: Theoretical and typological explorations*, ed. by Ekkehard König and Volker Gast, 105-168. Trends in Linguistics 192. Berlin: Mouton de Gruyter.

MOYSE-FAURIE, CLAIRE. 2003a. Les langues du Pacifique. Clio. Online: http://www.clio.fr/BIBLIO-THEQUE/les_langues_du_pacifique.asp.

MOYSE-FAURIE, CLAIRE. 2003b. The ergative features of Papuan and Austronesian languages. *Ergatividade na Amazônia II*. Villejuif: Centre d'Etudes des langues indigènes d'Amérique (CNRS, IRD), Laboratório de Línguas Indígenas (UnB).

MUYSKEN, PETER. 2004. *Bilingual speech: A typology of code-mixing*. New York: Cambridge University Press.

NESPOR, MARINA AND IRENE VOGEL. 1986. *Prosodic phonology*. Dordrecht: Foris.

NEYRET, JEAN-BAPTISTE M. 1974a. Belep-French dictionary. Unpublished manuscript. Canberra, A.C.T.: Pacific Manuscripts Bureau, Research School of Pacific Studies, Australian National University.

NEYRET, JEAN-BAPTISTE M. 1974b. French-Belep dictionary. Unpublished manuscript. Canberra, A.C.T.: Pacific Manuscripts Bureau, Research School of Pacific Studies, Australian National University.

NEYRET, JEAN-BAPTISTE M. 1974c. Grammar, hymns and church teachings in the language of Belep, New Caledonia. Unpublished manuscript. Canberra, A.C.T.: Pacific Manuscripts Bureau, Research School of Pacific Studies, Australian National University.

NICHOLS, JOHANNA. 1986. Head-marking and dependent-marking grammar. *Language 62* (1). 56–119.

NOMOIGNE, JEAN-YVES (Recorder). 1994. Traditional songs. Balade, Pouébo. Tjibaou Cultural Center DAT 94.10.

NOONAN, MICHAEL. 2007. Complementation. *Language typology and syntactic description, Second Edition, Vol. II: Complex constructions*, ed. by Timothy Shopen, 52-150. New York: Cambridge University Press.

O'BRIEN, R.G. 1981. A simple test for variance effects in experimental designs. *Psychological Bulletin 89*. 570–574.

ONISHI, MASAYUKI. 2004. Instrumental subjects in Motuna. *Non-nominative subjects, Vol. 2*, ed. by Peri Bhaskararao and Karumuri Venkata Subbarao, 83-102. Typological Studies in Language 61. Philadelphia: John Benjamins.

OVERSTREET, MARYANN. 1999. *Whales, candlelight, and stuff like that: General extenders in English discourse*. New York: Oxford University Press.

OVERSTREET, MARYANN. 2005. And stuff *und so*: Investigating pragmatic expressions in English and German. *Journal of Pragmatics 37*. 1845–1864.

OZANNE-RIVIERRE, FRANÇOISE. 1991. Incorporation of genitive relators in the languages of New Caledonia and the Loyalty Islands. *Currents in Pacific linguistics: Papers in Austronesian languages and ethnolinguistics in honour of George W. Grace*, ed. by Robert A. Blust, 321-338. Pacific Linguistics C-117. Canberra: Australian National University.

OZANNE-RIVIERRE, FRANÇOISE. 1992. The Proto-Oceanic consonantal system and the languages of New Caledonia. *Oceanic Linguistics 31*(2). 191–207.

OZANNE-RIVIERRE, FRANÇOISE. 1995. Structural changes in the languages of Northern New Caledonia. *Oceanic Linguistics* 34(1). 44–72.

OZANNE-RIVIERRE, FRANÇOISE. 1997. Spatial reference in New Caledonian languages. *Referring to space: Studies in Austronesian and Papuan languages*, ed. by Gunter Senft. Oxford: Oxford University Press.

OZANNE-RIVIERRE, FRANÇOISE. 2000. Terminologie de parenté proto-océanienne: Continuité et changement dans les langues kanak. *En pays kanak: Ethnologie, linguistique, archéologie, histoire de la Nouvelle-Calédonie*, ed. by A. Bensa and I. Leblic. Ethnologie de la France: Variation, Vol. 14. Paris: Maison des sciences de l'homme.

OZANNE-RIVIERRE, FRANÇOISE. 2004. The evolution of the verb 'take' in New Caledonian languages. *Complex predicates in Oceanic languages: studies in the dynamics of binding and boundedness*, ed. by Isabelle Bril and Françoise Ozanne-Rivierre, 331-345. New York: Mouton de Gruyter.

OZANNE-RIVIERRE, FRANÇOISE AND JEAN-CLAUDE RIVIERRE. 1989. The development of nasal vowels in languages from the northern area of New Caledonia. *Cahiers du LACITO* 4. 82-100.

OZANNE-RIVIERRE, FRANÇOISE WITH BAPTISTE BOIGUIVIE, SCHOLASTIQUE BOIGUIVIE AND ELIAN DEDANE. 1998. *Le nyelâyu de Balade*. Langues et cultures du Pacifique 12. Paris: Peeters.

PALMER, F.R. 2001. *Mood and modality, 2nd edn.* New York: Cambridge University Press.

PANDIT, IRA. 1986. *Hindi English code switching: Mixed Hindi English*. Delhi: Datta Book Centre.

PANOFF, MICHEL. 1976. Patrifiliation as ideology and practice in a matrilineal society. *Ethnology* 15 (2). 175–188.

PAWLEY, ANDREW. 1966. Samoan phrase structure: The morphology-syntax of a Western Polynesian language. *Anthropological Linguistics* 8 (5). 1–63.

PAWLEY, ANDREW AND LAWRENCE A. REID. 1976. The evolution of transitive constructions in Austronesian. *Working Papers in Linguistics* 8, 51-73. Honolulu: University of Hawai'i Press.

PAYNE, THOMAS E. 1997. *Describing morphosyntax: A guide for field linguists*. Cambridge: Cambridge University Press.

POPLACK, SHANA, DAVID SANKOFF AND CHRISTOPHER MILLER. 1988. The social correlates and linguistic processes of lexical borrowing and assimilation. *Linguistics* 26. 47–104.

PRINCE, ELLEN F. 1981. Toward a taxonomy of given-new information. *Radical pragmatics*, ed. by Peter Cole, 223-255. New York: Academic Press.

QUENÉ, HUGO AND HUUB VAN DEN BERGH. 2004. On multi-level modeling of data from repeated measures designs: A tutorial. *Speech Communication* 43. 103–121.

RAY, SIDNEY H. 1926. *A comparative study of the Melanesian Island languages*. London: Cambridge University Press.

REHG, KENNETH L. 1993. Proto-Micronesian prosody. *Tonality in Austronesian languages,* ed. by Jerold A. Edmondson and Kenneth J. Gregerson, 25–46. Oceanic Linguistics Special Publications 24. Honolulu: University of Hawai'i Press.

REHG, KENNETH. 2007. Does Hawaiian have diphthongs? And how can you tell? *Language description, history, and development: Linguistic indulgence in memory of Terry Crowley*, ed. by Jeff Siegel, John Lynch, and Diana Eades, 119-131. Creole Language Library 30. Amsterdam/Philadelphia: John Benjamins.

RIEHL, ANASTASIA KAY. 2008. *The phonology and phonetics of nasal obstruent sequences*. Ithaca, NY: Cornell dissertation.

RIVIERRE, JEAN-CLAUDE. 1973. *Phonologie comparée des dialectes de l'extrême-sud de la Nouvelle-Calédonie*. Paris: SELAF.

RIVIERRE, JEAN-CLAUDE. 1980. *La langue de Touho: Phonologie et grammaire du Cemuhi (Nouvelle-Calédonie)*. Langues et civilisations a tradition orale. Paris: Société d'études linguistiques et anthropologiques de France.

RIVIERRE, JEAN-CLAUDE. 1983. *Dictionnaire paicî-français*. Paris: SELAF.
RIVIERRE, JEAN-CLAUDE. 1993. Tonogenesis in New Caledonia. *Tonality in Austronesian languages*, ed. by J. A. Edmondson & K. J. Gregerson, 155-174. Oceanic Linguistics Special Publication. Honolulu: University of Hawaii Press.
RIVIERRE, JEAN-CLAUDE AND SABINE EHRHART WITH RAYMOND DIÉLA. 2006. *Le bwatoo et les dialectes de la région de Koné (Nouvelle-Calédonie)*. Selaf 435. Paris-Louvain-Dudley: Peeters.
ROLLE, NICHOLAS AND DONNA STARKS. 2014. Vowel length in Niuean. *Oceanic Linguistics 53* (2). 273–299.
ROMAINE, SUZANNE. 1995. *Bilingualism*. Oxford: Blackwell.
ROSS, DANIEL. 2016. Between coordination and subordination: typological, structural and diachronic perspectives on pseudocoordination. *Coordination and subordination: Form and meaning – Selected papers from CSI Lisbon 2014*, ed. by Fernanda Pratas, Sandra Pereira, and Clara Pinto, 209–243. Newcastle upon Tyne: Cambridge Scholars Publishing.
RUBINO, CARL. 2013. Reduplication. *The world atlas of language structures online*, ed. by Matthew S. Dryer and Martin Haspelmath. Leipzig: Max Planck Institute for Evolutionary Anthropology. Online:http://wals.info/chapter/27.
RUHLEN, MERRITT. 1973. Nasal vowels. *Working Papers on Language Universals 12*. 1–36.
RUSSMANN, STEFAN, YANN BARGUIL, PIERRE CABALION, MARINA KRITSANIDA, DANIEL DUHET, AND BERNHARD H. LAUTERBURG. 2003. Hepatic injury due to traditional aqueous extracts of kava root in New Caledonia. *European Journal of Gastroenterology & Hepatology 15* (9). 1033-1036.
SACIUK, BOHDAN. 1969. The stratal division of the lexicon. *Papers in Linguistics 1 (3)*. 464–532.
SAND, CHRISTOPHE AND PETER J. SHEPPARD. 2000. Long distance prehistoric obsidian imports in New Caledonia: Characteristics and meanings. *Comptes rendus de l'Académie des Sciences, Series IIA, Earth and Planetary Science 331* (3). 235–243.
SANKOFF, DAVID, SHANA POPLACK AND SWATHI VANNIARAJAN. 1990. The case of the nonce loan in Tamil. *Language Variation and Change 2*. 71–101.
SCHACHTER, PAUL AND TIMOTHY SHOPEN. 2007. *Language typology and syntactic description, Second Edition, Vol. I: Clause structure*, ed. by Timothy Shopen, 1-60. New York: Cambridge University Press.
SCHOOLING, STEPHEN J. 1990. *Language maintenance in Melanesia: Sociolinguistics and social networks in New Caledonia*. Publications in Linguistics 91. Dallas: Summer Institute of Linguistics and the University of Texas at Arlington.
SCHOOLING, STEPHEN J. 1992. The phonology of Yuanga. *Papers in Austronesian Linguistics*, ed. by H. Steinhauer and M.D. Ross. Canberra, A.C.T.: Dept. of Linguistics, Research School of Pacific Studies, Australian National University.
SCHOURUP, LAWRENCE C. 1972. Characteristics of vowel nasalization. *Papers in Linguistics 5*. 530–548.
SCHOURUP, LAWRENCE C. 1973. A cross-language study of vowel nasalization. *Ohio State Working Papers in Linguistics 15*. 190–221.
SCHÜTZ, ALBERT J. 1999. Fijian Accent. *Oceanic Linguistics 38* (1). 139–151.
SCOTT, NORMAN C. 1948. A study in the phonetics of Fijian. *Bulletin of the School of Oriental and African Studies 12* (3/4). 737–752.
SENFT, GUNTER. 1997. Introduction. *Deixis and demonstratives in Oceanic languages*, ed. by Gunter Senft, 1-14. Pacific Linguistics 562. Canberra: Australian National University.
SILVERSTEIN, MICHAEL. 1976. Hierarchy of features and ergativity. *Grammatical categories in Australian languages*, ed. by R. M. W. Dixon, 112–171. Canberra: Australian Institute of Aboriginal Studies.
SMITH, B. 1978. Temporal aspects of English speech production: A developmental perspective. *Journal of Phonetics 6*. 37–67.

Sperlich, Wolfgang B. 1997. *Tohi Vagahau Niue: Niue language dictionary*. Honolulu: University of Hawai'i Press and the Government of Niue.

Spriggs, Matthew. 1997. *The island Melanesians*. Cambridge: Blackwell.

Sproat, Richard. 1988. Bracketing paradoxes, cliticization and other topics: The mapping between syntactic and phonological structure. *Morphology and modularity: In honour of Henk Schultink*, ed. by Martin Everaert, Riny Huybregts and Mieke Trommelen, 339–360. Publications in Language Sciences 29. Dordrecht: Foris.

Stanford, James Norris. 2007. *Dialect contact and identity: A case study of exogamous Sui clans*. Ph.D. dissertation. Michigan State University.

Talmy, Leonard. 2007. Lexical typologies. *Language typology and syntactic description, Second Edition, Vol. III: Grammatical categories and the lexicon*, ed. by Timothy Shopen, 66-168. New York: Cambridge University Press.

Tay, Mary W.J. 1989. Code switching and code mixing as a communicative strategy in multilingual discourse. *World Englishes 8* (3). 407–417.

Thieberger, Nick. 2006. *A grammar of South Efate: An Oceanic language of Vanuatu*. Honolulu: University of Hawaii Press

Thomas, Nicholas, Allen Abramson, Ivan Brady, R.C. Green, Marshall Sahlins, Rebecca A. Stephenson, Friedrich Valjavec, and Ralph Gardner White. 1989. The force of ethnology: Origins and significance of the Melanesia/Polynesia division. *Current Anthropology 30* (1). 27–41.

Thompson, Sandra A. 2002. "Object complements" and conversation: Towards a realistic account. *Studies in Language 26* (1). 125–164.

Thompson, Sandra A. and Paul J. Hopper. 2001. Transitivity, clause structure, and argument structure: Evidence from conversation. *Frequency and the emergence of linguistics structure*, ed. by Joan L. Bybee and Paul J. Hopper, 27-60. Philadelphia: John Benjamins.

Thompson, Sandra A., Robert E. Longacre, and Shin Ja J. Hwang. 2007. Adverbial clauses. *Language typology and syntactic description, Second Edition, Vol. II: Complex constructions*, ed. by Timothy Shopen, 237-300. New York: Cambridge University Press.

Törkenczy, Miklós. 2004. *The phonotactics of Hungarian*. DSc dissertation, Eötvös Loránd University, Budapest.

Tschubby. 2018. Aire coutumière in Neukaledonien 2018. Image. Wikimedia Commons. Online: https://commons.wikimedia.org/wiki/File:Aire_coutumi%C3%A8re_in_Neukaledonien_2018.png Distributed under a CC BY-SA 3.0 license.

Van der Auwera, Johan and Ludo Lejeune, with Valentin Goussev. 2011. The prohibitive. *The world atlas of language structures online*, ed. by Matthew S. Dryer and Martin Haspelmath. Munich: Max Planck Digital Library, chapter 71. Online: http://wals.info/chapter/71.

Van Valin, Robert D., Jr. 2004. *An introduction to syntax*. Cambridge: Cambridge University Press.

Van Zanten, Ellen and Rob Goedemans. 2007. A functional typology of Austronesian and Papuan stress systems. *Prosody in Indonesian languages*, ed. by Vincent J. van Heuven and Ellen van Zanten, 63-88. Utrecht: LOT.

Wälchli, Bernhard. 2003. *Co-compounds and natural coordination*. Ph.D. dissertation, University of Stockholm.

Warner, William Lloyd. 1937. *A black civilization*. New York: Harper & Row.

Weber, Natalie and Lisa Matthewson. 2014. Reflections of complement type: The view from Blackfoot. *The art and craft of semantics: A Festschrift for Irene Heim*, vol. 2, MITWPL 71, ed. by Luka Crnič and Uli Sauerland, 275–298.

Whalen, D.H. and Patrice S. Beddor. 1989. Connections between nasality and vowel duration and height: Elucidation of the Eastern Algonquian intrusive nasal. *Language 65* (3).457–486.

Wohlgemuth, Jan. 2009. *A typology of verbal borrowings*. Trends in Linguistics. Berlin: Mouton de Gruyter.

ZUE, V.W. AND M. LAFERRIERE. 1979. Acoustic study of medial /t,d/ in American English. *Journal of the Acoustical Society of America 66* (4). 1039-1050.

ZWICKY, ARNOLD M. 1972. On casual speech. Papers from the eighth regional meeting, Chicago Linguistic Society, April 14–16 1972, 607–615.

ZWICKY, ARNOLD M. 1977. On clitics. Bloomington: Indiana University Linguistics Club.

ZWICKY, ARNOLD M. 1985. Clitics and Particles. *Language 61* (2). 283–305.

Index

absolutive
- arguments 24, 111, 139-141, 160-163, 169, 255, 265-266, 273-281, 285, 287, 289-293, 297-298, 316, 325-327, 331, 347-348, 355, 368-376, 379-380, 391, 394, 397-400, 408, 411, 429, 433-435, 466, 471, 493, 495-496, 500
- case, *see* case
- intransitive verbs 163, 266, 269-272, 276, 374-375, 391, 397, 410
- suffixes, *see* suffixes, absolutive

actual 431-432; *see also* focus
additive 235, 294-295, 332, 430, 432, 446, 450-451, 453-456
adpositions, *see* locatives
- adverbials 445-446
- conditional clauses 476-480
- linkers 472-476
- purpose clauses 468-471
- reason clauses 487-491

adverbs 147, 152-155, 250, 306, 312, 361, 440, 442
adversatives, *see* linkers
affectedness 215-216; *see also* completive
affixes, *see* suffixes
agentive 168-170
- reduced 302-304
aires coutumières, *see* coutume
Ajië 18, 108, 113, 268
alienable, *see* possessive constructions
alignment 24, 362-373
allophony 76-92
alveolar, *see* consonants
anaphoric determiners, *see* determiners
animacy 182, 184, 185, 192-194, 196-197, 212-213, 229-230, 243, 290-292
approximants, *see* consonants
arguments, *see* alignment

aspect 111, 154-155, 295, 304-319, 360, 419, 422, 440-441, 493
associative 211-214; *see also* quantifiers
Australia 1, 19, 87, 124, 164, 370, 445
- Yidiny 123-124
Austronesian 1, 3, 14, 16-17, 21, 35, 74, 178, 256, 302, 434; *see also* Oceanic
Balade 4, 11, 14-15, 19-22, 27, 30, 432, 510; *see also* Nyelâyu
Belema, *see* Belep
Belep
- Belema 1-15
- Belep Isles 1, 7, 18
- Belep Language Committee 20-22, 27, 29, 31-32, 98-99
- Teâ Belep 3, 8, 15, 241, 510
binomial, *see* linkers
borrowing, *see* language contact; words, loan
Caaàc 17-18, 35
cardinal 257-258; *see also* numerals
case 376-391
- absolutive 160, 269-272, 289, 297, 379-380
- dative 145, 192, 360, 376-377, 385-388, 441, 495
- genitive 24, 145, 272, 285, 298, 326, 328, 331, 355, 360, 382-385, 484-486; *see also* possessive
- instrumental 298-299, 377, 390-391
- locative 377, 388-390
- nominative 24, 266, 363, 368, 379, 381-382, 401
Catholic, *see* religion
causal, *see* linker
causatives 136, 172, 346, 373-374, 467
- morphological 297-301
- periphrastic 433-434
Cèmuhî 17-18
cessative 344-345

Index

clans 3-9, 13-15, 25, 167, 174
classifiers, *see* noun classifiers; numeral classifiers
clitics 142-147, 331-334, 348-354, 376-391; *see also* preface
    ditropic 24, 100, 124, 133, 160, 198-199, 207, 234, 285, 298-299, 355
    enclitic, *see* enclitics
    proclitic, *see* proclitics
    simple 143, 145, 156, 255, 263, 320, 408, 446, 448, 453, 472, 483
clusivity 241, 331, 392
comitative conjunctions 237, 239-240, 467
comparative 440-444
complementation strategies 463-495; *see also* pseudocoordination
complete phase, *see* phase shift
completive 155, 316-317; *see also* affectedness
compounding 108, 110, 115, 129, 139, 176-177, 191, 196, 203, 334-336, 354
conative 337-338
concessive 340-342
conditional clauses, *see* adverbials
conjunctions, *see* linkers
consonant inventory, *see* phonemes
consonants 37-45, 77-92
    alveolar 40-41, 51-53, 57-59, 63, 79-81, 83
    approximant 23, 25, 37, 39-42, 45, 59, 74, 77, 79, 81, 84, 88-89, 93, 98
    clusters 37, 49-50, 55-56, 59, 67, 101, 104, 116, 119, 132
    labial 37-39, 49-50, 56-60, 77, 98
    labiovelar 37-39, 49-50, 60, 77-78, 98
    nasal 23, 25, 35, 37, 44, 48, 55-60, 62-63, 69, 74, 76, 87, 97, 104, 129-131, 201, 282
    palatal 42, 51-54, 57-59, 63, 83
    prenasalized 25, 37, 39, 41, 44, 48, 54-58, 63, 74, 76, 99, 201, 282
    stop 23, 35, 37-43, 48-59, 63, 65, 74, 76-78, 83, 87-88, 93, 95, 99, 104, 114-115, 131-132, 179, 201, 282
    velar 43, 51, 53, 56-59, 85, 87; *see also* consonants, labiovelar
    voiceless 23, 35, 37, 45, 51-53, 56-59, 74, 77-86, 93, 95, 99, 104, 114-116, 119, 131-132, 179
constituent order, *see* words, order
continuative 305, 310-312, 325, 342-343, 493
coordination 155, 234-240, 242, 363, 367-368, 373-375, 445-465
correlational 446, 471-472
coutume 5, 10-13, 26, 175-176, 262, 308, 509, 512-513
    customary areas 3, 21, 30, 240
    Hoot ma Waap 4-5; *see also* phratry
custom, *see* coutume
customary areas, *see* coutume
dative, *see* case
definiteness 24, 231, 256, 260, 272, 355, 362-375, 381-383
deictic determiners, *see* determiners
deixis, *see* determiners
demonstrative pronouns, *see* pronouns
dependent possession, *see* possessive constructions
derivation 158-159, 165-178
desiderative 336-337, 468, 486-487
determiners 23, 216-231, 245, 351
    anaphoric 225-227
    deictic 221-225
    demonstrative 148, 228-231
    interrogative 220, 227-228, 403, 407
    numeric 138, 263-264
    relatives 497-499, 502
    suffixes 112, 128, 132-134, 142, 148-149, 159, 163, 210, 216-217, 220-226, 230, 243, 247-249, 251-252, 256, 351, 407, 436, 446, 490, 495, 497, 499
devoicing, *see* ingressive airstream

differential absolutive, *see* suffixes
diminished 305, 313-314, 360, 440-441
diphthongs, *see* vowels
directionals 24, 159, 217-220, 345, 347
    enclitics, *see* enclitics
    system of reference, *see* space
discourse markers 147, 156-158, 413-419, 446
disjunctive, *see* linkers
distal, *see* space
ditropic clitics, *see* clitics
Drehu, *see* Loyalty Islands
dual
    pronouns, *see* pronouns
    associative, *see* associative
dubitative 305, 315-316
duration, *see* vowels
dyadic 159, 166-168
Dyirbal 465
enclitics 23, 32, 93, 100; *see also* clitics
    directional 111, 113, 132-133, 138, 143, 159, 164, 217-218, 267-268, 306, 329, 345, 347-351
    ditropic, *see* clitics
    locational, *see* locational
    mood, *see* mood
endangerment 29-30
epenthesis, *see* vowels
equative constructions, *see* predicate nominals
ergative 20, 24, 362, 370-373
existentials, *see* predicates
extrametricality, *see* stress
Far North languages of New Caledonia 2-3, 17-20, 23, 37, 47, 49, 140, 263
Fijian 23, 56, 57-59, 67, 124, 141, 294, 319, 465, 503
focus 143, 147, 294-296, 332, 409-410, 428, 430-432
formatives 104, 112-113, 123-126, 141-142, 155, 158-159, 163, 165, 190, 295, 305, 326, 334, 376

France, *see* French
French 1, 3, 5, 7-9, 13, 15-16, 18-20, 25-30, 55, 74, 84-85, 94, 113, 115, 117-120, 126, 175, 256, 261-262, 286-287, 413
fusion 123
Fwâi, *see* Hienghène
gemination, *see* vowel
general extenders 163, 210, 214-215, 318; *see also* quantifiers
generic 183, 192-195, 268, 336, 443, 487; *see also* specific
genitive, *see* case
gnomic 305, 311-313, 325
habitual 305, 312, 315, 325, 343
hiatus, *see* vowels
Hienghène 15, 17-18, 36-37, 54, 362
Hoot ma Waap, *see* coutume
hosts, *see* clitics
Iaai, *see* Loyalty Islands
imperative 306, 310, 333, 355, 373, 375, 419-424
imperfective, *see* perfective
inalienable, *see* possessive constructions
inanimate, *see* animacy
inceptive 308, 339-340
inclusory, *see* linker
incomplete phase, *see* phase shift
independent possession, *see* possessive constructions
independent pronouns, *see* pronouns
Indonesian 465
inflection 158-165
information structure 226, 243, 245-248, 259-260, 263, 326, 396, 416, 495-497, 499
ingressive airstream 91-92
instrumental 170, 310; *see also* proclitics, derivational; case
interjections, *see* discourse markers
interrogative, *see* questions
interrogative pronouns, *see* pronouns
interrogative clefts, *see* focus
intonation 23, 25, 35, 72, 107

intonation units 71, 78, 92, 95, 135-136, 156-157, 229, 233, 236, 277, 292, 294, 329, 330, 332, 358, 378-379, 403-406, 414-416, 428, 432, 437, 440, 458-459, 472
intransitive; *see also* transitive
    absolutive-intransitive verb, *see* absolutive
    clauses 355-356, 362-368, 370, 371, 375, 379, 381, 394, 401, 493
    verbs 24, 138, 161, 265-269, 274, 280-290, 331, 336, 347, 370
irrealis 324-325; *see also* mood
iterative 305, 312, 315, 325
Jahai 222
Jawe, *see* Hienghène
juxtaposition, *see* coordination
Kanak 1, 3-5, 7, 11, 14, 16, 18, 20-21, 26-27, 30-31, 33, 41, 176, 190
Kastom, *see* coutume
kinship, *see* clans
Koumac 4, 15, 21, 30-31, 510; *see also* Nêlêmwa-Nixumwak
labial, *see* consonants
labialization 50, 60, 77
labiovelar, *see* consonants
Language Committee, *see* Belep
language contact 26-29, 41, 94, 113-121, 174; *see also* words, loan
Lapita, *see* Austronesian
Latin 113, 115-116, 119, 453
lengthening, *see* vowels
lenition 35, 78, 93-94, 96-97, 99-100, 104, 114-116, 119, 129, 131, 143-145, 177, 201
lexical strata 113-120
lexical stress, *see* stress
lexicalization, *see* derivation
linkers 155-156
    adverbial, *see* adverbial
    adversative 460-461
    binomial 231, 234-235
    causal 457-460
    conjunctive 448-456
    disjunctive 237, 418, 446, 456-457
    inclusory 237-239
    sequential 480-483
loan words, *see* words
locationals 100, 133, 143, 159, 164, 217-218, 241, 251, 272, 347, 351-354, 389
locative 328, 495; *see also* locationals
    case, *see* case
    nouns 206-209, 359, 361
    predicates, *see* predicates
    pronouns 244
Loyalty Islands 1, 18, 41
    Drehu 18, 41
    Iaai 18, 52
    Nengone 18
Maori 256
medial-distal, *see* space
medial-proximal, *see* space
missionaries, *see* religion
modality 24, 147, 162, 265, 336-347, 421, 425, 431, 464-465, 483-484, 492; *see also* mood
Mon-Khmer, *see* Jahai
mood 159-160, 162, 272, 294-296, 318-325, 332, 391-392, 437, 493
morphophonemic processes 23, 28, 35, 60-62, 71, 78, 93-97, 120-121, 131-133, 143-144, 150, 408
names
    language 20-22
    proper 3, 5-9, 115
    and words 123-125
nasal spreading 60, 76, 93, 97-99, 129-131, 143-144
nasal, *see* consonants
Ndumbea 18, 52, 56-57, 76
negation 24, 342, 397, 405, 413, 418, 422-428, 476-477, 486-487
Nêlêmwa-Nixumwak 13, 17-18, 23, 32, 35, 37, 39, 46-47, 52, 54-55, 68, 123, 140, 178-179, 196, 217, 230, 237, 239, 285, 319-320, 328,

336, 355, 362, 385, 406, 420, 434, 465, 496, 503
Nemi, *see* Hienghène
Nengone, *see* Loyalty Islands
neutralization 46, 60-62, 70, 76
New Caledonia 1-9, 11, 14-15, 17-23, 26-27, 30, 41 46, 115, 220; *see also* New Caledonian languages
New Caledonian languages 17-20, 23, 33, 35, 37, 46-47, 49, 52, 55, 68, 95, 98, 123, 147, 158, 176, 190, 196, 206, 217, 241, 256, 265, 336, 349, 362
nominative
    case, *see* case
    intransitive verbs 266-269, 367-368
    subject agreement proclitics 111, 147, 151, 159, 210, 213, 271, 294-295, 318, 320, 331-335, 357, 364, 367-368, 372, 419-422, 425, 430-431, 433, 450, 453, 455, 468, 493, 497
non-concatenative 178-179
nouns 159-161, 181-209, 359-360
    as a word class 148-150
    classes 23, 160, 181-190, 197
    classifiers 188, 202-206, 231
    phrases 231-240
    possessed 190-200
numerals 148-150, 181, 210, 217, 231, 256-264, 395
    classifiers 138, 262-264
    determiners, *see* determiners
Nyelâyu 1, 17-23, 27, 32, 35, 37, 39, 45-47, 52, 55, 62, 68, 98, 138, 168, 190, 196, 202, 217, 230, 248, 257, 265, 293, 355, 362, 496
Oceanic 16-17, 19-20, 32, 49, 57, 60, 67, 105, 141, 209, 256, 262, 285, 295, 385, 422
Or, *see* phratries
ordinal 159, 165-166, 256-264
orthography 20, 29, 32, 35-36, 61-62, 71, 98-99, 120, 125-127, 132, 141, 230
Paicî 17-18, 37, 42, 47, 55
palatal, *see* consonants

Papua 16, 124, 164, 223, 370, 434
    Yimas 124
parataxis, *see* coordination
passive 433, 435-436
paucal 241
    pronouns, see pronouns
pauses 127, 133, 139-140, 143, 145, 294, 333, 379, 415
perfect 304, 307-309
perfective 305, 320
periphrastic causatives, *see* causatives
personal pronouns, *see* pronouns, independent
phase shift 23, 32, 35, 71, 93-96, 100, 104, 108, 110, 132, 234, 258, 290, 336, 339, 488
phonemes 36-75, 119-120, 382-383
    consonant inventory 21, 35, 37-45, 102
    vowel inventory 46-47
phonetics, *see* allophony; consonants; vowels
phonotactics 50, 100-103, 110, 114, 119, 127, 179
phratries 3, 5, 21, 214, 240, 270, 398
pitch, *see* stress correlates
Pije, *see* Hienghène
plural
    pronouns, *see* pronouns
    associative, *see* associative
positional system of reference, *see* space
possessive
    constructions 110, 133, 135, 139, 148, 160, 173, 176-178, 181-209, 326, 360, 382-383
    locatives 206-209, 390
    suffixes, *see* suffixes
Pouébo 4, 17; *see also* Nyelâyu
Poum 4, 19, 21, 26, 30, 54, 429; *see also* Nêlêmwa-Nixumwak
predicates 151, 251, 265, 269, 360, 371, 391-402
    attributive 391, 401-403

locative 242, 392, 393, 399
existential 24, 258, 271, 371, 391, 397-401, 424, 497,
nominal 233, 255, 258, 355, 384, 391-397, 401, 408-409, 413, 424-427, 438, 467, 471-472, 475, 484-491
preface 124, 147, 162, 294-296, 318, 320, 332-333, 430-431, 453; see also clitics
prenasalized, see consonants
prestopped nasal 87
priests, see religion
proclitics 23, 32, 100, 141, 143, 145-147, 159
aspectual, see aspect
derivational 113, 126, 136-137, 165-176, 258, 271, 288, 304
subject agreement, see nominative
resultative, see resultative
progressive 304, 306-307
prohibitive, see negation; imperative
pronouns 240-256
demonstrative 142, 216-217, 228-229, 231, 243-255, 361, 382, 389, 391, 436, 499
independent 233, 237, 240-243, 375, 382, 392, 417
interrogative 240, 255-256, 403, 407-409, 412-413, 430
relative 217, 409, 495, 499-501
prosody 35, 50, 71, 104-112, 127, 420
prospective 324, 338-339
proximal, see space
pseudocoordination 24, 376, 433, 436, 446, 448, 465-475
punctual 305-306, 314-315, 323, 325, 360, 440-441
purpose clauses, see adverbials
quantifiers 257
suffixes 111, 132-133, 142, 148, 150, 159, 163, 209-215
questions 134-135, 139-141, 220, 227-228, 233, 242, 244, 355, 377-378, 403-419, 457

quotatives 251, 433, 436-437, 442, 467
realis 321-324; see also mood
reason clauses, see adverbials
reciprocals 172, 295, 301-302
reduced agentive, see agentive
reflexives 433-435
relative clauses 148, 150, 217, 231, 233, 244, 256, 359-360, 366, 409-410, 445-446, 465, 479, 487, 490-491, 495-502
religion 6, 15, 18-21, 30, 84, 115-116, 509
resultative
proclitics 168, 170-172
clauses 480
semantics 29, 319, 391
of clause combining 23-24, 283, 309, 365, 376, 393, 445-446, 465-471, 483-488
of morphological categories 160, 164, 166-167, 169, 173, 177-178, 202, 211-212, 216-217, 300, 377, 427
of noun classes 181-182, 185, 187, 190
roles 140, 240, 272, 280, 370, 373, 375, 383, 385, 388, 390
shifts 116-117, 284, 286, 334, 336
sequential, see linkers
serialization 335-347, 465, 492-495
simple clitics, see clitics
sociolinguistics 25-29, 64, 66, 84, 91, 476
sound symbolism 114, 179
South Efate 91, 93, 147, 319, 464-465, 503; see also Vanuatu
space 217-220; see also determiners
specificity 23, 140, 150, 161, 169, 193, 265-266, 269-270, 272-280, 287, 289, 328-329, 369, 373, 377, 390, 397
suffixes, see suffixes
stem modification 94, 161, 181, 184-185, 187, 189, 194-198, 200-202, 220, 243, 267, 280-285, 427
stops, see consonants
stress

correlates 35, 104-105, 107, 111
extrametrical 104, 111
lexical 104, 108, 112
penultimate 23, 35, 91, 97, 104-105, 107, 108-113, 120, 127-128
vowel lengthening 23, 69, 71, 90, 106, 110-111, 120, 128, 457
subjects 331-334, 373-376; *see also* nominative
subjunctive 305, 309-310
suffixes 3, 23, 32, 93, 111-113, 121, 123, 128-132, 138, 141-143, 145, 159-164, 172, 181, 196, 201, 216, 220, 230, 265, 280, 282, 285, 289, 293, 295, 347
    absolutive 111, 135-136, 140, 142, 145, 159, 162, 171-172, 190, 199, 209, 241, 270, 273-275, 277, 280, 282, 285, 287, 295, 297, 306, 325-330, 335, 354, 357, 364, 367, 369, 372, 374, 376, 380, 385, 391, 394-395, 400, 433, 434-435, 464, 500
    completive, *see* completive
    determiners, *see* determiners
    differential absolutive 135, 140, 150, 159, 272, 274, 280, 283, 285, 286, 287, 289-292, 295, 327
    possessive 112, 133, 135, 142, 145, 159-160, 168, 172, 183-185, 190-193, 202, 209, 240-241, 277, 387, 390, 443, 498
    quantifiers, *see* quantifiers
    specific 112, 135, 150, 159, 161, 169, 171, 192, 265-266, 269-270, 272-273, 276-279, 287, 289, 295, 327, 373
    valence 28, 135, 140, 159, 161, 280-288, 295, 327
syllables 23, 25, 35-46, 60, 68-72, 76, 90-91, 95-97, 100-112, 120, 127-129, 178-179, 280, 405
syndetic, *see* coordination
synthesis 123

Teâ Belep, *see* Belep
temporal 155, 208, 216, 220, 225-227, 384, 392, 437-440, 475-476, 480, 495
topicalization 149, 242, 258, 358, 375, 377, 428-430, 446, 452-453
transitive; *see also* intransitive
    clauses 331, 355-357, 362-372, 375-376, 379, 381-383, 443
    verbs 23-24, 134, 139-140, 152, 161-162, 265-266, 272-276, 280-290, 297, 326, 335-336, 347
    transitivization, *see* valence, patient
tripartite 24, 362, 368-370; *see also* alignment
valence 135, 140, 150, 159-161, 172, 265-266, 271, 327
    agent 295-304
    patient 280-289
    and voice 432-437
Vanuatu 10, 15, 27, 55, 256; *see also* South Efate
velar, *see* consonants
verbs 161-163, 172-176, 265-293
    as a word class 150-152
    groups 137, 141, 162, 171, 210, 265, 293-295, 306, 318, 320, 326, 329, 331-333, 336 355-357, 409, 419, 422, 424, 425, 430, 431, 441, 448, 453; *see also* verb phrase
    intransitive, *see* intransitive
    phrases 139-141, 152-154, 164, 169-170, 217, 165, 272, 293, 327, 329, 347-351, 389, 449, 473, 475, 492-494
    transitive, *see* transitive
Voh-Koné 17-18, 35, 54
voice, *see* valence
voiceless, *see* consonants
vowel inventory, *see* phonemes
vowels 23, 25, 35-36, 38, 46-47, 49-50, 54-55, 59-75, 77, 83, 88, 89, 90-92, 96-99, 101,

103-111, 127-129, 131, 198, 201, 220, 243, 247, 282, 351, 377, 381-382, 385, 387-388
    duration 69, 90, 104-107, 111,
    epenthesis 28, 104, 127-128, 132, 145, 220, 350
    hiatus 35, 46, 67-69, 71, 73-74, 96-99, 101, 106, 108-110, 132, 185, 195, 201, 220, 243, 247, 249, 251, 282, 387
    length 23, 35, 46, 50, 55, 68-71, 74, 90, 93, 105-107, 110-111, 120, 128, 457
    nasal 46-48, 62-63, 68, 74-75, 92, 97
    oral 46-48, 54-56, 62-65, 68, 71, 74-76, 97
Waap, *see* phratries
words 23-24, 99-100, 123-180
    classes 143, 147-165, 168, 173-174, 181, 231, 263, 295, 401, 447, 487
    definition 123-145
    grammatical 123-124, 127, 134-146, 179, 265, 294, 333, 335
    loan 20, 26-28, 113-120, 182, 188
    order 21, 24, 231, 334, 355-361, 403, 428
    orthographic 99, 125-126
    phonological 23, 51, 70, 77, 93, 104, 109, 111, 113, 127-143, 145, 154, 156, 177, 181, 190, 193, 240, 248, 252, 255, 265, 294-295, 332-333, 430-431, 453
    shape, *see* phonotactics
    stress, *see* prosody
Xârâcùù 18, 320
Xârâgurè 18, 434
Yidiny, *see* Australia
Yimas, *see* Papua
Yuanga 17-18, 35, 37, 47, 54, 263
zero-derivation 168, 173